THE KINGFISHER GEOGRAPHY ENCYCLOPEDIA

KINGFISHER

Kingfisher Publications Plc
New Penderel House
283-288 High Holborn
London WC1V 7HZ
www.kingfisherpub.com

First published by
Kingfisher Publications Plc in 2003
2 4 6 8 10 9 7 5 3 1

1TR/0803/C&C/CLSN(CLSN)/128CHMA

A CIP catalogue record for this book is available
from the British Library

ISBN 0 7534 0823 6

Printed in China

PROJECT TEAM

Project Director and Art Editor Julian Holland
Editorial Team Julian Holland, Lynn Bresler
Designer Nigel White
Commissioned artwork Julian Baker
Picture Research Caroline Wood
Maps Anderson Geographics Limited, Warfield, Berks

FOR KINGFISHER

Managing Editor Paula Borton
Art Director Mike Davis
DTP Manager Nicky Studdart
Senior Production Controller Deborah Otter

AUTHOR
Clive Gifford

CONSULTANT
Clive Carpenter

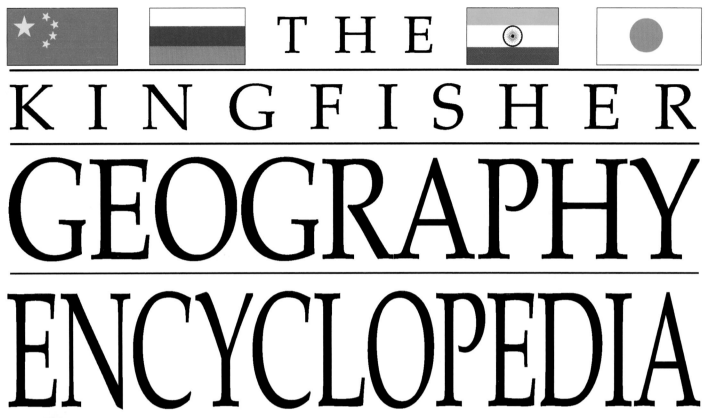

THE
KINGFISHER
GEOGRAPHY
ENCYCLOPEDIA

KINGFISHER

CONTENTS

CHAPTER 8

AFRICA

CHAPTER 9

OCEANIA AND ANTARCTICA

CHAPTER 10

READY REFERENCE

INTRODUCTION

Places that were remote to our grandparents are now visited regularly by tourists, while the world is brought into our homes by television. Although our planet is more accessible, it is also more vulnerable. You can explore our fast-changing world through the pages of *The Kingfisher Geography Encyclopedia*. Discover the challenges and environmental threats faced by Earth and its many nations.

Your encyclopedia is divided into ten sections. The Physical Earth describes how the planet was formed and then shaped by the forces of Nature, by water and ice, by wind and volcanoes. The variety of landscapes, climates and soils that influence how people live and the rich natural resources that offer opportunities are explored here.

The continents are surveyed, country by country, through eight thematic chapters. Clear mapping places each country in its broader setting, and shows its rivers and mountains as well as the major towns and cities. Concise fact boxes feature key information about each nation: its area and population, its capital, flag, languages and religions, trade and government system.

The unique story of each country is explained through a summary of its geography and recent history. From the densely populated industrial landscapes of western Europe and North America to the endangered rainforests of central Africa and the Amazon Basin, learn what makes each country special. The daily lives of people around the globe are pictured from the harsh desert margins of the Sahara to the icy wastes of Siberia, and from lush fertile farming lands of southeast Asia to the open savannah grasslands of east Africa.

The last section, Ready Reference, surveys climate, physical features, population, languages, trade, industry, international organizations and much more in a format that encourages quick and easy access. Ideal for projects and schoolwork, *The Kingfisher Geography Encyclopedia* is also your passport to an enjoyable journey of discovery around the world.

Clive Carpenter
Consultant

THE PHYSICAL EARTH

FORMATION OF THE EARTH

The Earth is part of the Solar System where nine planets orbit a star called the Sun. The Earth started life approximately 4.65 billion years ago.

At the centre of the Solar System is its biggest object, the Sun. It is the strong pull of the Sun's gravity that holds the Solar System together and controls the movement of the planets. There are nine planets in the Solar System. Earth is the third closest planet to the Sun, orbiting at an average distance of 149,600 million km. The Solar System is part of the Milky Way, a collection of star systems known as a galaxy.

The Milky Way is just one of what scientists estimate to be between 100 and 1,000 billion galaxies which occupy the Universe. The Universe consists of everything in space and space itself and is estimated to be between 12 and 14 billion years old. Many theories have been advanced to explain its origins. The most widely accepted is the Big Bang theory. This states that the Universe began when a gigantic explosion of energy started the process of forming matter, time and space. Huge forces were generated which saw the Universe expand with great energy; so much so, that the Universe is still expanding to this very day.

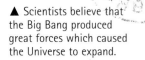

▲ Scientists believe that the Big Bang produced great forces which caused the Universe to expand.

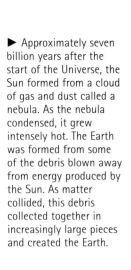

▶ Approximately seven billion years after the start of the Universe, the Sun formed from a cloud of gas and dust called a nebula. As the nebula condensed, it grew intensely hot. The Earth was formed from some of the debris blown away from energy produced by the Sun. As matter collided, this debris collected together in increasingly large pieces and created the Earth.

BIRTH OF THE SOLAR SYSTEM

Astronomers believe that the Sun formed around five billion years ago from a huge cloud of gas and dust. As the Sun began to shrink, it pulled more and more gas and dust into its centre. It became hotter and started to form a central orb surrounded by a spinning disc of gas and dust. Intense heat and energy were generated within the central orb. As the young Sun warmed up, it blew a wind of energetic particles through the spinning disc of gas and dust. This drove much of the disc's gases outwards where they cooled and over time formed the Solar System's largest planets, such as Jupiter and Saturn. The dust and ice left in the disc around the Sun gradually began to form rocky lumps; these collided and joined together. As the objects became bigger, the collisions grew more violent. Gradually these bodies formed into planets as dust and gas were drawn to them. The process of building up the planets took about 150 million years.

EARTH'S DEVELOPMENT

Earth began life as a sphere of dust, rocks and gases which were drawn together through the force of gravity. As Earth's size and mass increased, the pull of gravity gathered in more material and compressed it until it started to melt. Heavier, iron-rich materials moved towards the centre forming its dense core, while lighter materials began to form the outer layers. Earth started life as a waterless planet with temperatures too high to let water collect on its hot surface. Water vapour existed in the atmosphere and as the planet cooled, over 3.8 billion years ago, the vapour began to cool, condense and fall as rain. Rains that lasted thousands of years are believed to have formed rivers, lakes, early seas and oceans. Using fossil evidence, scientists estimate that the first life on Earth, single-celled blue-green algae, started around 3.5 billion years ago. Living things with more than one cell are believed to have emerged around 600 million years ago.

▲ The early Earth was a hot, fiery planet with volcanic activity and a surface of liquid rock spewing fumes and gases into the atmosphere. Some gases, mainly nitrogen and carbon dioxide, were prevented from drifting into space by Earth's gravity, forming the early atmosphere.

▲ A mangrove swamp in the Central American country of Belize. The Earth is the only known body in space able to support and sustain life.

EARTH'S ROTATION

As the Earth orbits around the Sun, it also rotates on its axis like a spinning top. These rotations bring day and night, and create the seasons.

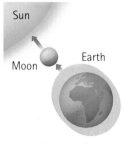

Spring tide

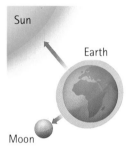

Neap tide

▲ As the Moon orbits the Earth, its gravity pulls water in the Earth's oceans towards it. The changes in water level that occur as a result are called tides. The strongest or spring tides occur when the Moon and the Sun, which also affects tides, pull in the same direction. Weaker neap tides occur when the Moon pulls at right angles to the Sun.

The Earth rotates on its axis at a constant rate as it orbits the Sun. The Earth spins eastwards on its axis which is why the Sun appears to rise in the east and set in the west. A complete 360 degree turn is called a planet's rotational period or day. Earth takes a fraction over 23 hours and 56 minutes to complete a rotational period.

The Earth is not quite a perfect sphere. It is slightly squashed with the diameter at its Equator approximately 38 km greater than its diameter from pole to pole. This is due to its rotation which forces material out towards the Equator. Earth, like the eight other planets in the Solar System, travels around the Sun along an elliptical, or oval, path called an orbit. The time taken to complete one orbit is known as a planet's orbital period or year. Mercury, the planet nearest to the Sun, takes 88 days to complete an orbit. In the case of the Earth, a complete orbit occurs every 365.26 Earth days.

▲ When the northern hemisphere is tilted towards the Sun, it is summer there. During this time, the North Pole is in sunlight for 24 hours a day.

EARTH'S TILT

The Earth's vertical axis is an imaginary line which joins its north and south poles. The Earth is tilted towards the Sun along its vertical axis at a constant angle. The Earth can be divided along the line of the Equator into two halves, a northern hemisphere and a southern hemisphere. The Earth's tilt creates the seasons. As one hemisphere is tilted more towards the Sun it experiences summer. In the other hemisphere, winter occurs. On or near 21 March and 23 September, the daylight hours experienced by the southern and northern hemispheres are equal. These dates are known as equinoxes.

The first day of winter is usually 21 December for the northern hemisphere and first day of summer in the southern hemisphere

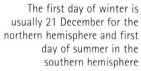

23 September is the first day of autumn in the northern hemisphere and the first day of spring in the southern hemisphere. The Sun is directly overhead at the Equator

SUN

▶ The two hemispheres of Earth experience opposing seasons as the Earth orbits the Sun on its tilted axis. From about 21 March to 21 September, the northern hemisphere is tilted towards the Sun and the seasons of spring and summer occur there, while the southern hemisphere has autumn and winter.

21 March sees the first day of spring in the northern and the first day of autumn in the southern hemisphere

21 June is the start of summer in the northern hemisphere and the first day of winter in the southern hemisphere

INSIDE THE EARTH

The Earth is made up of a series of layers that formed early in the planet's history. They include a central core, a mantle and a surface crust.

▲ Hot volcanic rocks underneath the Earth's surface boil and spurt out water and steam in the form of hot springs called geysers. Old Faithful is just one of over 3,000 geysers found in Yellowstone National Park in the United States. Each time it erupts, between 37,000 and 45,000 litres of hot water are expelled.

At the Earth's centre is its dense core which is largely made up of iron with a small amount of nickel and other elements. The core is divided into inner and outer regions. The outer core is kept molten or liquid by a temperature of approximately 3,360°C. The inner core's temperature is higher, in excess of 4,530°C, but is believed to be a solid, or acts like a solid, due to the intense pressure it experiences. Scientists estimate the pressure on the inner core to be four to five million times the pressure we experience on the Earth's surface. Together, the inner and outer core comprise 33.5 per cent of the Earth's mass. Lying above the outer core is the mantle, the layer which forms 66 per cent of the Earth's mass. The mantle is largely solid but with a temperature of over 1,300°C, it can deform and be distorted slowly.

Iron and oxygen are the most common components of the Earth. Iron is concentrated especially in the Earth's core. Compounds called magnesium silicates, made up of magnesium, silicon and oxygen, form most of the Earth's mantle.

Iron 36% — Oxygen 28.5% — Silicon 14% — Magnesium 13% — Nickel 2% — Calcium 1.9% — Sulphur 1.8% — Other elements 0.6% — Aluminium 0.4%

The final layer, the crust, floats on the mantle and is much thinner than the other layers. The crust comes in three types. Continental crust which forms land is usually between 30 and 50 km in depth, but in places can be just 20 km thick or bulge downwards beneath mountain ranges to depths of around 65 km. The transitional crust averages 15–30 km thickness. The oceanic crust found below oceans is thinner, usually between 5 and 15 km thick.

Oceanic crust averages 5–15 km thickness

Continental crust averages 30–50 km thickness

Molten rock rises to the surface

The mantle forms a 2,865 km thick layer

The inner core is estimated as 2,444 km in diameter

The outer core is 2,260 km thick

▶ Earth's different layers float on top of one another. The heaviest layer, the core, is at its centre and the lightest layer, the crust, is on the Earth's surface. The crust forms just 0.5 per cent of the Earth's total mass. The crust is rocky and brittle and can be fractured by earthquakes.

EARTH'S MAGNETISM

The Earth acts like a large magnet creating a magnetic field that extends out through the layers of Earth and into space.

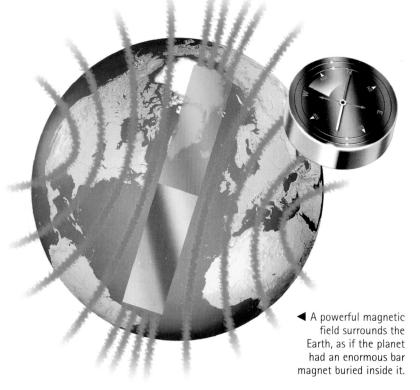

◀ A powerful magnetic field surrounds the Earth, as if the planet had an enormous bar magnet buried inside it.

An aurora is caused by particles of the solar wind which enter the Earth's atmosphere. The particles interact with gases in the atmosphere to create light energy. This aurora borealis, or northern lights, was seen in Alaska, USA.

The Earth's magnetic field originates in the molten outer core deep below the crust. There, electric currents churning and circulating through the molten material are believed to be behind the creation of Earth's giant magnetic field. The flow of electric currents in the core is continually changing, so the magnetic field produced by those currents also changes. The magnetic north and south poles move and are in different locations from the geographic poles. At the current time, magnetic north is about 966 km from the North Pole and magnetic south is around 1,500 km from the South Pole. The angle between a geographic pole and a magnetic pole is called magnetic declination. This is vital to know when navigating with a magnetic compass.

THE MAGNETOSPHERE

The Earth's magnetism generates a giant magnetic field that reaches out past the Earth's atmosphere and into space. It is called the magnetosphere and is irregularly shaped. The side facing the Sun extends approximately 60,000 km out from the Earth, while the side away from the Sun forms a long tail stretching a distance of over 1,000,000 km. The shape of the magnetosphere is influenced by the solar wind. This is the constant stream of high-energy particles produced by the Sun which moves at a speed of around 400 km per second. The magnetosphere helps to protect the Earth's atmosphere from the impact of the solar wind. If the Earth's magnetism did not exist, the solar wind would strip the Earth of its air, and the Earth would become incapable of supporting life. The Earth's magnetosphere is not unique. Space probes have detected magnetic fields surrounding the planets of Jupiter, Saturn, Uranus and Neptune.

▼ The shape of the Earth's magnetosphere is influenced by the Sun's solar wind. It compresses the magnetosphere on the side facing the Sun and sweeps it out into a long tail away from the Sun.

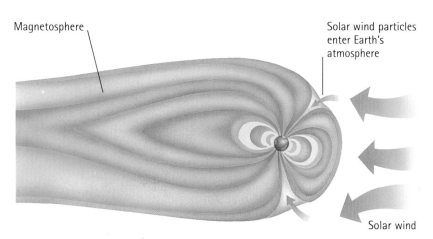

Magnetosphere

Solar wind particles enter Earth's atmosphere

Solar wind

CONTINENTAL DRIFT

The continents are on the move, carried by the Earth's crust which floats and drifts slowly on the mantle. This process is called continental drift.

1 Until around 200 million years ago, all land was part of one supercontinent which is known as Pangaea.

2 By around 110 million years ago, Pangaea had separated into a number of land masses. Africa and South America are already recognizable.

3 The continents today. Continental drift is continuing so that in around 50 million years from now, North America will separate from South America and be joined to the continent of Asia.

▶ There are seven major and nine minor plates covering the Earth. This map shows the positions of the seven major plates: Eurasian, African, Antarctic, Pacific, North American, South American and Indo-Australian. The arrows depict the directions in which the plates are currently moving.

The Earth's crust is not one piece but a number of giant slabs which move slowly around the planet's surface. These slabs are called plates and are propelled by convection currents created by heat from the Earth's core. This heat forces the mantle to rise and sink causing the plates above it also to move.

THEORY AND EVIDENCE

Geologists and fossil hunters had puzzled over how identical rock formations and fossils of species could be found in land masses thousands of kilometres apart. The theory of continental drift was first put forward by the German scientist, Alfred Wegener (1880–1930), in 1912. He stated that, over 100 million years ago, the continents as we know them today, emerged from the gradual break up of one supercontinent which he called Pangaea. Wegener's ideas were not widely accepted until the 1960s when advances in technology, including laser measurement systems and satellite imaging, supported his theory. Land masses are currently moving at an average rate of between one and ten centimetres per year. Over millions of years, continental drift has shaped the continents and many of their features.

The San Andreas Fault in California, USA, marks where the Pacific plate and the North American plate meet, slide and grate past each other.

PLATE TECTONICS

Plate tectonics is the study and theory of how the plates were created, move and their effect on the geography of the Earth. Over time, plates move apart from each other, grind and grate alongside each other or collide brutally into one another. In all cases, they help shape the Earth's land features. A boundary between two plates is known as a fault or fault line. Volcanoes and earthquakes frequently occur at fault lines where the crust is weak or is under extreme stress.

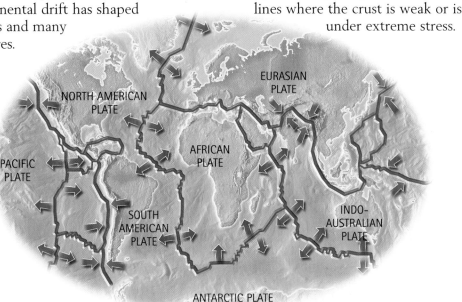

NORTH AMERICAN PLATE

EURASIAN PLATE

PACIFIC PLATE

AFRICAN PLATE

SOUTH AMERICAN PLATE

INDO-AUSTRALIAN PLATE

ANTARCTIC PLATE

EARTHQUAKES

Earthquakes are a trembling or shaking of the ground caused by the sudden release of energy stored in the rocks beneath the Earth's surface.

▲ This Ancient Chinese earthquake detector dates from around CE130. Earth tremors would cause balanced bronze balls to fall into the frogs' mouths.

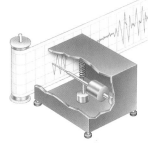

▲ A seismograph charts the intensity of Earth's vibrations using a pen held on a balanced pendulum and a roll of graph paper.

The Earth's crust is on the move and where the crust's plates meet, powerful forces produce large amounts of stress and energy. Plates rub up against each other, collide head on or one plate can be forced to dive down beneath another. Stresses and strains in the crust build up. When plates suddenly move or slip into a new position, the energy from the stress created can be released as an earthquake. The energy in an earthquake comes in the form of powerful disturbances, called seismic waves, which surge through rocks, moving and distorting them in the process. Earthquakes emit waves in all directions from the point where they start – known as the focus or hypocentre – less than 70 km below ground. The point on the surface of the Earth directly above the focus is called the epicentre. It is usually where the destructive effects of the earthquake are most felt. Some seismic waves travel deep underground through the body of the Earth. Other waves travel in a zone close to the Earth's surface.

P waves travel deep below the ground and stretch and squeeze rock particles as they progress

S waves also travel deep underground but move the rock from side to side

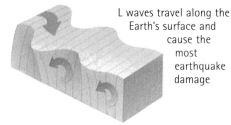

L waves travel along the Earth's surface and cause the most earthquake damage

▲ Different types of seismic waves travel by distorting rocks in different ways.

EARTHQUAKE LOCATIONS

Certain areas of the Earth are more prone to earthquakes than others, particularly regions which lie at the boundaries of the Earth's plates. The forcing together of the Eurasian, African and Australian plates, for example, creates a region of earthquake activity which has affected countries as far apart as Portugal, Iran and India. Earthquakes can also occur away from the boundaries of the Earth's plates. Some earthquakes are caused by volcanic activity. As molten rock works its way

▶ In August 1999, an earthquake measuring 7.4 on the Richter scale hit the cities of Izmit and Gölcük in the northwest of Turkey. It killed 17,118 people, injured a further 27,000 and made 200,000 people homeless. A second earthquake struck the region in November 1999. With its epicentre near the town of Düzce, it killed over 700 people and injured 5,100 others.

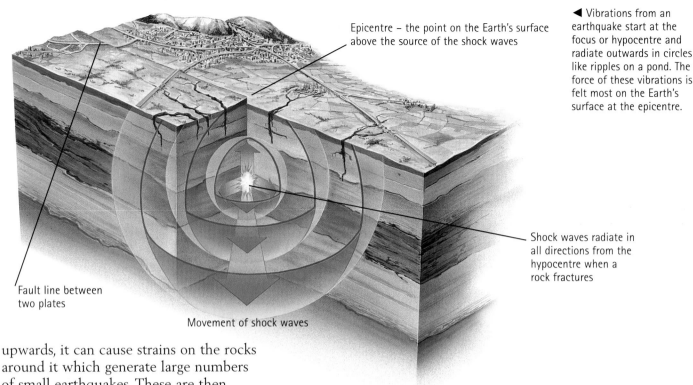

Epicentre – the point on the Earth's surface above the source of the shock waves

◀ Vibrations from an earthquake start at the focus or hypocentre and radiate outwards in circles like ripples on a pond. The force of these vibrations is felt most on the Earth's surface at the epicentre.

Shock waves radiate in all directions from the hypocentre when a rock fractures

Fault line between two plates

Movement of shock waves

upwards, it can cause strains on the rocks around it which generate large numbers of small earthquakes. These are then measured and used to predict the likelihood of a major volcanic eruption. Many earthquakes occur in the mid-ocean ridges (see pages 20–21) and account for five per cent of all of Earth's seismic activity. These earthquakes are measured by seismologists, but rarely affect people as they are so far from inhabited areas. A powerful earthquake sometimes occurs in the centre of a plate. The earthquake that struck the Gujarat region of India in 2001 was such an example. It caused great devastation, killing over 30,000 people.

AFTERSHOCKS AND TSUNAMIS

Further devastation can occur after the waves from a main earthquake have died away. Sometimes, an earthquake does not release all the energy built up in an area. This can cause smaller tremors, or aftershocks, after the main earthquake. Aftershocks can be deadly in an earthquake-hit area, creating even more destruction. Earthquakes can also produce giant ocean waves called tsunamis. These waves, which can also be created by volcanic activity, are believed to start when the ocean floor is tilted or moved during an earthquake. A set of fast-moving waves is created and can travel hundreds of kilometres across an ocean, reaching speeds of between 725 and 800 km/h. On

reaching shallow waters, the waves grow to as high as 15 m, destroying settlements on the coast. Most tsunamis occur in the Pacific Ocean.

MEASURING EARTHQUAKES

Two scales are used to measure earthquakes. The Mercalli scale measures the physical effects of earthquake activity on the Earth's surface. The Richter scale measures the energy produced by earthquakes on a scale of 1–10. At 3.5 on the Richter scale, the tremors are noticed by most people, at 4.5, some local damage can occur, while at 7.0 or above, a major earthquake has occurred.

▼ The blue dots show the sites of past major earthquakes. These are largely distributed along the fault lines marking the boundaries between the Earth's tectonic plates, shown in green. In these areas, the Earth's crust tends to be under the greatest pressure which can also give rise to large amounts of volcanic activity (see pages 10-11).

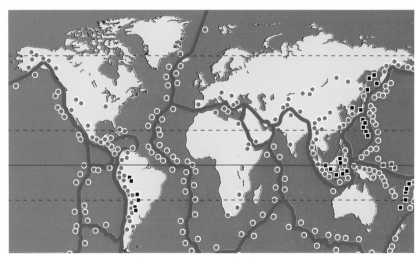

VOLCANOES

Volcanoes are openings in the Earth's crust which allow gases, ash and molten rock to rise up. This activity is called a volcanic eruption.

Deep underground in the Earth's mantle, high temperatures keep rock in a molten state called magma. Less dense than the solid rock that surrounds it, magma rises upwards and can collect in large reservoirs called magma chambers. As the rising magma nears the Earth's surface, the pressure on the magma decreases. This causes the gases held in the magma to expand. The magma is then forced up through openings in the Earth's surface creating a volcanic eruption. Once magma has erupted, it is called lava. Lava may erupt in explosive bursts or ooze and flow gently down slopes. Eventually, the

lava cools, forming rock and new rock formations. Volcanoes are located mainly in places where the Earth's crust is weakest, particularly at the boundaries between the Earth's plates. Some are found away from these boundaries in areas such as the Great Rift Valley in Africa where there is intense crust movement and above places called hot spots. These are locations where a rising plume of especially hot mantle rock is situated and melts the Earth's crust, forcing magma up towards the surface.

VOLCANO TYPES

The types of eruption and volcano vary and depend largely on the properties of the magma, including its composition and its consistency. Thin, runny lava, for example, allows gases to escape relatively easily. This tends to make the eruption less violent and the lava flows gently out of openings. Thin lava is also more likely to flow a great distance after reaching the surface before it cools, hardens and forms rock. As a result, it tends to form shallow-sloped shield volcanoes. Thick lava flows only a short distance before setting, to form steep-sided volcanoes. Thicker molten rock can trap gases and, if the gas content in the magma is high, the chance of a violent eruption is increased.

Explosive eruptions can propel ash, red-hot cinders, lava and pieces of rocks high into the atmosphere. Larger, more dense particles fall back to Earth but smaller

Fissure volcano

Dome volcano

Ash cinder volcano

Shield volcano

Caldera volcano

Composite volcano

▲ Many different volcano types can form depending on the type of lava and how the volcano erupts.

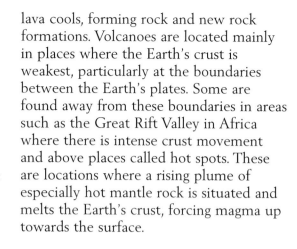

Volcanic cone

Fumaroles are volcanic openings which leak only gas or steam

Main cone – consists of layers of lava and cinders

◀ This composite volcano has steep slopes formed from layers of cinders and hardened lava that have emerged from previous eruptions. At the centre is a vertical opening called a vent. Smaller openings which branch off from the main vent are called side vents. Lying often several kilometres below is the supply of molten rock in the magma chamber.

Magma chamber

▲ Mount Etna is an active composite volcano on the island of Sicily in the Mediterranean Sea. At over 3,311 m in height, it is the highest volcano in Europe.

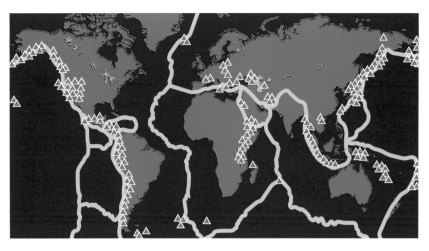

dust particles can travel high into the atmosphere where they may remain for months or years.

Many volcanoes are found underwater. Some are forced upwards by plate activity or erupt enough times to grow in height and rise above sea level to form volcanic islands. Curved chains of volcanic islands, called island arcs, are particularly common in the Pacific Ocean.

Volcanoes are classified as extinct, dormant or active. There are approximately 850 active volcanoes although fewer than 30 tend to erupt in a year. Dormant volcanoes have been quiet for many years, but may erupt in the future. After 600 years of inactivity, Mount Pinatubo in the Philippines erupted in 1991 sending ash over 15,000 m up into the atmosphere.

PEOPLE AND VOLCANOES

Some people choose to live and farm the slopes of volcanoes. The ash that has settled here is rich in minerals, making fertile growing land. Scientists monitor volcanic activity to predict eruptions and warn people in areas at risk. Seismometers detect Earth tremors caused by an impending eruption while tiltmeters and geodimeters measure changes in the land shape that may signal volcanic activity.

Bombardment from material thrown into the air from an eruption and the red-hot lava flow are not the only threats to people posed by volcanoes. Volcanic areas can also emit harmful gases in immense quantities. Heat from an eruption poses further threats in the form of large floods, when eruptions melt parts of nearby glaciers, and unstoppable mudflows.

▲ The triangles on this map show the location of active volcanoes around the world. Most volcanoes are found near plate boundaries (shown in yellow) or over hot spots.

▼ The Caribbean island of Montserrat suffered from serious volcanic activity in June 1997. A series of eruptions from both Soufrière Hills and Chance's Peak volcanoes destroyed the town of Plymouth, made thousands of islanders homeless and killed 19 people.

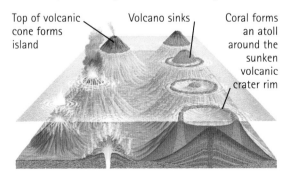

Top of volcanic cone forms island | Volcano sinks | Coral forms an atoll around the sunken volcanic crater rim

▲ Volcanic islands can form from a volcanic cone which rises above the ocean's surface. Sometimes, volcanoes sink and a new island type, called an atoll, is created from coral forming a ring where the volcanic crater lay.

ROCKS AND MINERALS

Rocks are the solid materials that make up the Earth's surface. They can be divided into three types – igneous, metamorphic and sedimentary.

▲ When basalt lava erupts from volcanic vents and cools, it shrinks and cracks and sometimes forms vertical columns. The Devil's Postpile consists of four- to seven-sided basalt columns and is found in the Sierra Nevada mountain range in California, USA.

Rocks consist of chemical compounds called minerals. There are many thousands of different minerals. Some are single elements, such as the metals gold and copper. Others are composed of a number of elements such as silicates which are compounds of silicon, oxygen and small amounts of other elements.

IGNEOUS ROCKS

Igneous rocks are formed from hot, molten rock material called magma which has cooled and turned solid. The type of igneous rock is determined by the chemical make-up of the magma and the rate at which it cooled and turned solid. Many igneous rocks, such as granite, are formed from magma buried deep within the crust of the Earth. These rocks cooled slowly and, as a result, contain large mineral crystals. Other igneous rocks, such as basalt and obsidian, are created by volcanic activity. They either form from magma which rose and filled cracks close to the Earth's surface or erupted onto the surface. In both cases, the magma of volcanic igneous rocks tends to cool rapidly and this creates very small crystals in rocks which give a fine grain or a glass-like appearance.

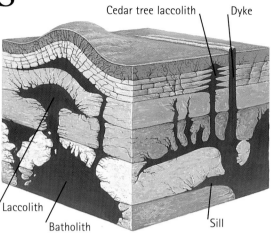

▲ Intrusive igneous rock is pushed up beneath overlying rocks as large masses that have already turned solid. Batholiths are large intrusions of igneous rock which push away or replace a vast amount of other rock. When an intrusion creates a mushroom shape, it is called a laccolith. A dyke is formed when magma fills a fracture in other rock and cools and turns solid. A sill occurs when magma intrudes between layers of sedimentary rock.

METAMORPHIC ROCKS

Metamorphic rock is rock that has been transformed from other metamorphic, sedimentary or igneous rocks. These form when extreme temperatures or pressures deep within the Earth alter existing rock without melting it or adding new substances to it. There are two main ways in which metamorphism can occur. Hot igneous rocks can force their way or intrude into an area. Heat from these igneous rocks bakes and transforms the surrounding rock. For example, limestone through heat can be turned into marble. Sandstone, a sedimentary rock, can through heat be turned into the metamorphic rock, quartzite. The second type of metamorphism tends to occur on a larger

▶ Heat from an igneous intrusion has turned some of the surrounding layers of limestone into marble (right). The pressures generated by mountain layers folding (left) can turn clay materials or shale into slate.

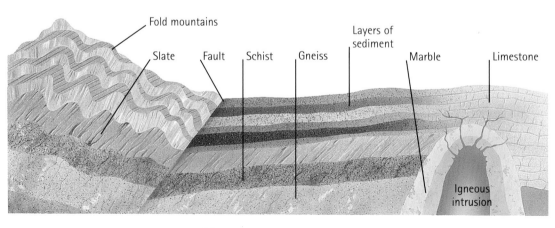

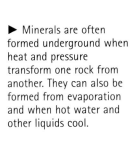

▲ Sedimentary rock can form clearly distinguishable rock layers or strata. These rocks form part of Death Valley in California, USA.

rock such as chalk. Chemical sedimentary rocks, such as gypsum, occur when water evaporates leaving behind minerals as a sediment. Clastic rocks make up 75 per cent of all sedimentary rocks. They are formed from other rocks which when exposed at the Earth's surface are worn away by a range of forces. These include wind, water, ice and frost as well as chemical reactions and the actions of plant roots. The material worn away from these rocks is transported by gravity, wind, water or ice and eventually is deposited as a layer or bed of sediment. Over time, the beds of sediment are slowly compacted by pressure as other material is deposited above them. Eventually the loose pieces of sediment join together, to form a solid sedimentary rock such as sandstone.

scale and involves huge pressures created by mountains forming and folding. Rocks such as mudstone and shale can be transformed under great pressure into metamorphic rocks such as slate, schist or gneiss.

SEDIMENTARY ROCKS

Although sedimentary rocks are only a small part of the entire Earth's crust they make up around three-quarters of the planet's surface rock. There are three types of sedimentary rock: biogenic, chemical and clastic. Biogenic sedimentary rocks consist of the skeletons and shells of millions of microscopic organisms which have been compressed over time to form a

GEMSTONES AND ORES

Minerals within rocks that are capable of being cut and polished are called gemstones. Certain gemstones, including rubies, opals and diamonds, are highly prized. Many minerals are concentrated in rocks as impure chemical compounds called ores. For example, aluminium is commonly found in the ore bauxite, while copper is frequently concentrated in an ore called malachite. Ores are mined and their valuable metal or other mineral is extracted from the rest of the ore using heat and chemical reactions.

▲ An open cast gold mine in Australia. Australia is the third largest producer of gold behind South Africa and the USA.

▶ Minerals are often formed underground when heat and pressure transform one rock from another. They can also be formed from evaporation and when hot water and other liquids cool.

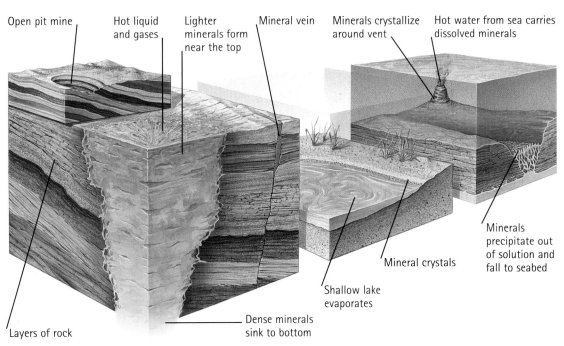

Open pit mine

Hot liquid and gases

Lighter minerals form near the top

Mineral vein

Minerals crystallize around vent

Hot water from sea carries dissolved minerals

Minerals precipitate out of solution and fall to seabed

Mineral crystals

Shallow lake evaporates

Dense minerals sink to bottom

Layers of rock

THE ROCK CYCLE

The rock cycle is a way of charting how rocks change from one type to another. Scientists measure this using geological time.

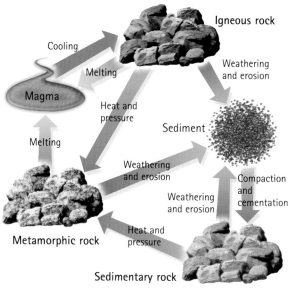

▲ This diagram illustrates the processes involved in the recycling and changing of rocks from one type to another.

Rocks are always changing. The minerals in them are constantly moved and acted upon by the environment. The upper part of the Earth – the mantle, crust and the surface – acts as a rock recycling system. The matter that makes up rocks is transported and transformed from one type of rock to another. The rock cycle shows the relationships between igneous, sedimentary and metamorphic rocks, and the ways they are formed and recycled. The basic rock cycle was devised by the Scottish geologist and naturalist, James Hutton (1726–1797). It starts with the formation of igneous rock when magma cools and solidifies. Particles of igneous rocks, worn away through erosion and weathering, are transported elsewhere and form deposits of sediment. These layers are compacted by the weight of layers above, and can become cemented together by minerals to form sedimentary rocks.

▲ Most sediments occur in marine environments which means that the majority of fossils found are of sea creatures. This fossil is of an ammonite, a group of hard-shelled sea creatures which existed between 400 and 65 million years ago.

Sedimentary rocks are formed at fairly low pressures and temperatures. They are most susceptible to further change when greater pressures and temperatures are applied. Those that become very deeply buried or involved in the processes of mountain building are often changed into metamorphic rocks. Yet more heat can turn solid metamorphic rock into a liquid or molten state, creating magma from which igneous rocks can form. The cycle is not always a simple progress between igneous, sedimentary, metamorphic and igneous again. For example, metamorphic rock can be worn away to create sedimentary rock. Another exception is that sedimentary rock can be heated to such extreme temperatures that it forms magma, which when it cools creates new igneous rock. All three types of rock can be worn away to generate sediment from which new sedimentary rock is created.

Rocks eroded by ice and frost

Magma (molten rock) underneath the Earth's surface

Mountain uplift creates pressures and heat creating metamorphic rocks

Igneous rock layer forms underneath the Earth's surface

River transports rock particles where they are deposited on the seabed

Sedimentary rock layer buried under other rock layers

Buried rock layer

▲ Deep underground, intense heat and pressure are at work, creating and transforming rocks. New rock is constantly being pushed towards the surface of the Earth while existing surface rocks are broken down. These rock fragments are carried and deposited in layers which may eventually become sedimentary rock.

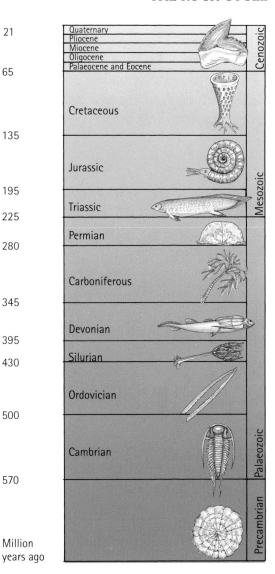

21	Quaternary		Cenozoic
	Pliocene		
	Miocene		
	Oligocene		
65	Palaeocene and Eocene		
	Cretaceous		Mesozoic
135			
	Jurassic		
195			
	Triassic		
225			
	Permian		Palaeozoic
280			
	Carboniferous		
345			
	Devonian		
395			
430	Silurian		
	Ordovician		
500			
	Cambrian		
570			
			Precambrian
Million years ago			

▲ Geological time is divided into four eras (right), three of which are then sub-divided into periods, each showing a different range of fossilized creatures.

FOSSILS

Fossils are the remains of dead plants and creatures that have settled in soft sediment which over millions of years has become sedimentary rock. Only the hard parts of living things, such as bones, teeth and shells, tend to become fossilized. As a result, soft-bodied creatures are rarely discovered. The fossil record has revealed valuable information about life on Earth millions of years ago. It has also provided scientists with an important method of comparing and dating rocks. This is because studies of fossils show that similar life forms existed at the same time in different parts of the world. The fossil record is one of a number of methods used to date rocks and geological features. Radiometric dating measures the levels of radioactive elements present in rocks. These radioactive elements decay at a constant rate providing a relatively accurate measure of the age of rocks in millions of years.

▲ At Bryce Canyon in Utah, USA, erosion has shaped a range of sedimentary rocks, including limestones and sandstones, into thousands of spires and pinnacles known as hoodoos.

▲ Where rock layers have lain largely undisturbed, it is possible to date rocks by their position. Younger rock layers tend to sit above older layers.

GEOLOGICAL TIME

Modern science estimates that the Earth is around 4.6 billion years old. Geological time is a way of presenting this huge span of time. Geological time is divided into a series of four eras which stretches back to the formation of the Earth over four billion years ago up until 570 million years ago. The Precambrian era represents over 80 per cent of the Earth's life but due to the constant changes in the rocks, it is the period from which the fewest fossil remains have been discovered. During the early Palaeozoic era, the first land plants grew and in time, the first forests formed, which would later decompose to create the world's coal reserves. The Mesozoic is the era during which the dinosaurs lived and died out.

MOUNTAIN BUILDING

Over millions of years, mountains have formed, risen and disappeared due to the actions of the Earth's crust, weathering and volcanoes.

Mountains are land masses which are steeply raised above the surrounding area. They are formed mainly through the movement and actions of the Earth's crust. The continental crust is made of hard rock but the immense pressures on the rock can cause softer rocks to bend into folds. The folds can be bent over, sink downwards and pile on top of each other like a crumpled blanket. Mountains can be formed from a sequence of folds, piling rock layers one on top of another. Rock layers subjected to severe forces can crack and break forming fractures and faults. Blocks of land can rise or sink between two faults, forming flat, steep-sided block mountains and long, deep rift valleys.

CONTINENTAL COLLISION

Continental drift (see page 7) sees the plates of crust move and drive into each other. The crust at the edges of the plates buckles and folds, and faults occur. Land often rises upwards forming many of the world's mountain chains. The most spectacular example of different plates driving towards each other to form mountains can be found in the Himalayas. There, over 60 million years ago, the Indian sub-continent started to head northwards pushing the Tethys Ocean ahead of it. Over a period of some 45 million years, the movement continued with the dense ocean crust pushed under the continental crust beneath Asia. Eventually, the Tethys Ocean disappeared, but masses

▲ The Wilder Kaiser mountain range is part of the Austrian Alps and features mountain summits between 1,900 and 2,400 m. It is a popular skiing and rock-climbing destination.

▲ Mount Aconcagua, rising to 6,960 m, is the highest mountain outside of Asia. Part of the South American Andes chain, the mountain is a long-dormant volcano.

A nappe is a large body of rock which has been moved around 2 km from its original position through faulting or folding

Recumbent folds are where the sides of a fold are pushed over so that it lies close to horizontal

Anticline occurs when folds form an arch

A basin or trough formed from folds is called a syncline

Fault

Block mountain or horst

Rift valley

▲ Parts of the Earth's crust are put under great pressure by the movement of plates and other activity. This pressure sees folds and faulting occur which shape the landscape in a number of ways and create a variety of features.

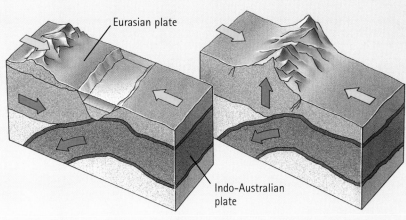

of sediment from its floor were scooped up and squeezed between the continents, helping to form the world's tallest mountain range.

ERUPTIONS AND EROSION

Some mountains form through other actions rather than directly through plate movements. Volcanic eruptions can form steep-sided, cone-shaped mountains such as Mount Vesuvius in Italy, Mount St Helens in the United States and Mount Fuji in Japan. More shallow-sloped volcanoes, called shield volcanoes, can still form mountains such as Mauna Loa and Mauna Kea in Hawaii. Dome mountains are caused by rising magma or igneous rock under the Earth's crust which thrusts at the rocks above with great force, lifting them into an arch shape. The Black Hills found in the American states of South Dakota and Wyoming are examples of dome mountains. Erosion can also help form mountains, not by lifting up existing land

but by wearing away softer rock, leaving a core of harder rock standing above the plains around it. Parts of the Ozark mountains in the American states of Arkansas and Missouri were formed in this way. Sometimes, a mixture of volcanic activity and erosion forms mountains. Magma which seeps into the crust may be uncovered by erosion to stand above the surrounding area as mountains. Scotland's Cairngorm Mountains, made of granite, are one such example.

RISE AND FALL

Mountains are far from permanent structures. They continually form, rise and then are worn down over millions of years. The eroding actions of wind, ice and water start to reduce mountains' size with rivers and glaciers transporting debris which they deposit as sediment. Eventually, mountains are worn down while new mountains are formed elsewhere.

▲ Long ago, the plate carrying the land we now call India collided with the plate carrying the rest of Asia (left). The sand, mud and soil on the ocean floor between the plates was slowly squeezed together and pushed up (right) to form the Himalayas.

▼ Fault-block mountains are formed when huge blocks of the Earth's crust are tilted on or pushed up along or near a fracture or fault line. These mountains lie near the Moab fault line in the American state of Utah.

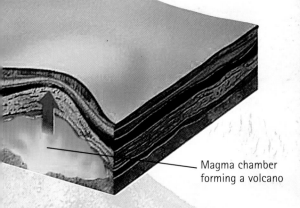

Magma chamber forming a volcano

RIVERS AND LAKES

Rivers and lakes have a great impact on the world. They shape the land and provide water and habitats for living things.

Rivers are large channels of water which carry water from high land towards areas at sea level. Rivers empty into seas, oceans and lakes. They carry water which comes from rainfall, snow, melting glaciers lakes and from water inside the Earth, called groundwater. Rivers vary greatly in length with the longest extending more than 6,000 km. They also vary in the volume of water they carry. The two biggest rivers (in volume), the Amazon in South America and the Congo in Africa, contain roughly 60 per cent of the world's river water.

Rising in Switzerland where it is fed by meltwaters from glaciers and snow, the River Rhine, here seen in Germany, flows approximately 1,390 km through Northern Europe before emptying into the North Sea.

A RIVER'S LIFE

Rivers tend to start life in higher altitude regions where they are fed by meltwaters from snow, ice or glaciers or from groundwater. When rain falls on high ground, some of the water disappears into the soil or seeps between cracks in the rocks. In places, the ground becomes saturated. The top of this saturated zone is called the water table. When the water table reaches the surface, groundwater can pour out forming a spring. Water from all sources is drawn by gravity towards sea level and trickles down slopes to form streams which act as tributaries, feeding rivers. The area of land from which a river collects water is called the drainage basin, and the shape of the river and its tributaries, the drainage pattern. This pattern depends on the type of soil and rock, how steeply the land slopes and earth movements under the ground. A young river flows

▼ A river starts in high altitude regions and flows through lands down towards sea level. As it makes its journey, the speed of its current, or water flow, slows and its effect on the landscape alters. As the river's flow slows on a flood plain, it deposits sediment.

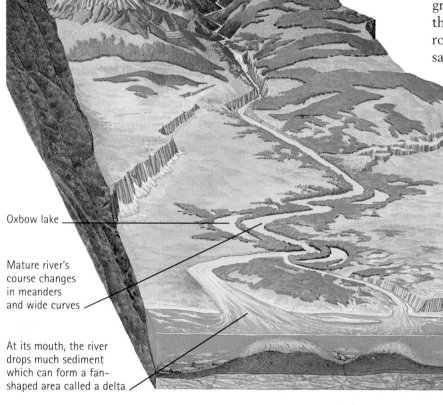

Mountain glacier feeds young river

Fast-moving young river carves out deep V-shaped valley

Oxbow lake

Mature river's course changes in meanders and wide curves

At its mouth, the river drops much sediment which can form a fan-shaped area called a delta

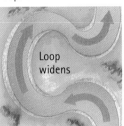

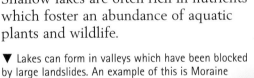

Meander

1 Some meanders will swell into broader loops than others

Loop widens

2 The neck of the loop may narrow as the loop develops

Oxbow lake

3 An oxbow lake forms from the old channel

▲ The Amazon river travels 6,448 km through South America before emptying into the Atlantic Ocean. More than 20 per cent of the freshwater that enters the seas and oceans every year comes from the Amazon.

▶ Oxbow lakes are horseshoe-shaped lakes once part of, and now lying near, a mature river.

fast and relatively straight, eroding and cutting through landforms (see page 22). As the river matures, it tends to carry more water, flow more slowly and is more likely to change its course in loops and bends called meanders. Finally, a river empties into a sea, ocean or large lake at its river mouth.

LAKES

A lake is a large quantity of standing water surrounded by land. Lakes form wherever water collects, particularly in dips or depressions in the ground, and does not drain away. Lakes can be formed in a variety of ways. Many, including the Great Lakes of North America, are the result of glaciers scooping out bedrock to form large basins. The deepest lakes are the result of movement of the Earth's tectonic plates which pushed material aside to create faults and depressions. Crater lakes form in the remains of meteorite craters or in the tops of extinct volcanoes. Artificial lakes can be created by humans deliberately damming rivers or valleys for fishing, irrigation or for generating electricity. Some lakes are created by the meandering of a mature or old river where a loop in the river is eventually cut off from the main course, forming what is called an oxbow lake. In geological terms, lakes are temporary features, forming in

many different ways and, in most cases, disappearing. The water in lakes can evaporate as the climate becomes drier or they can fill up with sediment leaving a bog or swamp in their place. Lakes make up a very small percentage of all the freshwater on Earth, but they make excellent habitats for plants and animals. Shallow lakes are often rich in nutrients which foster an abundance of aquatic plants and wildlife.

▼ Lakes can form in valleys which have been blocked by large landslides. An example of this is Moraine Lake in Banff National Park, Canada.

OCEANS AND SEAS

Water covers nearly 75 per cent of the planet's surface. Approximately 97.6 per cent of all Earth's water is contained in the world's seas and oceans.

▲ Coral reefs, such as this South Pacific reef, are formed near the ocean's surface by the remains of millions of creatures called polyps.

▼ The Pacific Ocean dominates a large portion of the Earth covering just over a third of the entire planet. It has a surface area of 181,000,000 km² including neighbouring seas. This is more than the total land area of all the continents put together.

All seawater was originally freshwater, but rain falling on land for millions of years has washed minerals, especially salt, from rocks into seas. Typically by weight, seawater is 96.5 per cent pure water, 2.9 per cent salt and 0.6 per cent other elements including calcium, fluoride, magnesium and potassium. The salt content, or salinity, of seawater can vary. Some seas such as the Baltic have a much lower salt content due to the large amounts of freshwater which run into them from rivers. Seas, such as the Dead Sea, which receive little rainfall and experience much evaporation, have a higher salt content. The world's rivers transport around three billion tonnes of salts into the water every year.

▼ Black smokers are vents found on the ocean floor which spout hot, mineral-rich waters. These provide nutrients for deep sea life forms such as tubeworms.

MOVING WATER

Waves, tides and currents move the water within the seas and oceans. Waves stir the ocean's surface and break in shallow waters, eroding, transporting and depositing debris. Tides caused by the gravitational pull of the Moon result in the oceans and seas rising and falling in a continuous cycle. There are four oceans spanning the planet: the Pacific, Atlantic, Indian and Arctic. These four bodies of water are interlinked and water circulates the Earth via ocean currents. Ocean currents are driven particularly by winds, but variations in water density and temperature also cause currents to flow. Ocean currents redistribute water and transfer the heat they absorb from the Sun's rays around the planet, influencing climate.

THE OCEAN LANDSCAPE

The edges of the continents slope down under the ocean to form continental shelves. These vary in width from a few kilometres to over 500 km and some are crossed by large depressions called submarine canyons. The continental shelves end at shallow depths of around 130 m. From there, continental slopes plunge sharply downwards meeting the ocean floor at the continental rise. Oceanographers estimate the average depth of the ocean floor or abyss to be 4,000 m. Large parts of the ocean abyss are relatively flat, forming abyssal plains broken by low hills and underwater

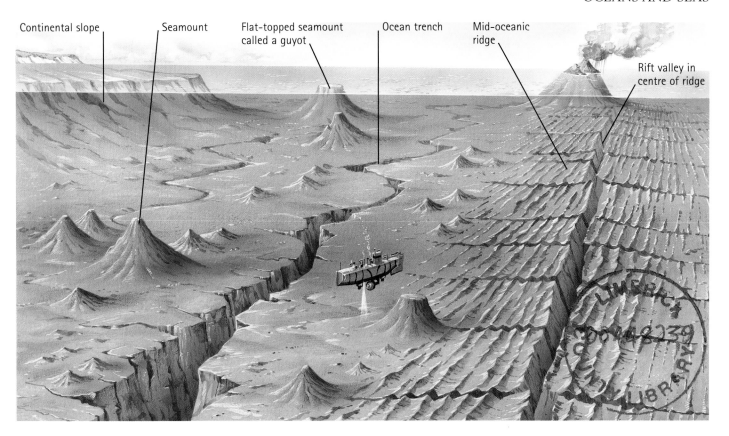

Continental slope

Seamount

Flat-topped seamount called a guyot

Ocean trench

Mid-oceanic ridge

Rift valley in centre of ridge

volcanoes, known as seamounts, which do not reach sea level. Where the plates of the Earth's crust collide, deep ocean trenches may form. These are often hundreds of kilometres wide, thousands of kilometres long and the deepest places on Earth. At 11,022 m below sea level, Challenger Deep, part of the Mariana Trench in the Pacific Ocean, is the deepest known place in the world's oceans.

A key feature of all ocean floors is the mid-oceanic ridge which are massive mountain ranges rising over 1,500 m from the ocean floor. These are formed by molten rock rising from the Earth's mantle. As it cools and hardens, the new ocean crust spreads out from the ridge in both directions. Where the ocean crust meets a continent, it tends to sink down, often forming an ocean trench.

MARINE LIFE

Seas and oceans teem with life. There are some 22,000 species of marine fish and thousands more plants and crustaceans. Most marine life exists in the top 100 m of the oceans which is called the euphotic zone. Sunlight penetrates this zone and is used by microscopic organisms called phytoplankton to convert light energy into food through a process called photosynthesis. Phytoplankton form the first link in marine food chains which support fish, crustaceans and marine mammals such as seals. Life exists even in the dark ocean depths. In regions below 1,000 m plants and creatures have adapted to living where little or no light reaches. Many are scavengers, relying on the sinking of dead plants and animals from upper ocean layers for their food.

▲ The landscape of the ocean floor is varied and contains a range of features. Trenches and ocean ridges are active volcanic and seismic zones.

Wind direction

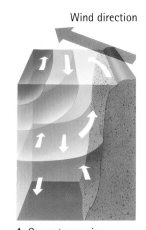

▲ Currents vary in temperature with depth. Sometimes, cold water rises as an upwelling to replace warmer surface water blown away from the coasts by winds.

◄ Waves begin as up and down movements caused by winds which turn into a circular motion as the wave advances. Waves topple over and break as they enter shallow water.

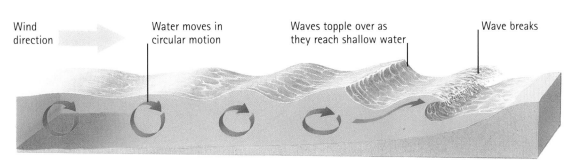

Wind direction

Water moves in circular motion

Waves topple over as they reach shallow water

Wave breaks

21

LANDSCAPING BY WATER

Rivers, seas, oceans and rainwater shape landscapes through erosion and by moving and depositing material to create new landforms.

▲ Wave action has eroded this limestone headland on the Dorset coast in southern England, to form a large arch, called Durdle Door. When the top of an arch collapses, the tall pillar of rock left behind is called a stack.

▼ The sea erodes landforms with its wave action compressing air in gaps and cracks in land, forcing rocks apart. Waves frequently undercut a cliff face at its base causing cliff falls.

Water moving downhill in streams and rivers carries with it any particles that it can move. This material helps erode, or wear away, the land it flows over, creating more loose material, some of which is also carried by the water. Near its source, a river tends to carve out steep v-shaped valleys. As a river matures, it usually erodes the sides of its banks, carving out wider valleys. When a river flows in a bend, its current is faster on the outside of the bend than on the inside. The faster flowing current continues to erode land while sediment is deposited on the inside edge.

When rivers meet harder rock that is more resistant to erosion, rapids and waterfalls can form. Although some waterfalls can form through faults and the action of glaciers (see page 25), most are the result of flowing water undercutting softer rock layers. The amount of eroded material a river can carry depends on the speed it travels. As a river matures, it tends to slow in speed and deposit the debris it carries as sediment. When an old-age river floods the lands either side of its course, it deposits much sediment, forming a flood plain. Over time, the build up of sediment can form fertile growing land such as the Nile flood plain in Egypt.

LANDSCAPING COASTLINES

Coastlines are constantly being shaped as they are broken down and built up by the action of waves. Waves exert great force on the landscape and the rocks, pebbles and sediment they carry and hurl against the land act as powerful eroding tools. Seawater is also slightly acidic and can rot and dissolve limestone and chalk rocks. Many coastlines are formed from a mixture of hard and soft rocks which erode at different rates. Soft rock is worn away into curved bays with hard rock left behind forming cliffs and headlands. Beaches are formed from some of the loose sediment and stone produced through coastal erosion and from material deposited by rivers as they flow into the sea. Beach material is pulled along

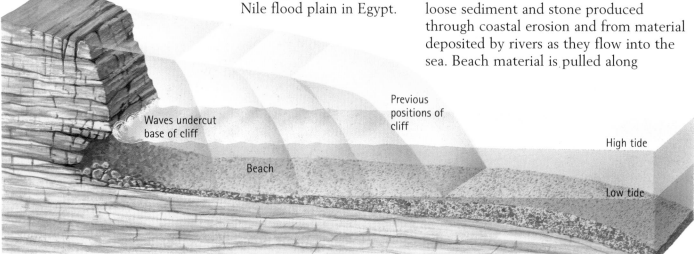

Waves undercut base of cliff

Previous positions of cliff

Beach

High tide

Low tide

▲ The Colorado river has landscaped the surrounding sandstone rock at Canyonlands National Park, USA, to form the spectacular Horseshoe Bend.

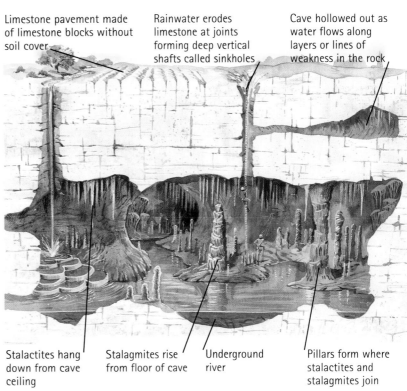

Limestone pavement made of limestone blocks without soil cover

Rainwater erodes limestone at joints forming deep vertical shafts called sinkholes

Cave hollowed out as water flows along layers or lines of weakness in the rock

Stalactites hang down from cave ceiling

Stalagmites rise from floor of cave

Underground river

Pillars form where stalactites and stalagmites join

sideways by the waves in an action called longshore drift. Breaks in the coastline cause this to push beach material out into the sea to form long, thin ridges called spits.

UNDERGROUND WATER
Water can pass through certain types of rock. Porous rocks, such as sandstone, have tiny spaces between their grains allowing

water to seep in. Permeable rocks, such as limestone, have gaps and fractures which water can travel through. Many cave systems are formed through the action of rainwater. As rain falls, it dissolves carbon dioxide from the atmosphere and becomes weakly acidic. Some rocks, especially limestone, can be dissolved by rainwater which gradually widens cracks and joints in the rock. Deep vertical tunnels called sinkholes are sometimes created and large caves are formed by the hollowing out of the underground rock.

▲ Acidic rainwater reacts with limestone dissolving the rock to landscape features underground. Stalactites and stalagmites are formed from minerals deposited by the water.

▼ Located on the border between Argentina and Brazil, the Iguaçu Falls are a spectacular series of waterfalls stretching over 4 km in width. Small, rocky and wooded islands divide the falls into 275 separate waterfalls.

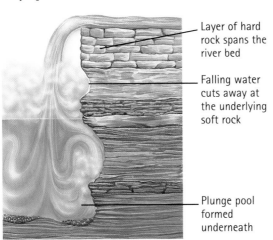

Layer of hard rock spans the river bed

Falling water cuts away at the underlying soft rock

Plunge pool formed underneath

▲ Waterfalls form when water erodes softer layers of rock downstream creating a sharp ledge. Over time, the the harder rock is eroded as well, creating a gorge.

LANDSCAPING BY ICE

Glaciers are giant rivers of ice which have the power to carve out large land features, form lakes and move soil and rocks hundreds of kilometres.

Ice covers a little more than 10 per cent of the Earth's land. During periods in the past, this figure was much higher. Long periods of colder, global climates, known as Ice Ages, have occurred a number of times in Earth's history. Scientists believe that the last Ice Age began around 3.5 million years ago. Glacial periods have occurred between 15 and 22 times in the last two million years. During the last Ice Age, ice sheets covered large parts of the northern hemisphere. Ice has receded from many of these areas and its effects on the landscape can be seen clearly. Ice wears down the surrounding rocks as it moves in large masses. The material deposited by ice has formed many lowland areas around the world.

▲ The white area shows the extent of the ice sheets which covered parts of the Northern Hemisphere during the last Ice Age. In places the thickness of the ice reached 3,000 m.

GLACIER FORMATION

Glaciers are large masses of ice that move slowly. There are around 100,000 glaciers found on all continents except Australasia. Glaciers form over time frequently in mountain valleys which receive heavy, repeated snowfall. Fresh snow is squashed together under pressure from successive layers to form a solid mass called firn. As more snow lands on top of the firn, air is pushed out, driving snow particles closer together. The grains melt and re-freeze, filling all remaining gaps until they form glacier ice. Once the depth of the

▼ Lowland areas which emerge from glaciers often contain a number of distinctive features formed through the action of the ice and the moraine it carried and deposited.

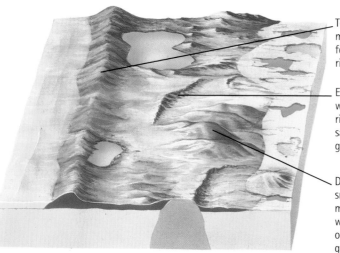

Terminal moraine forms large ridge

Eskers are winding ridges of sand and gravel

Drumlins are smooth mounds which often occur in groups

Meltwater

Terminal moraine

glacial ice reaches around 30 m, gravity forces the ice mass to begin to creep slowly down the valley.

MOVEMENT AND POWER

Glaciers advance slowly, usually at a rate of between one centimetre and one metre per day. At the base of the glacier, where the ice comes into contact with bedrock, the huge pressures generate heat which melts ice to form a layer of meltwater. This helps the glacier slide over the rock. Glaciers move with enormous force and erode the landscape below and to the sides. Water which refreezes in the rock underneath the glacier breaks pieces of rock loose which freeze into the bottom of

◀ The Moreno glacier, found in Argentina's Parque Nacional Los Glaciares, is one of the few major glaciers which is still advancing. The glacier's front face, approximately 5 km wide and up to 45 m high, moves forwards at a rate of around 30 cm per day.

▶ Snow falls feed the top of the glacier. At the lower, front end, the glacier melts forming cold meltwaters. As long as more snow continues to accumulate at the top than melts away at the bottom, the glacier will continue to advance.

Bowl-shaped hollow is called a cirque

Movement of glacier

Crevasses are cracks in the glacier which form when it moves around corners or over bumps

Lateral moraine

The front face of a glacier is commonly known as its snout

eroded so deeply that the mouths of smaller, tributary valleys are left high above the new valley floor. These are called hanging valleys and water can be seen cascading over them into the main valley as waterfalls. In lowland areas, much of the vast amount of moraine carried by glaciers is deposited as glacial drift. This consists of boulders, gravel, sand and clays and has shaped the Earth's surface greatly.

▼ Fjords are glaciated valleys that have been partly flooded by the sea. Geiranger Fjord in Norway is a 16-km long, U-shaped valley created by eroding actions of glaciation.

the glacier. These rocks scour and grind the land surface. Rock debris in glaciers is called moraine and can occur in the middle, at the front or to the sides of the glacier. As the glacier flows down the valley, it reaches a location where the temperature rises and it is no longer replenished by snowfall.

AFTER THE ICE
The landscape left behind after a glacier has retreated or disappeared is often altered. In highland areas, armchair-shaped hollows called cirques, jagged pyramidal peaks and sharp ridges between two glaciers, called arêtes, are often formed by the action of glaciers. Valleys where glaciers have flowed are eroded into a U-shape. In many instances, the valley is

LANDSCAPING BY WIND

Wind can have the power to alter landscapes by wearing away rock formations and by transporting sand and other particles.

▲ Wind erosion has bored through soft central rock to create an arch in Delicate Arch, Utah, USA.

The wind's ability to shape the land is particularly powerful in dry, desert regions where there are few plants and very little water to bind particles together. Finer, lighter particles are carried by winds and wear away rock formations to help form a range of landscape features. These include mesas, broad, flat-topped hills with steep sides, buttes which are smaller versions of mesas, pedestal rocks and archways. Winds can blow sands and other loose particles away from an area leaving the rocky pavement called hamada exposed. Wind forces sand grains to move via a series of short hops. As the grains land, they hit other grains, either

▲ These spectacular rock formations in Monument Valley, Utah, USA, are buttes formed by wind erosion.

bouncing off into the air themselves or forcing other grains to do likewise. This process is called saltation. Sand dunes form on lake shores, in deserts and sea shores. Different types of sand dune occur based on the wind direction, obstructions in the way and the sand supply. Where winds blow from one constant direction, large, crescent-shaped dunes called barchans often form. Star-shaped dunes occur where winds come from all directions.

Wind direction

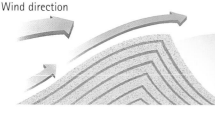

▲ Winds blow over the top, or crest, of the dune creating a steeper slope on its far side. When winds blow constantly, sand dunes tend to move in the same direction as the wind. A dune may travel as much as 30 m in one year.

▶ The Namib Desert stretches approximately 2,000 km through South Africa, Namibia and southern Angola. With virtually no rainfall or vegetation, vast seas of moving sand dunes have been formed and shaped by the winds.

SOIL

Soil covers much of the Earth's land surface and is vital for life. It provides the food and conditions which plants need to be able to grow.

Soil consists of particles of rocks and minerals, gases, water and humus – dead and decaying plant and animal matter. Soil is formed through many different processes of weathering and erosion which break up underlying bedrock into fragments of rock called regolith and, over time, into smaller particles. These are mixed with the decaying humus and bound together by moisture and by the roots of plants which extend down into the soil. Chemical reactions release many of the minerals in the rock particles which enrich the soil with nutrients vital for plant growth. These include calcium, potassium and magnesium. Bacteria, fungi and other small organisms help decompose, or break down the dead plant and animal matter on the ground surface or in the soil. This forms the nutrient-rich humus on which much plant growth depends.

Soils vary in type from place to place due to the climate, vegetation, the local rock types and other environmental factors. Soil is considered a renewable resource but it can easily be stripped of its nutrients. Most soils tend to be naturally fertile, but can be poisoned through pollution or exhausted through extensive farming which uses the soil's nutrients at a faster rate than can be replaced. Stripping land of its vegetation (see page 40) can result in rich layers of topsoil being washed or blown away, leaving the land infertile.

▲ Air and water in the soil are taken in by a plant's roots. Nearly half the volume of good agricultural soil, such as this ploughed field in Texas, USA, can consist of air and water.

Sandy

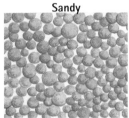

Clay

Loamy

▲ Sandy soils are rough, grainy, hold much air and allow water to drain rapidly. Clay soils consist of smaller particles which hold less air but retain much water. Loamy soils are a mixture of large and small particles which offer good growing conditions.

Larger soil creatures such as moles aid the movement of water and air through the soil as they burrow down, taking humus to deeper levels

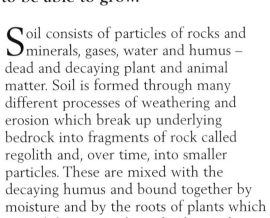

A well-developed soil will be full of millions of insects and billions of bacteria and micro-organisms

Earthworms are particularly efficient soil workers. They are able to pass both soil and organic matter through their guts, helping to break down humus and aerate the soil

▲ Soils are divided into a number of layers called horizons. The topsoil consists of the horizons nearest the surface and is most rich in humus. Below this comes the subsoil and, underneath the subsoil, the bedrock. Soil is home to millions of creatures which help the soil break down and release its minerals and contribute to the layers of humus when they die.

THE ATMOSPHERE

The Earth's atmosphere protects its surface from the extremes of space and is the cause of the planet's weather systems.

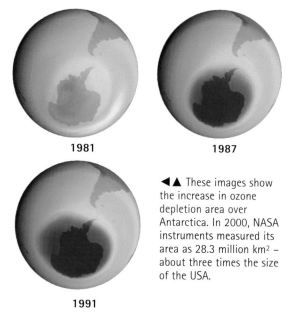

1981   **1987**

1991

◄▲ These images show the increase in ozone depletion area over Antarctica. In 2000, NASA instruments measured its area as 28.3 million km² – about three times the size of the USA.

Nitrogen 78%

Oxygen 21%

Argon and other gases 1%

▲ Air is a mixture of different gases including nitrogen (N) 78%, oxygen (O) 21%, argon (Ar) under 1% and water vapour which can vary from 0% to 7%. There are also trace amounts of hydrogen, methane, neon, carbon monoxide, helium, ozone, krypton and xenon.

▼ Viewed from space, Earth's atmosphere appears as a wispy, fragile arrangement of cloud masses. Yet the atmosphere protects life on Earth from many external hazards including the solar wind, the intense cold of space and ultraviolet and other harmful forms of radiation.

The Earth's atmosphere has evolved over millions of years. Volcanic eruptions helped form the earliest atmosphere which scientists believe produced much water vapour, nitrogen and carbon dioxide but little or no oxygen. As the atmosphere cooled, much of the water vapour condensed and fell to Earth to form the world's oceans. Oxygen only became an important part of the atmosphere once plant life was established. Plants are capable of capturing and converting light energy into stored energy in a complex process called photosynthesis. Oxygen is released into the atmosphere as a result of photosynthesis. The air contained in the atmosphere today provides creatures with oxygen to breathe and carbon dioxide which helps trap the Sun's energy to warm the planet. The atmosphere also recycles water and protects the planet from harmful radiation.

LAYERS OF ATMOSPHERE

The atmosphere can be divided into five different layers: the troposphere, stratosphere, mesosphere, thermosphere and exosphere. These layers merge into one another and vary according to the time of year, so only approximate measurements of their size can be given. The troposphere is the atmospheric layer closest to the ground. It extends between eight and 14.5 km up from the Earth's surface and is the most dense part of the atmosphere. Air circulates through this layer and almost all weather is generated within it. Temperatures in the troposphere vary from around 17°C to -52°C. The troposphere's temperature is at its highest near the ground where the air is heated by the Earth's surface. Climbing through this

layer, the air becomes thinner and less capable of holding onto heat. As a result, temperatures decrease on average at a rate of 5.5°C every 1,000 m. The stratosphere is drier and less dense than the troposphere and ends around 50 km above the Earth's surface. Together, the stratosphere and troposphere contain 99 per cent of the atmosphere's air. Extending from a height of around 85 km is the mesosphere, an atmospheric layer that is capable of reflecting radio waves. The thermosphere is also known as the upper atmosphere, and temperatures rise the higher one climbs through this layer, exceeding 1,700°C. Beyond the thermosphere is a boundary layer called the exosphere which extends and merges into space. The exosphere contains very little matter, just a small amount of hydrogen and helium.

OZONE LAYER

Ozone is found in the stratosphere, concentrated in a layer 20–30 km above the Earth. Ozone performs a vital function, absorbing and scattering much of the ultraviolet radiation which is produced by the Sun. This radiation is harmful to living things causing skin cancers and damaging plankton which form the base of the marine life food chain. A heavily

depleted area of the ozone layer over Antarctica was discovered in the late 1970s by the British Antarctic Survey. The main cause is believed to be the release of chlorofluorocarbon gases (CFCs) into the atmosphere. These gases are used as refrigerants, as solvents in the electronics industry and in aerosol cans. When CFCs enter the atmosphere, they react with the ultraviolet radiation which causes the chlorine in CFCs to destroy ozone molecules, converting them into oxygen. One molecule of chlorine can destroy up to 100,000 ozone molecules. International moves to ban the use of CFCs have occurred. However, any improvements take time as CFCs can last in the atmosphere for 50 to 100 years, and take five to ten years to reach the upper atmosphere where they are broken down.

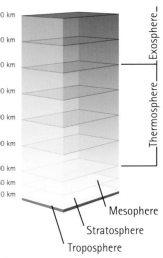

▲ The layers of the atmosphere flow into each other in transition zones called pauses. The tropopause, for example, is the zone between the troposphere and the stratosphere.

► The layers of the atmosphere rise upwards from the Earth's surface, held in place by the force of gravity. Within the different layers, a variety of different atmospheric features or phenomena can be witnessed.

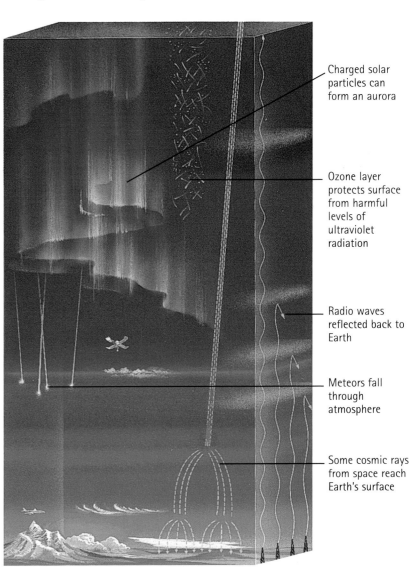

Charged solar particles can form an aurora

Ozone layer protects surface from harmful levels of ultraviolet radiation

Radio waves reflected back to Earth

Meteors fall through atmosphere

Some cosmic rays from space reach Earth's surface

CLIMATE

Climate is the general weather conditions which an environment experiences over a long period of time. Climates vary around the world.

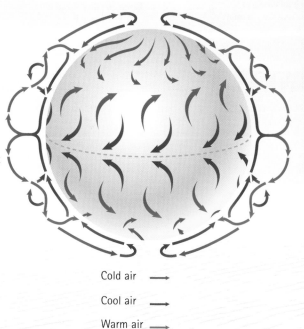

Cold air ———→

Cool air ———→

Warm air ———→

▲ Warm air rises at the Equator where sunlight is strongest and moves away from the Equator towards the poles drawing cool air behind it. Cold air near the poles heads in the opposite direction, from cold areas to warmer ones.

The Sun provides the Earth with the energy to support life while its heat drives the planet's weather systems. How the Sun's rays strike the Earth's surface help determine the temperature of an area which, in turn, affects its climate and weather patterns. The Earth's curved surface means that different parts of the planet receive differing amounts of the Sun's rays. Around the centre of the Earth, at the Equator, temperatures remain high and vary relatively little. This is because the Sun's rays strike almost directly all year and the Earth's tilt (see page 4) has little effect there. The further from the Equator, the greater the angle with which the Sun's rays strike the surface. This means that they have to travel through more of the Earth's heat-absorbing atmosphere and that their energy has to be spread over a wider surface area, lessening their warming effect. This is why the polar regions are also the coldest places on Earth.

Sun's rays

▲ The Sun's rays reach the Earth's surface at their most concentrated around the Equator. North and south from the Equator, they strike at a greater angle and their warming power decreases.

▼ The water cycle is heat-driven by energy from the Sun. Water evaporates from lakes, rivers and seas into the atmosphere. Plants also let water out into the atmosphere from their leaves. Warm, moist air cools as it rises over high land or meets cooler air. When the cooled air can no longer support all the water it holds as vapour, rain forms and falls to Earth. Water returns to vegetation and to lakes, rivers and seas, so completing the cycle.

CIRCULATING AIR

Three circles of winds, called circulation cells, blow around each hemisphere of the globe. The cold air in these winds sinks and spreads out until it reaches warmer regions where the air warms up, rises and flows back towards the poles. The Earth's constant spinning on its axis tends to bend or push winds to one side, a phenomenon known as the Coriolis effect. In the northern hemisphere, winds are pushed to the right of their intended direction. In the southern hemisphere, the winds are pushed to the left. As air moves, it creates differences in air pressure. When warm air rises, it leaves behind an area of lower air pressure. This is because the upward-moving air is not pressing down so hard on the Earth's surface. High air pressure areas are formed by air sinking and pressing down with greater force. High air pressure areas tend to bring hot, dry weather in summer and cold, dry weather in winter. Low pressure areas tend to bring clouds, rain or snow.

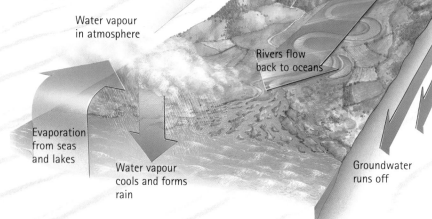

Rain and snow

Water vapour condenses and forms clouds

Transpiration from plants

Water vapour in atmosphere

Rivers flow back to oceans

Evaporation from seas and lakes

Water vapour cools and forms rain

Groundwater runs off

WATER'S INFLUENCE

The Earth's climate is affected by the oceans and their ability to absorb large quantities of the Sun's heat. The top 2 m of the ocean stores more heat than the whole of the atmosphere. Ocean currents carry much of this heat around the world and towards the poles, warming land masses and also the lower atmosphere above the ocean. One major ocean current, the Gulf Stream, carries warmth towards Northern Europe, helping to give that region a mild climate. Areas far inland from oceans tend to have more extreme temperature differences between their winters and summers. The amount of water present on the Earth's surface in its oceans, seas, lakes and rivers and in its atmosphere does not alter. Water, however, does change its state and its location in an endless sequence called the water cycle. Water is taken up into the atmosphere through evaporation and through the action of plants transpiring. Clouds form when warm air containing water vapour rises, cools and the vapour condenses to form millions of minute water droplets. Rain forms when these droplets collide with each other and form larger droplets too heavy for the clouds to support them.

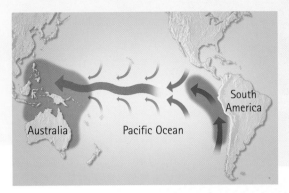

◀ Ocean currents affect the climates of regions and, occasionally, major currents can alter, leading to a large impact on climate. In the Pacific Ocean, surface ocean currents normally transport warmer water (shown in purple) westwards from South America towards Australia.

▶ El Niño is the name given to the occasional reversal in the currents of the Pacific Ocean. During El Niño, the warm current flows eastwards, causing floods in the Americas and reducing rainfall in southeast Asia, leading to droughts.

CLIMATE CHANGE

Although climate is the long term measure of weather conditions in an area, it is subject to change. Alternating long periods of hot and cold weather have occurred in the Earth's distant past many millions of years ago. More recently, in the 17th century, a cooler period occurred known as the Little Ice Age. It is believed to have been linked to a lack of dark patches on the Sun's surface called sun spots. Climate change is being closely monitored today as a result of concerns about global warming (see pages 40–41).

▼ The ground temperature of an area can be affected by how much its surface reflects or absorbs the Sun's energy, known as its albedo. Snow and ice in the Antarctic has a high albedo, meaning that most energy is reflected and little is absorbed.

▼ Waipoua forest, found in the Northland region of New Zealand, has a subtropical climate with warm temperatures and relatively high rainfall. These climatic conditions allow lush vegetation to flourish, including giant kauri trees standing between 35 and 40 m tall.

WORLD CLIMATE ZONES

Climates vary greatly around the world and influence what life exists in a region. A number of factors influence the climate of a location on Earth including altitude and its distance from seas and oceans. Climate zones are a way of mapping the world's climates.

A major factor in determining climate is a region's distance from the Equator. For example, while the regions nearest the Equator have a warm and wet tropical climate, the regions farthest from the Equator experience an intensely cold and dry polar climate. The temperate climate zone lies approximately halfway between the Equator and the poles. This climate zone features mild temperatures and moderate rainfall.

▲ Continental climate zones, such as central northern USA, tend to occur inland, long distances away from oceans. Their moderating effects on climate are negligible so continental climates tend to have large differences between summer and winter temperatures. These climate zones are also dry as the moisture carried by air from the oceans is lost as rainfall earlier in its journey.

▲ The Amazon rainforest is typical of tropical climates which are found close to the Equator. Heavy and prolonged rainfall and average temperatures above 25°C help produce lush plant growth which, in turn, provides food and habitats for a vast range of creatures.

Arctic Circle

NORTH AMERICA

Cheyenne
Pike's Peak

Tropic of Cancer

Equator

Manaus
SOUTH AMERICA

Tropic of Capricorn

Antarctic Circle

A   N

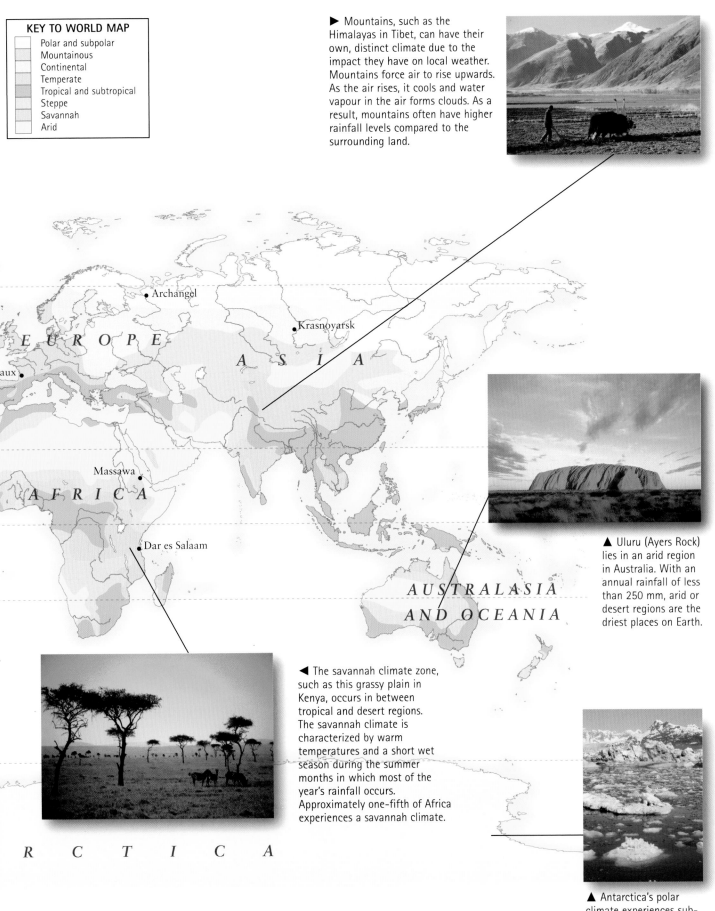

KEY TO WORLD MAP

- Polar and subpolar
- Mountainous
- Continental
- Temperate
- Tropical and subtropical
- Steppe
- Savannah
- Arid

▶ Mountains, such as the Himalayas in Tibet, can have their own, distinct climate due to the impact they have on local weather. Mountains force air to rise upwards. As the air rises, it cools and water vapour in the air forms clouds. As a result, mountains often have higher rainfall levels compared to the surrounding land.

▲ Uluru (Ayers Rock) lies in an arid region in Australia. With an annual rainfall of less than 250 mm, arid or desert regions are the driest places on Earth.

◀ The savannah climate zone, such as this grassy plain in Kenya, occurs in between tropical and desert regions. The savannah climate is characterized by warm temperatures and a short wet season during the summer months in which most of the year's rainfall occurs. Approximately one-fifth of Africa experiences a savannah climate.

▲ Antarctica's polar climate experiences sub-zero temperatures for most of the year.

EUROPE

ASIA

AFRICA

AUSTRALASIA AND OCEANIA

Archangel

Krasnoyarsk

eaux

Massawa

Dar es Salaam

R C T I C A

WEATHER

Weather is the name for the combination of conditions in the Earth's atmosphere and how these frequently change and behave.

▲ Sea mist shrouds the US city of San Francisco. Mist is a type of cloud close to the surface of Earth formed by the cooling of a moist air layer from the land or water below.

Three factors, the amount of water in the air, air temperature and air movement, are largely responsible for forming the many different types of weather. In some parts of the world, weather can vary little over a period of many days or weeks. In other regions, weather changes frequently.

PRECIPITATION AND STORMS

Water that falls on to the Earth's surface from clouds is called precipitation. Rain is the most common form, but there are others such as snow and sleet. Snowflakes form when water droplets freeze into ice crystals in clouds. If the freezing level is less than 300 m above ground level, the flakes do not have time to melt before reaching the ground and fall as snow. If the freezing level is much higher, the flakes tend to melt and fall as rain. Sleet is a mixture of snow and rain. It occurs when rain encounters a layer of very cold air close to the ground and some, but not all, the rain freezes. Thunderstorms occur in hot damp weather where water droplets rise quickly, hit colder air above and form tall, heaped

▲ Lightning is a massive discharge of electricity from one rain cloud to another or from the cloud to the Earth. This lightning storm was photographed in France. Electrically charged water particles occur in storm clouds with positive and negative charges. When they attempt to discharge or move to equalize their charges, they heat up the air to temperatures as high as 33,000°C which can generate lightning flashes and thunder.

▶ Clouds are classified by their appearance and their height above the Earth's surface. Medium-level clouds have their bases between 2,000 and 7,000 m. Below 2,000 m are low-level clouds while high-level cloud formations can extend up to an altitude of 14,000 m.

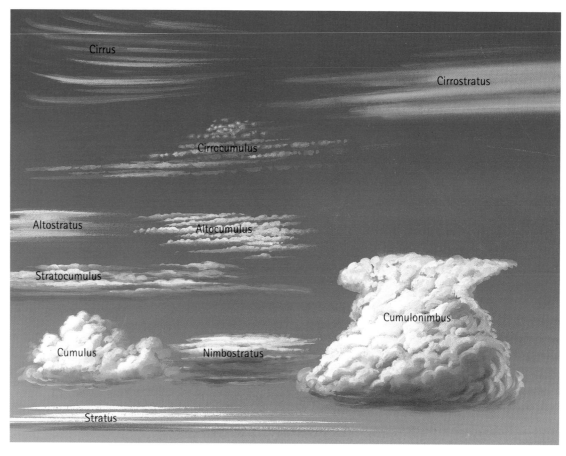

Cirrus

Cirrostratus

Cirrocumulus

Altostratus

Altocumulus

Stratocumulus

Cumulonimbus

Cumulus

Nimbostratus

Stratus

cumulonimbus clouds. A build-up of electrically charged particles in these clouds can generate lightning flashes and thunder. Tornadoes tend to form during violent thunderstorms when hot, fast-moving upward air currents meet a cold, downward air current. The hot and cold currents spiral round each other forming a tight funnel of clouds in which wind speeds can reach 480 km/h.

Powerful storms occur over the seas and oceans of equatorial regions. In the Atlantic and Caribbean they are known as hurricanes, in the Pacific as typhoons and elsewhere as cyclones. They involve the formation of an intense low pressure core which sucks in warm, moist air moving fast in spirals. As the air rises, the water vapour condenses and falls as torrential rain. A large amount of heat is emitted which makes the air rise even faster and increases the speed of the air moving in and around the storm. Reaching wind speeds of at least 199 km/h, they move relatively slowly allowing them to be tracked and warnings given to areas at risk.

◄ Tornadoes are narrow funnels of fast-moving air usually less than 300 m in width at ground level. They are hard to forecast as they are small, appear quickly and are usually short-lived.

MEASURING WEATHER

Weather details are measured and recorded using many instruments including barographs, which measure changes in air pressure, and anemometers which measure wind speed. Satellite imaging is used to track weather systems, radar helps detect cloud patterns and movements and computers assist in the analysis of weather patterns. Weather maps plot the movement of areas of high and low pressure and chart fronts where cold and warm air meets. Forecasting the weather can be difficult as the weather in one location can later influence weather in another area.

▲ Rainbows form when sunlight strikes water falling through the air at a certain angle, causing the colours of the visible light spectrum to be displayed.

◄ Hurricane Fran photographed by a weather satellite off the coast of the southeastern United States near Florida in 1996. Hurricanes are marked by huge cumulonimbus clouds which rapidly circle the hurricane's centre. Warm, moist air rises in a hurricane in a fast-turning spiral. Dry air sinks through the centre of the hurricane, known as the eye, where the weather is calm and the sky clear.

HUMAN IMPACT

Human beings have been on Earth only for a small fraction of its 4.6 billion year history. Yet they have transformed large parts of the planet.

▲ To generate electricity from falling water, hydro-electric power schemes often involve large dams built across rivers. The 221 m high, 379 m long Hoover Dam on America's Colorado river creates an artificial lake measuring 593 km² called Lake Mead.

CO₂ POLLUTION

Transport 70.6%

Others (waste disposal, chemical spray etc.) 12.3%

Fuel burning 10.3%

Industry 6.8%

▲ Carbon dioxide (CO_2) is emitted into the Earth's atmosphere by humans in a variety of ways.

▼ One of the largest and most crowded urban areas in the world, Mexico City is also one of the most polluted. Industry and over three and a half million vehicles generate serious air pollution.

The human race started life as hunter-gatherers roaming the land for food. Over time, people learned how to rear animals and grow crops. As people started to settle in one place they began to have a great impact on the geography and vegetation of their local area. Human beings are unique among Earth's creatures in being able to alter many aspects of their environment. Early changes were mainly concerned with making land suitable for growing crops such as clearing plots of trees, rocks and other obstructions and diverting water from nearby rivers, streams and lakes to irrigate crop fields.

EXPLOITING EARTH'S RESOURCES

As industries developed, the need for raw materials and fuels saw the start of people exploiting the Earth's resources. These include minerals, ores and fossil fuels such as coal. Large mines and pits have gouged the surface of the Earth as people have sought out building materials, precious metals and metal ores. Coal mines, oil wells and natural gas fields have exploited large quantities of the Earth's fossil fuel reserves. Most electricity is still generated by burning fossil fuels such as coal or oil in power stations. Plastics and many other artificial materials use petroleum products as a raw material. Oil, coal and metal ores are all known as non-renewable resources, and cannot be replaced at the rate at which humans are using them.

INCREASING POPULATION

The human population has boomed over the past two centuries; rising from between 700 and 800 million in 1800 to 6.2 billion in 2002. With this massive increase has come major changes in how

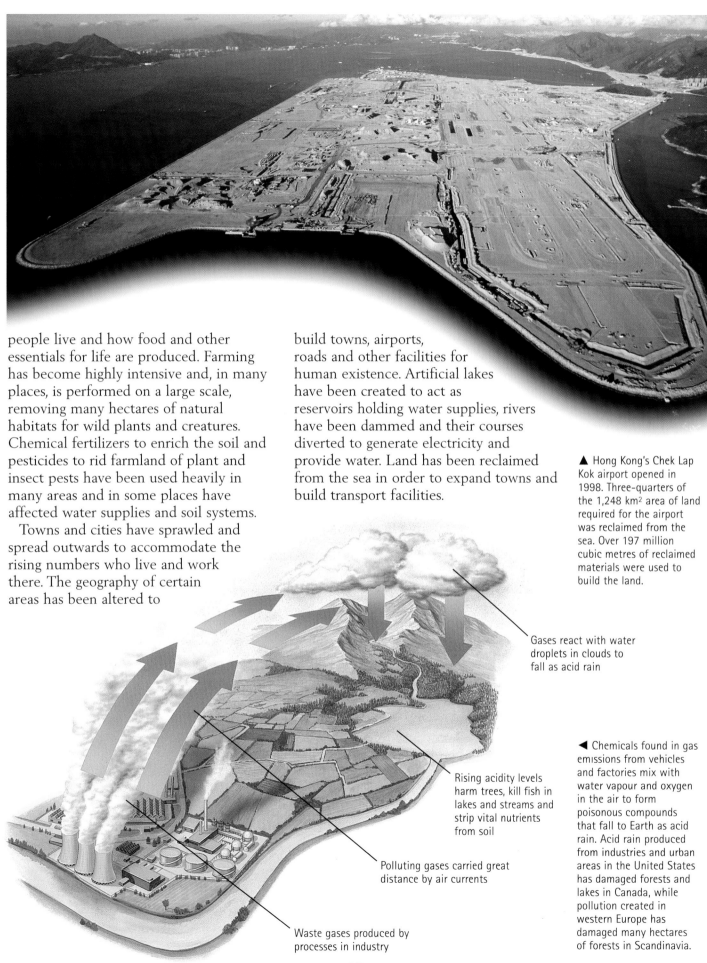

people live and how food and other essentials for life are produced. Farming has become highly intensive and, in many places, is performed on a large scale, removing many hectares of natural habitats for wild plants and creatures. Chemical fertilizers to enrich the soil and pesticides to rid farmland of plant and insect pests have been used heavily in many areas and in some places have affected water supplies and soil systems.

Towns and cities have sprawled and spread outwards to accommodate the rising numbers who live and work there. The geography of certain areas has been altered to build towns, airports, roads and other facilities for human existence. Artificial lakes have been created to act as reservoirs holding water supplies, rivers have been dammed and their courses diverted to generate electricity and provide water. Land has been reclaimed from the sea in order to expand towns and build transport facilities.

▲ Hong Kong's Chek Lap Kok airport opened in 1998. Three-quarters of the 1,248 km² area of land required for the airport was reclaimed from the sea. Over 197 million cubic metres of reclaimed materials were used to build the land.

Gases react with water droplets in clouds to fall as acid rain

Rising acidity levels harm trees, kill fish in lakes and streams and strip vital nutrients from soil

Polluting gases carried great distance by air currents

Waste gases produced by processes in industry

◄ Chemicals found in gas emissions from vehicles and factories mix with water vapour and oxygen in the air to form poisonous compounds that fall to Earth as acid rain. Acid rain produced from industries and urban areas in the United States has damaged forests and lakes in Canada, while pollution created in western Europe has damaged many hectares of forests in Scandinavia.

WORLD POPULATION GROWTH

The total human population of Earth passed six billion in the year 2000. This population is distributed unevenly throughout countries and regions of the world. Countries of similar land areas can contain greatly differing populations.

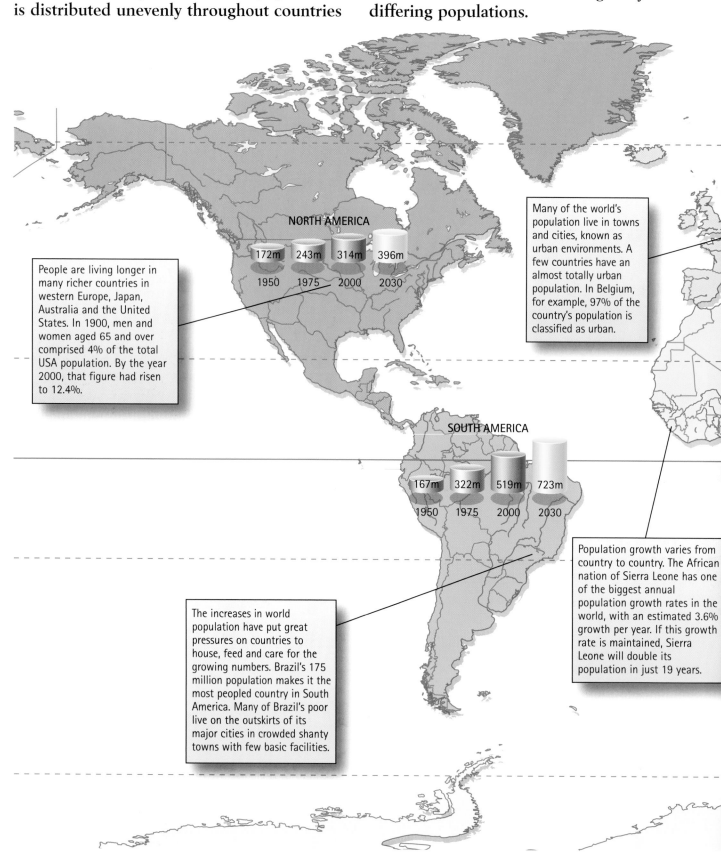

Many of the world's population live in towns and cities, known as urban environments. A few countries have an almost totally urban population. In Belgium, for example, 97% of the country's population is classified as urban.

People are living longer in many richer countries in western Europe, Japan, Australia and the United States. In 1900, men and women aged 65 and over comprised 4% of the total USA population. By the year 2000, that figure had risen to 12.4%.

NORTH AMERICA

172m — 1950
243m — 1975
314m — 2000
396m — 2030

SOUTH AMERICA

167m — 1950
322m — 1975
519m — 2000
723m — 2030

Population growth varies from country to country. The African nation of Sierra Leone has one of the biggest annual population growth rates in the world, with an estimated 3.6% growth per year. If this growth rate is maintained, Sierra Leone will double its population in just 19 years.

The increases in world population have put great pressures on countries to house, feed and care for the growing numbers. Brazil's 175 million population makes it the most peopled country in South America. Many of Brazil's poor live on the outskirts of its major cities in crowded shanty towns with few basic facilities.

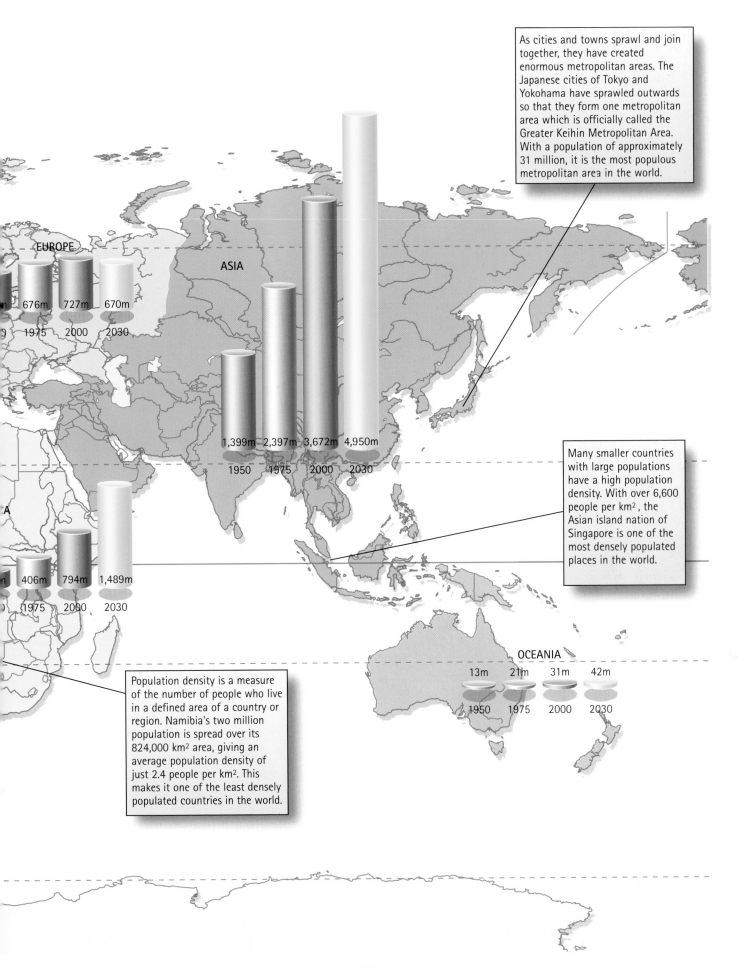

As cities and towns sprawl and join together, they have created enormous metropolitan areas. The Japanese cities of Tokyo and Yokohama have sprawled outwards so that they form one metropolitan area which is officially called the Greater Keihin Metropolitan Area. With a population of approximately 31 million, it is the most populous metropolitan area in the world.

EUROPE

676m 727m 670m

1975 2000 2030

ASIA

1,399m 2,397m 3,672m 4,950m

1950 1975 2000 2030

406m 794m 1,489m

1975 2000 2030

Many smaller countries with large populations have a high population density. With over 6,600 people per km², the Asian island nation of Singapore is one of the most densely populated places in the world.

OCEANIA

13m 21m 31m 42m

1950 1975 2000 2030

Population density is a measure of the number of people who live in a defined area of a country or region. Namibia's two million population is spread over its 824,000 km² area, giving an average population density of just 2.4 people per km². This makes it one of the least densely populated countries in the world.

THE FUTURE

The Earth in the early part of the 21st century continues to evolve and change. In some cases, changes are occurring due to human activity.

▲ Flood-prone countries such as Bangladesh are likely to be even more at risk if global temperatures continue to rise.

▼ When sunlight enters the atmosphere and strikes the surface, some of the Sun's energy is reflected back in the form of infrared radiation. Greenhouse gases tend to absorb this, trapping heat in the atmosphere.

Planet Earth is always changing. Mountains continue to rise, continents are still on the move, while wind, water and ice erode and shape rock formations. The climate also continues to change. At the current time, the Earth is warming up faster than in any period in recorded history. Many experts believe that global warming could see an average temperature increase of 2°C by 2060. Such an increase could result in great changes in weather patterns and local climates, increasing the extent of desert-like areas, harming land and sea ecosystems and turning some farmlands into wildernesses. A rise in sea levels due to the melting of parts of the polar ice caps and the thermal expansion of water may see coastal and low-lying areas of land reclaimed by the sea.

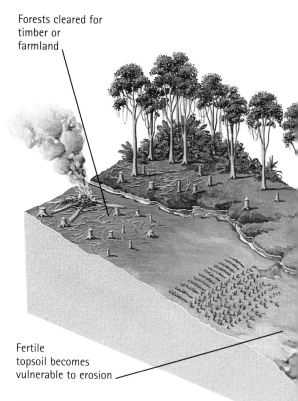

Forests cleared for timber or farmland

Fertile topsoil becomes vulnerable to erosion

▲ Desertification can occur in warm, dry regions removed of their plant cover. Without plant roots to bind the soil, the rainwater runs off the land quickly, soils bake hard and crack and become infertile desert-like areas.

ENHANCED GREENHOUSE EFFECT

Scientists believe that part of the change in climate is down to the enhanced greenhouse effect. Greenhouse gases, such as carbon dioxide, methane and nitrous oxide, are naturally present in the Earth's atmosphere. They perform a vital role, helping to trap some of the Sun's energy as heat and warming the planet's surface. The enhanced greenhouse effect sees more heat trapped as the result of an increase in the concentrations of greenhouse gases in the atmosphere. These have risen by as much as 25 per cent in the past 150 years. Deforestation and the burning of large quantities of fossil fuels, such as oil, in industry and by motor vehicles are believed to be the major causes.

DEFORESTATION

Forests are often described as the 'lungs of the planet' as they take in carbon dioxide from the air and generate much of the

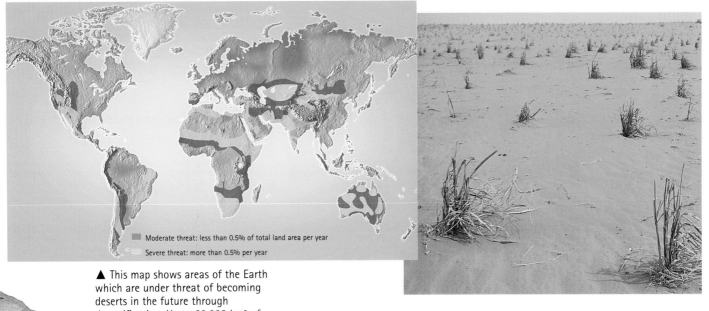

Moderate threat: less than 0.5% of total land area per year

Severe threat: more than 0.5% per year

▲ This map shows areas of the Earth which are under threat of becoming deserts in the future through desertification. Up to 60,000 km² of new desert are created every year.

▲ Desertification has seen deserts creep further into the northern part of the African nation of Sudan, removing farmland that was previously used for growing crops.

Land becomes dry, cracked and infertile

DESERTIFICATION

As the world climate has become hotter and drier, desertification, or the expansion of desert environments, has increased. Human activities such as deforestation and over-grazing livestock play a major part as well, resulting in ground losing its vegetation cover. The roots of trees and other plants bind soil together enabling water to be absorbed and further plant life to grow. As land is cleared of its vegetation, the topsoil is exposed to the elements and can be washed or blown away, clogging rivers with sediment. When topsoil is blown or washed away, water is no longer retained in the remaining soil, so that springs and wells dry up and fertile land becomes arid and desert-like.

▼ Non-polluting energy producing methods which use renewable resources, such as these Californian wind turbines, are to counter further pollution of the Earth's atmosphere.

oxygen in the Earth's atmosphere. Trees and vegetation also recycle water through the process of transpiration which releases water from the plants' leaves back into the atmosphere. Deforestation occurs when major tracts of forests are destroyed, either cut down for their wood or cleared to create more land for farming, to exploit mineral resources or to build new settlements. In the past 40 years, 45 per cent of the world's forests have disappeared, reducing the Earth's ability to convert carbon dioxide into oxygen, leaving more carbon dioxide in the atmosphere. Deforestation also removes vital habitats for living things. For example, the clearing of large areas of forest in Asia has reduced both the territory and the prey for tigers. An estimated 100,000 wild tigers were in existence at the start of the 20th century. Today that figure is fewer than 8,000.

MAP MAKING

Maps are graphical representations of the Earth which help record and communicate information about the world and help people to find their way.

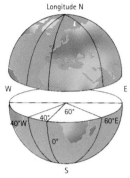

▲ Lines of longitude run from pole to pole over the Earth's surface. They are measured in degrees, east or west of 0° longitude.

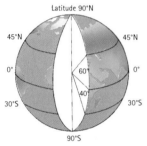

▲ Lines of latitude run around the Earth and are measured in degrees north or south from 0° latitude, also known as the Equator.

Since ancient times, people have been constructing maps. As people travelled greater distances and explored Earth more thoroughly, maps have become more accurate and detailed representations of the Earth. Maps are drawn to a scale which is often expressed as the ratio between the size of the map and the size of the area it represents. For example, a 1:100,000 scale map would portray a kilometre of the Earth as a centimetre on the map. Maps of the world may use a smaller scale with a centimetre equalling 100 km (1:10,000,000); town plans may use a far larger scale with 1 cm depicting 50 m (1:5,000).

LATITUDE AND LONGITUDE

To provide an accurate method of both map making and navigation, the Earth is criss-crossed with a grid of imaginary lines called latitude and longitude. Lines of latitude run around the Earth and lie parallel to the Equator. Lines of longitude run from pole to pole and are sometimes called meridians. The lines of latitude are

▲ Using a map and a magnetic compass, people are able to navigate their way around the Earth's surface.

measured in degrees north or south of the Equator. The North Pole has a latitude of 90° north, London is 51.5° north while Rio de Janeiro is 23° south. The lines of longitude are measured in degrees east or west of an imaginary line which runs from pole to pole and passes through Greenwich in London, known as the prime meridian. The Australian city of Sydney has a longitude of 151° east while Los Angeles is 118° west. Every place on Earth can be found by combining their longitude and latitude points.

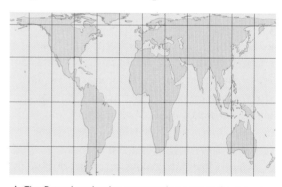

▲ The Peters' projection accurately portrays the extent of land area on maps but as a result, the shape of land masses is distorted.

▲ By combining their latitude and longitude locations, everywhere on the Earth's surface can be pinpointed on a map. For example, the Brazilian city of Rio de Janeiro lies at latitude 22°54'S and longitude 43°14'W.

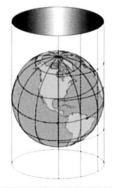

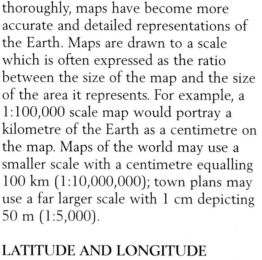

◄▼ Devised by the Flemish cartographer, Gerardus Mercator (1512–1594), the Mercator projection was one of the first widely used and relatively accurate map projections. However, it distorts the land area nearer the poles making those regions appear much larger than they actually are.

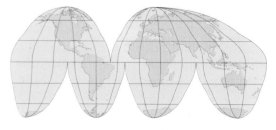

▲ The Homolosine map projects the Earth in irregular joined sections. It distorts land masses less than some other projections and is often used for global thematic maps.

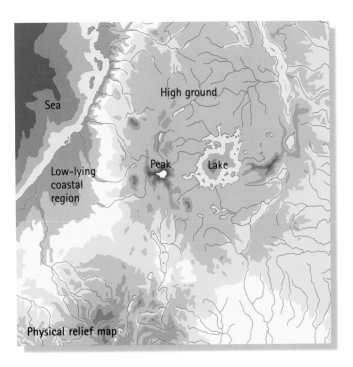

Sea

High ground

Peak

Lake

Low-lying coastal region

Physical relief map

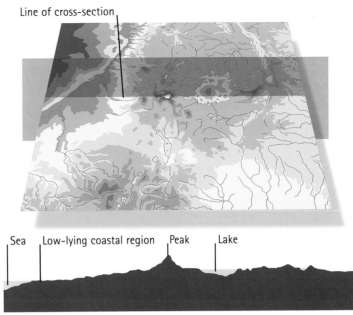

Line of cross-section

Sea | Low-lying coastal region | Peak | Lake

Cross-section through physical relief map

MAP PROJECTIONS

The Earth is a three-dimensional sphere while a map is usually a two-dimensional flat piece of paper. Map projections are ways in which cartographers convert the Earth's curved surface into a flat image. There are many different projections but all involve shrinking or stretching parts of the globe. Some projections, such as Peters', represent the relative land areas accurately, but distort the land shape. Others, such as Mercator's, distort the land area greatly. Some modern projections, such as Goode's Homolosine projection, have used mathematics to divide the Earth up into sections in order to convey more accurate land area and shape.

MAP TYPES

Different types of maps are constructed for a range of purposes. A political map shows the boundaries of the countries of the world. A physical map shows the natural features of the land using different colours or contour lines to show the varying elevations of land areas. A number of different maps and charts are produced to aid navigation, from hiking or cycling maps to maps depicting the main sea lanes for shipping. Maps can also be used to display types of data that varies throughout the world or a region. Thematic maps can show population density, or land use, for example.

MAPPING DEVELOPMENTS

Mapping the Earth is a task performed to this day. Modern cartographers use the many advances in technology that have occurred since World War II to produce highly detailed and accurate maps. Aerial photography, satellite imaging systems and other methods of remote sensing generate highly detailed data which can be analyzed by Geographical Information Systems (GIS). Running on powerful computers, GIS systems are able to produce maps layered with different information. These can be altered, updated and printed.

▲ A physical relief map shows the varying heights, or elevations, of the terrain in an area as well as physical features such as rivers and mountains. This map uses colours to represent different elevations, from purple (the highest points), through brown and yellow to green (the lowest points) on land. The lighter blues are used for more shallow waters and darker blues for the deeper.

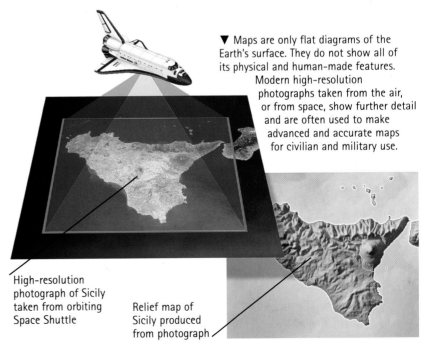

▼ Maps are only flat diagrams of the Earth's surface. They do not show all of its physical and human-made features. Modern high-resolution photographs taken from the air, or from space, show further detail and are often used to make advanced and accurate maps for civilian and military use.

High-resolution photograph of Sicily taken from orbiting Space Shuttle

Relief map of Sicily produced from photograph

43

THE PHYSICAL EARTH

A physical map of the world represents the Earth's evolving landscape, its mountain ranges, plains and deserts and its rivers, lakes and seas.

The Earth's major physical features are found on both land and deep underwater. The longest mountain range on Earth is actually underwater. The Mid-Ocean ridge consists of a series of ridges on the floor of the world's oceans and extends some 65,000 km in total length. Mountains form major physical features on all of the continents. The Alps are Europe's largest mountain range while the Rockies extend over 4,800 km through North America. While the world's highest mountain range is the Himalayas in Asia, the longest mountain range is the Andes, found on the western side of South America. With a length of 7,200 km, the Andes has an average elevation of 3,660 m.

ISLANDS

Thousands of islands dot the Earth's surface, including over 17,000 islands which form Indonesia and comprise the largest archipelago, or island chain, in the world. Islands vary in size from tiny rocky outcrops and coral atolls to giant land masses such as Madagascar and Borneo. Although Australia is an island, it constitutes most of the land of a continent and is known as a continental land mass. The largest island in the world is Greenland with an area of 2,175,000 km².

WATER FEATURES

Water has had a major influence in shaping the land. Water has eroded soft rock to form wide valleys or has, over millions of years, carved out deep gorges. The spectacular Grand Canyon in the USA is the world's largest gorge measuring 446 km in length and averaging 16 km in width. Moving water has also deposited fertile sediment on river banks and flood plains to create farmland. The ribbon of land either side of the world's longest river, the Nile, is where the vast majority of Egypt's population live.

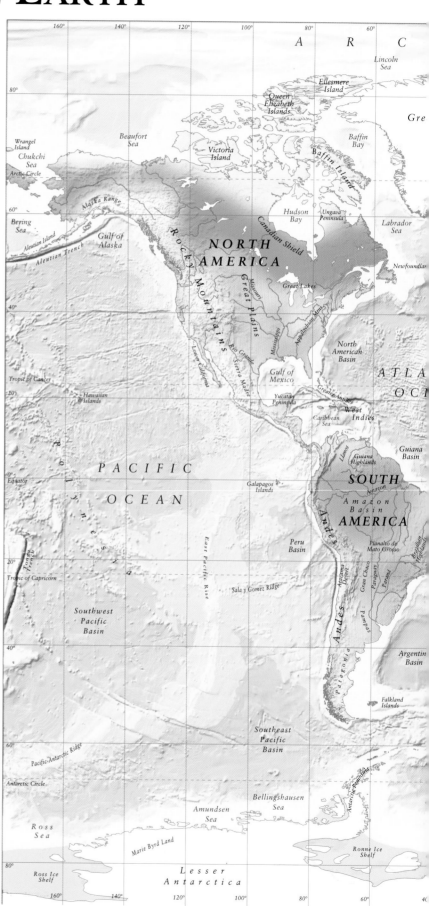

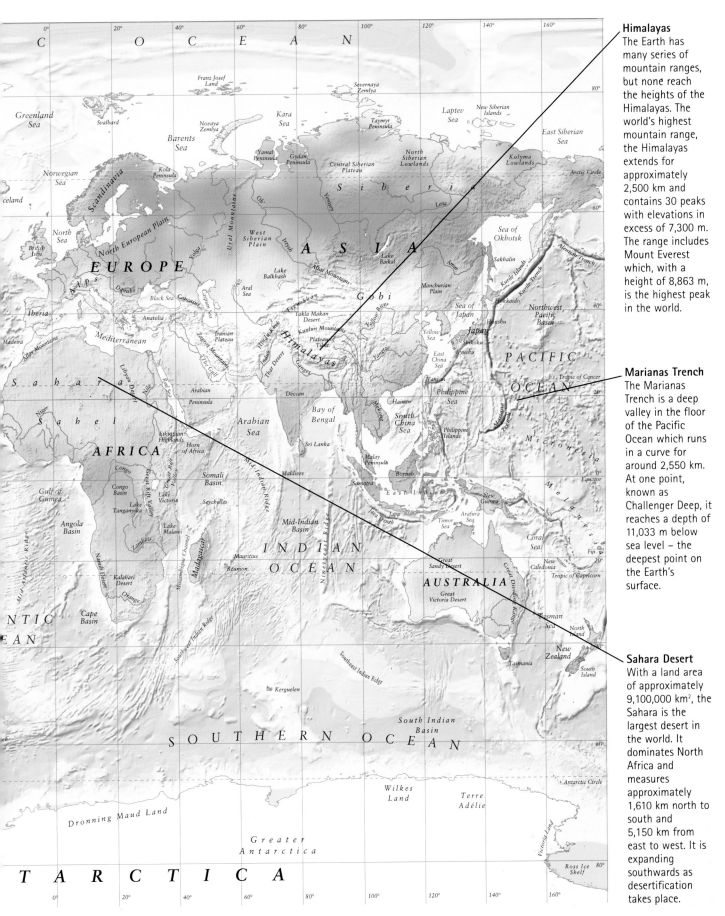

Himalayas

The Earth has many series of mountain ranges, but none reach the heights of the Himalayas. The world's highest mountain range, the Himalayas extends for approximately 2,500 km and contains 30 peaks with elevations in excess of 7,300 m. The range includes Mount Everest which, with a height of 8,863 m, is the highest peak in the world.

Marianas Trench

The Marianas Trench is a deep valley in the floor of the Pacific Ocean which runs in a curve for around 2,550 km. At one point, known as Challenger Deep, it reaches a depth of 11,033 m below sea level – the deepest point on the Earth's surface.

Sahara Desert

With a land area of approximately 9,100,000 km², the Sahara is the largest desert in the world. It dominates North Africa and measures approximately 1,610 km north to south and 5,150 km from east to west. It is expanding southwards as desertification takes place.

COUNTRIES OF THE WORLD

Every part of the Earth's land surface belongs to or is claimed by one of its 193 independent countries. The oldest country with defined borders is San Marino which was established in CE 301. East Timor became the newest independent nation in 2002.

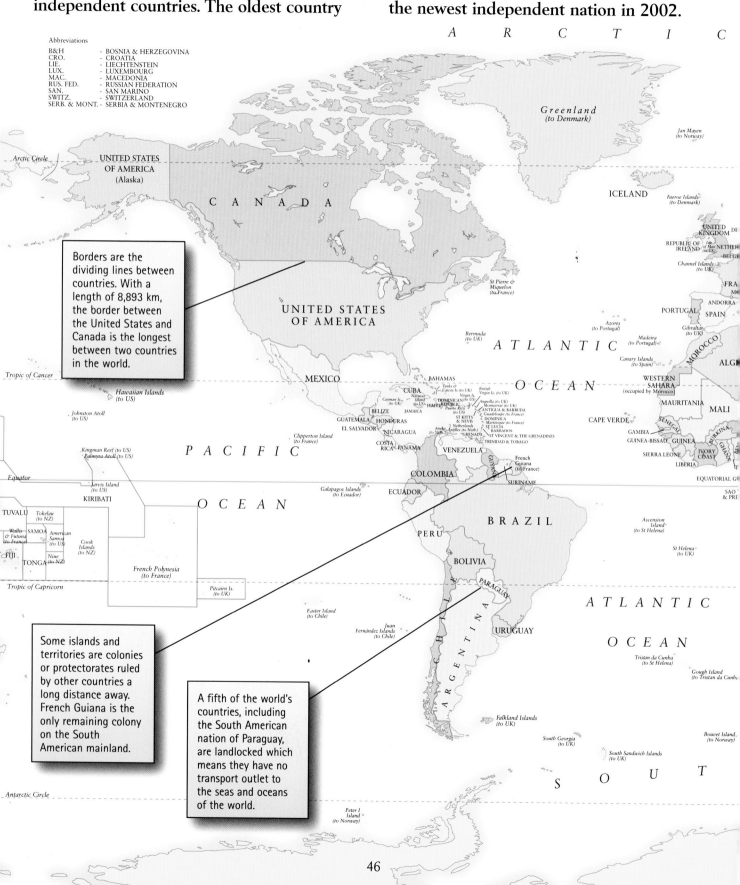

Abbreviations

B&H	- BOSNIA & HERZEGOVINA
CRO.	- CROATIA
LIE.	- LIECHTENSTEIN
LUX.	- LUXEMBOURG
MAC.	- MACEDONIA
RUS. FED.	- RUSSIAN FEDERATION
SAN.	- SAN MARINO
SWITZ.	- SWITZERLAND
SERB. & MONT.	- SERBIA & MONTENEGRO

Borders are the dividing lines between countries. With a length of 8,893 km, the border between the United States and Canada is the longest between two countries in the world.

Some islands and territories are colonies or protectorates ruled by other countries a long distance away. French Guiana is the only remaining colony on the South American mainland.

A fifth of the world's countries, including the South American nation of Paraguay, are landlocked which means they have no transport outlet to the seas and oceans of the world.

46

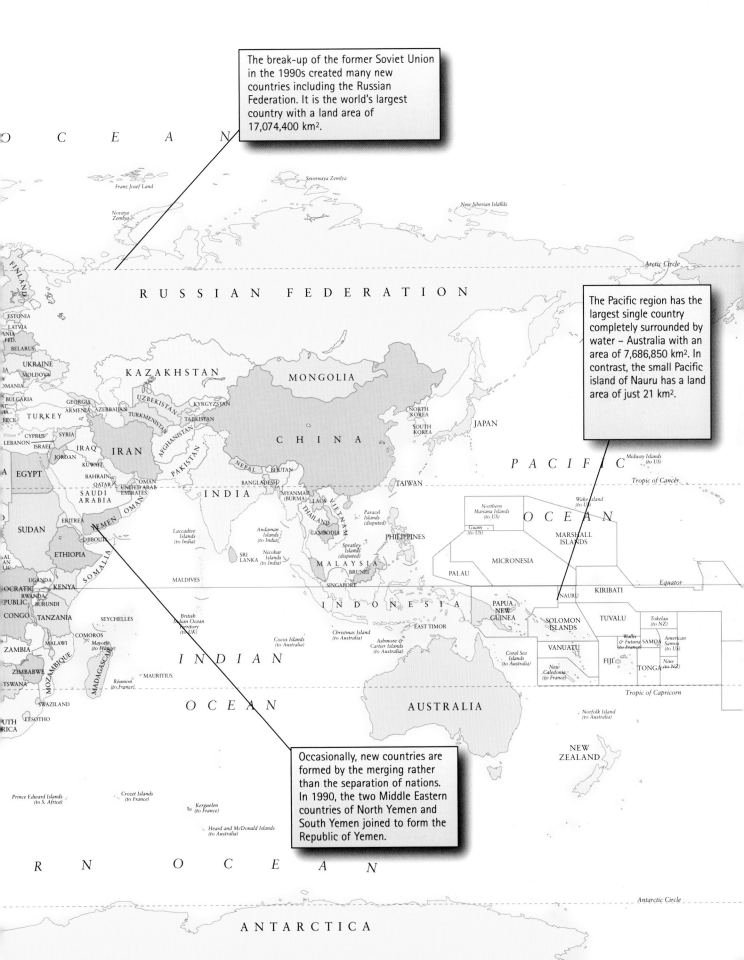

The break-up of the former Soviet Union in the 1990s created many new countries including the Russian Federation. It is the world's largest country with a land area of 17,074,400 km².

The Pacific region has the largest single country completely surrounded by water – Australia with an area of 7,686,850 km². In contrast, the small Pacific island of Nauru has a land area of just 21 km².

Occasionally, new countries are formed by the merging rather than the separation of nations. In 1990, the two Middle Eastern countries of North Yemen and South Yemen joined to form the Republic of Yemen.

EARTH STATISTICS

PLANETARY DATA

Estimated age	4.6 billion years	Orbital period (year)	365.24 days
Diameter at the Equator	12,756 km	Rotational period (day)	23 hours 56.1 minutes
Diameter at the poles	12,714 km	Average temperature	14°C
Circumference at the Equator	40,066 km	Surface area	510,066,000 km²
Circumference at the poles	39,992 km	Land area	148,647,000 km² 29.1%
Average distance from the Sun	149,597 million km	Total water area	361,419,000 km² 70.9%
Distance between Moon and Earth	384,400 km	Ocean area	335,258,000 km²

THE WORLD'S OCEANS BY AREA

Pacific	166,240,000 km²
Atlantic	86,560,000 km²
Indian	73,430,000 km²
Arctic	13,230,000 km²

THE WORLD'S MAJOR SEAS BY AREA

South China Sea	2,974,600 km²
Caribbean Sea	2,753,000 km²
Mediterranean Sea	2,503,000 km²
Bering Sea	2,268,200 km²
Gulf of Mexico	1,542,900 km²
Sea of Okhotsk	1,527,000 km²
East China Sea	1,249,000 km²
Hudson Bay	1,232,000 km²
Sea of Japan	1,007,500 km²
Andaman Sea	797,700 km²
North Sea	575,300 km²
Black Sea	461,900 km²

DEEPEST POINTS OF OCEANS AND SEAS

Pacific Ocean	11,022 m
Atlantic Ocean	8,605 m
Caribbean Sea	7,535 m
Indian Ocean	7,258 m
Gulf of Mexico	5,203 m
South China Sea	5,015 m
Mediterranean Sea	4,982 m
Arctic Ocean	4,665 m
Bering Sea	4,097 m
Sea of Japan	3,742 m

MAJOR RIVERS BY LENGTH

Nile, Africa	6,670 km
Amazon, South America	6,448 km
Chang Jiang (Yangtze), Asia	6,300 km
Mississippi-Missouri, North America	6,020 km
Yenisey-Angara, Asia	5,540 km
Huang (Yellow), Asia	5,464 km
Ob-Irtysh, Asia	5,409 km
Paraná-Rio de la Plata, South America	4,880 km
Congo, Africa	4,700 km
Lena, Asia	4,400 km
Amur-Argun, Asia	4,345 km

WORLD'S HIGHEST MULTIPLE WATERFALLS

Angel, Venezuela	979 m
Tugela, South Africa	947 m
Utigard, Norway	800 m
Mongefossen, Norway	774 m
Mutarazi, Zimbabwe	762 m
Yosemite, USA	739 m
Espelandsfoss, Norway	703 m
Ostre Mardola Foss, Norway	656 m
Tyssestregane, Norway	646 m
Cuquenán, Venezuela	580 m

MAJOR LAKES BY AREA

Caspian Sea, Asia-Europe	371,800 km²
Superior, North America	82,350 km²
Victoria, Africa	69,500 km²
Huron, North America	59,600 km²
Michigan, North America	57,800 km²
Tanganyika, Africa	32,900 km²
Great Bear, North America	31,800 km²
Baikal, Asia	30,500 km²
Malawi/Nyasa, Africa	29,600 km²
Great Slave, North America	28,500 km²

LARGEST ISLANDS BY AREA

Greenland	2,175,600 km²
New Guinea	821,030 km²
Borneo	744,366 km²
Madagascar	587,041 km²
Baffin	476,068 km²
Sumatra	473,607 km²
Honshu	230,448 km²
Great Britain	218,041 km²
Ellesmere	212,688 km²
Victoria	212,198 km²

HIGHEST MOUNTAINS BY CONTINENT

Asia, Mount Everest	8,863 m
S. America, Aconcagua	6,959 m
N. America, Mount McKinley	6,194 m
Africa, Mount Kilimanjaro	5,963 m
Europe, Mount Elbrus	5,633 m
Antarctica, Vinson Massif	4,897 m
Oceania, Puncak Jaya	4,884 m

WORLD'S 10 HIGHEST MOUNTAINS

Everest, Himalayas	8,863 m
K2, Karakorum	8,611 m
Kanchenjunga, Himalayas	8,598 m
Lhotse, Himalayas	8,511 m
Makalu, Himalayas	8,481 m
Cho Oyu, Himalayas	8,201 m
Dhaulagiri, Himalayas	8,167 m
Manaslu I, Himalayas	8,156 m
Nanga Parbat, Himalayas	8,156 m
Annapurna, Himalayas	8,091 m

10 LARGEST COUNTRIES BY AREA

Russian Federation	17,075,400 km²
Canada	9,970,610 km²
United States	9,629,091 km²
China	9,560,780 km²
Brazil	8,547,404 km²
Australia	7,682,300 km²
India	3,165,596 km²
Argentina	2,766,890 km²
Kazakhstan	2,717,300 km²
Sudan	2,505,815 km²

10 COUNTRIES WITH LARGEST HUMAN POPULATION

China	1,273,111,300
India	1,029,991,100
United States	278,058,880
Indonesia	228,437,870
Brazil	174,468,580
Russian Federation	145,470,200
Pakistan	144,616,640
Bangladesh	131,269,860
Japan	126,771,660
Nigeria	126,635,630
World Population	6,135,000,000

POPULATION OF WORLD'S LARGEST CITIES (URBAN AREAS)

Tokyo, Japan	29,950,000
New York, USA	21,199,000
Mexico City, Mexico	20,950,000
São Paulo, Brazil	17,834,000
Los Angeles, USA	16,374,000
Bombay (Mumbai), India	16,368,000
Seoul, South Korea	14,250,000
Osaka, Japan	14,190,000
Calcutta (Kolkata), India	13,217,000
Delhi, India	12,791,000
Buenos Aires, Argentina	11,931,000
Dhaka, Bangladesh	11,726,000
Cairo, Egypt	11,568,000
Jakarta, Indonesia	12,435,000
Lagos, Nigeria	10,878,000
Rio de Janeiro, Brazil	10,872,000
Manila, Philippines	10,492,000
Paris, France	9,654,000

HIGHS AND LOWS

DRIEST RECORDED PLACE ON EARTH
Calama, in Chile's Atacama Desert has zero average annual rainfall.

WETTEST RECORDED PLACE ON EARTH
Tutunendo, Colombia with 11,770 mm average annual rainfall.

COLDEST RECORDED TEMPERATURE
Vostok Station, Antarctica (-89°C)

HOTTEST RECORDED TEMPERATURE
Al' Aziziyah, Libya (58°C)

THE ARCTIC,
NORTH AND
CENTRAL AMERICA

THE ARCTIC

The Arctic is the area circling the North Pole and extending south to include the Arctic Ocean and the northernmost parts of three continents: Asia, Europe and North America. Surrounding the North Pole and extending outwards is a gigantic ice sheet, bigger than the whole of Europe. Much of this polar ice cap floats on the Arctic Ocean. The ice cap recedes in summer with large chunks breaking off to form icebergs. In winter, when the temperatures can fall as low as -60°C, it increases in size again. Despite the hostile climate and living conditions, the Arctic is home to a number of large mammals including the polar bear, walrus and seal. It has also been inhabited for thousands of years by peoples including the North American Inuits and the European Lapps.

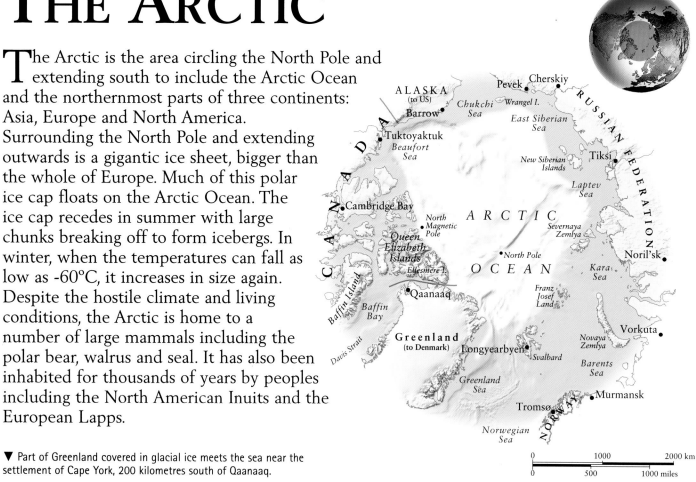

▼ Part of Greenland covered in glacial ice meets the sea near the settlement of Cape York, 200 kilometres south of Qaanaaq.

GREENLAND

Greenland is the world's biggest island. It is a
dependency of Denmark, but fifty times the size of it.
Much of the land is covered by a huge ice cap.

Area: 2,175,600 km²
Population: 59,800
Capital: Nuuk (13,700)
Main languages spoken:
Inuktitut, Danish
Main religion: Lutheran
Currency: Danish krone
Main exports: minerals,
(lead, zinc, coal, chrome,
copper), fish and fish
products
Government:
self-governing dependency
of Denmark

▼ The small village of
Savissivik lies on the west
coast of Greenland. It was
originally founded by Inuit
peoples who made iron
tools from the iron
contained in meteorites
discovered in the area.

Greenland lies mainly within the Arctic
Circle and its landscape is dominated
by a giant ice sheet which covers 80 per
cent of the island. The action of glaciers
has created a complex coastal landscape
with many fjords and offshore islands.
Almost all of Greenland's small population
live on the coast, particularly on the
southwestern side where the climate is not
as bitterly cold as is found in the interior.
Only one per cent of the island's total area
can be farmed; hardy vegetables such as
beets and turnips are grown and small
herds of sheep, goats and reindeer are
raised for their meat. The Arctic waters
around the coast provide good catches of
salmon, cod and prawns, and fish
processing is Greenland's major industry.
The island has no railways and only 150
km of roads. Dog sleds remain the main
form of land transport. The people of
Greenland are a mixture of descendants of
Inuit, Danish and Norwegian settlers.
Although Denmark is some 2,090 km
away, all Greenlanders are Danish citizens.
After a lengthy campaign, the island was
allowed to rule itself from 1979 onwards
although Denmark remains in control of
foreign affairs. A 31-member parliament
called the Landsting is elected every four
years. Following a referendum in 1982,
Greenland withdrew from the European
Union which it had joined in 1972.

NORTH AMERICA

The third largest continent, North America lies completely in the northern hemisphere. Its 25.3 million km^2 of land stretches deep into the Arctic Circle and extends southwards through Central America to join South America. The continent consists of three large countries: Canada, the USA and Mexico, and a cluster of smaller countries in Central America. Young, folded mountains run almost the entire length of the continent's western side and contain a number of volcanoes. This western area has been shaped greatly by the movement of the plates of the Earth's crust. Much of North America is uninhabited, especially the land in the far north, while many of the region's 444.8 million population live in large towns and cities. Fertile land exists throughout the continent and many of the countries have large reserves of minerals and fossil fuels. Economically, the continent is dominated by the USA, the world's richest and most powerful nation. The Central American nations tend to be poorer and reliant on trade and aid from the USA and, to a lesser extent, Canada and Mexico.

▲ The Chrysler Building was built between 1928 and 1930 and is just one of New York's many tall skyscrapers.

▼ A bison grazes on a grassy plain in Wyoming close to the Rocky Mountains. This 3,220 km long mountain chain runs from southwestern USA to British Columbia in Canada.

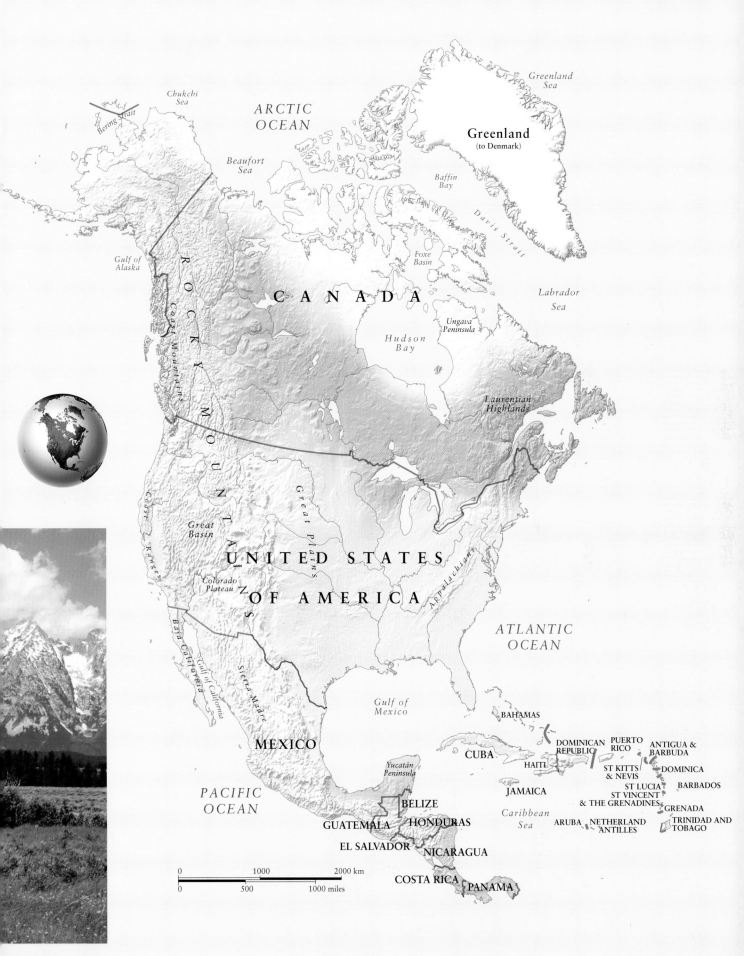

ARCTIC OCEAN

Chukchi Sea

Bering Strait

Greenland Sea

Greenland
(to Denmark)

Beaufort Sea

Baffin Bay

Davis Strait

Gulf of Alaska

C A N A D A

Labrador Sea

Foxe Basin

Ungava Peninsula

Hudson Bay

Laurentian Highlands

Great Basin

Great Plains

U N I T E D   S T A T E S

Colorado Plateau

O F   A M E R I C A

Appalachians

ATLANTIC OCEAN

Coast Ranges

Gulf of California

Baja California

Sierra Madre

Gulf of Mexico

BAHAMAS

MEXICO

Yucatán Peninsula

CUBA

DOMINICAN REPUBLIC

PUERTO RICO

ANTIGUA & BARBUDA

HAITI

ST KITTS & NEVIS

DOMINICA

PACIFIC OCEAN

BELIZE

JAMAICA

ST LUCIA
ST VINCENT & THE GRENADINES

BARBADOS

GUATEMALA

HONDURAS

Caribbean Sea

GRENADA

EL SALVADOR

NICARAGUA

ARUBA

NETHERLAND ANTILLES

TRINIDAD AND TOBAGO

COSTA RICA

PANAMA

0   1000   2000 km
0   500   1000 miles

Rocky Mountains

Coast Mountains

53

CANADA

With the longest coastline of any nation, Canada is a huge country which occupies the northernmost part of North America and extends deep into the Arctic Circle.

Area: 9,970,610 km²
Population: 31,000,000
Capital: Ottawa (1,064,000)
Main languages spoken: English, French
Main religions: Roman Catholic, United Church, Anglican
Currency: Canadian dollar
Main exports: motor vehicles, other machinery and transport equipment, mineral fuels, lumber, newsprint and wood pulp, and foodstuffs (particularly cereals)
Government: dominion, democracy

▼ The St Lawrence river runs from the most easterly of the Great Lakes, Lake Ontario, through the Canadian cities of Montreal and Quebec (pictured) before emptying into the Gulf of St Lawrence. The river provides a vital shipping link between the industrial centres of the Great Lakes and the Atlantic Ocean.

Canada is the second largest country in the world; only Russia is bigger. It has long coasts with the Arctic, Atlantic and Pacific oceans and shares two separate land borders with the USA. To the east it borders the US state of Alaska while its main border is to the south and extends over 6,400 km. Canada has a varied landscape which includes rugged mountain ranges, ice-covered wastes, fertile prairies and temperate lowlands and plains. Islands account for almost a sixth of its total land area with Baffin Island being the fifth largest island in the world.

A LAND OF LAKES AND TREES

Canada contains more lakes and inland waters than any other country in the world. Within its borders lie over 30 lakes with an area bigger than 1,300 km². Canada's longest river is the Mackenzie river which runs for 1,733 km, but the St Lawrence is the most important for trade and shipping. This river helps form more than 4,000 km of linked waterways connecting the Great Lakes to the Atlantic Ocean. It is estimated that as much as 25 per cent of the world's entire freshwater sources are found in Canada. Forests cover more than 35 per cent of the entire country. Trees such as pine, spruce, cedar and maple are especially common.

PEOPLE AND RESOURCES

Canada is one of the world's least densely populated countries with an average of fewer than four people per km². Vast areas, especially in the cold north, are unpopulated. Most people live in a relatively narrow belt in the southern part of the country where the climate is milder than the icy, harsh north. Although Ottawa is its capital, Canada's two largest cities are Toronto with 4,683,000 and Montreal with 3,426,000 populations respectively. Canada was settled by English and French speaking peoples. Today, people of European origin form more than two-thirds of its population. The country has rich mineral resources and large areas of fertile farmland.

▲ The Athabasca glacier lies in the northern Rocky Mountains and its meltwaters feed the 1,231 km long Athabasca river which runs though the Canadian province of Alberta. In the past, this river was an important transport route for fur traders.

ARCTIC OCEAN

Queen Elizabeth Islands

Ellesmere Island

Beaufort Sea

Banks Island

Baffin Bay

Victoria Island

Baffin Island

Mt Logan 5959m

Rocky Mountains

Mackenzie

Great Bear Lake

Foxe Basin

▲ The fox squirrel (*Sciurius niger*) is found in the western parts of Canada bordering the US states of Montana and Washington.

Coast Mountains

Great Slave Lake

C A N A D A

Lake Athabasca

Reindeer Lake

Hudson Bay

Ungava Peninsula

Labrador Sea

Labrador

Saskatchewan

Lake Winnipeg

Laurentian Highlands

St Lawrence

Newfoundland

St Pierre & Miquelon (to France)

Great OTTAWA

Lakes

ATLANTIC OCEAN

0   1000   2000 km
0   500   1000 miles

EASTERN CANADA

Eastern Canada includes the industrial and farming heartlands of Quebec and Ontario, Canada's biggest city, Toronto, and its seat of government in Ottawa.

▲ Canada's Parliament buildings are found in the eastern Canadian city of Ottawa. First opened in 1866, the buildings show British influence with the tower bearing a striking resemblance to the Houses of Parliament buildings in Westminster, London, UK.

▼ Built in 1976, the 553.34 m high CN Tower is the most notable landmark in the busy Ontario city of Toronto. The tower receives around two million visitors every year.

Canada is divided into ten provinces and three territories which are in the north. Six of these provinces form eastern Canada: Ontario, Quebec, New Brunswick, Prince Edward Island, Newfoundland and Labrador and Nova Scotia.

SHAPED BY GLACIERS

Canada was shaped mainly by glaciation. The glaciers that remain in the northern part of the country are remnants of a giant ice sheet which once covered the country. Glaciation is responsible for many of eastern Canada's distinctive geographical landmarks, from the low, rolling hills found on Prince Edward Island and Nova Scotia to the magnificent Niagara Falls which lie between Lake Erie and Lake Ontario. Eastern Canada is made up of three different geographical regions: the Canadian Shield, the Appalachian mountains to the east and, in between these two, a rich area of agricultural land called the Great Lakes–St Lawrence

lowlands. The Canadian Shield takes its name from the hard bedrock of gneiss and granite which lies underneath the surface. This rock is estimated to be over three billion years old. The shield occupies half of all of Canada. It extends southwards from the large inland sea called the Hudson Bay down through the provinces of Ontario and Quebec and reaches the northern shore of Lake Superior. Scraped by the advance and retreat of glaciers, the region contains many rivers and lakes and tends to have a thin soil which supports boreal forests containing evergreen trees.

THE ATLANTIC PROVINCES

The four Atlantic provinces are Prince Edward Island, Newfoundland and Labrador, New Brunswick and Nova Scotia. They are the smallest provinces of Canada and were also the first to be settled by Europeans. Large parts of these provinces are covered by the Appalachian mountains – an ancient mountain range which has been worn down by glaciers in the past to create low, rolling hills that are often heavily forested. Valleys full of fertile soil often lie between these hills and farming is a key industry in all four provinces. The smallest of all Canadian provinces is Prince Edward Island which lies in the Gulf of St Lawrence and has an area of just 5,660 km^2. Half of the island is covered in dense forests of both deciduous trees, such as the maple and the birch, and

▲ Seal Cove is a fishing village in the Atlantic province of New Brunswick. It is situated on Grand Manan Island in the Bay of Fundy.

coniferous trees such as the white pine. Farming and fishing are the most important industries for the island's 130,000-strong population. Around a quarter of the land is farmed with the most valuable products including dairy farming, fruit crops such as raspberries and blueberries, and vegetables such as peas, beans and potatoes. Newfoundland and Labrador is the newest Canadian province joining Canada in 1949 and consists of a mainland area, Labrador, and the large island of Newfoundland. Newfoundland has been the traditional centre of Canada's fishing industry. The Grand Banks area off the eastern coast of the island is a continental shelf which extends some 400 km. The arrival of a series of ocean currents there has helped to create one of the world's richest fishing grounds. Over-fishing has caused fish stocks to drop and there are now quotas in place which have harmed the local industry.

THE PROVINCES OF NEW BRUNSWICK AND NOVA SCOTIA

Lying between Quebec and the US State of Maine, New Brunswick is almost rectangular in shape with an area of 73,440 km². Large fishing grounds in the Bay of Fundy and the Gulf of St Lawrence as well as mines and some manufacturing factories, sustain many of the province's 513,000 people. With most of its land covered in forests, logging and timber products such as pulp and paper are a vital part of the province's economy. Forests also cover a large part of New Brunswick's eastern neighbour, the province of Nova Scotia. Bordering the Atlantic Ocean, Nova Scotia was home to the first permanent European settlement in Canada founded by French settlers in 1605. The province has a long history of ship and boat building which continues to this day supplemented by mining for coal and other minerals as well as fishing. Nova Scotia's largest settlement, Halifax, is a major port which can accept shipping all the year round.

▲ This hat shop in Québec displays its signs in both French and English. Canadian law gives its citizens the right to choose whether to receive many official services in English or French.

▼ Completed in 1959, the St Lawrence Seaway opened up a major shipping route from the Great Lakes to the Atlantic Ocean. In 2000, 2,978 vessels carrying over 35 million tonnes of cargo and thousands of passengers passed through the Montreal to Lake Ontario section alone.

THE POWERHOUSE PROVINCES

Ontario and the southern part of the province of Quebec are the agricultural and industrial powerhouses of Canada. Fifty per cent of all Canadians live in this region where approximately 70 per cent of all Canada's manufactured goods are made. The second largest province in terms of area, Ontario's population has risen 13 per cent in the past decade as more and more people flock to the industrial, commercial and governmental centre of the country. Curving round the shore of Lake Ontario is Canada's industrial heartland known as the Golden Horseshoe. Large steelworks, car-making, meat processing and ship and aircraft building factories exist in this region. They make use of the transport links provided by the lake and its connection to the Atlantic via the St Lawrence Seaway. Southern Ontario also has large stretches of prime agricultural land. Sixty per cent of revenue from farming is derived from livestock and much of the crop output of the region is used as fodder for farm animals. The two closest Great Lakes, Lake Ontario and Lake Erie, have a modifying effect on the climate, making it milder and

increasing the number of frost-free days. This allows a range of fruits to be grown including peaches and pears. In the southeastern corner of Ontario on the banks of Lake Ontario lies Toronto, Canada's largest city. Toronto is a cosmopolitan city with a booming population of over four million people.

CENTRAL GOVERNMENT

Ontario is also the home of Canada's national government in the capital city, Ottawa. The 1867 British North America Act united much of Canada but independence was only recognised in 1931. Canada is a federal union which means that power is divided between the provinces and the central government. The Canadian Parliament consists of two

houses: the Senate, whose members are appointed and serve until the age of 75, and the House of Commons whose members are elected once every five years or whenever Parliament is dissolved and a general election called.

FRENCH-SPEAKING CANADA

Canada has two official languages: English and French. This reflects the patterns of settlement which saw British and French arrivals from the 17th century onwards. Conflicts over territories and land rights saw a number of wars fought with the British gaining overall control but the French settlers remaining. Although French-speaking Canadians live in the Atlantic provinces and throughout Canada, they are concentrated in the province of Quebec, the area that French fur traders and farmers first settled. Around 90 per cent of Canadians who speak French as their first language live in Quebec. Lying to the east of Ontario, Quebec is blessed with many resources and good farmland. The province has rich mineral reserves and generates more electricity through hydro-electric power than any other province. On a number of occasions, Quebec has only narrowly resisted breaking away from the rest of Canada. Although the capital of the province is the city of Québec, its largest settlement is Montreal. A busy port and financial centre, the city stands on an island where two rivers meet and contains over three million people, most of whom speak French as their first language.

▼ The spectacular Horseshoe Falls in Canada is part of the Niagara Falls which extends into both Canada and the USA. Believed to have been formed around 12,000 years ago when glaciers retreated, around 5.5 million litres of water pass over Niagara Falls every second. It draws about 15 million visitors every year.

WESTERN CANADA

Rich in natural resources, western Canada features mountainous British Columbia and the three Prairie Provinces of Manitoba, Saskatchewan and Alberta.

▲ Grizzly bears are found in western Canada especially in more mountainous regions. They are one of the largest meat-eating land creatures, but they are an endangered species.

▼ Vancouver is Canada's third largest city and is situated on the Canadian mainland opposite Vancouver Island. It has a large natural harbour which has helped to make it the centre of British Columbia's sea trade.

Three of western Canada's four provinces are dominated by the Great Plains which run through large parts of Alberta, Saskatchewan and Manitoba. The plains feature fertile soils and large deposits of fossil fuels. Manitoba, the flattest of the three provinces, is known as the land of 100,000 lakes with many lakes being scoured out through glaciation. There are many rivers and lakes in the northern half of Saskatchewan, while the Rocky Mountains and their foothills extend into the southwestern corner of Alberta. The northern regions of all three provinces tend to be heavily forested and timber industries are a major contributor to the local economies. British Columbia is the only Canadian province with a Pacific coastline, and is more mountainous with two great mountain ranges running much of its length.

BRITISH COLUMBIA

British Columbia is separated from Alberta by the Rocky Mountains which run throughout its length and continue north into the Yukon territory. West of the Rockies lie heavily forested lands, natural grasslands and large numbers of lakes. Another mountain range, the Coast Mountains, define much of the province's coastal area with glaciation having carved out many islands and fjords. The Queen Charlotte Islands to the north and the 460 km-long Vancouver Island are the largest islands. The province's landscape is of great natural beauty and harbours much wildlife including grizzly and black bears, elks and waterfowl. This habitat is preserved in the form of 675 parks or protected areas which attract over 23 million visitors every year. A feature of the province is its great forests which contain a large percentage of Canada's merchantable wood – trees that can be used for timber, pulp, paper and other industries. Wood processing, mining, tourism and service industries are the biggest employers of the province's 3.9 million people. Most of the population live in the southwest with 60 per cent living in just two cities: Victoria and

▲ The Maligne river flows from the Canadian Rocky Mountains through Jasper National Park in the province of Alberta.

Canada's third-largest city, Vancouver. Victoria is the province's capital and is located on Vancouver Island. It is based on the site of the first permanent European colony established in 1843. Facing the Pacific and the Far East, British Columbia is increasingly trading and building commercial ties with Japan, Korea and other Asian nations. Although most people of the province are of British origin, there are also more than 60,000 inhabitants originally from India, around 200,000 native Americans, and North America's largest Chinese community outside San Francisco.

WARM SUMMERS – COLD WINTERS

Some distance from both the Pacific and Atlantic Oceans, the three Prairie Provinces have a continental climate. This means great differences between warm summer and cold winter temperatures. For example, Manitoba's largest city, Winnipeg, records average January temperature of -20°C and average temperatures in July are 20°C. In southwestern parts of Alberta, the closest of the three provinces to the Pacific, mild winds from the Pacific Ocean called the Chinook tend to raise the cold winter temperatures a little.

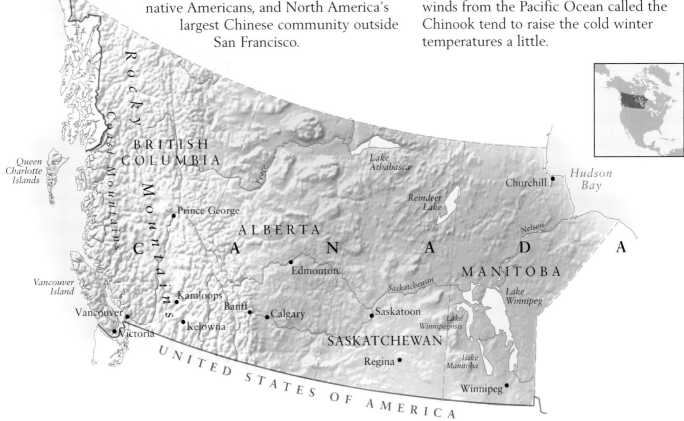

▲ Canada is the world's largest producer of barley, an important cereal crop. Over 90 per cent of the country's total production of 12.6 million tonnes is grown in western Canada. It is grown on Canada's Great Plains and harvested with automated machinery.

▼ Lying on the eastern slopes of the Rockies and famous for its spectacular mountain scenery, Banff National Park is Canada's oldest national park, first opened in 1883.

All three provinces receive low rainfall, averaging between 380 and 440 mm per year, but enjoy a large number of sunny days in both summer and winter. The town of Estevan in Saskatchewan is considered the sunshine capital of Canada with an average of over 2,500 sunshine hours per year. The most eastern parts of the fourth province, British Columbia, also feature a continental climate but much of this province has a climate affected greatly by its closeness to the Pacific Ocean. Warm, moist air from the Pacific not only helps to create milder winters but also brings heavy rainfall, between 1,300 mm and 3,800 mm per year.

FARMING AND FUELS

The warm summer conditions along with the large expanses of flat, fertile plains have made the three Prairie Provinces highly productive farming areas. Alberta, for example, is the largest beef producing province in Canada. Only 13 per cent is used within the state, half is shipped to other parts of Canada, while a further 30 per cent is traded with the USA. Saskatchewan produces over half of the wheat grown in Canada and also has large farmlands devoted to growing rye, flaxseed and other crops. Manitoba's central location in Canada has made it an important trading, transport and distribution centre for farming and food products. Around 60 per cent of its population live in and around the capital city of Winnipeg. Food production and packaging are major industries in all three provinces while fossil fuels are exploited particularly in Alberta, which supplies 90 per cent of Canada's natural gas needs, and Saskatchewan. Over 18,000 active oil wells in Saskatchewan produce around a fifth of Canada's total oil output.

NORTHERN CANADA

Northern Canada consists of three sparsely populated territories: Yukon, Northwest Territories and Nunavut. Four-fifths of these territories are wilderness areas.

▲ Northern Canada is the main home of the polar bear. Since 1973, hunting restrictions have helped its survival.

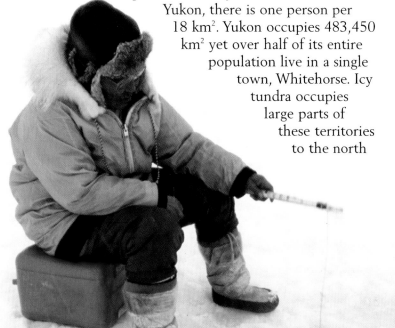

▼ Cutting a hole in the ice, this Inuit fisherwoman fishes for Arctic charr.

The three territories of Northern Canada are among the most sparsely populated regions in the world. In Northwest Territories and Nunavut there is one person for every 59 km² while in Yukon, there is one person per 18 km². Yukon occupies 483,450 km² yet over half of its entire population live in a single town, Whitehorse. Icy tundra occupies large parts of these territories to the north with permafrost widespread. Many of northern Canada's people are either native American Indians or traditional Arctic peoples such as the Inuit. Hunting, fishing, trapping, mining and forestry are the main sources of work.

NUNAVUT

The boundaries defining Canada's two territories were redrawn in 1999, creating the newly formed Nunavut territory. Nunavut is the most northerly region of Canada and includes the thousands of islands in the Arctic Ocean which form the Arctic Archipelago. Nunavut is a self-governing homeland for the Inuit people who form 85 per cent of the territory's total population of around 28,000. Nunavut means 'Our Land' in the Inuit language. More than a third of Nunavut's population is under 15 years of age.

UNITED STATES OF AMERICA

The USA is the third largest and the most powerful country in the world. A world leader in manufacturing industries, it has an abundance of natural resources.

Area: 9,629,091 km²
Population: 282,000,000
Capital: Washington DC (4,923,000)
Main languages spoken: English, Spanish
Main religions: Roman Catholic, Baptist, Methodist
Currency: US dollar
Main exports: machinery and transport equipment particularly road vehicles, chemicals, food, scientific and related equipment
Type of government: republic; democracy

▼ Independence Day in the USA commemorates the Declaration of Independence made in 1776. Held every 4th of July, it is celebrated with large firework displays such as this over Florida's largest city, Miami.

The United States of America gets its name from its administrative divisions. Each of its 50 states has its own courts and government which wield much local power. The mainland USA consists of forty-eight states which share borders and occupy the width of North America.It stretches from the Pacific Ocean to the Atlantic Ocean. Alaska, which borders western Canada, and the Pacific islands of Hawaii are the remaining two states. Two large mountain ranges dominate the country's landscape. To the west, the Rocky Mountains form a high altitude spine with some peaks rising to over 4,000 m. To the east, the Appalachian mountain system runs almost parallel with the Atlantic Ocean for approximately 2,400 km. These mountains are older, lower in height and large parts are covered in forest. In between, much of the land consists of giant plains crossed by many rivers. The USA's longest river is the Mississippi which together with its tributary, the Missouri, make up the third longest river in the world. To the north, the USA shares a border with Canada. Both countries share ownership of the series of lakes called the Great Lakes which runs along their border.

The United States is rich in natural resources from metals, such as lead and iron, to oil and timber. More than a fifth of the world's known reserves of coal lies within its borders. Large parts of the plains running through the centre of the country have fertile soils which are used for growing corn and other cereal crops on a massive scale, and as pasture for the USA's 100 million cattle.

The bald eagle is the national bird of the USA.

AMERICA'S PEOPLE

Peopled by native Americans for many thousands of years, the first Europeans arrived and settled particularly along its eastern coast in the 17th and 18th centuries. The American Revolutionary War (1775–1781) finally resulted in the new nation ridding itself of British rule. The new country encouraged settlers and immigrants for many decades and the USA today is a melting pot of different peoples and cultures. Approximately 69 per cent of people are of European origin with 13 per cent African Americans, 12 per cent Hispanics, four per cent Asians and two per cent native Americans.

▲ The USA's landscape varies greatly and includes flat, temperate grasslands, rugged mountains and arid wilderness regions such as this part of the US state of New Mexico.

▲ Giant redwood trees in Sequoia National Park, California can grow to a height of 100 m with a trunk diameter of up to 7 m.

EASTERN USA

The site of the first European arrivals to the United States, eastern USA is as rich in land resources as it is in history.

▲ The eastern seaboard of the USA has many excellent natural harbours around which ports and fishing settlements developed, such as Rockport on Cape Ann peninsula in Massachusetts.

▲ This marble statue of former US President, Abraham Lincoln, is the centrepiece of the Lincoln Memorial, a building located in Potomac Park in the capital city of Washington DC.

▼ The White House in Washington DC was designed by the Irish-American architect, James Hoban, and was originally called the Executive Mansion.

The eastern USA borders the Atlantic Ocean with a long, irregular coastline which, in places, is indented with many bays and inlets. Two eastern US states, Pennsylvania and New York, have shorelines with the two most easterly Great Lakes, Erie and Ontario. The geography of the region alters as one travels both south and inland. The Atlantic coastal plain broadens as the land runs southwards while inland lies the Appalachians mountain system. Running nearly parallel to the Atlantic coast, the Appalachians extend more than 2,400 km from the Canadian province of Quebec southwards through the eastern USA where they reach as far south as Alabama. They form many mountain ranges including the Green Mountains of Vermont, the Catskill Mountains found in New York state and the Blue Ridge Mountains which run through Georgia, North Carolina, West Virginia and Virginia. The Appalachians are some of the oldest mountains to be found anywhere in the world. Their heavily eroded formations are rich in mineral

deposits including coal, iron ore and zinc. The region includes the collection of six northeastern states known as New England as well as the mid-Atlantic states of New Jersey, Delaware, Maryland, Pennsylvania and Virginia. West Virginia sits inland and is the only one of the eastern states not to have a shoreline with either a Great Lake or the Atlantic Ocean. Some forest areas of these states have been cleared for farmland and for the many large towns and cities that house the region's 69 million people. However, 75 per cent of West Virginia, for example, is covered in trees while 60 per cent of Virginia, 55 per cent of Pennsylvania and 43 per cent of Maryland remain forested. Although there are extensive farmlands in many eastern

states, manufacturing industry and services are extremely important to state economies. In New Jersey, for example, agriculture accounts for only one per cent of the state's total revenue.

SETTLEMENT

The Appalachian Mountains played an important role in early European settlement of the USA. Their heavily forested heights formed an obstacle to travel further inland which prompted many to settle to their east, forming the first major colonies. The first successful English colony was established at Jamestown, now in the state of Virginia, in 1607. In 1620, English Puritans escaping religious persecution landed in what is now Massachusetts and founded Plymouth Colony. Most of the major events of America's colonial period, including the American War of Independence, took place in the eastern United States. The first major protest at British rule, the Boston Tea Party (1773), took place in Boston harbour in the state of Massachusetts; the important battle of Saratoga (1777) was fought in what is now New York state; and the US Constitution was framed in the city of Philadelphia in 1787. This document lays down the structure and powers of government in the USA and although there have been 27 amendments to its contents, much remains in place to this day.

▼ The autumn (fall) season in the states of New England sees the leaves of the deciduous trees there turn beautiful shades of orange, yellow and red. This autumnal scene is from Vermont.

GOVERNMENT

The US system of government splits powers between the 50 states and a national government called the federal government. Both state and national government have powers to collect taxes, borrow money, build roads and provide welfare services. In addition, the national government has powers to make foreign policy and treaties with other nations, provide military forces and print money. The offices of the federal government are also split with independence between the law-makers (the legislature), the law administrators (the executive) and the law interpreters and enforcers (the law courts). All three arms of the federal government have their headquarters in Washington, District of Columbia (usually shortened to DC). It was chosen in 1790 as the seat of national government. On the eastern banks of the Potomac River, Washington DC was originally a territory created by land donated from the two neighbouring states of Maryland and Virginia. Washington has developed into a major city where one-third of its permanent workers are employed by the federal government. The Capitol building in Washington DC is the home of Congress, the law-making body of the national United States and is split into two houses, the House of Representatives and the Senate. The members of both houses are chosen by public elections and both houses meet separately. Close by, is the Supreme Court, which makes the ultimate decisions on disputes in law. Pennsylvania Avenue links the Capitol building with the White House, the home of the president of the USA.

NEW ENGLAND STATES

Six northeastern states – Maine, New Hampshire, Rhode Island, Vermont, Connecticut and Massachusetts – are collectively known as the New England states. It was in this region that most of the earliest arrivals to the USA came ashore and settled in pioneer towns and villages. Some of the country's most highly regarded centres of learning have their

▲ The impressive 93.5 m high Statue of Liberty sits on a small island in the harbour of New York City. The statue was given by France to the USA in 1876 to celebrate 100 years of independence.

▼ Located at the meeting point of a number of rivers, including the 1,579 km long Ohio river, Pittsburgh is one of the busiest inland river ports in the entire USA.

▲ A night-time view over part of Manhattan, New York City sees how large skyscrapers including the Empire State Building (centre) shape the view of its skyline.

NEW YORK

Lying in the southeastern corner of New York state is the giant metropolis of New York. The city started life as a fur-trading post positioned on the mouth of the Hudson river. It is now one of the world's largest, busiest and richest cities and a world centre for finance and business. New York sits on both the mainland and a collection of 50 islands, the largest being Manhattan. For the past 200 years, it has been the main gateway into the USA and vast waves of immigrants have settled here giving it a mixed racial background. The 2000 census estimated the New York population to be 68 per cent white, 16 per cent black, 6 per cent Asian and Pacific islanders and 10 per cent other races.

▲ The world's largest market for the trading of securities, the New York Stock Exchange has traded from Wall Street in Manhattan since 1817.

homes in New England. These include Massachusetts Institute of Technology (MIT) and Harvard University in Massachusetts and Yale University in Connecticut. The New England states draw large numbers of tourists attracted to both the region's history and its rich landscapes of hills, mountains and picturesque forests of mainly deciduous trees. Rhode Island, with an area of 3,139 km², is the smallest state in the USA. The most northerly New England state, Maine, has over 85 per cent of its 86,156 km² of land covered in thick forests, while the state is also famed for its rugged, irregular coastline created mainly by glaciation in the last Ice Age. The highest peak in New England, Mount Washington (1,917 m), is found in northern New Hampshire close to the border with Maine.

▲ Baseball is one of the most popular sports in the USA. Here, at Camden Yards stadium in Baltimore, Maryland, the Baltimore Orioles play against the Boston Red Sox. Both teams are from the eastern United States.

MID-WEST AND THE GREAT LAKES

A major location for manufacturing and trade and home to the world's largest cereal farming operations, this region plays a major part in the US economy.

▲ Cities like Detroit and Chicago have been synonymous with manufacturing industries such as the production of motor vehicles. This Chicago-based Ford assembly plant turns out around 250,000 vehicles per year.

Most of the land that makes up the interior of the USA is part of a giant plateau that runs from the Rocky Mountains in the west across the interior of the country. Within it, there are a number of hill and mountain ranges including the Smoky Hills of Kansas and the Black Hills which lie in South Dakota and Wyoming. South and North Dakota and northwestern Nebraska are also home to a region of rugged, strangely shaped rock masses and hills called badlands. Unable to support more than sparse vegetation, they are caused by erosion assisted by short periods of heavy rains followed by long periods of drought. A large part of the interior consists of the Great Plains while a region called the Corn Belt, stretching from western Ohio west to the central part of Nebraska, is one of the largest crop growing regions in the world.

THE GREAT PLAINS

The Great Plains occupies a large area of southern Canada and extends south to cover the land east of the Rocky Mountains and west of the Mississippi

▲ Built on the southwestern shores of Lake Michigan, Chicago is the USA's third most populous city behind New York and Los Angeles. Its location makes it a vital junction for air, water and land transport.

river. In the USA the Plains include parts of North Dakota, South Dakota, Montana, Wyoming, Colorado, Nebraska and Kansas as well as parts of the southern states of Oklahoma, New Mexico and Texas. Much of the Great Plains region was once covered by a vast inland sea, and sedimentary deposits make up the rock strata which tend to lie horizontally underneath the land surface. The Great Plains was once one of the largest areas of grassland in the world supporting giant herds of bison estimated to total over 50 million. Much of the grassland featured a rich, fertile topsoil and was heavily exploited by farmers from the 19th century onwards. Years of over-farming and a lack of soil management saw the creation of large dust bowls as the topsoil eroded. However, modern farming and irrigation techniques have seen North America's grasslands return to intensive farming both in rearing vast herds of livestock and in growing cereal crops including rye, barley, alfalfa and wheat. A little over 75 per cent of the world's wheat exports are produced in this region.

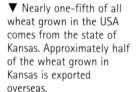

▼ Nearly one-fifth of all wheat grown in the USA comes from the state of Kansas. Approximately half of the wheat grown in Kansas is exported overseas.

▶ The bison is the largest land mammal in North America. Around 50 million bison roamed the central USA before the arrival of European settlers with firearms in the 19th century.

THE MISSOURI AND MISSISSIPPI

The Missouri river flows across the central USA. It is second in length only to the Mississippi which it flows into just north of the city of St Louis. Together, the Missouri and the Mississippi travel almost the length of the country and drain much of the central interior. The Mississippi remains an important transportation link with large barges and ships carrying bulk cargoes such as petroleum products, coal, sand, gravel and iron ore. The Missouri is harnessed by the Missouri River Basin Project to irrigate large areas of farmland and to provide energy via hydro-electric power stations.

THE GREAT LAKES

The Great Lakes were formed during the last Ice Age when glaciation helped to scour and hollow out increasingly broad and deep depressions from stream valleys. The resulting five large lakes hold an estimated 20 per cent of the world's freshwater and 90 per cent of the freshwater of the USA. Lake Michigan is the only one of the five Great Lakes which lies solely within the borders of the USA. The other four lakes – Erie, Ontario, Huron and Superior – span the border between the USA and Canada. They are all joined to form a giant drainage system. The water flows from Lake Superior, through the other lakes before entering the sea in the Gulf of St Lawrence. The lakes are large enough to have an effect on the climate of the land around them. They make the winters warmer and the summers cooler. Together, the lakes drain a region approximately three-quarters of a million square kilometres in size, known as the Great Lakes Basin. About one fifth of the United States' total population live within the area of the Great Lakes Basin.

▼ A shopping mall found in the city of Columbus. The state capital of Ohio since 1816, Columbus is Ohio's most populous city.

▲ The 192 m tall Gateway Arch in St Louis, Missouri commemorates the city's historic status as the gateway to the west.

▲ Mount Rushmore features 18 m high faces of four US Presidents carved into the rock.

THE GREAT LAKE STATES

The Great Lake States are considered to be Ohio, Michigan, Indiana, Illinois, Wisconsin and, sometimes, Minnesota. These states form the traditional industrial heartland of the USA where the majority of heavy engineering goods, such as motor vehicles and industrial machinery, are produced. Engineering and manufacturing industry grew up in the region in the 19th and 20th centuries. Raw material resources such as iron ore and coal were close to hand and the lakes allowed transport by boat over long distances. Large settlements sprang up on many shores of the Great Lakes acting as industrial centres, ports and trading communities. These have developed into some of the USA's largest cities, including Cleveland on Lake Erie, and Milwaukee and Chicago on Lake Michigan. Detroit, which sits on the Detroit river between Lake Erie and Lake Huron, became the world's foremost motor vehicle producing city. Large numbers of people, particularly new immigrants from overseas, especially Europe, and black people from the southern states, came to work in the industrial north. The mixture of cultures spawned new art and music forms including types of electric blues music originating in Chicago and soul music centred around Detroit. Economic problems in many heavy industries and cheaper competition from overseas have more recently forced the Great Lakes states to turn to other industries including finance, electronics and tourism. This is also an important farming region. More than 75 per cent of Illinois, for example, is devoted to farming with the state being the US's largest producer of soybeans. Wisconsin is known as a major dairy farming state, producing over 10 per cent of the USA's milk and large quantities of cheese.

▼ Millions of years of water and wind erosion have created the strange and spectacular rock formations found in the Badlands National Park, South Dakota.

NATIVE AMERICANS

Native American peoples had lived throughout much of North America for thousands of years before the arrival of European explorers and settlers. Although early contact tended to be peaceful, if wary, and linked to trade, gradually tensions built and conflicts occurred as the settlers wanted more land to farm and to exploit mineral resources. By the 19th century, crisis point had been reached. The buffalo herds on which many native American tribes depended had been killed in their millions and thousands of settlers, mainly from Europe, were pushing further west seeking to claim lands belonging to tribes. Wars erupted as the many different native American tribes sought to keep hold of all or part of their tribal lands. Many of these conflicts occurred in the Mid-west and in the states surrounding the Great Lakes. For example, the forced resettlement of the Sauk and Fox tribes resulted in the Blackhawk War of 1832 fought in Wisconsin and Illinois. Perhaps the most famous of all conflicts was the Battle of Little Big Horn (1876) between US cavalry, led by General Custer, and combined forces of Sioux and Cheyenne native Americans, led by Crazy Horse and Sitting Bull. It took place in the state of Montana and saw native American tribes overpowered by the settlers' forces. The 1890 massacre of Sioux men, women and children at Wounded Knee in South Dakota signalled the end of the conflict. Today, native Americans account for no more than two per cent of the country's total population. They are found in small numbers in all states, but the greatest numbers are in the four adjoining southern states of Oklahoma, New Mexico, Arizona and California. Each of the states has populations of over 200,000 native Americans.

▲ Yellowstone National Park was founded in 1872 and is the oldest in the USA. It is world famous for its hot springs, geysers, waterfalls and abundant wildlife. The park stretches across parts of Montana, Wyoming and eastern Idaho and is home to over 200 species of birds.

▲ Colorado's heavy snowfall on its mountains attracts thousands of skiers to resorts such as Powderhorn and Aspen.

THE SOUTH

The southern United States has a distinctive nature created by its landscape, its economy, culture and character of its inhabitants.

▲ The White Sands National Park lies in the south-west of New Mexico. These white gypsum sand dunes are shifted by winds to create ever-changing landscapes.

▲ New Orleans, Louisiana, is known for its rich mixture of cultural influences reflecting the periods when it has been a French and Spanish colony. Here, a jazz band strikes up in the Vieux Carré, also known as the French Quarter of the city.

▼ The Mesa Montosa lies in New Mexico. The river, the Rio Chuviscar, originates in this landform and eventually flows into the larger Rio Conchos across the border in Mexico.

The southern states of the USA have a varied geography and climate. Some have a warm, temperate climate, while others such as Louisiana and Florida have a subtropical climate with hot, humid summers and, in most places, mild winters. Much of the two most southerly states, Florida and Texas, remains warm all year round. In the states that surround the Gulf of Mexico, moderate to heavy rainfall is often increased by thunderstorms. On average, between five and eight tropical storms or hurricanes reach some part of the coast surrounding the Gulf every year.

THE LANDSCAPE

The Appalachian mountain chain extends into southern USA, reaching the states of North Carolina, Georgia and Alabama. Other major mountain ranges include the Cumberland Mountains and Plateau which cross eastern Tennessee, north Georgia and northeastern Alabama. The Ouachita Mountains are found to the west, spanning much of Arkansas and southeastern Oklahoma. Of the southern states, only New Mexico, Arkansas, Tennessee and Oklahoma do not have a coastline with either the Atlantic Ocean or the Gulf of Mexico. Florida has both, with the eastern side of its peninsula facing the Atlantic and its western side facing the warmer waters of the Gulf. Four more states border the Gulf. Louisiana and Texas have long coastlines, while Alabama and Mississippi have only small Gulf shores. West of Texas lies New Mexico where the Great Plains extends into the eastern third while much of the remainder consists of mountains and desert valleys.

THE MISSISSIPPI PLAINS AND DELTA

The Mississippi is the largest river in the region and also the longest in the USA. It flows south where it forms much of the border between Tennessee and Arkansas and the state of Mississippi's two western borders with Arkansas and Louisiana. The Mississippi meanders through the central southern states before its final journey through southern Louisiana after which it empties into the Gulf of Mexico near New Orleans at an average rate of 19 million litres per second. The Mississippi's final course has changed many times in the past few thousands years and has created a giant river delta measuring approximately 28,500 km². This is still expanding as more sediment is deposited by the river as it empties into the Gulf.

The power of the Mississippi to deposit sediment is not just seen at its delta. Large alluvial plains extend either side of the river as it flows through the southern states. These have been created over long periods of time and measure between 60 and 120 km in width. With the plains low-lying, the severe risk of flooding is countered in a number of ways, including storage reservoirs in the north of the river, dams and large embankments or levees which now run for an estimated 2,575 km along its length.

▼ An inhabitant of the Appalachian mountains region of the US state of North Carolina plays his banjo. Folk songs from the Appalachian mountains originated from Celtic folk music introduced by 18th and 19th century settlers from the British Isles.

▼ The Rio Grande runs for over 3,000 km, flowing through New Mexico and forming the border between Texas and Mexico. Here it flows through Big Bend National Park in Texas.

THE COTTON BELT

Cotton is the world's largest non-food crop and is used to make around half of all the world's textiles. In 2001, the USA was the world's second largest producer of raw cotton, most of it grown in the cotton belt which sweeps across the southern states. This region provides ideal climatic conditions for cotton which has been grown there since the time of the earliest European settlers. Today, much production has shifted west to California and Arizona but Mississippi, Arkansas, Louisiana and Texas are still leading producers.

SLAVERY

Cotton, tobacco, rice and sugarcane were major crops for the early European settlers in the southern states. As farms and plantations grew in size, farmers turned to slavery to create the large workforce required. Millions of black Africans were imported by slave traders into the southern USA. By 1790, black people comprised a third of the south's population. Controversy grew over the morality of slavery and the issue split the USA with the north opposing it. In 1860–1861, 11 southern states withdrew from the rest of the USA to form the Confederate States of America. This was the start of The American Civil War (1861–1865). The southern states lost the war and their economy suffered. Although slavery was abolished, conditions barely improved for many decades and many African Americans migrated to the industrial north.

▼ The American alligator lives in the swamplands of the southern US states of Alabama, Florida and Georgia. Adults can grow up to 3.6 m in length.

CHANGING ECONOMIES

Although traditional crops, such as cotton, are still grown in the region, the southeastern states of the USA have moved into other areas to strengthen their economies. Modern cash crops, such as soybeans and peanuts, have risen in importance while Alabama, North Carolina, Arkansas and Georgia are the leading US producers of poultry. Oil from the Gulf of Mexico and in the states of Louisiana and Mississippi helps supply raw materials to chemical and manufacturing industries. Engineering and electronics have grown in the region prompted, in part, by the US military and NASA, the national space agency. Tourism has become a major source of revenue, with the cities of New Orleans, Miami Beach and much of Florida providing top destinations for foreign tourists. Florida's wetlands, which cover almost a fifth of its land and include Everglades National Park, are a major attraction as are its beach resorts on both the Atlantic and Gulf coasts. Florida is a leading citrus fruit producer, and its all-year-round warm climate is attractive to retired Americans.

TEXAS

Texas is the second biggest state in the USA and is also the third most populous. Much of its western area lies within or near the Great Plains region. The state is one of the most important agricultural producers in the country and is a leading grower of a large range of crops, from watermelons to spinach. Cattle farming is a major industry and the state has many huge cattle ranches. Texas has developed separately from its neighbours due, in part, to its huge reserves of fossil fuels. Wealth from extracting these fuels, from processing oil and from the manufacturing industry, has financed the creation of large, modern cities including Dallas, Houston and Austin, the capital city of Texas.

▲ A NASA space shuttle blasts off from its launch site at Cape Canaveral on the east coast of Florida.

▼ These ranch hands herd cattle into a feedlot. A head count in 2000 revealed that Texas contained 15 million head of cattle.

WESTERN USA

From the high volcanic mountains of the north to the Grand Canyon and the flat, dry deserts in the south, western USA has a dramatic range of scenery.

▲ Convict Lake is found in the eastern Sierra Nevada mountains. The 1.3 km-long lake is named after an 1871 gunfight involving escaped prisoners on its shores.

Western USA is a land of contrasts. It contains major centres of population, including San Francisco and Los Angeles, as well as some of the least inhabited parts of the country. It is home to some of the most high-tech regions and centres in North America while other parts of its land are owned by native peoples who have lived there for thousands of years. Geographically, the region contains a number of the United States' highest and lowest as well as wettest and driest places. This part of the United States is made up of a number of distinct and quite different geographical regions. Inland, the giant Rocky Mountains separates much of western USA from states further east. They run through a large part of the state of Idaho before progressing deep into Canadian territory. To the south are large areas of mainly flat desert which stretch across the border and into northern Mexico. The large state of California has a complex geography partly created by a major fault line in the Earth's tectonic plates, called the San Andreas Fault. The Fault runs through approximately

▲ Organ Pipe National Park in Arizona is one of a number of national parks which preserve portions of the Sonoran Desert. The park, which covers over 132,000 hectares of land, is named after the rare organ pipe cactus.

1,050 km of the state. California has an enormous central valley flanked by the Sierra Nevada mountains to the east and ranges of coastal mountains to the west. Lower-lying areas of California are found in the central valley and along much of the Pacific coast, west of the coastal mountains, as well as to the southeast in flat, desert areas which includes the Mojave Desert. North of central California is the region known as the Pacific Northwest which runs from northern California through Oregon and Washington State. It features coastal ranges of mountains and the Cascade Range which is further inland. East of California and the Pacific Northwest, much of the landscape consists of what geographers call intermontane (between mountain) basins and plateaus, including the Great Basin (see page 81), bounded to the east by the Rockies.

◀ One of western USA's most notable landmarks, the Golden Gate suspension bridge, is found in San Francisco. Completed in 1937, the bridge's main span measures 1,280 m in length and is suspended from two cables hung from towers 227 m high.

CANADA

Seattle
Olympia
WASHINGTON
Mt. Rainier △
4392m
Portland
Salem
Columbia
Eugene

OREGON

Boise
IDAHO
Snake

Rocky Mountains

UNITED STATES

Reno   Great   Great
Carson City   Salt Lake   Salt Lake City
Sacramento
Basin
San Francisco
San Jose   NEVADA
OF AMERICA
UTAH
Fresno
Mt Whitney △
4418m
Las Vegas
Colorado
CALIFORNIA
Colorado
Plateau
Los Angeles
San Bernardino
ARIZONA
San Diego
Sonoran Desert   Phoenix

Tucson

PACIFIC OCEAN

Coast Ranges

Central Valley

Sierra Nevada

HOT AND COLD, DRY AND WET

To the north and south of western USA lie vastly different landscapes. Much of Arizona and parts of Nevada and southern California are covered in hot, arid deserts. The largest desert in the region is also the largest in the whole of North America. Called the Sonoran Desert, it covers an area of around 310,000 km² and extends from northwestern Mexico to include southwestern Arizona and southeastern California. Death Valley is an extremely dry desert area in California and Nevada which receives just 50 mm average rainfall a year. Here, the highest temperature ever was recorded in the USA: 56.7°C. In contrast, temperatures in the northern states of Idaho, Oregon and Washington are much lower, averaging between 7°C and 12°C and with a record low in Idaho of -51.1°C. These states are crossed by a series of mountain ranges with peaks above 4,000 m. Parts of Washington and Oregon are among the wettest places in the USA receiving more than 2,000 mm of rainfall every year. Large forests are found in all three states and forestry forms an important part of their economy.

◀ In less than a century, Los Angeles has grown from a town of 50,000 people to a metropolitan area which, in 2000, had 16,374,000 residents. It is famous as the home of Hollywood – the heart of the American film industry.

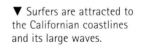
▼ Surfers are attracted to the Californian coastlines and its large waves.

CALIFORNIA'S INDUSTRIES

California is the state with the biggest population. It is home to 34 million people, a figure which has increased by 11 million in just 21 years. Many people are drawn to this western state for the glamour of its major film, music and entertainment industries, and its business opportunities. California is home to one of the largest and most profitable high-tech and computing regions in the world. Nicknamed Silicon Valley, this industrial region stretches a distance of over 40 kilometres along two valleys. Many leading computer manufacturers have their headquarters and research centres there, and Silicon Valley employs many thousands of people and generates hundreds of millions of dollars. Traditional industries in California, such as aerospace and ship-building, still exist. However light industries, such as electronics and service industries including entertainment, tourism and banking, are extremely important in the state's major cities of San Francisco and Los Angeles.

Over seven million people live in the metropolitan area of San Francisco, while the metropolitan area of Los Angeles is the largest urban area in western USA with a population of over 16 million people. Built on a large coastal plain, this cosmopolitan urban region is linked by a massive network of freeways which has created serious air pollution problems in the area. To the south of Los Angeles lies its port, called Los Angeles-Long Beach. It is the biggest cargo-handling port on the US Pacific coast.

▲ A field of mustard seed in California's Napa valley. California is also famous for its grapes which are used in its wine industry.

▲ Death Valley, in California, is a depression 86 m below sea level. It is the lowest point in the USA.

▼ Rows of slot machines and gambling tables abound in the many casinos found in the city of Las Vegas.

▲ Lying in Arizona, the Grand Canyon is one of the most famous geological features in the world. Carved out of the surrounding rock by the Colorado river, the canyon is over 440 km long and, in places, more than 1.6 km deep.

USA'S LEADING FOOD PRODUCER

If it were a nation, California would have a place in the world's top ten food producers. Half of the USA's fruit and vegetables and 15 per cent of its milk are produced within its border. California is also home to the largest single wine producer, Ernest Gallo, which produces around two million bottles a day. A number of reasons explain California's success as a farming area beyond rich, fertile soil. Much of the state has a warm, subtropical climate which allows long growing seasons. There are many variations in local climates depending on nearness to the Pacific and height above sea level. Different crops make use of these varying sub-climates, so that California grows more than 200 different foods. Much research and investment has led to the use of the latest technology and farming techniques as well as extensive irrigation schemes especially throughout the Central Valley which enables this dry region to produce half the state's farm output.

in size due to evaporation and the amount of water it receives. It is one of the saltiest freshwater lakes in the world. Industrial plants which extract and process the lake's salt are situated on its shores.

THE GREAT BASIN

The Great Basin covers an area of over half a million square kilometres. It occupies most of the state of Nevada, the western half of Utah as well as smaller parts of Oregon, Idaho and California. Widest in the north, the Great Basin narrows and decreases in height as it extends south. The basin consists of broad valleys and rugged mountain blocks. The Sierra Nevada mountain range to the west prevents winds carrying moist air from the Pacific Ocean reaching the basin. Most of the moisture falls as rain before reaching the basin. As a result, most of the Great Basin has a desert climate with total rainfall of between 150 and 300 mm per year. Natural plant and animal life is limited except in areas where artificial irrigation schemes bring water. The Great Basin is a region which features interior drainage. This means water from rivers and streams empties into desert flats and seeps underground rather than emptying into a sea or ocean. The region's largest lake is the Great Salt Lake in northern Utah. It is fed mainly by melting snow from mountains and from a number of small rivers. This shallow lake has an average area of about 4,400 km² but varies greatly

LIFE IN THE GREAT BASIN

Compared to many parts of the USA, the Great Basin is a hostile environment. Large parts of the Great Basin lie uninhabited but major towns and cities do exist. Much of the agriculture is concerned with raising cattle and sheep and only contributes a small amount to the area's economy. The region's greatest resource is its wealth of minerals. Mining for deposits of silver, gold and other metals helped develop settlements such as Carson City, the capital of Nevada. Today, Nevada remains the leading state producer of gold and mercury, while Utah is among the leading producers of silver, copper and iron ore. Salt Lake City is a major manufacturing centre. It is also home to the Church of Jesus Christ of Latter-day Saints – the Mormon religion whose pioneers established the city in the late 1840s. Much of Nevada's growth in cities and population is linked with the legalisation of gambling in 1931. Las Vegas opened its first casino in 1941 and, today, a population of 1.5 million people are reliant on its status as one of the world's leading gaming and gambling centres.

▼ Part of the Cascade Range which lies in the centre of Washington State, Mount Rainier is a dormant volcano which is clad in five major glaciers. With a peak 4,392 m above sea level, it is the third highest peak on mainland USA.

ALASKA

The largest and most northern part of the USA, the vast, icy wilderness of Alaska was bought from Russia in 1867.

▲ Built in the 1970s, the Trans-Alaska pipeline runs for 1,287 km carrying crude oil from Alaska's northern coast to the city of Valdez in the south.

▼ At 6,194 m above sea level, Mount McKinley is the highest point in the whole of North America. The mountain is known to native Americans as Denali which means 'the high one'.

Lying at the northwestern tip of the North American continent, Alaska is separated from the Russian Federation by the seas that course through the Bering Strait. The 1.59 million km² state includes frozen tundra to the north, large taiga forests, hundreds of small lakes and a southern peninsula which stretches out westwards. Beyond it lies the Aleutian islands, a long island chain. Alaska has a rugged geography with large mountain ranges bordering the Pacific as well as running inland. In total, the state has 39 mountain ranges which hold 17 of the 20 highest peaks in the entire United States.

PEOPLE AND ECONOMY

It was across the Bering Strait, at least 30,000 years ago, that the first peoples were thought to have entered North America. Descendants of these first arrivals include the Inuit and Aleut peoples who today make up around a tenth of Alaska's total population of 627,000. Oil and petroleum exploitation dominate the Alaskan economy producing nearly a third of its income. Forestry and fishing are the state's other key resources while tourism is also on the increase. Visitors are attracted to Alaska's harsh landscapes and its national parks which contain a rich range of wildlife including black, brown and polar bears and large herds of caribou (moose).

▶ Alaska is home to the world's largest population of grey wolves.

HAWAII

Hawaii is the name given to a group of 132 atolls and islands and the largest island in the group. In 1959, these Pacific islands became the 50th state of the USA.

The islands of Hawaii form a 2,400 km long arc through the Pacific Ocean. Some smaller islands are coral atolls, but most of the islands are the topmost parts of giant volcanoes which extend over 9 km up from the Pacific Ocean floor and break the water's surface. Only the volcanoes found on the island of Hawaii, known as the Big Island, are thought to be still active although the region experiences earthquake activity. The landscape of the Hawaiian islands is a dramatic mixture of volcanic peaks, steep cliffs, sandy beaches

▼ The fine weather, sandy beaches and excellent surfing in the waters of the Pacific attract many tourists from all over the world to the islands of Hawaii.

and deep valleys covered in forest. The climate is tropical with the northeast trade winds bringing rain, and large parts of the islands are covered in lush, tropical vegetation. Apart from Hawaii, there are seven other large islands. One of these, Oahu, is home to over two-thirds of the islands' 1,211,537 population as well as the islands' largest and capital city, Honolulu. The people of Hawaii are ethnically diverse with those of European (31 per cent), Japanese (20 per cent), Filipino (14 per cent) and Polynesian (13 per cent) descent the largest groups. Fishing is important to the economy in Hawaii; however, tourism is the islands' single biggest industry, worth more than 10 billion US dollars every year.

BERMUDA

The most northerly coral islands in the world, Bermuda lies in the Atlantic Ocean, some 900 km off the coast of the USA. It remains a British dependency.

Area: 53 km²
Population: 64,000
Capital: Hamilton (6,000)
Main language spoken: English
Main religions: Anglican, Methodist
Currency: Bermudian dollar
Main exports: fuel for shipping and aircraft, re-exported pharmaceuticals
Type of government: self-governing dependency of UK

Bermuda consists of more than 150 islands which have a base of volcanic rock with coral formations lying above. The population rely on collecting and storing rainfall for their water supply. The island chain has a mild, humid climate aided by the warm Gulf Stream ocean current. The islands are covered in rich vegetation including mangrove hedges and many flowering plants. Yet, there is very little agricultural land and flowering lilies are Bermuda's only agricultural export. Tourists, although falling in numbers throughout the 1990s, are still a major contributor to the economy with over 80 per cent of visitors coming from the USA.

The remainder of Bermuda's economy is reliant on service industries such as insurance. Discovered in 1503 by Spaniard, Juan Bermudez, the chain of islands came under British rule in 1684. Although still a dependency of the UK, Bermuda became self-governing in 1968. The population, who are mainly descendants of former black slaves or Portuguese or British settlers, enjoy a high standard of living and in 1995 rejected a move for full independence.

CENTRAL AMERICA

Bounded by the Pacific Ocean to the west and the Caribbean Sea to the east, Central America is a land bridge, known as an isthmus, which links the rest of North America with the South American continent. It is dominated by the country of Mexico, south of which lie a further seven countries: Belize, Guatemala, Nicaragua, El Salvador, Honduras, Costa Rica and Panama. Around 40 per cent of the land area of these countries is covered in rainforest which harbours a rich variety of wildlife. Much of Central America, from southern Mexico southwards, is mountainous and the region is one of the most active volcanic areas in the world. Water falling from high land is harnessed to generate almost half of the region's electricity via hydro-electric power. Farming is the main activity of the majority of Central Americans with many crops such as corn and beans grown on small family farms. Approximately half of all farm products are exported out of the region. The five most important export products are: coffee, cotton, sugar, beef and bananas. Central America has been inhabited by a series of ancient civilizations, including the Aztecs, Maya, Olmecs and Toltecs. The region has seen many wars and conflicts since the arrival of Spanish explorers in the 16th century.

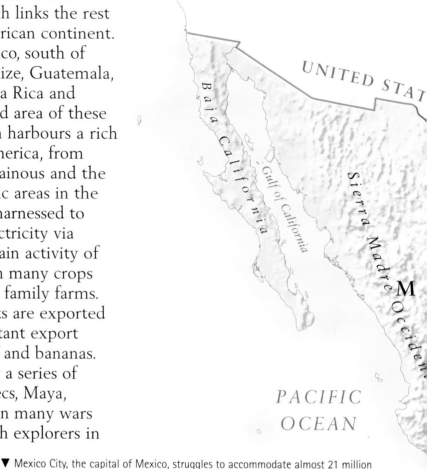

▼ Mexico City, the capital of Mexico, struggles to accommodate almost 21 million inhabitants. Many people live in slums without sanitation. The lack of environmental controls contributes to one of the world's worst air problems.

▲ The Mayan pyramid of Altun Ha in Belize is one of many ancient sites found in Central America. These places attract millions of tourists every year, providing the relatively poor region with much-needed income and employment.

ERICA

Río Grande

Sierra Madre Oriental

O

Gulf of Mexico

Yucatán Peninsula

■ MEXICO CITY

BELMOPAN ■

BELIZE

GUATEMALA

HONDURAS

GUATEMALA CITY ■

■ TEGUCIGALPA

SAN SALVADOR ■

NICARAGUA

EL SALVADOR

■ MANAGUA

Caribbean Sea

Lake Nicaragua

SAN JOSÉ ■

PANAMA CITY ■

COSTA RICA

PANAMA

COLOMBIA

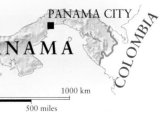

◄ The blue morpho butterfly with its spectacular metallic-blue wings is found in Costa Rica's forests and feeds mainly on fallen fruits.

0   1000 km
0   500 miles

MEXICO

About a fifth of the size of the USA with which it shares a major land border, Mexico is the most populous Spanish-speaking nation in the world.

Area: 1,958,201 km²
Population: 98,000,000
Capital: Mexico City (20,965,000)
Main language spoken: Spanish
Main religion: Roman Catholic
Currency: Mexican peso
Main exports: manufactures (including machinery and transport equipment), crude petroleum, agricultural goods (particularly sugar, fruit and meat)
Type of government: republic; democracy

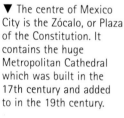

▼ The centre of Mexico City is the Zócalo, or Plaza of the Constitution. It contains the huge Metropolitan Cathedral which was built in the 17th century and added to in the 19th century.

Mexico is at its broadest to the north where it borders the USA. The country narrows as it runs in a curve south and eastwards. It ends in land borders with Guatemala and Belize and in a square-shaped peninsula jutting into the Gulf of Mexico called the Yucatán peninsula. The Yucatán is formed mainly of limestone rocks and is low-lying with an average height above sea level of only 30 m. Mexico has a second peninsula quite different in shape and landscape, Baja California. It extends south from the US state of California and runs some 1,225 km southwards creating the Gulf of California and bordering the Pacific Ocean on its western side. Much of Baja California consists of high mountain ranges of over 3,000 m.

THE CENTRAL PLATEAU

The centre of Mexico is a great, high plateau which is open to the north but bounded by two large mountain chains: the Sierra Madre Oriental to the east and

▲ Cancún is a major holiday resort found just off the east coast of the Yucatán peninsula. Growing from a small island village in the 1970s, it now has more than 30,000 hotel rooms and attracts tourists from around the world.

the Sierra Madre Occidental to the west. This plateau forms around half the total area of Mexico and slopes downwards from the west to the east. To the south, the plateau rises to form a region which is crossed by many mountains and volcanoes. Lying an equal distance between the cities of Veracruz and Puebla is Citlaltépetl, a volcano which is the country's highest point. On the far side of the mountain ranges from the central plateau, the land forms huge, low-lying coastal plains. The plains facing the Gulf of Mexico are fringed with swamps, lagoons and

▲ A busy market day for local Mexicans in the south of the country. Mexican markets, known as *mercados*, exist all over the country and are a major way in which goods are traded between local people.

sandbars. Mexico has relatively few major rivers and lakes. Its largest lake is Lake Chapala which covers approximately 1,080 km² and is found near Guadalajara, Mexico's second largest city. The country's longest river, the Rio Grande (also known as the Rio Bravo del Norte), forms over 2,000 km of border between the US state of Texas and Mexico before emptying into the Gulf of Mexico.

HOT AND COLD LAND

From mountain peaks permanently covered in snow to hot, dry deserts and lush, wet rainforest, Mexico has a varied range of landscapes and climates. Climate tends to change with both the height of the land above sea level and its latitude. Land below 910 m is known as tierra caliente (hot land), between 910 and 1,800 m, tierra templada (temperate land) and above 1,800 m, tierra fria (cold land). Mexico City, for example, lies in the tierra templada and has a cool, dry climate with only a small variation in temperature (averaging between 12 and 17°C) throughout the year. In the north of Mexico, temperature extremes are far greater and maximum temperatures can rise to over 45°C. This intense heat along with low rainfall, often below 250 mm a year, results in vast desert and semi-desert areas. Much of central and southern

Mexico is relatively dry as well, and it is only in the tropical regions to the far south and southeast of the country where rainfall is heavy. The wettest regions of Mexico are to the south and in the Yucatán; these areas can receive more than 3,000 mm of rainfall per year.

▼ Ancient Mayan peoples lived throughout large parts of Mexico and left behind many impressive structures and sites. This ancient Mayan pyramid is called the Temple of the Inscriptions. It is found at Palenque, 110 kilometres south-east of the city of Villahermosa.

▲ Mexico City has an estimated three million cars which are responsible for much of its air pollution.

▼ Fibres from the leaves of the sisal plant are used to make strong ropes which do not deteriorate quickly in salt water. Here, sisal leaves are harvested for a rope-making factory in the Yucatán peninsula's largest city, Mérida.

PLANTS AND ANIMALS

Mexico's wide range of landscapes and climate create habitats for a great variety of living things. Even in the hottest and driest desert areas in the north, plants such as yuccas and many species of cactus flourish, while insects, lizards, coyotes and armadillos also live in arid regions. Mexico has approximately 550,000 km² of forests which cover over 20 per cent of its land. In the hot and humid far south of the country, rainforests exist which provide habitats for monkeys, jaguars, anteaters and many species of birds and lizards. On the slopes of the Sierra Madre ranges and other mountains, large forests of pines and other coniferous trees grow below an altitude of around 4,000 m. Creatures that live in these mountainous forests include bears, wild pigs and ocelots. Due to continuing deforestation, many creatures in Mexico's forests are now endangered as their habitat is destroyed.

RESOURCES AND INDUSTRY

Agriculture, forestry and fishing make up less than 10 per cent of Mexico's economy. Much farming is conducted on a small scale but irrigation remains a problem. Coffee and sugar are Mexico's two most important food exports. The country has great reserves of many minerals, and is the world's leading producer of silver and one of the largest of zinc and lead. Mexico has the world's seventh largest reserves of oil, much of which is located offshore. Processing oil and natural gas, and manufacturing a wide range of products generate more revenue than any other sector. Manufacturing industries include food processing plants, paper mills and clothing factories. The country is also the world's tenth largest assembler of motor vehicles. A feature of Mexican industry, especially around Mexico City and near the US border, are Maquiladora industries. These are where well-known, brand-name products from one country are made under licence in another country where workforce costs are lower. In northern Mexico, there are more than 2,000 Maquiladoras producing clothes, computers, shoes and other goods.

▼ A train runs over a viaduct in the Copper Canyon in the Sierra Madre Occidental mountains.

▲ Iguanas are common throughout southern Mexico and in the southeast of the country they are sometimes smoked over an open fire and eaten as a delicacy.

mixed Spanish and native American origin, who form around 60 per cent of the population. The mixture of European and native groups contribute to Mexico's rich culture reflected in its music, art, textiles and its range of native foods and dishes, many of which use over 200 different species of chilli as flavourings.

UNITED STATES OF MEXICO

Mexico's full, official name is the United States of Mexico. The country is divided into 32 administrative regions – 31 states and a federal district located in its capital, Mexico City. This giant urban area has grown in size and population to extend beyond the federal district. Smaller settlements, once outside of the city, have been swallowed up as the metropolitan area has sprawled outwards. Nearly 21 million people are estimated to live in and around Mexico City, making it one of the world's largest urban areas. Over half of Mexico's industry is located in or near the city which is surrounded by mountains on all sides. These mountains trap the air around the city and increase the levels of air pollution caused by motor vehicles and industry. Air pollution is a serious health problem in Mexico City.

MEXICO'S PEOPLE

Mexico has been home to a number of ancient civilizations including the Olmecs, the Maya and the Aztec. The Aztecs settled in Mexico around CE 1200 and built their capital city, Tenochtitlán, on the site of present-day Mexico City. Most of the Aztec civilization was destroyed by Spanish explorers in the early 16th century. Called New Spain, Mexico was under Spanish rule until it became independent in 1821. Native Americans make up approximately 30 per cent of Mexico's total population of 98 million. The largest group are mestizos, people of

▼ The highest point in Mexico, and the third highest in North and Central America, Citlaltépetl is a dormant volcano standing 5,610 m above sea level.

GUATEMALA

Guatemala is a mountainous country which experiences both earthquakes and volcanic activity. It contains the largest continuous area of rainforest in Central America.

Area: 108,889 km²
Population: 11,000,000
Capital: Guatemala City (2,246,000)
Main languages spoken: Spanish, Mayan languages
Main religion: Roman Catholic
Currency: quetzal
Main exports: coffee, sugar, bananas, vegetable seeds, legumes
Type of government: republic; partial democracy

▼ Lying between Mazatenango and Guatemala City, Lake Atitlán fills part of a large sunken crater, or caldera, created by an enormous volcanic explosion.

Almost two-thirds of Guatemala is covered in mountains. There are two main mountain ranges which cross the country. To the north is a series of older mountains which have been heavily eroded, yet in some places still stand over 3,000 metres in height. To the south, the mountains are younger and contain over 30 volcanoes, three of which are still active. Soil mixed with volcanic ash has washed down from the mountains to create a narrow plain of excellent growing land along Guatemala's Pacific coast. Although it lies in the tropics, the cooler seas it borders and its range of high and low-lying land create a number of different climates. On the Pacific coast, temperatures tend to average over 30°C, while in the highlands above 1,800 m, temperatures between 10°C and 16°C are more common. The dry season is when most of the country's 850,000 tourists visit. Most tourists are from the USA and Mexico.

EL PETÉN

Approximately a third of Guatemala is made up of low-lying land in the northern region called El Petén. This area consists of plains and small, knobbly hills made largely of limestone rocks. Dense rainforest covers most of the region which provides habitats for a great variety of creatures including the jaguar. This big cat is the largest predator in Central America. Few rivers run through El Petén as most of the rainfall it receives drains underground. Transport links are sparse although a major road and airport connect the region's main town, Flores, with the rest of the country.

THE PEOPLE OF GUATEMALA

Guatemala was the centre of the ancient Maya civilization which flourished between CE 300 and CE 900. Almost half of all Guatemalans are descendants of the ancient Maya and other native Indian peoples, while just over half are mestizos – people of mixed Indian and European origins. Farming dominates the lives of 60 per cent of the workforce. Cereals and fruits are grown for local use and coffee is the most important export crop. The country is also one of the world's largest producers of cardamom seeds, a popular spice. After many decades of dictators ruling without elections and violent civil wars, Guatemala is currently peaceful but faces problems in healthcare and education. For example, 39 per cent of adult women cannot read or write.

◀ Approximately 1.7 per cent of Guatemala's rainforests, home to a large range of wildlife, is removed every year for their timber and to clear new land for farming.

BELIZE

Bordering the Caribbean Sea, the small country of Belize contains a varied mixture of landscapes and peoples. It became independent in 1981.

Area: 22,965 km²
Population: 240,000
Capital: Belmopan (8,100)
Main languages spoken: English Creole, English
Main religion: Roman Catholic
Currency: Belize dollar
Main exports: sugar, orange and grapefruit juice, bananas, fish, clothes
Type of government: dominion; democracy

▶ Keen-billed toucan

Known as British Honduras until 1973, Belize is a country of two distinct geographical halves. The northern half, which borders Mexico, is mainly low-lying and contains many swamps near the coast. The southern half begins with grassy savannahs and rises to mountain ranges. Over 40 per cent of Belize is covered in forests which flourish in the country's subtropical climate. The forests provide hardwoods such as mahogany, rosewood and chicle, the gum of which is used to make chewing gum. Off Belize's coastline is a chain of coral reefs and small sandy islands called cayes. Running for approximately 290 km, it is the largest coral reef in the western hemisphere. Several hundred thousand tourists visit Belize every year, mainly for its beaches and the reef, but also for its historic sites. Belize was once a part of the Mayan empire and many ancient sites remain. Its people are a mixture of many cultures with mestizos and creoles accounting for 75 per cent. More than half of the people live in rural areas where they work in forestry or grow sugarcane, citrus fruits, maize and rice. Although Belmopan is the official capital city, Belize City is much larger and around 20 per cent of Belize's total population live there.

▼ El Castillo is part of an ancient Mayan site found in the mountainous west of the country.

HONDURAS

The third largest country in Central America, Honduras is dominated by mountain ranges. It borders Nicaragua, Guatemala and El Salvador.

Area: 112,088 km²
Population: 6,000,000
Capital: Tegucigalpa (988,000)
Main language spoken: Spanish
Main religion: Roman Catholic
Currency: lempira
Main exports: coffee, bananas, shrimps and lobsters, zinc, frozen meat
Type of government: republic; partial democracy

Honduras has a long coastline with the Caribbean Sea and a short coast alongside the Pacific Ocean. The Caribbean coast features several important ports including Le Ceiba and, offshore, the Bay Islands which are popular tourist destinations. The country's lowland areas are found near the coasts and in large river valleys which criss-cross the highlands of Honduras. Much of the country is mountainous. The highest mountains are found in the western and central areas and were created by volcanic activity. In the hot, humid lowland areas, rainforests cover large stretches of land. On the mountains, forests of oak and pine trees dominate.

A DEVELOPING NATION

Honduras is less industrialized than its neighbours and its people are among the poorest in the Western world. Foreign aid and investment have helped to set up food processing plants as well as industries producing rum, cooking oil, cement and paper. The country's mountains contain vast deposits of metal ores, particularly silver, zinc, lead and gold. Underground mines have been excavated to extract these metals for industry. Most people farm land or work for owners of large plantations on which bananas, coffee and exotic fruits and flowers are grown for sale abroad. Honduras was once the world's leading exporter of bananas, and this crop still accounts for almost 25 per cent of the country's income. Much of the highland areas are unsuitable for farming, but the terrain allows 80 per cent of the country's electricity to be generated by hydro-electric plants harnessing the power of falling water.

▲ Discovered by Christopher Columbus in 1512, the Bay Islands lie in the Caribbean Sea off the north coast of Honduras and attract many tourists and divers.

► Many Hondurans work on plantations owned by foreign companies growing coffee and bananas. These women, employed by the US-owned Chiquita company, are washing bananas.

EL SALVADOR

The smallest nation in Central America, El Salvador's landscape is a mixture of lowlands and high volcanic mountains.

Area: 21,041 km²
Population: 6,000,000
Capital: San Salvador (1,522,000)
Main language spoken: Spanish
Main religion: Roman Catholic
Currency: colon and US dollar
Main exports: coffee, paper and paper products, clothing, pharmaceuticals, sugar
Type of government: republic; democracy

El Salvador is bordered to the east and north by Honduras and to the west by Guatemala. Behind its 320 km long coast with the Pacific Ocean, the land forms a narrow coastal plain before rising to a large central plateau dominated by several chains of mountains, some 20 volcanoes and deep valleys. More than 280 rivers and major streams flow across the country, mostly carrying water to the Pacific Ocean. Of all the Central America nations south of Mexico, El Salvador is the least-wooded country. In the past, much of the land would have been covered in trees, but many years of clearing the land for agriculture now mean that only around six per cent of the land remains forested.

▲ San Salvador is El Salvador's capital and largest city. The World Bank estimates that 48 per cent of the country's entire population live in extreme poverty. Many of these people live in slums in San Salvador and other cities.

NATURAL RESOURCES

El Salvador's mountainous backbone has been settled by native Indian peoples for many thousands of years. The slopes of the volcanic mountains were covered in nutrient-rich soils which have attracted farmers since earliest times. El Salvador has little in the way of mineral resources such as gold, iron or oil. The mountains and hills, however, do help to generate much of the country's electricity. Fast-falling water turns turbines in hydro-electric power plants to generate around two-thirds of El Salvador's electricity. A further 10 per cent is created by a large geothermal power plant. This taps into the heat below the Earth's surface.

RICH AND POOR

El Salvador is the most densely populated country in Central America with an approximate average of 300 people per km². The vast majority are mestizos – people of mixed native Indian and European descent. For many years, just 14 families owned 75 per cent of the country's land, but reforms are now handing over small plots of land to many people. After a devastating 13-year civil war which ended in 1991, the gap between rich and poor still remains large with wealth still concentrated in the hands of a few people. The USA is El Salvador's main trading partner responsible for 40 per cent of its imports and 20 per cent of its exports which include clothing, machinery and cash crops such as fruits, coffee and sugarcane.

▼ Pineapples are one of a number of fruits including avocados, mangoes and papaya grown in the rich soils of El Salvador.

NICARAGUA

Nicaragua is considered one of the most beautiful countries in Central America, but earthquakes and human conflict have left their mark.

Area: 130,000 km²
Population: 5,100,000
Capital: Managua (865,000)
Main language spoken: Spanish
Main religion: Roman Catholic
Currency: cordoba
Main exports: cotton, coffee, meat, chemicals, sugar
Type of government: republic; partial democracy

▼ Nicaragua's capital city, Managua, lies on the southern shore of Lake Managua. The city was badly damaged by earthquakes in 1931 and 1972. Parts of its centre have never been rebuilt.

Nicaragua has a varied landscape. The terrain changes dramatically across the country. The eastern region of Nicaragua, bordering the Caribbean Sea, is known as the Mosquito Coast. Partly covered in rainforest and featuring many lagoons and river deltas, this area is a coastal plain which extends over 70 km inland from the sea. The western side of Nicaragua has a drier climate and is mainly savannah grasslands and some forests. In between are two long chains of mountains which contain over 40 volcanoes. These volcanoes are partly responsible for the great amount of earthquake activity Nicaragua experiences. In 1992, for example, a large earthquake made 16,000 people homeless. Nicaragua has a tropical climate with a wet season between May and October. Parts of Nicaragua receive more than 3,100 mm of rainfall every year. The eastern side of Nicaragua has been hit by hurricanes on many occasions. In 1998, for example, Hurricane Mitch (which also devastated El Salvador and, particularly, Honduras) took the lives of over 1,800 Nicaraguans and also destroyed much of the country's banana, sugar and coffee crops.

LIVING NEAR THE LAKES

The southern part of Nicaragua is dominated by a giant basin in which lie Lake Managua and Lake Nicaragua, the largest lake in Central America. Lake Nicaragua is 177 km long and is 58 km at its widest point. The lake contains more than 400 islands and their picturesque location makes them popular visitor destinations. It is the only freshwater lake in the world to contain a number of sea fish, including swordfish and sharks. Research shows that these fish came from the Caribbean Sea and made their way to the lake via the San Juan river, one of four main rivers which flow from the lake. Most of Nicaragua's population lives and works in the lowlands between the Pacific Ocean and the shores of Lake Nicaragua and Lake Managua. The soil in this region is rich in nutrients and crops including cotton, maize, rice, bananas and beans are grown for local markets and for export.

TROUBLES

Nicaragua has suffered from many natural disasters such as hurricanes and earthquakes. It has also experienced many years of civil war, local conflicts and unrest. The Somoza family who ruled for over 40 years was overthrown in 1979 and the Sandinista government which replaced them was removed from power in 1990. Years of troubles have left Nicaragua's public services in poor condition, and shortages of food and clean water are common. To generate revenue, Nicaragua is developing more industries as well as exploiting its natural reserves of gold, silver and copper.

COSTA RICA

Costa Rica is one of the most peaceful and prosperous of the Central American nations. Growing coffee is the mainstay of rural life in this country.

Area: 51,100 km²
Population: 4,100,000
Capital: San José (970,000)
Main language spoken: Spanish
Main religion: Roman Catholic
Currency: Costa Rica colon
Main exports: bananas, coffee, textiles and clothing, fish, flowers
Type of government: republic; democracy

Costa Rica spans the width of the narrow Central America isthmus. The land on both coasts tends to be low-lying. The eastern side receives more rain than the western, but both coastal areas have a number of mangrove swamps and some white, sandy beaches. The land rises from the coasts in the centre and south of Costa Rica with high, rugged mountains created by volcanic activity. Between the main mountain ranges in the middle of the country lies a large plateau on which the majority of Costa Ricans live. The country has a tropical climate with relatively heavy rainfall. Its rainforests cover around a third of its land and help provide homes for an abundance of plant and animal life.

PEOPLE AND PROSPERITY

Costa Rica's population is unusual in the region in that they are mainly of European descent. Native Indians account for less than one per cent of the total population, while around three per cent of people are black. Agriculture occupies most of its workforce, with sales of bananas and coffee earning the country around 50 per cent of its income. Costa Rica generates the majority of its electricity using hydro-electric power. The mining of metal ores, particularly bauxite, is becoming more important, as is tourism. Since its 1948 civil war, Costa Rica has largely been a nation at peace. It has the

▲ Costa Rica was the first country in the region to grow and export coffee. Coffee growing on plantations supports around half of the population and has been the country's leading export for more than 100 years.

▲ The macaw is just one of the 725 different species of bird found within Costa Rica.

▶ A local fruit market in Costa Rica. Bananas are one of the country's major export earners.

most extensive welfare state in Central America. Compulsory education is free up to the age of 15 and Costa Rica is home to the University of Central America. The country has a well-developed healthcare system to which it devotes almost 25 per cent of its total expenditure. As a result, Costa Ricans have a life expectancy of just over 76 years, the best in Central America. The country does have economic problems. Reduced US aid, the rising price of imported oil, and falling prices for coffee and bananas, which it exports, have caused large debts to build up.

PANAMA

The small country of Panama links the continents of North and South America. Its 80 km long canal also links the Pacific and Atlantic oceans.

Area: 75,517 km²
Population: 3,000,000
Capital: Panama City (1,052,000)
Main language spoken: Spanish
Main religion: Roman Catholic
Currency: balboa. US currency is also legal tender
Main exports: bananas, shrimps, coffee, clothing, fish
Type of government: republic; democracy

Panama occupies a relatively narrow strip of land known as an isthmus bordered by the Caribbean Sea to the east and the Pacific Ocean to the west. Two sets of mountains run the length of Panama and between these ranges are many low-lying hills, lakes and over 400 rivers and streams. Panama has a tropical climate with particularly heavy rainfall on its eastern side. There, lush rainforests grow and Panama is home to over 2,000 species of tropical plants. On its western, Pacific side, the land tends to receive less rainfall and scrub forests are common. The scrub forests of Darien National Park, in the south of Panama, are virtually uninhabited and untouched by humans. Panama's coastline is indented by many bays and lagoons. In the Gulf of Panama on the Pacific side of the country lie a collection of over 100 small islands

THE PANAMA CANAL

One of the biggest engineering feats in the world, the Panama Canal was finally opened in 1914. The canal and its dredged entrances stretch 81 km through Panama and link the Atlantic and Pacific oceans. To travel between these oceans without using the canal involves a 12,000 km trip around the southernmost tip of South America. Over 14,000 individual journeys through the canal are made by shipping every year and the tolls that are paid are a major source of income for Panama. Traffic can travel in both directions and three sets of giant locks raise and lower the water level by 26 m during the journey. The canal was built by the USA which assisted Panama in obtaining independence from Colombia in 1903. At the end of 1999, after a 20 year handover period, full control of the canal was passed to Panama.

AN INTERNATIONAL GATEWAY

The Panama Canal has made the country an international gateway for shipping,

▲ Due to its shipping and banking interests and also because of the revenue collected from running the Panama Canal, Panama City, the country's capital, is one of the wealthiest cities in the entire Central American region.

trade and finance. Panama has a free trade zone around the canal and tax-free banking attracts customers from all over the world.

Panama also has one of the largest fleets of merchant ships in the world. Most of these ships are registered in Panama but are owned by foreign companies.

The warm climate and fertile soil allows the rural population of Panama to grow enough food for the country to be largely self-sufficient. Rice, corn and beans are the main staple crops with bananas, coffee and sugar grown for export abroad. Shrimps are also an important export.

▲ The Miraflores Locks on the Panama Canal raise or drop shipping 16.8 m, the difference between the elevation of the waters of Miraflores Lake and the Pacific Ocean.

THE CARIBBEAN AND SOUTH AMERICA

THE CARIBBEAN

The Caribbean islands form a broken bridge of land 3,200 km long between the South American country of Venezuela and the southeastern US state of Florida. The islands form a boundary separating the Atlantic Ocean from the Caribbean Sea. The region's climate is largely tropical with most islands experiencing a wet season between June and November. The Caribbean is also one of the regions most at risk from the threat of hurricanes. The Caribbean is comprised of three groups of islands. The Bahamas are the most northerly, the Lesser Antilles which include the islands of Antigua, Grenada and Trinidad & Tobago are the most easterly, while the Greater Antilles contain the largest islands such as Cuba, Jamaica and the large island of Hispaniola shared by the states of Haiti and the Dominican Republic. The region is named after some of the earliest known inhabitants of the area, the Carib people. In 1492, Christopher Columbus and his crew became the first European visitors when they landed in the Bahamas. He mistakenly thought he had reached Asia which led to the region being called the West Indies. In the centuries since Columbus's discovery, most of the Caribbean has seen colonial rule by the Spanish, French, British, Danish and Dutch.

► These Cuban workers are harvesting tobacco, a major crop in Cuba and several other Caribbean islands. Cuba with a land area of 110,861 km² comprises almost half the total land area of the Caribbean region.

◄ The landscape and climate of the US Virgin Islands make it a popular tourist destination. Sandy beaches often fringed with palm trees are to be found throughout the Caribbean.

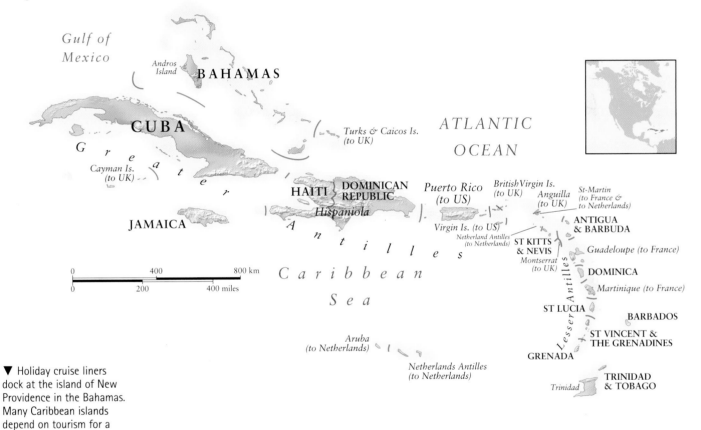

Gulf of Mexico

Andros Island

BAHAMAS

CUBA

G r e a t e r

Cayman Is. (to UK)

Turks & Caicos Is. (to UK)

ATLANTIC OCEAN

HAITI **DOMINICAN REPUBLIC**

Hispaniola

Puerto Rico (to US)

British Virgin Is. (to UK)

Anguilla (to UK)

St-Martin (to France & to Netherlands)

JAMAICA

A n t i l l e s

Virgin Is. (to US)

Netherland Antilles (to Netherlands)

ANTIGUA & BARBUDA

ST KITTS & NEVIS

Montserrat (to UK)

Guadeloupe (to France)

DOMINICA

Martinique (to France)

C a r i b b e a n

Sea

ST LUCIA

BARBADOS

ST VINCENT & THE GRENADINES

GRENADA

Lesser Antilles

0		400		800 km
0	200		400 miles	

Aruba (to Netherlands)

Netherlands Antilles (to Netherlands)

Trinidad

TRINIDAD & TOBAGO

▼ Holiday cruise liners dock at the island of New Providence in the Bahamas. Many Caribbean islands depend on tourism for a large part of their revenue.

CUBA

Cuba is the largest, most varied and one of the most beautiful of all Caribbean islands. Long but narrow, it lies just 144 km south of the US state of Florida.

Area: 110,861 km²
Population: 11 million
Capital: Havana (2,198,000)
Main language spoken: Spanish
Main religions: majority non-religious, Roman Catholic minority
Currency: Cuban peso
Main exports: sugar, minerals (nickel and chromite), fish products, tobacco
Type of government: republic; dictatorship

▼ This old steam train is carrying harvested sugarcane to a refinery. Sugar is an important export for Cuba, and in 2000, 36 million tonnes were produced.

Cuba extends approximately 1,260 km roughly east to west and its widest point measures 191 km. It is separated from mainland United States by the Straits of Florida and from the island of Hispaniola by the Windward Passage. Its nearest neighbour is Jamaica, 139 km away. Hundreds of natural bays, reefs and peninsulas give Cuba a shoreline of 3,735 km in length. Its territory includes one major island, the Isla de la Juventud (Island of Youth), and many tiny islets.

Cuba is less mountainous than its neighbours in the Greater Antilles, with around a quarter of its land covered in high elevations. The main mountain system of the Caribbean crosses southeastern Cuba where it is called the Sierra Maestra. Most of the remainder of Cuba is lowlands. Cuba is part of a limestone platform related to the limestone areas of the Yucatán peninsula in Mexico, in Florida and in the Bahamas. The country's longest river, the Cuoto, runs west to east and passes 20 km north of Bayamo. However, only small boats are able to navigate it.

▲ Tobacco grown in Cuba is used to make the country's world-famous cigars. In 1998, Cuba exported 180 million cigars. Only the most expensive are hand-rolled.

FARMING IN CUBA

About 80 per cent of Cuba's soil has been created by the action of rainfall on red limestone, producing deep, fertile soil. About 20 per cent of the land is covered with forests of pine and mahogany. Much of the remainder is pasture for the country's 4.6 million cattle or crop lands. Cuba has a mostly hot climate with heavy seasonal rainfall. Many crops flourish including rice, coffee, citrus fruits and tobacco which is used to make Cuban cigars. The country's chief crop, though, is sugar and has been so for over a century. Cuba is the world's third largest sugar producer, and sugar sales account for almost 50 per cent of its exports.

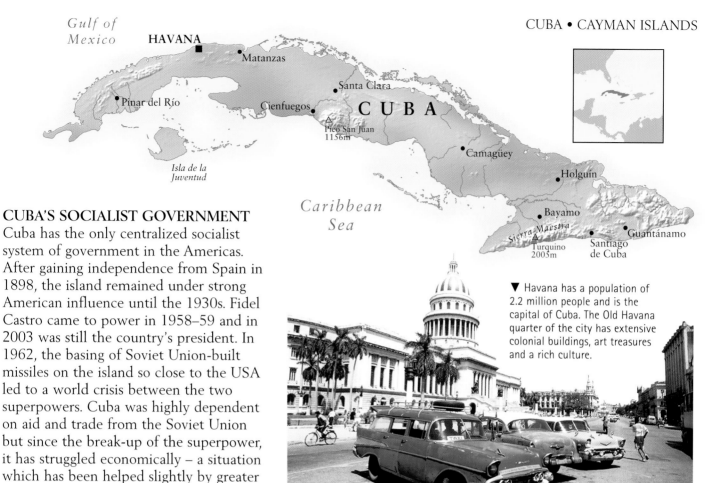

Gulf of Mexico

HAVANA

Matanzas

Pinar del Río

Santa Clara

Cienfuegos

C U B A

Pico San Juan
1156m

Isla de la Juventud

Caribbean Sea

Camagüey

Holguín

Bayamo

Sierra Maestra

Turquino
2005m

Guantánamo

Santiago
de Cuba

CUBA'S SOCIALIST GOVERNMENT

Cuba has the only centralized socialist system of government in the Americas. After gaining independence from Spain in 1898, the island remained under strong American influence until the 1930s. Fidel Castro came to power in 1958–59 and in 2003 was still the country's president. In 1962, the basing of Soviet Union-built missiles on the island so close to the USA led to a world crisis between the two superpowers. Cuba was highly dependent on aid and trade from the Soviet Union but since the break-up of the superpower, it has struggled economically – a situation which has been helped slightly by greater exploitation of its reserves of the metal, nickel, and increasing tourist numbers.

▼ Havana has a population of 2.2 million people and is the capital of Cuba. The Old Havana quarter of the city has extensive colonial buildings, art treasures and a rich culture.

CAYMAN ISLANDS

World-renowned for its beautiful beaches, the three islands that comprise the Caymans lie approximately 290 km northwest of Jamaica.

Cayman Islands
(to UK)

Little Cayman

Cayman Brac

Grand Cayman

George Town

Boddentown

Caribbean Sea

Area: 259 km²
Population: 35,000
Capital: George Town (25,000)
Main language spoken: English
Main religions: Anglican, Roman Catholic
Currency: Cayman Islands dollar
Main exports: manufactured consumer goods, turtle products
Type of government: self-governing dependency of UK

The Cayman Islands consist of Cayman Brac, Little Cayman and Grand Cayman, the largest of the group. All three islands are low-lying, feature excellent beaches and are fringed by spectacular coral reefs which are home to a rich range of marine life. Mangrove swamps cover a little under a third of the land although there are no natural streams on any of the islands. Among the vegetation on the islands are coconut palms, banana, mango and breadfruit trees. Turtles raised on a government turtle farm provide food, shell and leather which is sometimes fashioned into souvenirs for the Cayman's large number of tourist visitors. Cayman Brac is approximately 19 km long and 1.6 km wide. Its land is riddled with caves and dozens of shipwrecks which are popular sites for divers. Little Cayman is only around 8 km long and much of its area is given over to a wildlife sanctuary for iguanas and wild birds. More than half of the Cayman Islands' population is located in its capital, George Town, where more than 500 bank offices from many countries take advantage of the Cayman Islands' low levels of taxation. The Caymans were administered by Jamaica from 1863. When Jamaica became independent in 1962, they remained a British dependency. The governor of the islands who represents Britain works with a legislative assembly which consists of 18 members, 15 of whom are elected.

JAMAICA

Jamaica is a mixture of mountainous and lowland regions which are relatively densely populated. It lies about 145 km south of Cuba.

Area: 10,991 km²
Population: 3,000,000
Capital: Kingston (925,000)
Main language spoken: English
Main religions: Pentecostal, Roman Catholic, Seventh-Day Adventist
Currency: Jamaican dollar
Main exports: bauxite, agricultural products, food, beverages, tobacco
Type of government: dominion; democracy

▼ Kingston's bustling Coronation Market is where many Jamaicans sell a wide range of farm produce including peppers, bananas, tobacco, yams and mangoes. Jamaica grows almost the entire world supply of allspice.

Jamaica has beaches like many other Caribbean islands, but much of its land is mountainous. In the northwest, limestone rock forms a series of steep ridges and flat basins which have many sinkholes. To the northeast, the land rises to form the main mountain range of the island. Called the Blue Mountains, the highest of its summits, Blue Mountain Peak, is also the highest point in the Caribbean. The lowlands are largely covered in farms with sugar being the country's major crop. In 2000, around 2.5 million tonnes were produced. Agriculture employs about one-fifth of the Jamaican workforce and the island has over 440,000 goats and a similar number of cattle. Mining is one of Jamaica's most important industries. Bauxite – an ore from which aluminium is extracted – has been mined on the island since the 1950s and aluminium ore and products account for more than 60 per cent of the country's exports. Tourism is vital with over 1.5 million visitors to the island in 2001.

KINGSTON

Kingston is the capital of Jamaica and is the largest English-speaking city in the entire Caribbean. It is the centre of government of the island which is divided up into 14 parishes. The city was founded in 1692 after an earthquake destroyed much of the capital of the time, Port Royal. Kingston is situated on one of the largest natural harbours in the world and is overlooked by a highland area. The city is a busy port, a manufacturing centre for clothing and food processing, and a tourist destination for cruise liners. The city's architecture is a mixture of traditional colonial buildings, modern tower blocks, rich mansions and poor slum areas. Reggae music developed particularly in the deprived areas of Kingston and made reggae musician, Bob Marley, a world-famous Jamaican.

THE BAHAMAS

One of the most prosperous states in the region, the Bahamas are a collection of 700 islands plus 2,000 rocky islets located in the northwestern Caribbean.

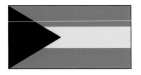

Area: 13,939 km²
Population: 303,000
Capital: Nassau (215,000)
Main language spoken: English
Main religions: Baptist, Roman Catholic, Anglican
Currency: Bahamian dollar
Main exports: petroleum re-exports, crayfish, machinery and transport equipment, salt
Type of government: dominion; democracy

An island archipelago, the Bahamas are spread over 233,000 km² of ocean with the nearest neighbouring land masses being the US state of Florida and, to the south, Cuba. Most of the islands are low-lying with mangrove swamps and reefs around their edges. The islands have no rivers, but many tropical plants, including orchids and jasmine, as well as a rich bird life. Thousands of tourists are attracted to the Bahamas for the scenery, beaches and warm climate. Average daily temperatures rarely slip below 18°C, even in winter. Only around 40 of the 700 islands are inhabited. Andros is the largest of the islands, while Grand Bahama is the site of much of the Bahamas' industry especially around the town of Freeport. Over half of the Bahamas' population lives in Nassau, its capital.

◄ Beautiful palm-fringed beaches, clear seas and a year-round warm climate attract visitors to the Bahamas.

TURKS & CAICOS ISLANDS

The Turks & Caicos are two island groups whose cays and islands rise more than 2,000 m from the sea floor. They are a British Crown Colony.

Area: 430 km²
Population: 17,000
Capital: Cockburn Town (5,000)
Main language spoken: English
Main religions: Anglican, Methodist
Currency: US dollar
Main exports: lobster, fish
Type of government: self-governing dependency of UK

The Turks & Caicos Islands are an extension of the Bahamas chain and consist of eight major islands and over 30 largely uninhabited cays. The two island groups are separated by a 35 km-wide trench, called the Turks Island Passage, which is over 2,200 m deep. Much of the land is sandy and rocky and covered in scrub and cactus. The Turks islands get their name from the turk's head cactus which grows on the islands. The climate is warm and constant, averaging between 24 and 32°C throughout the year. Rainfall averages between 540 mm and 720 mm per year, and drinking water is relatively scarce. Irrigation and careful management of the available water allows crops, including beans, corn and citrus fruits to be grown. In 1678, salt traders from Bermuda started to clear much of the island to create salinas – salt-drying pans – in which salt was dried and then taken on ships and traded. Salt remained a key industry until the 1960s, but today, tourism, fishing and financial services are the main sources of revenue.

HAITI

Occupying the western third of the tropical island of Hispaniola, Haiti has few natural resources and agriculture forms the basis of its economy.

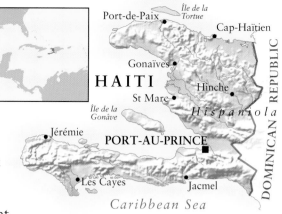

Area: 27,750 km²
Population: 7,820,000
Capital: Port-au-Prince (1,557,000)
Main languages spoken: French-Haitian Creole, French
Main religions: Roman Catholic, voodoo
Currency: gourde
Main exports: textiles and clothing, handicrafts, coffee, manufactures
Government: republic; dictatorship

Haiti is mountainous with five distinct mountain ranges separated by deep valleys and plains. The lowland areas are densely populated with around 80 per cent of the country's population living in rural areas. About a third of Haiti's land can be farmed and most farms are small plots on which families grow only enough to feed themselves. The most common subsistence crops are corn, bananas and cassava. Larger estates and plantations exist where crops including coffee, sisal and sugar are grown for export. Much of Haiti's farmland suffers from soil erosion and large tracts of its forest areas have been removed to create new farmlands and to produce charcoal. Ninety-five per cent of its people are descendants of black slaves employed

to grow sugarcane by Spanish and French colonial powers. In 1804, a slave revolt enabled Haiti to gain independence from France and it became the first independent nation in the Caribbean.

▶ Haitians are the poorest people in the entire Caribbean. Many live in slums such as Cité Soleil around the fringes of Haiti's capital city, Port-au-Prince.

DOMINICAN REPUBLIC

Occupying the western two-thirds of Hispaniola, the Dominican Republic is the second largest and second most populous country in the Caribbean.

Area: 48,433 km²
Population: 8,490,000
Capital: Santo Domingo (2,677,000)
Main language spoken: Spanish
Main religion: Roman Catholic
Currency: Dominican peso
Main exports: ferronickel, raw sugar, coffee, gold
Government: republic; partial democracy

The Dominican Republic is a mountainous country with large areas of fertile lands in valleys between the peaks and in the lower-lying lands near the coast. A wide range of crops is grown on these lands including tobacco, sugar and cocoa. In 2000, 1.29 million tonnes of fruits and berries were harvested. The Dominican Republic has the largest and fastest-growing economy in the Caribbean islands. Large reserves of ores containing nickel and gold are mined, while construction and telecommunications industries have expanded at a rapid rate. Tourism has also increased in importance with many holiday cruise ships stopping in its natural harbours. The country has established a number of

Free Trade Zones within its borders. Overseas companies employ more than 200,000 people making clothes, footwear and electronic goods. The land was twice visited by Christopher Columbus and the city of Santo Domingo was established in 1496 by his brother, Bartholomew. It is the oldest European settlement in the entire Americas. Today, Santo Domingo is the capital of the Dominican Republic with over 2.6 million inhabitants in its metropolitan area.

PUERTO RICO

The most easterly of the Greater Antilles Islands, Puerto Rico is a mountainous island with a tropical climate and a rich plant life.

ATLANTIC OCEAN

Puerto Rico
(to US)

San Juan

Bayamón

Carolina

Cerro de Punta
1338m

Caguas

Mayagüez

Cordillera Central

Isla de
Vieques

Ponce

Caribbean Sea

Area: 9,104 km²
Population: 3,809,000
Capital: San Juan (2,450,000)
Main languages spoken: Spanish, English
Main religion: Roman Catholic
Currency: US dollar
Main exports: chemicals and chemical products, food (particularly sugar, coffee and vegetables)
Government: self-governing dependency of USA

Puerto Rico is separated from the Dominican Republic by a stretch of the Caribbean called the Mona Passage. Part of a key shipping lane to and from the Panama Canal, the island has benefited from shipping and trade industries especially as its capital city, San Juan, is located on the site of one of the largest natural harbours in the Caribbean. Around three-fifths of the country is mountainous, with coastal lowlands in which dairy farming and coffee growing are the most important activities. The island was claimed by the explorer Christopher Columbus in 1493 and was a

Spanish colony until 1898 when the USA gained control. Many US businesses have invested in the island, and the economy is increasingly reliant on manufacturing and service industries. Eighty-nine per cent of the island's exports go to the USA.

▶ These Puerto Ricans are working in a rum distillery on the island. Rum uses sugar as its principal ingredient and the alcoholic drink is exported to many countries.

VIRGIN ISLANDS

Lying east of Puerto Rico, these islands form the economically strong dependency of the USA and the smaller, less prosperous British Virgin Islands dependency.

accounts for three-quarters of revenue. The economy of the US Virgin Islands is also largely based on tourism with more than a million visitors per year. Bought from Denmark by the USA in 1917, the US Virgin Islands consist of many small hilly volcanic islands. A giant oil refinery located on St Croix accounts for nearly all of the islands' exports.

Virgin Islands (US)

Area: 352 km²
Population: 109,000
Capital: Charlotte Amalie (28,000)
Main language spoken: English
Main religions: Baptist, Roman Catholic
Currency: US dollar
Main exports: refined petroleum, rum, watches, fragrances
Type of government: dependency of USA

British Virgin Islands

Area: 153 km²
Population: 21,000
Capital: Road Town (8,500)
Main language spoken: English
Main religions: Anglican, Roman Catholic
Currency: US dollar
Main exports: fish, gravel, fruit
Type of government: self-governing dependency of UK

The island group's capital, Road Town, is found on Tortola, the largest of the British Virgin Islands. Most of the islands are of volcanic origin with the exception of the second largest, Anegada, which is a coral and limestone atoll. The islanders engage in rum-making, raising livestock and fishing, but tourism

ATLANTIC OCEAN

British Virgin Islands
(to UK)

Anegada

Tortola

St Thomas

Road Town

Charlotte Amalie

St John

Virgin Islands
(to US)

St Croix

Christiansted

Frederiksted

Caribbean Sea

ST KITTS & NEVIS

The first British colonies in the Caribbean in the 1620s, St Kitts & Nevis is a federation formed by a pair of islands separated by a 3 km-wide channel.

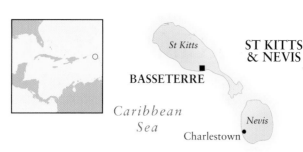

Area: 269 km²
Population: 41,000
Capital: Basseterre (18,000)
Main languages spoken: English, English Creole
Main religions: Anglican, Methodist
Currency: East Caribbean dollar
Main exports: electronic goods, sugar, foodstuff
Type of government: dominion; democracy

Both the islands of St Kitts & Nevis were formed by volcanic activity and both feature a high volcanic peak at their centre. The islands bask in a tropical climate with high rainfall but have been hit by a number of hurricanes which have caused widespread damage. Although much land has been cleared for farming, there are large areas of rainforest, wetlands and grasslands in which a great variety of plants and creatures live. St Kitts & Nevis has little mineral or energy resources. Almost all fuel for energy has to be imported, mainly in the form of oil from Mexico and Venezuela. St Kitts, the larger of the two islands, is also the home of the capital, Basseterre, which is an important port and receives much trade from cruise liners. Charlestown is the largest town on Nevis. Once inhabited by Carib and Arawak Indians, the population of St Kitts & Nevis is now almost entirely of African or mixed African-European descent. The islands gained independence from Britain in 1983, and in 1998 a vote for Nevis to withdraw from the federation just failed to gain the necessary two-thirds majority.

Below: A worker harvests sugarcane on the Caribbean island of St Kitts. Sugar is a major export earner for the federation of St Kitts & Nevis.

ANGUILLA AND MONTSERRAT

Anguilla is a flat limestone coral island while Montserrat is more mountainous and features seven active volcanoes. Both are British dependencies.

Anguilla

Area: 96 km²
Population: 8,000
Capital: The Valley (800)
Main language spoken: English
Main religions: Anglican, Roman Catholic
Currency: East Caribbean dollar
Main exports: lobsters, fish, livestock, salt.
Type of government: self-governing dependency of UK

Montserrat

Area: 98 km²
Population: 8,000
Temporary capital: Olde Town (2,000)
Main language spoken: English
Main religions: Anglican, Methodist
Currency: East Caribbean dollar
Main exports: electronic components, food, cattle
Type of government: self-governing dependency of UK

First occupied by British settlers in 1650, the present-day population of Anguilla is mainly descended from African and European peoples. Anguilla's income is derived from lobster fishing, salt mining and tourism. It has a dry sunny climate.

Montserrat's economy has been more varied than Anguilla's with vegetable farming, cotton growing and manufacturing industries producing local crafts, motor vehicle parts and electronic components. The island is dominated by a series of active volcanoes. In 1997, eruptions of the Soufrière Hills volcano east of Plymouth destroyed the capital.

ANTIGUA & BARBUDA

Colonized by Britain from the 17th century before becoming independent in 1981, Antigua & Barbuda is a nation almost totally dependent on tourism for income.

Area: 442 km²
Population: 68,000
Capital: St John's (38,000)
Main languages spoken: English, English Creole
Main religions: Anglican, Moravian
Currency: East Caribbean dollar
Main exports: re-exported petroleum products, fruit
Type of government: dominion; partial democracy

Antigua & Barbuda consists of three islands. Antigua is far and away the most important, being the largest and where an estimated 98 per cent of the population live. The remainder inhabit Barbuda, a low-lying coral island, while a tiny third island lies uninhabited. Unlike most of the other members of the Leeward Islands group, Antigua has no forests, few trees and no rivers. With only a few springs, droughts occur even though approximately 1,000 mm of rain falls every year. Few native animals exist but the islands are home to over 100 species of birds. After the closure of the sugar farming industry in the 1970s, the islands have come to depend on their beaches to lure tourists and on developing a finance and banking industry. Two military bases on Antigua have been leased to the USA. Ninety per cent of Antigua & Barbuda's population are the descendants of black slaves brought to the islands. The population has recently been increased by some 3,000 refugees fleeing a volcanic eruption on nearby Montserrat.

GUADELOUPE

Two contrasting islands, one a high-peaked volcanic island, the other a lower-lying coral island form the majority of the land of Guadeloupe.

Area: 1,780 km²
Population: 425,000
Capital: Basse-Terre (54,000)
Main language spoken: French
Main religion: Roman Catholic
Currency: euro
Main exports: bananas, sugar, rum, melons
Type of government: dependency of France

Guadeloupe is an archipelago made up of two major islands, Basse-Terre and Grande-Terre, and a number of smaller islands. On Basse-Terre, the summit of the active volcano, Soufrière, is one of the wettest landmarks in the Caribbean and can receive more than 8,000 mm of rain in a year. In contrast, the coastal areas of the islands tend to receive around 1,300 mm. While Basse-Terre is home to Guadeloupe's capital, Grande-Terre is more heavily populated with Pointe-à-Pitre being the main port and commercial centre. Guadeloupe depends heavily on tourism, and aid from France.

DOMINICA

A mountainous, volcanic island with many hot springs, Dominica has a great variety of wildlife and a large number of protected parks and reserves.

Area: 739 km²
Population: 73,000
Capital: Roseau (20,000)
Main languages spoken: French Creole, English
Main religion: Roman Catholic
Currency: East Caribbean dollar
Main exports: bananas, soap, fresh vegetables, limes
Type of government: republic; democracy

A high ridge forms the backbone of Dominica which slopes down towards the sea and contains over 300 rivers and streams. The mountains are covered in dense woodlands, thickets and rainforest, much of which is protected in a series of national parks and reserves. Dominica has a varied plant and animal life with over 130 species of birds. Many creatures, including opossum, iguanas, crabs and freshwater shrimps, are collected as food.

Much of the island's electricity is generated from a hydroelectric plant found in the centre of the island. Dominica was one of the few Caribbean islands whose native Indian inhabitants managed to hold off becoming a colony of a European nation until the late 18th century. Some 3,000 descendants of the Carib Indians still live on the island.

MARTINIQUE

Martinique is one of the most beautiful and rugged islands in the Caribbean with volcanic peaks, dense rainforests in the mountains and narrow fertile valleys.

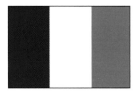

Area: 1,128 km²
Population: 384,000
Capital: Fort-de-France (134,000)
Main language spoken: French
Main religion: Roman Catholic
Currency: euro
Main exports: bananas, refined petroleum, rum, melons
Type of government: dependency of France

The island of Martinique has an average elevation of over 900 m above sea level. Narrow plains around the coast and a plain in the centre of the island are the only flat areas. Its highest point, the volcano, Montagne Pelée, destroyed the town of St Pierre, killing over 28,000 people, in 1902. Around a third of the island remains covered in forest with large amounts of tropical hardwoods. Colonized by the French in 1635, the island remains a dependency of France which maintains an oil refinery on the island in which crude oil from Venezuela and Trinidad & Tobago is processed and shipped elsewhere. The majority of its population are of either African or mixed African-European descent. Agriculture and service industries, particularly tourism, are the main sources of income.

ST LUCIA

Explored by Spain and then France, the volcanic island of St Lucia became a British territory in 1814 and became independent in 1979.

Area: 617 km²
Population: 154,000
Capital: Castries (59,000)
Main languages spoken: English, French Creole
Main religion: Roman Catholic
Currency: East Caribbean dollar
Main exports: bananas, other foodstuffs, live animals, chemicals and chemical products
Type of government: dominion; democracy

St Lucia's mountains are heavily wooded and contain many fast-moving streams and rivers. The legacy of its volcanic origins can be found at many points around the island. A volcanic crater and bubbling mud pools releasing sulphur gases are found at Soufrière, a town which is overlooked by twin volcanic peaks. To the south of the island lies an area that contains a chain of 18 volcanic domes and a number of craters. The island has many fine beaches, some of which in the southwest are covered in volcanic black sand. St Lucia is the second largest producer of bananas in the Caribbean. The seas around the island are exploited relatively heavily with 1,795 tonnes of fish, especially tuna, dolphin and kingfish, landed in 2000.

▼ Overlooking Jalousie Plantation harbour on the western side of St Lucia are the Pitons. These two volcanic domes have elevations of 798 and 750 m.

ST VINCENT & THE GRENADINES

St Vincent & The Grenadines consist of one main island, St Vincent, and the northern part of the chain of 600 islands and islets called The Grenadines.

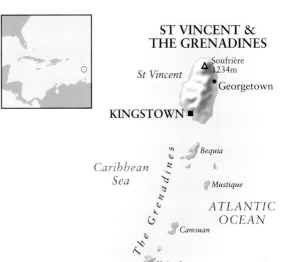

Area: 389 km²
Population: 115,000
Capital: Kingstown (27,000)
Main languages spoken: English, English Creole
Main religions: Anglican, Pentecostal
Currency: East Caribbean dollar
Main exports: bananas, flour, rice, manufactured re-exports
Type of government: dominion; democracy

◀ On Dominica, fishermen use seine nets to catch fish shoals which swim near beaches.

The island of St Vincent makes up 89 per cent of the area and 95 per cent of the population of the nation. The island is rugged with little flat land, and its northern third is dominated by an active volcano called Soufrière which erupted a number of times during the 20th century. The central and southern sections of the island fall sharply from mountainous heights to the sea, with rocky cliffs and black sand beaches on the eastern side. Most of the islands of The Grenadines are less rugged and tend to be surrounded by coral reefs. Several of The Grenadines, including Mustique and Bequia, have become exclusive resort islands for wealthy foreign visitors. Bananas are the most important farm crop and there are also small food processing, cement, clothing and rum-making industries. St Vincent & The Grenadines is less wealthy than many of its Caribbean neighbours and has high unemployment (22 per cent in 2001).

BARBADOS

The most easterly of all Caribbean islands, Barbados is some 34 km long with an economy based on agriculture, tourism and other service industries.

ATLANTIC OCEAN

BARBADOS

Speightstown

Mount Hillaby △ ● Bathsheba
340m

BRIDGETOWN ■ ● Crane

Area: 430 km²
Population: 269,000
Capital: Bridgetown (98,000)
Main languages spoken: English, Bajan (English Creole)
Main religions: Anglican, Pentecostal
Currency: Barbados dollar
Main exports: sugar, chemicals, food and beverages, construction materials
Type of government: dominion; democracy

Barbados is formed from coral limestone and is largely flat with a few rolling hills in the north. The west coast has a number of white sand beaches while the east coast has a rocky shoreline. Sugarcane production accounts for over 80 per cent of the cultivated land. Oil found on the island provides about a third of the country's energy needs. Founded in 1628, Bridgetown is the island's capital and commercial port. Ninety per cent of the population are of African descent and roughly one-third of Barbados' people, known as Bajans, live in or around Bridgetown. The original inhabitants of Barbados were Arawak Indians who are believed to have been driven off the island by the warlike Carib Indians around 1200. The island lay deserted until a colony was established in 1627 by British settlers. Barbados has been independent from the UK since 1966 and tourism now employs one-third of the workforce. Remnants of traditional British customs and buildings has earned it the nickname 'Little England' by its Caribbean neighbours.

▶ Cars head through an arch in Bridgetown, the capital of Barbados and the island's largest port.

GRENADA

Grenada consists of one major island and several of the southern Grenadine islands including Carriacou. It is famous for its spices and agricultural produce.

Carriacou

Caribbean Sea

GRENADA

Gouyave ● ● Mount St Catherine
△840m

ST GEORGE'S ■ ● Grenville

ATLANTIC OCEAN

Area: 344 km²
Population: 100,000
Capital: St George's (27,000)
Main languages spoken: English, English Creole
Main religions: Roman Catholic, Anglican
Currency: East Caribbean dollar
Main exports: fish, cocoa, nutmeg, bananas, clothing
Type of government: dominion; democracy

Grenada's geography is quite varied with a hilly interior covered in lush vegetation, deep valleys through which fast-flowing streams run, several mountain lakes and 45 beaches around its coastline. Its tropical climate features 1,500 mm of rainfall a year on its coasts and more than double that amount on the mountain slopes. Created by volcanic activity, the island has a rich, black soil in which many crops flourish. Grenada is known in the Caribbean as the 'Isle of Spice' and is the world's largest producer of nutmeg and mace. It also produces large amounts of cinnamon, cloves, pepper and ginger. Limes, cocoa and bananas are also grown. Grenada was a French colony from 1650 before it was captured by British forces in 1762. Gaining independence in 1974, two military coups, one in 1979, the second in 1983, were followed by US forces invading the island and establishing a new government.

Tourism has since become important after an international airport was built at Point Salines near the capital, St George's.

▲ A plantation worker separates strands of the spice, mace, from cloves.

TRINIDAD & TOBAGO

One of the few Caribbean nations with oil reserves, the two islands of Trinidad & Tobago are the most southerly islands in the Caribbean.

Area: 5,128 km²
Population: 1,295,000
Capital: Port of Spain (260,000)
Main languages spoken: English, English Creole
Main religions: Roman Catholic, Hindu
Currency: Trinidad & Tobago dollar
Main exports: petroleum, ammonia, iron and steel
Type of government: republic; partial democracy

Lying close to the coast of Venezuela, where the Orinoco river empties into the ocean, Trinidad is a geological extension of South America. Trinidad's major resources are fossil fuels. Large reserves of oil and natural gas have been exploited both on the island and just offshore. In the south-west of the island lies one of the world's largest sources of natural asphalt, used for road building. Unlike most Caribbean nations, Trinidad & Tobago's population comes from a great range of backgrounds. Those of African and East Asian descent each form around 40 per cent. There are also many people of European, Chinese and South American origin.

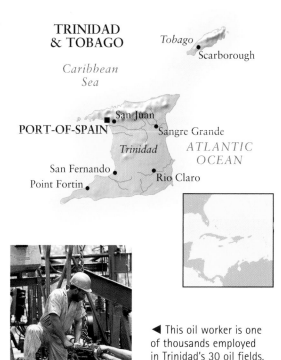

◄ This oil worker is one of thousands employed in Trinidad's 30 oil fields. In 1999, these produced a combined output of 46.8 million barrels.

NETHERLANDS ANTILLES AND ARUBA

The Caribbean dependencies of the Netherlands are clustered into two places – east of the Virgin Islands and just off the northern coast of Venezuela.

Netherlands Antilles

Area: 800 km²
Population: 217,000
Capital: Willemstad (119,000)
Main languages spoken: Dutch, Papiamento (in Curaçao and Bonaire), English (in Dutch Windward Islands)
Main religion: Roman Catholic
Currency: Netherlands Antilles guilder
Main exports: refined petroleum, consumer goods.
Type of government: self-governing dependency of the Netherlands

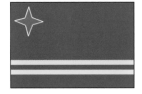

Aruba

Area: 193 km²
Population: 103,000
Capital: Oranjestad (21,000)
Main languages spoken: Dutch, Papiamento
Main religion: Roman Catholic
Currency: Aruban guilder
Main exports: refined petroleum, fish.
Type of government: self-governing dependency of the Netherlands

The Netherlands Antilles consist of two contrasting island groups. The islands of Curaçao and Bonaire lie off the Venezuelan coast while 800 km north, the second group, including Saba and St Eustasius, are found. Crude oil and petroleum products account for over

80 per cent of the Netherlands Antilles' imports and exports. The same industry is important to Aruba which lies just 25 km off the Venezuelan coast. Aruba is flat and its western side has been heavily developed for tourism. Agriculture is limited on the islands as soils are poor and water often limited, but peanuts and tropical fruits are among the crops grown.

► Willemstad with its Dutch-style buildings is the main town on Curaçao.

SOUTH AMERICA

South America is the fourth largest continent with a total surface area of 17,820,900 km². It extends from the Caribbean Sea southwards a distance of 7,400 km to Cape Horn, and its maximum width is 5,160 km. The Brazilian shield and the smaller Guyana shield to the north, as well as the Patagonian shield to the southwest, are the oldest geological parts of the continent. Running along the entire western edge of the continent is the much younger Andes mountain range with many peaks over 6,000 m. A large part of the interior is a series of basins in which three large rivers, the Amazon, the Orinoco and the Paraguay-Paraná, drain much of the continent's water into the Atlantic Ocean. The largest lowland region of South America is the enormous Amazon basin, the world's largest river basin, covering an area of over seven million km². Much of its extent is covered in lush tropical rainforest. South America has been inhabited for many thousands of years with advanced native cultures, including the Chavin, Moche, Chimu and Inca civilizations. The continent's population is now over 345 million, a figure which more than doubled between 1960 and 2000.

▲ These small houses are made of adobe mud bricks and lie on the shore of Lake Titicaca which straddles the border between Bolivia and Peru.

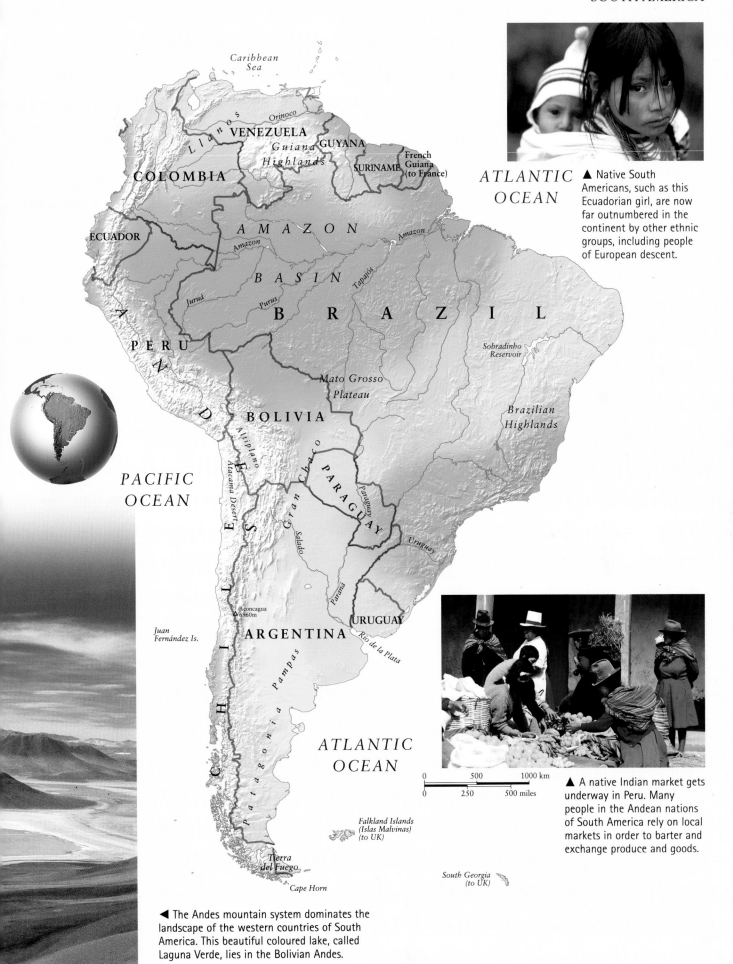

Caribbean
Sea

Orinoco

Llanos

VENEZUELA GUYANA

*Guiana
Highlands*

SURINAME

French
Guiana
(to France)

COLOMBIA

ECUADOR

A M A Z O N

Amazon

Juruá

Purus

B A S I N

Tapajós

Amazon

B R A Z I L

*Sobradinho
Reservoir*

P E R U

*Mato Grosso
Plateau*

*Brazilian
Highlands*

A

N

BOLIVIA

D

Altiplano

Atacama Desert

E

Gran Chaco

PARAGUAY

Paraguay

Salado

Uruguay

Paraná

S

△ Aconcagua
6960m

*Juan
Fernández Is.*

URUGUAY

C

H

ARGENTINA

Río de la Plata

Pampas

I

Patagonia

L

E

Paraná

**ATLANTIC
OCEAN**

*Falkland Islands
(Islas Malvinas)
(to UK)*

*Tierra
del Fuego*

Cape Horn

*South Georgia
(to UK)*

**PACIFIC
OCEAN**

*ATLANTIC
OCEAN*

▲ Native South
Americans, such as this
Ecuadorian girl, are now
far outnumbered in the
continent by other ethnic
groups, including people
of European descent.

0	500	1000 km
0	250	500 miles

▲ A native Indian market gets
underway in Peru. Many
people in the Andean nations
of South America rely on local
markets in order to barter and
exchange produce and goods.

◄ The Andes mountain system dominates the
landscape of the western countries of South
America. This beautiful coloured lake, called
Laguna Verde, lies in the Bolivian Andes.

NORTHERN SOUTH AMERICA

Northern South America is the widest part of the continent and includes the world's highest navigable lake, Lake Titicaca, which forms part of the border between Peru and Bolivia. It also includes the world's highest waterfalls in Venezuela and the mighty Amazon river. Second only to the Nile as the world's longest river, the Amazon drains a region of 7,050,000 km^2. The rainforests that cover the lands surrounding the river and its tributaries are some of the last major wild regions in the world, and contain the richest range of species of living things found anywhere on Earth. Brazil is the dominant country in terms of land area, population and economic importance. It shares a border with every country in the region with the exception of Ecuador and Chile. The lands bordering the Atlantic Ocean were the first to be explored and claimed as colonies of European nations. Although all of continental South America is now independent, with the exception of French Guiana, its colonial heritage is evident. English, Dutch, French and Portuguese are the official languages of Guyana, Suriname, French Guiana and Brazil respectively, while Spanish is the official language of the other nations.

▲ Around half of Ecuador's entire population are native Indians. The majority of native Indian peoples in northern South America can be found in the Andean countries of Peru, Bolivia, Colombia and Ecuador.

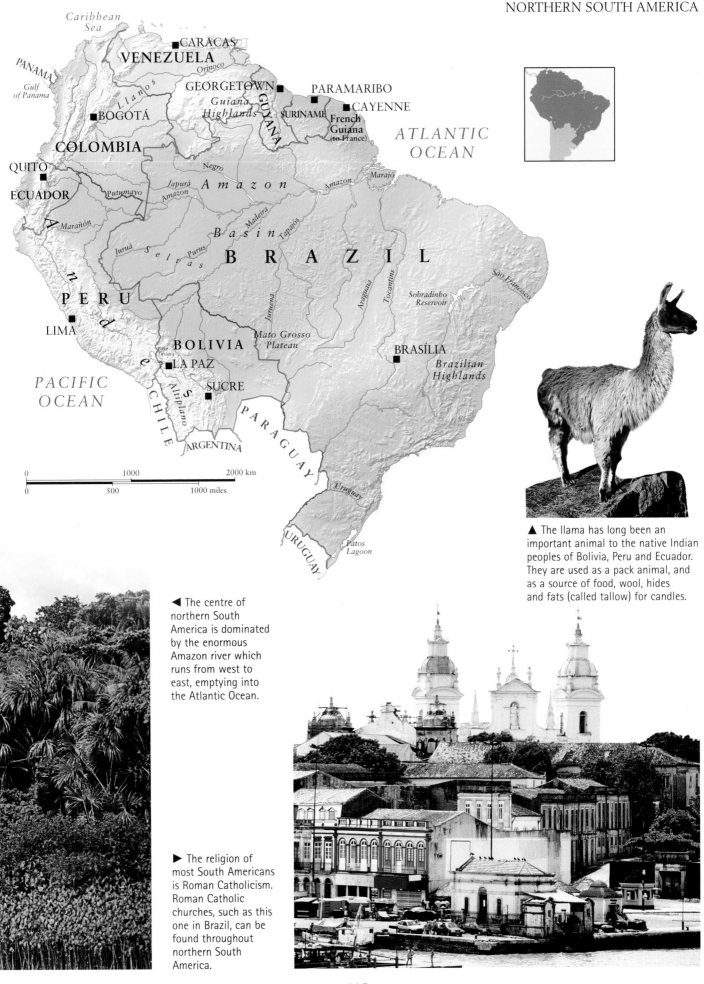

Caribbean Sea

CARACAS

VENEZUELA

PANAMA

Gulf of Panama

Orinoco

GEORGETOWN

PARAMARIBO

Guiana Highlands

GUYANA

SURINAME

CAYENNE

French Guiana (to France)

ATLANTIC OCEAN

BOGOTÁ

Llanos

COLOMBIA

QUITO

ECUADOR

Negro

Japurá

Amazon

Amazon

Marajó

Putumayo

A n d e s

Marañón

Juruá

Madeira

Purus

B a s i n

BRAZIL

Selvas

São Francisco

PERU

Tapajós

Juruena

Araguaia

Tocantins

Sobradinho Reservoir

LIMA

BOLIVIA

Mato Grosso Plateau

BRASÍLIA

Brazilian Highlands

LA PAZ

Lake Titicaca

SUCRE

Altiplano

PACIFIC OCEAN

CHILE

PARAGUAY

ARGENTINA

Uruguay

URUGUAY

Patos Lagoon

| 0 | | 1000 | | 2000 km |
| 0 | 500 | | 1000 miles | |

▲ The llama has long been an important animal to the native Indian peoples of Bolivia, Peru and Ecuador. They are used as a pack animal, and as a source of food, wool, hides and fats (called tallow) for candles.

◀ The centre of northern South America is dominated by the enormous Amazon river which runs from west to east, emptying into the Atlantic Ocean.

▶ The religion of most South Americans is Roman Catholicism. Roman Catholic churches, such as this one in Brazil, can be found throughout northern South America.

VENEZUELA

During the 20th century, Venezuela underwent a transformation from one of the poorest South American countries to one of the wealthiest.

Area: 912,050 km²
Population: 23,610,000
Capital: Caracas (3,783,000)
Main language spoken: Spanish
Main religion: Roman Catholic
Currency: bolivar
Main exports: petroleum and petroleum products, basic manufactures, bauxite, aluminium, chemicals
Type of government: republic; partial democracy

▼ The flat, grassed plains of the Llanos in central Venezuela provide good grazing ground for large livestock herds. The cattle ranchers, or cowboys, are called llaneros.

Venezuela shares borders with Brazil to the south, Colombia to the west and Guyana to the east. Its coastline meets the Caribbean Sea in the northern part of the country and the Atlantic Ocean to the east in which lie around 70 islands belonging to Venezuela. Mainland Venezuela has a number of geographical regions. In the centre are low-lying plains covered in grassland vegetation called the Llanos. The rugged granite Guiana Highlands are situated in the south and southeast and are only sparsely inhabited. Much of the northern portion of Venezuela is made up of a series of narrow coastal plains and large mountains including two branches of the Andes. These define part of the Venezuela-Colombia border and include the country's highest peak, Pico Bolivar (5,007 m). In between these two mountain ranges lie the swampy lowlands surrounding Lake Maracaibo. Most of the Llanos and Guiana Highlands are drained by the 2,740 km-long Orinoco river.

▼ An oil terminal on the edge of Lake Maracaibo. Although Venezuela has many other mineral resources, crude and refined oil account for almost four-fifths of the revenue made through exports.

OIL AND LAKE MARACAIBO

Lake Maracaibo is actually a large inlet of the Caribbean Sea lying in northwestern Venezuela. It extends southwards from the Gulf of Venezuela for approximately 210 km. Many rivers flow into this stretch of water, some of which are also important transport routes for shipping. The waters in the northern part of Lake Maracaibo are salty and stagnant as the tides mix seawater with freshwater. In the southern portion of the lake, the water is fresh. An eight-kilometre bridge spans the

▼ Angel Falls is the waterfall with the highest drop in the world. The falls, which are located in the Guiana Highlands, drop a vast 979 m.

outlet of the lake. The discovery of oil reserves in and around the lake has transformed the Venezuelan economy. The first productive oil well was drilled in 1914, and many foreign-owned companies helped develop the oil fields until the oil industry was nationalized in 1975. The oil reserves are immense and one of the largest supplies outside the Middle East. Venezuela produces approximately 3.2 million barrels of oil per day and oil refining, processing and shipping industries have grown up around the area. Two large cities, Cabimas – on the shoreline of Lake Maracaibo – and the port of Maracaibo, have flourished as a result.

▲ The Orinoco river flows from the Guiana Highlands through the Llanos before emptying into the Atlantic Ocean.

▼ Caracas is a modern-day city with towering office blocks yet large shanty towns housing the poor are to be found on the nearby hills.

HISTORY AND PEOPLE

Venezuela was inhabited by native Indian peoples for many centuries before the arrival of European explorers and settlers. Until the early 19th century, Venezuela was controlled by Spain which imported Asian and African slaves to work the lands. An independence movement grew in the late 17th and early 18th centuries. Led by the Venezuelan general, Simón Bolivar, victory was finally achieved over Spanish forces whereupon, in 1821, Venezuela along with Ecuador and Colombia became the republic of Great Colombia. In 1830, Venezuela withdrew from Great Colombia and became a nation in its own right. The population of Venezuela reflects its colonial past, with people of mixed native American and European descent (mestizos) making up two-thirds of the population. Only two per cent of the population comprises unmixed native Americans. A small number of native Americans still maintain their traditional way of life deep in Venezuela's forests. The most notable group is the Yanomami who live in the remote forests of the Orinoco river basin in southern Venezuela and over the border, in northern Brazil. There are between 10,000 and 17,000 Yanomami in existence; around a third of the population died in skirmishes with gold prospectors and miners in the 1970s or from diseases introduced by these outsiders. In 1991, Brazil set up a 93,000 km² homeland for the Yanomami but many remain inside Venezuela's borders.

CITY DWELLERS

Venezuela is a country of vast tracts of uncultivated land. Grasslands occupy half of the country, and forests of different types cover about two-fifths. Less than five per cent of the land is cultivated although this farmland produces large amounts of staple crops, including bananas, maize and rice. Around 15 million cattle, 4.5 million pigs and 4 million goats are also raised. The majority of Venezuela's people live in cities and towns – around 87 per cent of the population is considered urban. The largest city is the capital, Caracas, which has existed for more than four centuries.

GUYANA

Guyana means 'land of many waters' in local native Indian language reflecting the many rivers which cross its area. It gained independence from the UK in 1966.

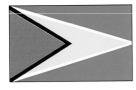

Area: 215,083 km²
Population: 761,000
Capital: Georgetown (225,000)
Main languages spoken: English Creole, English, Cariban
Main religions: Hindu, Roman Catholic, Anglican
Currency: Guyana dollar
Main exports: sugar, gold, rice, bauxite, timber
Type of government: republic; democracy

Guyana is a country of dense rainforests in its interior, many parts of which have been barely touched by humans. Ninety per cent of its people live on a relatively narrow coastal plain bordering the Atlantic Ocean. Parts of this plain have been formed by land reclaimed from the sea, creating over 200 km of dykes and canals. Rice, sugar, coconuts, corn and coffee are grown on the coastal plain which is never more than 64 km in width. Guyana's longest river is the Essequibo which measures 1,010 km and is partly navigable by small boats along stretches of its length. Diamond dredging industries occur on parts of many of Guyana's rivers while mining for bauxite is Guyana's chief mineral resource. The Dutch were the first colonial power to reach Guyana, where they established settlements along the Essequibo river in 1615. They grew a range of crops including sugarcane and cocoa and imported slaves from Africa. During the early 19th century, Britain took over the

Dutch colonies of Berbice, Demerara and Essequibo, which became British Guiana in 1831. Slavery was outlawed in 1834, and the great need for plantation workers led to a large influx of immigrants, mainly from the Indian subcontinent. Today, about half of the population is of East Indian descent and about 43 per cent are of African descent.

▲ A Guyanan forestry worker in the process of felling a tree. Forests cover around four-fifths of the country's land.

► Situated in central Guyana, Kaieteur Falls are between 90 and 105 m at their top and fall 226 m. Over time, the falls have eroded a gorge around 8 km long.

SURINAME

Previously called Dutch Guiana, the independent republic of Suriname has a small population that is one of the most varied in South America.

Area: 163,270 km²
Population: 417,000
Capital: Paramaribo
(205,000)
Main languages spoken:
Sranan, Hindi, Dutch
Main religions: Hindu,
Roman Catholic, Sunni
Islam
Currency: Suriname
guilder
Main exports: bauxite,
shrimps and fish, rice,
aluminium
Type of government:
republic; democracy

▼ Suriname's largest
industry, the mining,
processing and exporting
of the aluminium ore,
bauxite, forms the basis of
its economy. Here, barges
carrying bauxite arrive at
Suralco Refinery.

Suriname consists of three distinct geographical areas: a coastal plain which is narrow and marshy in places, a small plateau area which is covered in savannah grasslands and woodlands and a vast tract of dense rainforest. The rainforest makes up around 90 per cent of the country and few roads penetrate it. Unlike its immediate neighbours, French Guiana to the east and Guyana to the west, Suriname has a number of huge lakes including one of the largest artificial lakes in South America just south of Brokopondo, created by damming a river for hydro-electric power. Only a small area of Suriname's land is given over to agriculture with rice being the major crop. The British established plantations on the banks of the Suriname river in 1651 and founded the settlement on which Suriname's capital city, Paramaribo, now lies. In 1667, Britain and the Netherlands exchanged lands in the Americas. The English swapped their territories in Suriname. In exchange they received the territory of New Amsterdam which is now known as New York in the USA. The Dutch imported many slaves to work on plantations, not just from Africa, but from many parts of Asia and this has given the country its varied cultural background. Around 37 per cent of the population are Asian Indians while 31 per cent are Creoles and 15 per cent are of Indonesian origin. There are also sizeable populations of Chinese and the descendants of native tribes. The Netherlands granted Suriname independence in 1975 but remains a major aid donor and provides 80 per cent of its tourists. Many Surinamese have emigrated to the Netherlands. The country has suffered from a lack of political stability with the military often intervening in affairs.

FRENCH GUIANA

An overseas department of France, French Guiana consists of a narrow belt of flat land at the coast which rises to higher ground blanketed in lush rainforest.

Area: 86,504 km²
Population: 181,000
Capital: Cayenne (66,000)
Main language spoken: French
Main religion: Roman Catholic
Currency: euro
Main exports: timber and wood products; bauxite
Type of government: dependency of France

French Guiana is situated on the northeast coast of South America and is bordered by Brazil to the south and the east and by Suriname to the west. An area bounded by the Maroni river is under dispute between Suriname and French Guiana. Most of the country is covered in rainforest which rises from low elevation near the coast, to mountains which lie on the frontier with Brazil. The rainforest region is largely uninhabited by humans but has a rich wildlife, including many species of monkey, tapirs, anteaters, ocelots and caimans, a relative of the crocodile family. French Guiana has a tropical climate with high humidity and heavy rainfall especially in its interior. The heaviest rain falls from January to June and average rainfall in the country's capital, Cayenne, on the coast, is approximately 3,800 mm. Cayenne is the country's largest town and its chief port. French Guiana exports bananas, sugar, aluminium ores and timber. With only one per cent of the country's land devoted to agriculture, many foods have to be imported.

The French first established a colony at Cayenne in 1637 and French Guiana remains the last remaining colony on mainland South America. From 1852 for almost a century, it was notorious as the place where France sent its most hardened convicts. Penal colonies were established at Cayenne and on a nearby small islet in the Atlantic Ocean known as Devil's Island. Most of French Guiana's population live near the coast and are people of mixed white, native American and black African origin called Creoles. Small numbers of native Americans live in the rainforests and highlands of the country's interior, largely untouched by modern life.

▲ Almost nine-tenths of French Guiana is covered in rainforest which provides timber, oils, fibres and foods for many of the dependency's population.

▲ An Ariane 4 rocket blasts off from Kourou satellite launch base in French Guiana in May 2002. Kourou is the launch site for European Space Agency projects and the town nearby has grown to become the second largest in French Guiana.

COLOMBIA

Colombia is troubled politically, but it is a country blessed with rich wildlife, fertile growing land and large mineral resources.

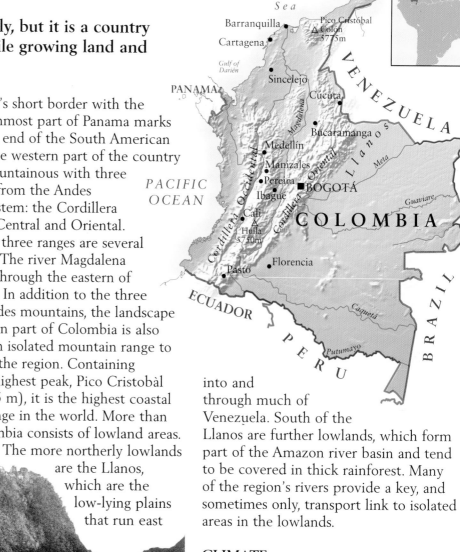

Caribbean
Sea

Barranquilla

Cartagena

Gulf of
Darién

PANAMA

Sincelejo

Cúcuta

Bucaramanga

Medellín

Manizales

Pereira

Ibagué

BOGOTÁ

Cali

Pasto

Florencia

Pico Cristóbal
Colón
5775m

VENEZUELA

Llanos

Meta

Magdalena

Cordillera Occidental

Cordillera Oriental

Guaviare

COLOMBIA

Huila
5750m

PACIFIC
OCEAN

BRAZIL

Caquetá

ECUADOR

PERU

Putumayo

Area: 1,141,568 km²
Population: 42,320,000
Capital: (Santafé de) Bogotá (6,803,000)
Main language spoken: Spanish
Main religion: Roman Catholic
Currency: Colombian peso
Main exports: petroleum products, coffee, chemicals, textiles and clothing. (The illegal export of cocaine and marijuana produces the greatest revenue.)
Type of government: republic; partial democracy

Colombia's short border with the southernmost part of Panama marks the northern end of the South American continent. The western part of the country is mostly mountainous with three large ranges from the Andes mountain system: the Cordillera Occidental, Central and Oriental. Between the three ranges are several large valleys. The river Magdalena flows north through the eastern of these valleys. In addition to the three chains of Andes mountains, the landscape of the western part of Colombia is also marked by an isolated mountain range to the north of the region. Containing Colombia's highest peak, Pico Cristobàl Colòn (5,775 m), it is the highest coastal mountain range in the world. More than half of Colombia consists of lowland areas. The more northerly lowlands are the Llanos, which are the low-lying plains that run east into and through much of Venezuela. South of the Llanos are further lowlands, which form part of the Amazon river basin and tend to be covered in thick rainforest. Many of the region's rivers provide a key, and sometimes only, transport link to isolated areas in the lowlands.

CLIMATE

As the country lies close to the Equator. Colombia's climate is mainly tropical with little change throughout the year. However, there is much variation in temperature and rainfall according to altitude and also according to location near the mountain ranges, some of which cast a rain shadow over nearby lowlands. Above about 3,000 m, the climate is cold with temperatures ranging from -18 to 13°C. Mountain peaks in the Andes which extend above 4,500 m are permanently capped in snow and ice. Generally, Colombia receives moderate to heavy rainfall with no completely dry season.

◀ Colombia's capital city, Bogotá, sprawls over a sloping plain at the base of two mountains. The city features two of the oldest universities in South America: the University of Santo Tomás (founded in 1580) and the Xavier Pontifical University (founded in 1622).

▼ A large coffee plantation near the city of Manizales in western Colombia. Founded in 1848, Manizales is a major trading and transport centre for coffee, cocoa and gold.

▲ This stone statue, one of several hundred created by an unknown civilization, is found in San Augustin Archaeological Park near the source of the Magdalena river.

RICH PLANT AND ANIMAL LIFE

Colombia is home to a huge range of plant and animal life and is considered one of the most biodiverse countries in the world. Over 130,000 species of plant have been identified within its borders and it has as many different animal species as Brazil, which is ten times its size. Larger creatures include the jaguar, spectacled bear, ocelot, tapirs and many species of monkeys. Colombia also has more than 1,500 bird species, thought to be the most of any nation. Deforestation for cattle ranching, for farmlands and for Colombia's timber industry saw 1.3 million hectares of forests cleared between 1990 and 1995.

COLOMBIA'S RESOURCES

Colombia has large mineral resources including copper, lead and mercury: 21,000 kg of gold were recovered in 2000, mainly from many small mines, while emerald gemstones are mined in an area northeast of Bogotá. The country has large reserves of fossil fuels; Colombia has the biggest reserves of coal in South America,

while its oil fields produce an average of 800,000 barrels per day. Most of its oil fields are found in the Magdalena Valley and near the border with Venezuela. Despite the abundance of fossil fuels, 70 per cent of Colombia's electricity, used to fuel its many industries, comes from hydro-electric power plants making use of the many rivers flowing at speed down its mountains.

AGRICULTURE

Agriculture employs over 30 per cent of the Colombian workforce, with coffee being the most important cash crop. Other important crops are bananas, cotton, maize, rice and potatoes. Unfortunately, the crop believed to generate the most revenue is coca (used to make cocaine) and cannabis. Colombia is one of the world's largest producers of these drugs which are illegal in most countries. The power of the producers of illegal drugs has added to the already significant problems with keeping law and order in the country. Colombia has been in a state of near civil war for decades.

ECUADOR

Ecuador is the smallest of the Andean countries but has a varied landscape. It also owns the world-famous Galapagos Islands in the Pacific Ocean.

Area: 269,178 km²
Population: 12,157,000
Capital: Quito (1,750,000)
Main languages spoken: Spanish, Quechua
Main religion: Roman Catholic
Currency: US dollar
Main exports: petroleum, bananas, shrimps, coffee, cocoa
Type of government: republic; partial democracy

▼ Quito is located on the slopes of a volcano in a valley among the Andes. The oldest of all South American capital cities, Quito has many well-preserved Spanish colonial buildings, including 86 churches.

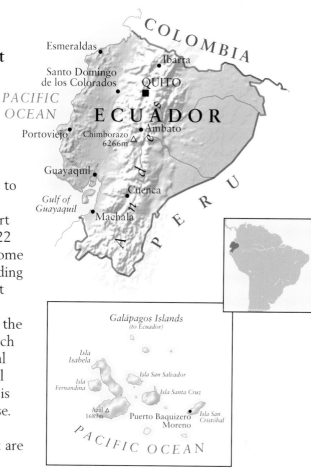

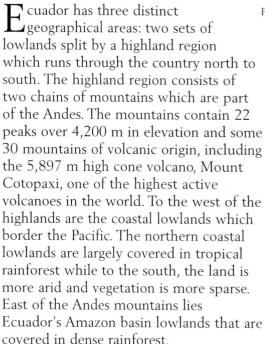

Ecuador has three distinct geographical areas: two sets of lowlands split by a highland region which runs through the country north to south. The highland region consists of two chains of mountains which are part of the Andes. The mountains contain 22 peaks over 4,200 m in elevation and some 30 mountains of volcanic origin, including the 5,897 m high cone volcano, Mount Cotopaxi, one of the highest active volcanoes in the world. To the west of the highlands are the coastal lowlands which border the Pacific. The northern coastal lowlands are largely covered in tropical rainforest while to the south, the land is more arid and vegetation is more sparse. East of the Andes mountains lies Ecuador's Amazon basin lowlands that are covered in dense rainforest.

ECUADOR'S ECONOMY

Ecuador's economy is based largely on agriculture, fishing and oil. Over 310,000 tonnes of fish are caught every year although over-fishing now threatens certain marine life. Ecuador's oil industry produces around 400,000 barrels a day which make oil the single largest export earner. Ecuador's rugged countryside allows it to produce over 70 per cent of its electricity from hydro-electric power plants. A number of metals are mined while the government of Ecuador controls a large salt mining industry. Guayaquil in the south of the country is Ecuador's main industrial centre and its biggest port. Quito in the north remains the governmental and cultural capital.

PEOPLE

Like all of the Andean nations, Ecuador was colonized by the Spanish and only obtained independence in the 19th century. Wars with Peru between 1904 and 1942 saw the country lose much territory. Unlike most South American countries, the native American population is large; pure-blooded Quechua Indians make up 25 per cent of the population. Most speak the Quechua language used in the times of the Inca civilization. People of mixed European and native American descent make up a further 65 per cent of the population. Ecuador is the most densely populated South American country with an average of approximately 48.5 people per km².

GALAPAGOS ISLANDS

Ecuador's major island territories lie around 1,000 km from its coastline in the Pacific Ocean. The Galapagos Islands comprise 19 islands and many islets and rocks, most of which are formed from lava piles. Lava rock forms the islands' shorelines with higher ground containing most of the islands' plant

▲ Around 60 per cent of Ecuadorians live in towns and cities. The country's most populous city, Guayaquil, contains over two and a half million people.

life. Although some remains of Inca pottery have been found in places, the Galapagos are believed to have been uninhabited for most of their existence. Isolated from other land masses, the islands are home to a large number of unusual species of plant, and creatures not found elsewhere. Most of the Galapagos Islands' animals are thought to have originated long ago in South and Central America, but they have adapted and evolved into separate species. For example, the marine iguana is the only lizard which swims and feeds on seaweeds. Other unusual creatures include flightless cormorants and giant tortoises which can weigh over 250 kg and are believed to be the longest-living land creatures. Ecuador has had to control visitor numbers to the islands to conserve their future well-being. Laws ban further settlement and development.

▲ Found on the Galapagos Islands, the giant tortoise can grow to lengths of just over a metre, weigh over 250 kg and live for over 100 years.

▼ Ecuadorians herd some of the country's 2.1 million sheep down from the slopes of the inactive volcano, Chimborazo, the country's highest point. Permanently snow-capped from around 4,600 m upwards, the volcano gets its name from the Quechua Indian for 'mountain of snow'.

PERU

Peru is the third largest country in South America and has a long Pacific Ocean coastline. The interior features the Andes and rainforest.

Area: 1,285,216 km²
Population: 25,662,000
Capital: Lima (7,061,000)
Main languages spoken: Spanish, Quechua, Aymará
Main religion: Roman Catholic
Currency: new sol
Main exports: copper, fish and fish products, zinc, coffee, petroleum, lead
Type of government: republic; democracy

Peru can be divided into three geographical regions: the coast, a jungle interior and, between them, the highlands or sierra. Peru's narrow coastal region runs the entire length of the country, some 2,410 km. Facing the Pacific Ocean, this region is largely dry although many of the valleys near the coast are farmed using modern irrigation techniques. In contrast, the jungle interior receives heavy rainfall – as much as 3,800 mm in places. This region covers more than half of Peru's land and is divided into highland and lowland regions. The highland area is found on the eastern flanks of the Andes at altitudes between 490 and 2,800 m. Covered in thick rainforest, the lowland area is part of the Amazon river basin and includes Peru's longest rivers, the Ucayali and the Marañón. These rivers join 80 km south of Iquitos to help form the Amazon river.

PERUVIAN HIGHLANDS
The Peruvian highlands cover approximately 30 per cent of Peru and consist of large numbers of mountain peaks, over 170 of which rise above 4,850 m.

Temperatures vary with altitude and can range from -7 to 21°C. This region has a mixture of arid areas and some fertile growing land, usually found in deep valleys. Most people who live there either work in mining industries extracting the many metal ores or practise subsistence farming. The area is also home to Lake Titicaca, a large lake of over 8,300 km² which, at an altitude of over 3,800 m, is the highest navigable lake in the world.

▼ Local Aymará native Americans fish the waters of Lake Titicaca. The Aymarás use boats built out of reeds and rushes in the same way as their ancient ancestors.

PEOPLE OF THE INCA EMPIRE

Peru has been home to a number of ancient native cultures including the Nazca, Chimú and Chavín civilizations. The country was also at the centre of the great Inca empire which had its capital at Cuzco in southern Peru. Despite great destruction by the Spanish, many remains of the Incas' former glory lie throughout Peru, and are one of the biggest draws for the one million tourists who visit the country each year. While around 37 per cent of Peru's population are people of mixed European and native American descent, the largest population group are native Americans who comprise 45 per cent of Peruvians. Spanish was the sole official language until 1975, when Quechua, a language of native Americans, was also made an official language. Aymará, another important native American language, was added in 1980.

POLITICS AND ECONOMY

Exploiting oil and natural gas, and mining metal ores are major industries in Peru. The country ranks as one of the world's leading producers of silver, lead and copper. Agricultural land is relatively limited, but the use of terraces cut into the mountain and hillsides, and irrigation in dry coastal areas allows a range of crops to be grown, especially maize, sugarcane, rice and potatoes. Fishing is a major industry but, along with farming, has been hit by the change in weather patterns known as El Niño (see page 31) which has reduced fish stocks off the coast of Peru and caused large floods and landslides to damage harvests. Further hardships have hit Peru's population, 50 per cent of which the UN estimates live below the poverty line. Economic troubles saw inflation rise to over 7,000 per cent at one point while guerrilla wars in the recent past have claimed more than 23,000 lives.

▲ A Peruvian market draws traditionally dressed local native Indian people to sell and trade produce and goods.

▼ Known as the Sacred Valley of the Incas, many ancient sites, including the city of Cuzco, the large stone fortress of Sacsahuamán and Machu Picchu are found here.

BOLIVIA

Most of the people of Bolivia, one of the poorest
South American nations, live on a high plateau between
the Andes mountain ranges called the Altiplano.

Area: 1,098,581 km²
Population: 8,274,000
Capitals: La Paz (1,477,000)
and Sucre (194,000)
Main languages spoken:
Spanish, Quechua, Aymará
Main religion: Roman
Catholic
Currency: boliviano
Main exports: zinc,
soybeans, petroleum, gold,
natural gas, tin
Type of government:
republic; democracy

Bolivia is a landlocked country
with no sea or ocean coastline.
It borders five South American
countries – Peru and Chile to the
west, Brazil to the north and east and
Paraguay and Argentina to the south.
The largest expanse of water is formed
by Lake Titicaca which sits on the
country's border with Peru. The country's
most notable highland areas consist of two
mountain ranges which run roughly south
to north through the western side of the
country. The more westerly of these two
mountain ranges includes a number of
active volcanoes, and its steep slopes and
high peaks are the least inhabited part of
Bolivia. The more easterly range in which
Bolivia's twin capital cities of La Paz and
Sucre are situated, is more densely
populated. Its eastern slopes are densely
covered by forest. This region is the
wettest part of the Bolivian Andes,
receiving
around
1,350 mm
of rain
per year,
mostly
falling in
just three
months of
the year. To
the north and
the east, the
land descends
into part of a
vast lowland area
called the Oriente.
This is made up of
low alluvial plains,
large swamp areas
and tropical forests.

◀ Life in rural areas is
often very harsh. Almost
half of the Bolivian
workforce grow crops or
raise livestock for a living.

THE ALTIPLANO

Lying between the two Andean mountain
ranges running through Bolivia is a large
high altitude plateau called the Altiplano.
Approximately 800 km long, the plateau
is over 320 km wide at its broadest point.
The Altiplano is a series of basins lying at
around 3,650 m above sea level. Lake
Titicaca and Lake Poopo occupy two of
the basins while salt flats inhabit several
others. The northern half of the region
receives moderate rainfall while the
southern region is dry. Most rain comes
during summer thunderstorms in January
and February. Cold winds sweep the entire
plateau, keeping average temperatures
under 12°C with sub-zero temperatures
during winter. The land has a thin soil, and
grasses, scrub bushes and small trees are
the main vegetation.

This harsh landscape actually provides
homes for the majority of Bolivians. Many
live in towns, work in the mining region
based around Oruro or farm the land and
raise herds of alpacas and llamas.
Successive Bolivian governments have
urged people to move from the Altiplano
to the Oriente, where the discovery of
fossil fuels and the possibility of large-
scale forestry and growing tropical crops
could provide a boost to the country's
economy. The population has increased
especially in and around the main town of
the Oriente, Santa Cruz, but most people
who live on the Altiplano are reluctant to
leave the homelands of their ancestors.

▲ Most crops grown in Bolivia are traded in markets and consumed within the country. These include maize, potatoes, wheat and soybeans.

▼ The imposing San Francisco Church is found in La Paz. At an elevation of between 3,250 and 4,100 m, La Paz is the highest capital city in the world. More than two-thirds of all Bolivia's manufacturing industry is based in La Paz.

MINING AND NATURAL GAS

The Spanish explorers who came to Bolivia in the 16th century discovered reserves of silver and the mine established at Potosi became famous as the world's largest. The boom in silver production came and went and now Bolivia, independent from Spanish rule since the middle of the 19th century, relies on other mining industries to prosper. The country has reserves of a number of minerals but has not invested in exploiting them all. Large scale tin production, which first started in 1895, replaced silver as the main metal mined. For the first half of the 20th century, Bolivia was the world's largest tin producer and still ranks as one of the top ten countries. Other metals are mined including zinc, tungsten, uranium, copper and lead. Almost half of Bolivia's electricity is generated by hydro-electric power schemes but the country also has reserves of oil and natural gas. Natural gas is Bolivia's biggest export and accounts for over 50 per cent of the money Bolivia earns from abroad.

LIVING IN BOLIVIA

Many Bolivians are poor and struggle to make a living. The country once had a Pacific coastline but lost the land during the 1879–1885 war with Chile. It then lost further important territory in the Chaco War (1932–1935). Its isolated position in South America, poor transport links due to the rugged geography of the land, and frequent changes of government have not aided development. While there is wealth in the larger towns and cities, life in rural areas tends to be harsh. Doctors and healthcare services are hard to find outside of the towns and cities, and many children are not immunized against diseases. Many Bolivian farmers have turned to cultivating coca even though it makes the illegal drug cocaine.

BRAZIL

The largest country in South America, Brazil has a rapidly industrializing economy, growing population and incredibly rich wildlife and mineral resources.

Area: 8,547,404 km²
Population: 169,800,000
Capital: Brasilia (2,043,000)
Main language spoken: Portuguese
Main religions: Roman Catholic, Candomblé
Currency: real
Main exports: iron and steel products, non-electrical machinery, iron ore, road vehicles, wood and wood products, coffee
Type of government: republic; partial democracy

▼ Brazil has outlawed much deforestation that occurs in the Amazon basin. However, laws are hard to police in such a huge area and illegal forestry to recover valuable tropical hardwoods accounts for much deforestation occurring in the Amazon.

Brazil shares a border with every country in South America with the exception of Chile and Ecuador. The country is a federal republic which is divided up into 26 separate states and a federal district based in the city of Brasilia. The country has a great variety of landscapes over its huge area but there are a small number of major geographical regions. To the north and east, where Brazil borders four other South American countries, lie the Guiana Highlands which run into Suriname and Guyana. This region of mountains and valleys include Pico da Neblina. With an elevation of 3,014 m, this mountain is the country's highest peak and was only discovered in 1962. Most of northern and western Brazil is home to a large part of the Amazon basin, containing the Amazon and its hundreds of tributary rivers as well as the largest rainforest region in the world. In the centre and south of the country are the Brazilian Highlands. This area is a large plateau of ancient rock which is divided

▲ The ornate opera house at Manaus was built in 1896. Situated on the Negro river, Manaus is the capital of Amazonas State and home to half the state's population.

by low mountain formations and has been weathered over thousands of years to create deep river valleys. Much of the Brazilian Highlands are covered in scrubland or forests.

THE AMAZON BASIN

Although the giant basin and rainforest through which the Amazon runs lie in a number of South American countries, the river's greatest extent is located in Brazil.

ATLANTIC
OCEAN

▲ Found in many parts of central and southern America, but most common in Brazil, the jaguar is the largest wild cat species in either North or South America.

The Amazon basin covers over a third of Brazil and large parts of the rainforest-covered region remain unsurveyed or have only been recently explored. The Amazon forest contains the largest single reserve of biological organisms in the world. No one knows how many species of living thing exist in the Amazon, but scientists estimate the number could be as high as five million which could equal almost a third of the entire world's living organisms. What is not in doubt is that the Amazon basin is extraordinarily rich in wildlife. At one time, around five million native Americans lived in the Amazonian rainforests but this number is closer to

200,000 today. The major tribes still inhabiting the Amazon include the Tikuna, the Yanomami which are also found in Venezuela, the Xavante and the Guajajara.

DEFORESTATION IN THE AMAZON

The rainforest is shrinking, occasionally due to forest fires but mainly due to human impact. Deforestation to clear lands for mining, farming or for the timber and other products has seen more than 15 per cent of the entire rainforest destroyed since the early 1970s. As much as 35,000 km² have been lost in individual years. Deforestation of the Amazon has become an international issue with aid programmes and initiatives designed to slow or halt the cutting down of trees. Yet, governmental plans to construct a massive dam and road network to help develop industry may threaten far greater areas of the rainforest.

▲ Rio de Janeiro's carnival is a massive festival billed as the largest party in the world and features parades, music and dancing.

▼ Standing on Corcovado peak, 787 m above sea level, the statue of Christ the Redeemer looks over the major Brazilian city of Rio de Janeiro.

A COFFEE AND MINING GIANT

No country produces more coffee than Brazil. The world leader, Brazil produced 1.27 million tonnes of this lucrative crop in 2001, most of which was exported. Sugarcane, beans, cocoa, maize and oranges are also major export crops and many more, including potatoes, cotton, tobacco and rice are grown. Brazil has some of the richest mineral deposits in the world, although their full extent is not known as the entire country has yet to be surveyed. Brazil has iron ore reserves estimated at a minimum of 48 billion tonnes and large reserves of other metal ores including bauxite, lead, nickel and manganese. Ninety per cent of the country's electricity is generated by hydro-electric power plants. Brazil's resources are used by the country's giant manufacturing industry to produce large quantities of products including motor vehicles, chemicals, clothing and textiles.

BRAZIL'S CLIMATE

Brazil has a generally warm and humid climate but with great variation in local areas. Cities on plateaus, such as Brasilia, have mild climates with average daily temperatures of around 19°C. Cities on the coast, such as Rio de Janeiro, have warmer climates. The hottest part of Brazil is the northeast where in the dry season between May and November temperatures above 38°C are often recorded. Most of Brazil receives moderate rainfall with parts of the Amazon basin the wettest areas.

BRAZIL'S PEOPLE

Almost half of Brazil's population are under 20 years of age and the population has more than tripled in the last 60 years. Brazilians are a mix of different origins

with the native Americans who first settled the country now comprising less than one per cent of the population. Most of the early European settlers were Portuguese and, from the 16th to the 19th century, they brought between three and four million black Africans to Brazil as slaves. People of mixed descent from European, African and native American backgrounds comprise the majority of Brazil's population. Brazil also has the largest population of Japanese outside of Japan. Arriving mainly as poor farmers in the 1920s, over two million people of Japanese origin now live in Brazil. Massive migration from rural to urban areas has occurred. Some Brazilians are very wealthy but income is distributed with huge inequalities and millions are desperately poor. Large shanty towns surrounding major cities see people living in squalor with little water or sanitation.

BRAZILIAN CITIES

Unlike many South American countries, Brazil has many major cities: São Paulo is the country's most populous city, while Rio de Janeiro is its most famous city internationally and its cultural centre.

Neither is the official capital of the country, a role given to the purpose-built city of Brasilia. In the 1950s, as part of initiatives to encourage people to move into the Brazilian interior, a new capital city was constructed. Brasilia now houses the national seat of government and many foreign embassies. The largest Brazilian city, however, is also one of the country's oldest colonial settlements, São Paulo. Founded in 1554 on a plateau 760 m above sea level, São Paulo has boomed in the last 120 years as first, coffee growing and exports and, later, industry, brought wealth and employment to the region. Today, it is at the centre of an urban area which houses approximately 17,834,000 people. This makes it the most populous urban area in South America and the third largest in the world. Lying some 75 km inland from the Atlantic Ocean, São Paulo is home to more than 20,000 industrial plants and factories and is also the financial centre of Brazil. If São Paulo is Brazil's biggest city, then Rio de Janeiro is certainly its most well known internationally. A major tourist and business destination, Rio was the capital until 1960 but remains a major metropolis and the entry point for most of the country's 5.3 million tourists that arrive every year.

▲ Poverty and housing shortages mean that many millions of Brazilians live with little water, sanitation or other basic facilities in shanty towns, known as favelas, that surround the country's major cities.

▼ Located in the modern capital city of Brasilia, the National Congress building forms part of the official parliamentary buildings of Brazil.

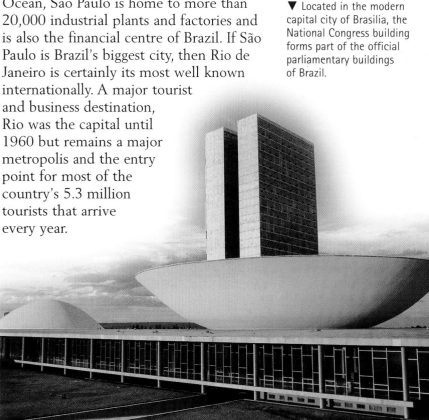

SOUTHERN SOUTH AMERICA

The four nations that make up southern South America contrast in size, shape and geography. The geography varies from the seemingly endless flat plains of the Pampas to the spectacular and rugged Andes mountain system. The region's climate varies just as greatly, from the rainless hot deserts of northern Chile to the icy wastelands of extreme southern Argentina. Running along the western coast is Chile, 4,300 km long but rarely more than several hundred km wide. Smaller and more compact are the landlocked nation of Paraguay and the smallest country in southern South America, Uruguay. Argentina is the largest country in the region and the second largest in the continent. Together, the four countries have an area of approximately 4,106,000 km². However, vast areas of land are sparsely inhabited or uninhabited. In contrast to the Andean nations, native American peoples in all of these countries, except for Paraguay, make up very small proportions of the population. Most of them can trace their descent back to European settlers in the past four centuries. Traditionally important, farming remains the backbone of the economy of the region although, with the exception of Paraguay, the nations of southern South America are increasingly dependent on industry and services for revenue.

▲ The Torres del Paine National Park lies in the extreme south of Chile more than 2,500 km south of the country's capital city, Santiago. It is renowned for its unspoilt mountain and river scenery.

PERU
BOLIVIA
PARAGUAY
BRAZIL

PACIFIC
OCEAN

Atacama Desert

Gran Chaco
Pilcomayo
Paraguay
Salado

ASUNCIÓN ■

Paraná

URUGUAY

△ Aconcagua
6960m

SANTIAGO ■

BUENOS AIRES ■
MONTEVIDEO ■
Río de la Plata

ARGENTINA

Pampas
Colorado
Río Negro

Chiloé I.

ATLANTIC
OCEAN

Patagonia

| 0 | | 500 | | 1000 km |
| 0 | 250 | | 500 miles | |

Strait of Magellan
Tierra
del Fuego

Cape Horn

▼ Cattle and livestock raising is important in all four
southern South American countries. The Pampas region is
an area of flat plains found in Argentina, large parts of
which are used to raise the country's huge herds of cattle
and sheep. In 2000, Argentina had approximately
58 million head of cattle and 15 million sheep.

PARAGUAY

A relatively unknown and isolated country,
Paraguay is divided into two geographical regions.
The eastern half is the more populous.

Area: 406,752 km²
Population: 5,496,000
Capital: Asunción (998,000)
Main languages spoken:
Guaraní, Spanish
Main religion: Roman
Catholic
Currency: guaraní
Main exports: soya flour,
cotton, oilseed and
vegetable oil, timber
Type of government:
republic; partial democracy

▼ Oxen are used as beasts
of burden throughout rural
Paraguay. Ninety per cent
of the country's roads are
unpaved and car ownership
is low; 14 vehicles per
1,000 of the population
compared to 140 per 1,000
in Argentina.

Paraguay's borders are
largely created by rivers such
as the Parana, Paraguay and the
Pilcomayo which form much of the
border with Argentina. The Paraguay
river also divides the country into two
quite different geographical regions. To
the east, is the Paraneña region which
increases in elevation forming a series of
low-lying mountains near the border with
Brazil. To the west lies the Chaco region.
This is a huge plain averaging around
125 m in altitude above sea level. It covers
more than 60 per cent of the country and
in the summer rainy season, large parts are
flooded and become temporary
swamplands. Paraguay's people are mainly
descendants of native Americans.
Agriculture is the key occupation of much
of Paraguay's workforce. Half of the
country's population live in rural areas
growing a wide range of crops including
cotton, sugarcane, wheat, bananas and
sweet potatoes. Livestock raising,
especially cattle, is very important.

There are over nine million cattle reared
on the grasslands as well as sheep and
horses. Paraguay is much less industrialized
than its neighbours. However, forestry, is a
major industry worth seven per cent of
the country's exports. Asunción is
Paraguay's capital and its largest city.
Founded by Spanish settlers in 1537, it is
built on low-lying hills overlooking the
Paraguay river at the point where it joins
the Pilcomayo river. It is the chief
manufacturing city of the country.

URUGUAY

The smallest country in southern South America, Uruguay is a land of rolling plains and low-lying hills. Much of this land is given over to raising livestock.

Area: 176,215 km²
Population: 3,341,000
Capital: Montevideo (1,370,000)
Main language spoken: Spanish
Main religion: Roman Catholic
Currency: peso
Main exports: meat and other animal products, live animals, textiles and clothing, vegetables
Type of government: republic; democracy

Uruguay is one of the few countries in South America which does not have a tropical or subtropical climate. Its location some distance from the Equator and position facing the Atlantic Ocean give the country a warm temperate climate with relatively high rainfall (around 950 mm per year) and average temperatures of 10°C in winter and 22°C in summer. Cold wind storms called pamperos can occur during winter but few parts of Uruguay ever experience frost. The natural vegetation is tall prairie grasslands with relatively few forest areas. Almost 90 per cent of the country is suitable for agriculture but only a tenth of this land is used for growing crops such as maize, wheat and rice. Much of the remainder supports the giant herds of livestock, particularly cattle and sheep, which roam Uruguay's plains. For such a relatively small country, Uruguay is a major sheep farming nation and the world's second largest exporter of wool.

Uruguay's people bear few traces of the original native American inhabitants. Less than 10 per cent of the population are either solely or part native American. The vast majority of people are immigrants from Europe or from Brazil and Argentina. Uruguay's capital city, Montevideo, sprawls along the northern banks of the Rio de la Plata and is the centre of Uruguayan business and food and wool processing industries. Large-scale migration from the

▲ A market stall in the Barrio Reus district of Montevideo, Uruguay's capital city. Montevideo is Uruguay's main port and the site of its state university.

country to the city means that around half the entire country's population live in or close to the city. Uruguay was the first South American country to establish a state welfare system and has a high level of literacy (97 per cent) and healthcare.

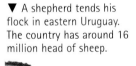

▼ A shepherd tends his flock in eastern Uruguay. The country has around 16 million head of sheep.

CHILE

Chile is a nation of natural extremes in its landscapes and especially its climate. Volcanoes, icy wastelands and temperate plains are all part of this highly developed country.

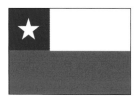

Area: 756,626 km²
Population: 15,050,000
Capitals: Santiago (6,039,000). Valparaiso (811,000) is the legislative capital
Main languages spoken: Spanish, Araucanian
Main religion: Roman Catholic
Currency: peso
Main exports: copper, iron ore, zinc, silver, food products, paper and paper products
Type of government: republic; democracy

▼ Founded in 1849, Punta Arenas lies on the stretch of water, known as the Straits of Magellan, which links the Atlantic and Pacific Oceans. The city's 116,000 inhabitants work in industries processing and transporting oil, mutton, wool and timber.

Chile shares borders with Argentina, Peru and Bolivia and has the longest Pacific coastline of any South American country. Some 3,700 km west of its coast in the southern Pacific Ocean lies Easter Island which is owned by Chile. Several other small islands in the Pacific are also under Chilean control. Chile owns the western part of the island group of Tierra del Fuego in the extreme south of the continent.

A CHANGING LANDSCAPE

About 4,300 km long but averaging only 175 km in width, Chile's landscape is dominated by the Andes mountains which run the entire length of the country. Northern Chile includes one of the driest places in the world, the Atacama desert. Parts of this arid area have never received any recorded rainfall. South of this area lies a large temperate region where most of Chile's towns, cities and agricultural land are found. The southern central region of Chile is renowned for its natural beauty containing many lakes and large areas of forest. As one progresses further south, the mild climate gives way to a cold, windswept region. Rainfall is high here reaching as much as 4,065 mm per year. Cape Horn is the most southerly point of both Chile and the South American continent and is just 650 km away from Antarctica.

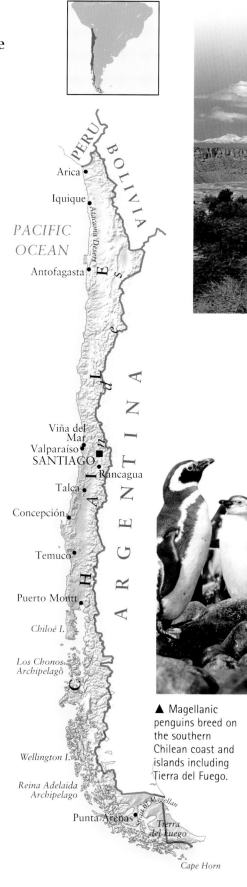

▲ Magellanic penguins breed on the southern Chilean coast and islands including Tierra del Fuego.

▲ The Atacama desert is one of the driest places on Earth. Here there are salt mines and copper reserves which are exploited by the largest open-pit mine on Earth.

THE CHILEAN PEOPLE AND ECONOMY

The great majority of Chile's people are mestizos. Native Americans make up about one-tenth of the total population and most live in the Andes in northern Chile and along the southern coast. Nearly 90 per cent of all Chileans live in central Chile, with more than one-third living in and around the capital city of Santiago. Valparaiso is the country's main port.

The exploitation of minerals, including salt and metals, are major industries in the country with Chile remaining the world's largest producer of copper. Agriculture in the centre of the country produces fruit crops for export and provides grapes for a flourishing and world-famous wine industry. The fast-flowing rivers found in the Andes have been harnessed for hydro-electric power to generate just over half of Chile's electricity.

▶ Located 55 km north-east of Puerto Montt, Mount Osorno is 2,652 m high and is just one of hundreds of volcanoes found within the Andes that run through Chile. A cone volcano with its topmost part covered in glaciers, Osorno is a young volcano which last erupted in the 1830s.

ARGENTINA

The second largest country in South America, Argentina's territory includes large areas of rich pastures on which some of the largest cattle herds in the world graze.

Area: 2,766,890 km²
Population: 37,030,000
Capital: Buenos Aires (11,931,000)
Main language spoken: Spanish
Main religion: Roman Catholic
Currency: peso
Main exports: meat, wool, cereals, manufactures, machinery and transport equipment
Type of government: republic; partial democracy

▼ Ushuaia is the capital of the Argentinian province of Tierra del Fuego, Antarctica and South Atlantic Islands. Founded in 1884, and with around 29,000 inhabitants, Ushuaia lies at a latitude of 54.8°S, making it the most southerly large settlement in the world.

Forming the southeastern part of South America, Argentina is a large plain which rises in elevation from the Atlantic Ocean westwards to the country's border with Chile. There, some of the highest peaks of the Andes are found including Aconcagua with an elevation of 6,960 m. The Andean region of Argentina is sparsely inhabited by miners and sheep herders. To the north, where Argentina borders Bolivia and Paraguay, lies the Gran Chaco region which contains large forested areas and swamplands. South of this are the large rolling plains of the Pampas region within which lies Argentina's largest city, Buenos Aires. Further south, lies Patagonia, a vast, inhospitable region shared with Chile.

CLIMATE

Because Argentina is a long country – approximately 3,330 km from north to south – its climate varies greatly. In the north, there is a small tropical region to the northeast while the Gran Chaco has subtropical temperatures. Most of Argentina has a temperate climate which gets colder the further south one travels. Rainfall varies greatly, with Argentina's capital city, Buenos Aires, averaging about

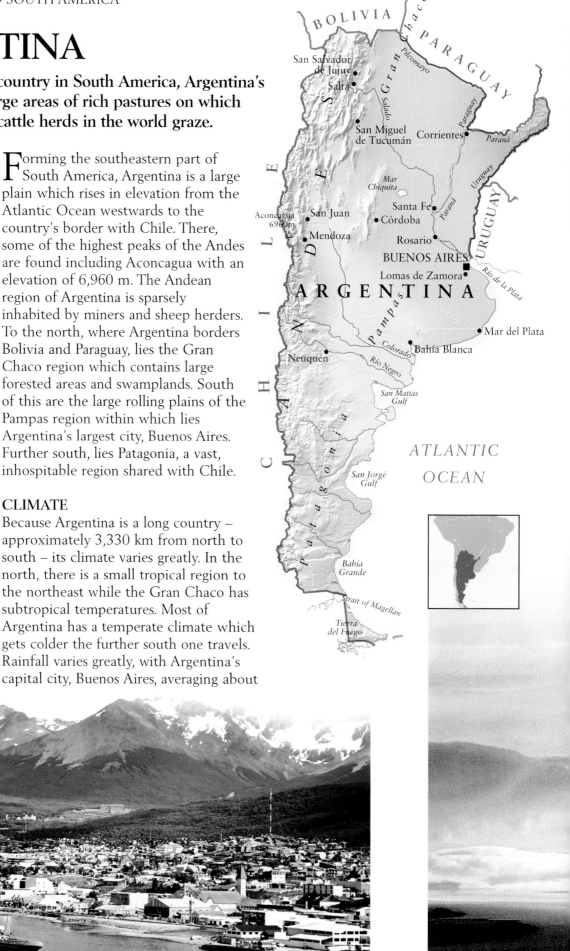

▲ Argentina is one of the foremost polo-playing nations. Many of the world's best polo ponies are thoroughbred horses from either Argentina or the southwestern USA.

▼ Southern Patagonia has a cold and very dry climate with less than 250 mm of rainfall per year. The region is split between Chile and Argentina.

950 mm per year. To the south and the west, far less rain falls and the semi-arid climate restricts the types of plants that can grow there. In the Argentinian Andes, hot dry winds, called zondas, travel across the mountains absorbing moisture but not forming clouds and rain.

PATAGONIA

The southernmost region of Argentina, Patagonia is a vast, frequently windswept plain, with an area of approximately 777,000 km². Much of the region experiences a dry climate but the northern portion of the region is warm enough to be able to support large farms growing alfalfa grass, vegetables and some fruit, as well as massive flocks of sheep. Argentina has approximately 13.7 million head of sheep, many millions of which are found in Patagonia. Tourism has become important in the region. Argentina has more than 20 national parks, a number of which are located in Patagonia along with wildlife reserves and other protected areas. However, Patagonia's biggest impact on the country's economy is increasingly due to its reserves of oil, natural gas and coal as well as metal ores such as iron, tungsten, lead and gold.

▲ Buenos Aires is Argentina's largest city and became its capital in 1816. The city is a major transport terminus in South America, the largest railway centre and the continent's largest port.

THE PAMPAS

The Pampas get their name from a Quechua Indian word meaning 'flat surface' and are a vast series of largely treeless plains which cover much of central Argentina. The region is split into two, based on climate. The Humid Pampas runs from the coast inland and receives moderate to heavy rainfall. The soils are deep, heavy and rich. Further inland, the Dry Pampas is a larger area but supports fewer people and has less crop-growing land. Originally covered in grassland vegetation, much of the Pampas region has been turned into farmland with massive pasture lands and ranches for the country's huge herds of cattle which number over 49 million.

▲ Argentinian ranchers, known as gauchos, herd cattle across the plains of the Pampas. A national symbol of Argentina, the gauchos were originally nomadic cowboys who traded herds of cattle and horses. Many gauchos now work as cattle hands on individual ranches.

ARGENTINA'S HISTORY AND PEOPLE

Argentina received its name, meaning 'land of silver' from Spanish explorers who reached the region in the 16th century. In 1580, Spaniards established a colony on the site of what would become the major city of Buenos Aires. After repelling an attempted British invasion in 1806–1807, the country declared independence from Spain in 1816 and there began a long internal conflict for power. A series of fierce battles with the country's native American population occurred in the 1870s and resulted in a major decline in their number. Today, there are an estimated 700,000 native Americans living in Argentina. Waves of immigrants from Europe, particularly Italy, Spain and the United Kingdom, and the Middle East, particularly Syria and Lebanon, arrived in the late 19th and early 20th centuries. These transformed the country's agriculture and its infrastructure such as railways and ports. As a result, Argentina has a different mix of peoples compared to most South American countries with particularly strong Italian-Argentine, British-Argentine and Jewish communities. Until the economic crisis of 2002, a relatively large number of Argentinians enjoyed a high standard of living compared to the rest of South America. The crisis has forced many into poverty; the United Nations estimates that 53 per cent of Argentinians live below the poverty line while a quarter of the country lives in extreme poverty.

▼ Considered one of the natural wonders of South America, Iguaçu Falls lie in the northeast of the country. They are four times the width of North America's Niagara Falls and fall a distance of 72 m.

SOUTH ATLANTIC ISLANDS

Lying in the icy waters of the south Atlantic Ocean is a number of largely barren, ice-covered islands which include South Georgia and the South Sandwich Islands.

S outh Georgia is the largest of the south Atlantic islands and lies some 1,300 km southeast of the Falkland Islands. Largely covered in ice, it is mountainous with a rugged coastline. The small population consists mainly of military personnel and scientists, who reside in a small settlement formerly used by whalers. The South Sandwich Islands are a group of six glacier-covered volcanic islets 760 km southeast of South Georgia. British ownership of these islands and South Georgia is disputed by Argentina.

▲ The third largest penguin species, the gentoo penguin is found on the South Sandwich Islands where it nests on rocky shorelines.

ST HELENA AND DEPENDENCIES

A small, isolated collection of islands makes up the British dependency of St Helena and includes the islands of St Helena, Ascension and Tristan da Cunha.

Ascension Island
(to St Helena)

Georgetown • The Peak 859m

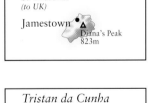

St Helena
(to UK)

Jamestown • Diana's Peak 823m

Tristan da Cunha
(to St Helena)

Edinburgh • Queen Mary's Peak 2160m

Inaccessible I.

Nightingale I.

Area: 411 km²
Population: 7,000
Capital: Jamestown (1,500)
Official language: English
Main religion: Anglican, Baptist
Currency: local issue of UK pound
Main exports: canned and frozen fish, handicrafts
Government: dependency of UK

A rugged mountainous island created by volcanic activity, St Helena sits in the South Atlantic Ocean about 1,920 km from the west coast of Africa. Large cliffs face the ocean on its north, east and west sides while deep valleys are carved into its mountainous interior. About a quarter of the island's population live in Jamestown, a natural harbour and port for shipping. Potatoes, maize and flax are grown, but most of the economy is subsidized by the United Kingdom with additional revenue generated through the port. Ascension lies

▲ St Helena was the last place of exile for the French leader, Napoleon Bonaparte.

over 1,130 km northwest of St Helena and is used as a military base. Its rugged volcanic landscape provides habitats for thousands of sea turtles and sooty tern birds. The small population of the volcanic islands of Tristan da Cunha grow potatoes and catch crawfish. The main island is dominated by a volcano which last erupted in 1961 causing the island to be evacuated.

▶ The slopes of Green Mountain on Ascension is one of the few places where fruit and vegetables are grown on the island.

FALKLAND ISLANDS

Located in the southern Atlantic Ocean, the Falkland Islands are a dependency of the UK. Their ownership is disputed by Argentina which calls them Islas Malvinas.

Falkland Islands (to UK)

Area: 12,170 km²
Population: 2,000
Capital: Stanley (1,800)
Main language spoken: English
Main religion: Anglican
Currency: pound
Main exports: sheep products, fish
Type of government: dependency of UK

▼ With a permanent population of around 20 people, Port Howard is the second largest settlement on West Falkland island. It is the base of Port Howard Farm which has around 45,000 sheep.

The Falklands consist of two main islands, East and West Falkland, and approximately 200 smaller islets. The two major islands are hilly and their coastlines are heavily indented with many drowned river valleys which form natural harbours. The climate is cool, very windy and wet. Average winter temperatures are 1.7°C while the average summer temperature is approximately 9.4°C. Rain falls on around 250 days of the year with almost constant winds averaging 31 km/h. The islands' vegetation reflects the harsh conditions with few trees and mainly grasses and low-lying scrub bushes. The grasslands act as pasture for the main farming activity on the island which is rearing sheep. East Falkland is the site of the islands' biggest settlement, Stanley. Ninety per cent of all Falkland islanders live in this town which contains the islands' only hospital. Many of the older buildings in Stanley were constructed from locally quarried stone and timber salvaged from shipwrecks. Timber today is just one of many items which has to be imported. Situated on the site of a large natural harbour, Stanley is the main terminal for imports of food, coal, oil and clothing, and exports of wool and sheepskins. A dependency of the United Kingdom, disputes over the ownership of the islands with Argentina have rumbled on for many decades. Negotiations came to crisis point in April 1982, with the invasion of the islands by Argentina. A bloody ten-week war ended with UK military forces reoccupying the islands. In 2002, the United Nations called on both countries to re-enter negotiations over the islands' future.

EUROPE

EUROPE

Europe is considered an individual continent but it is actually part of the Eurasian land mass which extends eastwards through Asia. Its landscape varies from icy, rugged mountain ranges such as the Alps, to temperate woodlands and warm regions, particularly around the Mediterranean Sea. Europe is the second smallest continent and its land area is not that much greater than the country of Australia. However, its population of close to 700 million makes it the second most populous continent and the most densely populated of all. The birthplace of modern industry and exploration, a number of European countries, particularly Spain, France, Britain, Portugal and the Netherlands, claimed lands all over the world as colonies from the 15th century onwards. Rich in history which extends back thousands of years, Europe has many divisions of language and nationality and over 60 native languages. The continent has seen much conflict and changing boundaries. The most recent redrawing of borders came in the 1990s with the reunification of East and West Germany into one nation, the splitting of Czechoslovakia into Slovakia and the Czech Republic and the break-up of the former country of Yugoslavia into a series of states. Europe's largest nation is also its most easterly. The Russian Federation emerged from the break-up of the Soviet Union in the early 1990s.

▲ The capital of the Russian empire for over two centuries, St Petersburg is the Russian Federation's second-largest city. It is located on the delta of the River Neva and contains many elaborate buildings including this church, the Church of Our Saviour.

◄ Many countries of southern Europe border the Mediterranean Sea which provides thousands of tonnes of fish every year. They are sold at markets such as this one in Marseille in the south of France.

0 250 500 miles
0 500 1000 km

Novaya Zemlya

Barents Sea

North Cape

Norwegian Sea

Vesterålen
Lofoten

Kola Peninsula

White Sea

N O R W A Y

S W E D E N

FINLAND

Gulf of Bothnia

RUSSIAN

FEDERATION

Ural Mountains

▲ The red deer is found mainly in woodland areas in northern Europe.

Gulf of Finland

Saaremaa

ESTONIA

orth ea

DENMARK

Gotland

Öland

Baltic Sea

Bornholm

LATVIA

LITHUANIA

Russ. Fed.

HERLANDS

GERMANY

UXEMBOURG

POLAND

BELARUS

CZECH REPUBLIC

SLOVAKIA

Carpathians

UKRAINE

MOLDOVA

WITZ.

LIECH.

AUSTRIA

SLOVENIA

HUNGARY

ROMANIA

Sea of Azov

Caspian Sea

L P S

ACO

SAN MARINO

CROATIA

BOSNIA-
HERZEGOVINA

CRIMEA

Caucasus

Apennines

Adriatic Sea

SERBIA AND
MONTENEGRO

BULGARIA

Black Sea

Corsica

VATICAN CITY

an

ITALY

MACEDONIA

ALBANIA

Sardinia

Tyrrhenian Sea

GREECE

Aegean Sea

Ionian Sea

Peloponnese

Sicily

Rhodes

MALTA

Crete

▶ Europe is one of the most industrialized continents and this steel-making plant is located in the Ruhr Valley in western Germany's central and southern territory, one of the largest industrialized regions in the world.

NORTHERN EUROPE

Northern Europe includes a varied collection of countries from the large economic powerhouses of Germany, France and the United Kingdom to the tiny nation of Luxembourg. Much of the region's landscape has been shaped by glaciation. This has left behind land features such as Norway's complex coastline made up of over 100,000 islands and fjords. The three largest islands in the region are Iceland and the two islands which comprise the United Kingdom and Ireland. All three islands are located in the north Atlantic. Much of northern Europe was once covered in forests but a growing population and the demands of industry have cleared much of the land. The largest forests remain in Norway, Sweden, Denmark, Finland and Germany. Although large parts of northern Europe are farmed, the economies of most of the region's countries are dominated by manufacturing industries and services such as banking. These have helped to give the majority of the region's people a high standard of living. Most of the countries receive large numbers of tourists. France is the world's leading destination with over 75 million visitors every year. Most of the countries in the region are members of the European Union which has its major centres in France, Belgium and Luxembourg.

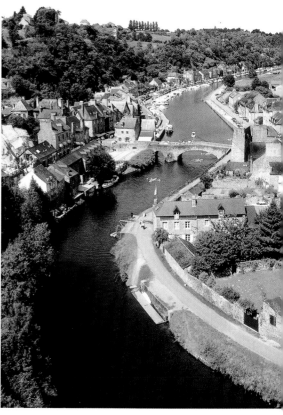

▼ Northern Sweden is home to some of the last large wilderness areas in northern Europe. The region contains over 1,000 km² of virgin fir and pine forests.

▲ Northern Europe is criss-crossed by rivers and many of the region's towns grew up along a river bank. This is the market town of Dinan in northwestern France.

ICELAND
REYKJAVIK

North Cape

Vesterålen
Lofoten

N O R W A Y
S W E D E N
FINLAND

RUSSIAN FEDERATION

*Norwegian
Sea*

*ATLANTIC

OCEAN*

*Faeroe Is.
(to Denmark)*

Shetland Is.

Outer Hebrides

Orkney Is.

Gulf of Bothnia

OSLO

HELSINKI

Gulf of Finland

Vänern

STOCKHOLM

UNITED
KINGDOM

*North
Sea*

Vättern

Gotland

REP. OF
IRELAND
DUBLIN

DENMARK
COPENHAGEN

Öland

*Baltic
Sea*

*Celtic
Sea*

Bornholm

LONDON

NETHS.
AMSTERDAM

Elbe

English Channel
*Channel Is.
(to UK)*

THE HAGUE

BERLIN

POLAND

BELGIUM
BRUSSELS

GERMANY

*Bay of
Biscay*

PARIS

Seine

Loire

LUX.
LUXEMBOURG

Rhine

CZECH
REPUBLIC

FRANCE

SWITZ. LIECH.

AUSTRIA

Garonne

Mont Blanc
4810m △

*Massif
Central*

Rhône

A L P S

ITALY

SPAIN

Pyrenees

ANDORRA

MONACO

*Ligurian
Sea*

*Mediterranean
Sea*

*Corsica
(to France)*

0	250	500 km
0	125	250 miles

▶ A windmill in the Netherlands. In contrast to the rugged
scenery of Scandinavia, the Low Countries of Belgium,
Luxembourg and the Netherlands are flat and barely rise
above sea level.

149

NORWAY

A mountainous and rugged country, Norway is the most northerly and westerly of the mainland Scandinavian nations and one of the most sparsely populated in Europe.

Area: 386,958 km²
Population: 4,478,000
Capital: Oslo (764,000)
Major language spoken: Norwegian
Main religion: Evangelical Lutheran (Church of Norway)
Currency: Norwegian krone
Main exports: petroleum and natural gas and their products, machinery and transport equipment, metals and metal products
Type of government: kingdom; democracy

▼ The first major discovery of oil was made at the Ekofisk field in the North Sea in 1969. Large oil terminals, such as this Statoil terminal, assist in processing and export.

Norway is a long, narrow country which runs northeast to southwest along the Scandinavian Peninsula and broadens out to the south where it borders the North Sea. An extended portion of the North Sea, called the Skagerrak, separates Norway from Denmark; it shares a long land border with Sweden and much shorter, northerly borders with Finland and the Russian Federation. Norway's territory also includes the island of Jan Mayen and the island group of Svalbard in the Arctic Ocean. The Norwegian mainland consists of a large number of high plateaus called vidder. These are often very mountainous and in the far north are still covered in glaciers. The Norwegian people live mainly in settlements along the coast including the important cities of Bergen, Trondheim and Stavanger, or in the southeast of the country where the capital city of Oslo is located.

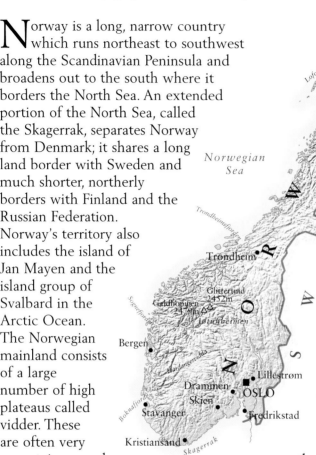

A COUNTRY OF WATER

Norway's western coastline is so indented that in a country which measures 2,650 km in length, the coastline measures 21,347 km. Along most of the coastline's length lie hundreds of islands collectively known as the skerryguard. These islands provide some shelter from the open sea allowing Norwegian peoples to use the fjords and bays as excellent natural harbours. Most of this coastline is kept free of ice, despite lying in northern latitudes, due to the warm Gulf Stream current. Much of the country's landscape has been shaped by the various periods of glaciation. Norway has hundreds of rivers and streams which criss-cross the country as well as thousands of lakes. The largest lake is Lake Mjøsa (Mjoesa) which covers an area of 368 km² and is situated in the southeast of the country, approximately 70 km north of Oslo. The lake often freezes during the winter months.

FARMING, FORESTRY AND FISHING

Only approximately three per cent of Norway's land can be farmed and most of this lies in the southeastern part of the country. Fodder crops, grown to feed livestock, such as hay, some cereals including rye, oats and barley, and root vegetables are the most common crops. Pigs, sheep and cattle are all raised. Over a quarter of its land remains covered in forests and wood pulp and paper industries are as important as farming. No part of Norway is too far from the sea and Norwegians have long relied on the sea for fishing, transport, port trade and boat and shipbuilding industries. Norway has one of the largest fleets of merchant shipping in the world and its fishing industry, despite depletion of many fishing grounds, still catches about 2.6 million tonnes of fish every year.

AN OIL-RICH NATION

Norway's traditional industries have declined in favour of light industries including furniture making, electronics and oil and chemical processing. The discovery of large reserves of oil and natural gas off the Norwegian coast in the 1960s made a great difference to the country's economy. Today, Norway is Europe's largest oil producer, producing around 3.2 million barrels per day. As Norway generates 99 per cent of its own electricity from hydro-electric power, it is able to export a large proportion of its oil. This has helped to give its population one of the highest standards of living in the world with low unemployment and extensive social services.

▲ The spectacular Holmenkollen ski jump, near Oslo, is the world's oldest and the site of Norway's annual ski festival held in March.

▼ The fishing village of Nusfjord on the island of Flakstadøya, one of the Lofoten islands, is located at the site of a picturesque natural harbour created by the process of glaciation.

SWEDEN

Sweden has a highly developed welfare state and advanced industries which help give its population a very high standard of living.

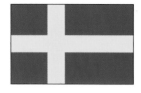

Area: 449,964 km²
Population: 8,883,000
Capital: Stockholm (1,661,000)
Major language spoken: Swedish
Main religion: Lutheran (Church of Sweden)
Currency: Swedish krona
Main exports: machinery and transport equipment (mainly motor vehicles and electrical machinery), paper products, chemicals, iron and steel products
Type of government: kingdom; democracy

The kingdom of Sweden is the largest of the three Scandinavian countries and also the most populous. Its eastern coast faces the Gulf of Bothnia and the Baltic Sea while its much shorter western coast is an outlet to the North Sea. Sweden's main land border is with Norway and to the west the country is mountainous just like its neighbour. To the northwest, the Kölen Mountains contain Sweden's highest points. In central, eastern and southern regions, the landscape is less rugged and consists largely of plateaus and gently rolling lowlands. Periods of glaciation have left behind many lakes. Sweden has more than 4,000 lakes over 1 km² in size while its largest, Lake Vänern, occupies 5,585 km². Sweden also has many rivers, most of which flow eastwards, emptying into the Gulf of Bothnia and the Baltic Sea.

USING THE LAND
Around half of Sweden is covered in forests, most of which are situated to the north. Sweden exploits this huge resource and is a leading producer of paper and timber products with many timber processing factories along its eastern coast.

Less than seven per cent of the country is suitable for farming, but intensive techniques mean that Sweden is able to be self-sufficient in a number of crops

▼ The northern area of Sweden is part of a region called Samiland (Lapland) which extends into Norway, Finland and Russia. Samiland has an Arctic climate and dog sleds are still used in areas for transport.

◄ The long waterfront street of Strandvagen in central Stockholm links the Old Town (Gamla Stan) with Diplomat Town, part of the city so-called because it contains many foreign embassies.

including wheat, barley and potatoes, as well as rearing large herds of pigs and cattle. Sweden generates 53 per cent of its electricity from hydro-electric power. Much of this energy is used to power industries, some of which use locally extracted minerals. Sweden has large reserves of iron ore and other metals but lacks coal or oil reserves and has to import these from Norway, Russia and elsewhere.

SWEDEN'S CITIES

Sweden's largest city, Stockholm, has been the capital for over 600 years. Built on a series of islands linked to the neighbouring mainland by a mixture of ancient and modern bridges, it is one of the most elegant and picturesque capital cities in the world. It is also Sweden's second biggest port and the country's largest industrial area with machine making, advanced telephone and computer technologies, printing, chemicals and metalworking

industries. Stockholm is home to the country's national law-making body, the Riksdag. Just outside Stockholm is the official residence of the country's monarchy. Sweden's largest port is the city of Gothenburg found on its western coast. Located on the southernmost tip of Sweden, Malmö is a major port and trading centre likely to increase in importance since a 15.5 km transport link, called the Øresund Fixed Link, was completed in 2000. This major engineering feat comprises 3.5 km of tunnel, 7.8 km of bridge and 4 km of man-made islands linking Malmö to the capital city of Denmark, Copenhagen. It provides Sweden with a direct rail and road link with mainland Europe, building on its attempts to integrate more fully into Europe since joining the European Union in 1995.

▲ A member of the Sami peoples, formerly known as Lapps, in traditional dress. There are around 80,000 Sami found in Sweden, and also Finland, Norway and Russia.

▼ The city of Gothenburg lies on the western coast of Sweden and is the largest port in Scandinavia handling 33.5 million tonnes of cargo in 2001.

FINLAND

Finland is a low-lying country of lakes and forests. Physically isolated and remote from much of Europe, Finland joined the European Union in 1995.

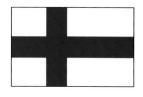

Area: 338,145 km²
Population: 5,195,000
Capital: Helsinki (957,000)
Major languages spoken: Finnish, Swedish
Main religion: Evangelical Lutheran
Currency: euro
Main exports: metal products and machinery, paper and paper products, chemicals and chemical products
Type of government: republic; democracy

Lying between Russia to the east and Sweden to the west, Finland also shares a land border with Norway to the north. The western coast of Finland faces Sweden separated by the Gulf of Bothnia. The Gulf of Finland, to the south, flows into the Baltic Sea and separates Finland from the small Baltic nation of Estonia. Most of Finland is relatively level with an average elevation of between 120 and 190 m. The coast of Finland, although not quite as indented with fjords as Norway, is still marked by thousands of mainly small islands. Many of these are found in the southwest where an island chain called the Turun or Turku archipelago extends westwards and joins the Åland Islands. The Åland Islands are made up of over 6,500 rocky reefs and granite islands of which only 35 are inhabited. The landscape of Finland was massively altered by glaciation in the past. Experts estimate that glaciers, several kilometres thick, forced the Earth's crust downwards by many metres. Since the glaciers and their weight have gone, much of Finland is rising up from the sea at rates of as much as 1 cm per year.

THE LAND OF THE MIDNIGHT SUN

The northern part of Finland, a little over a quarter of its territory, lies within the Arctic Circle. It is the hilliest region of the country and rises into mountains to the northwest, close to the border with Norway. In its most northerly region, the sun does not set for 73 days in the summer and shines for 24 hours a day. This gives the region its nickname of 'The Land of the Midnight Sun'. In the same area, during the dark winter period called Kaamos in the Finnish language, the sun does not rise above the horizon for 51 days.

▲ A member of the Sami people fishes in the Arctic by cutting a hole in the ice through which he can extend his fishing line.

LAKES AND FORESTS

Finland's scenery is dominated by large tracts of forests which are found over three-quarters of its land. More than 1,100 species of trees and plants are found in Finland. While some deciduous trees, such as aspen and elm, are found in the south, the vast majority of its trees are coniferous and include pine and spruce. These forests provide habitats for a range of wildlife including wild geese and swans and mammals including the Arctic fox, lynx and wolf. Finland's forests are far and away its most important natural resource. In 2000, almost 30 per cent of money gained from exports came from its forests including timber, young trees, wood chippings and paper. Lacking large reserves of coal and oil, wood is one of only two naturally occurring fuels. The other is peat which is mainly found in large peat bogs in the northern third of

◀ Reindeer differ from other species of deer in that both males and females have antlers. Reindeer are herded by the Sami (formerly Lapp) peoples found in Finland and elsewhere in Scandinavia. Their skins are used to produce clothing, boots and tents while their meat and milk are a source of food. Reindeer are also used as pack animals in some isolated regions.

▲ Part of the harbour area found in Finland's capital city of Helsinki.

the country. Finland has about 87,000 lakes which make up around ten per cent of its land area. The largest of its inland waterways is Saimaa in southeastern Finland which measures approximately 4,400 km². Part of a complicated network of natural waterways, which includes 120 other lakes containing a total of 14,000 islands, the waters of the Saimaa flow to Lake Ladoga in Russia, the largest lake in Europe.

HISTORY AND INDUSTRY

Positioned between Sweden and Russia, Finland has been governed by both of these nations for long periods of its history. From 1323 to 1809 it was under Swedish rule before becoming a territory of Russia until 1917, when it declared its independence. Finland's capital city was founded in 1550. It was moved to its present position on a small peninsula extending out into the Gulf of Finland in 1640. Helsinki has traditionally relied on its position as an important port, although all except one shipping channel is icebound from January to April or May every year. In the 20th century, Finland developed an advanced industrial economy. Metal extraction and metalworking industries, along with engineering and electronics, account for just over half of all the money made through exports. Helsinki is its industrial and commercial centre and also the home of the 200-member Finnish Parliament, called the Eduskunta. Its area includes almost 20 per cent of the country's population.

▼ Koli National Park is located on the western shore of Lake Pielinen approximately 95 km east of Kuopin. The Koli hills are remnants of a mountain chain which formed almost 2 billion years ago. Over 120,000 visitors a year come to admire the views and hike through the trails that line the park.

DENMARK

The smallest and most densely populated of the Scandinavian countries, Denmark consists of a peninsula and 406 islands.

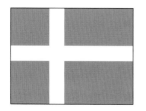

Area: 43,094 km²
Population: 5,293,000
Capital: Copenhagen (1,386,000)
Major language spoken: Danish
Main religion: Evangelical Lutheran
Currency: Danish krone
Main exports: machinery, pig meat, pharmaceuticals, furniture, textiles and clothing
Type of government: kingdom; democracy

Mainland Denmark occupies the Jutland Peninsula which extends north from Germany almost 340 km into the North Sea. The portion of the North Sea which lies between Sweden and Denmark's eastern coast is called the Kattegat, while the arm of the North Sea which separates Norway from northwest Denmark is called the Skagerrak. In the south of Jutland, Denmark has a 68 km long border with Germany. The Jutland Peninsula makes up around 70 per cent of Denmark's land area. The remainder is made up of a large series of islands mostly found to the east of Jutland. The country has responsibilities for two self-governing territories: the Faeroe Islands and the world's biggest individual island, Greenland.

A LOWLAND, TEMPERATE COUNTRY

Denmark is one of the lowest and flattest countries in the world. Almost the whole of the country is low-lying with an average height of only 30 m above sea level. The 588 km² island of Bornholm, lying east of Denmark in the Baltic Sea, is an exception as it is covered with rocky hills. The western coast of Jutland is indented with lagoons, spits and sandbars. Fjords cut into parts of the eastern coast. The largest fjord, Limfjorden,

slices right through the northern part of the Jutland Peninsula and broadens out into a complex series of inland waterways. Denmark's climate is temperate with mild summers where temperatures can reach 25°C and cold, rainy winters where the average daily temperatures hover around freezing point. Winter temperatures are up to 10°C warmer than average for this latitude. The warming effect of the Gulf Stream which sweeps northwards along the west coast of the country is the reason for Denmark's milder than typical climate.

▲ The Tivoli Gardens is a large area of gardens in the centre of Copenhagen which was opened in 1843. It includes concert halls, cafés, flower gardens and an amusement park.

► Nyhavn Canal in Copenhagen is lined with picturesque buildings, many dating back to the 16th century. Most immigrants to Denmark and just over a quarter of the entire Danish population live in or around Copenhagen. The city is situated on the island of Sjaelland.

A FARMING NATION

Denmark's manufacturing and service industries are very important to the economy although the country has few mineral resources. Almost two-thirds of its land is used for farming. Centuries of cultivation has improved the land's ability to grow crops, particularly cereals, of which wheat, followed by barley and rye, are the most important. Much of Denmark's farmland is used to support livestock, particularly pigs and cattle. In 2000, Denmark had 11.6 million pigs, 1.85 million cattle and produced over 4 million tonnes of barley. It also has a large fishing fleet of around 2,500 vessels which catch over one million tonnes of fish every year.

THE DANES

Denmark has been occupied for thousands of years but took its name from the Danes, a people from Sweden, who colonized the region in around CE 500. Denmark's oldest town, Ribe, 25 km southeast of Esbjerg, was an international trading centre as far back as CE 850. The Danish people almost entirely stem from the Danes and other Scandinavian peoples who make up 96 per cent of its population. Communities of people of German origin are found close to Denmark's border with Germany and there are small numbers of Turks, Iranians, Pakistanis and some refugees from countries such as the former Yugoslavia and Somalia. Denmark's people enjoy one of the highest standards of living in the world.

▲ The south Denmark island of Fyn has large expanses of fertile land on which cereal crops and fruit are grown. Together with a number of neighbouring islands, Fyn makes up a Danish county with a population of almost half a million.

FAEROE ISLANDS

Lying in the North Atlantic Ocean midway between Norway, Iceland and Scotland, the Faeroes are a group of islands which are a self-governing territory of Denmark.

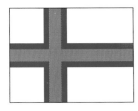

Area: 1,399 km²
Population: 46,000
Capital: Tórshavn (16,700)
Major languages spoken: Faeroese, Danish
Main religions: Evangelical Lutheran, Plymouth Brethren
Currency: Faeroese krone
Main exports: fish and fish products
Type of government: self-governing dependency of Denmark

The Faeroe Islands are clustered closely together separated by deep fjords. The islands were shaped by volcanic action and subsequent erosion has created sharp cliffs and towering stacks on a number of the islands, and deposited a relatively thin layer of soil in many places. Almost constant high winds mean that the islands have few naturally occurring trees although some have been planted in artificially sheltered areas. Large flocks of seabirds are found on the islands' coasts while a thick grass layer in many areas provides food for sheep. However, the majority of Faeroe islanders are engaged in fishing industries. The seas around the islands are rich in fish including cod and haddock, and the prospects of offshore oil

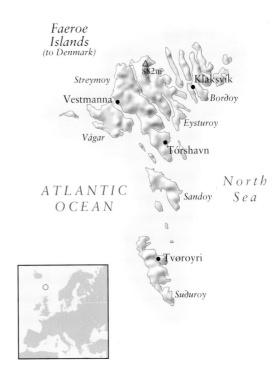

exploration have increased following an agreement signed in 1999 between Denmark and the United Kingdom.

ICELAND

Lying in the North Atlantic Ocean, Iceland is a young, volcanic island. Its population relies largely on the fishing industry for trade.

Area: 102,819 km²
Population: 282,000
Capital: Reykjavik (171,000)
Major language spoken: Icelandic
Main religion: Evangelical Lutheran
Currency: Icelandic krona
Main exports: frozen fish, shrimps and lobsters, salted fish, fresh fish, aluminium
Type of government: republic; democracy

ATLANTIC OCEAN

Iceland is just 287 km east of Greenland and 798 km northwest of Scotland. Most of its landscape consists of a rocky plateau dotted with mountains. Its entire area averages between 600 and 950 m in height above sea level. Around 15 per cent of the land is covered in ice or snowfields. The coastline is indented with deep bays, steep cliffs and fjords on the east and northwest, while the south coasts tend to be more low-lying. Geologically, Iceland is a very young country still in the process of formation. The island sits on a major geological fault – the mid-Atlantic rift – which makes it one of the most volcanically active countries in the world.

THE ICELANDIC PEOPLE
Celtic peoples from Ireland and Norse peoples from Scandinavia were Iceland's first settlers, and almost all of the country's population are descendants of these peoples. The island was controlled first by Norway, and then Denmark,

▲ Sea fishing contributes more than 70 per cent of all export income to the Icelandic economy. The biggest customers are the United Kingdom and Germany.

before becoming independent in the 20th century. Almost all electricity and much heating is generated by abundant hydro-electric and geothermal power.

▲ Thermal springs are found in various parts of Iceland and are harnessed to heat many buildings. Erupting hot water springs, called geysers, got their name from an example found on Iceland called Geysir.

▶ More than half of Iceland's population live in Reykjavik, its capital city. The centre of Iceland's fishing and fish processing industries, Reykjavik is also home to Iceland's one university and the world's oldest ongoing law-making body, the Althing (established in CE 930).

BRITISH ISLES

Located off the northern coast of mainland Europe, the British Isles are a group of two large and a number of small islands. The largest of the islands, Great Britain, is divided up into three countries: England, Scotland and Wales which, with Northern Ireland, form the United Kingdom. The Republic of Ireland occupies the remainder of the second largest island which is separated from Great Britain by the Irish Sea. For a relatively small land mass, the British Isles features a wide range of landscapes from low-lying wetlands in East Anglia and bogs and marshes in Ireland, to rolling hills in England and Wales and rugged mountain ranges in the highlands of Scotland. Ireland was part of the United Kingdom from 1800 to 1922 when the Irish Free State was established as an independent member of the British Commonwealth. Ireland became a republic in 1937 and, in 1949, left the Commonwealth.

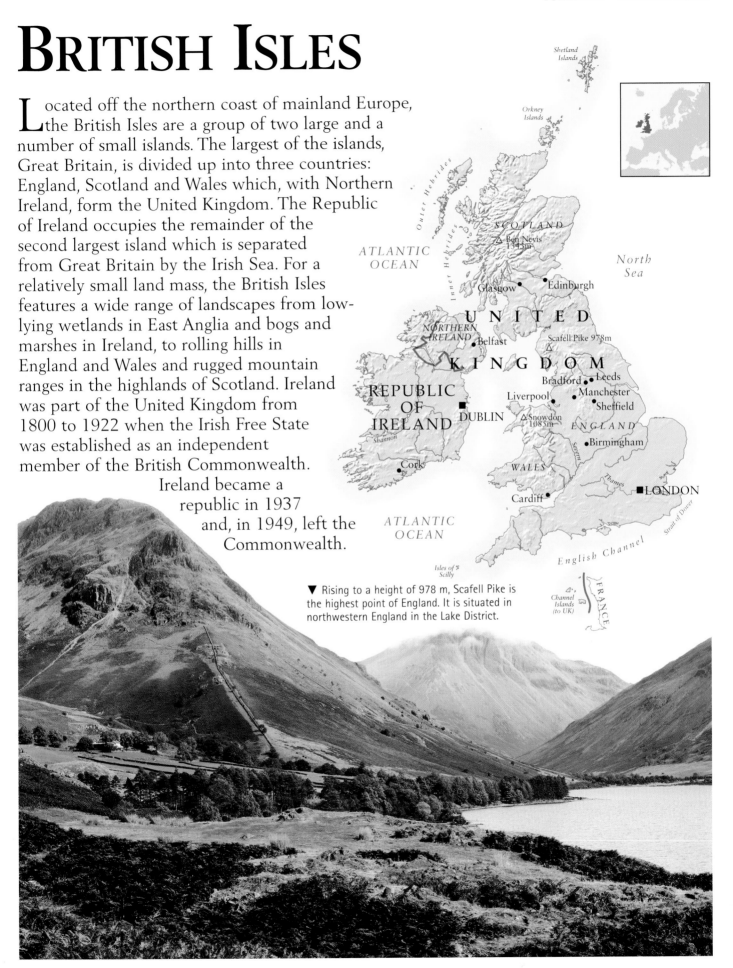

▼ Rising to a height of 978 m, Scafell Pike is the highest point of England. It is situated in northwestern England in the Lake District.

IRELAND

One of the most westerly European nations, the Republic of Ireland occupies much of the island of Ireland and consists of farmland, lakes and mountains.

Area: 70,285 km²
Population: 3,917,000
Capital: Dublin (1,009,000)
Major languages spoken: English, Irish (Gaelic)
Main religion: Roman Catholic
Currency: euro
Main exports: machinery and transport equipment, chemical products, food products (particularly dairy products and meat), manufactures
Type of government: republic; democracy

The Republic of Ireland is located on the most westerly part of the Eurasian land mass and, like Great Britain, was once part of the European mainland. Great Britain and Ireland became separated only around 11,000 years ago with the melting of glaciers and the rising of sea levels. Ireland's landscape consists of a large central plain almost completely surrounded by highlands near the coast. The plain is relatively low, averaging around 90 m in height and broken in many places by low hills, lakes and rivers. The country's main river is the Shannon which rises in the north of the country and forms a long estuary south of Limerick. A broad, slow-moving river, at 372 km in length the Shannon is the longest in the British Isles.

THE EMERALD ISLE

Ireland's climate is moderated by the warm waters of the North Atlantic Drift which help to make the winters milder than other places of a similar latitude. The average daily temperature in winter is between 4.5 and 7°C – as much as 14°C warmer than comparable places of similar latitude. The opposite effect occurs in summer, when average temperatures are

▲ Found in the centre of Dublin, St Patrick's Cathedral was founded in 1191 although a church had lain on its site since the 5th century. At 91 m in length, St Patrick's is one of the largest cathedrals in Ireland.

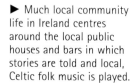

▶ Much local community life in Ireland centres around the local public houses and bars in which stories are told and local, Celtic folk music is played.

▲ A sheep market in the town of Ballinrobe, 25 km south of Castlebar in County Mayo. In 2001, there were over 5.3 million sheep in the Republic of Ireland.

kept to a relatively cool 15 to 17°C. With the warming ocean currents and Atlantic winds comes plenty of rain. It tends to rain on two out of three days throughout the year and average rainfall can be as high as 2,500 mm in the mountains of the southwest. This heavy rainfall helps promote the thick grass, moss and wild plants and flowers which cover much of the country and give it the nickname, the Emerald Isle. Peat bogs, which occupy around ten per cent of the land, are homes for rare wild plants but are threatened due to peat's continued use as a fuel to generate power and also as a fertilizer. Many small mammals including stoats, hares and foxes, along with over 120 species, of native birds inhabit the country.

TRADITIONAL LIFE

The whole of Ireland has a long tradition of settlement stretching back at least 9,000 years. Around 2,400 years ago, Celts arrived from mainland Europe. Since that time, Ireland was often isolated from the rest of Europe – for example, it was never part of the Roman Empire – which led to its people developing a rich and different culture and language called Gaelic. English has taken over from Gaelic as the most widely spoken language and, although still taught in schools, is only the first language of a dwindling number of people in rural areas. Other elements of Irish culture still flourish in Celtic art, literature and various forms of music.

▶ Found on the western coast of Ireland, the Cliffs of Moher are a series of shale and sandstone cliffs which reach heights in excess of 200 m.

A CHANGING ECONOMY

For a long period, Ireland's economy relied on traditional methods of agriculture with crops such as sugar beet, potatoes and cereals. Pigs were kept in their hundreds of thousands, while sheep grazed on the pastures of the mountain slopes and cattle were reared in the centre and south of the country. Agriculture remains important, but Ireland's economy is changing dramatically. Farming has been modernized with financial assistance from the European Union of which the country is a part. Less than seven per cent of its workforce is now employed in agriculture. Many more work in new manufacturing industries such as electronics and computing, and in food, drink and clothing industries. Ireland's beautiful landscape, its history and culture have been heavily promoted to foreign visitors and in 2000, over 6.7 million tourists came to the country.

▲ An Irish peat cutter removes chunks of peat which have been used for many centuries as a fuel. Peat is the remains of dead, rotted plants which have been squeezed together. When it is burned, peat generates heat. Several power stations in Ireland are powered by peat.

UNITED KINGDOM

A union of four countries: England, Scotland, Wales and Northern Ireland, the densely populated United Kingdom lies off the coast of northwest Europe.

Area: 244,088 km²
Population: 58,789,000
Capital: London (8,201,000)
Major language spoken: English
Main religions: Anglican, Roman Catholic, Methodist
Currency: pound sterling
Main exports: electrical equipment, chemicals, road vehicles, petroleum and petroleum products
Type of government: kingdom; democracy

▲ The London Eye wheel towers 135 m over the River Thames. Over 15,000 passengers can travel in its pods each day.

▲ London was the first city to have an underground railway. The London Underground opened in 1863 and now serves more than 260 stations.

▶ The prehistoric stone circle of Stonehenge in southern England was built between 3200 and 1000 BCE. It is one of the most important prehistoric monuments in Europe.

The United Kingdom's territory consists of the island of Great Britain, a northeastern portion of Ireland and a large number of smaller islands off its coast. Due to the warming effect of the Gulf Stream, the country has a temperate climate with relatively high rainfall and milder winters than usual for its latitude, . Its location, at a point where many seas and air currents meet, means that its weather is extremely changeable. In general, the south of the country tends to be warmer and the west of the country tends to receive more rainfall.

A VARIED LANDSCAPE

For such a small area, the landscape of the UK has great variation from lowland areas barely above sea level to rugged mountain ranges in Scotland, Wales and the north of England. Around half of Scotland consists of the Highlands and a large number of islands off its coast, while Wales's landscape is dominated by the Cambrian mountains which run through much of the principality from north to south. Northern Ireland is a region of rolling plains with some low mountains. The north of England features hill and low mountain ranges, while most of the rest of the country is relatively flat with occasional areas of gentle hills.

The UK has a large number of rivers criss-crossing its land: most of the major cities are sited on rivers, for example London is located on the Thames and Newcastle is on the Tyne. The longest river is the Severn (354 km) which flows from central Wales to southwest England. Scotland's heavily indented coastline and its many lakes, known as lochs, reveal the past action of glaciers

which have greatly shaped the country's landscape.

Glaciation also scoured out river valleys to form the lakes in the scenic Lake District of northwest England. The Lake District is also home to England's

▼ At a height of 244 m, Number One, Canada Square, known as the Canary Wharf Building, is the tallest in the United Kingdom. It is a landmark in the Docklands area of London which has been re-developed since the 1980s from old, disused docks and warehouses to a major financial, media and business centre.

highest point, Scafell Pike. Mount Snowdon is the highest point in Wales, while Ben Nevis is the highest point in Scotland and the whole of the British Isles. The UK's largest lake is Lough Neagh in Northern Ireland which is located just 20 km west of Belfast.

FLORA, FAUNA AND FARMING

Most of the UK was once covered in woodland but thousands of years of human settlement and activity have reduced these areas dramatically. Although replanting schemes have been in place since the early 20th century, the UK has one of the lowest levels of tree cover in Europe. Coniferous trees, such as pine, are found in Scotland, while the most common trees elsewhere are beech, ash, oak and chestnut. The largest animal found in the wild is the red deer in Scotland and on Exmoor in southwestern England. Smaller mammals include foxes, voles, shrews, mice and squirrels. The hedgerows, moors and coasts of the UK provide habitats for many species of birds but all fauna and much of the UK's rich collection of wild flowers have suffered from habitat destruction and air and water pollution. Around seven per cent of the UK is under a degree of protection as National Parks. These include Snowdonia in North Wales, the Lake District and areas of the North York Moors, 15 km south of Middlesbrough. Much of the UK is farmed with belts of cropland and large areas of pastures on which livestock herds are grazed. Although only one per cent of the workforce is employed in agriculture, the UK is self-sufficient in 60 per cent of all types of food and animal feed.

▲ Canals such as the Trent and Mersey in the Midlands of England (opened in 1777) were built to transport materials and goods during the Industrial Revolution. Today, the majority of canals are used for leisure cruising.

▲ Sitting on a giant volcanic rock which towers over Scotland's capital city, Edinburgh Castle has been the main Scottish royal fortress for many centuries.

THE FIRST INDUSTRIALIZED NATION

The United Kingdom was the first country in the world to undergo an industrial revolution. Based on industries including coal, iron, steel and textiles, the UK became wealthy through inventing and pioneering machinery and factory processes used in industry. However, coal mining, steel working, ship-building and other heavy industry have been in decline for many years. In their place have come fast-growing service industries and high tech companies, medicine and chemical manufacturers, industrial research and engineering. Aided by large offshore oil and natural gas reserves, the UK is the fourth biggest economy in the world today and is a major international trading power.

CROWDED ISLANDS

The United Kingdom is Europe's fourth most populous nation after Russia and Germany, yet is less than half the size of France which has a smaller population. Population density is around 250 people per km² with 90 per cent living in or around major towns and cities. In the past century, the urban areas of the UK have sprawled outwards, creating both new towns, such as Milton Keynes, midway between London and Birmingham, and large urban areas, called conurbations, such as the many towns around Birmingham. The majority of the population of each of the three countries of Great Britain is situated in the south. The south coast of Wales includes the cities of Swansea, Cardiff and Newport, while Scotland's two largest cities of Glasgow and Edinburgh are both south of the Highlands. The southeast is the most densely populated portion of England and is dominated by London.

Founded by the Romans in CE 43, London is one of the world's foremost cities. Its prosperity today is founded mostly on services such as insurance, finance and trading while its many historic buildings and parks attract millions of tourists every year.

▼ The United Kingdom has the largest energy resources of any member of the European Union, most of which is in the form of oil and natural gas situated off the country's east coast in the North Sea.

◄ The Millennium Stadium is the national stadium of Wales and hosts concerts and sports events. It has a sliding roof and seats over 72,000 spectators.

▲ Over 11 million cattle, including this Highland breed, were reared in the UK – before the outbreak of foot and mouth disease in 2001 caused more than a million to be destroyed.

▲ The symbol of the Celtic cross is found as standing signs and statues particularly in Scotland and Northern Ireland.

▼ The Giant's Causeway on the north coast of Northern Ireland was formed over 50 million years ago from volcanic lava which cooled to form over 40,000 basalt pillars.

THE UK PEOPLE

In the past, the UK's position as an island nation lying close to mainland Europe saw it undergo periods of both isolation and invasion. Migration by Celtic peoples, occupation by the Romans and waves of invasion and settlement by Danes, Saxons, Vikings and the Normans, have all left their mark. Most of the UK population are descended from these invaders and settlers. Sizeable communities of other ethnic groups do exist, including peoples from former British colonies in Africa, the Caribbean and south Asia as well as Chinese, Jewish and European peoples. Although Celtic languages still exist, especially in Wales, the dominant language is English which is primarily a blend of Anglo-Saxon and Norman French.

FOUR COUNTRIES IN ONE

The UK has a complex political history. England and Wales were united by the 16th century while the 1707 Act of Union formed the Kingdom of Great Britain including Scotland. For a period from 1801 to the 1920s, Great Britain and the whole of Ireland were ruled as one nation. Wales, Scotland and Northern Ireland have their own national identity, different elements of culture and a degree of government devolved away from the UK national government based in London. In 1999, the Scottish Parliament and the National Assembly for Wales were opened, giving these two countries more control over

their own affairs. The Northern Ireland Assembly, held in the city of Belfast, has been beset by problems between the Protestant majority and the Catholic minority. The UK head of state is officially the monarch, but power is held by the Prime Minister, usually the leader of the majority political party in the House of Commons at Westminster in London.

A COLONIAL POWER

From the 17th to the 20th century, the UK was a major colonial power, with the British Empire laying claim to territory on every continent and exploiting its colonies' resources and peoples in order to grow wealthy and powerful. Most of its former colonies are now independent, but are part of a loose alliance of states known as the Commonwealth. The UK still owns a number of dependencies as far afield as the Falkland Islands in the South Atlantic, and the Turks & Caicos in the Caribbean. Closer to home are the Isle of Man, lying between Ireland and Great Britain, and the Channel Islands lying off the northern coast of France. Both of these dependencies have their own legal systems but the UK government is responsible for their external affairs. The UK continues to exert international influence through its close relationship with the USA, and as a member of the European Union.

BELGIUM

One of the three Benelux countries (with Luxembourg and the Netherlands), Belgium is an industrialized nation in which 97 per cent of its people live in urban areas.

Area: 30,528 km²
Population: 10,239,000
Capital: Brussels (1,076,000)
Major languages spoken: Dutch (Flemish), French, German
Main religion: Roman Catholic
Currency: euro
Main exports: machinery and transport equipment, chemicals (particularly plastics), food, diamonds, iron and steel, textiles
Type of government: kingdom; democracy

The north of Belgium has a similar landscape to the Netherlands. It is a flat coastal plain, barely rising more than a few metres above sea level and is laced with river deltas and canals. Most of the coastline is marked by a belt of giant sand dunes which are among the largest in Europe. South of the coastal plain is a central plateau region which contains the country's best farming land, while the southeastern area of the country is part of the Ardennes region, a rocky, heavily forested region with an average elevation of 460 m. Belgium's main river, the Meuse, is linked with other rivers and canals, giving the country almost 1,600 km of inland waterways, most of which can be travelled by large boats.

A TRADING NATION

Belgium's location between a number of European countries plus its access to the oceans via the Scheldt estuary, on which lies the port of Antwerp, has made it a major trading nation. Belgium's manufacturing industries include metalworking, steel, cloth and carpet making and heavy engineering. Much of the electricity required by these industries is supplied by nuclear power which generates almost two-thirds of Belgium's electricity. Lacking large reserves of raw materials, Belgium imports many of them raw and exports finished or semi-finished goods. Millions of tonnes of imports and exports pass through the port of Antwerp. Situated some 80 km inland from the North Sea, Antwerp is one of the largest ports in Europe.

▲ Work on building the City Hall in Belgium's capital city of Brussels started in 1402. The imposing tower is 96 m high.

▶ The Atomium stands in the Heysel Exhibition Park in Brussels and has become a symbol of the city. Designed for the 1958 World's Fair, the 120 m high structure is an aluminium model of a carbon molecule magnified 165 billion times.

LANGUAGE FRONTIERS

Belgium is divided into three federal districts which reflect, in part, its centuries old language frontiers between its Flemish or Dutch-speaking people, known as Flemings, and its French-speaking peoples called the Walloons. Flanders, its northern district, is principally home to the Flemings while the southern district, Wallonia, is populated mainly by French-speakers. Bilingual signs in both Flemish and French are common throughout the country while to the extreme east of the country lives a small German-speaking minority. The third district, the land in and around Brussels, its capital city, has a mixed population. Brussels is home to one-tenth of Belgium's population and is an international business centre. The city is also the administrative centre of the European Union and home of the major headquarters of the North Atlantic Treaty Organisation (NATO).

▲ The picturesque city of Ghent located in western Belgium, lies at the joining point of two rivers. These rivers, along with many canals, criss-cross the city dividing it into many small islands linked by more than 200 bridges.

LUXEMBOURG

A tiny nation bordering Germany, the Netherlands and France, Luxembourg is a centre for finance and for the European Court of Justice.

Area: 2,586 km²
Population: 440,000
Capital: Luxembourg (112,000)
Major languages spoken: Letzeburgish, Portuguese, German, French
Main religion: Roman Catholic
Currency: euro
Main exports: machinery and transport equipment, plastics and rubber, textiles, processed food
Type of government: grand duchy; democracy

Luxembourg's landscape can be divided into two areas. The northern third consists of densely forested hills and many narrow valleys with fast-flowing streams. The southern two-thirds have a more gentle landscape of meadows, vineyards and woodland. The southwest is heavily industrialized with large iron and steel works and some chemical and food processing plants.

The people of Luxembourg enjoy the highest standard of living in Europe. Nearly a third of Luxembourg's workers are foreigners, many of them employed by the over 200 banks, including the European Investment Bank, which are based in the country. Luxembourg is also home to the European Court of Justice. Most of the country's population speak two or three languages. French is the main language used in the courts, while German is the language used in newspapers and literature. For centuries, Luxembourg was ruled by other countries and it did not finally regain complete independence until 1890.

THE NETHERLANDS

Lying between Germany and Belgium with a long North Sea coastline, the Netherlands is one of the lowest-lying countries in the world.

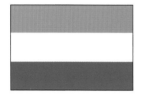

Area: 41,526 km²
Population: 15,987,000
Capitals: Amsterdam (1,121,000); The Hague - seat of government (701,000)
Major languages spoken: Dutch, Frisian
Main religion: non-religious (more than one-third), Roman Catholic, Dutch Reformed, Calvinist
Currency: euro
Main exports: machinery and transport equipment (particularly motor vehicles), food (mainly meat and dairy products), chemicals and chemical products, petroleum
Type of government: kingdom; democracy

Geographically, the Netherlands can be divided into two regions, the Low Netherlands to the north and west and a smaller region of gently rolling land called the High Netherlands to the southeast. The average elevation of the High Netherlands is below 50 m. Because the Netherlands has no high hill ranges or mountains, the climate varies little from area to area with only a slight difference in temperatures and rainfall between the coast and inland areas. The Netherlands has a temperate maritime climate shared by much of northwestern Europe. Winters are mild while summers are kept cool by westerly winds. Rainfall averages around 730 mm per year.

BELOW SEA LEVEL
The country derives its name from the Dutch for low-lying land and around a quarter of its land lies below sea level. Much of the Netherlands has been reclaimed from the sea or fortified to stop rivers submerging the surrounding area. From the 13th century onwards, barriers were built to stop water getting in and windmills were used to pump excess water out. By the 19th century, the Netherlands had over 9,000 windmills. Polders are areas of drained land surrounded and protected by embankments called dikes. Today, there are over 5,000 polders in the Netherlands, the largest of which was the result of the Zuyder Zee works during which the inland sea, the Zuyder Zee, became a lake and 1,650 km² of land were created.

▶ Opened in 1996, the Erasmus Bridge provides a link over the river at the major European port of Rotterdam. Rising to a height of 139 m and spanning a width of 800 m, the bridge took seven years to construct. Its steel deck contains lanes for motor vehicles, a tram track, two footpaths and two cycle paths.

▲ 10,150 hectares of fruit, vegetables and flowers were grown under glass in the Netherlands in 2000. Over a tenth of this (1,155 hectares) is devoted to growing peppers which are shown here being harvested for export.

Without dikes and dams, the most densely populated part of the Netherlands, around half of the country's land area, would be submerged by the North Sea and the country's rivers.

EUROPE'S LARGEST PORT

Located at the centre of the most industrialized and populated area in the world is the port of Rotterdam. Originally a fishing village, Rotterdam was seriously damaged in the two world wars but has since developed into the world's largest port and a major oil refining and trading centre. It has a prime location, 30 km inland from the North Sea, and lies at the mouths of two important European rivers, the Rhine and the Meuse. Tens of thousands of cargo barges, loaded and unloaded at Rotterdam, travel the Rhine, taking raw materials and goods into France, Germany and the heart of Europe. In 2000, 397 million tonnes of goods travelled through Dutch ports, particularly Rotterdam. Shipping is not the only way goods are transported. Giant pipelines carry oil and petroleum products to other parts of the Netherlands, to Antwerp in Belgium and also to Germany.

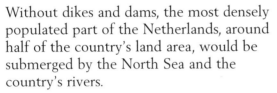

▶ The picturesque city of Amsterdam with its well-preserved buildings, 160 canals and hundreds of bridges is a popular tourist destination for foreign visitors.

THE DUTCH PEOPLE

The Netherlands is one of the world's most densely populated nations, with 395 people per km^2. A proportion of the country's population are immigrants from Turkey, Morocco and former Dutch colonies including parts of Indonesia, Suriname and the Netherlands Antilles. Half of the country is farmed and Dutch farming is among the most advanced and intensive in the world. The Netherlands has one of the 20 largest and most powerful economies based on its transport and trade services, including tourism and the engineering, chemical and electronics industries.

GERMANY

The third largest economy in the world, Germany lies at the heart of Europe and is a vital part of the European Union.

Area: 357,021 km²
Population: 82,220,000
Capital: Berlin (4,064,000)
Major language spoken: German
Main religion: Evangelical Lutheran, Roman Catholic
Currency: euro
Main exports: road transport equipment, chemicals and chemical products, other machinery, electrical equipment, plastics
Type of government: republic; democracy

Germany extends from the Alps in the south to a northern coastline which borders both the North Sea and Baltic Sea, a maximum distance of 876 km. The country's territory extends into islands in both seas, most notably the islands of Rügen, Hiddensee and Fehmarn in the Baltic, and the East and North Frisian Islands in the North Sea. The country shares 3,621 km of borders with nine countries: France, Luxembourg, the Netherlands and Belgium to the west, Switzerland and Austria to the south, Denmark to the north and Poland and the Czech Republic to the east.

▼ Heavy industry, such as this chemical works near the River Elbe, remains an important part of the German economy although services and light industries such as electronics contribute more to the economy.

LOWLANDS AND UPLANDS

Germany's landscape is varied, including heavily forested hills and mountains, plains and lakes, and many winding rivers. The

country can be split into three main geographical regions. A large lowland belt lies to the north and stretches from the Netherlands to Poland. It contains dry, sandy plains with moors and heaths. The second major geographical area is the Central Uplands which divides northern Germany from the south. It consists of a number of hill and mountain ranges, river valleys and plateau areas. Its highest point reaches 1,142 m above sea level. The southern part of Germany consists mainly of hills and mountains, the lower slopes of which are heavily forested. Part of southern

Germany lies in the Alps mountain system and is known as the Bavarian Alps.

GERMANY'S FORESTS

Germany is a heavily populated industrial country but it is large enough to also include huge areas of relatively untouched forests. Around 30 per cent of Germany is forested and around a third of this area is covered with deciduous trees such as beech, oak and birch while the remainder consists of firs, pines and other coniferous trees. Half of all Germany's forested areas is owned by the state or by the local community while farmers and forestry companies manage and harvest fast-growing coniferous trees for timber, paper and other wood-based products. The Bavarian Forest in the southeast of Germany is the largest mountain forest in western Europe. Germany's most famous forest, the Black Forest, is to the southwest of the country and covers an area of over 5,100 km² and attracts thousands of tourists from Germany and elsewhere to view its scenery and picturesque lakes.

▲ A horseshoe bend in the Saar river. This river starts its life in the northern Vosges mountains of France and meanders in a northwesterly direction through Germany before becoming a tributary of the Mosel river.

▼ A major financial and commercial centre which hosts many international trade fairs every year, Frankfurt is also the home of the European Central Bank. The city's airport is also among the busiest in Europe.

A GOOD FARMING CLIMATE

Germany is situated in the moderately cool zone between the Atlantic Ocean and the continental climate in eastern Europe. Nearly all of the country features a temperate climate, with rainfall occurring throughout the year and long periods of overcast skies even when rain does not fall. The country has an average annual temperature of 9°C and sharp changes in temperature are rare although there is a great difference between the seasons. In the winter, the average temperature is between 1.5°C in the lowland areas and -6°C in the mountains. In the warmest month of the year, July, temperatures are between 18°C in low-lying regions and 20°C in the sheltered valleys of the south. In parts of the southern region of Germany called Bavaria, occasional warm winds called Föhns pass over the northern Alps and can cause abrupt melting of snow. With a long growing season free of frost, over 700 mm of rainfall a year and few extremes of temperature, Germany has a good climate for many forms of farming. The country is home to 27 million pigs, 14 million cattle and 103 million chickens and is one of the world's top ten producers of cereal crops such as barley. Despite less than three per cent of the country's population being employed in growing crops, Germany is also a major producer of potatoes and other root vegetables as well as hops used to make beer. Food and drink processing is one of the largest employers in Germany with the country being the second largest beer brewer after the USA and one of the top ten wine producers in the world.

▲ The New Town Hall with its ornate tower lies in the Marienplatz in the heart of the city of Munich. In the Middle Ages, this square was the site of markets, festivals and tournaments.

▼ The distinctive buildings of the Markplatz (market place) in the medieval town of Rothenberg, around 65 km south of Nuremberg.

THE RHINE AND OTHER RIVERS

Germany's biggest river is the Rhine which flows from the Alps in Switzerland through or along the boundaries of Austria, Liechtenstein, France, Germany and the Netherlands before emptying into the North Sea. A broad river, the Rhine acted as a natural boundary in historic times and is now a vital transport link. Giant barges carrying millions of tonnes of cargo travel its length. In 1992, the 171 km long Main-Donau-Kanal was opened. This links the Danube, which flows through eastern Europe, with the Rhine allowing heavy cargoes to be carried right through the centre of Europe. Apart from the Rhine and Main, a further ten major rivers flow through Germany. These include the Elbe, Ems and Main. All are navigable along most of their length and provide important transport links for the industries that are found along their banks.

East Germans help to break down the Berlin Wall in 1989. A landmark in the history of Germany, the Berlin Wall had divided Germany into two nations for over 35 years. Most of the wall is now dismantled but some parts have been preserved, most notable of which is the East Side Gallery. This 1,316 m long stretch features 106 paintings.

INDUSTRY AND ENVIRONMENT

Germany's modern wealth and power is founded on its manufacturing and processing industries, many of which are located in the Ruhr in the west of the country, one of Europe's centres of heavy industry. Consequently, Germany is the second largest exporter in the world. Manufacturing industry employs a quarter of the German workforce and ranges from producing household electrical goods to heavy factory machinery. It was the third largest producer of motor vehicles during the 1990s. Germany has greatly suffered from pollution and environmental damage with almost 50 per cent of the trees of the Black Forest affected by acid rain. The country was one of the first industrialized nations to take environmental problems seriously and the Green Party now holds a large number of seats in the Bundestag – the German Parliament. Pressure from the Green Party and environmental groups has resulted in Germany's tightening its pollution controls and starting to phase out its nuclear power stations.

▲ Designed by architect Carl Gotthard Langhans and completed in 1791, the Brandenberg Gate in Berlin lay close to the border separating the former East Germany and West Germany. Since reunification in 1990, the 19 m high gateway has become a symbol of the united Germany.

▼ A shipyard building container vessels in Stralsund in northeast Germany. Located on an inlet of the Baltic Sea, Stralsund was founded in the 13th century and passed through Swedish control before becoming part of Prussia in 1815.

A giant beer hall in Munich is in full swing as the city's Oktoberfest celebrates Germany's food, drink and entertainment.

The church of Ramsau, is situated in the mountainous area of southeast Germany. It lies close to a mountain lake.

TRANSPORT AND CITIES

Germany has excellent land, sea and air transport links. More goods and people travel by road than any other mode of transport. Germany has over 650,000 km of roads including 11,400 km of motorways. Many of the country's major cities are linked by high-speed rail links along which InterCity Express (ICE) trains travel at 280 km/h. Regular flights between the major cities take little more than an hour. Germany has a large fleet of ocean-going merchant shipping which sails from ports such as Bremen and Hamburg, the country's biggest port and fourth largest urban area.

CONFLICT AND DIVISION

Germany has spent many more years as separate states than it has as one nation. Around 3,000 years ago, a number of tribes settled in the Rhine and Danube river valleys. The Romans named the area Germania, after one of these tribes, the Germani. Until the 19th century, the region was home to many different states but in 1871 was unified into one nation. Germany suffered greatly after its defeat at the end of World War I in 1918. Under Adolf Hitler, the country was again defeated at the end of World War II in 1945. Germany was then divided into four zones occupied by the UK, France, the USA and the Soviet Union. By 1949, the occupation zones had become two separate nations. The Soviet occupation zone became the German Democratic Republic or East Germany. The Federal Republic of Germany or West Germany comprised the three remaining zones. Both nations joined the security organizations of their previous occupying powers – West Germany was a part of NATO while East Germany belonged to the Warsaw Pact. Germany was reunited in 1990 after the break-up of the Soviet Union. West Germany's 11 lander or states were joined by five new additions from East Germany: Brandenburg, Mecklenburg-West Pomerania, Saxony, Saxony-Anhalt, and Thuringia. Since then, Germany has had to deal with the economic and social issues that come with reuniting two sets of people who have spent more than 40 years living apart.

FRANCE

The largest country in western Europe, France has a long history of political, economic and cultural influence which continues to this day.

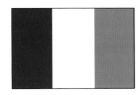

Area: 547,030 km²
Population: 59,060,000
Capital: Paris (9,645,000)
Major language spoken: French
Main religions: Roman Catholic, Sunni Islam
Currency: euro
Main exports: machinery and transport equipment, agricultural products (particularly food and wine), chemical products, plastics
Type of government: republic; democracy

▼ The TGV high-speed train travels at speeds of up to 300 km/h linking Paris with major cities throughout France.

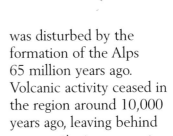

Sixty per cent of France lies below 250 m in elevation. Much of this land consists of gently rolling plains with occasional rocky outcrops and hills and large river valleys. To the northwest of the country, the regions of Brittany and Normandy are more hilly and have heavily indented coastlines. France contains a number of distinct highland areas. To the northeast, the Vosges are a series of gently rounded summits over 200 million years old. South of the Vosges are the Jura mountains which extend into Switzerland and reach 1,710 m at their highest point. The Jura and Vosges are dwarfed by the French Alps found in the east of France. Peaks include Mont Blanc, the second highest in Europe. The south-central highland plateau, called the Massif Central, was formed some 300 million years ago. Covering about 15 per cent of the country, it was disturbed by the formation of the Alps 65 million years ago. Volcanic activity ceased in the region around 10,000 years ago, leaving behind many extinct cones, outcrops and pointed hills called puys. A number of France's major rivers begin their life in the Massif Central including the Loire. This and other rivers, including the Seine and the Rhône, have carved out large valleys and have helped to create fertile lands.

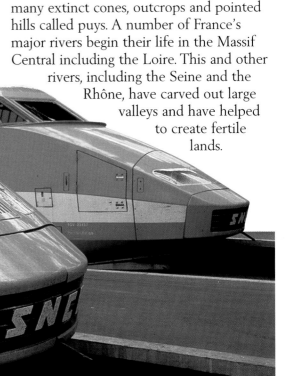

▲ A major landmark in Paris and symbol of France, the Eiffel Tower was built between 1887 and 1889 out of 7,300 tonnes of wrought iron. Breathtaking views of Paris greet those who ascend the 300 m high tower.

▼ The spectacular Mont St Michel is a rocky islet in the Gulf of St Malo cut off from the mainland of northwestern France at high tide. The islet has been the site of a monastery since CE 966 and the church on the summit was first built in the 11th century.

FRANCE'S BORDERS AND TERRITORY

France's other significant mountain range, the Pyrenees, acts as a natural border to the southwest separating France from Spain. To the southeast, near the French city of Nice, France surrounds the tiny principality of Monaco. The remainder of France's land borders are to the east with Belgium, Luxembourg, Germany, Switzerland and Italy. France is divided into 96 departements and four overseas departements: Réunion in the Indian Ocean, Martinique and Guadeloupe, both in the Caribbean Sea, and French Guiana in South America. In addition, there are overseas territories which include French Polynesia, New Caledonia, Wallis and Futuna Islands, St Pierre and Miquelon, Mayotte and Clipperton Island. France also lays claim to a portion of the continent of Antarctica. Corsica, the fourth largest island in the Mediterranean, is part of France. Two-thirds of Corsica consist of granite-based mountains with over 20 peaks rising more than 2,000 m in elevation. The island has a population of approximately 251,000 people.

THE FRENCH COASTLINE

France is situated on the western side of continental Europe with long north and west-facing coastlines as well as a coastline with the Mediterranean. This location has enabled France, in the past, to grow strong as a trading and colonial power. To the north, France borders the North Sea and the English Channel. Northern ports such as Le Havre handle large amounts of shipping, particularly passenger ferries. At its narrowest point, in the Straits of Dover, France and the UK are no more than 30 km apart. 1994 saw the opening of the Channel Tunnel (Eurotunnel) which runs underneath the English Channel, providing a rail link between the two countries. Nearly all of France's Atlantic coastline lies to the west within the large, sweeping Bay of Biscay close to towns such as Bordeaux which have developed as ports. The Mediterranean coastline is a major tourist destination and includes resort towns such as Cannes 16 km from the city of Nice.

FRANCE'S CLIMATE

The climate of France is temperate but with some regional variations. In the north and west of the country, winds from the Atlantic bring large amounts of moisture in the air, changeable weather and help produce cool summers and mild winters. The region around Paris known as Paris basin or Île de France has a more continental climate. The area receives heavy rainfall in spring and autumn and, sometimes, thunderstorms in summer. In eastern France and in the Massif Central region, the temperature range is greater between winter and summer. In the south of the country, particularly in the southeastern region of Provence, a warmer, Mediterranean climate prevails. Average daily temperatures here range between 17°C and 29°C in summer while only very rarely falling below zero in winter. Southern France can feel the effects of the Mistral – a strong, cold, dry wind which can blow for several days at a time, reach speeds of over 130 km/h and cause damage to crops. The amount of precipitation varies greatly throughout France with some northern lowlands receiving less than 300 mm and some mountain areas receiving over 1,300 mm of rain per year.

FARMING AND FOOD

France is one of the biggest agricultural producers and exporters in the world. A great variety of crops are grown, from cereals and root vegetables to asparagus, silk, flax and tobacco. Over 20 million cattle and close to 300 million poultry are also reared. Fruit-growing is widespread and much of the output of grapes, apples and other fruit is used to make drinks and sauces. France is a renowned producer of wines and spirits, usually named after their region or area of production such as Burgundy or Bordeaux. The French have developed a rich and diverse cuisine which varies from region to region. Along the eastern coast, fish-based dishes are common and every region has its own variety of pastries and rich breads, meat dishes, desserts and cheeses. France is the second largest producer of cheese in the world.

▲ A field of lavender in the southern region of Provence. Lavender grows to between 60 cm and 90 cm in height and is cultivated in many places in France for its sweet-smelling oil used in perfumes and potpourri.

▲ A cellarman attends racks of champagne at the Veuve Clicquot vineyards. This luxury sparkling wine gets its name from the Champagne region close to the city of Reims.

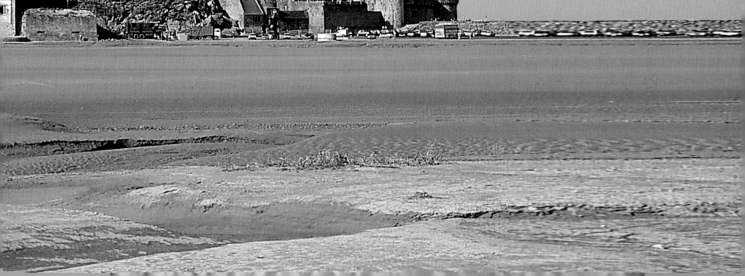

▲ The European Parliament building in Strasbourg, in northeast France, opened in 1999. Members of the European Parliament are elected by voters of countries in the European Union.

▼ Outdoor eating and drinking at pavement cafés is a feature of life in France. This café is located on the Champs Elysées, a famous broad avenue in Paris, which runs from the Arc de Triomphe, a distance of 1.88 km.

INDUSTRY AND THE ENVIRONMENT

Although it was slow to industrialize, France has become a major industrial power since World War II. It has been aided by large reserves of minerals, including some of the richest deposits of iron ore in Europe. Coal, particularly from the north and the east, was once plentiful but is dwindling. France is one of the countries most committed to using nuclear power to supply its electricity needs. Seventy seven per cent of its electricity is generated from nuclear power plants. The country is a key engineering centre of Europe with many companies devoted to producing machinery, cars and defence products. The water and air pollution caused by some of these industries have had a detrimental effect on the country's environment. France's 15 million hectares of forest and woodland has suffered some acid rain damage but not as much as some of its eastern neighbours.

THE CULTURAL CAPITAL

As the world's most popular visitor destination with over 75 million arrivals in 2000, tourism is a vitally important part of the French economy. People travel all over France to visit its many attractions: from the pilgrimage centre of Lourdes at the foot of the Pyrenees, and its winter ski resorts in the Alps to the unspoilt countryside of its river valleys and the warmth and glamour of coastal towns such as Nice. Paris is the number one destination. More than France's capital, the city exerts a dominant influence in government, business and culture over the rest of the country. Paris dwarfs all other French cities. Its metropolitan area is home to a fifth of the country's people and is around more than seven times more populous than France's next largest city, Marseille. The Île de la Cité is a small island on the River Seine first populated by a Celtic tribe over 2,200 years ago. Paris has since grown up around this point with the river winding its way through the city. The city has had a long and turbulent history. It was occupied during both World Wars and became the focal point of the French Revolution (1789–1799) which overthrew the succession of kings and queens who had ruled France for over 1,300 years. The legacy of France's long history can be found throughout Paris in such famous sites as Notre Dame, the Sorbonne university and the Louvre museum.

FRANCE'S PEOPLE

Over 90 per cent of French people were born in the country, are white and speak French. In the distant past, France was a trading crossroad and was settled by waves of different peoples including Celts, Visigoths from Italy and Vikings. The Ancient Greeks started a trading colony in what is now the major city and port of Marseille over 2,600 years ago while much of France later came under the control of the Roman Empire. A colonial power in the 18th–20th centuries, much of North Africa, parts of West Africa, the Caribbean, Southeast Asia and many

islands in the Pacific all came under France's colonial rule. Although almost all of its colonies are now independent, large numbers of people from former French colonies, particularly from North Africa, are now resident in France along with sizeable communities of Portuguese, Italian, Spanish and Turkish peoples.

▲ French cakes and confectionery are frequently enjoyed by the French and visitors alike. This confectionery stall is part of a market in the city of Nice in southeast France.

MONACO

Monaco borders the Mediterranean Sea and is otherwise completely surrounded by France. The country has a largely rugged landscape and a mild climate.

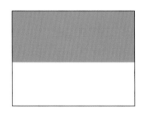

Area: 2 km²
Population: 34,000
Capital: Monaco-ville (34,000)
Major languages spoken: French, Monegasque
Main religion: Roman Catholic
Currency: euro
Main exports: chemicals, plastics, electronic goods
Type of government: principality; democracy

Although since 1964 land reclaimed from the sea has increased its area by 20 per cent, Monaco remains the second smallest nation in the world. Less than a quarter of Monaco's population were born in the country. Its population has grown due to a large number of celebrities, business and sports people settling there attracted by low taxes. Light industries including cosmetics and clothing are dwarfed in economic importance by the nation's banks and insurance industries. Monaco has been ruled by one family, the Grimaldis, for over seven centuries. The National Council of 18 elected members

helps run the country along with the current head of the Grimaldi family, Prince Rainier III.

▶ Attracted by Monaco's mild climate and its status as a tax haven, millionaires have made their homes among the luxury apartments that overlook the Mediterranean Sea.

CENTRAL EUROPE

The region of central Europe consists of a number of small to medium size nations as well as the larger country of Poland and the tiny state of Liechtenstein. Much of the region lies on the North European plain and is of a relatively low elevation, but to the south of the region is found central Europe's principal mountain range, the Alps. Stretching in an arc measuring almost 1,200 km, the highest and most densely populated mountain range in the whole of Europe is found through much of Switzerland and Austria as well as extending into France, Italy, Slovenia and the extreme south of Germany. The most important river in the region is the Danube which starts its life in Germany's Black Forest, but flows through Austria, Hungary and Slovakia before continuing through eastern Europe and emptying into the Black Sea. Politically, the region has seen great change in both ancient and more modern times. Only Switzerland, which has remained neutral since 1815, has stayed out of the many wars, conflicts and border changes that have occurred in the region. Today, the nations of central Europe all have mixed economies where agriculture and food processing remains important but have been overtaken by industry and services particularly tourism.

▲ Central Europe's major river, the Danube, is pictured here (top) flowing through the Hungarian capital city of Budapest. Under Soviet influence until 1991, Hungary now has a growing tourist industry.

▼ Approximately 70 million tourists visit central Europe every year with Switzerland and its spectacular mountain scenery one of the region's leading destinations.

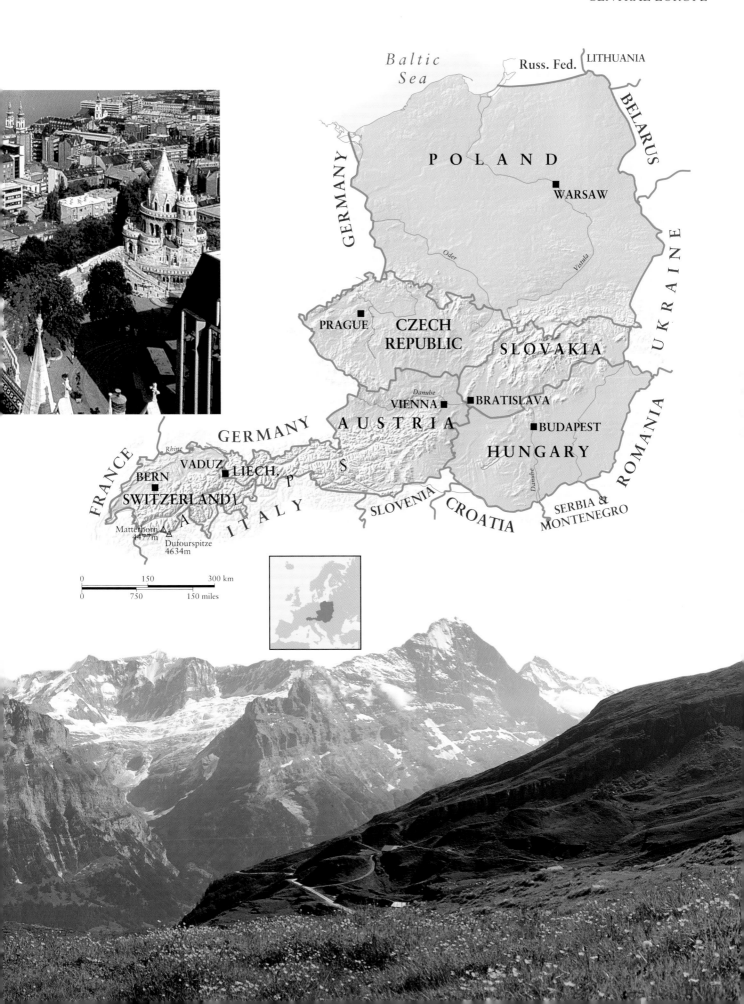

Baltic Sea

Russ. Fed. LITHUANIA

BELARUS

GERMANY

P O L A N D

■ WARSAW

Oder

Vistula

UKRAINE

PRAGUE ■

CZECH REPUBLIC

SLOVAKIA

Danube

VIENNA ■

■ BRATISLAVA

GERMANY

A U S T R I A

■ BUDAPEST

HUNGARY

Rhine

FRANCE

VADUZ

■ LIECH.

A L P S

ROMANIA

BERN ■

Danube

SWITZERLAND

I T A L Y

SLOVENIA

CROATIA

SERBIA & MONTENEGRO

A

Matterhorn △ 4477m

△ Dufourspitze 4634m

0   150   300 km

0   750   150 miles

SWITZERLAND

The most mountainous country in the whole of Europe, Switzerland's people speak a number of languages and enjoy a prosperous life.

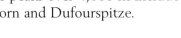

Area: 41,285 km²
Population: 7,288,000
Capital: Berne (Bern) (317,000 urban area)
Major languages spoken: German, French, Italian, Romansch
Main religions: Roman Catholic, Calvinist, Lutheran
Currency: Swiss franc
Main exports: machinery, electronics, chemical products, precision instruments, watches, jewellery
Type of government: republic; democracy

Switzerland borders France to the west, Lichtenstein and Austria to the east, Germany to the north and Italy to the south. It has a landscape of high mountain peaks and lush green valleys and plateaus, with around 20 per cent of its land covered in forests. The country's main rivers, which include the Rhine and the Rhône flow in different directions and finally empty into three different seas, the North Sea, the Mediterranean and the Black Sea. To the west, winds from the Atlantic Ocean carry much moisture and cause rainfall. In the east, the climate is drier and with sharper differences in temperature. Generally, the lower-lying areas of plains and valleys enjoy a temperate climate while the low-lying region south of the Alps receives warmer weather.

THE MOUNTAINS OF SWITZERLAND
Over two-thirds of its area is covered in two sets of mountain ranges. Lying to the west, the Jura mountains form a natural border between Switzerland and France. Between the Alps and the Jura mountains lies the Swiss Plateau, a region with an average elevation of 395 m and dotted with many low hills. The country is home to a fifth of the entire Alps mountain system which runs roughly east to west across

much of the south and central regions. The Alps are at their most spectacular along Switzerland's southwestern border with Italy. Famous peaks over 4,000 m include the Matterhorn and Dufourspitze.

FARMING, TRADE AND TRANSPORT
Swiss farming and industry have had to adapt to its landscape and location in order to prosper. The terrain makes farming difficult, yet the Swiss people are self-sufficient in certain farm products including beef, dairy products and wheat. Swiss dairy products including cheeses and chocolate are exported around the world. Apart from fast-flowing rivers to generate hydro-electric power, Switzerland has few

▼ The Reuss river in the Swiss city of Luzern is crossed by seven bridges. The town is a German-speaking centre.

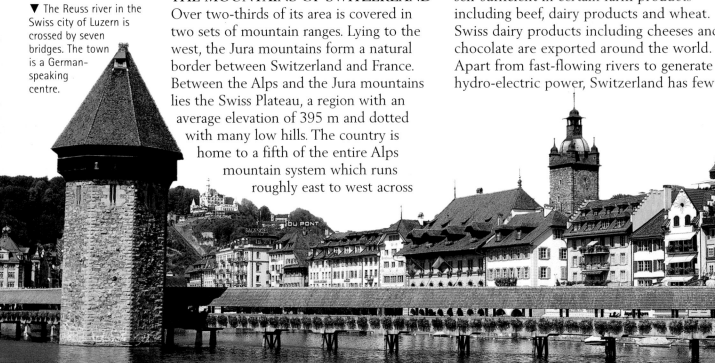

natural resources for industry. The country relies on importing raw materials, processing them and using them for manufacturing goods, particularly small items of high value including watches, medicines, electronics, scientific instruments and handicraft products. Transporting raw materials in and finished goods out of the country relies on rivers and especially good road and rail links. Switzerland has worked with other nations to build a number of road and rail tunnels through its mountainous borders. Although Switzerland is landlocked, it has a national fleet of over 170 merchant vessels which operate from foreign ports or from Basel, a city located on the Rhine.

MANY LANGUAGES

Even though Switzerland is a small country, its people speak a variety of languages. German is spoken by 65 per cent of the population, French by 18 per cent and Italian by four per cent. Swiss-German is quite different from regular German but, because it is not a written language, regular German is used for newspapers and other print media. French is most often spoken and used in and around Geneva and in the west of the country. Romansch is the fourth official language although it is only spoken by less than two per cent of the population.

A NATION APART AND AT PEACE

Switzerland has remained neutral in wars and conflicts for almost two centuries. Internally, the country has remained stable and grown wealthy as a financial and banking centre. These and other service industries employ over half of the workforce. The country has become home to a number of major world organizations, including the Red Cross and the World Health Organization, both of which have their headquarters in the city of Geneva. The European headquarters of the United Nations is also sited in Switzerland although the country only voted to join the UN in 2002. The year before, over three-quarters of voters rejected the proposal to join the European Union.

▲ Switzerland's famous Emmenthal cheese is pressed for around 20 hours and the holes found in the cheese occur due to gases trapped inside.

▼ The town of Lauterbrunnen is located 100 km east of Lausanne in a steep river valley which contains famous waterfalls, including the Trümmelbach and the Staubbach Falls.

AUSTRIA

Famous for its mountain scenery and its historic and cultural sites, Austria is a landlocked country dominated by the foothills and mountains of the Alps.

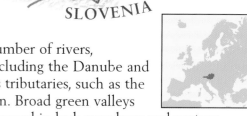

Area: 83,858 km²
Population: 8,065,000
Capital: Vienna (1,825,000)
Major language spoken: German
Main religion: Roman Catholic
Currency: euro
Main exports: machinery and transport equipment, chemicals, paper and paper products, iron and steel
Type of government: republic; democracy

▼ Traditional dancing at a winter ball in Vienna. The winter ball season is a major part of Viennese social life and lasts for around seven weeks from New Year's Eve onwards.

Austria lies north of Italy and Slovenia and south of Germany and the Czech Republic. The Alps sweep across much of its extent covering more than two-thirds of its land area. The mountain barriers are broken in many places by passes, including the Brenner Pass, 30 km south of Innsbruck and a major route between Austria and Italy. The country has a temperate continental climate with temperatures varying according to altitude. Summers tend to be relatively short and mild, while winters are cold and last three months or more in the valleys. Austria is crossed by a number of rivers, including the Danube and its tributaries, such as the Inn. Broad green valleys covered in lush meadows and pasture frequently separate the mountains while dense forests cover large portions of the mountains' lower slopes. Almost all of the croplands in Austria are situated in the northeast while dairy farming is common in the mountain valleys.

ELECTRICITY AND INDUSTRY

The fast-flowing rivers and mountainous landscapes help Austria generate vast amounts of hydro-electric power enabling it to sell excess energy to neighbouring countries. More than 70 per cent of Austria's electricity is generated this way, much of which is used by industry to produce iron, steel and aluminium. Such raw materials are used in manufacturing industries to build ships, machine tools and motor vehicles. A feature of Austrian industry is the large number of factories and companies making and selling craft goods including porcelain, fine glassware, jewellery and traditional clothing. Much of Austria's industry is

centred around Vienna, the capital of the country. Around a fifth of the country's population live in Vienna which is counted as one of the nation's nine Bundesländer or provinces.

HISTORY AND GOVERNMENT

People have lived in Austria since prehistoric times but the country rose to prominence from the 13th century onwards under the rule of one family, the Hapsburgs. The country became the centre of a vast empire which at its peak included Hungary and much of other nations such as Spain and the Netherlands. The cities of Vienna and Salzburg became major European centres of culture and the arts. Two world wars devastated the country and left it occupied by Soviet, US, British and French forces. Austria regained its independence in 1955 and, in 1995, joined the European Union.

▲ The Tirol province of Austria is highly mountainous with over 300 peaks above 3,000 m in elevation. Between the peaks are lakes, dense forests and lush meadows which attract many walkers in summer and winter sports enthusiasts in winter. The largest city in the Tirol is Innsbruck with a population of around 183,000.

LIECHTENSTEIN

The world's sixth smallest nation, Liechtenstein is perched between the Rhine river and the Alps. Its neighbour, Switzerland, provides many of its services.

Area: 160 km²
Population: 33,000
Capital: Vaduz (5,100)
Major language spoken: German
Main religion: Roman Catholic
Currency: Swiss franc
Main exports: machinery and transport equipment, metal products, dental products, hardware
Type of government: principality; democracy

Liechtenstein is not as mountainous as its neighbours, Austria and Switzerland. During winter it may experience heavy snowfall and sub-zero temperatures but its summer is warm with maximum temperatures as high as 28°C, allowing grapes and corn to be cultivated. On the plain near the Rhine river, livestock is reared. First formed in 1719, the tiny principality has managed to stay independent and has flourished, giving its inhabitants one of the highest standards of living in the world. Low tax rates have attracted foreign businesses and banking, while sales of postage stamps generate almost a tenth of the country's income. Liechtenstein has no airport; the nearest is found in the Swiss city of Zurich. Like its neighbour, Switzerland, Liechtenstein is not a member of the European Union.

HUNGARY

A landlocked country in central Europe, Hungary has a mixed economy and one of the most beautiful capital cities in Europe.

Area: 93,030 km²
Population: 9,810,000
Capital: Budapest
(1,975,000 urban area)
Major language spoken: Hungarian
Main religions: Roman Catholic, Reformed Church
Currency: forint
Main exports: industrial goods, consumer goods, machinery, food (cereals, meat and dairy products)
Type of government: republic; democracy

The Danube river divides Hungary into two regions. To the east lies the Great Plain or Great Alföld which covers more than half of Hungary. Although mountains lie along its northern border, the Great Plain is a mainly low-lying region crossed by Hungary's second major river, the Tisza. West of the Danube is a hilly region called Transdanubia. It contains the Bakony Mountains which are close to Lake Balaton, the largest freshwater lake in central Europe. Hungary has a continental climate with cold, cloudy winters, late summers and heavy rainfall in the spring and summer.

FROM AGRICULTURE TO INDUSTRY
The black-coloured soils of the Great Plain are extremely rich in nutrients. Coupled with its mild, dry climate in which rainfall is heaviest during the growing season, Hungary's farms have flourished. Fruit-growing, wine-making and cereal and vegetable planting are the biggest users of cropland. Hungary was a mainly agricultural country until World War II when its industries started to grow, in part aided by financing from the Soviet bloc of communist nations to which Hungary belonged from 1949 to 1989. Steel-making, aluminium and cement production were among the largest industries with leather goods, cars, factory machinery and fertilizers also important. Unchecked industrial development in some of the regions generated a great deal of air and water pollution. Lake Balaton and stretches of the Danube are heavily polluted while deciduous forests which consist mainly of beech and oak have also suffered.

▼ The Elizabeth Bridge is one of many bridges that cross the Danube river linking both sides of the city of Budapest. The bridge was first completed in 1903 and then rebuilt between 1961 and 1964.

THE MAGYARS

Hungary was in the past a larger country, with large minorities of Germans, Croats and Romanians but its land area shrunk after World War I when it lost its border provinces. Today, over 95 per cent of Hungarians are Magyars, descendants of a mixture of tribes which moved to and settled in Hungary over 1,100 years ago. The ancient Magyars had a strong culture, much of which is still kept alive today especially in the towns and villages of the Great Plains. There, aspects of traditional life from weaving and embroidery to traditional dress, folk stories and music can still be found.

BUDAPEST – QUEEN OF THE DANUBE

Hungary's capital and largest city, Budapest, is, in fact, an amalgam of three individual cities with long histories: Obuda became the first centre of Hungary in the 10th century; Buda on the western bank of the Danube was the former royal capital of the Hungarian empire; Pest on the eastern bank grew as a centre of trade and industry, and for long periods was under the control of German rulers. In 1849, the first bridge across the Danube connecting Buda and Pest was opened, uniting the cities. Budapest is ten times larger than the second largest Hungarian city, Debrecen, which lies in a farming region in eastern Hungary. Budapest is home to universities and colleges which teach more than half of all Hungarian students while it attracts over two-thirds of the money invested in Hungary by foreign companies. Known as the Queen of the Danube, the city attracts many of the country's 15 million tourists.

▶ Built between 1880 and 1902, the tall, domed parliament building in Budapest is 268 m long and 123 m wide.

▲ A father and son play Romany folk music on their violins on the banks of Lake Balaton. Situated approximately 90 km southwest of Budapest, Lake Balaton measures 598 km^2 and is central Europe's largest freshwater lake.

CZECH REPUBLIC

A small, hilly country at the centre of Europe, the peoples and settlements of the young Czech Republic have a long history.

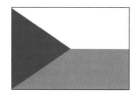

Area: 78,864 km²
Population: 10,293,000
Capital: Prague (1,179,000)
Major languages spoken: Czech, Moravian
Main religion: non-religious (nearly half), Roman Catholic
Currency: Czech koruna
Main exports: manufactured goods (including textiles), industrial machinery, motor vehicles, chemicals, fuel
Type of government: republic; democracy

▼ Prague Castle has a long history but today is the home of the President of the Czech Republic.

On 1 January 1993, the former federal republic of Czechoslovakia was dissolved and two new nations created: the Czech Republic and Slovakia. The Czech Republic is the larger, more populous and more industrialized of the two nations. It is actually the most industrialized of the former communist nations of central Europe. The country is landlocked and lies 322 km from the Adriatic Sea and 326 km from the Baltic. It shares borders with four nations: Germany to the west and north, Poland to the north and east, Austria to the south and Slovakia to the southeast. Mountain ranges form a large part of its borders, including the Carpathians which separate the country from Slovakia, and the Sudeten Mountains which run west of the city of Ostrava and form most of the border with Poland. Most of the country inside this ring of low mountains consists of a large basin called the Bohemian Massif. The country is split into two regions: to the east lies Moravia and to the west lies Bohemia.

COLD WINTERS AND WARM SUMMERS

The Czech Republic has a humid, continental climate and does not experience the modifying effects of ocean air masses. As a result, winters tend to be colder and summers warmer than in other European nations at similar latitudes. Easterly winds from Siberia force the temperatures down to below freezing during winter and snowfalls are often heavy on the high ground. A little under two-thirds of the country is covered in forests particularly of spruce, pine and beech trees, and 14 million m³ of timber was produced in 2001. Farming has been modernized and cereal crops and root vegetables are the most widely grown. In 1999 there were 30,000 km² of cultivated land.

MODERNIZING OLD INDUSTRIES

For over a century, the Czechs have relied on heavy industry based around their large deposits of coal, reserves of copper, lead and zinc and their central trading location in Europe. With economic independence in 1993 came the realization that many of their industries were neither modern nor efficient enough to compete in the world market. Successive Czech governments have spent large amounts of revenue as well as securing loans to modernize many of their industries. Foreign companies have been keen to invest in the country with its skilled workforce and stable government. The Czech Republic's single largest industry is engineering, followed by food production, electronics, chemicals, rubber, asbestos, and iron and steel. The country's biggest trading partner is Germany which accounted for 40 per cent of its exports and 27 per cent of its imports in 2001.

THE CZECH REPUBLIC'S HERITAGE

The Czech Republic has only been in existence for little more than a decade and Czechoslovakia, the country of which it was once part, was only established in 1918. However, the Czech people have a long history of settlement in the area dating back 1,500 years. The modern-day capital of the country, Prague, was a major European city by the 14th century and flourished as a centre of culture, the arts and learning for over 500 years. Much of Prague's older buildings and town layout have survived many conflicts, including the two World Wars and Soviet occupation. It is one of the most beautiful capitals in Europe and is a major tourist destination. The Czech Republic has developed its tourism industry so that now almost six million foreign visitors arrive every year.

▲ The Budweiser brewery in the southern Czech Republic town of České Budejovice. Situated close to the Vltava river, the town has been a centre of the beer brewing industry for 700 years.

▼ Located in the south of the Czech Republic around 40 km south of the city of Brno, the Palava Hills form a Biosphere Reserve in which the country's woodlands and other wild plant and animal life are officially protected.

POLAND

A large nation in northern central Europe, Poland's present borders were fixed in 1945 after the end of World War II.

Area: 312,685 km²
Population: 38,644,000
Capital: Warsaw (1,900,000)
Major language spoken: Polish
Main religion: Roman Catholic
Currency: zloty
Main exports: manufactures, machinery and transport equipment, consumer goods, food (particularly poultry, eggs, pork, fruit and vegetables)
Type of government: republic; democracy

The Republic of Poland borders seven other nations. Its land consists mainly of plains with low hills to the north, while the southern third of the country is mainly occupied by highland areas. Along the country's southern border are the Carpathian mountains. The Tatras, a mountain range within the Carpathians, is a protected national park and contains peaks over 2,400 m in height. The range is one of 28 national parks within Poland's borders.

A CHANGEABLE CLIMATE

Poland essentially has a warm summer and a cold winter, but its location means that its climate is influenced by many different air fronts which lead to variable, changeable weather. Cold polar air from Russia and Scandinavia meets warmer air currents from south of the country as well as air currents from the west. Poland is sometimes described as having six seasons with its spring and autumn periods both split into two different sets of climatic conditions.

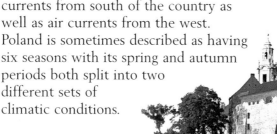

The annual average rainfall is about 600 mm, but there is much variation. The central lowlands receive around 450 mm while in the mountain regions, rainfall can be as high as 1,450 mm. In winter, snow covers most of the mountainous areas of Poland and around half of the plains.

▼ Wawel Castle lies in the city of Kraków, one of the most ancient settlements in Poland. The castle overlooks the Vistula river and, for centuries, was the site where Polish kings were crowned.

The largest city in northern Poland, Gdansk is a major shipbuilding and boat and ship repair centre on the Baltic Sea coast.

CHANGING BOUNDARIES

The name Polska, or Poland, has applied to part of northern central Europe which has changed its area and boundaries many times. It originally came from a people known as the Polaine who settled the lowlands between the Oder and Vistula rivers in the 10th and 11th centuries. At its peak in the 15th century, Poland's extended borders made it the largest country in Europe. Three centuries later, in the period 1772–1795, it ceased to exist as its territory was divided up by the major powers of Austria, Prussia and Russia. Poland received its independence from Russia in 1918 but was again overrun in 1939 prompting the onset of World War II. Part of the communist Soviet Bloc in the mid to late 20th century, the country was the first in central and eastern Europe to break from communist rule in 1989. The following year, the leader of the Solidarnosc (Solidarity) trade union, Lech Walesa, became President. Poland is expected to join the European Union in 2004.

▲ Found in the Old Town Square in Warsaw, the statue of the fighting mermaid with raised sword and shield is called Syrenka. A national symbol, images of Syrenka are found on city buildings throughout Warsaw.

▼ Lying 14 km southeast of Kracow are the Wieliczka salt mines. Comprising a vast network of 2,148 chambers and passages totalling 320 km in length, many of the older chambers are decorated with sculptures carved out of rock salt. Worked since the 13th century, these are the oldest operational salt mines in Europe.

POLAND'S RIVER SYSTEMS

Poland has over 4,000 km of navigable rivers and lakes which have been historically important as transport and trade routes. The Oder river starts in the Czech Republic but flows through the west of Poland forming part of its border with Germany. Over 900 km long, it is joined by a canal to the Vistula or Wisla – Poland's longest river. The Vistula is navigable for almost all of its 1,047 km length from the Carpathian mountains to the Gulf of Danzig. Many of Poland's important cities, including Kraców and the capital, Warsaw, lie on its banks.

PEOPLE AND WORK

Poland has substantial mineral and agricultural resources. It has the world's fifth largest reserves of coal in addition to deposits of copper, sulphur, zinc, lead and silver. Its industrial region around Katowice is one of Europe's largest. The main agricultural crops are cereals such as barley, wheat, potatoes, sugar beet and hay. The country contains approximately eight million beef and dairy cattle and 19 million pigs. Around 30 per cent of Poland is covered in forests but the thriving forestry industry has been damaged by high levels of air and water pollution from heavy industries.

SLOVAKIA

A small, landlocked country in central Europe, Slovakia was formed from the separation of the two halves of Czechoslovakia in 1993.

Area: 49,036 km²
Population: 5,379,000
Capital: Bratislava (429,000)
Major languages spoken: Slovak, Hungarian
Main religions: Roman Catholic, Slovak Evangelical
Currency: Slovak koruna
Main exports: semi-manufactured products, machinery and transport equipment, chemicals, manufactures, food
Type of government: republic; democracy

Slovakia is bordered by five nations: Poland, Austria, the Ukraine, Hungary and the Czech Republic. Much of the country is mountainous to the north and west while the southern region consists of fertile lowlands on which crops such as corn, wheat and potatoes are grown. Slovakia has a continental climate with warm summers and cold winters. Eighty six per cent of the country's people are Slovaks – a distinct ethnic group which has lived in the region for more than 1,000 years. People of Hungarian origin make up a further 11 per cent of the population, reflected in the fact that Slovakia's capital, Bratislava, was the capital of the Kingdom of Hungary from the 16th to 18th centuries.

INDUSTRY AND ENVIRONMENT

Slovakia has reserves of copper, lead, iron and lignite (brown coal) but has to import most of its oil and natural gas. Hydro-electric power from plants located on the Váh and other rivers provides an important source of energy while Slovakia is also building nuclear power stations. A large scale hydro-electric project at Gabcíkovo, 40 km southeast of Bratislava, which involved damming the Danube river, has caused environmental concerns. Slovakia has high levels of industrial pollution which have affected its forests and inland waterways. Around three in ten of all Slovakian workers are employed in industries such as iron- and steel-making and motor vehicle manufacture. Many thousands more work in food processing factories producing products such as beer and sheep's cheese. Most of the country's industry is centred around the capital city, Bratislava, or to the southeast around the city of Kosice.

▶ The Tatra or Tatry mountain range is the highest range of the Carpathian mountains which lie along the Poland–Slovakia border. The range consists of more than 300 peaks and its lower slopes are heavily forested with pine and spruce trees which provide habitats for creatures including bears and eagles. A popular year-round leisure destination, visitors come to hike its mountain trails and to view its many picturesque mountain lakes.

SOUTHERN EUROPE, THE BALKANS, THE CAUCASUS AND ASIA MINOR

SOUTHERN EUROPE

Most of southern Europe is dominated by the Mediterranean Sea. Of the larger nations, only Portugal, facing the Atlantic, does not have a significant Mediterranean coastline. With a length of 3,880 km and a total area of 2,503,000 km², the Mediterranean is the world's largest inland sea. It is almost landlocked and is joined to the Atlantic Ocean only through a narrow channel called the Straits of Gibraltar which measures between 13 and 27 km in width. The Mediterranean is a relatively young sea; 50 million years ago, it was all dry land. Movement of the tectonic plates in the region still occurs and is responsible for the volcanic activity found in and around Italy, and for earthquakes which have damaged parts of southern European countries such as Italy and also the Balkan nations close to the Mediterranean, including Greece and Macedonia. Important since ancient times as a trading and transport route, many of the great European civilizations have begun their life in or around the Mediterranean. The sea influences the climate of the region which, except for mountainous areas such as the Italian Alps and the Spanish Pyrenees, experiences mild winters and warm to hot summers with relatively low rainfall. This climate has a major effect on the lifestyles and work of the people of southern Europe, helping to make agriculture and tourism major industries.

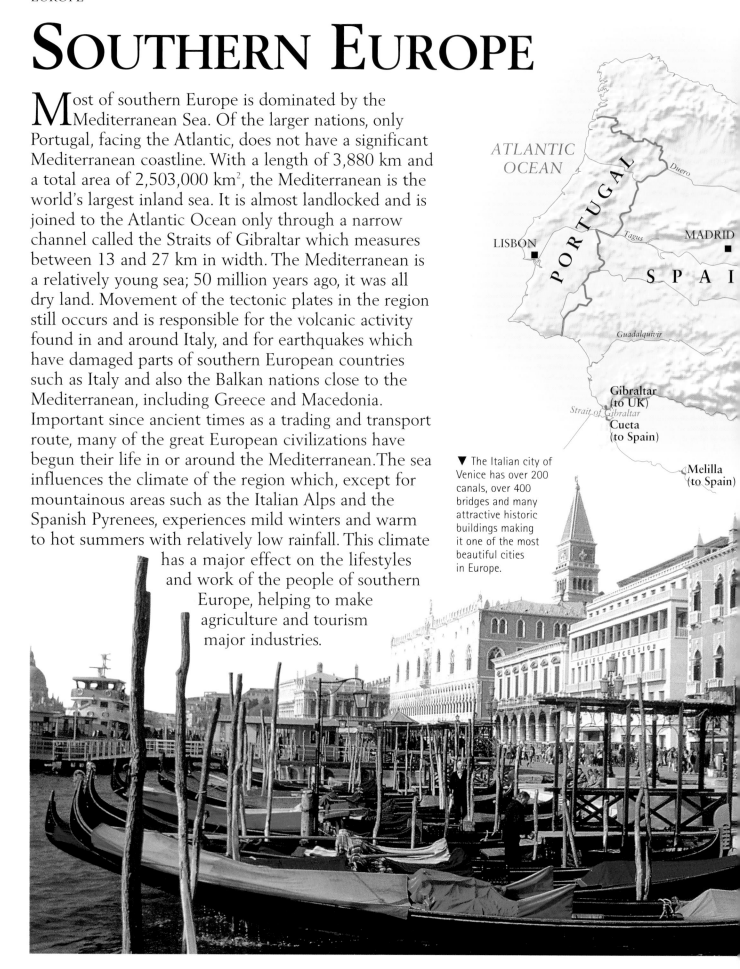

ATLANTIC OCEAN

PORTUGAL

LISBON

Duero

Tagus

MADRID

S P A I

Guadalquivir

Gibraltar (to UK)

Strait of Gibraltar

Cueta (to Spain)

Melilla (to Spain)

▼ The Italian city of Venice has over 200 canals, over 400 bridges and many attractive historic buildings making it one of the most beautiful cities in Europe.

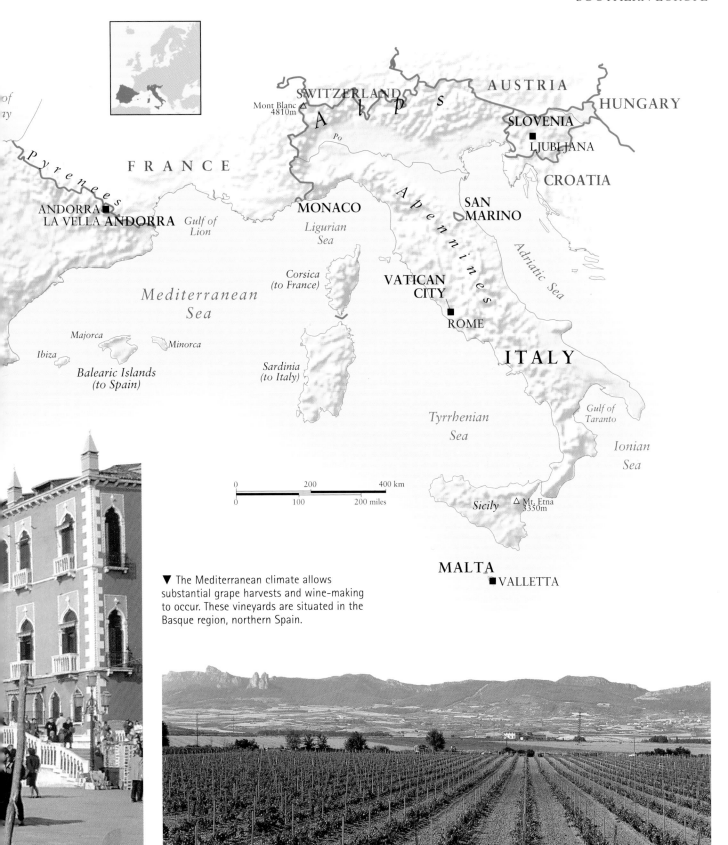

▼ The Mediterranean climate allows substantial grape harvests and wine-making to occur. These vineyards are situated in the Basque region, northern Spain.

SPAIN

The fourth largest nation in Europe, Spain was once the centre of a giant colonial empire and possesses a rich culture, history and fine architecture.

Area: 504,782 km²
Population: 40,847,000
Capital: Madrid (5,087,000)
Major languages spoken: Castilian (Spanish), Catalan, Basque, Galician
Main religion: Roman Catholic
Currency: euro
Main exports: transport equipment, agricultural products, machinery
Type of government: kingdom; democracy

Spain is the fifth most populous nation in Europe. It shares land borders with Portugal, Gibraltar and two nations in the Pyrenees mountains: France and Andorra. Spanish territory includes the Balearic and Canary Islands and three smaller island groups off the coast of Africa. Spain has a long Atlantic coastline to the north and northwest of the country and, on its eastern side, it borders the Mediterranean Sea.

CLOSE TO AFRICA

Spain occupies four-fifths of the Iberian Peninsula, the European land mass closest to Africa. It is separated from North Africa by the Straits of Gibraltar – the Mediterranean's narrow outlet to the Atlantic Ocean. Spain administers two small areas in the north African country of Morocco called Ceuta and Melilla. Close to the straits on the Spanish mainland is the British dependency of Gibraltar. This 6.5 km² territory is home to 25,000 people, most of whom are engaged in tourism and shipping. Spain and the UK have been contesting the dependency's sovereignty for many years. A referendum in November 2002 saw Gibraltarians vote in favour of staying as part of the UK but negotiations are expected to continue in the future.

THE MOUNTAINS AND THE MESETA

Spain has a number of large mountain ranges, which cross different parts of the country, and a huge central plain called the Meseta which occupies almost half of the Spanish mainland. To the north lie the Pyrenees and westwards, the Cordillera Cantabrica mountains which run close to Spain's

▲ Flamenco originated in southern Spain in the 18th century and is an exciting mixture of dance, guitars and percussion instruments.

northern coastline with the Atlantic before veering southwards towards northern Portugal. To the east, mountains run southeast from the Cordillera Cantabrica towards the Mediterranean Sea while south of the central plain lies the Sistemas Béticos. The Meseta covers an area of around 210,000 km² and has an average elevation of 700 m. It contains the oldest geological features of the Iberian Peninsula. Much of the plain is treeless and water is drained by two major rivers, the Duero and the Tagus, and their tributaries. A series of block mountains called Sistema Central occurs in the middle of the Meseta. There is a marked difference in soil quality between the east and west parts of the Meseta. The underlying limestone rocks of the eastern plains have been weathered to form richer soils and provide good agricultural areas.

CLIMATE AND FARMING

Most of Spain has an essentially warm Mediterranean climate which varies with altitude and with location. While temperatures in parts of northern Spain fall below zero in winter, Málaga, on the south coast, has an average daily winter temperature of 13.9°C. Most of the country receives less than 600 mm of rainfall

a year and droughts frequently occur in the Meseta. Farmers in many regions rely on irrigation systems to get water to their fields and the problem of desertification is growing. Spain was traditionally an agricultural nation growing a wide range of crops from sugar beets and cereals to citrus fruits and grapes. The country has industrialized rapidly in the past four decades, but farming and food processing remain very important. Spain is also one of the world's leading wine-makers.

▲ The Guggenheim museum was opened in the industrial city of Bilbao in 1997 and within a year had received 1.3 million visitors. Covered in titanium sheets, it is a supreme example of modern architecture.

▼ These Spaniards are harvesting grapes near the southern city of Málaga. In the year 2000, Spain produced just over six million tonnes of grapes.

▲ The layout of the city of Toledo is dominated by the Alcázar, a fortress-palace built in the 14th century and renovated on several occasions since. Toledo lies in central Spain on the River Tagus not far from Madrid.

▼ The giant cone of the volcano, El Tiede, lies at the centre of Tenerife, the largest of the Canary Islands. El Tiede reaches an elevation of 3,718 m and is the highest point in the islands and Spain.

A VARIETY OF CULTURES

Until the 15th century, many waves of settlement had helped to make Spain a patchwork of different states with varying cultures. After the Roman conquest of the native Iberian peoples came settlers and invaders from northern Europe as well as Muslim peoples from north Africa. Between the 9th and 14th centuries, the land was a flourishing centre of Islamic arts, culture and science which influenced the architecture and society for centuries afterwards. Spain, itself, has been very influential in European art, architecture, literature and music, and traditional artforms and entertainments have survived to this day. Several regions of Spain have maintained their own distinct culture and identity including the Basques in northern

Spain, and the Catalans in the east and northeast of the country. After the Spanish Civil War (1936–1939), Spain was ruled by a dictator, General Francisco Franco, until 1975. During his leadership, minority languages and customs were banned. Separatist movements in the Basque region and Catalonia, which had existed before Franco's rise to power, strengthened in their demands for independence from Spain. Democratic elections and a new constitution were established in the late 1970s. The separatist movements still exist, and Basque, Catalan and Galician languages are all taught in schools.

CITY LIVING

With a move to more manufacturing and service industries has come a migration of Spaniards from the countryside to towns and cities. Around three-quarters of Spaniards now live in towns and cities of which Madrid is the biggest as well as being the capital and seat of government. Unusually for a European capital city, Madrid, which sits in the centre of the Meseta, is neither located on one of the country's major rivers nor on the coast, like Barcelona, Spain's second largest city. Barcelona is a major Mediterranean port and the centre of a large and densely populated industrial centre.

A MAJOR COLONIAL POWER

In the late 15th century, Spain became united as one nation under the rule of Queen Isabel and King Ferdinand. At around the same time, some of the first major explorations of other continents by Spanish sailors were underway. These resulted in Spain building up a large colonial empire. By 1600, Spain controlled parts of North and South

America, much of Central America and a number of Caribbean islands. The Spanish Empire also included Portugal, the Netherlands, Austria and parts of France, Germany and Italy. Conflicts from the mid-17th century onwards caused Spain to lose its European territories by 1714 and, by 1850, almost all of its South American colonies.

A TOURISM GIANT

Spain is one of the world's top five tourist destinations and, in 2000, the revenue from tourism was over 30 billion US dollars. Half of all visitors come from Germany and the UK, lured by the warm climate, the beaches of the Mediterranean, particularly those of the Costa del Sol, Costa Blanca and Costa Brava, and major cities of culture and history such as Barcelona, Madrid and Valencia. The country's two main island groups – the Balearics in the Mediterranean and the Canary Islands in the Atlantic – have also become major tourist destinations. The Canaries are the remains of steep-sided volcanic cones and their land is rugged with relatively sparse vegetation. Year-

round sunshine and mild winters not only attract many tourists, but also enable bananas and tomatoes to be grown for export. The Balearics include the islands of Majorca, Minorca and Ibiza, which have become popular holiday destinations. Development on a massive scale has transformed large parts of both groups of islands and led to environmental concerns.

▲ Café-goers sit and enjoy the views found in the Plaza Mayor in the centre of Spain's capital, Madrid. The plaza was built in the early 17th century and was originally used by royalty to watch plays, bullfights and royal pageants.

ANDORRA

A small, mountainous principality in the Pyrenees, Andorra has existed as a separate state since 1278 and relies on tourism and its status as a tax haven.

Area: 468 km²
Population: 66,000
Capital: Andorra la Vella (36,000)
Major languages spoken: Catalan, Castilian, French
Main religion: Roman Catholic
Currency: euro
Principal exports: motor vehicles, electrical machinery
Type of government: co-principality; democracy

Andorra lies in the eastern Pyrenees, bordering both France and Spain. Its land consists of sharp mountain peaks, mountain slopes and a series of valleys. Andorra has a large number of natural sources of hot water known as thermal rock springs. Summers are dry and relatively warm but in winter, snowfall and cold temperatures mean that its mountain slopes are covered with snow for many months. Only four per cent of its land can be cultivated; much of the remainder is forested. Andorra relies on its snowfall to lure winter visitors in their millions. Visitors at other times are attracted by its charm and tranquillity. Andorra's heads of state are the co-princes – French and

Spanish authorities who in modern times have been the Spanish Bishop of Urgel and the French President. In 1993, Andorra introduced a new constitution which gave its inhabitants free elections and the right to join trades unions. In the same year, Andorra joined the United Nations, although France and Spain still remain responsible for its defence. Native-born Andorrans make up only around 30 per cent of the population. Most of the remainder are immigrants from France and Spain. Andorra la Vella is the highest capital in Europe.

PORTUGAL

Lying on the far west of southern Europe, Portugal is a long rectangular-shaped country. It is one of the most rural countries of western Europe.

Area: 92,391 km²
Population: 10,318,000
Capital: Lisbon
(2,900,000)
Major language spoken: Portuguese
Main religion: Roman Catholic
Currency: euro
Main exports: textiles and clothing, machinery and transport equipment, footwear, cork, chemicals
Type of government: republic; democracy

▼ Built on seven hills around the estuary of the River Tagus, Lisbon is a major European city and important deep water port.

Portugal occupies the southwestern part of the Iberian Peninsula and shares borders in the north and the east with Spain, while facing the Atlantic Ocean to the south and west. Northern Portugal is mountainous, the highest part is a highland region which in winter is snow-covered and popular for skiing. Much of the forests which cover around 35 per cent of the country are also found in the north. Portugal's major river, the Tagus, rises in western Spain and divides Portugal into its northern and southern regions. The Douro and the Guadiana rivers, both of which also rise in Spain, are the other major rivers. South of the Tagus, the land is much flatter and more low-lying. Much of it consists of vast plains which are divided from the south coast by a mountain range. The south coast region, known as the Algarve, is popular as a tourist destination.

TRADITIONAL FARMING

Around ten per cent of its population are engaged in farming, while nearly a quarter live in rural areas. The dry soils and climate of the southern part of the country have allowed olives, grapes and fruits to flourish and Portugal is renowned worldwide for production of table wine and two fortified wines, madeira and port, named after the city of Oporto. Cereal grains are grown and

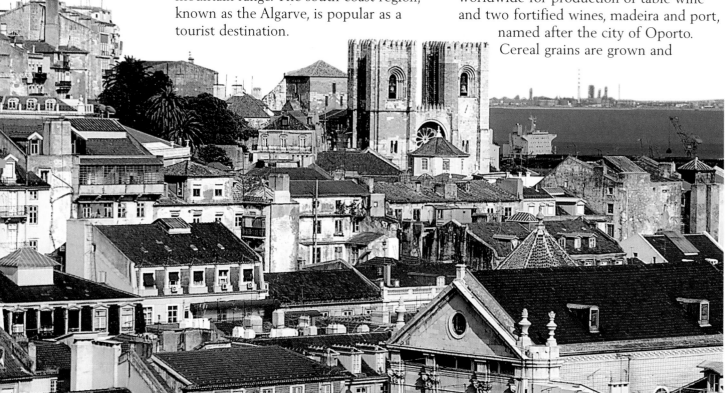

◀ Over 12 million tourists visit Portugal every year and a large proportion of them come to the Algarve region in the south of the country. It is renowned for its wide sandy beaches and warm climate.

▲ This distinctively styled pottery is from Sintra, a small collection of towns and villages on the slopes of the Sintra Mountains about 24 km from Lisbon.

livestock are raised on the flatter uplands, as well as on the plains near the coast. Traditional agricultural methods are still practised in large parts of Portugal. As a result, wild birds and animals have been able to flourish without losing their natural habitats. In the last 20 years, Portugal has undergone major economic change. In particular, it has increased its levels of light manufacturing industries including clothing, footwear, and paper and food processing.

A SEAFARING NATION

Portugal's long coastline with the Atlantic has meant that, for hundreds of years, many of its people have relied on fishing and trade to make a living. This is still partly the case today, with major ports such as Lisbon and Oporto and large fishing fleets. Trawlers fish the Atlantic for cod, hake, mackerel, halibut and anchovies, while sardines account for a third of all fish catches. In more shallow waters near the coast, oysters and other shellfish are harvested. From the 15th century onwards, Portuguese explorers travelled the world and the country became a colonial power with colonies in Africa, the Caribbean, South America and Asia. In 1999, Portugal relinquished control over the last European colony to be found in the Far East when it handed Macau over to China. Today, most of Portugal's trade is conducted with other members of the European Union.

▶ Portugal is the world's leading producer of cork, the thick bark of a particular evergreen oak tree which grows in abundance in the country.

ISLANDS AND ADMINISTRATION

Portugal first won its independence from Moorish Spain in 1143 and was ruled by a monarch until 1910 when it became a republic. Portugal is divided into seven administrative regions which include the Atlantic island groups of Madeira and the Azores. Madeira consists of three small islands and one main island on which is located its capital, Funchal. Covered in subtropical and tropical plants, Madeira, a popular holiday destination, is around 1,000 km southwest of Portugal. The Azores are a group of nine volcanic-formed islands and smaller islets. They lie just over 1,200 km due west of Lisbon.

ITALY

Unified as one country in 1860, Italy is now a major European industrial country with a large agricultural base.

Area: 301,277 km²
Population: 56,306,000
Capital: Rome (2,630,000)
Main language spoken: Italian
Main religion: Roman Catholic
Currency: euro
Principal exports: machinery and transport equipment, electrical machinery, precision machinery, chemicals, textiles, clothing and shoes, processed metals
Type of government: republic; democracy

▼ The city of Naples was founded around 2,600 years ago by the Ancient Greeks. Today, it is one of Italy's largest ports and the centre of industry in southern Italy.

Much of Italy extends into the Mediterranean Sea as a long peninsula. It is bordered by five different nations to the north: France, Switzerland, Monaco, Austria and Slovenia, while within its territory are two tiny independent states, San Marino and the Vatican City. In the northeast of the country is Italy's largest plain, the Plain of Lombardy, which is drained by Italy's longest river, the 652 km long River Po. Running along the western coast of Italy from Genoa in the north to Naples are a series of lowlands separated by mountains, plains and peaks. This region, along with the Plain of Lombardy, have Italy's most fertile soil and are the most densely populated parts of the country.

HILLS, MOUNTAINS AND VOLCANOES

Much of Italy is covered by hills and mountains. To the north, and part of the Alps, lie the Dolomites, so named because many of their peaks are topped with formations of dolomite rock. On the southern side of the Alps is a series of large lakes including Lago di Como, Lago di Garda and Lago Maggiore. Fast-flowing rivers and streams are harnessed to provide northern Italy with around half of its electricity needs. Along the eastern part of the country, running from north to south over almost

the entire length of the country, is the Apennine Mountains. These mountains form the backbone of the country and rise to a height of over 3,000 m in the Gran Sasso Range, east of the capital city of Rome. A fault line running through the western coast to Sicily features several active volcanoes, including Etna in Sicily and Mount Vesuvius close to Naples.

SICILY

Italy's territory includes Sicily, the largest island in the Mediterranean which is separated from the southwestern tip of the mainland by the Straits of Messina. Most of Sicily is a plateau of between 200 and 500 m in elevation with higher mountains to the north and several isolated volcanic peaks. The most famous of these is Mount Etna which rises to 3,350 m and is Europe's highest active volcano. Sicily's warm, dry climate allows large crops of citrus fruits, grapes and olives to be grown despite the island often suffering drought . Fishing is extremely important to the island economy with around a quarter of all Italian fishing vessels based in Sicily. The island is also one of the world's leading producers of sulphur while other mineral deposits include iron and coal.

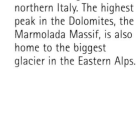

▲ The Marmolada Massif is part of the Dolomites mountain range in northern Italy. The highest peak in the Dolomites, the Marmolada Massif, is also home to the biggest glacier in the Eastern Alps.

▼ Tomato pickers hard at work harvesting their crop. Italy is the second largest grower of tomatoes in the world and processes much of its crop into sauces and pastes used in Italian cuisine.

▲ One of the most famous architectural features of Rome is the Scalinata della Trinità dei Monti or Spanish Steps. Constructed in the early 18th century, the steps are a magnet for tourists and outdoor artists and lead to the 16th century church of Trinità dei Monti at the top.

heartland of the country producing, among other things, chemicals, iron and steel, electrical consumer goods, textiles and over a million motor cars per year. Major industrial cities in the north, including Milan and Turin, are home to giant Italian companies such as Fiat and Olivetti. Northern Italy is one of the most prosperous regions in the whole of Europe which is in marked contrast to the south of the country which is poor and with high unemployment. There, among its terrain of rugged hills and dry soils, traditional methods of agriculture and small scale industries remain the dominant way of life. Poverty has forced many southern Italians to migrate to the north and around two-thirds of the country's population live in cities and towns.

SARDINIA

North of Sicily, the island of Sardinia is also mountainous with its best farmland in the southwest of the island where a large plain is situated. Cereals, olives, tobacco and grain are the chief crops, while the mining industry extracts lead, copper, zinc and salt from the island. Sardinia's population of over 1.5 million lives in a number of towns mostly situated around the island's coast. The island's capital is Cagliari, which is also the principal port of Sardinia.

NORTH-SOUTH DIVIDE

Italy is divided into 20 administrative regions but geographers and economists talk of two Italys: the north and the south. Particularly since World War II, the north has become the industrial

ITALY'S ATTRACTIONS

Italy is one of the world's top five tourist destinations with its warm Mediterranean climate, its scenic lakes and mountains, remains of ancient Rome and its ski resorts in winter. In 2001, 41 million tourists flocked to Italy to experience its amazingly rich history, culture and cuisine. Italy's cuisine is varied and extensive with hundreds of regional dishes and more than 50 different cheeses. The country is also the second largest wine producer in the world. Over 100,000 historical sites are found throughout Italy, a legacy of the country's past historic wealth and power as the centre of the Roman Empire and, from the 14th century onwards, the birthplace of new thinking in science, philosophy and the arts called the Renaissance. As the home of opera as well as dozens of influential artists, architects, writers and composers, Italy's culture is world-renowned.

► Italy is one of the foremost manufacturers of motor vehicles in Europe and the distinctive red Ferrari, Europe's most famous make of luxury sports car. Ferrari was formed in 1939 by Enzo Ferrari and has run a successful Formula One team since the 1940s.

SAN MARINO

The third smallest nation in Europe, San Marino was established in the 4th century and is totally surrounded by Italy. It relies on tourism for much of its income.

Area: 61 km²
Population: 27,000
Capital: San Marino (4,400)
Main language spoken: Italian
Main religion: Roman Catholic
Currency: euro
Principal exports: wine, wheat, woollen goods, furniture, ceramics
Type of government: republic; democracy

Located in central Italy in the Apennine mountain range, San Marino is a tiny country with a maximum length of around 14 km. Its landscape is dominated by Monte Titano which has three individual peaks. Each of these peaks is topped by a medieval fortress: la Rocca, la Cresta and Montale. The land to the northeast of the mountain slopes gently towards the Romagna plain while to the southwest there are a number of hills. Several large streams run through San Marino including the Ausa and Marano. The country is crowded with an average population density of over 450 people per km². Hewn out of the steep slopes of Monte Titano is the nation's capital, also called San Marino.

Agriculture and stone quarrying were important in the past but, today, San Marino relies on tourism for around three-fifths of its income. The spectacular location of its settlements and their history, along with the mild climate, lure 2.5 million tourists within its borders every year. Three-quarters of these are Italians and many tourists arrive via the Italian city of Rimini, where San Marino's nearest airport is located.

VATICAN CITY

The world's smallest independent state, the Vatican City is encircled by the city of Rome. It is home to the head of the Roman Catholic church, the Pope.

Area: 0.44 km²
Population: 860
Capital: Vatican City (860)
Main languages spoken: Italian, Latin
Religion: The Vatican is the headquarters of the Roman Catholic Church
Currency: euro
Exports: none
Type of government: theocracy

The Vatican City lies near the River Tiber and is cut off from Rome by its medieval walls. All food, goods and energy supplies have to be imported. The Vatican City's economy is unlike any other nation in the world. Money comes from investments and from the churches and followers of Roman Catholicism around the world. In addition, admission charges and sales of literature and souvenirs to the hundreds of thousands of tourists who visit provide a large proportion of the state's income. The Vatican's form of government is a theocracy. The person elected Pope for life by the Roman Catholic Church has supreme powers for the country's laws and government. Security is the task of the 100-strong Vatican army called the Swiss Guard.

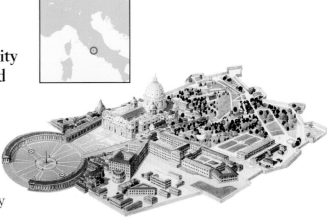

► Built in the 16th century, St Peter's Basilica in the Vatican City is one of the world's largest religious buildings.

SLOVENIA

Part of former Yugoslavia, Slovenia is a small, scenic and mountainous country which gained its independence in 1991.

Area: 20,273 km²
Population: 1,948,000
Capital: Ljubljana (257,000)
Main language spoken: Slovene
Main religion: Roman Catholic
Currency: tolar
Main exports: machinery and transport equipment, chemicals, foodstuffs
Type of government: republic; democracy

▼ A market in progress in the Slovenian city of Ljubljana. Located on the banks of two rivers, the city has been a major transport centre for many centuries. Today, it is an industrialized city with large heavy engineering and paper, soap and chemical works.

Slovenia borders Italy to the west, Hungary to the east, Austria to the north and Croatia, to the south. The country has a small 46.6 km long coastline with the Adriatic Sea. Much of the northern and western parts of Slovenia are occupied by mountains which are heavily forested on their lower slopes. Almost half of Slovenia is covered in forests which still provide habitats for small numbers of bears, wolves and lynx. The eastern portion of the country lies on a barren limestone plateau. Over millions of years, the erosive actions of rainwater in this region have formed some of the most impressive cave systems in Europe, including the 19.5 km long Postojna caves.

Slovenia has a continental climate with cold winters and warm summers. Forty-five per cent of the country's population live in small farming communities where cattle and sheep rearing are the most important activities. In the northeast of Slovenia, where the climate is warmer, wine-making is an important industry. Brown coal, lead, zinc and uranium are among the minerals found within its borders and Slovenia has a small but flourishing manufacturing industry. Despite being ruled by other nations for long periods of their history, the Slovenian people, over 85 per cent of whom are descendants of Slavs, have retained much of their rich culture and crafts skills. Slovenia's people enjoy relatively high standards of living, healthcare and education. The country has the lowest number of prisoners as a proportion of its population, with just 630 in jail in 2001.

MALTA

Strategically located in the Mediterranean Sea between Europe and North Africa, Malta has been an important trading centre for over 2,000 years.

Gozo
Rabat
(Victoria)

Comino

Mediterranean
Sea

Sliema
Rabat
Birkirkara

VALLETTA

MALTA

Malta

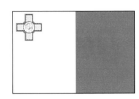

Area: 316 km²
Population: 389,000
Capital: Valletta (201,000)
Major languages spoken:
Maltese, English
Main religion: Roman
Catholic
Currency: Maltese lira
Principal exports:
machinery and transport
equipment, manufactures
(mainly textiles, clothing
and footwear), chemicals
Type of government:
republic; democracy

The Maltese archipelago consists of three inhabited islands, Malta, Gozo and Comino, and two uninhabited islands. They lie in the middle of the Mediterranean Sea around 90 km south of the Italian island of Sicily and over 250 km from the coast of North Africa. Malta is the largest of the islands. Measuring 27 km by 14.5 km at its greatest extent, the island's 137 km long coastline is rocky and contains many low cliffs, bays and natural harbours. There is also a number of sandy beaches which, along with its warm, dry climate and its long history, attract over one million holidaymakers every year. Away from the coast, Malta's landscape is one of mainly low hills with small farming fields cut into the hill slopes as terraces. Crops including feed for livestock, flowers and citrus fruits

are grown on these terraces. Malta has no rivers, and little surface water. It relies on desalination plants which produce fresh water from seawater for its water supply. Lying northwest of Malta and linked by a regular ferry service, the island of Gozo is less populated but with more fertile soils in which grapes, other fruits and vegetables are grown. The Maltese islands' strategic location has seen them occupied by the ancient Phoenicians, Greeks, Romans, Normans, Arabs and Turks. The last colonial power to control Malta was Britain from which Malta became independent in 1964. Shipping and trade remain vitally important to the Maltese economy. Malta has few natural resources and has to import fuel, raw materials and many foodstuffs.

▼ Lying on the southeastern coast of Malta, the harbour and town of Marsaxlokk has been a site of the Maltese fishing industry for many centuries.

THE BALKANS

The Balkans gets its name from the Balkan Peninsula which juts into the Mediterranean Sea. The peninsula's coastline faces Italy across the Adriatic Sea on its western side and terminates to the south with the fragmented coastline of Greece and its many island groups. The Mediterranean Sea reaches its deepest off the coast of Greece where a maximum depth of 4,982 m has been recorded. Balkan comes from the Turkish word for mountains, and mountains and rugged hills are a major feature of the region's landscape. Much of the region was part of the Turkish Empire for many centuries. As it declined in the late 19th and early 20th centuries, rivalries between different ethnic groups in the territory north of Greece led to new states being formed. After World War I, a large portion of the Balkans was combined into a new nation which became known as Yugoslavia. The tensions between the different ethnic groups in Yugoslavia turned into direct conflict with fierce fighting and thousands of deaths after the break-up of that country in 1991. Today, the region contains a number of new or young nations in an uneasy peace, seeking to rebuild after war and create stable societies.

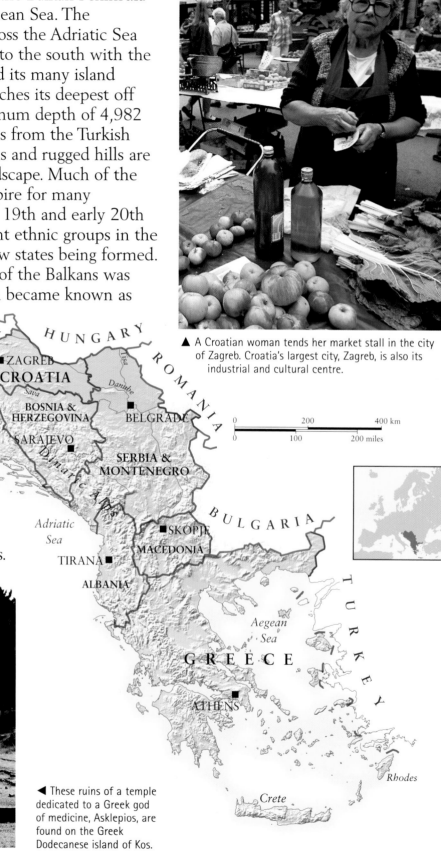

▲ A Croatian woman tends her market stall in the city of Zagreb. Croatia's largest city, Zagreb, is also its industrial and cultural centre.

◄ These ruins of a temple dedicated to a Greek god of medicine, Asklepios, are found on the Greek Dodecanese island of Kos.

CROATIA

Founded in 800 and part of Yugoslavia during much of the 20th century, Croatia lies on the crossroads between central Europe and the Mediterranean.

Area: 56,542 km²
Population: 4,437,000
Capital: Zagreb (779,000)
Major language spoken: Croat (Serbo-Croat)
Main religions: Roman Catholic, Serbian Orthodox
Currency: kuna
Principal exports: basic manufactures, machinery, chemicals, fuels, food
Type of government: republic; democracy

▼ The ancient historic town and port of Dubrovnik is one of the most scenic settlements in the whole of Croatia. Originally founded in the 7th century, it is overlooked by Mount Srjd and features heavily fortified stone city walls.

Croatia borders Slovenia and Hungary to the north while its eastern border with Serbia is partly defined by the River Danube. Croatia wraps around the northern and western sides of Bosnia & Herzegovina and extends along the Adriatic Sea with one 20 km break to give Bosnia & Herzegovina a short Adriatic coastline. The remaining Croatian territory, which includes the city of Dubrovnik, is cut off from the rest of Croatia and has a short border with Serbia & Montenegro. The western part of Croatia is known as Dalmatia and is a rocky and relatively barren land. There, changes in sea level have drowned mountain valleys, creating many steep islands and small, rocky peninsulas. This western part of Croatia experiences a Mediterranean climate while the remainder of the country's climate is continental with colder winters. Croatia's large river, the Sava, flows into the Danube. Around a fifth of the country is devoted to agriculture, with the most fertile region being in the east. Pigs, chickens and dairy cattle are reared while cereal crops cover almost two-thirds of the land. Other important produce includes sunflower seeds, soybeans and sugar beets. The country has rich mineral resources including oil and coal and now, following the damaging conflicts of the 1990s, much aid and investment is being introduced into rebuilding its former industries.

BOSNIA & HERZEGOVINA

Bosnia & Herzegovina became independent of Yugoslavia in 1992, and is now rebuilding after a devastating civil war.

Area: 51,129 km²
Population: 3,972,000
Capital: Sarajevo (360,000)
Major languages spoken: Serb and Croat (both dialects of Serbo-Croat)
Main religions: Sunni Islam, Serbian Orthodox, Roman Catholic
Currency: marka
Principal exports: food, timber, basic manufactures
Type of government: republic; partial democracy

▼ The city of Mostar is surrounded by high, barren mountains. Formerly home to Roman Catholic Croats, Bosnian Muslims and Serbs, the city was heavily damaged during the civil war and today, Serbs no longer live there.

Bosnia & Herzegovina lies in the Balkans bordering Serbia & Montenegro and Croatia. The country's rugged landscape is very mountainous in the north while to the south there are flatter, more fertile, regions. Cereal crops and flax are grown in the north while tobacco, fruits and cotton are important in the south. Large parts of the country lie on a barren limestone plateau. Underground rivers flow through this area and there are many mineral springs. Almost half of the country is covered in forests of oak, beech and pine trees. Since the time of the Roman Empire, many different religious and cultural groups have settled here. The country's main ethnic groups today are Croats, Serbs and the largest group, ethnic Bosnians, most of whom are Muslims. Following the savage civil war, many people emigrated and the population dropped by a quarter. The country is now made up of two self-governing states, the Muslim-Croat Federation and the Serbian Republika Srpska. Bosnia & Herzegovina is now trying to revive its industries.

SERBIA & MONTENEGRO

A union of two semi-independent republics both of which were a part of the former Yugoslavia, Serbia & Montenegro have a varied landscape and climate.

Area: 102,173 km²
Population: 10,640,000
Capital: (Serbia) Belgrade (1,295,000)
Capital: (Montenegro) Podgorica (131,000)
Major language spoken: Serb
Main religions: Serbian Orthodox, Sunni Islam, Montenegrin Orthodox
Currency: (Serbia) dinar; (Kosovo) euro; (Montenegro) dinar, euro
Principal exports: basic manufactures, food, machinery and transport equipment, chemicals
Type of government: republic; partial democracy

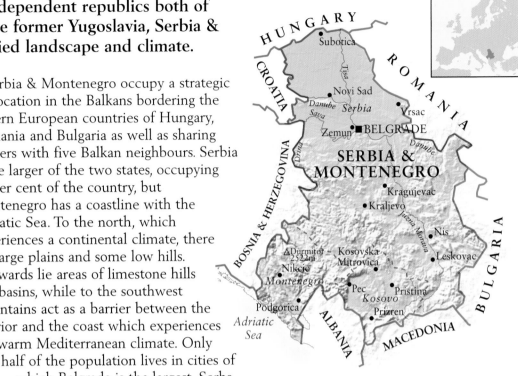

Serbia & Montenegro occupy a strategic location in the Balkans bordering the eastern European countries of Hungary, Romania and Bulgaria as well as sharing borders with five Balkan neighbours. Serbia is the larger of the two states, occupying 86 per cent of the country, but Montenegro has a coastline with the Adriatic Sea. To the north, which experiences a continental climate, there are large plains and some low hills. Eastwards lie areas of limestone hills and basins, while to the southwest mountains act as a barrier between the interior and the coast which experiences a warm Mediterranean climate. Only half of the population lives in cities of which Belgrade is the largest. Serbs are the biggest ethnic group comprising around 60 per cent of the population with Muslim Albanians making up around 17 per cent. Almost all of the five

▼ Serbian refugees from Kosovo work on a farm in the central region of Serbia & Montenegro.

per cent of the population who are Montenegrins live in Montenegro. The country's resources allow it to produce all the electricity that it needs from large coal reserves and hydro-electricity. Serbia & Montenegro also has large reserves of bauxite, iron, copper and lead. Industries have been disrupted by the bitter civil war. Its ending may have brought a degree of peace but as yet, little prosperity. The country's people are among the poorest in Europe with as many as two-thirds living below the poverty line.

MACEDONIA

A landlocked nation of great scenic beauty, the former Yugoslav republic of Macedonia was once at the heart of the ancient Greek Empire.

Area: 25,713 km²
Population: 2,024,000
Capital: Skopje (444,000)
Major languages spoken: Macedonian, Albanian
Main religions: Macedonian Orthodox, Roman Catholic
Currency: dinar
Principal exports: basic manufactures, machinery and transport equipment, food products, chemicals
Type of government: republic; partial democracy

Macedonia is bordered by Bulgaria, Albania, Serbia & Montenegro and Greece. Much of the country is covered in steep-sided hills and mountains with deep valleys and large forested areas. Macedonia has 34 mountain peaks that exceed 2,000 m and four major lakes, of which Lake Ohrid is the largest. Macedonia's longest river, the Vardar, runs for 301 km through the country. It starts in the northwest and flows into southern Greece, where it is called the River Axiós, before draining into the Aegean Sea. The country's capital and largest city, Skopje, lies on the Vardar. Rebuilt after an earthquake destroyed much of the city in 1961, Skopje is an important market centre for neighbouring farmlands. It is also the country's main industrial region where metal production and metalworking, chemicals and assembling goods are key industries. Sheep and chickens are the most common livestock, while there are over 80,000 beehives producing honey and beeswax.

▼ A Macedonian man sews United Nations' patches on military uniforms. Around 1,000 United Nations Peacekeepers were stationed in Macedonia from the 1990s onwards.

One of Macedonia's most thriving industries is alcohol production. In 2000, the country produced more than 135 million litres of wine, 150 million litres of brandy and over 800 million litres of beer. A part of the former nation of Yugoslavia, Macedonia became independent in 1991, but there followed disputes with Greece over its name and flag which led to its adopting the temporary name of the Former Yugoslav Republic of Macedonia. Two-thirds of the country's population are Macedonian Slavs, while Albanians comprise 23 per cent. There are small populations of Turks, Serbs and Romany peoples. Tensions between its different ethnic groups and an influx of many refugees from other Balkan countries are among the country's most pressing problems.

ALBANIA

One of the poorest and least developed nations in Europe, Albania remained isolated from the outside world for much of the 20th century.

Area: 28,748 km²
Population: 3,113,000
Capital: Tirana (279,000)
Major language spoken: Albanian
Main religions: Sunni Islam, Albanian Orthodox
Currency: lek
Principal exports: manufactured goods, chromium and copper, food and tobacco, manufactures
Type of government: republic; partial democracy

▼ Founded in the 17th century and lying on the Ishm river, Tirana is Albania's capital and largest city.

Albania is found on the western part of the Balkan Peninsula facing the Adriatic Sea with Serbia & Montenegro to the north, Macedonia to the east and Greece to the south. The country can be divided into two geographical regions. To the west is an area of coastal lowlands. Although some of this land is marshy, much of it contains fertile soils and is heavily farmed, as well as being the most densely populated part of the country. Much of the rest of Albania consists of highlands and mountains. Albania's major rivers begin their life in the mountains and flow in a westerly direction emptying into the Adriatic.

Half of the country's workforce is employed in agriculture with wheat, corn, potatoes and sugar beet being the major crops, while there are some 1.9 million sheep. Albania's population is one of the least mixed in Europe with only two per cent of people not ethnic Albanians. Much of the 20th century was spent in isolation from the rest of the world under a communist dictatorship. As a result, the country is less developed and despite its reserves of metals, gas and oil, its industry and economy lags behind the rest of Europe. Albania's people are among the poorest in Europe and many young Albanians emigrate to seek work. There are more ethnic Albanians abroad than in the country.

GREECE

Greece is one of the oldest civilizations in Europe, although it only gained independence from Turkey in 1832.

Area: 131,957 km²
Population: 10,940,000
Capital: Athens
(3,193,000)
Major language spoken: Greek
Main religion: Greek Orthodox
Currency: euro
Principal exports: textiles, food, beverages and tobacco, petroleum products, minerals, cotton
Type of government: republic; democracy

▼ Lying on the Saronic Gulf, the city of Piraeus first served as a port for the city of Athens, some eight km inland, almost 2,500 years ago. Developed in the 20th century, Piraeus is now Greece's largest port.

Greece is a highly fragmented land mass, with a heavily indented coastline that measures over 4,000 km. The country occupies the southernmost part of the Balkan Peninsula and curves round the northern and eastern edge of the Aegean Sea. The country's land borders are to the north with Albania, Macedonia, Bulgaria and Turkey. Two large gulfs almost split the southern portion of the mainland, the Peloponnese Peninsula, from the rest of mainland Greece. Much of the country consists of highland areas. The Pindus mountains is Greece's largest mountain range. Greece's mountains are young and are still being built which results in many earthquakes. Most of Greece has a Mediterranean climate with mild, rainy winters with average daily temperatures rarely below 10°C and subtropical, dry and warm summers. Temperatures are cooled slightly by a system of seasonal breezes popularly known locally as the Meltemia. Greece's northern forests are home to wildcats, roe deer and small numbers of brown bears, lynx and wild boar. Jackals and wild goats are found in the south. Much of Greece, especially its western wetlands, are visited in winter by flocks of migratory birds.

FAMILY FARMING

Only 22 per cent of Greece's territory consists of arable land. The rest is rocky scrubland, mountain or forest. Greek agriculture employs almost one-fifth of the country's workforce despite poor soils and soil erosion in places. It has received much assistance from the national government and the European Union which Greece joined in 1981. Most farms are small and family-owned and warm weather crops including olives, grapes and citrus fruits are grown. The leading export crop is tobacco, with cotton, olive oil and Greek cheeses also important. Sheep and goats are reared while fishing is strictly controlled to protect the Mediterranean Sea from over-fishing.

THE GREEK ECONOMY

One of the poorer members of the European Union, Greece relies on tourism and agriculture for a major part of its economy. The country has poor mineral reserves, with some exceptions such as bauxite. Its industries have been built up since World War II and include textiles, cement, telecommunications and processed foods. The Greek merchant fleet is the largest home-owned fleet of vessels in the world and shipbuilding and trading services are a major part of the Greek economy.

THE ISLANDS OF GREECE

One-fifth of Greece's land area consists of more than 2,000 islands, of which only 154 are inhabited. These are divided into many groups including the Ionian Islands to the west, and the Cyclades to the southeast. A number of Greece's islands lie just off the coast of Turkey, the country with which Greece has had territorial disputes. With an area of 8,336 km², Crete is the largest of the Greek islands and the fifth largest in the Mediterranean. Three mountain ranges run across the island forming a spine, and create the deep and scenic gorges for which Crete is famous. Home to the Minoan civilization from 3500 BCE, Crete was also one of the major birthplaces of the Ancient Greek civilization which became centred around the modern day capital of Athens. The Olympic Games, which started in Ancient Greece over 2,500 years ago are set to return to Athens in 2004.

▲ A crowded pedestrian crossing in the bustling city of Athens. As a result of thousands of people migrating from the countryside to the capital city of Greece, Athens has a high population density and suffers badly from heavy air pollution.

▼ The remains of hundreds of Ancient Greek buildings can be found throughout Greece. This theatre at Epidaurus once held around 2,000 spectators.

EASTERN EUROPE

astern Europe stretches westwards from the eastern part of the Russian Federation, bordered by the Ural Mountains, to the Baltic states of Latvia, Lithuania and Estonia in the north of Europe, and the countries of Belarus, Ukraine, Moldavia, Romania and Bulgaria to the south. Two seas provide vital trading links for the region: the Baltic Sea to the west and the Black Sea to the south. While mountain chains exist in parts, much of eastern Europe is part of the Great European Plain which extends deep into western Russia. Although the soil is poor in some parts of the plain, in other regions it is fertile enough to support extensive cereal crop farming especially in the Ukraine and western Russia. All the countries of this region were, until the late 1980s, either part of the former Soviet Union or a member of the communist power bloc of countries controlled by that nation. Most of the countries of eastern Europe are seeking to modernize their industry to compete with the countries of western Europe and closer ties between both halves of the continent are being forged. The Baltic states of Latvia, Lithuania and Estonia will join the European Union in 2004. Bulgaria and Romania hope to join in 2007.

▼ St Basil's Cathedral stands in Red Square in the centre of Moscow, the capital of the Russian Federation. Completed in 1679, the church was built to commemorate the military conquests of the Russian Tsar known as Ivan the Terrible.

▼ Transylvania, in Romania, consists of a high plateau surrounded by mountains. The region is extensively farmed and contains reserves of minerals such as coal, silver and gold.

Novaya Zemlya

Barents Sea

Ural Mountains

Pechora

Kola Peninsula

White Sea

NorthernDvina

FINLAND

Lake Onega

Lake Ladoga

RUSSIAN

FEDERATION

Kama

■ TALLINN
ESTONIA

Volga

LATVIA
RIGA ■

MOSCOW ■

LITHUANIA
Russ. Fed.

■ VILNIUS

Volga

■ MINSK

Ural

BELARUS

POLAND

Don

KIEV ■

Dnister

UKRAINE

SLOVAKIA

Carpathians

HUNGARY

MOLDOVA
■ CHISINĂU

Dnieper

Sea of Azov

Caspian Sea

ROMANIA

CRIMEA

ELBRUS
△5642M

BUCHAREST ■

Danube

Black Sea

Caucasus

SERBIA & MONTENEGRO

BULGARIA

■ SOFIA

MACEDONIA

TURKEY

GREECE

0		400		800 km
0	200		400	miles

ESTONIA

Dense forests, low hills and a lengthy coastline are key features of the smallest and most northerly of the three Baltic states.

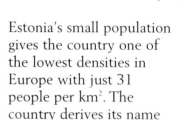

Area: 45,227 km²
Population: 1,377,000
Capital: Tallinn (404,000)
Major languages spoken: Estonian, Russian
Main religions: Non-religious (over 60%), Lutheran, Estonian Orthodox
Currency: kroon
Main exports: chemicals and mineral fuels, food products, textiles and clothing, wood and paper
Type of government: republic; democracy

▲ Tallinn dates back to the 13th century when crusading knights built a castle on the site. The city has developed and retained many charming historic buildings which have survived fire and wars. Tallinn is visited by several hundred thousand foreign tourists every year.

Estonia borders its Baltic state neighbour of Latvia to the south and the Russian Federation to the east. It faces the Baltic Sea to the west and an arm of the Baltic called the Gulf of Finland to the north. Estonia is a low-lying country with two-thirds of its land below 50 m in elevation. Its land is crossed by around 7,000 streams and rivers as well as more than 1,000 lakes, which together make up around five per cent of the country's area. Lake Peipus is Estonia's largest lake. It forms much of the Estonian border with Russia and is Europe's fifth largest freshwater lake. A further ten per cent of Estonian territory comes in the form of islands lying a short distance off its Baltic coastline. The two largest islands are Saaremaa, where livestock raising is the main activity, and Hiiumaa on which most of its workforce, many of whom are of Swedish origin, fish for a living. Trees cover around 45 per cent of the country and provide habitats for many creatures, as well as the raw materials for Estonia's large timber, furniture-making and paper industries. Metalworking, engineering and the mining and processing of oil shale into fuels and chemicals are the country's chief industries.

Estonia's small population gives the country one of the lowest densities in Europe with just 31 people per km². The country derives its name from a people called the Ests who settled in the region around 2,000 years ago. Around two-thirds of the population are native Estonians whose language and descent are closely related to the Finns. Russians form the largest minority group comprising 28 per cent of the population. Seven out of ten Estonians live in major towns and cities such as the capital, Tallinn, the industrial city of Narva and Pärnu, a popular summer holiday resort with a warmer climate than most of the country.

► A sailing boat in the choppy waters of the Bay of Tallinn. The waterfront of Estonia's capital city is in the background.

LATVIA

Latvia is the most industrialized of the Baltic states. A flat, wooded and marshy country, it uses its coastline for trade and for fishing.

Area: 64,610 km²
Population: 2,375,000
Capital: Riga (783,000)
Major languages spoken: Latvian, Russian
Main religions: Non-religious (about 60%), Lutheran, Roman Catholic
Currency: lat
Main exports: timber and paper products, textiles, food and agricultural products, machinery
Type of government: republic; democracy

▼ Lying on the southern shore of the Bay of Riga, the city of Riga is Latvia's major port and home to around a third of the entire country's population.

Latvia is a low-lying country with 98 per cent of its territory below 200 m in elevation. It borders Belarus and the Russian Federation to the east, and a large part of its coast curves round to form much of the Gulf of Riga. Sheltered from the Baltic by the large Estonian island of Saaremaa, the Bay of Riga provides warm water harbours including Liepája, Ventspils and the country's largest port and capital city, Riga. Latvia has thousands of small rivers and streams, only 17 of which are longer than 90 km. The longest is the Daugavapils which begins its life in northwestern Russia and flows through Latvia emptying into the Gulf of Riga. Frozen from December to April and with a series of rapids and shallows, the river is not navigable by large shipping. It is, however, used to provide hydro-electricity and to float timber to transport it from

Latvia's wooded interior to the ports on its coast. Over half of Latvia's forests consists of pine woods while forests of oak are also common. Trees cover around 40 per cent of the country's land and contribute to a sizeable timber industry. Apart from peat from the bogs which cover almost one-tenth of the country, and limestone and dolomite rocks for building, Latvia has few natural resources. It is reliant on the Russian Federation for imports of oil and other fuels although oil has recently been discovered in the east of the country. Dairy and livestock farming occupy many Latvians in rural areas while three-quarters of its people live in towns and cities. Around 57 per cent of the population are Latvians, with Russians forming a large minority of over 30 per cent. Smaller minorities of Ukrainians, Belarussians and Poles exist.

INDEPENDENCE AND GOVERNMENT

Latvia has been ruled by foreign powers including Sweden and, later, Poland, for most of its history. In the 18th century, the country was absorbed into the large Russian Empire of Peter the Great. It seized independence in 1919 and remained so until the Soviet Union took control after World War II. Since independence in 1991, the country has restored the 1922 constitution, and the government is headed by a president elected by the Saeima, a 100-member parliament elected by free vote for terms of four years. Latvia is to join the European Union in 2004.

LITHUANIA

The most southerly of the Baltic states, Lithuania has a short west facing coastline. Most of its people work in heavy industry or farming.

Area: 64,610 km²
Population: 3,484,000
Capital: Vilnius (580,000)
Major languages spoken: Lithuanian, Russian
Main religion: Roman Catholic
Currency: litas
Main exports: textiles, chemicals, mineral products, machinery
Type of government: republic; democracy

▼ Lithuanians pray in front of the altar of a church containing an icon of the Virgin Mary. Around 72 per cent of Lithuanians are Roman Catholic.

Lithuania borders Latvia to the north, Belarus to the south and east, and Poland to the southwest. Its land is mainly a series of plains and low hills dotted with many lakes and crossed by over 20 rivers. The largest river, the Neman, is around 937 km long and drains much of the country. Lithuania's short coastline with the Baltic is the location of much of the world's amber, the fossilized resin from prehistoric trees used in jewellery. It is also the site of the Courland Spit, a 95 km long bank of sand dunes stretching south from the port of Klaipeda and enclosing the Courland Lagoon. Over a quarter of the country is forested and it has five national parks and four national wildlife reserves. Lithuania was a powerful independent state 700 years ago but from the 16th century onwards it became part

of Poland and, later, Russia. It declared independence in 1918 only to become occupied by the Soviet Union from 1944 until 1991 when it again achieved independence. Native Lithuanians comprise 82 per cent of the population. Poles and Russians (around seven per cent each) make up the largest minorities.

LATVIA

Siauliai

Klaipeda

Penevezys

Baltic Sea

LITHUANIA

Courland Lagoon

Neman

Kaunus

RUSSIAN FEDERATION

VILNIUS ■

Alytus

POLAND

BELARUS

BELARUS

A flat, low-lying nation with many lakes in the north and large marshlands in the south, Belarus became independent from the former Soviet Union in 1991.

Area: 207,546 km²
Population: 10,236,000
Capital: Minsk (1,719,000)
Major languages spoken: Belarusian, Russian
Main religions: non-religious (nearly 50%), Belarusian Orthodox, Russian Orthodox
Currency: Belarusian rouble
Main exports: trucks and tyres, diesel fuel, synthetic fibres, refrigerators, fertilizer, milk and dairy products
Type of government: republic; dictatorship

The mountain range which runs diagonally through Belarus forms a ridge which divides the country into two areas of lowlands. The northern area has a number of gentle hills and many of the country's 11,000 small lakes. South of the ridge lies a large marshy plain drained by the River Pripet and its tributaries. This region comprises the largest area of un-reclaimed marshland in Europe. To the west, where Belarus borders Poland, lies the Belovezhskaya Forest. Much of this forest is protected to create Europe's largest nature reserve, the home of the otherwise rare Wisent or European bison.

DEVASTATED TWICE

Over two million Belarusian people lost their lives during World War II which devastated many of its towns and cities. In 1986, the Chernobyl nuclear plant, in neighbouring Ukraine, exploded and 70 per cent of the radioactive fallout landed on Belarus territory. Close to three million people were seriously affected and soil, streams and rivers were contaminated. Around 15 per cent of the country's forests and 20 per cent of its farmland remains too radioactive for their products to be used. The cost of cleaning up the region, rehousing people and dealing with the long-term effects of the world's biggest nuclear accident has put severe strain on the country's health service and economy despite aid from other nations and charities.

▼ A monument overlooks part of the Belarusian city of Minsk. The nation's largest settlement, almost all of Minsk was reconstructed from 1944 onwards. The city has barely changed since independence.

A DECLINING ECONOMY

An estimated one-fifth of the country's workforce is engaged in agriculture but industry contributes more to the economy. When part of the former Soviet Union, many heavy industrial factories and processing plants were built in Belarus to process the raw materials extracted from other parts of the Soviet Union, especially the Ukraine. As an independent nation and one with relatively few mineral resources, Belarus has struggled since independence. It has largely kept its old Soviet-style economy and has privatized or modernized very little of its industry to make it more competitive in the world market. As a result, production has declined and the country faces huge economic problems. Its main industrial centre is in and around the capital city, Minsk. There, many products including farm machinery, motor vehicles, machine tools and electrical goods are manufactured and assembled. The country retains close ties with Russia which it relies on for around three-fifths of its imports and almost half of its exports. Russia provides over one billion US dollars in aid, through relief from debts and cheap supplies of oil and gas.

UKRAINE

Bordering the Black Sea to the south, the Ukraine is one of the most economically powerful of the former Soviet states.

Area: 603,700 km²
Population: 48,416,000
Capital: Kiev (2,750,000)
Major languages spoken: Ukrainian, Russian
Main religions: non-religious (about 55%), Ukrainian Orthodox (Russian Orthodox), Ukrainian Orthodox (independent)
Currency: hryvnia
Principal exports: ferrous metals, machinery, minerals, chemicals
Type of government: republic; partial democracy

▼ A combine harvester gathers and processes a cereal crop in the Ukraine. The country is one of the world's leading producers of cereals such as wheat and is the largest producer of sugar beets.

The Ukraine is the second largest of the former states of the Soviet Union, second only in land area and population to the Russian Federation. Most of the Ukraine consists of fertile plains, known as steppes, and plateaus. Much of the northern part of the country is covered in dense forests largely consisting of pine, oak and spruce. Mountains are found only to the west of the country and in the Crimean peninsula which juts out into the Black Sea. The Ukraine has a long shoreline with the Black Sea and also borders the Sea of Azov which measures approximately 37,555 km². Shallow and with low salt levels due to the large number of rivers which deposit freshwater, the Sea of Azov is almost entirely landlocked. It has just one marine opening to the south connecting it with the Black Sea. The Ukraine generally has a continental climate with warm summers and cold winters, especially in the east of the country. The Crimean coastline, however, has a Mediterranean climate with hotter summers. The levels of rainfall vary greatly depending on the region, with more rain in the north and west of the country, and heavy snowfalls in the country's mountainous areas.

RICH IN MINERALS

An estimated five per cent of the entire world's mineral reserves are found within the Ukraine. The country has the world's largest reserves of manganese and titanium and the third largest iron ore reserves. In 2000, the Ukraine produced over 26 million tonnes of iron ore. Despite declining dramatically since independence, the metals industry remains the Ukraine's most important single industrial area. It contributes approximately one-fifth of its GDP and one quarter of all its exports. The country has giant coal reserves, the largest of which are situated to the east around the city of Donets'k. However, it has only small oil and gas reserves and has to import over four-fifths of these fuels for its energy needs.

EASTERN EUROPE'S CEREAL GIANT

The Ukraine has extremely rich soil and its millions of hectares of flat land allow a range of cereal crops to be grown in bulk. Formerly known as 'the breadbasket of the Soviet Union', the Ukraine has traditionally produced a huge surplus of agricultural and food products which it exported to other parts of the former Soviet Union, or to countries in eastern Europe. In the late 1980s, the Ukraine contributed over a quarter of the entire Soviet Union's agricultural output. However, since independence farm

production has plummeted to under half of 1991 levels. Some of the Ukraine's farmland was contaminated by the radioactive fallout from the 1986 nuclear plant disaster at Chernobyl. Industries linked to agriculture, such as producing factory machinery and processing foods, tend to be outdated and struggle to keep up with demand. As a result, there are often shortages of certain basic foods. A number of foreign companies have started operations within the Ukraine looking to modernize parts of its industry and utilize its trained and educated workforce. Since independence in 1990, the population, 73 per cent of which are of Ukrainian descent with 22 per cent comprising Russians, have seen the gap between rich and poor increase greatly.

▲ Ukrainian coal miners work at the pit face. The Ukraine has large coal reserves, enough to sustain production at the current rate for at least 300 years.

MOLDOVA

Moldova is the smallest and most densely populated of the former Soviet republics. The country is landlocked and is one of the poorest nations in Europe.

Area: 33,700 km²
Population: 4,380,000
Capital: Chisinau (655,000)
Major languages spoken: Romanian (Moldovan), Russian, Ukrainian, Gagauz
Main religions: non-religious (over 45%), Romanian (Moldovan) Orthodox, Russian Orthodox
Currency: Moldovan leu
Principal exports: food and agricultural goods, machinery, textiles, metals
Type of government: republic; partial democracy

Moldova is surrounded on three sides by the Ukraine, while to the west it shares a border with Romania. The country is low-lying with an average elevation of only 140 m, but much of its land is hilly. Hundreds of short streams and rivers cross the land, the longest being the Dneister which flows through the east of Moldova and empties into the Black Sea in the Ukraine.

A FARMING NATION

Over seven-tenths of Moldova's land is covered in a rich black soil which can be farmed. Wheat, tobacco, maize and sunflower seeds are among the main crops, while grapes tend to be grown in the south of the country. Moldova's wine-making industry is one of the few industries which has flourished since the country gained independence in 1991. Agriculture is the leading employer of Moldova, providing work for 39 per cent of the country's workforce and generating many of its exports. Food processing accounts for 42 per cent of the country's industrial output. With only limited mineral resources and poor transport links, the country's economy has struggled and Moldavians are among the poorest people in Europe. Moldova was once a part of Romania and almost two-thirds of its people are of either Moldavian or Romanian descent. Two large minorities – Ukrainians and Russians – make up a further quarter of the population. Many of the Russians and Ukrainians live east of the River Dniester in an autonomous republic within Moldova.

▲ A church wedding takes place in the country's capital city of Chisinau. Many Moldavians are followers of the Romanian Orthodox Church.

► Moldavians harvest potatoes in a small field. Most agriculture in Moldova is farmed by co-operatives of people working together.

ROMANIA

Achieving independence in 1878, Romania is a country with a Black Sea coastline. Its land is a mixture of mountains and lowlands.

Area: 237,500 km²
Population: 21,698,000
Capital: Bucharest (1,922,000)
Major languages spoken: Romanian, Hungarian
Main religion: Romanian Orthodox
Currency: leu
Main exports: textiles, mineral products, chemicals, machinery, footwear
Type of government: republic; democracy

Romania borders Hungary to the northwest, the Ukraine to the north, Moldova to the east, Bulgaria to the south and Serbia & Montenegro to the west. It also has a strategically important coastline on the Black Sea. The Danube river flows along most of the border with Bulgaria, providing an important transport route for inland shipping. The Danube forms a large delta as it empties into the Black Sea.

MOUNTAINS, FORESTS AND FARMING

Much of north and central Romania is covered by two large mountain ranges. Running east to west are the Transylvanian Alps which include the country's highest point, the 2,544 m high Mt Moldoveanu. North of these mountains is a large, hilly plateau which is bordered to the north and east by the Carpathian Mountains. Forests cover over a quarter of the country and provide home for a wide range of wild animals, including wolves, deer, bear, wild boar and lynx. Forty-five per cent of Romania's land is suitable for agriculture.

NATURAL RESOURCES

Most of the raw materials for Romania's industries are imported and its once-important oil and natural gas reserves are fast dwindling. Romania's major natural resources are its fertile soils and its fast-moving rivers which are harnessed for hydro-electricity generation. The country also has deposits of lead, zinc and sulphur. Much of Romania's industrial and agricultural exports are transported out of the country's biggest port called Constanta. Lying in the northeast, the city of Iasi has a population of over 320,000 making it Romania's second city after Bucharest, the capital.

▼ A large portion of Bucharest was demolished in the 1980s to build the huge Palace of the People (now Parliament Palace). Even though parts of the building remain incomplete, it is the second largest administrative building in the world behind the United States' Pentagon.

BULGARIA

A mountainous country bordering the Black Sea in southeastern Europe, Bulgaria has had a long and colourful history.

Area: 110,993 km²
Population: 7,974,000
Capital: Sofia (1,096,000)
Major languages spoken: Bulgarian, Turkish
Main religions: non-religious (over 40%), Bulgarian Orthodox, Sunni Islam
Currency: lev
Principal exports: chemicals and plastics, food, beverages and tobacco, textiles
Type of government: republic; democracy

Bulgaria is a country with varied scenery. Plateaus, plains, hills and mountains are all found in its territory. The two largest mountain ranges are the Balkan Mountains, which run west to east through the centre of the country, and the Rhodope Mountains to the southwest. Bulgaria's climate is temperate with marked differences between the four seasons. To the south and around the Black Sea, the temperatures are milder in winter and warmer than average in summer, reaching a daily average of 29°C in July and August.

A COUNTRY IN TRANSITION

Bulgaria was ruled by the Turkish Ottoman Empire from the late 14th century until 1878 before becoming fully independent in 1908. A communist ally of the former Soviet Union until 1990, the country has since become a multi-party democracy. Its economy is recovering after major crises in 1995, 1997 and 1999, and Bulgaria is still readjusting to economic independence which has meant that cheap supplies of high quality coal, oil and iron from the Soviet Union are no longer available. Farming and industry are in the process of being reorganized to become more competitive and tourism is being promoted. Eighty-four per cent of the country's population are Bulgars – ethnic Bulgarians – while ten per cent are of Turkish origin. There are also smaller minority groups, including Macedonians and Roma peoples. Seventy per cent of people live in towns and cities.

▲ There are an estimated 1,000 wolves living in the wild in remote parts of Bulgaria. Other large mammals found in the country include wildcats, elks and bears.

▶ Bulgaria's National Assembly building lies in the centre of its capital city of Sofia. It was built in three stages between 1884 and 1928 from plans by the Austrian architect, Yovanovich.

RUSSIA

The world's largest nation, the Russian Federation bestrides two continents and eleven time zones. Its people are undergoing great change to their way of life.

Area: 17,075,400 km²
Population: 146,934,000
Capital: Moscow
(9,107,000)
Major languages spoken:
Russian, Tatar, Ukrainian, Chuvash, Bashkir, Chechen, Mordovinian
Main religions: non-religious (over 70%), Russian Orthodox, Sunni Islam
Currency: rouble
Main exports: fuels and lubricants, ferrous and non-ferrous metals, machinery and transport equipment, chemicals, precious metals, timber and forestry products
Type of government: republic; partial democracy

Russia is a gigantic nation extending almost 10,000 km west to east and more than 4,000 km north to south at its greatest extent. Vast plains cover much of Russia's territory while mountain ranges are found mainly in the eastern and southern regions. The Ural Mountains running north to south divide western, European Russia from eastern, Asian Russia. Much of Russia experiences a continental climate although there is great variation both in climate and vegetation in such a vast country with large temperate regions, giant forests and vast tracts of icy wastes to the north. The country has large areas of fertile farmlands and a great wealth of mineral resources. It is one of the world's leading producers of fossil fuels and a wide range of metals. The largest and most powerful republic of the former Soviet Union, Russia has had to deal with a number of political and economic problems since its emergence in 1991.

▲ With an area of 73,000 m², the giant Red Square is the focal point of the city of Moscow. On its west side lies the tomb of the communist leader, Lenin, in front of which a changing of the guard ceremony is occurring.

WESTERN RUSSIA

The most economically powerful part of the Russian Federation, western Russia is the home of the country's largest cities and most of its productive farmland.

▲ The ornate marble halls of a Moscow underground railway station. The Moscow Metro was built in the 1930s and carries over six million passengers every day.

Western Russia borders Kazakhstan, Georgia and Azerbaijan to the south and has coastlines with both the Caspian and Black seas. To the west, the country borders Ukraine, Belarus, Latvia, Lithuania and Finland and, to the far north, Norway. Its territory includes the enclave of Kalingrad which is separated from the rest of Russia by Lithuania and Latvia. Western Russia is mostly part of the Great European Plain which increases in width eastwards.

THE KOLA PENINSULA AND BARENTS SEA

The highest elevations of western Russia are found in the Caucasus in the southwest and in the Kola Peninsula which faces the Barents Sea to the east. The Barents Sea is a shallow arm of the Arctic Ocean and is subject to freezing during winter. However, warm waters from the Gulf Stream keep a coastal shipping lane open throughout the year. Western Russia's two largest islands, which form the archipelago called Novaya Zemlya, are found in the Barents Sea. Perched on the Kola Peninsula is the strategically important port of Murmansk. A major Russian naval base, the city also has fishing, ship-building and marine research facilities.

THE URAL MOUNTAINS

The Great European Plain extends east until it reaches the Ural Mountains. Formed by continental drift which forced Siberia and Europe together, the Urals are around 250 million years old. Erosion has worn these mountains down so that they now have an average elevation of 600 m. The Urals are, however, rich in important minerals including coal, iron ore, platinum, lead, chromium and copper. West of the southern Urals, a number of industrial cities including Perm and Ufa have sprung up through extracting and processing these minerals and developing manufacturing industries.

THE FERTILE TRIANGLE

The vast majority of Russia's farmland lies in western Russia in what is called the fertile triangle. The fertile triangle extends from the Black Sea to the Baltic along Russia's western borders and stretches from the area of the city of St Petersburg southeast to the southern Ural Mountains. In the fertile triangle, vast quantities of

▼ The Kremlin was founded as a fortress within the city of Moscow in 1156. Rebuilt on several occasions it is now used as the central seat of the Russian government.

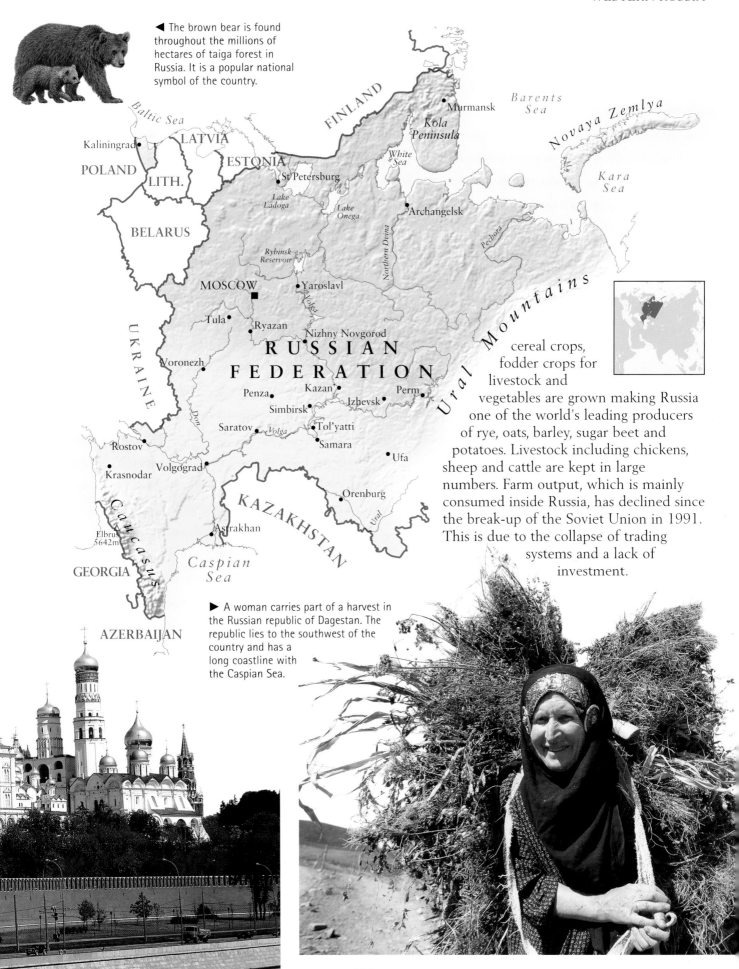

◀ The brown bear is found throughout the millions of hectares of taiga forest in Russia. It is a popular national symbol of the country.

cereal crops, fodder crops for livestock and vegetables are grown making Russia one of the world's leading producers of rye, oats, barley, sugar beet and potatoes. Livestock including chickens, sheep and cattle are kept in large numbers. Farm output, which is mainly consumed inside Russia, has declined since the break-up of the Soviet Union in 1991. This is due to the collapse of trading systems and a lack of investment.

▶ A woman carries part of a harvest in the Russian republic of Dagestan. The republic lies to the southwest of the country and has a long coastline with the Caspian Sea.

▲ A large area of apartment buildings offers accommodation for some of Moscow's nine million inhabitants. Apart from being Russia's largest and most politically dominant city, Moscow is also the spiritual centre of the Russian Orthodox Church.

TWIN CITIES OF POWER

Russia has a long history of settlement and has been a powerful force in Europe and Asia for hundreds of years. Two cities have been its capital and centre during this period – Moscow and St Petersburg. The first Russian leader to use the title of Emperor was Peter the Great who founded the city of St Petersburg in the early 18th century. The city became the home of the Tsars – the Russian royal family – from 1713 onwards. Its position connected to the Baltic Sea by the Gulf of Finland, enabled St Petersburg to rise as a trading power and become a major cultural centre of eastern Europe. Today, St Petersburg is Russia's second largest city, the home of many large industries especially in engineering, chemicals and ship-building, and its largest seaport. A system of rivers and artificial inland waterways links St Petersburg south to the Caspian Sea and also to the White Sea and Volga river.

Moscow was founded as a city in 1138 and was the capital of Russia prior to the establishment of St Petersburg. It became the capital again in 1918 after communist forces toppled the Tsar and came to power. For 70 years, Moscow was the capital city of the former Soviet Union. During this period its industry boomed and it produced around one-sixth of the entire Soviet Union's industrial output. Moscow has sprawled into a giant city and is the home of both the leader of the country, the President, and the highest legislative body, the Federal Assembly.

Over three-quarters of Russia's population live in Moscow, St Petersburg and other urban areas found in western Russia.

▼ Nizhniy Novgorod is a major transport terminus and industrial centre producing cars, aircraft and electrical goods. It lies on the River Volga. The Volga is navigable along almost all of its 3,531 km length and is the longest river in Europe.

EASTERN RUSSIA

Russia, east of the Ural Mountains, is a sparsely populated land of mountains, rivers and icy wastes where huge resources remain largely untapped.

▲ A train on the Trans-Siberian railway passes by Lake Baikal. The lake holds 85 per cent of all of Russia's lake water and around a fifth of the entire world's. The Trans-Siberian railway runs a huge distance of 9,297 km from Moscow to Vladivostok on eastern Russia's Pacific coast. In the late 1990s, the entire trip took six days.

East of the Ural Mountains, Russia stretches over 5,000 km eastwards to a long coastline with the Pacific Ocean. Eastern Russia borders three nations to the south: Kazakhstan, Mongolia and China. Most of the Russian territory near Mongolia and China is part of a series of mountain ranges including the Yablonovyy and Stavonoy ranges.

Geographically, eastern Russia is often divided into four broad regions: the southern mountain ranges mentioned above, the West Siberian Plain, the Central Siberian Plateau and the Russian Far East. Each of these regions is vast, has large tracts of barely inhabited territory and much variation in rock formations, landscape and vegetation.

THE SIBERIAN PLAIN

To the east of the Urals is the vast West Siberian Plain. This area stretches about 1,900 km from west to east, and about 2,400 km from north to south. It covers an area of more than 2.5 million km². Over half of the plain lies at elevations below 100 m and only in the south does the land rise above 250 m. Much of the plain is poorly drained and consists of some of the world's largest swamps and flood plains. Important cities include Omsk and Chelyabinsk which is sited near the Urals in a rich coal-mining region. The long Yenisey river flows broadly south to north, a distance of 3,540 km where it completes its journey, discharging over 19 million litres of water per second. Together with its tributary, the Angara, the two rivers flow 5,540 km. The valley it has formed acts as a rough dividing line between the West Siberian Plain and the Central Siberian Plateau.

▲ Eastern Russia has vast, untapped oil reserves but oil exploitation of much of the region is beset with problems of transportation and the hostile climate.

▼ A camp of Koryak nomads is pitched amidst the icy tundra of northeast Russia. The Koryak continue traditional ways of living, mainly herding reindeer and hunting for furs. Koryak peoples who live on the coast fish, especially for crab.

THE CENTRAL SIBERIAN PLATEAU AND FAR EASTERN RUSSIA

The Central Siberian Plateau is, in fact, several plateaus lying between 300 and 700 m in elevation. Mountains border the plateaus to the south and much of the east. The region is rich in mainly untapped mineral resources.

Far Eastern Russia has a complex geography consisting of many mountain ranges formed in different ways. A major feature of the region is the Kamchatka Peninsula which juts southwards into the Sea of Okhotsk, itself an arm of the Pacific Ocean. The peninsula has many volcanic peaks, some of which are still active. The highest is the 4,750 m high Kliuchevskoi volcano, the highest point in the Russian

Far East. Along with the Caucasus in the southwest of Russia, Kamchatka is one of Russia's main areas of earthquake activity. The volcanic chain continues from the southern tip of Kamchatka through the Kuril Islands. This island chain extends for approximately 1,200 km ending close to Hokkaido – the northern island of Japan. The islands contain 100 volcanoes of which around a third are either dormant or active. Some of the southernmost Kuril Islands have their ownership disputed by Japan. Located on the far south of the Far Eastern Russian mainland, the city of Vladivostok is the largest in the region. Founded as a military naval outpost in 1860, Vladivostok now has a population in excess of 620,000. It is an important port and a base for fishing and whaling fleets.

TUNDRA AND TAIGA

Eastern Russia's main zones of vegetation vary with latitude and run from north to south. To the south are steppes, plains of grassland which form eastern Russia's best farmland. The northernmost reaches of Russia, stretching the entire width of the country, consist of tundra. These are largely icy and treeless plains with very cold winters and limited plant life. South of the tundra are large belts of forests called taiga. These are the world's largest forest regions and consist of coniferous trees such as Siberian cedar, fir, pine and larch.

RIVERS AND LAKES

Russia is crossed by over 100,000 rivers; most of the longest are found in the east. The Ob-Irtysh river system, for example, flows a distance of 5,409 km from western China north through Siberia, before emptying into the Arctic Ocean. Approximately 84 per cent of Russia's surface water is located east of the Urals in its rivers and lakes. The largest lake, Lake Baikal, is found in central south Siberia. Measuring 620 km and varying between 15 and 80 km in width, the lake reaches a depth of 1,637 m, making it the world's deepest freshwater lake.

RUSSIA'S PEOPLE

Russia's population is a striking multi-cultural mix in both eastern and western portions of the country. When it was the dominant part of the Soviet Union throughout much of the 20th century, ethnic Russians made up around 50 per cent of its population. Many republics of the Soviet Union containing other ethnic groups started to press for independence during the 1980s. Reforms such as glasnost (openness) and perestroika (restructuring) were introduced by the Soviet Union's leader, Mikhail Gorbachev. They were attempts to modernize the way the country was run and give some of these republics more control. However, by December 1991, the Soviet Union split into 15 independent republics of which the Russian Federation is the largest. Ethnic Russians now comprise 82 per cent of the population but there are large minority groups including over 5 million Tatars – Islamic peoples who descended from the Mongols who invaded Russia over 750 years ago. In total, over 120 different nationalities and ethnic groups are found within the country's borders. Russia's people have faced much change in the past. They are currently witnessing further, enormous and often difficult change to the way their country and businesses are run. Health and other social services are in crisis and crime is rising. Most Russians are having to deal with a drop in their standard of living.

▲ A woman watches a helicopter run by the state airline, Aeroflot, depart from a landing site near her isolated village in the far east of Russia. In many isolated parts of eastern Russia, air transport is the only way to travel outside the local area.

THE CAUCASUS AND ASIA MINOR

A land bridge between Europe and Asia since prehistoric times, the region that includes the Caucasus and Asia Minor has a long and complex history. Wave after wave of armies, traders and settlers have passed through the region which is bounded by three different seas: the Mediterranean, the Black Sea and the Caspian Sea. As a result, there is a large number of different ethnic groups, languages and cultures found in the region. The area's largest and most populous nation is Turkey which straddles the traditional boundaries that separate Asia from Europe. East of Turkey, lie three countries – Georgia, Armenia and Azerbaijan – which sit between the Black Sea and the Caspian Sea. These three nations, all part of the former Soviet Union, are sometimes collectively known after the pair of mountain ranges which dominate their territory, the Caucasus. The land of the Caucasus nations is rugged yet fertile in places. Many of the mountain slopes are covered in coniferous trees while a large number of rivers crosses the land emptying into the Black Sea, the Caspian Sea or the Sea of Asov to the north. Large mineral deposits including oil, natural gas and various metal ores are found throughout the region.

▲ The massive extinct volcano of Mount Ararat straddles the border between Turkey and Armenia and has a diameter of approximately 40 km at its base. The mountain has two peaks, the higher of which lies in Turkey and reaches an elevation of 5,137 m.

GEORGIA

A mountainous country bordering the Black Sea, Georgia was a part of the former Soviet Union until 1991.

Area: 69,492 km²
Population: 4,989,000
Capital: Tbilisi (1,253,000)
Major languages spoken: Georgian, Russian, Armenian
Main religions: non-religious (over 40%), Georgian Orthodox, Sunni Islam
Currency: lari
Principal exports: food products, ferrous metals, textiles, chemicals
Type of government: republic; partial democracy

Georgia borders Turkey, Armenia and Azerbaijan to the south and the Russian Federation to the north. The Caucasus mountains define the country's northern border and are home to its highest point, Mt Shkhara. The southern part of Georgia is crossed by the Lesser Caucasus Mountains. Sandwiched between the two mountain ranges are lower-lying lands including the valley of the country's major river, the Kura. Lower-lying areas also exist to the east and the west of the country. To the west, the region close to the Black Sea was formerly swamps and wetlands but much land has been reclaimed. This region now forms the most productive farmlands of Georgia. The warm moist climate in that area allows citrus fruit, tea, grapes and tobacco to be grown. Further inland, less rain falls and the climate is continental with cold winters. Glaciers and snow cover the upper reaches of most of the Caucasus Mountains. Large woodlands of birch, beech and oak grow over the lower mountain slopes. Almost two-fifths of the country is forested.

A CROSSROADS

Despite its rugged terrain, trade routes through Georgia have been travelled for thousands of years. The country's status as a crossroads resulted in its highly diverse population. Ethnic Georgians comprise around 70 per cent of the population, but there are also around 100 different ethnic groups in the country. Tensions between groups, especially in the Abkhazia region in the northwest of the country which sought independence from Georgia, led to conflict in the 1990s and weakened an economy trying to develop to compete in the world market. Most Georgian people live in poverty although improving transport links, encouraging tourism and exploiting the country's largely untapped oil reserves bring hope of improvement in the quality of their life.

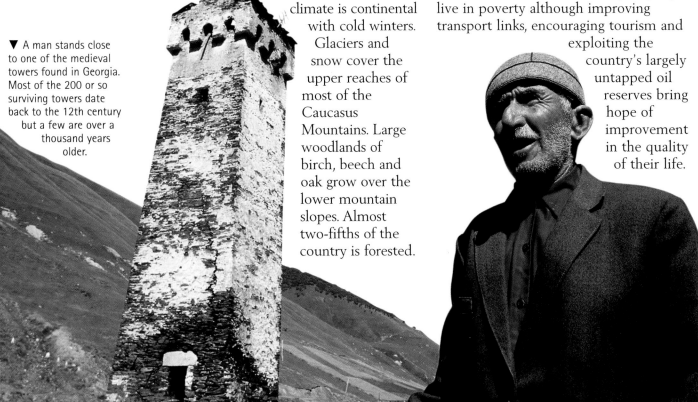

▼ A man stands close to one of the medieval towers found in Georgia. Most of the 200 or so surviving towers date back to the 12th century but a few are over a thousand years older.

ARMENIA

Once the smallest republic of the former Soviet Union, Armenia is a landlocked, mountainous country with an average elevation of around 1,800 m.

Area: 29,800 km²
Population: 3,803,000
Capital: Yerevan (1,250,000)
Major languages spoken: Armenian, Azeri
Main religion: Armenian Apostolic Orthodox, Shia Islam
Currency: dram
Principal exports: jewellery, various machinery and equipment, minerals, textiles
Type of government: republic; partial democracy

▼ Armenian peasants dig in potato fields in northern Armenia. Potatoes, along with wheat, tobacco and other vegetables, are the main crops grown in the country.

Armenia is one of the most rugged countries in the whole of Eurasia with large mountains and steep-sided valleys. Many smaller rivers and streams cross the land and provide the country with hydro-electric power. There are also many waterfalls, river rapids and mountain lakes. Armenia's largest lake, Lake Sevan, lies in the Caucasus Mountains and measures approximately 1,360 km². It holds over 85 per cent of all the standing water found in Armenia. Parts of the country are susceptible to earthquakes; in 1988, one devastated the country's second largest city of Gyumri. Armenia was one of the most industrialized and wealthiest states in the former Soviet Union with a variety of industries, including machine building, chemicals, canned goods and leatherware. Since independence in 1991, Armenia has been in conflict with Azerbaijan over Nagorno Karabakh, an area of Azerbaijan with a largely Armenian population. The cost of war included fuel shortages which damaged many of the country's industries. Armenia's transport and communications links are old and in need of repair and modernization in many places. Its capital city, Yerevan, is one of the oldest cities still in existence with archaeological evidence of settlement for more than 5,000 years. Ethnic Armenians make up more than 90 per cent of the country's population. There are more people of Armenian descent living abroad.

AZERBAIJAN

A mountainous and oil-rich country, Azerbaijan has been beset by economic difficulties and territorial disputes.

Area: 86,600 km²
Population: 7,734,000
Capital: Baku (1,727,000)
Major languages spoken: Azeri, Russian
Main religion: Shia Islam, Sunni Islam
Currency: manat
Principal exports: petroleum and petroleum products, cotton, machinery, food products
Type of government: republic; partial democracy

Azerbaijan is ringed by mountains on almost all sides except to the east where it borders the Caspian Sea. To the north lie the Russian Federation and Georgia, Iran lies to the south and Armenia to the west. Azerbaijan and Armenia's border is complex with enclaves of both nations surrounded by the lands of the other and some territory disputed. The largest disputed area, Nagorno Karabakh, was the subject of violent conflict during the 1990s. The Greater and Lesser Caucasus mountain ranges run through Azerbaijan and the fast-flowing rivers that flow down the mountain slopes are not only harnessed to generate electricity, they are also diverted and used for water reservoirs and irrigation systems. Parts of Azerbaijan, particularly the peaks of the Caucasus Mountains and the extreme southeast of the country, receive heavy rainfall but much of the remainder of the country is warm and dry, receiving less than 300 mm of rain a year. Irrigation enables the farmers to grow cereal crops, tobacco, grapes and cotton. Agriculture remains the biggest employer in the country.

Unlike its Caucasus neighbours, the people of Azerbaijan are mostly Muslims. They are descended from peoples who conquered the territory more than 900 years ago. The country not only has large natural gas reserves but also great deposits of oil.

▲ Azerbaijan fishermen bring in their catch from the Caspian Sea. In 2001, 8,488 tonnes of fish were caught in the Caspian.

▼ A century ago, Azerbaijan was the world's leading producer of oil but the industry declined as oil was discovered in many other places in the world.

TURKEY

A large country with extensive mountains and long coastlines, Turkey straddles the point where southern Europe and Asia meet and has a long history.

Area: 779,452 km²
Population: 67,804,000
Capital: Ankara (3,550,000)
Major languages spoken: Turkish, Kurdish
Main religion: Sunni Islam
Currency: Turkish lira
Principal exports: textiles and clothing, iron and steel, electrical and electronic machinery, fruit
Type of government: republic; partial democracy

Geographically, Turkey's territory is found in both Asia and Europe. Although 97 per cent of its land lies in Asia and is known as Anatolia or Asia Minor, the country is generally accepted as part of Europe, takes part in many European organizations and has applied to join the European Union. Turkey is a country of rugged highland areas with a large central plateau. Four-fifths of the country lies over 500 m in elevation and the key lowland areas are found on the coasts. Most of Turkey is part of the great Alpine-Himalayan mountain belt and several large ranges run east to west through the country. A highland area runs along the Black Sea coastline and the Taurus Mountains are found in the south of the country. Mostly composed of limestone, these mountains contain many caves, potholes and underground streams. The far east of Turkey is home to both the country's highest point, Mount Ararat, and its largest lake, Lake Van, with an area of 3,713 km². Turkey lies on a major fault line and often experiences severe earthquakes.

SURROUNDED BY SEAS

Nearly all of Turkey's northern border is a 1,595 km long coastline with the Black Sea. To the south and the west of Turkey are the Mediterranean and Aegean seas. Its Aegean coastline is heavily indented and contains many of the country's 159 islands. To the northwest of the country lies the Sea of Marmara which is connected to both the Black Sea and the Aegean through two narrow straits. The Sea of Marmara separates the European part of Turkey from the Asian part. The sea has an area of 11,140 km².

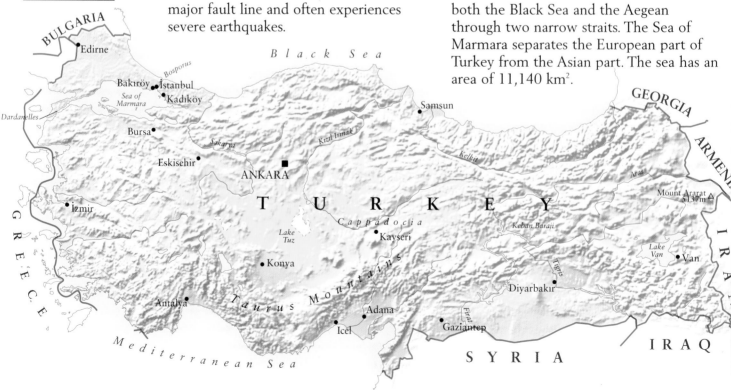

◄ Hagia Sophia lies in Turkey's most populous city, Istanbul. Completed in the 6th century, the church is one of the finest artefacts from the Byzantine civilization. Once known as Constantinople, Istanbul served as the capital of both the Byzantine and Ottoman empires in the past.

fruits and nuts. Almost half of the workforce is engaged in farming, and Turkey is self-sufficient in many basic foods. Turkey is also relatively rich in mineral deposits including coal, oil and a number of metals. Thirty-eight per cent of the country's electricity is generated by hydro-electric power, particularly from fast-flowing rivers such as the Tigris.

▲ Turkish men enjoy their tea drinking in the Youth Park in the city of Ankara. The country's second largest city, Ankara became its capital when Turkey was formed in 1923.

WHERE WEST MEETS EAST

Turkey's strategic location, at the point where the three continents of Africa, Asia and Europe are closest, has meant that the region has been travelled and settled since ancient times. Its land has seen the birth of many civilizations including the Ancient Hittites, Persians, Romans and Arabs. Turks today are descended from these and other peoples, and make up the majority of the population with the largest minority being Kurdish peoples.

▼ The stepped terraces of Pammukale in southwest Turkey attract many visitors who bathe in their hot waters. The limestone terraces have been formed over thousands of years from calcium-rich springs.

CLIMATE AND COUNTRY

Turkey has a range of climates based largely on altitude and closeness to the sea. The land bordering the Black Sea has hot summers and mild winters with high humidity and relatively heavy rainfall. In the Mediterranean and Aegean regions, the climate is equally warm but drier with most rainfall in winter. Further inland, the country experiences a dry, continental climate. The range of climates allows a variety of crops to be grown including cereals, cotton, tobacco,

CYPRUS

The third largest island in the Mediterranean, Cyprus is situated 80 km south of the Turkish coast. The country is currently divided into Greek and Turkish sectors.

CYPRUS

Area: 9,251 km², of which 3,355 km² are in the Turkish-controlled zone
Population: 786,000, including Turkish 'settlers' in the north
Capital: Nicosia (235,000)
Major languages spoken: Greek, Turkish
Main religions: Greek Orthodox, Sunni Islam
Currency: Cyprus pound; Turkish currency is used in the Turkish Cypriot area
Principal exports: Re-exported cigarettes and electronic equipment, ship's stores, clothing, potatoes
Type of government: republic; democracy

▼ This orchard is located in the Troodos Mountains in the southwest of Cyprus. The island's warm climate allows a large range of fruits to be grown.

Cyprus consists of a central plain with mountains to the south and north of the island. The largest mountain chain, the Troodos Mountains, covers much of the southwest of the island. Much of Cyprus's forests have been cleared and scrub grass and bushes are the most common vegetation. The island has no permanent rivers. Pasture lands used to graze sheep, goats and pigs cover one-tenth of the land area. The main crops grown include wheat, potatoes, tobacco and grapes which are used in Cyprus's wine-making industry. The island enjoys a warm Mediterranean climate with an average annual temperature of 20.5°C. Average annual rainfall is less than 500 mm although parts of the Troodos Mountains can receive 1,050 mm.

A DIVIDED ISLAND

Cyprus has been a colony of a number of nations including Greece, Egypt and the Ottoman Empire. Greek Cypriots make up about 78 per cent of the population with almost all of the remainder of Turkish descent. Cyprus became independent from the United Kingdom in 1960 but, in 1974, Turkey invaded the island and gained control of its northern third. It later established the Turkish Republic of Northern Cyprus, but this has not been recognized by the rest of the world. Cyprus has remained divided with a permanent United Nations peacekeeping force based there. Although the Turkish territory contained most of Cyprus's industrial centres, it is the south of the island which has improved its economy, particularly through tourism with around 2.7 million visitors arriving in 2000.

ASIA

ASIA

Covering an area of 44.6 million km², Asia is the world's largest continent. It is geologically active with many of the world's most active volcanoes within its territory, particularly to the east where the continent faces the Pacific Ocean. Asia is also home to many of the planet's physical extremes, including the lowest point, the Dead Sea in Jordan, and the highest point, Mount Everest in the Himalayas. Central Asia is considerably more mountainous than other continents with the Himalayas just one of many ranges. To the south, the most notable features are several major peninsulas: the Arabian Peninsula to the west, the Indian subcontinent, and the Indochina peninsula which extends into the South China Sea, and the large island archipelagos found in Southeast Asia. Every form of climate and vegetation zone is present in this continent, from icy tundra and large arid deserts to tropical rainforests and highly fertile plains and river valleys. Around 16 per cent of Asia is covered in forest with the largest to be found in Siberia, China and southeast Asia. Although parts of Tibet, Siberia and a region of Saudi Arabia are virtually unpopulated, the continent is also home to the world's two most populous nations – China and India. Approximately one-third of the entire world population is found within their borders. Although the people in Asia's most developed nations, such as Japan, enjoy a high standard of living, many are desperately poor.

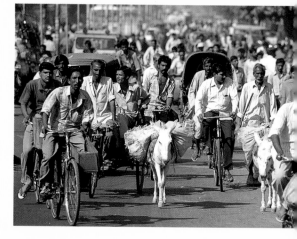

▲ Bicycles and beasts of burden constitute most of the traffic in this busy street in the northern Indian city of Jaipur.

▼ Nomadic peoples herd horses in the isolated countryside of Mongolia. Nomadic peoples travelling with herds of livestock comprise just over 40 per cent of Mongolia's population.

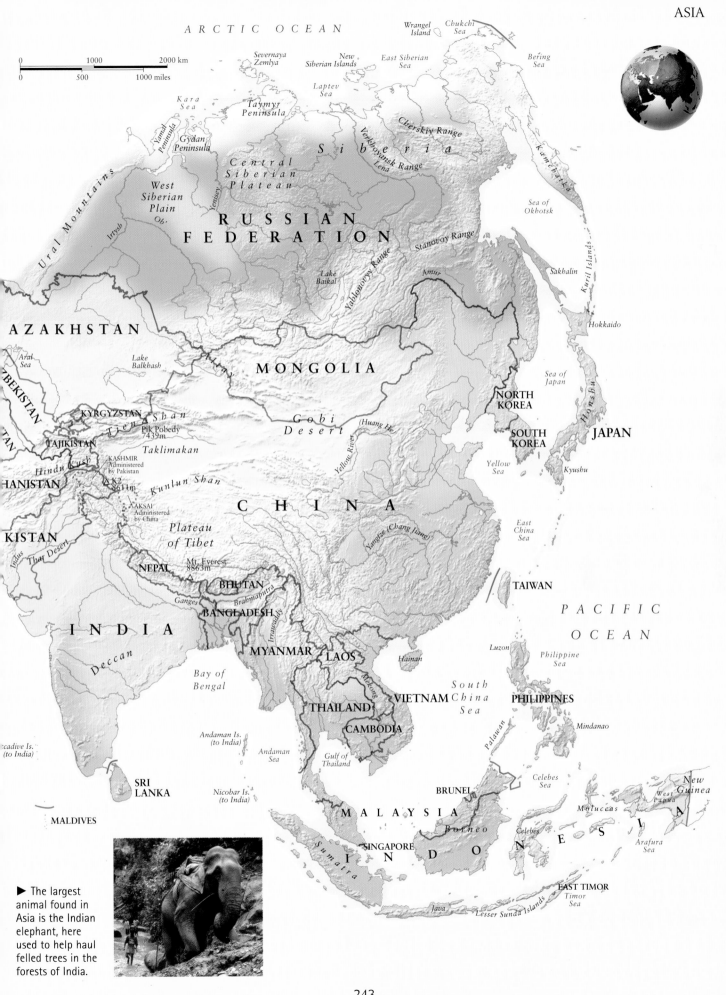

ARCTIC OCEAN

Wrangel
Island

Chukchi
Sea

Severnaya
Zemlya

New
Siberian Islands

East Siberian
Sea

Bering
Sea

0   1000   2000 km

0   500   1000 miles

*Kara
Sea*

*Taymyr
Peninsula*

*Laptev
Sea*

Cherskiy Range

*Yamal
Peninsula*

*Gydan
Peninsula*

*Central
Siberian
Plateau*

S i b e r i a

Kamchatka

*West
Siberian
Plain*

Yenisey

Ob

**RUSSIAN
FEDERATION**

Verkhoyansk Range

Lena

Stanovoy Range

*Sea of
Okhotsk*

Ural Mountains

Irtysh

*Lake
Baikal*

Yablonovyy Range

Amur

Sakhalin

Kuril Islands

Hokkaido

AZAKHSTAN

*Aral
Sea*

*Lake
Balkhash*

Altai

MONGOLIA

*Gobi
Desert*

(Huang He)

*Sea of
Japan*

Honshu

**NORTH
KOREA**

ZBEKISTAN

KYRGYZSTAN

Tien Shan

Pik Pobedy
7439m

Taklimakan

Yellow River

**SOUTH
KOREA**

JAPAN

TAJIKISTAN

*Yellow
Sea*

Kyushu

HANISTAN

Hindu Kush

KASHMIR
Administered
by Pakistan

△K2
8611m

Kunlun Shan

C H I N A

*East
China
Sea*

KISTAN

AKSAI
Administered
by China

Indus

Thar Desert

*Plateau
of Tibet*

Yangtze (Chang Jiang)

Mt. Everest
8863m
△

NEPAL

*PACIFIC
OCEAN*

BHUTAN

Brahmaputra

TAIWAN

Ganges

BANGLADESH

I N D I A

Irrawaddy

MYANMAR

LAOS

Hainan

Luzon

*Philippine
Sea*

Deccan

*Bay of
Bengal*

Mekong

*South
China
Sea*

VIETNAM

PHILIPPINES

THAILAND

Mindanao

Andaman Is.
(to India)

CAMBODIA

*Andaman
Sea*

*Gulf of
Thailand*

Palawan

*cadive Is.
(to India)*

*Celebes
Sea*

**SRI
LANKA**

Nicobar Is.
(to India)

BRUNEI

*New
Guinea*

Moluccas

*West
Papua*

MALDIVES

M A L A Y S I A

Borneo

Celebes

A

*Arafura
Sea*

Sumatra

SINGAPORE

I N D O N E S I A

EAST TIMOR

Java

Lesser Sunda Islands

*Timor
Sea*

► The largest
animal found in
Asia is the Indian
elephant, here
used to help haul
felled trees in the
forests of India.

MIDDLE EAST

The Middle East has been the birthplace of many important civilizations and major world religions such as Christianity, Judaism and Islam. Much of the region's terrain is hostile with large sand or rocky deserts and rugged mountain regions. Smaller areas of fertile lands exist around coastlines and in river valleys and basins. Much of the region was underdeveloped until the discovery of vast reserves of oil in the early 20th century. The Middle East now produces over a third of the world's daily oil output and many countries have been transformed by oil revenue. Although the region has an ancient history, many of the national boundaries are relatively new, drawn up by particular Western colonial powers in the early and mid-20th century. Partly as a result, the region has had a turbulent recent history with disputes over land and resources as well as conflict between different religious groups. The latest conflict in Spring 2003 saw international forces invade Iraq.

In 1948, Israel was founded in Palestine as a Jewish homeland. The Palestinians rejected a UN proposal to divide Palestine between them and Israel. In the ensuing war, Israel ejected hundreds of thousands of Palestinians from their land. This led to five wars and terrorist attacks by Palestinians upon Israel. In 1967, Israel occupied Gaza and the West Bank, where Israelis have since founded settlements. The UN regards the occupation and settlements as illegal. In 1993, the Palestinians recognized Israel and Israel gave them limited self rule in the West Bank and Gaza. However, the peace process has stalled and Israel has reoccupied most Palestinian territory. Some Palestinians continue terrorism, while Israel refuses to abandon its illegal settlements. The international community, including the United States, recognizes the right of the Palestinians to their own independent state in the West Bank and Gaza.

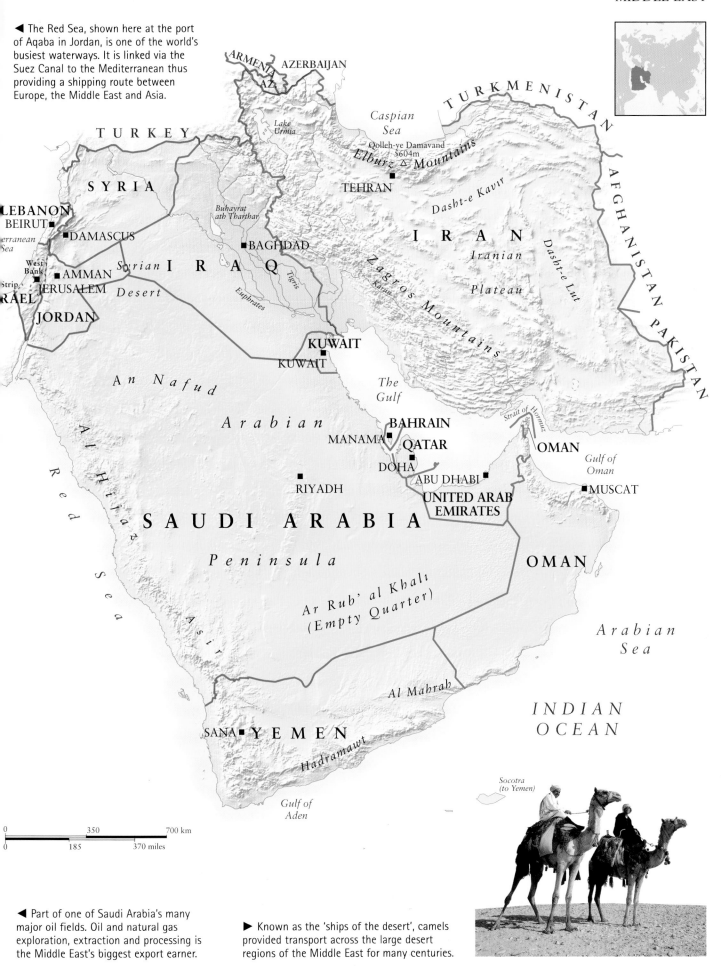

◄ The Red Sea, shown here at the port of Aqaba in Jordan, is one of the world's busiest waterways. It is linked via the Suez Canal to the Mediterranean thus providing a shipping route between Europe, the Middle East and Asia.

◄ Part of one of Saudi Arabia's many major oil fields. Oil and natural gas exploration, extraction and processing is the Middle East's biggest export earner.

► Known as the 'ships of the desert', camels provided transport across the large desert regions of the Middle East for many centuries.

245

SYRIA

A large Arab nation, Syria borders Turkey, Iraq, Lebanon, Jordan and Israel. The latter has occupied Syrian territory in the Golan Heights since 1967.

Area: 185,180 km², including areas of the Golan Heights occupied by Israel
Population: 16,729,000
Capital: Damascus (1,663,000)
Main languages spoken: Arabic, Kurdish
Main religions: Sunni Islam, Shia Islam, Uniat Christian Churches
Currency: Syrian pound
Main exports: crude petroleum and petroleum products, vegetables and fruit, cotton, textiles and fabrics
Type of government: republic; dictatorship

Syria consists of three main geographical regions. The most westerly is a coastal plain which contains the country's best farmland and is home to the majority of its population. Syria's Mediterranean coastline extends some 180 km between the borders of Turkey and Lebanon and is the location of the two major ports of Tartus and Al Ladhiqiyah. Dividing much of the coastal plain from the interior are mountain ranges and several fertile basins in which large cities have developed. East of the mountains lie plateaus and a great expanse of rock and gravel desert. The Syrian Desert makes up over half of the country and extends into Jordan, western Iraq and northern Saudi Arabia. The desert is bounded to the north by a region of fertile land through which the Euphrates river flows. A dam built on the river generates almost 35 per cent of the country's electricity.

▲ A textile printer at work in a souk in the city of Aleppo. With a population of 1,583,000, Aleppo is Syria's second largest city.

AGRICULTURE
Syria was a predominantly agricultural nation until the early 1960s, when large-scale state industries were developed. Agriculture still employs 40 per cent of the workforce with some 48,150 km² of croplands in which barley, wheat, olives, tobacco, fruit and vegetables are grown.

The most important cash crop is cotton. Nearly all crop farming depends on irrigation systems as, even in the wettest regions, most rain falls in winter. Large parts of the country north of the Syrian Desert are not cultivated but are used as pastures for Syria's 14.5 million sheep and 1.1 million goats.

POWER AND INDUSTRY
The areas in and around the Syrian cities of Damascus, Aleppo and Homs have become the chief industrial centres. In these regions, oil and tobacco are processed, chemicals produced, cotton-based textiles are woven and a wide range of handicrafts including

▼ Huge olive groves span low Syrian hills. In 2001, Syria produced around 26 per cent of the world's olive oil.

silk, leather and glass goods are made. The development of Syria's oil industry has made it, since 1974, the country's largest export earner. In 2001, it accounted for 68 per cent of the country's exports. A series of oil pipelines crosses Syria linking it to Iraq, Jordan and to the Mediterranean coast.

ARAB PEOPLES

Syria has been settled continuously for many thousands of years by different civilizations including the Egyptians, Hittites, Babylonians and Persians. Although Syria was part of the Ottoman Empire from the 16th century until 1918, its modern population is largely descended from Arab peoples who conquered the country in the 7th century and ruled for

800 years. Over 90 per cent of the population are of Arab descent with the largest minorities being Kurds, found near the Turkish border, and Armenians. Syria's capital, Damascus, is one of the world's oldest surviving cities and claims to be the oldest continuously inhabited capital city in the world. Situated in the southwestern corner of the country, Damascus is located at the border of a fertile plain and at the foot of mountains which divide Syria from Lebanon.

▲ Lively markets, known as souks, are a feature of towns in Syria and other Arab nations. This large, bustling Souk al-Hamidiye is found in Damascus.

ISRAEL

Established as a homeland for the Jewish people in 1948, Israel stands apart from the rest of the Middle East with which it has been in conflict since its formation.

Area: 20,400 km² excluding areas annexed by Israel (East Jerusalem and the Golan Heights)
Population: 6,369,000, including Golan Heights and East Jerusalem
Capital: Jerusalem (658,000). Jerusalem is not recognized as the capital of Israel by the international community
Main languages spoken: Hebrew, Arabic
Main religions: Judaism, Sunni Islam, various Uniat Christian Churches
Currency: new sheqel
Main exports: machinery and transport equipment, cut diamonds, chemicals, clothing, food and beverages
Type of government: republic; democracy

I srael is located at the eastern end of the Mediterranean Sea and is bordered by Egypt, Lebanon, Syria, Jordan and the occupied territories of Gaza and the West Bank. Its most southerly point is a short Red Sea coastline which has been developed as a tourist centre. The country has a variety of landscapes including hills which run from the north into its centre, and a large depression, part of the Great Rift Valley, along its most eastern lands. Israel's coastal plain runs parallel to the Mediterranean and is bordered by stretches of fertile farmland extending up to 40 km inland. This plain contains over half of Israel's population, most of its industry and much of its agriculture. To the south lies the dry and rugged Negev Desert.

ISRAEL'S ECONOMY AND PEOPLE

Although agriculture has been developed using advanced techniques and irrigation, the country's economy is dominated by service, defence and manufacturing industries. Israel is a major world centre for the cutting and polishing of gems and has large computing, machine making and chemicals industries. Tourism, although declining since the late 1990s, has been important, with visitors attracted by the warm climate and the religious history of a land which holds importance for three of the world's major religions: Islam, Christianity and Judaism. In the 1990s, Israel's economy expanded, partly due to the mass immigration of large numbers of highly skilled Jews from the former Soviet Union. They joined a

▼ A gardener plants a tree at a kibbutz. Some farms in Israel are organized as kibbutzim, settlements and communities in which people share their income and property.

highly mixed population consisting of approximately 80 per cent Jews and 20 per cent Arab peoples. An open immigration policy to Jewish people around the world has resulted in Jews from over 100 countries settling in Israel.

AID, TRADE AND CONFLICT
The USA maintains a strong relationship with Israel. It is its largest trading partner, and the US donates more aid to Israel than any other nation. Israel trades heavily with a number of European countries but very little with its immediate Arab neighbours. The country has been in political and sometimes military conflict with these neighbours over

its territory and very existence. A series of wars since Israel's formation saw Israel occupy parts of the neighbouring countries. The Gaza Strip on the Mediterranean coast was once part of Egypt. The West Bank and East Jerusalem were once part of Jordan, while the Golan Heights was previously Syrian territory. Israel's strained relationship with its Arab neighbours and the violence between Jews and Palestinians means that over a quarter of the national budget is spent on defence. The major issue remains the fate of the Palestinian peoples who were expelled from their territory when Israel was formed in 1948. They seek their own homeland in the West Bank and Gaza.

▲ A dry river bed in the hostile Negev Desert. Covering over half of Israel's territory, the Negev holds less than seven per cent of the country's population. Hot and dry, the landscape becomes more rugged and rises in elevation to the south.

▼ Jerusalem is Israel's third largest city. In 1950, Israel proclaimed Jerusalem as its capital although the United Nations does not recognize this and almost all countries maintain their embassies in the coastal city of Tel Aviv.

LEBANON

Occupying a narrow strip of land along the eastern coast of the Mediterranean Sea, Lebanon is a nation which is rebuilding after a prolonged civil war.

Area: 10,452 km²
Population: 3,282,000
Capital: Beirut (1,100,000)
Major language spoken: Arabic
Main religions: Shia Islam, Sunni Islam, Druze, Greek Orthodox, Maronite Christian
Currency: Lebanese pound
Main exports: re-exports, paper products, food and live animals, machinery and transport equipment
Type of government: republic; dictatorship

Lebanon is a small country bordered to the south by Israel and on its north and eastern sides by Syria. The country consists of a coastal plain which rises to a pair of mountain ranges in the east. Between these mountain ranges lies a large, fertile valley, the Bekaa. Lebanon has two main climatic zones. Its coast with the Mediterranean experiences warm, dry summers and rainy yet mild winters. Inland, in the Bekaa valley, the summer months are hot and dry. The Litani river runs through the valley and is harnessed to provide hydro-electricity as well as irrigation for both the southern part of the valley and, via a mountain tunnel, water for part of the coastal plain. Compared to many countries in the region, Lebanon receives relatively high rainfall. Farming is a key occupation both in the coastal plain and in the Bekaa with crops including cereals, vegetables and a large range of fruits.

▲ The majestic cedars of Lebanon, some of which are 1,500 years old, are a national symbol. Much of Lebanon was once covered in huge forests but these now occupy less than eight per cent of its land.

CIVIL WAR AND RECONSTRUCTION
The site of ancient Phoenician cities, built over 3,000 years ago, Lebanon was a prosperous nation and a commercial and trading centre. Beirut, its capital city attracted many tourists. The country's complex ethnic background contains many different Christian and Muslim groups. Tensions between religious groups were responsible for a lengthy civil war which started in 1975 and devastated much of the country. Stability in the 1990s has allowed foreign aid and government spending to rebuild the country.

▶ New hotels and apartment buildings, viewed from a beach café, show how Beiruit is re-developing and attracting back large numbers of tourists after many years of devastating conflict.

JORDAN

Lying between Saudi Arabia, Israel, Syria and Iraq, the almost landlocked small Arab kingdom of Jordan became fully independent in 1946.

Area: 91,860 km²
Population: 5,230,000
Capital: Amman (1,307,000)
Major language spoken: Arabic
Main religion: Sunni Islam
Currency: Jordanian dinar
Main exports: chemicals and chemical products, re-exported petroleum, phosphate fertilizers, potash, fruit, vegetables and nuts
Type of government: kingdom; limited democracy

Jordan has three distinct geographical regions: the Jordan Valley to the west, an eastern desert region and between them, an area of highlands and plateaus. Western Jordan has a Mediterranean climate with hot, dry summers, cool, wet winters and two short transitional seasons. The remaining three-quarters of the country has a largely desert climate with less than 250 mm of rainfall per year. Water shortages are a major problem in Jordan, which also lacks large oil and other major mineral reserves, with the exception of phosphates which with fertilizer and potash are the country's major exports. Less than five per cent of its land is capable of supporting crops which include tomatoes, fruits, wheat and olives. Sheep are the country's most important livestock with an estimated 1.6 million head in 2002. Jordan lost around a fifth of its industrial production and much of its best farmland following the Israeli occupation of the West Bank in 1967. About three-quarters of its people, many of them displaced Palestinians, live in cities, including Amman, the capital.

THE JORDAN VALLEY

Part of the Great Rift Valley of Africa, the Jordan Valley extends down the entire western flank of the country. The valley contains the Jordan river which is heavily exploited to irrigate the surrounding land and provide water for the local population. The Jordan flows into the Dead Sea which, at 408 m below sea level, is the lowest point on the surface of the Earth.

▲ Tourism is a major source of revenue for Jordan and many visitors flock to see the ruins of the ancient city of Petra. Petra's stunning buildings, including this tomb known as the Treasury of the Pharaohs, are carved out of red sandstone cliffs.

▶ Lying on the Gulf of Aqaba, an arm of the Red Sea, the city of Aqaba is Jordan's only port. It is also used as a base for divers who visit the rich coral reef marine life further south in the gulf.

IRAQ

Iraq is a nation of mountains, deserts and fertile plains. It has been in conflict with the international community for over a decade.

Area: 438,317 km²
Population: 23,115,000
Capital: Baghdad (4,478,000)
Main languages spoken: Arabic, Kurdish
Main religions: Shia Islam, Sunni Islam
Currency: Iraqi dinar
Main exports: crude petroleum and petroleum products
Type of government: republic; dictatorship

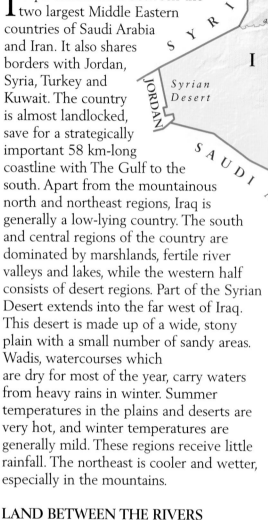

Iraq is sandwiched between the two largest Middle Eastern countries of Saudi Arabia and Iran. It also shares borders with Jordan, Syria, Turkey and Kuwait. The country is almost landlocked, save for a strategically important 58 km-long coastline with The Gulf to the south. Apart from the mountainous north and northeast regions, Iraq is generally a low-lying country. The south and central regions of the country are dominated by marshlands, fertile river valleys and lakes, while the western half consists of desert regions. Part of the Syrian Desert extends into the far west of Iraq. This desert is made up of a wide, stony plain with a small number of sandy areas. Wadis, watercourses which are dry for most of the year, carry waters from heavy rains in winter. Summer temperatures in the plains and deserts are very hot, and winter temperatures are generally mild. These regions receive little rainfall. The northeast is cooler and wetter, especially in the mountains.

LAND BETWEEN THE RIVERS

Iraq covers a region known in ancient times as Mesopotamia, a Greek word meaning land between the rivers. The two major rivers which flow through Iraq are the Tigris and the Euphrates. Where the two rivers meet, in the far south of the country, lies an area of marshy lowlands covered in reeds and palm trees. Further north, the land between and on either side of these two large rivers consists of fertile plains criss-crossed by many natural and artificial waterways and lakes. For over 6,000 years, this region has been cultivated and seen settlement by a number of ancient civilizations

▲ An image of Saddam Hussein, Iraq's leader from 1979 until the US-led invasion of Iraq in 2003, adorns a Baghdad street.

► Situated in a suburb of Iraq's capital, Baghdad, the Kadhimain Mosque was built in 1515 and is decorated with gold minarets and ornate designs.

including the Sumerians, Babylonians and the Assyrians. Today, this region is where most Iraqis live. Many are engaged in agriculture either rearing livestock or growing cereal crops and a large range of fruits. Before the 1991 Gulf War, Iraq produced 80 per cent of the world's dates.

OIL AND WAR

Oil was first discovered in Iraq in 1927 and since that time, the country has become one of the world's leading oil producers. Before 1990, the country rose to become the world's third leading oil producer. Iraq also has one of the world's largest reserves of sulphur, an element widely used in industry. Much of the oil revenue was channelled into building a large military force. Iraq invaded Iran in 1980 and by the time a cease-fire was struck in 1988, over 300,000 Iraqis had lost their lives. Two years later, the country occupied the small oil-rich state of Kuwait. In 1991, a coalition of nations led by the USA pushed Iraq's forces out of Kuwait. Following United Nations sanctions after the Gulf War, Iraq was only able to use its massive oil reserves for domestic use until 1996 when limited and supervised exports were allowed. As a result, the country's gross national product (GNP) was cut by half. Damage inflicted on the country during the Gulf War and the subsequent embargoes on trade have

▼ Ill-treatment of the Kurdish minority by the Iraqi government has generated thousands of refugees. Here, a Kurd from Iraq sits in a refugee camp inside the Turkish border.

disrupted both agriculture and industry. As a result, widespread poverty and hardship has been created especially among the poorer sections of Iraqi society. Iraq, under the strict leadership of Saddam Hussein, remained isolated and at odds with much of the rest of the world. In March 2003, an international coalition force led by the United States invaded Iraq. Within four weeks, the coalition forces had captured much of the country and had toppled Saddam Hussein from power. The future for Iraq remains uncertain as the country undergoes rebuilding.

▼ A group of Iraqi Arab women walk in front of a bomb-damaged building in the capital city of Baghdad. Iraqis are predominantly Arab peoples with Kurds the one large minority.

IRAN

The most populous and second largest nation in the Middle East, the Islamic Republic of Iran is a rugged country with massive fossil fuel deposits.

Area: 1,638,057 km²
Population: 66,129,000
Capital: Tehran
(8,900,000)
Main languages spoken:
Farsi (Persian), Azeri,
Kurdish
Main religions: Shia
Islam, Sunni Islam, Bahai
Currency: rial
Main exports: petroleum
and natural gas, carpets,
pistachios, iron and steel
Type of government:
republic; dictatorship

Iran is bordered by seven nations and has coastlines with three large seas: the Gulf of Oman, The Gulf and the Caspian Sea. The country's main geographical features are several large mountain ranges and a giant plateau. Lying in the centre of the country, the Iranian Plateau extends eastwards into central Asia. Around 1,220 m in elevation, the plateau is hot, dry and contains two large deserts in the northeast and east: the Dasht-e Kavir (180,000 km² in area) and the Dasht-e Lut (over 166,000 km²), which occupy most of the northeast and east of the central plain. There are a large number of climatic regions throughout Iran. Yet, although the northern mountains bordering the Caspian Sea receive heavy rainfall, Iran is a country in which precipitation is relatively scarce and dependent on the seasons.

▲ One of hundreds of carpet workshops found in the central Iranian city of Esfahan. The city is a centre of textile mills processing cotton, silk and woollen cloth for manufacturing clothing and carpets.

IRANIAN MOUNTAINS

Iran's longest mountain range – the Zagros – stretches from the northwest of the country close to the border with Armenia southwards and southeastwards along The Gulf where it ends near the Strait of Hormuz which link The Gulf and the Gulf of Oman. Its terrain includes many

peaks over 3,000 m while many of its deep valleys are fertile and are farmed. The Elburz mountain range runs along the southern shore of the Caspian Sea. The highest of its peaks is Qolleh-ye Damavand (5,604 m), Iran's highest point. The northern slopes of the Elburz mountains are densely covered with deciduous trees, forming the largest area of vegetation in Iran. Many of Iran's seasonal rivers start in these mountains and flow north into the Caspian Sea. The country's capital city, Tehran, is located on the southern slopes of the Elburz mountains at a height of around 1,070 m.

AN OIL ECONOMY

Iran's economy is closely tied to its natural resources; 85 per cent of its export revenues are derived from oil and gas. Iran contains about eight per cent of the known global oil reserves, and nearly one-fifth of the world's total reserves of natural gas. Under modernizing schemes introduced by Shah Mohammad Reza Pahlavi – the country's monarch from 1953 to 1979 – Iran developed oil processing and transport industries at a number of large ports on its Gulf coast including Bandar-e' Abbas and Abadan. Industries such as chemicals, textiles, machinery and cement production were also developed.

REVOLUTION AND WAR

The Iranian people are deeply religious and all aspects of life are heavily influenced by the Islamic faith. In 1979, the Shah was overthrown in a revolution and Iran was declared an Islamic Republic. Iran outlawed many Western influences and enforced a strict code of Islamic law. In 1980, the country was invaded by Iraq and in the ensuing eight-year-long war, over 400,000 Iranians died. The country's support for strong Islamic rule elsewhere has brought it into conflict with some of its Middle Eastern neighbours as well as Western nations.

▲ A petroleum refinery found in the city of Abadan. Located at the northernmost end of The Gulf, Abadan is a major centre of oil processing and transport.

▼ Iranian farmworkers prepare to gather in harvested crops. Agriculture contributes one-fifth of GDP with important crops including wheat, barley, rice, sugar beets, tobacco and wool.

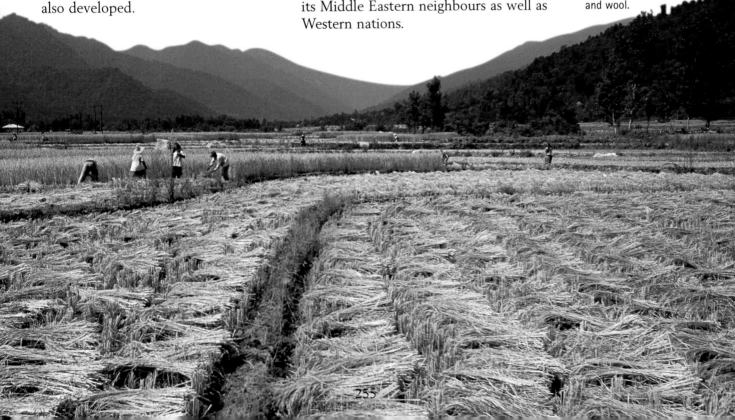

SAUDI ARABIA

The desert kingdom of Saudi Arabia covers much of the Arabian Peninsula and is the largest and wealthiest of the oil-producing nations of the Middle East.

Area: 2,240,000 km²
Population: 21,607,000
Capital: Riyadh
(2,776,000)
Major language spoken: Arabic
Main religion: Sunni Islam
Currency: riyal
Main exports: petroleum, petrochemicals, natural gas
Type of government: kingdom; dictatorship

Saudi Arabia borders seven countries and is connected to an eighth, Bahrain, by a causeway. The country is about one quarter the size of the USA and has 2,640 km of coastline, approximately 1,760 km with the Red Sea to the west and the remainder with The Gulf. A narrow coastal plain between 15 and 65 km in width extends along the Red Sea coast and a range of mountains runs further inland and parallel to this plain. These mountains increase in height as they extend southwards reaching the country's highest point, on the slopes of Jabal Sawda (3,133 m). A large plateau stretches out to the northeast of Saudi Arabia, reaching a maximum height of 1,800 m and dropping in altitude as it slopes down towards The Gulf in the east. To the south and southeast, Saudi Arabia contains the world's largest continuous sand desert, the Ar Rub' Al-Khali, or Empty Quarter. In parts of this hostile environment, rain has not fallen for years.

▲ Excess gas is burned off at an oil well in Saudi Arabia. Oil and natural gas are transported around the country to refineries and ports via over 17,000 km of pipelines.

WATER AND AGRICULTURE
Saudi Arabia's climate is generally hot and dry. Temperatures can reach 50°C in summer days although nights are cool, and frosts occur in winter. Rainfall is generally low; the capital city, Riyadh, receives an average of 85 mm per year although the Asir Mountains tend to receive three to four times as much. Saudi Arabia's generally dry climate means that the country has no permanent rivers or large lakes. Agriculture has traditionally been restricted to livestock herded by nomadic Bedouin Arabs, with crops only grown in the mountainous Asir region in the southwest of the country

and in the oases which dot the desert landscape north of the Empty Quarter. Massive desalination works where the seawater is processed, the salt removed and freshwater created have helped generate millions of litres of water. Desalination along with irrigation projects in recent times have helped reclaim many square kilometres of desert and turn it into fertile land. As a result, Saudi Arabia's farming sector is growing. The country's leading crops are wheat, barley, dates, dairy products and a range of fruits. Sheep, goats and camels are the most commonly reared livestock.

WORLD'S BIGGEST OIL PRODUCER

Oil was first discovered in Saudi Arabia in 1936, and in 2002, an estimated 10.5 million barrels per day were produced. The country has the world's largest oil and natural gas reserves; an estimated quarter of the entire world's oil deposits. As a result, oil revenues not only dominate the country's economy, making up over 90 per cent of exports, they also give the country great importance in the global economy. Its oil region lies primarily in the east along The Gulf. The enormous revenues from oil have been used to build modern cities, develop infrastructure, ports, hospitals and schools to bring electricity to towns. It has also been used to develop other industries such as chemicals, metal working and medicines.

INDEPENDENCE AND GOVERNMENT

Although the region has a long history and has been settled for thousands of years, the actual kingdom of Saudi Arabia is a relatively young nation. It emerged in the early 20th century as Abd al-Aziz ibn Saud (1882–1953) conquered successive territories in the Arabian Peninsula, beginning with Riyadh in 1901 and ending largely in 1920 with the incorporation of the region of Asir. The year 1932 saw the formation of the kingdom of Saudi Arabia by Abd al-Aziz ibn Saud. Descendants of the Saud family continue to run the country with absolute power invested in the monarch. In 1993 the current monarch, King Fahd, introduced political reforms creating a Consultative Council of 60 members who advise the king. A bill of rights was also established and power was given to local governments of the 13 provinces into which Saudi Arabia is divided. However, Saudi Arabia still remains a nation dominated by one family who make all key political appointments. There are no political parties and strong media censorship is imposed. Satellite television, for example, was banned in 1994 while there are strict rules regarding the Internet and religion.

▼ Two Saudis engage in falconry, the training of falcons or hawks to capture wild animals or birds. Falconry is now a sport enjoyed by wealthy Saudis. It is carefully regulated to protect endangered species on which falcons prey.

▼ A Bedouin camel train winds its way across the Saudi Arabian desert. Many Bedouins are no longer nomadic and now work in the oil industry or have settled in cities.

THE BIRTHPLACE OF ISLAM

The world's second-largest religion has its origins within Saudi Arabia. The founder of Islam, the prophet Muhammad (c.CE 570–632), was born in the city of Mecca, about 70 km inland from the Red Sea port of Jeddah. The Islamic calendar begins in CE 622, the year of the hegira, or Muhammad's flight from Mecca. He returned to capture the city in CE 630 and it is now the holiest city in the Islamic world. Every Muslim strives to make the religious pilgrimage, known as a hajj, to Mecca once in their lifetime and millions of Muslims visit Mecca every year. There, they attend the Great Mosque or al-Haram, a religious place of worship large enough to hold 300,000 people. In the centre of the Great Mosque's courtyard lies the Kaaba, a small building in which is housed the Black Stone of Mecca. It is the holiest shrine in the entire Islamic world. Medina, 340 km north of Mecca, is also a holy city and houses Muhammad's remains in a tomb. Saudi Arabia is run as a strict Muslim state in which Islamic law, the Sharia, is paramount. Women have no role in public life, are prevented from taking jobs in many fields, apart from teaching and healthcare, and cannot hold a driving licence. Strict Islamic punishments for certain crimes are enforced, generating criticism from international human rights groups.

▲ Saudi stock traders monitor prices of companies' shares in their business suite in the city of Riyadh. The Saudi Arabian Stock Market is now the largest in the Arab world.

▼ Pilgrims at the Great Mosque at Mecca surround the Kaaba, the holiest place on Earth to Muslims.

A REGIONAL SUPERPOWER

As the wealthiest of the Middle East nations, Saudi Arabia has strong ties and much influence with both its Arab neighbours and the Western world. This has increased as the country has grown richer and made more contributions to military and economic operations in the Middle East. It has also funded a number of aid and investment projects in the Gulf and Middle East region, and frequently contracts US, Japanese, French and British companies for defence and civil engineering projects. Many Saudis are sent abroad to Europe and North America to complete their higher education.

KUWAIT

Dwarfed by its neighbours of Saudi Arabia, Iraq and Iran, Kuwait is an intensely oil-rich nation still recovering from the effects of the 1990 Iraqi invasion.

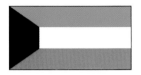

Area: 17,818 km²
Population: 2,228,000
Capital: Kuwait City (1,636,000)
Major language spoken: Arabic
Main religion: Sunni Islam, Shia Islam
Currency: dinar
Main exports: petroleum and petroleum products (accounts for 94 per cent of exports)
Type of government: emirate; limited democracy

Kuwait is located on the northernmost end of The Gulf. Its territory includes a number of islands in The Gulf most of which are uninhabited. The country's landscape is flat and almost featureless. It consists largely of a rolling sandy plateau which rises to the west to an elevation of 289 m near the country's borders with Saudi Arabia and Iraq. Average annual rainfall is around 125 mm, there is little surface water and the country relies on advanced desalination projects for water. Fertile soil is minimal. The one major exception is the oasis at Al Jahrah 50 km west of Kuwait City. The remaining few areas of natural vegetation occur in salt marshes in the northeast and along parts of the coast. Green areas in Kuwait's large towns and cities have been created using imported soil. Fishing is the country's only major food-related industry with shrimp the most profitable catch.

OIL, INVASION AND REBUILDING

Beneath Kuwait's barren, featureless land lie enormous oil and smaller, but still significant natural gas deposits. Kuwait has an estimated 10 per cent of the world's proven reserves of crude oil and, in 2002, produced approximately 2.2 million barrels per day. This is a recovery from a major slump which followed the invasion of the country by Iraq in 1990. The Iraqi invasion and subsequent war in which an international coalition forced Iraqi troops to withdraw proved to be both an economic and ecological disaster. In 2003, Kuwait became a base for large numbers of international coalition forces which invaded Iraq.

▼ An oil worker in Kuwait works on one of the country's many modern oil rigs. Kuwait's oil industry employs thousands of foreign workers mainly from southern Asia and other Arab nations.

BAHRAIN

Lying in The Gulf between Qatar and Saudi Arabia, the small kingdom of Bahrain consists of one large and a number of smaller islands.

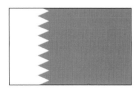

Area: 694 km²
Population: 651,000
Capital: Manamah (205,000)
Major languages spoken: Arabic, languages of the Indian subcontinent
Main religions: Shia Islam, Sunni Islam
Currency: dinar
Main exports: petroleum and petroleum products, basic manufactures
Type of government: kingdom; dictatorship

Bahrain Island, the nation's main land area, has a rocky centre and is linked to the Saudi Arabian mainland by a large causeway. The island's climate is hot and extremely dry with no more than 100 mm of rainfall annually. Imported soil, irrigation and drainage schemes have helped Bahrain grow some fruit and vegetables. Bahrain was the first Gulf state to start producing oil in commercial quantities but the nation's reserves are heavily depleted and may run out in the next 10–20 years. Investment in other industries, including aluminium production, chemicals and plastics has occurred, while many educated Bahrainis work in flourishing service industries such as insurance and banking. The country, run by the powerful al-Khalifa family, owns a quarter of the region's Gulf Air airline. Bahrain came under the protection of the United Kingdom in the 19th century and declared itself independent in 1971. English is still widely spoken by both the Arab population and the large communities of foreign workers.

▶ Part of the large business district in Bahrain's capital city, Manamah. The city is connected to the nearby island of Al Muharraq on which the country's airport is located.

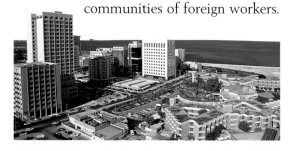

QATAR

The emirate of Qatar occupies a peninsula jutting out into The Gulf. It is a flat, dry desert land with particularly high reserves of natural gas.

Area: 11,427 km²
Population: 599,000
Capital: Doha (446,000)
Major languages spoken: Arabic 40 per cent, various languages of the Indian subcontinent
Main religion: Sunni Islam
Currency: riyal
Main exports: petroleum and natural gas, chemicals
Type of government: emirate; dictatorship

Qatar shares land borders with the United Arab Emirates and Saudi Arabia. Much of Qatar consists of rolling desert with some low hills to the west facing the coast. Rainfall is very low, less than 100 mm per year, and tends to fall only in heavy storms during winter. Some freshwater is tapped from underground sources, but Qatar relies on desalination plants which process seawater into freshwater. Little land is suitable for farming but irrigation schemes do allow melons, tomatoes and aubergines to be cultivated. Fishing off the peninsula coast is important locally with around 5,000 tonnes caught per year. Qatar has one of the smaller reserves of oil in the Middle East but has the world's third largest natural gas deposits.

A NATIVE MINORITY

Only one in five of the country's population was born in Qatar. Since oil production began, great numbers of foreign workers have been employed in Qatar, especially peoples from Iran, Pakistan and India. The native peoples are descendants of nomadic Bedouin Arabs. Now, over 80 per cent of native Qataris live in cities, and many small villages and settlements lie abandoned. Ruled by the ath-Thani family, Qatar has grown very wealthy from its oil and natural gas reserves. The country's population has a high standard of living with no income tax, and free health and education services.

UNITED ARAB EMIRATES

A federation of seven states or emirates, the United Arab Emirates lies on The Gulf and is a dry desert land prosperous from gas and oil revenues.

Area: 83,600 km²
Population: 2,441,000
Capital: Abu Dhabi (399,000)
Major languages: Arabic, various languages of the Indian subcontinent, English
Main religions: Sunni Islam, Shia Islam, Hinduism
Currency: dirham
Main exports: crude and refined petroleum, natural gas, manufactures, dates
Type of government: confederation of sovereign emirates; dictatorship

The United Arab Emirates is a land of mainly low-lying desert and salt flats with an average elevation of under 150 m. To the east, the land rises sharply to a height of 1,527 m along the border with Oman. The country has a long coastline with The Gulf and a short coast facing the Gulf of Oman. The waters in this latter gulf are much deeper and richer in nutrients and support a vibrant fishing industry. In 2001, 115,000 tonnes of fish were caught. The country is extremely dry with as little as 50 mm of rainfall per year rising to 150 mm per year in the mountainous areas. Agriculture is only possible via irrigation.

The United Arab Emirates formed in 1971 as a federation comprising the seven emirates of Abu Dhabi, Dubai, Sharjah, Ajman, Umm Al Qaiwain, Ras Al Khaimah and Fujairah. Formerly known as the Trucial States, the federation was formed after British forces left the region. Abu Dhabi was the largest of the former states in land area and is home to the country's political capital city of the same name. Along with the sizeable city of Dubai, these are the two main industrial centres of the country. Oil extraction and processing dominates the country's economy. The United Arab Emirates has approximately nine per cent of the world's proven reserves of oil and produces around 2.5 million barrels a day. The world's largest artificial port, 30 km south of the city of Dubai, has become a major transport terminus for the Gulf nations. The United Arab Emirates has used some of its oil revenue to develop other industries including finance, metal production and tourism, as well as providing high quality transport links and other services for its people. The citizens of the UAE have the highest per capita income in the entire Arab world and pay no income tax.

▲ The United Arab Emirates is largely self-sufficient in many fruits including dates, here being harvested from palm trees.

▶ The New Souk market building (right) sits in front of a Muslim mosque in the city of Sharjah. The city's population has increased 20 times over since 1968 as foreign workers, predominantly male, have arrived to work in the oil and other industries. Today, over two-thirds of the entire country's population are male.

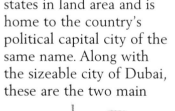

OMAN

Located strategically at the entrance to The Gulf, Oman has large oil reserves but is one of the least developed of the Gulf states.

Area: 309,500 km²
Population: 2,542,000
Capital: Muscat (350,000)
Major languages spoken: Arabic, Baluchi
Main religions: Ibadiyah Islam, Sunni Islam, Shia Islam
Currency: rial
Main exports: petroleum (accounts for over 80 per cent of exports), re-exports
Type of government: sultanate; dictatorship

▼ This rugged mountain landscape is found in the Musandam Peninsula, an enclave of Oman separated from the rest of the country by territory belonging to the United Arab Emirates.

The terrain of Oman is dominated by a vast desert plain which covers over three-quarters of the country. In the north lie mountains which rise to heights of over 3,000 m. The narrow coastal plain that is fertile in places is separated from the desert interior by a range of hills which runs southwest parallel to the Arabian Sea. The country has a 2,092 km long coastline with both the Gulf of Oman and the Arabian Sea. The coastline has a variety of terrain from deep fjords, long sandy beaches, mangrove lagoons, coral reefs and rocky islets. There are no major rivers or lakes in Oman and, with a warm, dry climate with less than 110 mm of rainfall per year, there is little agriculture. It is reliant on irrigation and concentrates on export crops such as limes and dates. Fishing is important, especially to Omani peoples living in small coastal settlements. Oman is ruled by a sultan who appoints a cabinet and council of regional representatives. The country has no political parties or law-making assembly. Oil dominates the economy and was first discovered in Oman in 1964.

The country started large scale oil production three years later. From 1970 onwards, Oman has undergone a rapid transformation. Previously, there were few schools, few communications links and only 10 km of paved roads. Using oil revenues, Oman, under the leadership of Sultan Qaboos, has developed a modern infrastructure and public services. This process is still continuing. For example, 100 new schools have been built since 1996 and the country's literacy rate has risen rapidly to nearly 80 per cent.

YEMEN

A union of two former nations, Yemen is the newest country in the Middle East. It occupies the rugged and arid southwestern corner of the Arabian Peninsula.

▼ A goatherder tends his flock in front of a hill topped with an old fortress in Al Mahwit Province, the smallest of Yemen's 18 administrative divisions.

Area: 527,970 km²
Population: 18,112,000
Capital: Sana (1,410,000)
Major language spoken: Arabic
Main religion: Sunni Islam
Currency: rial
Main exports: petroleum (over 90 per cent of exports), food and live animals, crude minerals
Type of government: republic; dictatorship

Yemen shares land borders with Oman to the east and Saudi Arabia to the north, both of which were finally agreed in the period 1992–2000 after disputes. Yemen's territory also includes a small number of islands, the largest of which is Socotra with an area of 3,579 km². The country has coastlines with both the Red Sea and the Gulf of Aden which flows out into the Indian Ocean. Yemen's location has been strategically important since ancient times with Aden a major port for over 2,000 years. The country's landscape is varied and consists of a semi-desert plain facing the Red Sea that then rises to form mountains and plateaus which are cut by deep valleys. East of the central region, the landscape is rugged desert and mountains. Rainfall varies depending on location with the southern coast receiving less than 100 mm per year while up to 750 mm falls in the western mountain region. The wettest area of Yemen is also the most highly populated, with Sana, the largest city and capital, and other major towns such as Ibb and Ta'izz.

The vast majority of Yemenis are Muslim Arabs and the population is one of the most rural of all Arab nations. More than half of the workforce is engaged in agriculture, often farming small plots of land. Ancient terraces cut into the mountain sides provide extra farmland. Wheat, millet and other cereal crops are vital staple foods along with citrus fruits, tomatoes and some vegetables. The main cash crops for export are coffee and cotton. Mocha coffee has been exported from Yemen for 1,200 years. Today, oil is the dominant export accounting for the majority of the country's export revenue. Yemen was formed in 1990 when the Yemen Arab Republic (North Yemen) and the People's Democratic Republic of Yemen (South Yemen) unified. The newly formed nation supported Iraq during the 1991 Gulf War and reprisals followed with Saudi Arabia and Kuwait expelling many Yemeni migrant workers. This has had a severe effect on the economy with over 30 per cent unemployment. A civil war between northern and southern forces broke out in 1994 but, since that time, an uneasy peace has held.

▲ A Yemeni market which trades and sells qat. The leaves of this evergreen shrub have a mild stimulating effect when chewed, a popular practice in Yemen.

CENTRAL ASIA

A region of extremes in terrain, Central Asia lies south of the Russian Federation and borders the Middle East to the west and Pakistan and China to the east. People, particularly nomadic livestock herders and traders, have lived in the area for many thousands of years. Part of the region lay on the Silk Road, an overland route used since 100 BCE to carry goods, especially silk, between China and Europe. Yet, today, most of Central Asia is hampered by a lack of transport facilities due to its mountainous and desert terrain, and its general lack of ocean ports. Kazakhstan and Turkmenistan have coastlines with the inland Caspian Sea, but the other nations of the region are landlocked. The entire region is a long distance away from the world's oceans and experiences a continental climate with great extremes in temperature. Generally, Central Asia is dry and water is at a premium. Irrigation is vital to most crop-growing but is placing great strains on freshwater lakes and rivers. Further environmental problems of desertification and pollution caused by industry and nuclear facilities have attracted great concern. Five of the six countries of Central Asia, Kazakhstan, Turkmenistan, Uzbekistan, Kyrgyzstan and Tajikistan, were all former republics of the Soviet Union, but became independent in 1991. The Russian Federation continues to exert influence on the region as a major trading partner and Russians make up large minorities in a number of the countries.

▲ Travelling through a mountain pass, these Afghanistan traders are carrying opium. The United Nations estimates that Afghanistan grows more than 60 per cent of the world's illegal supplies of opium.

▼ This fisherman plies his trade on the Aral Sea which straddles the border between Uzbekistan and Kazakhstan. Falling water levels have caused extinction of most of the fish species and devastated the fishing economy of the area.

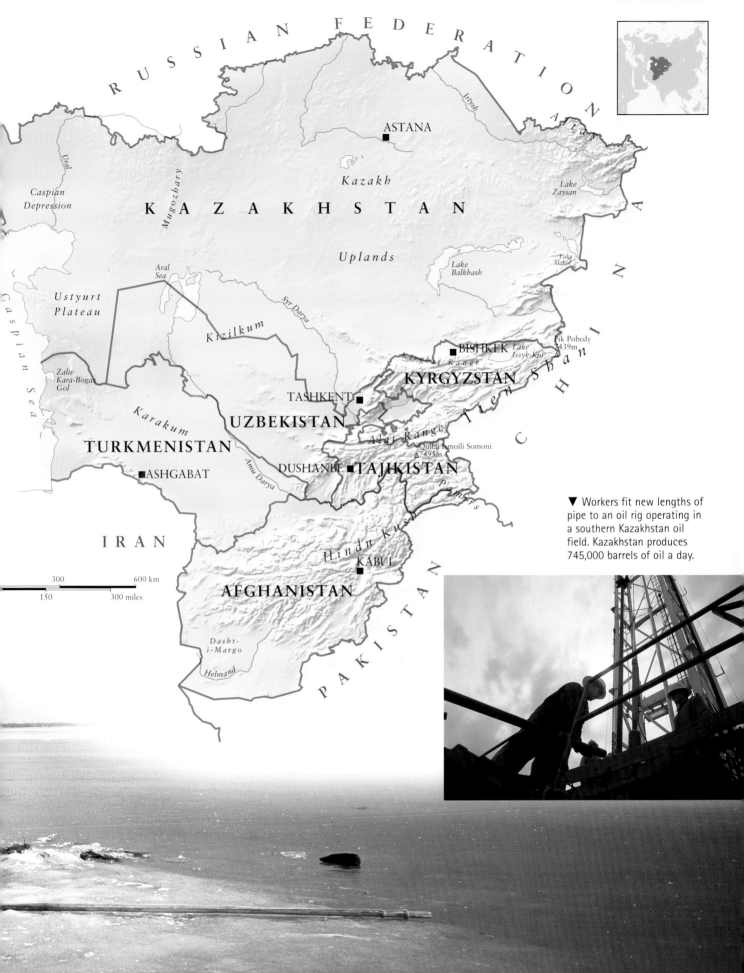

RUSSIAN FEDERATION

■ ASTANA

Kazakh

KAZAKHSTAN

Ural

Caspian Depression

Mugozhary

Irtysh

Altay

Lake Zaysan

Uplands

Lake Balkhash

Lake Alakol

Aral Sea

Ustyurt Plateau

Kizilkum

Syr Darya

Zaliv Kara-Bogaz Gol

BISHKEK *Lake Issyk-Kul*

Pik Pobedy 7439m

Kirghiz Range

KYRGYZSTAN

Tien Shan

C h i n a

TASHKENT ■

Karakum

UZBEKISTAN

Alaj Range

Qullai Ismoili Somoni 7495m

TURKMENISTAN

Amu Darya

DUSHANBE ■ TAJIKISTAN

Caspian Sea

ASHGABAT ■

Pamirs

IRAN

Hindu Kush

KABUL ■

AFGHANISTAN

Dasht-i-Margo

Helmand

PAKISTAN

▼ Workers fit new lengths of pipe to an oil rig operating in a southern Kazakhstan oil field. Kazakhstan produces 745,000 barrels of oil a day.

300   600 km
150   300 miles

KAZAKHSTAN

The biggest of the Central Asian states and the ninth largest country in the world, Kazakhstan is a land of desert and plains with vast mineral reserves.

Area: 2,717,300 km²
Population: 14,952,000
Capital: Astana (313,000)
Main languages spoken: Kazakh, Russian
Main religions: Sunni Islam, non-religious (about 40 per cent), Russian Orthodox
Currency: tenge
Main exports: oil and natural gas, rolled ferrous metals, refined copper, cereals, coal
Type of government: republic; dictatorship

▲ A Soyuz-Fregat rocket launch occurring at the Baikonur Cosmodrome. The site of the former Soviet Union's space launching programme, it lies approximately 200 km northwest of the city of Qyzylorda.

Much of Kazakhstan's vast area consists of grassy plains, known as steppes, which cover the north and some of the central regions of the country. The south and south-central regions of the country are covered by desert while to the extreme east and south the land rises to form several high mountain ranges. This area features the country's highest point, Mount Khan Tangiri (6,995 m). In contrast, the western part of the country which borders the Caspian Sea has a low point of 28 m below sea level. Kazakhstan has a continental climate with great extremes of temperature and rainfall. The mountains to the east, for example, can receive an annual average rainfall of 1,500 mm. Most of the country receives between 200 mm and 400 mm while parts of the central desert region receive no more than 100 mm. Much farming relies on irrigation from the country's rivers and lakes. The largest lake entirely in Kazakhstan is Lake Balkhash which has an area of 17,400 km². Russians form 29 per cent of the nation's people and there are large minorities of Ukranians, Tatars and Uzbeks. The

▲ Founded in 1824 as a fortress settlement, Kazakhstan's capital city of Astana has been known as Akmolinsk, Tselinograd and Aqmola in the past. Its status is a duty free tax zone to encourage foreign investment.

Kazahks are the biggest ethnic group in the country making up almost half of the population. Historically, most Kazahks lived a nomadic life, but during the 20th century many were forced to settle in one place. Mining is the largest industry, while agriculture remains important. Kazakhstan has enormous reserves of many minerals including lead, zinc, chromium and tungsten as well as coal, iron ore and nickel. Large oil and natural gas deposits are found in the Caspian Sea and the country has formed partnerships with foreign companies to exploit these reserves.

UZBEKISTAN

Uzbekistan is the most populous country in Central Asia. It has huge mineral resources but its infrastructure is limited and many of its people are poor.

Area: 447,400 km²
Population: 25,155,000
Capital: Tashkent (2,210,000)
Major languages spoken: Uzbek, Russian, Tajik, Kazakh
Main religions: Sunni Islam, Russian Orthodox
Currency: som
Main exports: light industrial products, petroleum and natural gas, machine-building equipment, food
Type of government: republic; dictatorship

▼ Since 1960, the Aral Sea has shrunk in area by approximately 40 per cent due to overuse of the rivers which have fed it for thousands of years. In addition to the stranded boats, the salt and sand left behind has made the surrounding land unsuitable for agriculture.

Uzebekistan is one of only two countries in the world which are doubly landlocked – that is surrounded by other landlocked countries (Liechtenstein is the other). Approximately a third of the country's territory consists of mountains and foothills to the east and southeast, where they merge with the mountain ranges of neighbouring Kyrgyzstan and Tajikistan. Most of the remainder consists of dry desert plains. Uzbekistan's continental climate is characterized by low rainfall levels of between 200 mm and 400 mm across the country. Farming tends to rely on irrigation and occurs mainly to the east and in the fertile river valley of the Amu Darya which feeds the Aral Sea. Overuse of river and lake water for irrigation has caused severe ecological problems. Cotton is the most important crop followed by tobacco, fruit and vegetables but the country produces only a third of the cereals it requires and has to import the rest. Uzbek peoples comprise 80 per cent of the population, with Russians making up five per cent, Tajiks three per cent,

▲ Uzbekistan is one of the world's leading producers of cotton.

Kazakhs four per cent and Tatars two per cent. The country's population is concentrated in the south and east of the country. Many live in towns and cities which date back many centuries. Samarqand is one of the oldest cities in Central Asia. Tashkent is the country's capital and the centre of Uzbekistan's manufacturing and heavy industry which includes car and aircraft production, farm machinery and jewellery using gold from several large mines in the Kizilkum desert.

TURKMENISTAN

The least populous of the Central Asian nations, Turkmenistan is an isolated, largely desert nation with large natural gas reserves.

Area: 488,100 km²
Population: 4,459,000
Capital: Ashgabat (640,000)
Major languages spoken: Turkmen, Uzbek, Russian
Main religion: Sunni Islam
Currency: manat
Main exports: natural gas and oil products (nearly 70 per cent of exports), cotton, textiles
Type of government: republic; dictatorship

Four-fifths of the land of Turkmenistan consists of the large, flat Karakum desert, famous for its black sands, which experiences maximum temperatures in excess of 50°C. Turkmenistan has a very dry climate with extremes of temperature; in winter temperatures can fall below -30°C. The country's principal river, the Amu Darya, flows through the eastern part of the country. Near the country's border with Afghanistan, some of its waters are diverted along a 1,100 km irrigation canal westwards to Ashgabat. The Karakum Canal is the world's largest irrigation canal and brings water to farmlands along its route enabling cotton, wheat, silk and fruit among other crops to be grown. Many people in the country suffer health problems due to the scarcity of clean water. Turkmenistan's largest city, Ashgabat, was completely destroyed by an earthquake in 1948 but has since been rebuilt and is the country's capital. It is well known as the centre of the country's cotton and textiles industries. However, these are second as an export earner to oil and natural gas production.

TAJIKISTAN

The smallest and poorest of the Central Asian nations, Tajikistan is also the most mountainous. Over half of the country lies above 3,000 m.

Area: 143,100 km²
Population: 6,118,000
Capital: Dushanbe (582,000)
Major languages spoken: Tajik, Uzbek, Russian
Main religions: Sunni Islam, Shia Islam
Currency: Tajik rouble
Main exports: aluminium (over one half of exports), electricity, cotton fibre, fruit, vegetable oil
Type of government: republic; dictatorship

Mountains cover more than 90 per cent of Tajikistan with the highest peaks found in the Pamirs in the southeast of the country. Mountain glaciers feed many streams which allows the country to generate surplus electricity to support both its own aluminium industry and to export to neighbouring nations. Only six per cent of the country is farmed. Irrigation allows parts of the country's lowlands to be used to grow a range of crops including cotton, fruit and mulberry trees. Tajikistan has substantial reserves of a number of minerals including mercury, silver, gold and over a tenth of the world's proven reserves of uranium. However, the mountainous terrain makes mining and transport extremely difficult. The country is named after the Tajik people who are descended from Iranians and comprise over 64 per cent of the country's population. The Uzbeks are the largest minority group who comprise 25 per cent. Most of the country's people are followers of the Islamic religion. A civil war following independence in 1991 and the emigration of highly skilled Russian workers are key causes of a decline in the country's industries. Over 80 per cent of the population live in poverty with poor healthcare facilities.

KYRGYZSTAN

A mountainous republic, Kyrgyzstan is the most rural of the Central Asian nations. The country's economy relies on mining its extensive mineral deposits.

Area: 198,500 km²
Population: 4,699,000
Capital: Bishkek (762,000)
Major languages spoken: Kyrgyz, Russian, Uzbek
Main religions: Sunni Islam, non-religious (about one quarter)
Currency: som
Main exports: food products, light manufactures, metals, machinery
Type of government: republic; dictatorship

◀ A yurt formed from a frame of wooden poles covered in cloth acts as a portable summer home for nomadic livestock herders in Kyrgyzstan.

Kyrgyzstan's landscape is dominated by mountains which extend through much of the country and into neighbouring China. The highest peaks in these snow and ice-covered mountains rise to over 7,000 m in elevation. Overlooked by the Tien Shan mountains in the east of the country lies Ozero Issyk-Kul', one of the world's largest mountain lakes and the fourth deepest in the world. The country experiences a continental climate with average daily temperatures in the valleys reaching 27°C in July and -4°C in January. Large reserves of many minerals including gold, coal, iron, zinc, mercury and natural gas are found within its mountainous terrain. Despite less than seven per cent of the land being suitable for farming, agriculture employs larger numbers of people than any other sector. The rearing of sheep and the herding of cattle, goats and horses, all for their meat and milk, is widespread and helps make the country self-sufficient in basic foodstuffs.

AFGHANISTAN

A mountainous nation, Afghanistan has been torn apart by conflict over the past 25 years. Most of its people live in poverty.

Area: 652,225 km²
Population: 22,720,000
Capital: Kabul (2,450,000)
Main languages spoken: Pashto, Dari (Persian), Uzbek
Main religions: Sunni Islam, Shia Islam
Currency: afghani
Main exports: dried fruit and nuts, carpets and rugs, wool and hides, cotton
Type of government: republic; dictatorship

▼ Afghanistan's forbidding mountainous landscape has hampered transport and trade and leaves many small settlements isolated.

Nearly three-quarters of Afghanistan is covered in mountains and highland areas. Principal among its mountains is the Hindu Kush range which extends some 800 km through central Afghanistan and into Pakistan and Tajikistan. The highest peaks here rise to over 7,000 m and the average altitude of the region is approximately 4,300 m. The Hindu Kush forms a natural and imposing barrier between the country's northern plains, its major farmlands, and the rest of the country.

South and southwest of the Hindu Kush lies a flat plateau with an average height of approximately 1,000 m. Most of this plateau is covered in desert. The soil here supports little life except for the immediate lands around the rivers which run through the region. Chief among these is the Helmand river, Afghanistan's longest, which begins its life

approximately 80 km south of Kabul and flows through the Dasht-i-Margo Desert into Iran. Afghanistan's climate varies with elevation but, generally, the country experiences cold winters and hot summers in which temperatures in the southern deserts can exceed 45°C. The whole of the country receives low levels of rainfall; the average annual precipitation is around 300 mm. Drought sometimes causes serious problems for the country's farmers.

AFGHAN PEOPLE

Afghanistan has a long history going back over 5,000 years and its people come from a range of origins: the main groups are Pashtuns, Tajiks, Hazaras and Uzbeks. Over 30 languages are spoken and many Afghans speak their own local language as well as one of the two official languages. Ninety-nine per cent of the population are Muslims. Most Afghans are rural people who depend on farming to live. The flat northern plains and foothills are where the majority of crops including corn, rice, wheat, cotton and nuts are grown. Many Afghans keep sheep and goats that provide milk as well as wool for making rugs, one of the key crafts of the country. Several million Afghans still live nomadic lives tending small herds of livestock.

A SUCCESSION OF WARS

Afghanistan's strategic position between Central Asia and the Indian subcontinent has seen it invaded and fought over a number of times in its past. In 1979, the Soviet Union invaded the country to support an unpopular government and a lengthy war was fought between Soviet and government forces and the mujahideen – rural tribesmen supported by the United States and Pakistan – which continued for 10 years. Further conflicts between different Afghan groups occurred before a strict Islamic group, the Taliban, came to power in 1996. The Taliban was deposed by the United States and its allies in 2001. These conflicts have left behind a devastated nation, with many towns in ruins and landmines killing or maiming 80 people every month. In the past, Afghans were self-sufficient in wheat and other basic foodstuffs, but a third of its farmland has since been destroyed and many people are reliant on food aid. Less than ten per cent of the population have access to clean water and around a quarter of Afghan children die before they reach five years of age.

▲ A school for female students in Kandahar which opened in January 2002. Afghanistani women have a literacy level of 21 per cent – the lowest level in the world.

SOUTH ASIA

South Asia is one of the oldest centres of permanent human settlement and the birthplace of several of the world's major religions. Extremes of terrain and climate are found in South Asia; from the permanently snow-capped peaks of the towering Himalayas to the giant, very low-lying flood plains which are found in India and comprise most of Bangladesh. Large parts of the region are subject to monsoon winds which bring heavy rainfalls in the summer, but can also bring floods and storms. However, massive crop failures are caused if the rain fails. Over one-fifth of the world's population live in South Asia, many in abject poverty as fast-growing populations outpace countries' abilities to provide for their people. The region is dominated by the large and populous nation of India. Two of its neighbours, Pakistan and Bangladesh, were formerly parts of India when it was under British rule. These two nations are predominantly peopled by Muslims while Hindus are the majority in India and Nepal, and Buddhists in Sri Lanka and Bhutan.

▲ Completed in 1978 after 20 years of work, the Karakoram Highway runs for 800 km through some of the most hostile terrain in Asia to link China with the Pakistan city of Islamabad.

▼ Hindu Indians bathe in the Ganges, the holy river for South Asia's large Hindu population.

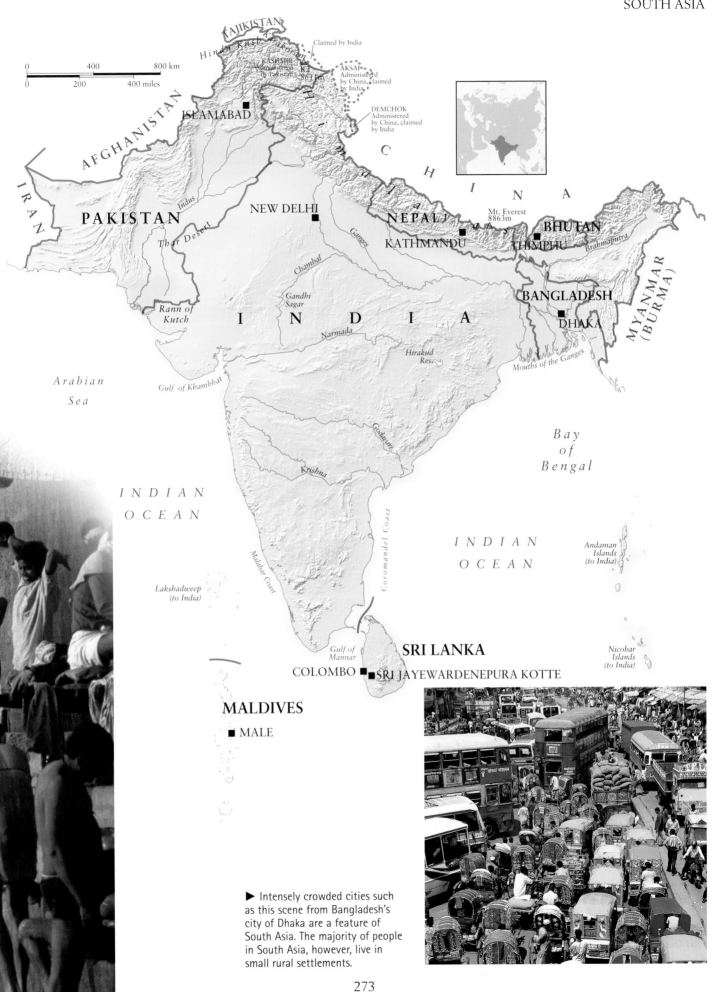

0   400   800 km
0   200   400 miles

TAJIKISTAN
Hindu Kush Karakoram
Claimed by India

KASHMIR
Administered
by Pakistan
K2
8611m
AKSAI
Administered
by India, claimed
by India

DEMCHOK
Administered
by China, claimed
by India

AFGHANISTAN

ISLAMABAD

IRAN

PAKISTAN

Indus

Thar Desert

NEW DELHI

C H I N A

NEPAL

KATHMANDU

Mt. Everest
8863m

BHUTAN

THIMPHU

Brahmaputra

Ganges

Chambal

Gandhi
Sagar

I N D I A

Narmada

BANGLADESH

DHAKA

MYANMAR
(BURMA)

Rann of
Kutch

Hirakud
Res.

Mouths of the Ganges

Arabian
Sea

Gulf of Khambhat

Godavari

Bay
of
Bengal

Krishna

I N D I A N

O C E A N

I N D I A N

O C E A N

Andaman
Islands
(to India)

Malabar Coast

Coromandel Coast

Lakshadweep
(to India)

Nicobar
Islands
(to India)

Gulf of
Mannar

SRI LANKA

COLOMBO   SRI JAYEWARDENEPURA KOTTE

MALDIVES

MALE

▶ Intensely crowded cities such
as this scene from Bangladesh's
city of Dhaka are a feature of
South Asia. The majority of people
in South Asia, however, live in
small rural settlements.

273

PAKISTAN

The Islamic Republic of Pakistan borders Afghanistan, Iran and India. It is a country of dramatic and contrasting scenery, people and cultures.

Area: 796,095 km²
excluding 83,716 km² of
the Pakistani-held areas of
Kashmir and the disputed
Northern Areas (Gilgit,
Baltistan and Diamir)
Population: 156,483,000
Capital: Islamabad
(529,000)
Major languages spoken:
Urdu, Punjabi, Pashto,
Sindhi, Siraiki
Main religions: Sunni
Islam, Shia Islam, Ismaili
Islam
Currency: Pakistan rupee
Main exports: textiles,
clothing, rice, leather
goods, fish, cotton
Type of government:
republic; limited
democracy

The landscape of Pakistan is partly divided by the Indus river system which enters the country in the northeast and flows southwards before emptying into the Arabian Sea. The Indus Plain, found mostly along the eastern side of the river, varies in width between 80 km and 330 km and is the most densely populated and farmed region of Pakistan. A series of mountain ranges including the Toba Kakar Range dominate the northern regions of the country and Pakistan is crossed by part of the Thar Desert in the southeast. The country's climate varies greatly according to elevation and region but most of Pakistan suffers from scarce rainfall with droughts being common.

FARMING AND INDUSTRY
Around 44 per cent of the working population is involved in agriculture. Pakistan produces many crops, is self-sufficient in cereals and is one of the world's leading

▲ A bustling street in the city of Faisalabad in northeast Pakistan. Faisalabad is a major transport terminus and industrial centre with engineering works, cotton, sugar and flour mills and large textiles factories.

producers of cotton which provides the raw material for a giant textiles industry. However, farming faces a number of environmental challenges including salt waterlogging of the soil, droughts and floods. Although around 60 per cent of Pakistanis live in rural areas, the country has a number of large cities. Lahore is a major distribution and trading centre for the surrounding heavily industrialized areas. Hyderabad is a centre of heavy industry, while Karachi, lying on the coast, is Pakistan's chief port and the most populous city of all. Manufacturing industry, services and mining a range of minerals are all major employers in the country.

INDEPENDENCE AND POLITICS
The lands that now comprise Pakistan have been invaded and controlled by many different peoples including Persians, Huns, Turks and Arabs. European traders started to travel the area in the 16th century and by the mid-18th century, the region, including the territory of both India and Pakistan, was under British rule. Demands for independence grew until 1947 when the

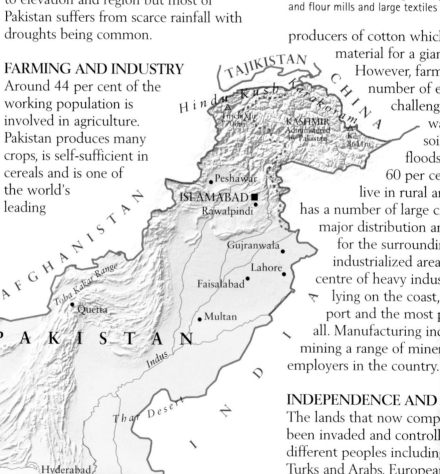

region was partitioned into India, containing mainly Hindus, and a separate Muslim nation of East and West Pakistan. Separated by 1,600 km of land, cultural and political differences grew between the two Pakistans leading to war in 1971 with East Pakistan becoming the independent nation of Bangladesh. Pakistan has experienced much political instability with military coups, political assassinations and rule by the army for many years. A serious dispute over the region of Jammu and Kashmir on the northern border between India and Pakistan has existed since 1947.

PAKISTAN'S PEOPLE

The people of Pakistan are a racial mixture of various groups who have moved to and settled in the region over thousands of years. The five largest ethnic groups are Punjabis, Pashtuns, Sindhis, Balochis and muhajirs. Punjabis comprise approximately 48 per cent of Pakistan's population and their language is the most commonly spoken. Sindhis are the second-largest group making up around 12 per cent of the population. When Pakistan was separated from the Hindu state of India in 1947, millions of Muslims left India to settle in Pakistan. These people and their descendants are the muhajirs who tend to speak Urdu. Ninety-seven per cent of Pakistanis are Muslim. While a wealthy elite, of mainly Punjabis, live in considerable luxury, a large proportion of Pakistan's population barely survive. The country has one of the lowest access rates to doctors, hospitals and essential medicines in the world. Malaria, tuberculosis and other diseases are common, and food and water shortages are widespread.

▲ Sugar cane being harvested in the province of Sind in southeast Pakistan. In 2000, Pakistan produced about 46.2 million tonnes of sugar cane.

▼ Distinctive trucks wait for the road ahead to clear on the mountainous Karakoram Highway. This road took the efforts of over 24,000 workers to complete.

INDIA

Home to over a billion people, India is a vast and diverse country with much variety and richness in culture. India is also the world's largest democracy.

Area: 3,287,263 km²
Population: 1,027,000,000
Capital: New Delhi (12,791,000)
Main languages spoken: Hindi, Telegu, Bengali, Marathi, Tamil, Urdu, Gujarati, Kannada, Malayam, Oriya, Punjabi, Assamese, English
Main religions: Hinduism, Sunni Islam, Shia Islam, Sikh
Currency: rupee
Main exports: agricultural products, cut and polished diamonds and jewellery, clothing, machinery and transport equipment, metals with iron and steel, cotton
Type of government: republic; democracy

India is the seventh biggest country in the world and the second most populous. It shares borders with six countries, mostly to the north and including Myanmar, Nepal and Bhutan. India surrounds the country of Bangladesh on three sides and is involved in long-running disputes over territory with its two other neighbours, Pakistan to the northwest and China to the north. Its landscape is incredibly varied with dry desert regions, lush wet highlands, vast plains and plateaus. The country is also home to a large part of the world's youngest and highest mountains – the Himalayas. The Himalayas and their foothills form a massive geological barrier across almost all of northern India extending a distance of over 2,300 km. They were formed and continue to rise due to the immense forces which are pushing the Indian subcontinent northwards towards China. Extending south from the highlands region, much of India consists of a giant peninsula jutting out into the Indian Ocean. The Arabian Sea lies to the west of India and to the east lies the Bay of Bengal.

THE NORTHERN PLAINS
Lying south of the Himalayas is a huge belt of flat land known as the northern plains. Much of this land surface has been formed by rivers, including the Ganges and Brahmaputra, depositing sediment on great flood plains and deltas, creating extremely rich and fertile soils. Many of India's rivers start their life in the Himalayas, among them the Ganges.

▼ Situated in Kashmir in northwest India, Lake Dal is known for its beautiful location, its lotus flowers and for its striking lake dwellers who live in wooden houseboats and tend floating gardens.

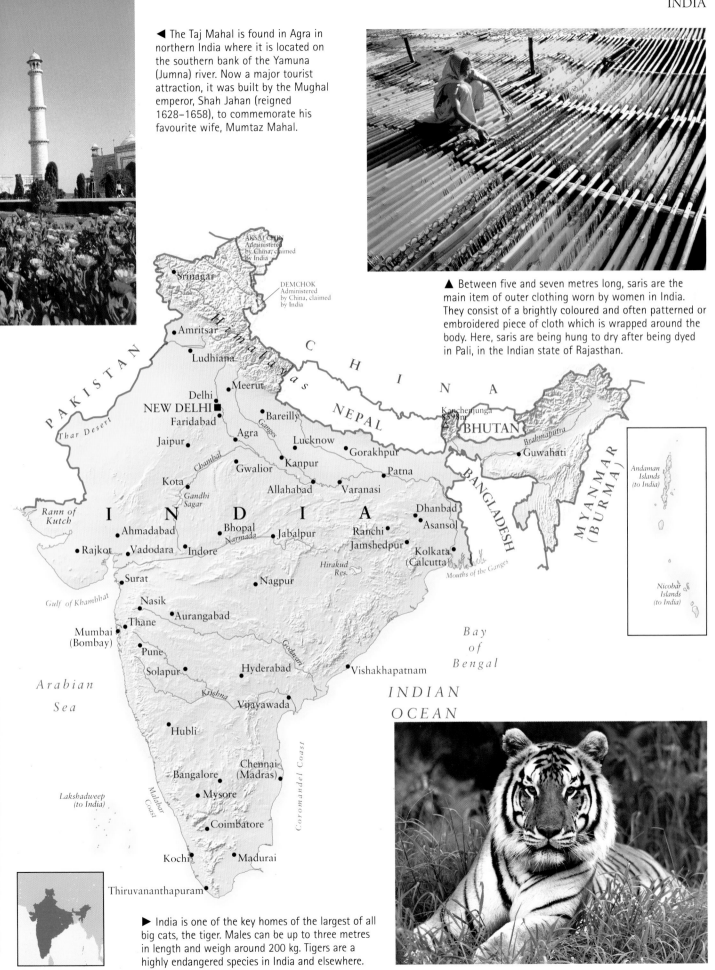

◄ The Taj Mahal is found in Agra in northern India where it is located on the southern bank of the Yamuna (Jumna) river. Now a major tourist attraction, it was built by the Mughal emperor, Shah Jahan (reigned 1628–1658), to commemorate his favourite wife, Mumtaz Mahal.

▲ Between five and seven metres long, saris are the main item of outer clothing worn by women in India. They consist of a brightly coloured and often patterned or embroidered piece of cloth which is wrapped around the body. Here, saris are being hung to dry after being dyed in Pali, in the Indian state of Rajasthan.

► India is one of the key homes of the largest of all big cats, the tiger. Males can be up to three metres in length and weigh around 200 kg. Tigers are a highly endangered species in India and elsewhere.

▲ An Indian guide to the city palace of Jodhpur. Located in northwest India, the city is a major trading centre for the surrounding farmlands and is famous for its handicraft products including ivory, glass, cloth and leather goods.

▼ A reminder of British rule in India, Mumbai's Victoria Station was completed in 1887 and was built on the site of the first train route in Asia which opened in 1853.

The wide, slow-moving Ganges river is just over 2,500 km long, and drains almost a quarter of the country. The Ganges has created the wide, flat Gangetic Plain which lies in both India and Bangladesh. This region is heavily populated and farmed by millions of Indians who rely on water from the river. A largely low-lying region, it is subject to flooding and typhoon storms. In marked contrast to the plains, the arid Thar Desert lies to the northwest and crosses the Indian-Pakistan border. South of the plains is the Deccan plateau, an area of around 600 m average elevation which covers much of central and southern India. Either side of the plateau are coastal mountains. India has a highly varied plant and animal life, from arctic plants in the high mountains to tropical flowers, rhinoceros, tigers and many other cats. The country provides habitats for more than 1,100 species of birds.

FARMING AND FISHING
Agriculture is the backbone of India's economy. It employs approximately 61 per cent of the workforce directly, as well as providing raw materials for some of the country's other key industries particularly

▲ Indians with camels cross part of the Thar Desert. Just over one million camels are used as the main beast of burden in the dry, desert regions of India.

textiles, jute and sugar industries. Although much farming is largely conducted in ways unchanged for centuries, advances in technology, fertilizers and irrigation have seen more and more land come under cultivation. Almost 600,000 km² of land is now irrigated by canal or well systems and over half of India's land is cultivated. Massive farms and plantations do exist, growing cash crops such as coffee, tea, cotton and jute. Yet, thousands of farms are tiny – less than one-tenth of a square kilometre in size – and many rural families struggle to grow enough to feed themselves. Fishing is carried out around all of India's coastline and also in its major rivers. Sea fishing accounts for more than two-thirds of catches. Most fishing is conducted in simple unmotorized vessels although the Indian government is investing in ocean-going trawlers.

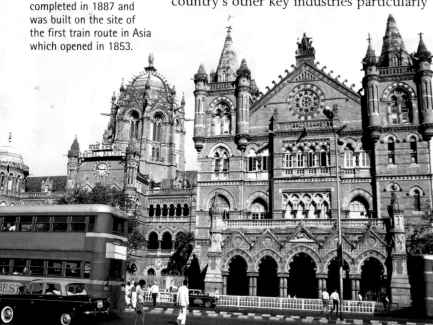

livestock raising is an important part of the country's agriculture with many of the country's 220 million cattle and 94 million water buffalo used as beasts of burden and sources of milk.

MINING AND INDUSTRY

India has great reserves of many minerals from oil and coal to zinc, copper, silver and gold. It has developed a number of sizeable industries based on its natural resources, including large scale steel production and engineering industries. Millions of Indians are employed in the textiles industry, mostly in small scale businesses. Helped by foreign investment in the 1990s, India built up large computer software, telecommunications and other modern industries. Based in and around the city of Mumbai (Bombay), India's film industry, nicknamed Bollywood, produces more films per year than anywhere in the world.

▼ Hindus bathe in the Ganges river in the northern city of Varanasi. Formerly known as Benares, Varanasi is home to more than 1,500 religious buildings. Hindus believe that bathing in the Ganges cleanses them of sin.

RICE AND SPICES

India has more land devoted to growing rice than any other country in the world and became self-sufficient in rice production in the late 1970s. It is now the world's second largest rice exporter. India is also one of the world's largest producers of a number of other crops including sugarcane, tea, cotton, maize, pulses and wheat. A major grower of many of the world's spices, India is justly renowned for its rich cuisine and the enormous variety of regional dishes. In contrast, most Indians have a simple diet. Many eat little meat, but

A MASSIVE POPULATION

With around two per cent of the world's land area, India supports some 15 per cent of the world's population. Although it is still a predominantly rural country, India has an urban population of over 250 million and two of the top ten largest metropolitan areas in the world: Mumbai with 16.4 million people and Kolkata (Calcutta) with 13.2 million people. Extremes of wealth and poverty are often seen side-by-side. India's well-off middle classes number over 150 million yet under four per cent of Indian households have an annual income of more than 2,500 US dollars. The United Nations estimates that 25 per cent of the population live below the poverty line, many in city slums or without any home.

▲ Pilgrims flock to the Har Mandir Sahib or Golden Temple in Amritsar, the most sacred shrine to followers of the Sikh religion. Originally built in 1604 and rebuilt in the 19th century, the Golden Temple sits on a small island surrounded by the Pool of the Nectar of Immortality called Amrita Sar from which the city gets its name.

LANGUAGE, RELIGION AND CASTE

The country has been peopled since prehistoric times and waves of different invaders and settlers have been absorbed, giving the country a rich culture. This is reflected in the two official, 17 recognized and several hundred more languages spoken in the country of which Hindi is the most widely used. Although 81 per cent of the people are Hindu, India is also home to one of the world's largest Muslim populations numbering over 120 million. The varied religions found in India include over 20 million Christians, around 20 million Sikhs as well as Buddhists, Parsis and Jains. A complex caste system exists in India in which people are placed in one of around 3,000 social class positions which limit where they can work, who they can interact with and who they can marry. Despite government reforms, the caste system remains an important factor in Indian life.

THE WORLD'S LARGEST DEMOCRACY

India gained independence from British rule in 1947 and established its present constitution in 1949. The country is a multiparty democracy with an electorate of

◄ Farmers plough rice paddy fields in the southeastern Indian state of Tamil Nadu. Indian farmers rely on the monsoon season from June to November for water to irrigate their crops.

619.5 million, making it the largest in the world. India has a federal form of government with 28 states, each with a large amount of control over their own affairs and seven union territories with less control. Each state is headed by a governor who is appointed for a five-year term by the country's head of state, the President. The Prime Minister is the holder of most political power in India. He and his Council of Ministers are responsible to the parliament which is based in New Delhi. India's parliament consists of two chambers, the Rajya Sabha (Council of States) and the Lok Sabha (House of the People).

JAMMU AND KASHMIR

Jammu and Kashmir is a region on the northern borders of India and Pakistan. Famous for its natural beauty, the region is home to K2 (or Mt Godwin Austen), at 8,607 m the world's second-highest mountain, and around 12 million people. Both India and Pakistan claim the region as a part of their own territory. After several armed conflicts, the area was separated with the eastern region including the vale of Kashmir, Jammu and Ladakh administered by India. The potential for conflict to flare up into full-scale war remains, with both countries having tested nuclear devices in the 1990s. Partly as a result of the ongoing problems over Jammu and Kashmir, defence spending is high. India keeps one of the world's largest military forces made up of 1.3 million personnel.

▲ A crowded train operates on part of India's enormous railway system. Approximately 63,700 km of track link the country and carry millions of passengers and millions of tonnes of cargo.

▼ Simla lies on the southern slopes of the Himalayas and was the summer capital of British India between 1865 and 1939. In 1971, a meeting of Indian and Pakistani leaders formed the Simla Agreement dividing Jammu and Kashmir.

BANGLADESH

Lying on the Bay of Bengal bordered by India and Myanmar, Bangladesh was formerly West Pakistan before it gained its independence in 1971.

Area: 147,570 km²
Population: 129,155,000
Capital: Dhaka (11,726,000)
Major language spoken: Bengali
Main religions: Sunni Islam, Hinduism
Currency: taka
Main exports: clothing, jute manufactures, fish and prawns, hides and leather
Type of government: republic; limited democracy

Much of the land of Bangladesh is a low-lying flood plain formed by two large rivers, the Ganges and the Brahmaputra. These and other rivers carry meltwaters from the Himalaya mountains southwards to empty into the Bay of Bengal. Few places in the world are more susceptible to floods than Bangladesh. Some parts of the country can receive over 5,000 mm of rainfall annually and approximately two-thirds of the land is flooded for part of the year. The floods often result in great loss of life, crops, and property damage. The coastal regions of Bangladesh are also prone to cyclones. These intense storms can generate seven-metre-high waves and wind speeds of over 240 km/h. The rich soils created by sediment left by rivers in the delta region and a long growing season create fertile farming conditions.

Bangladesh is the world's leading producer of jute, a natural fibre particularly used in making rope, string, baskets and rough forms of paper. Sugarcane and tea are other important crops grown for export. However, most of the agriculture in the country is on a small scale and many Bangladeshi farmers struggle to grow enough food to feed their families. Rice is the most important crop along with pulses such as lentils and a range of vegetables. Over 1.1 million tonnes of fish, mainly freshwater varieties, are caught each year. The water which damages Bangladesh's land and threatens its people is also harnessed to irrigate farmlands in the dry season and to generate electricity. In the past, Bangladesh's mineral reserves were untapped. However, recent discoveries of large natural gas reserves are now being exploited with pipelines carrying the gas to the major industrial centres of Dhaka and the major port of Chittagong.

▼ A traffic jam of pedestrians and bicycle rickshaws occupies a crowded street in Dhaka, the capital of Bangladesh. However, around 80 per cent of Bangladeshis live in small rural villages.

NEPAL

Home of Mt Everest and many other Himalayan peaks, the kingdom of Nepal has developed a financially important tourist industry.

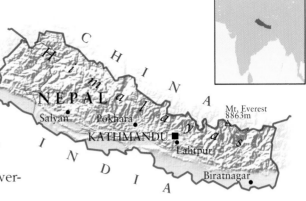

Area: 147,181 km²
Population: 23,078,000
Capital: Kathmandu (1,022,000)
Major languages spoken: Nepali, Maithili, Bhojpuri
Main religions: Hinduism, Buddhism
Currency: Nepalese rupee
Main exports: basic manufactures, textiles and clothing, food
Type of government: kingdom; limited democracy

▶ Offerings are left at the Swayambunath temple, a Buddhist temple near the capital city of Kathmandu. Only eight per cent of the Nepalese population are Buddhists. Eighty-six per cent are Hindus.

Four-fifths of Nepal is covered in mountains with eight of the world's ten highest peaks within its borders. To the south of the country, the land is lower-lying and forms an area of plains and marshlands which runs over the border with India. This region contains both hardwood and bamboo forests which provide homes for tigers, leopards and some elephants. Most of Nepal's population live in these southern plains or in the large central valley in which the country's largest city, Kathmandu, is found. Farming dominates the economy with most Nepalese engaged in growing crops and rearing livestock such as goats and buffalo. Nepal's landlocked and mountainous location has made large scale industry hard to develop. Carpets and textiles are the main manufacturing industries. Nepal once attracted half a million tourists a year to its mountains,

and historic and religious sites but recent numbers have fallen due to instability and attacks by rebel groups. Nepal is a poor country in which over a third of its population is undernourished.

BHUTAN

A mountainous landlocked kingdom surrounded by China and India, Bhutan remains one of the most isolated and unknown of all nations.

Area: 46,500 km²
Population: 2,124,000
Capital: Thimphu (45,000)
Major languages spoken: Dzongkha (Bhutanese), Nepali, Assamese
Major religions: Buddhism, Hinduism
Currency: ngultrum
Main exports: electricity, cement, timber, fruit and vegetables
Type of government: kingdom; dictatorship

The northern part of Bhutan is located in the Great Himalayas with mountain peaks rising to elevations of over 7,300 m. In the centre of the country are the lower-lying Lesser Himalayas. Between many of these mountain peaks are wide, fertile valleys. The only portion of Bhutan that is not mountainous is the Duars Plain which is a narrow strip along the southern border largely covered in dense forest. The people of Bhutan are among the most rural in the world. Only seven per cent are estimated to live in towns and around 93 per cent are dependent on farming. Sheep and cattle are reared while yaks, used for transport, meat and wool, are herded on colder

mountain slopes. Only 42 per cent of the country's adults are able to read and write and the country's industries and infrastructure remain under-developed. India is Bhutan's key trading partner, accounting for 77 per cent of imports and 94 per cent of exports. Bhutan is a strongly traditional Buddhist society. Until 1999, TV was banned and tourism still remains restricted.

SRI LANKA

A British colony until 1948, Sri Lanka is a pear-shaped island lying just off the coast of India. However, since 1983, its people have experienced a violent civil war.

Area: 65,610 km²
Population: 19,410,000
Capitals: Colombo, the administrative capital, and Sri Jawardenepura Kotte, the legislative capital (combined population 1,260,000)
Main languages spoken: Sinhala, Tamil
Main religions: Buddhism, Hinduism, Sunni Islam, Roman Catholic
Currency: Sri Lankan rupee
Main exports: textiles, clothing, tea, diamonds, coconut products
Type of government: republic; limited democracy

▼ Much of Sri Lanka's tea is grown on large plantations in the central highlands where cooler temperatures allow the tea plants to grow slowly and with more flavour. In 2000, 283,760 tonnes of tea were grown.

Sri Lanka's main geographic feature is an extensive area of rugged highlands in the central and southern parts of the island. These include peaks rising up over 1,500 m, steep river gorges and large plateaus. North of the highlands, the land consists of more gently rolling plains criss-crossed by a number of rivers. Lying close to the Equator, the island has an essentially tropical climate while the central highlands are cooler and temperate. Sri Lanka has an average 1,200 mm of rainfall per year but parts of the southwest of the country can receive between two and three times more. This wet zone is also the most densely populated part of the country. Sri Lanka has no fossil fuel reserves, relying instead on hydro-electricity to supply 68 per cent of its electricity needs. It does have reserves of iron ore and graphite and is a major source of a number of semi-precious and precious gemstones. Around 36 per cent of the population work in agriculture. The most common crop is rice which is grown primarily as a local food source. Almost three million tonnes of rice were produced in 2001, yet the country has to import more rice and many other foodstuffs. Only

12 per cent of Sri Lanka's farmland is used to grow tea but the country is the world's largest tea exporter.

SINHALESE AND TAMIL PEOPLES

Sri Lanka's population consists largely of two peoples: the Sinhalese who are mainly Buddhist and comprise around 74 per cent of the population and the Tamils, most of whom are Hindus, who make up around 18 per cent. Both peoples have inhabited Sri Lanka for over 1,400 years. Tensions between them spilled over into violent civil war from 1983 onwards. Many Tamils, especially in the north and east of Sri Lanka, want an independent state. Conflict between government forces and the Tamil rebel group called the Liberation Tigers of Tamil Eelam (Tamil Tigers) has seen over 60,000 deaths and large military forces which have been a major drain on the Sri Lankan economy. In 2002–2003, cease-fire talks promised more autonomy for the Tamils.

INDIAN OCEAN ISLANDS

The third largest of the oceans, the Indian Ocean extends from the eastern coast of Africa east to the Australian coast. A number of islands is contained in its waters; most are considered geographically to be part of the continent of Africa, although they have been settled by people of both African and Asian descent. The exception is the Maldives island group which is considered part of Asia. Apart from Madagascar which has an area larger than the European country of France, the remaining islands tend to be relatively small. Lush vegetation is found on many islands yet the terrain often allows only small areas of land to be farmed. Tourism, encouraged by the palm-fringed beaches of the islands, is the biggest growing industry.

MALDIVES

A chain of over 1,200 coral islands of which around 200 are inhabited, the Maldives lies southwest of India. Fishing dominates the economy of these isles.

Area: 298 km²
Population: 270,000
Capital: Male (74,000)
Main language spoken: Dihevi
Main religion: Sunni Islam
Currency: rufiyya
Main exports: fish, clothing, textiles
Government: republic; dictatorship

The Maldives consists of a 760 km long series of island groups in the Indian Ocean. All the islands are low-lying, with none over two metres in height and many are under threat from rising sea levels due to global warming. Many have sandy beaches fringed with lush palms and other vegetation. The islands lie in the tropical zone and have a hot climate with an average temperature of 26.7°C. Moist, seasonal winds known as monsoons blow across the islands bringing an annual average 1,520 mm of rain, mainly between May and August. The two major naturally growing food resources on the islands are coconut palms and breadfruit trees. However, the islands' most important resource is its rich marine life. Over 107,000 tonnes of fish, especially tuna, were caught in 2002. Along with a growing tourism industry, fishing accounts for the greater part of the Maldives' exports.

▼ A typical small, low-lying island in the Maldives.

MALE

M A L D I V E S

MADAGASCAR

The fourth largest island in the world, Madagascar lies in the Indian Ocean. It is a poor country best known for its many unique plant and animal species.

Area: 587,041 km²
Population: 15,492,000
Capital: Antananarivo (1,053,000)
Main language spoken: Malagasy
Main religions: traditional beliefs, Roman Catholic, Protestant Church of Madagascar
Currency: CFA franc
Main exports: coffee, vanilla, shrimps, cotton, cloves
Type of government: republic; limited democracy

Madagascar was once part of the African continent from which it split approximately 50 million years ago. Its current position is around 400 km east of Africa separated by the Mozambique Channel. Highlands run north to south through the island and drop sharply to the east. To the west, they descend more gently to a coastal plain. Nearly all of Madagascar was once covered in forests but much of the land has now been cleared. Areas of the island are covered in a rich, red soil which is suitable for farming. Isolated from mainland Africa, over three-quarters of the island's species of plants and animals are not found anywhere else in the world. Large amounts of foreign aid have been targeted to protect many of these species and their habitats which are under threat from deforestation and soil erosion.

MADAGASCAR'S PEOPLE

The island's people are of a range of origins, with the largest groups descendants of Indonesian peoples believed to have settled on the island over 1,000 years ago. Today, most Madagascans are engaged either in agriculture or in industries which process livestock and crops into products including foods, sisal rope, sugar and textiles. The main staple food is rice while cassava, beans, taro and bananas are widely grown. Over 10 million head of cattle exist on the island, many of which are a type of humped cattle called zebu. Madagascar is one of the poorest countries in the world. It struggles to import enough food to help feed its population which is growing at a rate of three per cent every year. Health and education services are also under-developed although there have been recent successes in reducing the levels of diseases such as malaria.

► Lemurs are a member of the primate family which includes monkeys, apes and humans. They are only found naturally in the wild on Madagascar. Forty distinct species of lemur have been catalogued.

COMOROS

An island archipelago lying between the eastern coast of Africa and Madagascar, Comoros is a poor nation; its population is reliant on fishing and farming.

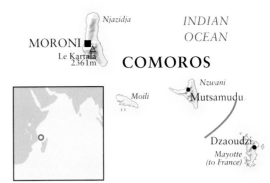

Area: 1,862 km²
Population: 714,000
Capital: Moroni (36,000)
Major languages spoken: Comorian, French, Arabic
Main religion: Sunni Islam
Currency: Comorian franc
Main exports: vanilla, ylang-ylang, cloves
Type of government: republic; limited democracy

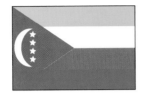

Volcanic action has created the three major islands and the small number of islets that comprise Comoros. Mayotte, a neighbouring island to the east, remained a dependency of France after the Comoros became independent in 1974. Njazidja is the largest and the youngest island in the archipelago. Its highest point, Le Kartala, is an active volcano. The islands have over a dozen bird species and several animals not found anywhere else in the world. These include Livingstone's flying fox, a giant fruit bat with a wing span of over one metre. Most Comorians fish or farm small areas of land, growing cassava, rice and sweet potatoes for food, and coffee, vanilla and other crops for export. Despite three-quarters of the workforce being engaged in farming or fishing, over half of all food is imported.

SEYCHELLES

Consisting of 105 islands lying 1,600 km from the east coast of Africa, the Seychelles was formerly a British colony before achieving independence in 1976.

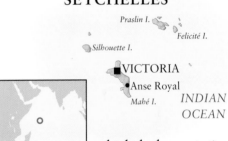

Area: 455 km²
Population: 77,000
Capital: Victoria (25,000)
Major languages spoken: Creole, English, French
Major religion: Roman Catholic
Currency: Seychelles rupee
Main exports: canned tuna, re-exported petroleum products, other fish and fish products, prawns
Type of government: republic; limited democracy

▼ Tourists attracted to unspoilt scenery and beaches in the Seychelles help fuel the tourism industry which employs over 30 per cent of the islands' workforce.

The Seychelles consists of two different types of island formations. The Mahé group are mainly granite while the remaining islands are largely formed from coral. The granite islands rise to heights of over 600 m and many contain small streams. In contrast, the coral-based islands rarely rise above nine metres and tend to have no freshwater. Forty-six of the islands are inhabited but 98 per cent of the population live on the four main islands: Mahé Island, Praslin, Silhouette and Felicité. Mahé is the largest and most populous of the Seychelles. The islands have a tropical climate with heavy rainfall in the highest areas. Many are covered in thick, lush vegetation and, in places where land has been cleared for farming, crops such as tea, cinnamon, tobacco, banana and sweet potatoes are cultivated. Many tropical fruits also grow on the islands, including avocados, mangoes, papaya and pineapples. The Seychelles has no mineral resources but the islands' two greatest natural resources are the fish-rich seas and the white sandy beaches. The beaches, abundant wildlife and warm climate have enabled the Seychelles to attract over 125,000 tourists every year. As a result, the islanders have a relatively high standard of living.

RÉUNION

A French overseas departement, Réunion is an island in the Indian Ocean. Its inhabitants rely on growing sugarcane, tourism and financial aid from France.

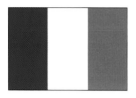

Area: 2,510 km²
Population: 699,000
Capital: St-Denis (158,000)
Major languages spoken: French, Creole
Main religion: Roman Catholic
Currency: euro
Main exports: sugar, machinery, lobsters
Type of government: dependency of France

Réunion is the largest of the Mascarene Islands which lie in the western Indian Ocean. The island is located around 180 km southwest of Mauritius and around 680 km east of Madagascar. Volcanic in origin, most of Réunion's landscape consists of mountains which rise to their highest point of 3,069 m, at Piton de Neiges in the centre of the island. The climate is tropical although cooler at higher altitudes and there is much variation in rainfall. On the south and eastern sides, rainfall is extremely heavy and can exceed 4,000 mm per year while on the north and western sides, rainfall can be lower than 1,000 mm per year. The island sometimes suffers from powerful tropical storms. The island was uninhabited when it was discovered by Portuguese explorers in the 16th century. In 1643, it was claimed by France who named it Bourbon and imported slaves from Africa to work on sugar plantations. Renamed Réunion in 1793, the island became an overseas departement of France in 1946. Réunion's economy has relied on agriculture for many years, particularly sugarcane which has been the island's major crop for over a century. Other export products include rum, vanilla and essences used in perfumes. The island's inhabitants are of mainly mixed African, Asian and French descent.

MAURITIUS

Mauritius is an island republic in the Indian Ocean. Once a colony of the Netherlands, France and then Britain, it achieved independence in 1968.

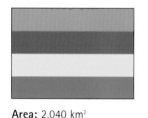

Area: 2,040 km²
Population: 1,179,000
Capital: Port Louis (168,000)
Major languages spoken: French Creole, Bhojpuri, English, Hindi, Tamil
Main religions: Hinduism, Roman Catholic, Sunni Islam
Currency: Mauritius rupee
Main exports: clothing, sugar, yarn, pearls
Type of government: republic; democracy

▶ Sugarcane plantations cover half the cultivated land and make up 30 per cent of the country's export earnings.

Mauritius lies approximately 800 km east of the large island of Madagascar and consists of one large, dominant island with the name, Mauritius, and a number of smaller islands. Formed by volcanic activity, Mauritius has a mountainous southern region, a central plateau and a lower-lying plain in the north. Traditionally reliant on sugarcane growing and processing, Mauritius has broadened its range of industries. Its white sand beaches and coral reefs together with its tropical climate have attracted many foreign tourists. It has developed hydro-electric power to provide energy for industries such as clothes making and electronic goods. Sixty-eight per cent of the population are Indo-Mauritians, mostly descendants of Indian labourers brought to the island in the 19th century. People of mixed descent known as Creoles comprise 27 per cent while there are also significant minorities of Europeans and Chinese.

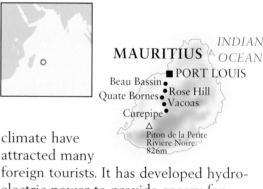

EASTERN AND
SOUTHEAST ASIA

EASTERN ASIA

A region of great extremes in landscape and peoples, eastern Asia consists of a large mainland area which borders the Russian Federation, Kazakhstan and Kyrgyzstan to the north. The mainland has a long easterly-facing coastline with the northern Pacific Ocean. In the Pacific are the island nations of Taiwan and Japan, while the peninsula containing North and South Korea juts out into the ocean waters. Geographically, eastern Asia is dominated by China, the most populous and fourth largest country in the world. The highest part of the region is the Plateau of Tibet to the southwest where heights exceed 5,000 m and rise higher to the south where it is bordered by the Himalayas. Directly north of this rugged mountain region lies the Taklimakan, a huge and bleak sand desert. The region's largest desert, the Gobi, occupies a vast part of Mongolia and northern China. A number of major rivers flow through eastern Asia, including the Huang He or Yellow river and the Chang Jiang or Yangtze river. To the east and southeast, the landscape becomes less hostile and is more easily farmed. It is this area and on eastern Asia's islands where the majority of the region's people live. Historically, most of the countries of this region kept themselves isolated from the rest of the world, but the 20th century saw great change. Japan, South Korea and Taiwan modernized and developed large manufacturing and trading industries and strong links with the global economy. China is currently in the process of great change, while Mongolia is also undergoing economic change. Only North Korea remains largely isolated from the rest of the world.

KAZAKHSTAN

Altai

KYRGYZSTAN

TAJIKISTAN

PAKISTAN

INDIA

NEPAL

BHUTAN

Tien Shan

Tarim Basin

Taklimakan Desert

Kunlun Shan

Himalayas

C
P
of

0   500   1000 k
0   250   500 miles

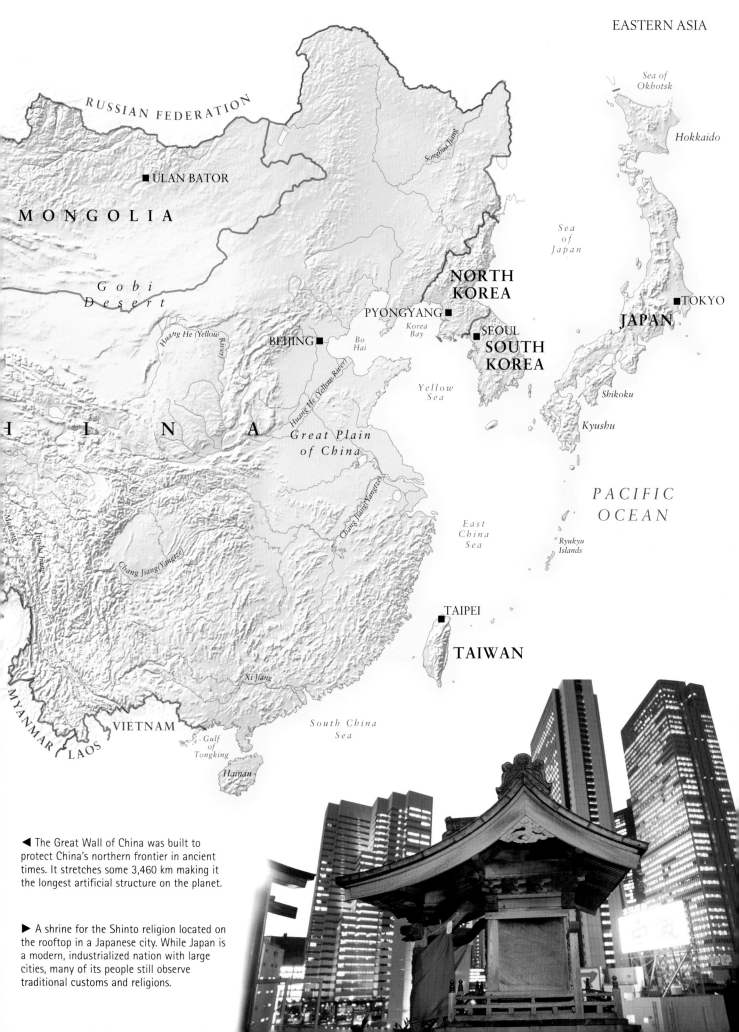

RUSSIAN FEDERATION

■ ULAN BATOR

M O N G O L I A

G o b i
D e s e r t

Songhua Jiang

Sea
of
Okhotsk

Hokkaido

NORTH
KOREA

PYONGYANG ■

Korea Bay

*Sea
of
Japan*

■ TOKYO

JAPAN

Huang He (Yellow River)

BEIJING ■

*Bo
Hai*

SEOUL ■
SOUTH
KOREA

*Yellow
Sea*

Shikoku

C   H   I   N   A

Huang He (Yellow River)

*Great Plain
of China*

Kyushu

Chang Jiang (Yangtze)

PACIFIC
OCEAN

Mekong

*East
China
Sea*

*Ryukyu
Islands*

Nu Jiang (Salween)

Chang Jiang (Yangtze)

TAIPEI ■

TAIWAN

Xi Jiang

*South China
Sea*

MYANMAR
LAOS

VIETNAM

*Gulf
of
Tongking*

Hainan

◀ The Great Wall of China was built to
protect China's northern frontier in ancient
times. It stretches some 3,460 km making it
the longest artificial structure on the planet.

▶ A shrine for the Shinto religion located on
the rooftop in a Japanese city. While Japan is
a modern, industrialized nation with large
cities, many of its people still observe
traditional customs and religions.

301

CHINA

The home of advanced civilizations stretching back over 5,000 years, the People's Republic of China is the world's most populous and fourth largest country.

Area: 9,560,780 km²
Population: 1,284,960,000
Capital: Beijing (7,336,000)
Main languages spoken: Chinese (Guoyo), Wu, Cantonese, Xiang, Min
Main religions: non-religious majority, Chinese folk religions (including Daoism)
Currencies: yuan, Hong Kong dollar (legal only in Hong Kong) and pataca (legal only in Macau)
Main exports: machinery and equipment, textiles and clothing, footwear, toys and sports goods, minerals and metal products, electrical goods and office equipment
Type of government: republic; dictatorship

▼ The waterfront of Hong Kong with its many high-rise offices and apartment buildings reflects the former British colony's status as one of the world's leading trade, banking and finance centres. In 1997, control of Hong Kong was handed back to China.

China has a 14,500 km long Pacific coastline and land borders of some 22,000 km with a total of 14 other nations. With massive variation in climate and landscape, China can be broadly divided into three key regions: the southwest, the east and the north, and the northwest. The southwest is a cold, mountainous area containing the world's highest plateau, the Plateau of Tibet. Much of this region consists of frozen wastes, marshlands and salt lakes and is sparsely inhabited. The eastern region of China is where the majority of the country's vast population resides. Much of eastern China is at elevations below 400 m although highland regions do exist. Many rivers criss-cross its land which, over time, have created large flood plains and deltas which are fertile farming areas. The largest of China's rivers, and the longest in Asia, is the Chang Jiang or Yangtze river: 700 tributaries flow into the Chang Jiang as it completes its 6,300 km journey flowing essentially eastwards from the Kunlun Shan mountains through central China, before emptying into the Pacific just north of Shanghai. The northwestern regions of China are largely highlands

marked by large desert basins and some mountains. East of these areas, the giant Gobi Desert extends through northern central China. Desert covers about 27 per cent of China and is increasing at an annual rate of 1,550 km² due to deforestation and over-use of dry soils on farms near desert areas. Winds from the north generate giant sandstorms which envelop towns and cities, hamper transportation and damage farmland. A 70-year project called the Great Green Wall seeks to plant millions of trees along the southern borders of the Gobi to help bar the further spread of desert.

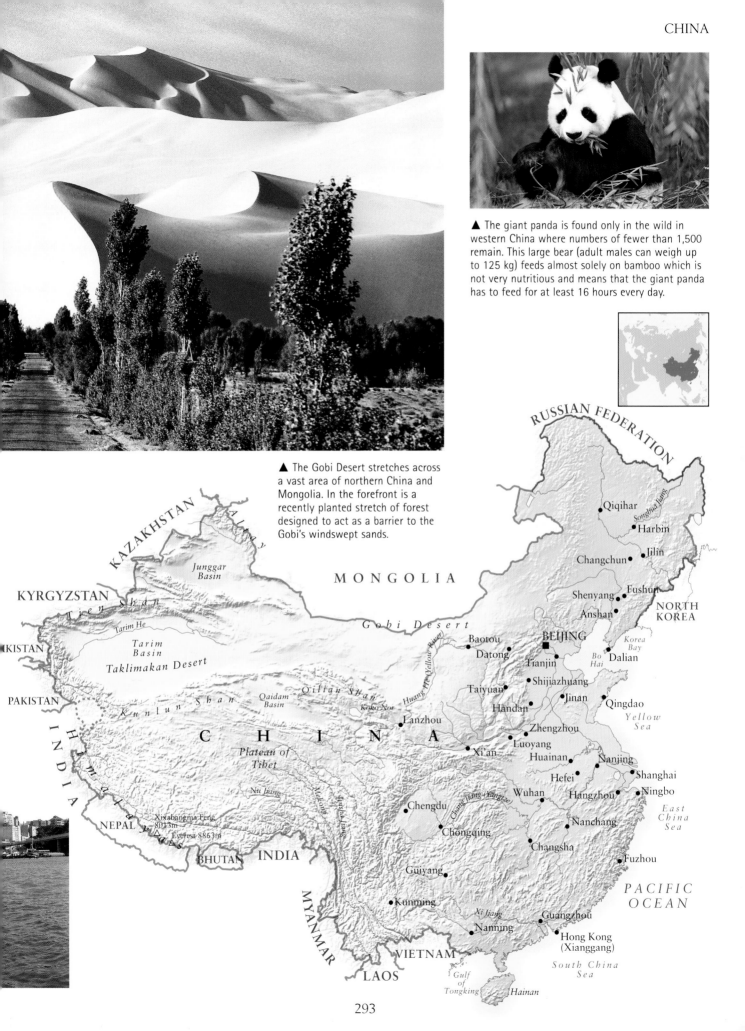

▲ The giant panda is found only in the wild in western China where numbers of fewer than 1,500 remain. This large bear (adult males can weigh up to 125 kg) feeds almost solely on bamboo which is not very nutritious and means that the giant panda has to feed for at least 16 hours every day.

▲ The Gobi Desert stretches across a vast area of northern China and Mongolia. In the forefront is a recently planted stretch of forest designed to act as a barrier to the Gobi's windswept sands.

RUSSIAN FEDERATION

Qiqihar

Harbin

Changchun · Jilin

Songhua Jiang

Shenyang · Fushun

Anshan

NORTH KOREA

MONGOLIA

KAZAKHSTAN

Altay

Junggar Basin

Gobi Desert

Baotou

Datong

BEIJING

Korea Bay

Dalian

KYRGYZSTAN

Tien Shan

Tarim He

Tarim Basin

Taklimakan Desert

Qilian Shan

Qaidam Basin

Koko Nor

Huang He (Yellow River)

Tianjin

Bo Hai

Taiyuan

Shijiazhuang

Jinan

Qingdao

Handan

Lanzhou

Zhengzhou

Yellow Sea

KISTAN

PAKISTAN

Kunlun Shan

Luoyang

Xi'an

Huainan

Nanjing

C H I N A

Plateau of Tibet

Hefei

Wuhan

Shanghai

Hangzhou

Ningbo

Nu Jiang

Mekong

Yangtze Jiang

Chang Jiang (Yangtze)

Chengdu

Nanchang

East China Sea

INDIA

Himalayas

NEPAL

Xixabangma Feng 8013m

Everest 8863m

Chongqing

Changsha

BHUTAN

INDIA

Guiyang

Fuzhou

MYANMAR

Kunming

Xi Jiang

Guangzhou

PACIFIC OCEAN

Nanning

Hong Kong (Xianggang)

VIETNAM

LAOS

Gulf of Tongking

Hainan

South China Sea

CHINA'S CLIMATE

China's climate varies greatly over its large area. Temperatures increase from north to south, and rainfall increases from northwest to southeast. Northeast China has a continental climate with warm and humid summers, long cold winters and rainfall under 750 mm per year. The central lowlands contain the hottest areas of China, and has an annual rainfall of 750 to 1,100 mm. The south is wetter, while the extreme subtropical south experiences the monsoon. The northwest is arid, continental and has cold winters. Western China experiences an extreme climate due to its altitude and long distance from the sea. Rainfall is low and most of Tibet has ten months of frost.

A FARMING GIANT

Around half of China's workforce is engaged in agriculture. A third of all cultivated land is sown with rice, which dominates farming in southern China and is the country's key staple food. Other cereal crops, particularly wheat, maize, millet and barley, are also vital along with oil seeds, soy beans, root vegetables, sugarcane and sugar beet. China is also one of the world's leading growers of a number of crops including peanuts, cotton and tea. China's livestock numbers are enormous

▼ Located 370 km northwest of Guangzhou, the spectacular scenery around the settlement of Guilin has been formed by erosion of the limestone rock. Many tall pinnacles covered in vegetation exist, along with extensive and beautiful cave systems.

◄ Water buffalo are popular beasts of burden in China, especially in the wetter, rice-growing regions. In 2001, there were an estimated 24 million water buffalo in the country.

with 500 million pigs, 610 million ducks and 3,600 million chickens. Fish is also a vital part of the Chinese diet. Unusually, most of the annual catch of 36 million tonnes is freshwater fish from rivers, lakes and fish farms.

MINING AND INDUSTRY

China has enormous mineral resources within its borders and is the world's leading producer of coal, graphite and a number of commercially valuable metals including titanium and tungsten. Mining also extracts large amounts of other metals particularly iron ore, tin, copper and bauxite, the ore from which aluminium is made. Much of the country's iron ore is concentrated in the northeast, which remains the centre of the heavy metals industry. Oil production in 2002 was around 3.2 million barrels per day although older oilfields in the east of the country have dwindling reserves. Energy supplies are

heavily reliant on burning coal which has led to high levels of pollution in the cities. Since coming to power, the communist government has made massive attempts to build up China's industries to compete in the world's markets. Steel making and metal working industries, processing oil into chemicals, artificial fibres and plastics and the manufacture of fertilizers, heavy machinery, farm machinery and railway and motor vehicles are all major industries. China's textiles industry is the world's largest, employing an estimated 4.1 million workers in 2001. Since the late 1980s, China has opened its borders to foreign investment and joint ventures with other countries. Although the economy is planned by the state, many businesses are now in private hands and are thriving. However, economic growth and prosperity has occurred mainly to the east and in coastal areas. In many other parts of China, particularly the west, the population contends with poor transportation, undeveloped industries and a lower standard of living.

▲ Located in China's capital city of Beijing, the Temple of Heaven was traditionally where Chinese emperors used to pray to the gods for good harvests. Built in the 15th century, this beautiful temple was constructed from wood without using nails.

▼ A centre of trade in Asia before the communists came to power, the bustling city of Shanghai is again attracting foreign visitors and trade.

▲ Over six million people live in the small, but heavily built-up, Special Autonomous Region of Hong Kong. It is one of the world's most densely populated areas.

▼ Since it was built in the 17th century, the breathtaking Potala palace has been the traditional home of Tibet's spiritual leader, the Dalai Lama, who now lives in exile.

COMMUNIST CHINA

While China makes large reforms to advance its economy in line with the world market, changes to the strict way the country is run have been minimal. The Chinese Communist Party (CCP) was formed in 1921 and came to power in 1949 after a bitter struggle with nationalist forces over a period of two decades. This struggle culminated in a four-year-long civil war (1945–1949) in which an estimated 12 million people died. The CCP, under its leader Mao Zedong, embarked upon a huge series of reforms to transform much of China's economy and society. Some have been successful, such as improving education, healthcare and developing new infrastructure and industries. Women's role in society has been improved and China has grown as an economic power. Other policies, such as the Great Leap Forward in the late 1950s, proved disastrous. An attempt to reorganize China's rural people into farming and industrial communes saw harvests fall and an estimated 20 million people die of starvation. Communist China has also practised much

censorship of the media and abused human rights to quell criticism. The Cultural Revolution (1966–1976) saw chaos and thousands of people executed. In more recent times, student uprisings have also been violently suppressed.

A FIFTH OF ALL PEOPLE

In 1949 there were an estimated 500 million people in China. Fifty years later, that figure

◄ Construction work continues on the Three Gorges Dam across the Chang Jiang river. This enormous two km wide dam is a part of the world's biggest hydro-electric power scheme scheduled to open in 2009. It is being built to generate enormous quantities of electricity and to let large ships sail into China's interior. Environmentalists are concerned at the vast area of the river valley which will be flooded, displacing over 1.5 million people.

had more than doubled to over 1.2 billion. Managing and feeding almost a fifth of the world's people is a massive task, and China has sometimes embarked upon methods which are criticized by the outside world. For example, to curb the high birth rate China introduced very strict one child per family policies in the 1970s. Greater family planning has resulted in a low birth rate but still over 11 million Chinese babies are born every year. The continued rise in China's population is due mainly to the dramatic increase in life expectancy. Since 1950, better healthcare and the eradication of certain diseases has resulted in life expectancy more than doubling to just over 70 years. Despite industrialization and the growth of massive cities, approximately two-thirds of China's population is rural. During its rule, the communist government has attempted many policies to prevent the migration of rural peoples to its towns and cities, but city sizes are still increasing. China has more large cities than any other nation, with 36 having a population of over one million.

▼ Chinese women work on an assembly line building electronics equipment. Electronics and electrical goods manufacture are fast-growing industries in China. Around 36 million TV sets were produced in China in 2002.

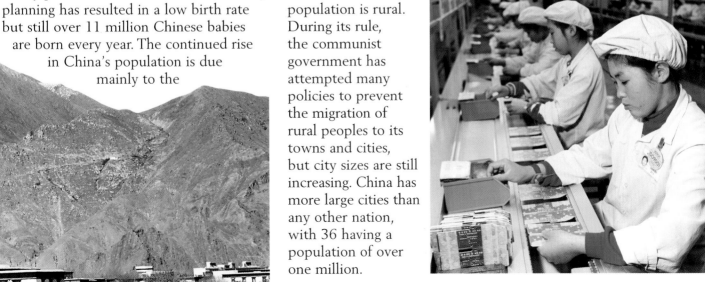

▲ Bordering Myanmar, Vietnam and Laos to the south, and Tibet to the west, the Chinese province of Yunnan is a region of plateaus and mountains.

▼ Discovered in 1974, the Terracotta Army is a collection of more than 6,000 full-size statues of soldiers and animals made from terracotta clay. An astonishingly large and beautiful collection of sculptures, the figures were designed to guard the tomb of the emperor Shi Huangdi who ruled in the third century BCE.

PEOPLE, RELIGION AND HISTORY

China contains over 55 different ethnic groups but an estimated 93 per cent are of Han Chinese origin. The largest minority, the Zhuang, are related to the Thai peoples and number over 15.5 million. There are also approximately 8.6 million Hui and 7.2 million Uyghur peoples. Many of the largest populations of ethnic minorities are found in the border areas of China. Just over half of the Chinese people consider themselves non-religious, while one-fifth practise one of many forms of traditional folk religion. In addition, there are millions of Chinese who follow Buddhism, Islam, Taoism and various forms of Christianity. Over 3,000 years ago, the Zhou Dynasty arose during which time the teachings of the philosopher Confucius (551–479 BCE) became important and influence Chinese society to this day. The short-lived Qin Dynasty (221–206 BCE) saw the unification of much of China and the building of the Great Wall along the country's northern frontier. The Han (202 BCE–CE 220), Tang (618–907) and Song (960–1279) dynasties were times of great advances in science and the arts. The Mongols completed the first foreign conquest of the Chinese Empire in the 13th century and were followed by the Ming Dynasty and then China's last dynasty, the Qing, which ended in 1912 when the country became a republic.

AUTONOMOUS REGIONS

China has a number of autonomous regions in which a degree of local rule has been granted. Inner Mongolia to the north, Guangxi Zhuang to the south and Xinjang Uyghur to the northwest are three of the largest of these regions but, in each, dissent against Chinese rule has often been suppressed with force.

The best-known autonomous region of China is Tibet in the southwest. Cut off from neighbouring areas by giant mountain chains on three sides, ethnic Tibetans make up over 90 per cent of the total population of 2–3 million. Tibetans developed their own form of Buddhism led by the Dalai Lama as their national and spiritual leader. By turns independent or under Chinese rule for much of its existence, China invaded Tibet in 1950–1951. Since that time, there has been much religious persecution of the Tibetan people with many Buddhist monasteries, books and artworks destroyed.

On the southern coastline of China is the former British colony of Hong Kong, which was returned to China in the late 1990s. It is an important trading centre and it has been made a Special Autonomous Region with some control over its own affairs.

TAIWAN

Officially known as the Republic of China, this large island lies 165 km off the coast of mainland China. Taiwan is in dispute with China over its independence.

Area: 36,179 km² including Quemoy and Matsu islands
Population: 22,167,000
Capital: Taipei (4,606,000)
Main languages spoken: Chinese, Min, Hakka
Main religions: Chinese folk religions (including Daoism), Buddhism
Currency: Taiwan dollar
Main exports: non-electrical machinery, electrical machinery, plastic articles, textiles, synthetic fibres, chemicals
Type of government: republic; democracy

▼ A food stall in a night market in Taiwan's largest city, the capital, Taipei. Since World World II, Taiwan has undergone rapid urbanization.

Taiwan consists of Taiwan Island and a number of smaller islands including Pescadores. More than 60 per cent is mountainous with over 150 peaks above 3,000 m. Many of the mountain slopes are covered in forests. Most Taiwanese live along the broad and fertile coastal plains to the west and the south. Taiwan has heavy annual rainfall with a tropical climate in the south and a subtropical climate in the higher elevations in the north. Agriculture contributes less than two per cent of Taiwan's income with the major crops being rice, maize, pineapples and bananas. The Taiwanese fishing industry is important and exports mainly to Japan.

ECONOMIC SUCCESS

Taiwan has relatively few mineral resources and is not an oil producer, but has become an economic success. Land reforms in the 1950s gave many farm workers control of land while former land owners were encouraged to set up in business.

Taiwan is a strong industrial nation with four-fifths of its industry devoted to manufacturing a wide range of products, particularly electrical and electronic goods, textiles, plastics and motor vehicles. Since the early 1990s, Taiwan has been one of the world's top five producers of computer hardware. The Taiwanese people have one of the highest standards of living in Asia.

TAIWAN AND CHINA

Formerly called Formosa, Taiwan became part of the Chinese Empire in 1624 and for half a century (1895–1945) was ruled by the Japanese. In the late 1940s, the communist takeover of China saw almost two million people flee to Taiwan. The former leader of China, Chiang Kai-shek, refused to recognize the Communist Party government and established his own administration on the island. Mainland China still considers Taiwan as one of its provinces and, in 1971, Taiwan lost its seat at the UN. Today, only a small number of countries recognize Taiwan as an independent nation and the country's relationship with China dominates politics. With one of the world's top ten largest armies, a great proportion of the government's expenditure goes on defence.

MONGOLIA

A large, remote country of mountains, plains and deserts, Mongolia was once the centre of a mighty empire. Today, this isolated nation is one of the poorest in Asia.

Area: 1,566,500 km²
Population: 2,373,000
Capital: Ulan Bator (760,000)
Main language spoken: Mongol
Main religion: Buddhism (lamaism)
Currency: tugrik
Main exports: mineral products (particularly copper), live animals, textiles (cashmere and wool), animal products (including hides)
Type of government: republic; democracy

Mongolia is surrounded by the Russian Federation to the north and China to the south. Much of its land consists of a plateau lying between 900 m and 1,500 m in elevation. This plateau is broken up by mountain ranges especially to the west where the Altai mountains rise to heights of above 4,000 m. Large grass-covered prairies exist in the northeast and the northwest of the country supporting flocks of sheep and herds of goats, cattle and horses. Central and southeastern Mongolia are covered by the hostile Gobi Desert. This giant desert measures over 1,600 km west-to-east and over 950 km north-to-south. Its surface consists largely of rock and gravel. To the southeast, the Gobi is extremely arid and supports little life. Elsewhere in the Gobi, tough grass, scrub and thorn bushes provide scanty vegetation and feeding for the herds and flocks of Mongolia's nomadic desert dwellers. Water comes from the occasional shallow lake and watering holes.

CLIMATE, RESOURCES AND PEOPLE
Mongolia's climate is harsh with great extremes in which the temperature can vary as much as 30°C in a single day. Summers tend to be short, cool to mild with low rainfall and have many clear days. Winters are long and bitterly cold with temperatures ranging between -15°C

▶ This Mongolian farmer cuts and harvests hay using Bactrian camels to pull his simple plough. Over 350,000 camels are kept in the country, mainly as beasts of burden.

◄ A small child fetches water from a frozen river near the Mongolian capital city of Ulan Bator.

and -30°C. Especially severe winters, called Zud, can devastate livestock on which many Mongolians depend. Agriculture and the processing of agricultural products into foods, cloth and leather goods is a vital part of the Mongolian economy. Mongolia is also rich in a number of minerals including iron ore, coal, copper, lead and tungsten. The country's harsh climate and isolated location have so far prevented much of its mineral resources from being exploited.

From 1206 onwards, Mongolia was the centre of the great Mongol Empire which extended throughout much of Asia and was feared for its fierce horse-riding warriors. Today the people live in one of the most undeveloped nations in Asia. Transport links are sparse and often in disrepair. The country has just 1,600 km of paved roads, no highways and limited water and rail links. Many Mongolians have given up their rural way of life and have moved to towns. An estimated 36 per cent live below the poverty line.

▼ Nomadic Mongolian herders take a meal inside their large portable tent-like home called a yurt.

NORTH KOREA

North Korea is run by a communist government which has kept this mountainous country isolated since the Korean Peninsula was partitioned in 1948.

Area: 122,762 km²
Population: 24,039,000
Capital: Pyongyang (2,741,000)
Main language spoken: Korean
Main religions: non-religious majority; traditional beliefs, Chondogyo
Currency: won
Main exports: minerals, metallurgical products, armaments, agricultural products
Type of government: republic; dictatorship

▼ A political festival in progress in a stadium in North Korea's capital city of Pyongyang. Only people who are loyal to the strict communist regime are allowed to live in the city.

The Democratic People's Republic of Korea occupies the northern half of the Korean Peninsula. Four-fifths of its land is mountainous with many slopes covered with forests of coniferous trees. The mountains rise in elevation to the north where Pektu-San (2,744 m), the country's highest peak, is located. Most of the east coast of the country is steep and rugged with few islands. To the west, the slopes are more gentle and end in plains and a network of river estuaries. The country's lowlands, comprising one-fifth of the land, are found mainly in the west and are where most of its people live. Farming is also concentrated here and the country's major crops are rice, maize and other cereals, potatoes and other vegetables. North Korea has a continental climate, with hot summers and cold winters. The climate is influenced by both the cold winds from Siberia and the monsoon winds from east Asia. During the summer months, the monsoon brings much of the country's rainfall.

AN ISOLATED COMMUNIST NATION

Since its formation, North Korea has been run by a strict communist government with the military exerting a powerful influence. The state owns nearly all farms and industries, and distributes the wealth among its people. In practice, loyal members of the Korean Workers Party (KWP), the only political party allowed by law, benefit more than others. The country's media is largely state-controlled and opponents of the government are

◀ Opened in 1984, the Mansudae Assembly Hall in Pyongyang is one of the major governmental buildings of North Korea. It is used to hold sessions of the Supreme People's Assembly.

often dealt with harshly. While other communist nations have changed greatly, North Korea has remained apart and largely isolated. Trade and communications with the rest of the world are limited. This closed nation has recently opened its borders to aid and limited foreign investment as its economy has declined. Important industries in North Korea include the mining of coal, iron ore, tungsten, zinc and other metals, and heavy and engineering industries producing refined metals, machinery and chemicals. The country produces almost two-thirds of its electricity from hydro-electric power but shortages are common. From 1995 to 1999, successive droughts and floods damaged vast tracts of farmlands and brought famine to North Korea in which as many as two million people died. Chronic food shortages remain.

NORTH AND SOUTH RELATIONS

The Korean Peninsula has a long history of settlement and civilization before coming under first, Chinese, and by 1910, Japanese, control. In 1948, the peninsula was partitioned into two separate nations. Two years later, North Korea launched an invasion of South Korea in an attempt to unify Korea under a single communist government. The Korean War (1950–1953) was a bitter conflict in which North Korea was supported by China and South Korea by a coalition of forces, mainly from the USA. By the end of the war, over a million Koreans and many thousands of foreign troops had died. Relations between the two nations have remained difficult with many incidents since this time. Despite a summit meeting between the two countries' leaders in 2000, the first time they had ever met directly, there remains considerable tension between North and South. At the end of 2002, North Korea started to reactivate part of its nuclear programme, leading to fears that it was to embark on creating nuclear weapons.

▼ A class for North Korean schoolchildren is held outdoors. North Korean schooling starts with pre-school kindergartens. Education emphasizes science and technology, and English is compulsory as a second language for students above the age of 14.

SOUTH KOREA

Occupying the southern half of the Korean Peninsula, South Korea industrialized rapidly and is now one of Asia's most powerful nations.

Area: 99,392 km²
Population: 45,985,000
Capital: Seoul (14,250,000)
Main language spoken: Korean
Main religions: non-religious majority; Buddhism, various Protestant Churches
Currency: won
Main exports: electronic products, machinery and transport equipment (including motor vehicles), steel, ships, textiles, clothing and footwear
Type of government: republic; democracy

Over two-thirds of South Korea is mountainous with the largest lowland areas to the west and the south. South Korea's western coastline is indented and most of the country's 3,000 islands lie off this coast in the Yellow Sea. The largest of Korea's islands is Cheju, south of the mainland. With a subtropical climate, many fruits are grown here and the island attracts tourists to its spectacular scenery. Ullung, the largest island off the eastern coast, serves as a major fishery base. In 2002, a total of 2.7 million tonnes of fish were caught by South Korean vessels. The country's one land border is with North Korea to the north. It features the demilitarized zone or DMZ, a four km-wide strip of land which runs from the west to east coasts of the peninsula. Thousands of troops from the forces of the two countries are stationed on either side of the DMZ. Tensions remain high between the two nations.

▼ Sungnyemun or the South Gate was originally a grand entrance to the capital city of Seoul and is the oldest wooden structure in the city. Seoul was also the capital of Korea from the late 14th century until 1948.

THE KOREAN PEOPLE

The population of the Korean Peninsula is unique in southeast Asia in that it is made up almost entirely of one single ethnic group which has lived in the region for over 2,000 years. Between 1950 and 1990, the country's population more than doubled. Vast numbers of people, particularly the young, moved to South Korea's cities, and now around 80 per cent of the population are urban. Farming is still important in rural areas with rice, potatoes and cereals the biggest crops. The country's high population density has created environmental pressures with serious air pollution in some cities.

AN ECONOMIC MIRACLE

South Korea had a largely agricultural and under-developed economy before the 1960s. From 1962 onwards, a series of five-year plans sought to build up the country's manufacturing industries, assisted by investment from foreign companies and aid, particularly from Japan and the USA. South Korea's economy boomed as a result, growing by around nine per cent every year between 1970

and the early 1990s. The country has become a giant in manufacturing areas such as ship-building, motor vehicle manufacture, high-tech electronics and computers. Much of the industry is run by massive enterprises known as chaebol or conglomerates such as Samsung or Hyundai. Most of its major industrial centres are located on or near the coastline, allowing shipping to import many fuels and raw materials and to transport manufactured goods all over the world. The country's biggest port is Pusan which is also South Korea's second largest city after Seoul. South Korea has relatively few mineral resources apart from raw materials used in the cement, glass and ceramics industries. It is not an oil producer but refines crude oil imported from other nations. Around 38 per cent of its electricity is generated using nuclear power.

▲ Cranes at Hyundai Heavy Industries' giant ship-building yard in the city of Ulsan. The world's largest ship-builders, Hyundai Heavy Industry account for about 15 per cent of the global ship-building market. South Korea is the world's 12th largest trading nation.

▼ South Korean border guards in the heart of the demilitarized zone (DMZ), a heavily armed border zone separating North and South Korea.

JAPAN

The island nation of Japan lies on the western edge of the Pacific Ocean. A land of ancient and rich culture, the country has become a world economic superpower.

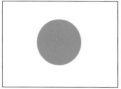

Area: 377,819 km²
Population: 126,926,000
Capital: Tokyo (29,950,000)
Main language spoken: Japanese
Main religions: Buddhism, Shinto
Currency: yen
Main exports: motor vehicles, electrical and electronic equipment (particularly semiconductors and computers), office machinery, chemicals, scientific and optical equipment, iron and steel products
Type of government: empire; democracy

Japan is an island archipelago which extends over 2,900 km in a roughly north-south direction. It is separated from mainland Asia to the west by the Sea of Japan. The country's territory includes more than 1,000 smaller islands and four main islands which are from north to south: Hokkaido, the most rural, Honshu, the largest, Shikoku, and Kyushu. South of Kyushu, the Ryuku island chain, including Okinawa island, arcs in a southerly direction towards Taiwan. Japan's four main islands are located close enough for them all to be linked by tunnels, bridges or causeways. Together, they comprise almost 98 per cent of Japan's land mass and are where the vast majority of Japanese live.

Japan's climate is varied in part due to the fact its land covers some 17 degrees of latitude. Winds from Siberia and cold ocean waters influence the climate of Hokkaido and northern Honshu where summers are short and winters long and severe, with plenty of snowfall. Hokkaido's largest city, Sapporo, is a renowned winter sports centre. Southern Honshu, Shikoku and Kyushu enjoy longer, warmer and more humid summers and milder winters partly created by warmer Pacific winds and the warm, fast-moving Kuroshio ocean current which travels northeast from the Philippines. Typhoons can strike between June and October. The heavy rains and fierce winds can damage houses and crops. The Ryuku islands experience a subtropical climate. Precipitation, too, varies greatly with Hokkaido the driest region averaging just over 1,000 mm per year. In contrast, central Honshu's mountains can receive 3,800 mm per year.

JAPANESE FLORA AND FAUNA

Japan has a rich plant life with over 17,000 species. Forests cover over 60 per cent of the land, particularly coniferous forests, although great parts of Honshu are covered in deciduous trees. Larger land animals include bears, wild boar, deer and one species of monkey, the Japanese macaque. Over 400 species of birds exist.

VOLCANOES AND EARTHQUAKES

Japan is located on the meeting point of three of the Earth's tectonic plates and its landscape has been shaped by plate movement for millions of years. Japan's terrain is largely mountainous with coastal plains on which nearly all of the country's cities are located. More than 200 volcanoes exist, of which 77 are considered active. Examples of the volatility of the Earth's crust below can be seen both in the numerous hot water springs and occasional tsunami which tend to strike the country's eastern coast. An estimated 800–1,000 earthquakes strike Japan every year.

▲ A bullet train on the Shinkansen high-speed railway line passes by a rice paddy – a typical Japanese scene of the traditional alongside the modern. The Shinkansen trains offer some of the most rapid land transport in the world reaching speeds in excess of 260 km/h.

▼ Hikone Castle, one of the best preserved in Japan, lies on the eastern shore of Lake Biwa, some 53 km northeast of Kyoto. Construction of the castle began in 1603 and the city of the same name grew up around it.

◀ A national symbol of Japan, the spectacular volcanic cone of Mt Fuji lies approximately 100 km west of Tokyo. With a height of 3,776 m, it is Japan's highest point. Although it has not erupted since 1707, Mt Fuji is not considered extinct and could erupt again in the future.

▲ A Japanese rocket is assembled at a Mitsubishi Heavy Industries factory. Japan is one of the small and exclusive group of nations which has launched space vehicles. Its first satellite was launched in 1970 and the Nozomi space probe is expected to reach Mars in 2004.

AGRICULTURE AND FISHING

Although only around 13 per cent of the country is suitable for cultivation, advanced, intensive farming and irrigation methods and government support have enabled Japan to be self-sufficient in its key staple foodstuff, rice. More than 40 per cent of the cultivated land is devoted to rice production but other crops are grown including potatoes, sugar beet, onions, cucumbers and mandarin oranges. Fish and seafood are a major part of the Japanese diet and the country's fishing fleet is one of the biggest in the world. Japan has also developed large aquaculture or fish farming techniques.

PEOPLE AND CITIES

Japan's rugged landscape means that little more than a fifth of its area is habitable, yet the country is the ninth most populous in the world. People tend to live in densely populated towns and cities, especially on Honshu which accounts for four-fifths of the population. The capital, Tokyo, in which 29.9 million people live, is the

world's largest metropolitan area. Ninety-nine per cent of Japanese share the same ethnic and cultural background. Small minorities of Koreans, a native people of northern Japan called the Ainu and small handfuls of foreign workers also exist. Japan has a rapidly ageing population. By 2000, 17 per cent of its people were aged over 65.

A RICH AND UNIQUE CULTURE

Most Japanese practise Buddhism as a religion, but also follow some traditions of the Shinto religion. For long periods of history, Japan has remained isolated from the rest of the world,

▼ A busy street scene at the heart of the world's largest metropolis, Tokyo. The city was known by the name of Edo until 1869 when it became the capital of Japan.

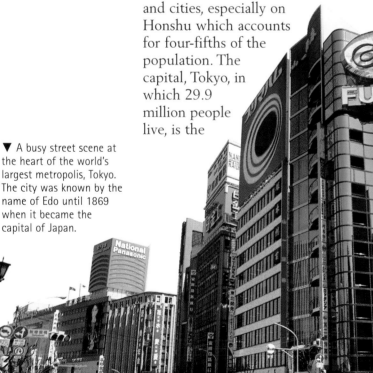

absorbing influences from afar. This, along with its cramped living conditions, has given rise to a complex series of manners and ways of behaving. Respect for elders, superiors and companies is strong, and many ceremonies and traditions exist that are unique to the country. Japan's art, literature, music and drama are strong and world-renowned, and the Japanese are among the world's most avid readers: 70 million newspapers are sold every day and around 1.5 billion books every year.

A DYNAMIC ECONOMY

Japan first industrialized in the late 19th century, retaining its own culture but borrowing industrial ideas from the West. At around the same time it started to expand its empire, fighting wars with China and Russia, and capturing much territory in east Asia. In World War II, Japan was aligned with Germany and suffered a devastating defeat, surrendering after atomic bombs were dropped on Hiroshima and Nagasaki. Japan rebuilt its economy embracing new technology. Forced to disband its costly military forces and helped by foreign aid, the Japanese economy boomed until the 1990s. By that time, it had become the second wealthiest and technologically most advanced economy in the world. Japan owns more than half of the world's industrial robots and has heavily invested in higher education and research. It is one of the world's leading producers of many goods, as well as chemicals, textiles and steel. Government works closely with industry, many workers are employed for life and many Japanese companies trade with each other in relationships called Keiretsu which make it difficult for foreign companies to sell into Japan. In the past, Japan has been ruled by clans, emperors and rival feudal lords called Shoguns. Japan still has an emperor, but his position is mainly ceremonial and power lies with the Prime Minister and the parliamentary ruling party, the Diet.

▲ Ritsurin Park is one of the largest and most beautiful of Japan's many traditional gardens. It was built during the Edo Period (1603–1868) and covers an area of 780,000 m².

▼ The traditional Japanese thatched roofed housing, known as Gassho-zukuri, has made Shirakawa village a UNESCO World Heritage site and a popular destination for tourists from Japan and abroad.

SOUTHEAST ASIA

Lying east of India and south of China, southeast Asia consists of a mainland region and over 15,000 islands stretching through the Indian and Pacific Oceans. Over 13,000 of these islands form the nation of Indonesia and the biggest island in the region, Borneo, which is the third largest in the world. Lying on the meeting points of three of the Earth's major tectonic plates – the Eurasian, Indian-Australian and Pacific – much of the mainland is mountainous while the majority of the islands have been formed through volcanic action. The region remains one of the most volcanically active on Earth. Southeast Asia has been settled for thousands of years and there is a great diversity of languages and culture. Buddhism is the most popular religion among the peoples of the mainland nations, while Islam is practised by around two-fifths of southeast Asians, in part due to the large Muslim population in Indonesia. Sizeable Christian and Hindu communities also exist in the region. From the 16th and 17th centuries into the 20th century almost all of southeast Asia was under rule by the colonial powers of Britain, France, Portugal and the Netherlands. While war and conflict have devastated some of the nations of this region, most have developed modern, industrial and service economies which have brought prosperity and has led to the growth of large, modern cities.

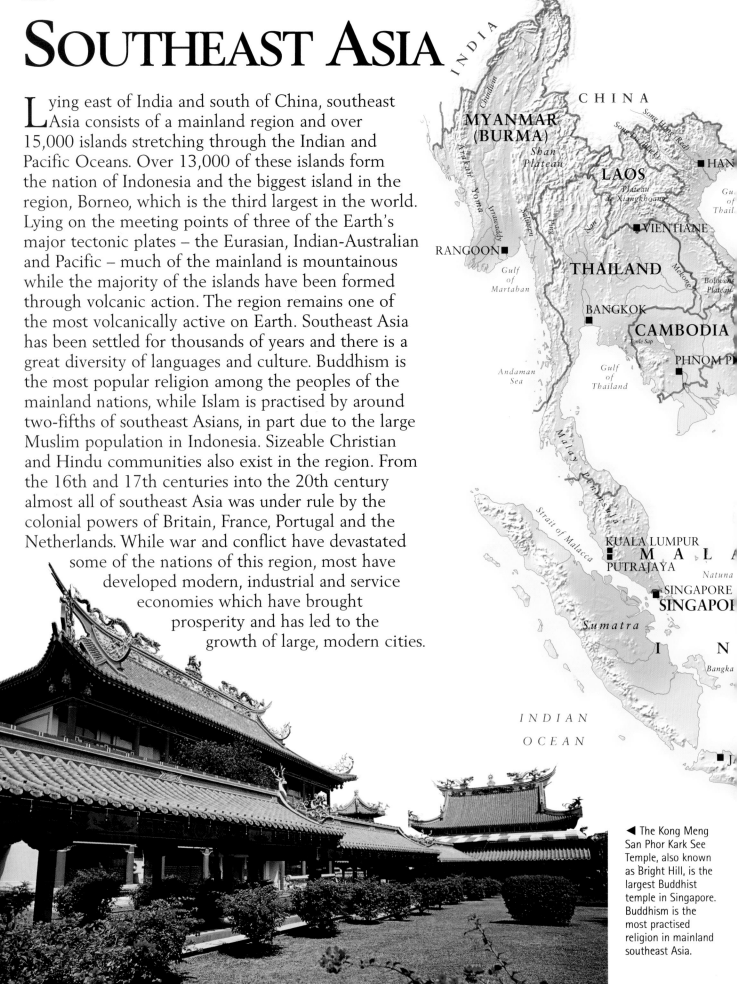

◄ The Kong Meng San Phor Kark See Temple, also known as Bright Hill, is the largest Buddhist temple in Singapore. Buddhism is the most practised religion in mainland southeast Asia.

▲ Floating markets, such as this one in Bangkok, are found in many cities of southeast Asia. Small wooden boats paddled by market sellers on rivers and canals sell an array of products including clothing, hot meals, fresh fish, fruit and vegetables.

▲ A worker tends a rice field on the Indonesian island of Bali. Rice is the single most important crop in southeast Asia and in many places two crops are grown each year. The region experiences a tropical climate with heavy rainfall in most areas.

Luzon Strait

Luzon

PACIFIC

OCEAN

■ MANILA

Mindoro

Samar

PHILIPPINES

Panay   *Leyte*

M

*South
China
Sea*

Cebu

Palawan

Negros

*Sulu
Sea*

Mindanao

*Philippine
Sea*

Balabac Strait

ERI BEGAWAN

BRUNEI ■

*Celebes
Sea*

A

I A

Sarawak

Borneo

O   N   E   S   I   A

Manadao

*Molucca
Sea*

Moluccas

Halmahera

Papua

New Guinea

**PAPUA
NEW
GUINEA**

Celebes

Seram

Makassar Strait

*Banda
Sea*

*Kepulauan
Kai*

*Kepulauan
Aru*

*ava
Sea*

*Flores
Sea*

*Kepulauan
Tanimbar*

*Arafura
Sea*

0   500   1000 km

0   250   500 miles

Bali Lombok Sumbawa Flores

DILI ■

**EAST
TIMOR**

Lesser Sunda Islands

Sumba   *Timor*

▶ Many southeast Asian cities, such as Malaysia's largest, Kuala Lumpur, have developed and grown at a rapid rate in the past 50 years.

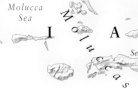

THAILAND

One of the most peaceful and stable of southeast Asian nations, Thailand is a rapidly industrializing country with a large tourist industry.

Area: 513,115 km²
Population: 60,607,000
Capital: Bangkok (7,642,000)
Main languages spoken: Thai, Lao, Chinese (Guoyo)
Main religion: Buddhism
Currency: baht
Main exports: electrical machinery (particularly computers and transistors), non-electrical machinery, seafood and live fish, clothing, rice, plastics
Type of government: kingdom; democracy

▼ Wat Phra Si Sanphet is a beautiful Buddhist monastery found in Ayutthaya, the ancient capital of Thailand.

A series of mountain ranges cross Thailand and are at their highest and most extensive in the north. The Khorat Plateau, to the northeast, comprises over a quarter of the country's land area. This flat, relatively barren land is the poorest region of the country. The fertile central plains are the most densely populated part of Thailand. This region includes the Bangkok metropolitan area and is known as Thailand's Rice Bowl. The country produced over 24 million tonnes of rice in 2002 and is one of the world's top three exporters of rice. South of the central plains is the part of Thailand that occupies the Malay Peninsula and includes a number of beautiful islands and beaches. Tin mining, rubber cultivation and fishing are also found in this region. Thailand's annual fish and shellfish catch in 2001 was 3.49 million tonnes. The country experiences a warm and wet tropical climate with the peninsula in the south receiving almost twice the rainfall of central and northern areas. Thailand is rich in natural resources. Among the known mineral deposits are tin, coal, gold, lead, zinc and precious gemstones. Oil production is minimal but Thailand exploits its natural gas reserves. Around 28 per cent of the country is forested with large, valuable hardwood forests especially in the north and coastal areas. Many species of animal, including elephants, leopards, tigers, crocodiles, gibbons and 50 species of snakes inhabit the jungles and forests.

INDUSTRIALIZATION AND MIGRATION

Thailand has industrialized greatly since the 1970s and 1980s, with electronics and textiles the key industries while the service sector is dominated by tourism, with over nine million tourists every year. The gap in the standard of living between people in urban and in rural areas has widened dramatically leading to a large migration of the population into Thailand's towns and cities. Bangkok,

◄ Thailand's capital city, Bangkok, has exploded in population numbers and size in the past 40 years. The MBK shopping and entertainments centre in the heart of Bangkok is just one of many modern developments in the city.

in particular, is straining under the vast increase in population with some of the worst traffic congestion and pollution anywhere in the world. The first stage of Bangkok's mass transit system was opened in 1999, and initiatives are attempting to relocate industries away from Bangkok.

THE KING AND HIS PEOPLE

Seventy-five per cent of the people of Thailand are Thai, a people believed to have originated in southwest China who moved to southeast Asia around 2,000 years ago. The Chinese are the largest minority group, making up around 14 per cent of the population and there are smaller numbers of Malay Muslims, Cambodians and Vietnamese. The hills of the far north and northeast are home to approximately 650,000 tribespeople with their own culture and language. Unlike many southeast Asian nations, there is relatively little tension between ethnic groups. Buddhism, a religion practised by 95 per cent of Thais, is a powerful force for peace. In 1932, a new constitution moved much political power from the monarch to the people. However, the country's King Bhumibol has remained as monarch since 1946 and wields great influence. He is the world's longest-serving head of state.

▼ A floating restaurant on the banks of the Mae Nam Khwae Noi river, known in English as the River Kwai. The river rises on the border with Myanmar west of Nakhon Sawan. It is known outside of the country for the bridge built across it by Allied prisoners of war during World War II.

MYANMAR (BURMA)

Beset by political troubles, Myanmar is an agricultural nation with large tracts of hardwood forests. It is one of the least known of all southeast Asian countries.

Area: 676,577 km²
Population: 45,611,000
Capital: Rangoon (4,100,000)
Main languages spoken: Burmese, Shan, Karen, Arakanese
Main religion: Buddhism
Currency: kyat
Main exports: clothing (more than half of all exports), food and live animals, wood and wood products, precious stones
Type of government: republic; dictatorship

Myanmar is bordered by Bangladesh, India, China and Thailand. It is a highly mountainous country with giant and largely impassable mountain ranges running in a horseshoe shape along its western, northern and eastern sides. Lower mountains are also found in more central areas. The mountains reach their highest in the northern range where the peak of Hkakado Razi reaches 5,881 m making it the highest point in southeast Asia. Enclosed within the horseshoe of mountain ranges are the country's lowland areas comprised mainly of valleys and deltas of the rivers Chindwin and Irrawaddy. The rich, fertile soils and the monsoon climate in this region make it

the centre of the country's agriculture, employing the majority of Myanmar's people, growing principally rice, pulses, maize and sugarcane. Myanmar extends south occupying a narrow western strip of the Malay Peninsula. Its coastlines tend to be rocky with some good natural harbours. The Irrawaddy is the country's principal river. It originates in the Chinese region of Tibet and flows north-to-south through almost the entire length of Myanmar. Navigable for over 1,400 km, it is an important transport route, especially for the movement of timber.

◀ Myanmar labourers cut and transport bamboo for a government project. Bamboo is used as an important building material for houses especially in the countryside.

▼ One of over 2,000 Buddhist pagodas found in the village of Pagan. An historic centre of Myanmar in the past, Pagan was founded in 849 on the banks of the Irrawaddy river and lies about 500 km north of Rangoon.

OVER-EXPLOITATION OF RESOURCES

Almost half of Myanmar is forested and the supplies of teak and other hardwoods are among the country's most valuable resources, though at severe risk from over-exploitation. Along the coasts there are tidal mangrove forests and, in the mountainous north, pine forests. The country has a varied wildlife including rare creatures such as red pandas, rhinoceros and tigers – the latter two species are sometimes killed to make medicinal products. A number of minerals are mined, including copper, lead and silver, and also sapphire and ruby gemstones. Industry is limited, under state control and mainly confined to processing farming and timber products.

A BUDDHIST STRONGHOLD

Myanmar was the first country in southeast Asia where the words of the Buddha were spread, and Buddhism, today, is the religion of almost nine-tenths of the population. Buddhism has a great influence on the everyday life of most of Myanmar's population, with Buddhist temples the centre of most villages and small towns. Many Buddhists in Myanmar also believe in certain spirits of the forests, mountains and trees called Nats for which they build houses and hold festivals. Small minorities of Christians, Muslims and Hindus also exist in the country.

INEQUALITIES AND CONFLICT

Burmans comprise about 68 per cent of the population with smaller numbers of many ethnic groups including Shan, Karen, Kachin, Mon and Chin peoples. Largely ruled by the military since independence, internal conflict between the majority Burmans and these minority groups has been widespread and violent. Opposition is not tolerated and human rights abuses are frequent.

▼ Over 100 different species of tree are commercially exploited in Myanmar's forests, such as this one 50 km west of the city of Tanggyi. Teak wood is the single most important commodity.

VIETNAM

Vietnam is a country of great river deltas, mountain chains and coastal plains. Its people endured long periods of war and oppression during the 20th century.

Area: 331,041 km²
Population: 79,832,000
Capital: Hanoi (1,074,000)
Main languages spoken: Vietnamese, Tho, Tai
Main religions: Buddhism, Roman Catholic
Currency: dong
Principal exports: crude petroleum, fish and fish products, coffee, rice, rubber
Type of government: republic; dictatorship

▼ Vietnamese fishermen use small, simple boats to navigate West Lake near the capital city of Hanoi. In 2001, approximately 1.4 million tonnes of fish, crab and prawns were caught mainly from the South China Sea but some from inland rivers and streams. However, many freshwater and marine fishing grounds are now in danger of being overfished.

The Socialist Republic of Viet Nam is a long, S-shaped country which borders China to the north and has a 3,200 km long coastline. The northwest of the country is mountainous with the country's highest point, the peak of Fan Si Pan, reaching an elevation of 3,142 m. Almost two-thirds of the country is dominated by highlands with the crest of this mountain range forming most of Vietnam's long westerly border with Laos and, further south, Cambodia. Much of the mountain slopes are forested or have been cleared to create plantations growing tea, rubber and coffee. Vietnam is one of the world's five largest exporters of coffee. To the east of the highlands, the land forms a long coastal plain bordering the Gulf of Tongking and the South China Sea. Fishing is important to many Vietnamese living on this plain.

Vietnam has a mainly tropical climate with warm to hot temperatures and heavy rainfall. Seasonal monsoon winds bring rains and occasional typhoons during the summer and autumn. In the mountainous north, the climate is subtropical with cooler temperatures.

TWO RIVER DELTAS

The narrow strip of land that links the north of the country to the south is vulnerable to typhoons, and a series of sea-dykes protects many villages from the worst weather. Vietnam's large and fertile river deltas (the Red or Song Hong river in the north and the Mekong in the south) are where rice production and a large proportion of the country's population are concentrated. Agriculture is the mainstay of Vietnam's economy and rice is the dominant crop. Despite a large migration to cities, the Vietnamese population is still one of the most rural in southeast Asia with fewer than a quarter living in urban areas.

20TH CENTURY WARS

Vietnam was home to a number of ancient civilizations before being dominated by China for many centuries. The country came under French rule in the 19th century but this ended in the French Indochina War (1946–1954). Vietnam was then partitioned into northern and southern halves as a temporary measure. Tension between the communist north and the largely anti-communist south mounted and in 1964 a full-scale war erupted. The conflict involved hundreds of thousands of troops from the USA and other nations. The 1973 cease-fire saw the US withdraw its troops and in 1975 the South Vietnamese capital of Saigon fell to northern forces. Vietnam has since been run by a staunchly communist government.

REPAIR AND RENOVATION

Repairing the extensive damage done to much of the country during the Vietnam War has been a major undertaking. Over seven million tonnes of bombs were dropped during the conflict, towns and cities were devastated, and unexploded land mines are still a threat. Five per cent of Vietnam's forests were destroyed and almost 50 per cent damaged by chemical weapons, which stripped trees of their leaves. Since 1986, the country has pursued an economic policy called 'doi moi', meaning renovation. Investment from foreign companies was sought, trade links with other nations have been engaged, private enterprise has been encouraged and, in 2000, the country's first stock exchange opened. Industry is largely concentrated in the north while Vietnam produces some 300,000 barrels of oil per day. In the 1990s, Vietnam started to encourage tourists from non-communist nations and, in 2001, around 2.1 million tourists visited the country, attracted by its history, culture and areas of natural beauty.

▲ A busy market in Ho Chi Minh City. The city was once the capital of South Vietnam. Known as Saigon before reunification, it is Vietnam's largest city with a population of over three million and is also a major shipping port.

CAMBODIA

Cambodia is a land of great history and natural beauty which has been beset by conflicts throughout the latter part of the 20th century.

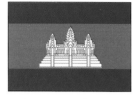

Area: 181,035 km²
Population: 11,168,000
Capital: Phnom Penh (1,078,000)
Main language spoken: Khmer
Main religion: Buddhism
Currency: riel
Main exports: logs and sawn timber, clothing, rubber, rice, fish
Type of government: kingdom; dictatorship

The centre of Cambodia is a large low-lying basin, the Tonle Sap, surrounded by a broad plain which is drained by the country's biggest river, the Mekong. To the southeast of the basin lies the Mekong delta which extends into Vietnam before the river reaches the South China Sea. To the north and the southwest of the basin lie several mountain ranges, while in the northeast of Cambodia are highlands. These merge into the highlands in the centre of the country which extend into Vietnam. In the centre of the basin lies southeast Asia's largest lake, also called Tonle Sap. This shallow lake varies enormously in size. At its smallest, it measures about 2,700 km² with depths of between one and three m. During the wet monsoon season, between June and November, the high waters of the Mekong feed into the lake, greatly increasing its size to around 10,300 km² and its depth to between nine and 14 m.

THAILAND

LAOS

Sisophon
Monkol Borey
Bardambang
Siem Reab
Stoeng Treng
Lumphat

CAMBODIA

Tonle Sap

Kampong Thum
Kracheh
Senmonorom

Kampong Chhnang
Phnum Aoral
1810m

PHNOM PENH

Kampong Cham

Gulf of Thailand

Mekong

VIETNAM

Takeo

Preah Sihanouk

USING ITS NATURAL RESOURCES

Cambodia is poorly endowed with mineral reserves but, in contrast, the country has relatively rich resources from the natural world. These include plentiful fish from its rivers and lakes which are often fermented or salted to preserve them. The well-watered lowlands of Cambodia allow rice farming to dominate the country's agriculture. Nearly 80 per cent of all cultivated land is given over to rice, with other crops including mangoes, bananas and pineapples. Rubber, grown in the east of the country, is an important cash crop along with corn, pepper, sesame and cassava. A large proportion of the country is covered in forest, much of it tropical hardwoods such as teak and mahogany. However, deforestation is one of the most serious problems facing the country with as much as half of its tree cover having disappeared in the past 35 years.

FROM KINGDOM TO KHMER ROUGE

Cambodia came under French rule in the 19th century. Regaining independence in 1954, the country underwent a period of stability before exploding into conflict from the late 1960s onwards. Following the Vietnam War which enveloped the region, a violent communist regime called the Khmer Rouge swept to power. Between 1975 and 1979, as many as 1.5 million people were murdered including much of the country's professional class of workers. The Khmer Rouge were ousted and Cambodia is now a kingdom again. However, ongoing conflicts and changes of government have continued with the result that Cambodia is one of Asia's poorest countries.

▲ Houses on stilts stand in the waters of Tonle Sap lake where many Cambodians engage in carp rearing and fishing. Fish is a major part of many Cambodians' diet.

▼ Constructed during the reign of King Suryavarman II, the 12th century ruler of the Khmer Kingdom, Angkor Wat is a gigantic Hindu temple built of stone and measuring 1,000 m in length.

LAOS

The most sparsely populated nation in southeast Asia, Laos is an isolated, poor and mountainous nation ruled by a communist government.

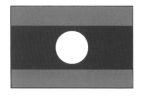

Area: 236,800 km²
Population: 5,433,000
Capital: Vientiane (190,000)
Main languages spoken: Lao, Khmer
Main religions: Buddhism, traditional beliefs
Currency: kip
Main exports: wood products, garments, electricity, coffee, tin
Type of government: republic; dictatorship

▼ Laotian farmers tend vegetables grown in the rich soil of the banks of the Mekong river. Over half of the country's population lives in the lowland areas of Laos, especially along the banks of the Mekong.

The Lao People's Democratic Republic shares borders with five nations: Vietnam, Thailand, Cambodia, Myanmar and China. About 70 per cent of its land is mountains which run northwest to southeast, and reach their highest elevation in the north of the country at Mount Bia, with an elevation of 2,819 m. Approximately 55 per cent of Laos is covered with forests of different types. In the north, these are mostly tropical rainforests while to the south, tropical vegetation mixes with deciduous hardwood trees such as teak and rosewood. Large tracts of bamboo jungle can also be found in the south. Despite timber from these forests being one of Laos' principal exports, the forests help support a wide and varied range of wildlife including tigers, leopards, panthers and wild oxen called gaurs. Laos has a tropical monsoon climate with two distinct, wet and dry, seasons. The wet season runs from between May and October with rainfall almost every day and high humidity levels. During this period between 1,300 and 2,300 mm of rain falls in the central regions of the country. In the south, rainfall can reach over 3,000 mm.

THE MEKONG RIVER

Much of Laos' westerly border with Thailand and Myanmar is formed by the winding Mekong river which extends over 1,800 km through Laos. Most of the country's major towns and cities are located on the Mekong, which can be navigated by boat south of the city of Louangphrabang. The people of Laos belong to over 65 different ethnic groups, with very diverse customs and lifestyles. The vast majority of Laotians work the land, mainly growing rice as well as sweet potatoes and maize. Rearing livestock including water buffalo and pigs is important, as is the illegal growing and selling of opium poppies. The lands adjacent to the Mekong make up the most

extensive lowland area in Laos and are the site of much of the country's farming.

LANDLOCKED AND ISOLATED

Laos is the only landlocked country in southeast Asia. Its rugged terrain of mountains and forests along most of its borders have held back the country's industrial, transport and trading development with neighbouring nations. Laos has no railways, and roads are few in number and of generally poor quality. Most of the country's freight is transported by river, especially along the Mekong. Prior

to 1994, foreign visitors to Laos arrived largely by air as there was no major road link to other countries. The Australian-funded Friendship Bridge was opened in 1994. It spans the Mekong river at Vientiane, the country's capital city, and links Laos to Thailand by road. Until very recently, the country was as isolated politically as it is

geographically. After more than two decades of internal power struggles, Laos became a one-party communist state in 1975 and restricted its foreign relations to a few communist nations, especially Vietnam. From 1986, the country started slowly to re-integrate with the world community and its largest single trading partner today is Thailand. Laos is reliant on foreign aid and investment while its industry remains undeveloped and its mineral resources unexploited. Around ten per cent of babies die before reaching adulthood and Laotians have a low average life expectancy of 54 years.

▲ Buddhist monks collecting food in the morning from the local people for their one meal of the day. Buddhism is the religion of around 60 per cent of Laotians.

▼ A Khmu tribe family sit round the fire in their two-room house prior to dinner. The Khmu mainly live in small villages on mountain slopes near the Thailand-Laos border. They survive on subsistence agriculture, supplemented by fishing, hunting and trading.

BRUNEI

The Sultanate of Brunei is located on the northwest coast of the island of Borneo. Gaining independence in 1984, the country is rich in fossil fuel reserves.

Area: 5,765 km²
Population: 333,000
Capital: Bandar Seri Begawan (230,000)
Main languages spoken: Malay, Chinese, English
Main religion: Sunni Islam, Buddhism
Currency: Brunei dollar
Main exports: crude petroleum, natural gas, petroleum products
Type of government: sultanate; dictatorship

Brunei faces the South China Sea to the north and shares a border with Malaysia which divides Brunei into two. The country consists of a narrow coastal plain lined largely with mangrove swamps while the interior rises to form hill ranges mainly covered in rainforest. The country's highest point, Pagon (1,850 m), lies in the southeast of the country. Within Brunei's border are 33 islands which make up 1.4 per cent of the country's total land area. Most of these islands are uninhabited and are important breeding grounds for certain endangered species of birds, flying foxes and monkeys. Brunei has a tropical climate with rainfall averaging over 2,000 mm per year and a narrow temperature range averaging between 24° and 31°C. Most streams and rivers flow north to the coast. This includes the Belait river, the longest in the country, which runs close to the country's western border. A large proportion of Brunei, almost 80 per cent, is covered in rainforest. This lush tree cover is filled with animal life including Asian elephants, leopards, many species of monkeys and numerous reptiles and birds.

▼ Oil exploitation in Brunei is mainly concentrated offshore. Brunei's oilfields produce approximately 194,000 barrels of oil per day.

OIL AND BRUNEI'S PEOPLE

By the 16th century, Brunei was an independent sultanate, or kingdom, controlling almost the entire island of Borneo. Following a decline in influence it became a British protectorate in 1888. The indigenous peoples of Brunei now comprise just six per cent of the population. People of Malay descent make up two-thirds of Brunei's population and there are large minorities of Chinese and Indians. Much of Brunei's non-indigenous and non-Malay population arrived when oil was found in 1929. The exploitation of the country's large oil and natural gas reserves completely dominates the economy of this small nation. Oil revenues have made the country's leader, Sultan Muda Hassanal Bolkiah, one of the wealthiest people in the world. The people he rules have also benefited from the oil revenues with a generally high standard of living. There is no income tax, and there are high levels of medical care and education, and subsidized food and housing. However, political parties were banned in 1988 and all government workers are banned from political activity. Although Brunei's mixed population follows a number of religions, the country is more inclined to its state religion of Islam.

SINGAPORE

An island city-state, Singapore is one of the most prosperous and modernized of Asian countries with a standard of living equal to Western Europe.

Area: 660 km²
Population: 3,567,000
Capital: Singapore (3,567,000)
Main languages spoken: Chinese, English, Malay, Tamil
Main religions: Buddhism, Chinese folk religions (including Daoism), Sunni Islam
Currency: Singaporean dollar
Main exports: machinery and transport equipment, consumer goods, chemicals, petroleum products
Type of government: republic; limited democracy

Singapore lies just off the southernmost tip of the Malay Peninsula, separated from Malaysia by a narrow body of water. The two countries are linked by a causeway carrying road and rail links. The country consists of one major island, Singapore Island, and a collection of 60 smaller islands. Singapore's land is mostly flat and low-lying with several small hills. A network of small streams runs through the main island, but Singapore remains reliant on neighbouring Malaysia for some of its freshwater supplies. Lying near the Equator, the country has a tropical climate with an average annual temperature of 27.2°C and heavy rainfall, averaging over 2,420 mm per year, especially between November and March. Singapore was once covered completely in rainforest, but much of the land has been cleared and swamps and marshlands drained and reclaimed. Now, only five per cent of the land remains forested, much of this lying in protected reserves. Singapore was barely settled before a British colonial administrator, Sir Stamford Raffles, founded Singapore City in 1819 as a trading post. Singapore grew as a port and naval base following the opening of the Suez Canal in 1869. The country is now one of the most densely populated nations in the world, with Chinese immigrants making up approximately 77 per cent of the population and Malays (14 per cent) and Indians (seven per cent) the largest minorities. Although Singapore has to import all fuel and raw materials, the country has vibrant manufacturing industries, particularly electrical and electronic goods. The country also has large oil refining and chemicals industries.

▲ In 2001, 146,265 vessels arrived at the port of Singapore, making it the busiest port in Asia.

► Singapore's high-rise financial district is the financial capital of the region. Over a quarter of the country's income is derived from financial and business services.

MALAYSIA

A multi-ethnic nation with rich natural resources, Malaysia has had one of southeast Asia's fastest-growing economies in the past 30 years.

Area: 329,758 km²
Population: 23,275,000
Capitals: Kuala Lumpur – legislative and diplomatic capital (2,220,000)
Putrajaya – administrative capital (7,000)
Main languages spoken: Malay, Chinese, Tamil, Iban
Main religions: Sunni Islam, traditional Chinese folk religions, Hinduism
Currency: ringgit
Main exports: electronic equipment, machinery and transport equipment, petroleum and petroleum products, wood and wood products, rubber, textiles, chemicals
Type of government: elective monarchy; limited democracy

► Kek Lok Si Buddhist temple is situated at Ayer Itam on the island of Penang. The temple features gardens, shrines, a turtle pond and the 30 m high pagoda of Ten Thousand Buddhas.

Malaysia is divided into two geographical areas separated by the South China Sea and lying some 650 km apart. Peninsula Malaysia occupies the southern portion of the Malay Peninsula bordering Thailand to the north and close to the islands of Singapore to the south. It accounts for about 40 per cent of the country's land mass and is divided by several central mountain chains with poorly drained lowlands to the south, a narrow, forested belt to the east and broader, fertile plains to the west. The western plains are the most densely populated and developed pàrt of Malaysia. In contrast, the two states of Sabah and Sarawak which make up East Malaysia, over 600 km away, are barely developed. Home to around 20 per cent of the country's population, the land of East Malaysia consists of a coastal plain with many swamps, rising to densely forested hills and valleys before rising further to mountains. At 4,101 m, Mount Kinabalu in Sabah is the country's highest peak.

TROPICAL CLIMATE AND WILDLIFE
Malaysia has a tropical climate with warm to hot temperatures and high humidity. The west coast of Peninsula Malaysia experiences a rainy season from September through to December while the east coast, as well as East Malaysia, has its rainy season from October to February. The country has an extremely biodiverse environment in which some 8,000 different flowering plants exist.

◀ A short distance from the coast of Sabah, the island of Pulau Sipadan is a coral sea mount covered in dense jungle and surrounded by seas containing rich marine life.

▼ The 452 m high Petronas Twin Towers in Kuala Lumpur are the world's tallest buildings. Completed in 1996, the towers are the headquarters of the national oil company of Malaysia.

East Malaysia has one of the largest and most varied bird populations in the world, and elephants, rhinos, leopards, tigers, orang-utans and gibbons are among its larger animal species. Attracted by its wildlife, highland and rainforest scenery, climate and beaches along the peninsula coast, some 10 million tourists visited Malaysia in 2001.

ABUNDANT NATURAL RESOURCES

Much of Malaysia's economic success is due to its rich natural resources. Oil deposits, particularly offshore of Sabah and Sarawak, are large, allowing Malaysia to produce over 800,000 barrels of oil per day. Sizeable deposits of natural gas also exist, and metal ores including tin, bauxite, copper and gold are mined. Much of Peninsula Malaysia's forests have been cleared for plantations, farmland and settlements. The East Malaysia state of Sarawak still contains some of the largest and oldest original tropical forests on Earth. However, deforestation is the country's biggest environmental issue with logging one of Malaysia's prime industries. The country is the world's largest exporter of tropical hardwood, logs and sawn timber, mostly from Sarawak. The World Bank estimates that trees are being felled at three times the rate they can be replaced.

SUBSISTENCE AND PLANTATION FARMING

Agriculture is a declining sector of the Malaysian economy but it still employs approximately 18 per cent of the workforce. A large number of agricultural workers are smallholders farming their own plots of land. Rice is the most common staple food but the country is not self-sufficient and must import it. Vast plantations growing tea, tropical fruits, sugarcane and especially cocoa and rubber dominate farming for export. Malaysia is one of the world's top ten cocoa producers and was once the world's largest rubber producer. The country still ranks as one of the top five largest producers of natural rubber. This is despite production declining due to labour shortages, with workers increasingly becoming employed in the country's growing manufacturing industries. Many plantation owners are switching to other crops – palm oil in particular – which is possible to grow and harvest using machinery.

THIRTEEN STATES, MANY PEOPLES

Malaysia has been inhabited for over 30,000 years and is now a melting pot of different ethnic groups and cultures. The

▲ These unusual, knife-like limestone pinnacles rise above the densely forested slopes of Gunung Mulu, Sarawak's largest national park.

▼ Malaysia is the world's largest producer of palm oil used in the manufacture of soaps, ointments, margarine and cooking oils. This plantation worker is loading oil palm fruit bunches into a skip for transport to a refinery.

► Logging is a massive industry in Malaysia despite concerns about deforestation. To counter this there have been moves away from selling raw timber to manufacturing furniture. This now accounts for a quarter of all Malaysia's exports from wood and wood products.

Orang Asli are the original native people of Peninsula Malaysia who now number just over 60,000. Larger numbers of indigenous peoples exist in East Malaysia. This includes the Iban, Bidayuh and Kadazan, the most numerous of some 30 different peoples, who together comprise approximately nine per cent of Malaysia's total population. Approximately 48 per cent of Malaysians are Malays, while 34 per cent are of Chinese and eight per cent of Indian origin. In addition, there are an estimated one million immigrants, mostly from the Philippines and Indonesia working mainly in low paid industries. Islam is the national religion of Malaysia although religious freedom and toleration means that almost all the world's major religions are practised in the country. Tensions between the traditionally wealthier Chinese and the Malay peoples has seen, since 1970, positive discrimination in education, jobs and business in favour of Malays.

A DEVELOPING SUCCESS STORY

In the early 1970s, 70 per cent of Malaysia's exports consisted of rubber and tin. In just 25 years, the economic situation has completely changed, so that over 75 per cent of exports are now manufactured goods. The rapid growth of industry in Malaysia since the 1960s was, in part, down to the New Economic Policy

▲ Malaysia has become a major oil and natural gas producer with its fields off the coast of Sarawak and Sabah yielding around 800,000 barrels a day.

metals, the production of electrical and electronic equipment, motor vehicles and chemicals. Today, Malaysia is one of the world's leading exporters of high-tech components such as computer chips and hard disk drives. George Town and towns and cities around Kuala Lumpur are the key centres for the country's booming computing industry. Peninsula Malaysia is home to the vast majority of the country's industry and has seen living standards rise for much of its population.

(NEP) introduced in 1970 following large, violent riots in the country. It aimed at changing the country's economic structure where businesses had traditionally been owned by the Chinese population, and developing a range of new industries. Over a quarter of Malaysia's labour force is now employed in manufacturing, especially the processing of export commodities such as rubber, tin, oil, wood,

ADVANCED DEVELOPMENT BY 2020

Although Malaysia is developing rapidly and is much wealthier than in the past, it still suffers economic and social problems. A major economic crisis in 1998 slowed growth dramatically and there are shortages of skilled workers in some industries. Away from the cities and especially in East Malaysia, many people's standard of living has not risen greatly and a large number remain below the poverty line. Major government policies to complete Malaysia's transformation into an advanced nation by 2020 include greater technical education, improved healthcare and the use of advanced technology. A new city has been developed, Putrajaya, to be the new administrative capital, 35 km south of Kuala Lumpur.

▼ The Cameron Highlands in Perak Province, on the western coast of Peninsula Malaysia, are the centre of the country's tea plantations such as the Sungai Palas Estate.

INDONESIA

A gigantic island archipelago, Indonesia is a sprawling
land of great natural and human diversity and the
fourth most populous nation in the world.

Area: 1,904,413 km²
Population: 206,265,000
Capital: Jakarta
(12,435,000)
Main languages spoken:
Bahasa Indonesia
(Indonesian Malay),
Javanese, Sundanese,
Madurese, Minang
Main religions: Sunni
Islam, various Protestant
Churches
Currency: Indonesian
rupiah
Main exports: crude
petroleum and natural gas,
electrical goods, plywood,
processed rubber, clothing
Type of government:
republic; limited
democracy

Indonesia consists of over 13,660 islands
which extend around one-eighth of the
Earth's circumference. Sumatra is the most
westerly of the larger islands and is
separated from western Malaysia and
Singapore by the Strait of Malacca. Papua,
occupying the western part of the island
of New Guinea, is Indonesia's most
easterly territory. The vast majority of the
population live on five islands: Java,
Sumatra, Papua, Celebes and Kalimantan –
the Indonesian part of the island of
Borneo. The country experiences a tropical
climate with a small temperature range
between the seasons due to the islands'
location near the Equator. Temperatures
mainly differ with height, with only some
highland areas of Papua receiving snowfall.
Rainfall varies more with the highest
amount of rainfall occurring in the
mountainous regions of Kalimantan,
Sumatra, Celebes and Papua, which
receive in excess of 3,000 mm per year.
Most lowland areas receive between
1,600 mm and 2,200 mm.

▲ At 2,392 m, Mount Bromo on the eastern end of the island of Java is one of the highest active volcanic peaks on the island.

Jazirah Doberai

Papua

Puncak Jaya
5030 m

Pegunungan Maoke

A

New Guinea

Kepulauan Aru

PAPUA NEW GUINEA

Arafura Sea

INDONESIA'S VOLCANOES

Much of Indonesia's land has been shaped by volcanic activity, with most islands featuring a mountainous interior. The ashes, lava and mud flows from successive eruptions have helped create fertile soils in many places. Indonesia's territory contains over 128 active volcanoes with Java containing 22. Of Indonesia's volcanoes, none is more famous than Krakatoa. Located between Java and Sumatra, Krakatoa generated the largest explosion in recorded history when it erupted in 1883. The gigantic explosion destroyed three-quarters of the island, was heard 4,000 km away in Brisbane, and showered volcanic debris as far away as Madagascar on the other side of the Indian Ocean. Earthquakes also strike the country with 2,000 people killed on the island of Flores in 1992.

▼ Located on the northwest coast of Java, the city of Jakarta is the country's commercial and financial centre. A sprawling urban area, much of which lies on a low flat plain subject to swamping, Jakarta is southeast Asia's most populous urban area.

329

over 82 per cent of the country was covered in forest. Cutting down forests to clear land and for logging gradually increased throughout the 20th century as Indonesia developed large paper, timber and wood pulp industries. Deforestation throughout the late 1990s was at an estimated rate of 20,000 km^2 per year, placing hundreds of species, such as the orang-utan, under threat of extinction. More than half of all timber produced is estimated to come from illegal logging.

ASIAN AND AUSTRALASIAN ANIMALS

Indonesia spans the dividing line between two of the world's major animal communities, the Asian and the Australasian. As a result, Australasian creatures such as the echidna, cockatoo and bandicoot can be found on the most easterly islands, while the more northerly and westerly land masses contain Asian species including tigers, the Asian elephant and the tapir. The isolated location of many of Indonesia's islands has resulted in many species unique not only to Indonesia but to individual islands. These include the world's largest lizard, the 4 m long Komodo dragon, which is only found on two small islands – Rinca and Komodo – off the west coast of Flores.

▲ This worker is tapping the trunk of a rubber tree to release liquid latex. Producing over 1.6 million tonnes of rubber in 2002, Indonesia is one of the world's three dominant rubber producers.

▼ A series of terraces cut into a hillside in Bali is occupied by rice paddies. Rice is the staple diet of most Indonesians and in 2002, 51 million tonnes were produced.

ASIA'S LARGEST TROPICAL RAINFORESTS

The tropical climate, high rainfall and fertile soils of Indonesia are largely responsible for the vast array of natural life found throughout Indonesia. There are thousands of plant and animal species, although many are now under threat. Indonesia has the largest tracts of virgin rainforest in the world outside of the Amazon. At the start of the 20th century,

▲ The Krakatoa volcano is found between the islands of Java and Sumatra and was the site of a gigantic eruption in the 19th century. Giant tsunami (tidal waves) as high as 40 m were a major cause of the death toll which reached over 36,000. Minor eruptions continue to this day.

LIVING OFF THE LAND AND SEA

Since ancient times, the peoples of Indonesia have made great use of their rich and diverse natural environment. Many thousands of different plant species, for example, are known to be used in traditional herbal medicine known as Jamu. Over 2,000 years ago, Indonesian peoples in the coastal areas were already using irrigation systems to grow rice, while peoples in the interior tended to practise slash-and-burn agriculture where forest areas were cleared and crops planted. Although less than 20 per cent of Indonesia is under cultivation, the country produces vast amounts of many different crops. Rice is the key staple food but after periods of self-sufficiency, Indonesia now has to import much rice to feed its growing population. Other vital crops include cassava, maize, soybeans, peanuts and sweet potatoes. For such a populous nation, livestock herds are relatively small with around 15 million goats, 12 million cattle and 10 million pigs. Chickens, however, are kept in large numbers; there were over a thousand million in Indonesia in 2002. Many Indonesians who farm smallholdings near rivers, lakes or the coast also fish part-time. Large-scale sea fishing has increased with Japanese assistance.

▼ The striking Buddhist monument of Borobudur is found on Java. It was built between 778 and 850 and hidden by volcano ash and vegetation from around the 10th century until it was discovered in the 19th century.

▲ A small river settlement in West Sumatra.

▼ Indonesian tea pickers at work. In 1998, Indonesia grew 166 million tonnes of tea, approximately six per cent of the entire world market.

INDONESIA'S RESOURCES

Much of Indonesia's farmland is devoted to growing cash crops on large plantations. Indonesia is one of the world's top three rubber producers, the third largest grower of coffee and a leading producer of coconuts, tobacco, cacao and a number of spices. Apart from the resources provided by the living world, Indonesia has large mineral reserves. The country has rich deposits of tin, copper, gold, bauxite and nickel. In addition, Indonesia is the world's largest exporter of liquefied natural gas (LNG) and has relied on oil reserves to generate much export income. In 2001, Indonesia produced 1.4 million barrels per day but oil production is declining. Concerns that Indonesia will soon become an importer of fuels has led to fossil fuel exploration of remote areas and the possibility of more geothermal and hydro-electric energy plants being built.

RAPID INDUSTRIALIZATION

Although agriculture and the exporting of raw materials have dominated the economy, Indonesia has industrialized rapidly in the past 35 years. Larger industries, mainly controlled by the state, process metals, oil, wood and wood products, and produce chemicals, cement, glass, rubber goods, machinery and fertilizers. Indonesia has also become involved in high-technology fields such as electronics and aerospace. The country has a large textile industry including batik, a technique for hand-printing cloth. Despite the country's vast resources and growing industries, the Indonesian economy is fragile with political instability, high unemployment and large foreign debts. Progress has not occurred evenly with Java and its neighbouring islands the most economically developed but with great poverty elsewhere.

PEOPLE AND HISTORY

Indonesia had been settled for thousands of years before it came under Dutch control at the end of the 17th century. In 1945, Indonesia declared itself independent, an act recognized by the Netherlands in 1949 after a violent conflict. Indonesia is the most populous nation in southeast Asia and its population has grown dramatically throughout the 20th century. Despite family planning campaigns, the country's population is growing by around three million people every year. Overcrowding on the most populous islands resulted in transmigration whereby over 3.5 million people were relocated in less populated parts of the country. This created some new jobs but also damaged the traditional cultures. Indonesia's people come from around 300 different ethnic groups speaking over 250 distinct languages. The Javanese, the largest ethnic group in Indonesia, represent 45 per cent of the population. Traders from India brought Hinduism and Buddhism to Indonesia almost 2,000 years ago while Islam reached Sumatra in the 13th century. This religion spread throughout much of Indonesia and there are now over 175 million Muslims making it the world's largest Islamic country. Conflict between different ethnic and religious groups have blighted Indonesia since independence. Governments have tried to suppress the traditional cultures of many local ethnic groups which has increased conflict. East Timor became independent of Indonesia in 1999 while strong independence movements exist especially in Papua and northern Sumatra. The number of tourists drawn to Indonesia rose rapidly in the 1980s and 1990s but have since been harmed by ongoing political instability. In 2002, terrorist bombs on Bali caused nearly 200 deaths, damaging the country's tourism prospects further.

▲ Two of Kelimutu's three beautiful coloured lakes. Kelimutu is a volcano located on the island of Flores, east of Java, and is at the centre of one of Indonesia's national parks.

▼ Members of the Organisasi Papua Merdeka (OPM) in their traditional dress on Papua. A collection of different tribal groups, the OPM has been fighting for Papua's independence from Indonesia since the 1960s.

EAST TIMOR

The first new nation of the 21st century, East Timor was finally recognized as an independent country in May 2002 after a long and violent struggle.

Area: 14,874 km²
Population: 885,000
Capital: Dili (56,000)
Main languages spoken: Tetum, Portuguese
Main religions: Roman Catholic, Sunni Islam
Currency: US dollar
Main exports: timber (sandalwood), coffee, marble
Type of government: republic; limited democracy

▼ Two East Timorese farm workers gather in a harvest. The people of East Timor are a diverse mixture of more than 15 ethnic groups including some Indonesians and Chinese. Many are Roman Catholic reflecting the long period as a Portuguese colony.

The island of Timor lies in the Malay Archipelago. East Timor occupies the eastern half of the island, the island of Palau Kimbing and the enclave of Ambeno (also known as Oe-Cusse). This lies on the northern coast of the remainder of Timor which is part of Indonesia.

East Timor has a mostly mountainous landscape with elevations rising inland to 2,963 m. In the north, the mountains rise almost immediately from the sea while in the south, there is a wide coastal plain which is broken up by river deltas and swampland. The country has a tropical climate with temperatures remaining high throughout the year but with great variations in rainfall. The southern side of the island tends to receive more rainfall and the foothills are covered in bushes and trees, including eucalyptus. The northern side is more arid and droughts can occur in the long dry season between May and November.

SUBSISTENCE AND CASH CROP FARMING

The people of East Timor largely rely on farming, with corn the most important staple food, followed by rice, cassava, millet and sweet potato. Buffalo, cattle, goats and poultry are kept and traded. Outside the main settlements, much trade occurs through barter. A number of cash crops are grown including coffee, coconuts, cloves and sandalwood trees. The sandal oil extracted from the tree is used in soaps and perfumes. Australian-funded investigations have shown that offshore reserves of oil and natural gas exist.

BLOODSHED AND INDEPENDENCE

Portugal colonized the island in the 16th century and East Timor remained a colony until 1975 when the Portuguese withdrew. Within ten days, Indonesian forces invaded and declared East Timor part of Indonesia. Massive human rights abuses occurred and over 100,000 East Timorese died resisting the Indonesian occupation. In a referendum on East Timor's future in 1999 almost four-fifths of the vote supported independence. East Timor was administered by the UN for almost three years after armed groups supported by the Indonesian military, killed hundreds and destroyed much of the country's largest city, Dili. Much aid and investment has since poured into East Timor.

THE PHILIPPINES

The sprawling island nation of the Philippines occupies the northernmost part of the Malay Archipelago and lies in the western Pacific Ocean.

Area: 300,076 km²
Population: 76,499,000
Capital: Manila (10,492,000)
Main languages spoken: Filipino (Tagalog), English, Cebuano, Iliocano
Main religions: Roman Catholic, Sunni Islam
Currency: Philippine peso
Main exports: electronic equipment (particularly computer peripherals), machinery and transport equipment, clothing, coconut oil, wiring
Type of government: republic; democracy

The Philippines consists of 7,107 islands, only a fraction of which are inhabited. Luzon to the north and Mindanao to the south are by far the largest, and comprise two-thirds of the country's total area. A further nine islands have land areas in excess of 2,500 km². Only two-fifths of the islands are named and only 350 of the islands have an area more than 1.6 km². The islands are volcanic in origin and are the peaks of a partly submerged mountain chain. Their terrain is rugged, with the highest point on the island of Mindanao where Mount Apo reaches 2,954 m.

A DIVERSE LAND AND PEOPLE

The Philippines lies in the tropics and has a hot and humid year-round climate with an average annual temperature of 27°C and average rainfall of 2,030 mm per year. However, there is much variation in temperature and rainfall based on location and elevation. About 45 per cent of the country is under cultivation and about a third remains forested, despite logging, much of it illegal, and slash-and-burn agriculture. There are over 10,000 species of tree, shrub and fern, the most common of which are palms and bamboos. There are also more than 700 species of birds and many species of amphibians and reptiles. Rice and corn are the most common staple foods but a wide range of crops are grown for both local consumption and export. Over 100 different ethnic groups live in the country and a vast range of languages and dialects are spoken. While Filipino is the official language, English is widely used for commercial and governmental purposes. Over 80 per cent of the population are Roman Catholic while a large Muslim minority of around 15 per cent are found particularly on the island of Mindanao.

▼ The capital city of Manila is at the heart of a sprawling metropolis which contains five individual cities and houses more than 10.4 million people.

▲ Many Filipino people, especially those who live on smaller islands, survive through fishing. In 2002, over 2.1 million tonnes of fish were caught off the Philippines.

▼ The San Guillermo Parish Church lies in the settlement of Bacolor, 60 km northwest of Manila. Founded in 1576, the church was severely damaged by a mud flow caused by an eruption of Mount Pinatubo in 1991.

NATURAL DISASTERS

As part of the Pacific's Ring of Fire, the Philippines lies on some of the most geologically active parts of the Earth's crust. The country regularly experiences earthquakes, including one in 1990 which struck the northern part of the island of Luzon, taking the lives of 1,600 people and leaving over 100,000 homeless. The islands also have an estimated 20 active volcanoes including Mount Pinatubo, on Luzon, which after six centuries of lying dormant erupted severely in 1991. The people of the Philippines also have to contend with floods, landslides and relatively frequent typhoons (known as hurricanes in the Atlantic) which tend to occur during the wet season, particularly from September to December. In 2002, the United Nations Office for Civilian and Humanitarian Affairs (OCHA) released statistics showing that the Philippines was the most disaster-prone nation on Earth. Some 757 natural disasters struck the Philippines between 1900 and 2001.

AN HISTORIC TRADING CENTRE

The Philippines came under Spanish colonial rule in 1521 when they were named Felipinas in honour of Spain's then ruler, Philip II. Lying in a strategic location between Asia and the New World of the Americas, the Philippines grew as a trading and transport hub. Spain's colonial rule lasted until the USA gained possession after victories in the Spanish-American War of 1898 and the Philippine-American War (1899–1901). After occupation by Japan during World War II, the Philippines became an independent republic in 1946. Ferdinand Marcos came to power in 1965 and he suppressed all political opposition. The Marcos regime was finally overturned in 1986 and despite bouts of corruption and political scandal since, the Philippines is now an emerging democratic nation. The brutal years of the Marcos rule, and corruption and natural disasters since, have acted as a brake on the Philippines' economic growth. Manufacturing industries such as textiles, electronics, chemicals and machine parts are growing but there is great poverty and overcrowded slums in many cities.

AFRICA

AFRICA

The second largest continent, Africa holds around one-fifth of the Earth's total land area. It is bordered by the Mediterranean and Red seas as well as two oceans, the Atlantic and the Indian. Off its Indian ocean coastline lies the world's fourth largest island, Madagascar (see p.286). Africa's landscape is varied; from the world's largest desert, the Sahara, in the north, to lush tropical jungles and rainforests in the centre of the continent. Africa is home to an amazing variety of wildlife including the world's largest land animals, such as the African elephant, the rhinoceros and the giraffe. Africa has a rich and diverse human population consisting of more than 3,000 different ethnic groups. Much of Africa was ruled in past centuries as colonies of major European powers, such as Britain, France and Belgium. They divided up the land with little regard for ethnic boundaries and territories. Today, Africans live in many nations, most of them obtaining independence in the last fifty years. Many of these are the least developed in the world and have been blighted by ethnic conflict, civil war and natural disasters including drought, famine and disease.

▲ These Nigerian women transport goods for market by foot to the town of Ikere-Ekiti in southwestern Nigeria. The vast majority of Africans live in rural areas and depend on farming in order to make a living.

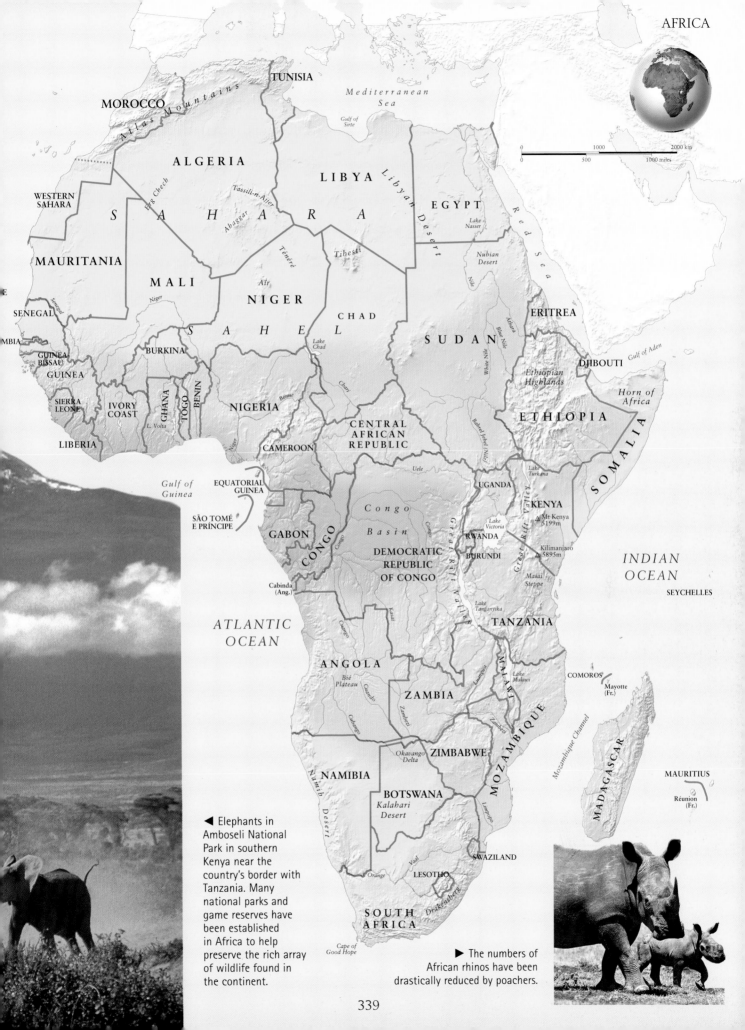

MOROCCO

TUNISIA

Atlas Mountains

Mediterranean Sea

ALGERIA

LIBYA

EGYPT

Gulf of Sirte

WESTERN SAHARA

S   A   H   A   R   A

Reg Chech

Tassili-n-Ajjer

Libyan Desert

Lake Nasser

MAURITANIA

Abaggar

Ténéré

Tibesti

Nubian Desert

MALI

Aïr

NIGER

CHAD

Nile

SUDAN

Red Sea

ERITREA

SENEGAL

Niger

S   A   H   E   L

Lake Chad

Bahr el Nile

White Nile

Blue Nile

Atbara

Ethiopian Highlands

Gulf of Aden

DJIBOUTI

GAMBIA

GUINEA BISSAU

BURKINA

Chari

SUDAN

GUINEA

IVORY COAST

GHANA

TOGO

BENIN

NIGERIA

Bénue

CENTRAL AFRICAN REPUBLIC

Horn of Africa

SIERRA LEONE

L. Volta

ETHIOPIA

SOMALIA

LIBERIA

Niger

CAMEROON

Uele

Gulf of Guinea

EQUATORIAL GUINEA

UGANDA

Lake Turkana

KENYA

△ Mt Kenya 5199m

SÃO TOMÉ E PRÍNCIPE

GABON

CONGO

Congo

Congo Basin

Congo

Great Rift Valley

Lake Victoria

RWANDA

△ Kilimanjaro 5895m

BURUNDI

INDIAN OCEAN

DEMOCRATIC REPUBLIC OF CONGO

Masai Steppe

SEYCHELLES

Cabinda (Ang.)

Kasai

Lake Tanganyika

TANZANIA

Cuango

ATLANTIC OCEAN

ANGOLA

Great Rift Valley

MALAWI

Lake Malawi

COMOROS

Mayotte (Fr.)

Bié Plateau

Cuando

ZAMBIA

Luangwa

Zambezi

Cubango

Zambezi

MOZAMBIQUE

MADAGASCAR

MAURITIUS

NAMIBIA

Okavango Delta

ZIMBABWE

Mozambique Channel

Réunion (Fr.)

Namib Desert

BOTSWANA

Kalahari Desert

Limpopo

◄ Elephants in Amboseli National Park in southern Kenya near the country's border with Tanzania. Many national parks and game reserves have been established in Africa to help preserve the rich array of wildlife found in the continent.

SWAZILAND

Orange

LESOTHO

Vaal

SOUTH AFRICA

Drakensberg

Cape of Good Hope

► The numbers of African rhinos have been drastically reduced by poachers.

NORTHWEST AFRICA

The four nations and one disputed region which comprise northwest Africa occupy a strategic location between the rest of Africa, western Europe and the Middle East. Much of the region borders the Mediterranean Sea to the north while the massive desert region of the Sahara lies to the south and covers the majority of the land area of Algeria and Libya. Running through Morocco, a small part of Algeria and into Tunisia is the region's principal mountain range, the Atlas Mountains. The majority of the peoples of northwest Africa are of Arab descent following invasions into the region between the 7th and 11th centuries. More than 85 per cent of the population of northwest Africa live on the narrow coastal plain that borders the Mediterranean. Here, the climate is hot and dry in summer, and warm and relatively wet in winter, providing conditions in which land can be farmed. Isolated water wells and oases in the interior support the small number of people who live there. The region includes the former colony of Western Sahara, almost all of which has been occupied by Morocco since 1979. Bordering the Atlantic Ocean, a large proportion of Western Sahara's population consists of settlers from Morocco encouraged to move there by the country's government. Most of the native Sahrawi peoples of Western Sahara now live in exile in Algeria.

▲ The Tuareg are a native people of the Sahara desert who for many centuries controlled the trade across much of the Sahara. Tuareg people today live in Algeria, Tunisia, Libya, Burkina and Mali.

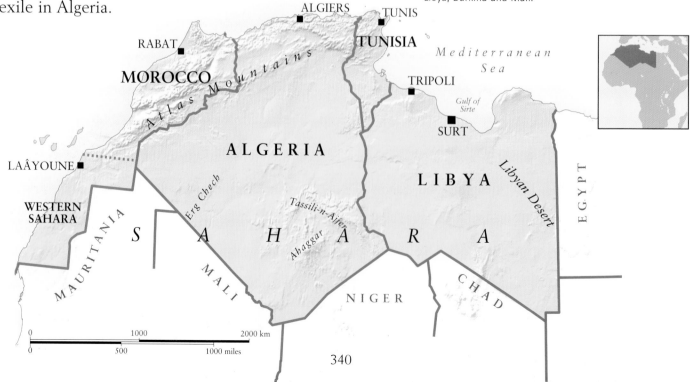

MOROCCO

The rugged and mountainous kingdom of Morocco faces Spain across the Straits of Gibraltar. It gained independence from France and Spain in 1956.

Area: 458,730 km² excluding the disputed Western Sahara territory or 690,275 km² including the Western Sahara
Population: 28,351,000
Capital: Rabat (1,336,000)
Main languages spoken: Arabic, Berber
Main religion: Sunni Islam
Currency: dirham
Main exports: phosphates, food (particularly fruit, wine and vegetables), consumer goods
Type of government: kingdom; limited democracy

▼ The lively central square, Djemaa el-Fna, of the city of Marrakech. Located inland on a fertile plain, the city was founded in the 11th century and is an important transport and trade centre.

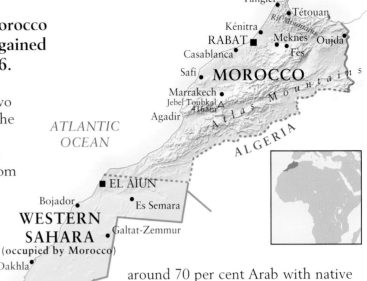

Morocco's land contains two large mountain chains. The Rif Mountains run along the Mediterranean coast while the higher Atlas Mountains run from southwest to northeast and in places are heavily forested. A large amount of snow and rainfall falls on these mountains, and this water flows through a network of streams. To the south and southeast lies part of the Sahara desert. Around 50 per cent of the Moroccan workforce is engaged in farming and fishing. Cereals, sugarcane and sugar beets, dates, olives and citrus fruits are key crops, while large herds of sheep and goats are kept. Fishing is important with over three-quarters of a million tonnes of fish caught every year. The country's location on both the Mediterranean and Atlantic coasts has seen a number of large ports develop including Casablanca, the country's most populous city. Morocco's population is around 70 per cent Arab with native Berber peoples comprising 29 per cent. Almost all of the population is Muslim. Morocco controls around three-quarters of the world's reserves of phosphates, substances which are an important ingredient of fertilizers, metal-cleaning agents, toothpastes and detergents. Morocco has some deposits of coal, iron ore, lead and other metals, while oil was discovered in the desert area to the northeast in 2000. Tourism has become an increasingly important industry, vital to Morocco's economy. The country's warm climate, beaches, scenery, and its ancient cities such as Fès, Tangier and Marrakech attracted 4.1 million tourists in 2002.

ALGERIA

Algeria won independence from France in 1962 after a bitter struggle. Its land is dominated by the Sahara desert, and its economy by oil and natural gas production.

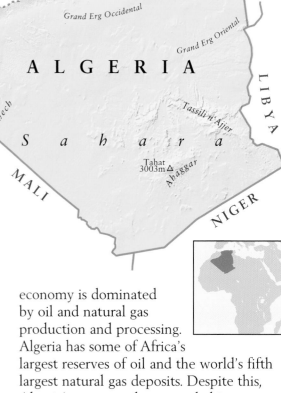

Area: 2,381,741 km²
Population: 31,736,000
Capital: Algiers (2,136,000)
Main languages spoken: Arabic, Berber
Main religion: Sunni Islam
Currency: Algerian dinar
Main exports: crude petroleum, natural gas, refined petroleum
Type of government: republic; dictatorship

▼ Located deep in the Sahara desert, 430 km east of Mount Tahat, the oasis of Djanet is the main settlement in the southeast of Algeria. Droughts in recent times have forced many desert herders and some farmers to abandon their traditional lives and look for work in the cities.

The narrow and hilly coastal plain bordering the Mediterranean Sea contains most of Algeria's best farmland and is also where most of the country's people live. Separating this area from the desert interior are the Atlas Mountains and high, barren plateaus. South of these mountains lies the Sahara desert which occupies more than four-fifths of the country's land area. Coastal areas in Algeria have a warm temperate climate with average rainfall of around 1,000 mm per year. In contrast, areas deep in the Sahara may not see rainfall for years. Three-quarters of Algeria's people are Arabs, almost one-quarter are of Berber descent and around one per cent are European. Ninety-nine per cent of the population are Muslims. The main crops grown in Algeria's farmlands are cereals, figs, dates, olives and a variety of fruits and vegetables. Although farming engages around one-quarter of the workforce, the country's economy is dominated by oil and natural gas production and processing. Algeria has some of Africa's largest reserves of oil and the world's fifth largest natural gas deposits. Despite this, Algeria's economy has struggled in recent times with high food prices, over 30 per cent unemployment and clashes between terrorists and military groups.

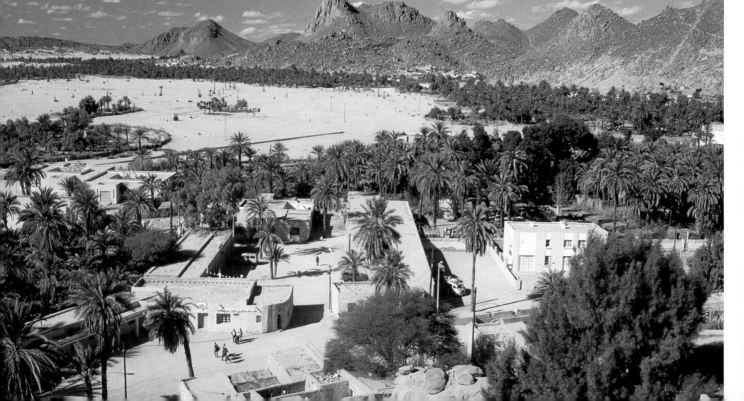

TUNISIA

The smallest nation in northwest Africa, Tunisia is sandwiched between Algeria and Libya and has a historically important Mediterranean coastline.

Area: 163,610 km²
Population: 9,586,000
Capital: Tunis (1,600,000)
Main language spoken: Arabic
Main religion: Sunni Islam
Currency: Tunisian dinar
Main exports: clothing and accessories, machinery and electrical apparatus, phosphates
Type of government: republic; dictatorship

▼ A livestock market is held each week at Douz, 110 km west of Gabès. Douz is the largest of Tunisia's desert oasis settlements and has a population of around 15,000. Every year the town hosts the International Festival of the Sahara which draws performers and artists from across northern Africa.

Mountainous and very green in the north, Tunisia becomes flatter and drier towards the south. The Atlas Mountains extend into the northern portion of Tunisia forming two ranges which contain the country's highest point, the peak of Jabal ash-Shanabi with an elevation of 1,544 m. A mountainous plateau extends northeast, sloping down towards the coast. Towards the south, lies a region of salt lakes, some of which are below sea level. South of these lakes, the land becomes part of the Sahara desert with isolated watering holes and settlements. The large lake of Shatt al Jarid lies in the centre of the country. In the north is the country's most fertile farming area. Compared to its neighbours, a far greater proportion of Tunisia can be farmed using irrigation. However, periodic droughts have a massive effect on farm output. Cereals, citrus fruits, olives and vegetables are key crops while herds of sheep, goats, cattle and camels are kept. Tunisia has a mixed economy in which farming, manufacturing, mining and tourism all play their part. Much of the country's manufacturing industry has been developed since independence from France in 1956, and is based around

Tunis, its largest city. Steel-making, food processing, chemicals and leather goods are among the leading manufacturing areas, while phosphates, lead and oil are the most important mined products. Separated from the island of Sicily by just 160 km of sea, Tunisia has had much contact with Europe for over three millennia. The Phoenicians established colonies in the country over 3,000 years ago. The city of Carthage, located close to Tunis, became the centre of a major Mediterranean power until it was overthrown by the Romans in 146 BCE. Ancient remains from these civilizations along with Tunisia's many sandy beaches and warm climate attracted 5.1 million visitors in 2002.

LIBYA

Libya is a sparsely populated desert nation whose people have benefited from its large oil reserves.

MEDITERRANEAN SEA

Az Zawiyah · TRIPOLI ■
TUNISIA · Al Khums · Al Marj · Tubruq
· Misratah Gulf of · Benghazi
Surt
SURT ■

ALGERIA

LIBYA

Great Sand Sea

EGYPT

Sahara

NIGER

CHAD

△ Bikku Bette 2267m

Area: 1,759,540 km²
Population: 5,605,000
Capitals: Tripoli (1,200,000) – official and diplomatic capital. Surt (40,000) – legislative and administrative capital
Main language spoken: Arabic
Main religion: Sunni Islam
Currency: Libyan dinar
Main export: crude petroleum
Type of government: republic; dictatorship

▼ A desert oasis in the Sahara desert. Large amounts of water lie underneath the surface of the land in south and southeast Libya. The Great Man-Made River Project, one of the largest engineering works in the world, transports water from this region to the cities on the coast.

The Great Socialist People's Libyan Arab Jamahiriya borders Tunisia, Algeria, Niger, Chad, Sudan and Egypt, and has a long coastline with the Mediterranean. Most of its people live in towns and cities situated on or close to the coast. Small, isolated settlements exist southwards in the Sahara and in the northeastern arm of the desert. Less than one per cent of the land is under cultivation, with barley, tobacco, dates, figs and grapes being grown. Livestock, particularly sheep, goats and poultry, is more important than crop growing. Until the discovery of oil in the 1950s, Libya was a desperately poor nation reliant on aid and imports of food to enable its people to survive. Oil output today is around 1.5 million barrels per day and crude oil makes up 99 per cent of all Libya's exports. Oil revenue has enabled the government to establish a welfare state in which education and healthcare are free, although under-resourced and less common in rural areas. It has also enabled Libya to build up its military forces. Libya invaded part of its southern neighbour, Chad, in the 1970s, but its forces were driven out in 1987. Ruled since 1969 by a dictator, Colonel Gaddafi, Libya's economy and people suffered as the result of United Nations' sanctions for the country's link with terrorism. These were lifted in 1999.

NORTHEAST AFRICA

Northeast Africa is a geographically varied region through which two of Africa's greatest features run – the Great Rift Valley and the River Nile. The Nile flows through Sudan and Egypt before emptying into the Mediterranean and provides vital water in an otherwise dry region. The Great Rift Valley is the largest split in the Earth's surface and cuts through much of Ethiopia and into the nations south of this region. The rugged terrain surrounding the Great Rift

▲ These Sudanese girls live in Camp Riang Aguer, Bahr-al Gazal, a makeshift camp in southern Sudan for people displaced from their home areas through conflicts. The camp holds more than 4,000 people.

Valley makes Ethiopia the region's most mountainous country and the home of northeast Africa's highest peaks. Ethiopia is the only nation in the region not to have a coastline with either the Red Sea or the Indian Ocean. Shipping passes along these stretches of water and through the Suez Canal in the north to gain access to the Mediterranean Sea and the nations of Europe. Northeast Africa's natural life varies greatly from the plant-rich wetlands of southern Sudan to the Sahara and other large desert areas throughout the region. Northeast Africa's climate is generally characterized by low rainfall which has led to prolonged droughts and famine in many of the nations. Millions of people have starved to death or remain undernourished, susceptible to life-threatening diseases and reliant on foreign aid for their existence. The countries that comprise this region have been heavily influenced by their proximity to the Middle East and many of their people are either Muslims or Christians. While Egypt has maintained prosperity and a degree of stability, the remaining nations of northeast Africa have all suffered in recent times from wars and internal conflict.

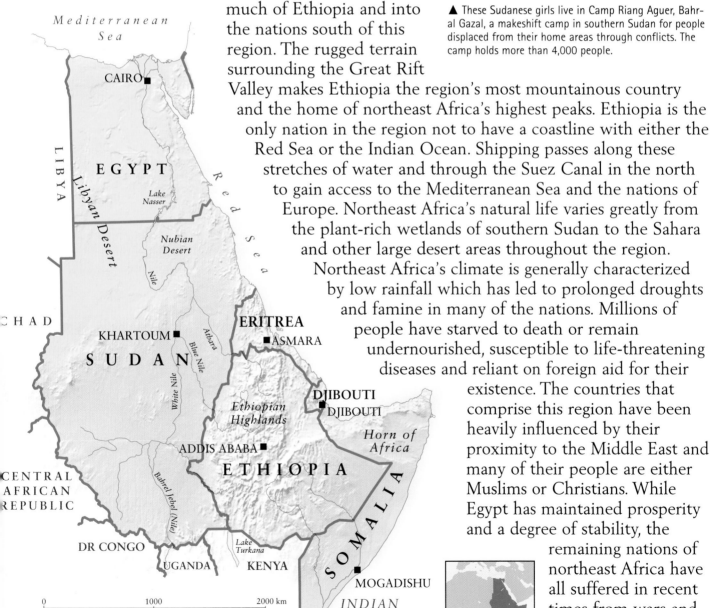

EGYPT

The birthplace of the great Ancient Egyptian civilization, Egypt captivates and fascinates people to this day.

Area: 997,739 km²
Population: 68,470,000
Capital: Cairo
(11,568,000)
Main language spoken: Arabic
Main religions: Sunni Islam, Coptic Christian
Currency: Egyptian pound
Main exports: petroleum and petroleum products, cotton yarn and textiles, basic manufactures, clothing
Type of government: republic; dictatorship

▼ The Ancient Egyptian Pyramids near El Gîza are among the most majestic monuments to the great Ancient Egyptian civilization. For almost 3,000 years a largely unbroken line of pharoahs presided over an empire in which culture, arts, science and technology all flourished.

Egypt is roughly square in shape with long coastlines to the north and east. The Sinai Peninsula lies between the main body of Egypt and Israel and the Gaza territory to the northeast. It is separated from the rest of Egypt by the Gulf of Suez and the Suez Canal, the artificial waterway which links the Mediterranean to the Red Sea. The northern part of Sinai consists of sandy desert while the southern portion is mountainous and contains the country's highest point, Jabal Katrina (2,629 m). Over 90 per cent of Egypt's land is very dry desert which is split into two regions by the Nile. The Libyan Desert is a low-lying series of gravel and sand plateaus. There are no rivers or streams, and rain that does fall gathers in depressions forming temporary salt lakes. A smaller desert to the east is more rugged and contains mountains and plateaus that end in cliffs facing the Red Sea.

A DESERT CLIMATE

Egypt experiences a dry climate and even the wettest parts of the country – the coastal strip bordering the Mediterranean – receive less than 220 mm of rainfall per year. Most of Egypt receives less than 100 mm per year, while in some desert areas, rain may not fall for years. The mountains of Sinai often receive snow in winter and the meltwaters are collected for use in the hot, dry summer. Egypt's deserts experience dramatic temperature swings. When the sun rises, sand and rock begin to heat, radiating warmth into the dry air. Daytime temperatures can reach over 50°C. When the sun sets, the desert cools rapidly. Temperature changes of over 37°C have been recorded in one 24-hour period.

THE NILE RIVER

The world's longest river, the Nile, flows over 1,500 km south to north through Egypt before emptying into the Mediterranean. North of the city of Cairo, the Nile divides into two branches which, through depositing sediment, have created the wide and fertile Nile Delta. Since ancient times, the people of Egypt have been dependent on the Nile for water, transport and for the fertile soils of the banks either side of the river known as the Nile Valley. Today, the vast majority of the population live on just four per cent of Egypt's land, the Nile Valley or Nile Delta regions. Agriculture provides work for almost a third of Egyptians with the fields close to the Nile among the highest-yielding in the world. Cotton, maize, wheat, sugarcane, rice and a large range of vegetables and fruits are the leading crops.

EGYPT'S RESOURCES AND INDUSTRY

The Nile is Egypt's greatest natural resource, yet Egypt also has a variety of mineral deposits, including gold, uranium, phosphates and iron ore. Oil and natural gas are the most important minerals, with Egypt being Africa's fourth largest oil producer behind Nigeria, Algeria and Libya. Almost a quarter of the country's workforce now works in manufacturing industries, particularly processing the crops grown and minerals extracted within its borders. Egypt's cotton, textiles and clothing industries are its largest employers after the government while oil refining, fertilizers, cement and refined sugar are also major industries. Large numbers of small businesses produce pottery, perfume and handicrafts, which are sold to the over four million tourists who visit every year.

THE EGYPTIAN PEOPLE

Ninety-eight per cent of Egyptians are descendants of either the native Ancient Egyptian population (Hamites) or of Arabs who conquered Egypt in CE 642 and settled in the region. Before the Arab invasion, most Egyptians had been Christians but the Arab settlers introduced the Islamic religion and today, over 90 per cent of Egyptians are Muslims. Egypt's population is growing at a fast rate, with around 1.2 million babies born every year. This is putting great pressure on both Egypt's economy and the already densely populated habitable land. Large cities such as Alexandria, its major seaport, and, the largest of all, Cairo, are being forced to grow rapidly in size.

▲ The Nile has been a major transport route through Egypt for over 5,000 years. The river is formed by three major tributaries: the Atbara, the White Nile which flows from Lake Victoria in Uganda, and the Blue Nile which begins life in the Ethiopian highlands. The Nile's waters have been harnessed near Aswan to generate massive amounts of hydro-electricity. This, along with increasing demand for irrigation, has caused the river's level to drop significantly.

SUDAN

The largest African nation, Sudan has distinctly different northern and southern halves. The peoples of these two regions have been in conflict for many years.

Area: 2,505,815 km²
Population: 29,490,000
Capital: Khartoum (2,920,000)
Main languages spoken: Arabic, Dinka, Nubian languages, Beja, Nuer
Main religions: Sunni Islam, traditional beliefs, various Christian churches
Currency: Sudanese dinar
Main exports: cotton, sheep and lambs, sesame seed, gum arabic, gold
Type of government: republic; dictatorship

▼ This Sudanese nomad tends his herd of cattle, some of the over 38 million head that exist in the country. Around two million Sudanese are nomads making a living through herding cattle, sheep and goats.

With the exception of small areas of highlands, Sudan is mostly a land of flat plains. The northern part of the country is split by the River Nile into the Libyan Desert to the west and the Nubian Desert to the east. The clay plains in the centre of the country support dry savannah which give way to giant swamplands and rainforest in the south. The lands around the two key tributaries of the Nile, the Blue and White Nile, are the most fertile farming areas of the country. Sudanese people come from more than 500 different tribes, clans and groups. Around two-thirds live in rural areas and depend on agriculture, which is often hit by droughts, to survive. Cotton is the main cash crop, while a range of food crops including wheat, millet and sorghum are grown. The people of northern Sudan are mainly of Arab origin and follow the Islamic religion. Some non-Arab peoples in the north have also become Muslims. The people of southern and central Sudan are predominantly black Africans who practise traditional African religions, or are Christians. Conflict and civil war have dogged Sudan since independence in 1956, particularly through attempts by Muslims to impose their values on the southern population.

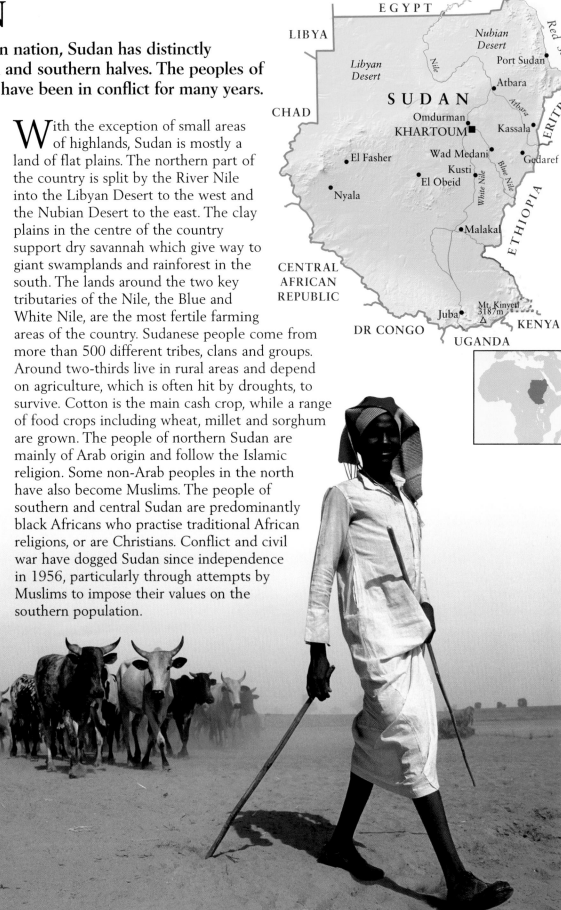

SOMALIA

Formed in 1960 from Italian and British Somaliland colonies, Somalia is drought and war-ridden and is one of the poorest nations in the world.

Area: 637,657 km²
Population: 10,097,000
Capital: Mogadishu (900,000)
Main languages spoken: Somali, Arabic
Main religion: Sunni Islam
Currency: Somali shilling
Main exports: sheep and goats, bananas, camels and cattle
Type of government: republic; no effective national government

Somalia's land generally consists of rugged plains and plateaus. Much of the country is very dry, receiving between 50 and 150 mm of rainfall per year. Bananas and other fruit along with maize, sugarcane and cotton are grown in the southwest. More than half of the population are nomadic, wandering with herds of animals in search of grazing lands. Industry, limited to processing leather and food goods, largely halted in the 1990s. In 1991, a 22-year-long military dictatorship was overthrown and since that time the country has been in political turmoil. Severe droughts and famines along with vicious tribal fighting have added to the troubles of an already desperately poor people.

ETHIOPIA

Formerly called Abyssinia, Ethiopia is one of the world's oldest nations and one of the only parts of Africa not to have been a European colony.

Area: 1,127,127 km²
Population: 65,892,000
Capital: Addis Ababa (2,424,000)
Main languages spoken: Amharic, Oromo, Tigrinya, Gurage, Somali
Main religions: Ethiopian Orthodox, Sunni Islam, traditional beliefs
Currency: birr
Main exports: coffee (accounts for nearly two-thirds of exports), animal hides, pulses, petroleum products
Type of government: republic; limited democracy

Ethiopia is dominated by highland areas divided by the Great Rift Valley which runs from north to south. Three-quarters of its land are above 1,400 m in elevation. Lake Tana, which lies in the north of the country, is northeast Africa's largest lake. To the east lies a semi-desert plain, and north of this is one of the hottest places on Earth, with temperatures reaching 50°C. Rainfall varies greatly, usually with elevation, but is often not enough to prevent devastating droughts. Over 80 per cent of Ethiopians are rural and rely on farming to survive, with coffee the key cash crop and livestock herding vital for domestic food. Ethiopia is one of the least developed and poorest nations in the world. Frequent droughts, famine and war have all damaged the economy and created great suffering among the country's people.

▼ A cascading waterfall on the Blue Nile river as it runs through Ethiopia. The Blue Nile, known as Abay to Ethiopians, is a major tributary of the Nile.

ERITREA

One of the youngest African nations, Eritrea became independent from Ethiopia in 1993. The country has a 1,000-km-long coastline with the Red Sea.

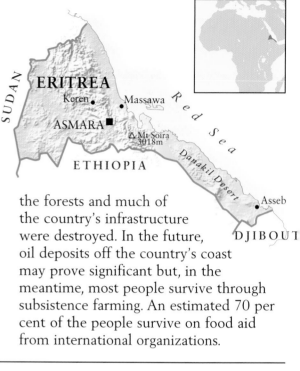

Area: 93,679 km²
Population: 3,850,000
Capital: Asmara (358,000)
Main languages spoken: Tigrinya, Arabic, Afar
Main religions: Sunni Islam, Ethiopian Orthodox
Currency: nakfa
Main exports: raw materials (including animal hides), food products, manufactures (including footwear and textiles)
Type of government: republic; dictatorship

Eritrea's land consists of a hot, dry coastal plain which rises to form areas of highland plateaus with an elevation of between 1,500 and 2,450 m. Rainfall is higher in the highland areas but is still relatively low and the country suffers from drought at times. Handed to Ethiopia by the United Nations in 1952, Eritreans embarked upon a 30-year-long war of independence in which many hundreds of thousands of people died, and the forests and much of the country's infrastructure were destroyed. In the future, oil deposits off the country's coast may prove significant but, in the meantime, most people survive through subsistence farming. An estimated 70 per cent of the people survive on food aid from international organizations.

DJIBOUTI

A small nation, Djibouti is a dry desert land which lies at the entrance to the Red Sea. Its capital, also called Djibouti, is a major regional port.

Area: 23,200 km²
Population: 638,000
Capital: Djibouti (450,000)
Main languages spoken: Somali, Arabic, Afar, French
Main religion: Sunni Islam
Currency: Djibouti franc
Main exports: re-exports, live animals
Type of government: republic; limited democracy

Mountainous to the north with low plains to the centre and south, most of Djibouti's land is hot desert broken by occasional oases and salt lakes. Rainfall is highest in the mountains but even here rarely exceeds 320 mm, while most of the country receives less than 150 mm per year. Rearing livestock is the chief farming activity but close to three-quarters of the people live in or around the city of Djibouti. The country's economy is highly dependent on the port's strategic location at the junction of the Red Sea and the Gulf of Aden. Much of Djibouti's income is derived from port trade as it is the main outlet for landlocked Ethiopia's coffee crop and other produce. Djibouti became independent from France in 1977 and still relies on aid from that country. Unemployment is high, poverty is common and tensions between the country's two main peoples, the Issas and the Afars, have resulted in occasional conflict.

► Salt is extracted from Lake Assal in the centre of Djibouti. At 157 m below sea level, the lake is the lowest point in Africa.

WEST AFRICA

Most of the land that comprises west Africa lies below 1,500 m in elevation and much of its territory consists of plains. Three large nations, Mauritania, Mali and Niger, lie to the north – much of their land area is part of the Sahara desert. Further south, the land and vegetation run from semi-desert to savannah and, furthest south, there are large but shrinking tropical rainforests. South of these three desert giants are nations whose land is among the most densely populated in Africa. All, except Burkina, Mali and Niger, have coastlines with the Atlantic Ocean. The majority of the region's rivers, including its largest, the Niger, empty into this ocean. West Africa was the home of large and flourishing civilizations hundreds of years before European explorers and traders arrived on its shores. The region became subject to rule and exploitation of its resources and people by European colonial powers. Millions were sent abroad to work as as slaves, and the region became seriously depopulated. Today, west Africa comprises 16 nations and the island republic of Cape Verde. Relatively rich in mineral and natural resources, the region includes a number of countries which are developing large scale industries.

▲ A woman grinds grain into flour using a pole called a pestle in the west African country of Niger. Although a number of west African nations have developed large manufacturing and service industries, agriculture still remains the biggest single employer.

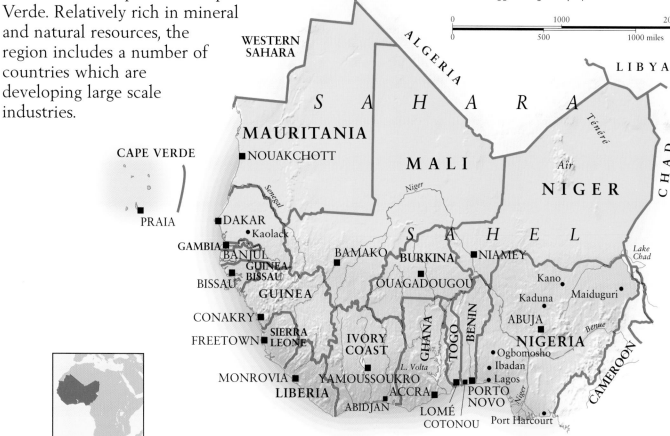

CAPE VERDE

Lying off the west coast of Africa, the island group of Cape Verde became independent of Portugal in 1975. Over half of the people live on the island of São Tiago.

Area: 4,033 km²
Population: 435,000
Capital: Praia (95,000)
Main languages spoken: Portuguese, Crioulo (Portuguese Creole)
Main religion: Roman Catholic
Currency: Cape Verde escudo
Main exports: shoes, clothing and textiles, fish and fish products, salt, bananas
Type of government: republic; democracy

CAPE VERDE

The ten islands and five islets that comprise Cape Verde are of volcanic origin and contain one active volcano, Pico do Cano, which at 2,829 m is also the island's highest point. Rainfall (less than 250 mm per year), vegetation and wildlife are all relatively sparse on these rugged islands, most of which are mountainous. Farming is only possible in limited areas in valleys using irrigation and the islands have to import much of their food. The fishing industry is the country's biggest export earner. Ports at Porto Novo and Mindelo are used by ocean shipping as refuelling stops which also brings in revenue. Aid, mainly from the European Union, has helped to improve healthcare and education.

MAURITANIA

The largely desert nation of Mauritania received its independence from France in 1960 and since that time has increased its ties with the Arab world.

Area: 1,030,700 km²
Population: 2,548,000
Capital: Nouakchott (612,000)
Main languages spoken: Arabic, Wolof, Tukulor
Main religion: Sunni Islam
Currency: ouguiya (the world's only non-decimal currency)
Main exports: iron ore, fish and fish products
Type of government: republic; limited democracy

▶ Imraguen fishermen gather in a catch of golden mullet at the Banc d'Arguin National Park off the coast of Mauritania. Imraguen fishermen have fished this area for thousands of years.

Like Mali, which it borders to the south and east, most of Mauritania lies within the Sahara desert. Only its southern lands and some areas of its Atlantic coast are capable of supporting varied vegetation. Farming is mainly confined to the valley along the border area with Senegal where millet, pulses and dates are among the crops grown. The rich fishing grounds off its coastline make fish and fish processing one of the country's major exports behind iron ore which accounts for 60 per cent of exports. The country also has some of the world's largest gypsum deposits. Fishing and mining account for over 99 per cent of its earnings from exports. The majority of Mauritania's population are either Moors, a north African people, or of mixed Arab origin. Black Africans of many different ethnic groups make up around 30 per cent. Ethnic tensions and occasional conflict exist between the Moors, who are dominant in politics, and the black minority.

MALI

Once the centre of a great Saharan trading empire, Mali is a landlocked, underdeveloped country in which droughts and famine have created widespread poverty.

Area: 1,248,574 km²
Population: 11,234,000
Capital: Bamako (1,056,000)
Main languages spoken: Bambara, French, Fulani, Senufo
Main religions: Sunni Islam, traditional beliefs
Currency: CFA franc
Main exports: cotton and cotton products, live animals, gold
Type of government: republic; democracy

▶ Droughts and political boundaries have forced many of the Saharan nomadic Tuareg peoples to settle in towns and cities.

Almost half of Mali's land is part of the Sahara desert while semi-arid sand areas cover much of the rest of the country. Mountains rise to the south and hydro-electric dams on the River Niger provide 57 per cent of the country's electricity. Mali's fast-growing population is concentrated in the southern part of the country and is reliant on the Niger for water for crop irrigation as well as for the rich fish stocks it holds. Deforestation and desertification are rife and less than ten per cent of the country's people have access to adequate sanitation. Most people are rural farmers and livestock herders. The key industries of the country are cotton growing and, increasingly, mining for gold and other minerals.

NIGER

Niger is a poor, mainly desert, country. The majority of its people live in a semi-fertile southern strip bordering Nigeria and, to the southwest, the River Niger.

Area: 1,186,408 km²
Population: 10,730,000
Capital: Niamey (627,000)
Main languages spoken: Hausa, Djerma-Songhai, French, Tuareg
Main religions: Sunni Islam, traditional beliefs
Currency: CFA franc
Main exports: uranium, livestock, cowpeas
Type of government: republic; democracy

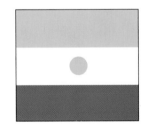

The northern two-thirds of Niger are part of the Sahara desert which is spreading southwards as desertification continues. Ninety per cent of the population work in agriculture, although less than four per cent of the land can be cultivated. Herding livestock is a major occupation while others fish the Niger river and Lake Chad to the southeast. Niger was one of the world's leading producers of uranium, used in atomic energy, but demand has dropped, creating large debts. Coal, phosphates, tin and salt are also mined. Niger's population is ethnically diverse. The largest group is the Hausa, who make up more than half of the population, and the Djerma comprise around 23 per cent. Other large minorities include the Tuareg, many of whom live a nomadic life in the north. The average life expectancy in Niger is just 42 years.

SENEGAL

The former French colony of Senegal lies on the bulge of western Africa, bounded by the Atlantic Ocean, Mauritania, Mali, Guinea, and Guinea-Bissau.

Area: 196,712 km²
Population: 10,050,000
Capital: Dakar (1,905,000)
Main languages spoken: Wolof, French, Fulani, Serer
Main religion: Sunni Islam
Currency: CFA franc
Main exports: fish and crustaceans, chemicals, peanut oil, phosphates
Type of government: republic; limited democracy

▼ Senegalese women carry a harvest of fingers of millet in baskets perched on top of their heads. Millet is a staple grain used in stews and many Senegalese meals.

Senegal is a largely flat and low-lying country with an average elevation below 200 m and sandy soils. Higher land is only found in the extreme southeast where mountains rise to elevations above 500 m. Senegal has a hot, tropical climate with rainfall getting progressively higher towards the south. As a result of this there is dry savannah in the north and considerably more lush areas of rainforest in the south. Four major rivers cross the country including the large Sénégal river which forms most of the country's border with Mauritania. The Sénégal floods every year and deposits fertile sediment over a large area on which a number of crops are grown. Nearly 70 per cent of the workforce are employed in farming. The country is encouraging greater growing of crops like sugarcane, cotton, rice and vegetables to reduce its reliance on the

single dominant crop of peanuts. The country's population consists of seven main ethnic groups with the Wolof making up nearly 45 per cent. Compared to many neighbouring countries, Senegal is relatively wealthy. It has well-developed transport and communications systems and a relatively large industrial sector. Senegal's capital and largest city, Dakar, is located on the Cape Verde peninsula which contains mainland Africa's most westerly point.

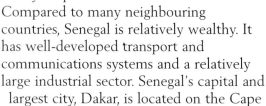

THE GAMBIA

Surrounded by Senegal on three sides, the Gambia is the smallest nation on the west African mainland and at no point measures more than 80 km wide.

▲ Formerly a naval port, the Gambia's capital city of Banjul is located on Banjul Island. This road, Independence Drive, connects the city to the mainland.

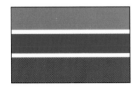

Area: 10,689 km²
Population: 1,411,000
Capital: Banjul (270,000)
Main languages spoken: Malinké, Fulani, English
Main religion: Sunni Islam
Currency: dalasi
Main exports: re-exports (mainly to Senegal), fish and fish products, groundnuts, processed food
Type of government: republic; limited democracy

The Gambia is dominated by the River Gambia which runs east to west through the entire country and divides it in two. Most of its land is savannah grassland with some forested areas and swamplands close to the river and the coast. Rice and peanuts are the two largest crops. Gambia's industry is mainly limited to processing farm products. The country has a tropical climate with a short rainy season between June and October. Gambians come from many different ethnic groups and around 90 per cent are Muslims. Many rural Gambians are migrating to towns where incomes are often three or four times higher than in rural areas. There, they work in service industries, transport and tourism. The country's capital city, Banjul, is located on

a deep natural harbour, one of the best on the whole west coast of Africa. Revenue from tourists, most of whom come from the UK, Germany and other European nations, is the fastest growing part of the country's economy.

GUINEA-BISSAU

Guinea-Bissau, one of the poorest nations in west Africa, has been beset by internal strife since its independence from Portugal in 1974.

Area: 36,125 km²
Population: 1,213,000
Capital: Bissau (195,000)
Main languages spoken: Portuguese, Crioulo (Portuguese Creole), Fulani
Main religions: traditional beliefs, Sunni Islam
Currency: CFA franc
Main exports: cashews, timber, cotton, fish
Type of government: republic; limited democracy

Guinea-Bissau has a heavily indented coastline and its territory has more than 60 offshore islands including the Bijagos Islands, which lie in the Atlantic Ocean. The landscape consists of a coastal plain split by many river estuaries. The land rises to a low plateau in the interior with highlands to the northeast close to the country's border with Guinea. Guinea-Bissau has a tropical climate with heavy rainfall. Mangrove swamps and tropical jungle cover much of the land near the coast. Much of the land in the interior is savannah. Guinea-Bissau's forests contain commercially valuable hardwood trees, and the country has mineral deposits of tin, bauxite and copper as well as possible reserves of oil offshore.

None of these resources has been seriously exploited. The population generally makes a living through subsistence farming. Fishing is also important. Around 50 per cent of the people follow traditional African beliefs, around 45 per cent are Muslim and the rest are Christian. Most of the population are below the poverty line, 66 per cent cannot read and around 11 per cent of all babies die before reaching adulthood. The country is heavily reliant on foreign aid.

GUINEA

Independent since 1958, Guinea is a poor country and reliant on foreign aid despite being rich in mineral reserves.

Area: 245,857 km²
Population: 7,430,000
Capital: Conakry (1,093,000)
Main languages spoken: Fulani, French, Malinké, Susu
Main religions: Sunni Islam, Roman Catholic
Currency: Guinean franc
Main exports: bauxite, alumina, gold, coffee, diamonds, fish
Type of government: republic; dictatorship

Guinea consists of four varying regions: the wet coastal plain, the northwestern Fouta Djallon hill region, the northern dry lowlands, and the hilly, forested area of the southeast. Guinea is one of the wettest countries in west Africa and its largest city, Conakry, receives over 4,295 mm of rain per year. Many crops are grown including rice, cassava, pineapples and peanuts. Guinea has more than 30 per cent of the world's reserves of bauxite ore from which aluminium is smelted. Bauxite makes up over 75 per cent of all exports. The country remains poor and underdeveloped with large numbers of refugees fleeing from conflict in neighbouring countries.

SIERRA LEONE

Founded in 1787 for freed African slaves, Sierra Leone became independent in 1961. Scarred by war and political instability, the country is extremely poor.

Area: 71,740 km²
Population: 4,854,000
Capital: Freetown (553,000)
Main languages spoken: Krio (English Creole), Mende, English
Main religions: Sunni Islam, traditional beliefs
Currency: leone
Main exports: diamonds, rutile/titanium ore, cocoa, coffee
Type of government: republic; limited democracy

Sierra Leone's land consists of a swampy, coastal plain which rises to a plateau and mountains to the northeast. The capital, Freetown, is located on a rocky peninsula, overlooking one of the world's largest natural harbours. Savannah grassland is found in the northern interior with dense rainforest in the south. Valuable tropical hardwoods, including teak and mahogany, as well as wildlife including chimpanzees, monkeys and numerous bird species are under threat from heavy deforestation. In the 1990s, an estimated three per cent of Sierra Leone's forests were cut down each year. Two-thirds of the country's workforce are involved in subsistence farming, with rice the largest staple crop. After a devastating civil war in the 1990s, Sierra Leone now relies heavily on foreign aid. The country remains unstable and under threat of more conflict. Its people, comprising more than 20 ethnic groups, are among the world's poorest with just one doctor per 15,000 people.

▶ A group of Sierra Leonean women tie-dye cloth to make a traditional form of brightly patterned cloth called gara.

LIBERIA

Liberia was founded in 1847 by freed African slaves from the USA. The majority of its population are engaged in subsistence farming.

Area: 111,370 km²
Population: 3,154,000
Capital: Monrovia (440,000)
Main languages spoken: Krio (English Creole), English, Kpelle
Main religions: traditional beliefs, Sunni Islam, various Protestant churches
Currency: Liberian dollar (the US dollar is also in circulation as legal (tender)
Main exports: iron ore, rubber, timber, diamonds, gold
Type of government: republic; dictatorship

Liberia's land includes a rocky coastline with lagoons and sand bars and a coastal plain on which the majority of its population live. This plain rises to a series of plateaus and low mountains. With an elevation of 1,381 m, Mount Wuteve, near the border with Guinea, is Liberia's highest peak. One-fifth of the country is forested. Between 1990 and 1997, a bloody civil war destroyed much of Liberia's economy. Before the war, giant rubber plantations and large scale iron ore mines accounted for most of its exports. Since the conflict, the country, which had previously retained close ties with the USA, has struggled to maintain peace. Liberia has the world's largest registered fleet of shipping but almost all of the vessels are owned by foreign companies.

▼ Digging for diamonds – Liberia is one of the world's top 20 diamond producers.

TOGO

A long narrow country with a mixture of coastal swamps, plateaus and low mountains, Togo stretches from the Gulf of Guinea some 515 km into west Africa.

Area: 56,785 km²
Population: 4,629,000
Capital: Lomé (375,000)
Main languages spoken: Ewe, French, Kabye, Watyi
Main religions: traditional beliefs, Roman Catholic, Sunni Islam
Currency: CFA franc
Main exports: cotton, re-exports, phosphates, coffee
Type of government: republic; limited democracy

Nearly 65 per cent of Togo's workforce are engaged in agriculture. Most of the country's food is grown on smallholdings and farms with staple crops such as cassava, yams, sorghum, maize and plantains. Minerals, particularly phosphates, have become the country's leading export earner and mining is the country's main industry. The capital city, Lomé, is also a major regional port. The people of Togo come from many ethnic groups. Tensions exist between the two largest groups – the Kabye in the north and the Ewe in the south. Fifty-one per cent of the population practise traditional African religions while 29 per cent are Christians.

▲ This Togolese woman is at a market selling yams which are eaten as a vegetable, ground into a flour, or boiled and eaten as a paste with soup.

IVORY COAST

The Republic of Côte d'Ivoire, or the Ivory Coast, is a large, square-shaped west African nation with a tropical climate and large areas of fertile land.

Area: 320,783 km²
Population: 14,786,000
Capitals: Yamoussoukro (245,000) – official capital; Abidjan (3,110,000) – diplomatic and administrative capital
Main languages spoken: French, Akan, Malinké, Kru
Main religions: Sunni Islam, Roman Catholic, traditional beliefs
Currency: CFA franc
Main exports: cocoa, coffee, wood and wood products, petroleum products, fish products
Type of government: republic; limited democracy

▼ Yamoussoukro's Basilica of Our Lady of Peace was modelled on St Peter's Basilica in Rome and is one of the largest Catholic churches in the world. It took three years to build and cost over 300 million US dollars.

The Ivory Coast consists of an extensive plateau rising gradually from sea level to an elevation of almost 500 m. The country's coast is not easily navigable as it is fringed with lagoons, sand bars and swamps with some cliffs and bays to the east. A canal, completed in 1950, links the country's major city, Abidjan, to the sea so that ocean-going shipping can dock. The northern part of the country is largely savannah grassland with mountains to the northwest, while the centre is dominated by heavy rainforest which supports a rich array of wildlife. Much forest clearance has occurred in the centre and south-central regions of the country.

Farming is the chief occupation of the Ivory Coast's workforce. While many people grow only enough to feed their families, much of the country's farming is conducted on a larger scale. The Ivory Coast is one of the world's top five producers of cacao beans used to make chocolate and cocoa. It is Africa's leading coffee producer and also grows cotton, palm oil and rubber for export. Yamoussoukro, near the country's largest lake, Lac de Kossou, was declared the country's capital in 1983 but many government offices remain located in Abidjan, the country's major port, commercial centre and its most populous city. Compared to many of its west African neighbours, the Ivory Coast has had a stable political past. It became independent from France in 1960, and was ruled for 33 years by a single President, Houphouet-Boigny. During the 1960s and 1970s, the country's economy flourished with financial assistance from France. Expensive projects were undertaken, including the building of some of the world's largest churches and mosques. But, in the 1980s, the economy took a downturn. Today, the Ivory Coast is struggling to repay giant foreign debts. Forty per cent of its people are foreigners who were attracted to the country's former prosperity. Tensions between native and foreign-born people have led to much instability since 1999.

GHANA

Once the centre of ancient empires, Ghana is one of the most developed countries in west Africa. Its economy is based mainly on agriculture and mining.

Area: 238,533 km²
Population: 20,212,000
Capital: Accra (1,390,000)
Main languages spoken: Hausa, English, Akan, Mossi
Main religions: traditional beliefs, Sunni Islam, Roman Catholic
Currency: cedi
Main exports: gold, cocoa, other food products, timber, electricity
Government: republic; democracy

▼ A traditional wooden boat known as a pirogue travels along the Volta river. The Volta river and lake system provide almost 10 per cent of the country's total fish catch of over 440,000 tonnes.

Ghana is a low-lying nation in west Africa. Half of its land lies below 150 m and its highest point, Afadjato (880 m), is located in the eastern hills near the border with Togo. Much of the country's landscape is formed by the basin of the Volta rivers. The northern region is drained by the Black Volta and White Volta rivers which join to form the Volta. This river is crossed by the Akosombo hydro-electric dam in the southeast of the country which forms one of the world's largest artificial lakes, Lake Volta. Almost all of Ghana's electricity is generated via hydro-electric power. Ghana has a tropical climate with daily temperatures tending to range between 21 and 32°C. There are two rainy seasons, from March to July and from September to October. Rainfall varies greatly throughout the country ranging between 1,000 mm in the north to 2,050 mm in the southeast. In the north, large areas are savannah, while a mixture of savannah and rainforest covers the centre and south of the country. Much of the original vegetation has been cleared for farming and by the country's large timber industry. Ghana is one of Africa's leading timber exporters, and cocoa is its chief export crop. Ghana was a British colony until 1957 and had been known as the Gold Coast. The country lives up to its former name, being the second largest producer of gold in Africa, producing around 80,000 kg in 2002. It also has diamond, bauxite and manganese mines. Ghanaians have suffered from political instability and corruption with long periods of rule by the military.

NIGERIA

The most populous country in Africa, Nigeria is home to several hundred different ethnic groups. This large nation is rich in natural resources, especially oil.

Area: 923,768 km²
Population: 111,506,000
Capital: Abuja (212,000)
Main languages spoken: Hausa, Yoruba, Ibo, English, Fulani
Main religions: Sunni Islam, various Protestant Churches, traditional beliefs, Roman Catholic
Currency: naira
Main exports: crude petroleum (over 90 per cent of exports), cocoa beans, rubber, textiles
Type of government: republic; limited democracy

Nigeria's coast consists of a number of long sandy beaches broken by mangrove swamps where rivers meet the sea. The Niger river, which enters the country in the northwest and flows through the western region of Nigeria, is the country's major river system. As the Niger heads towards the coast it fans out to form Africa's largest river delta, some 36,000 km² in area. High rainfall in the river valleys and along the coast enables a large range of crops to be grown. Along the river flood plains, rice is a common crop. From the coastal region, which extends up to 100 km inland, the land becomes hilly and largely covered in forest before rising to the Jos Plateau in the centre of the country. North of this are savannah plains which are the largest areas of farmland in the country. The savannah gets drier and becomes semi-desert and desert in the far north.

AN OIL DEPENDENT ECONOMY
Nigeria is rich in natural resources including tin, iron ore, coal, limestone, zinc and lead. Chief among its mineral reserves, though, are oil and natural gas. Nigeria is one of the world's leading crude oil producers, extracting approximately two million barrels per day. Oil accounts for over 90 per cent of the country's

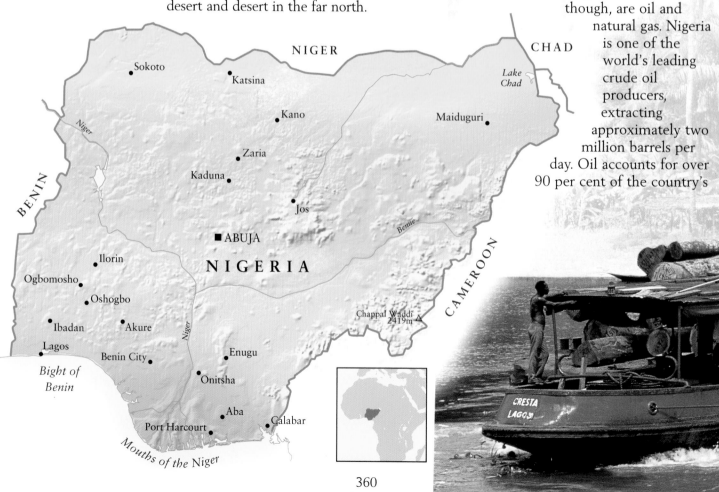

360

including sorghum, millet, maize, yams, taro and rice. The country's fast-growing population means that Nigeria has to import a large amount of its food.

MANY DIFFERENT PEOPLES

Nigeria has a long history, not just of settlement, but of empires and city-states long before the region was colonized by European powers. Peoples such as the Hausa in the north, the Ibo (Igbo) in the southeast and the Yoruba, based around the city of Ife in the southwest, had formed well-organized kingdoms centuries before European arrivals. The Hausa, Yoruba and Ibo peoples make up over half of the country's population. The remainder belong to over 250 different ethnic groups which not only contribute to Nigeria's extremely rich culture and arts, but has also divided the country along both ethnic and language lines. In addition, there is a religious divide with people in the north predominantly Muslim while those in the south are mainly Christian or practise traditional African beliefs. Keeping so many different peoples with different cultures and beliefs together in one single nation has proved difficult, especially as the divide between the Muslim north and the rest of the country is increasing. Since independence in 1960, Nigeria has had to contend with much conflict within its borders, including a civil war (1967–1970) when the Ibo peoples tried to break away and form their own nation of Biafra. There have been more years of rule by military dictatorships than elected civilian governments and the country to this day maintains an uneasy peace.

◄ Lagos is the most important city in Nigeria with a fast-growing population rivalling Cairo for the title of Africa's largest city. The country's chief port, around half of the entire country's manufacturing industry is based in or around Lagos.

exports, but the wealth generated has only benefited very few as corruption is rife. In addition, the reliance on a single commodity means that the economy is severely affected by changes in oil prices. In comparison to oil, Nigeria's natural gas and other mineral deposits are underexploited. Agriculture employs 70 per cent of the country's workforce and cocoa, rubber and textiles are the chief exports. However, the vast majority of farming is performed on small family farms growing staple foods

▼ A tugboat manoeuvres a raft of logs along one of Nigeria's rivers. Logging is a major industry in Nigeria with the majority of the wood being used by Nigerians as firewood.

BURKINA

Burkina is a landlocked country lying on the fringe of the Sahara. Severe droughts and desertification have recently increased the nation's difficulties.

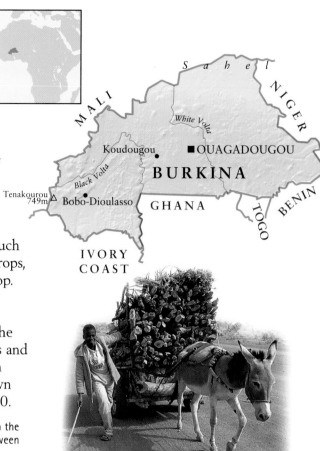

Area: 274,122 km²
Population: 12,603,000
Capital: Ouagadougou (710,000)
Main languages spoken: Mossi, French, Fulani, Gurma
Main religions: Sunni Islam, traditional beliefs, Roman Catholic
Currency: CFA franc
Main exports: cotton, live animals, gold, hides and skins
Type of government: republic; limited democracy

Most of Burkina is flat, with some rolling hills and woodlands in the southwest. The north of the country is dry and frequent droughts afflict most of the country. The majority of the population are farmers who live in the south and grow either food crops such as rice, cereals and vegetables or cash crops, including cotton, the leading export crop. Goats, sheep and cattle are herded but livestock numbers have been severely decreased by droughts. The Mossi are the largest of Burkina's many ethnic groups and were the traditional rulers of the region before it became a French colony, known as Upper Volta, between 1895 and 1960.

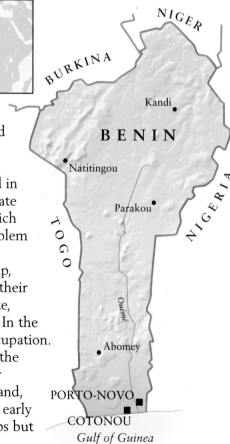

▶ A Burkinan man guides his cart carrying wood in the Sahel region. The Sahel is a dry transition zone between the Sahara and more lush grasslands to the south.

BENIN

Formerly known as Dahomey, Benin is a small west African nation which stretches north some 670 km from the Gulf of Guinea to the Niger river.

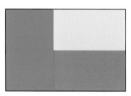

Area: 112,622 km²
Population: 6,097,000
Capitals: Porto-Novo (218,000) – official; Cotonou (650,000) – diplomatic and administrative
Main languages spoken: Fon, French, Yoruba, Adja
Main religions: traditional beliefs, Roman Catholic, Sunni Islam
Currency: CFA franc
Main exports: cotton yarn, re-exports of manufactures, petroleum
Type of government: republic; democracy

Benin's sandy 121-km-long coastal strip is indented with lagoons and mangrove swamps. North of this region is a fertile plateau which contains large marshlands. The plateau gradually rises and is crossed in the centre of the country by mountains. Benin's climate is tropical but with relatively low average rainfall which is highest in the south. Desertification is a major problem in the northern region. The people are a mixture of different ethnic groups with the Fon, the largest group, making up just under 40 per cent. The people make their living mainly through subsistence farming. Rice, maize, cassava, millet and yams are among the crops grown. In the north, goat, sheep and cattle herding is the major occupation. For more than six centuries, the city of Abomey was the centre of a prosperous kingdom before coming under French control. Independence was achieved in 1960 and, in 1975, the country changed its name to Benin. The early years of independence saw a number of military coups but multiparty elections were restored in the 1990s.

CENTRAL AND EAST AFRICA

Central and east Africa straddles the Equator and much of the land of the 14 nations that occupy this region experiences a tropical climate. The region is divided in two by a giant split in the Earth's crust called the Great Rift Valley with uplands on either side of the valley. A chain of lakes runs along the Rift Valley, while between the two branches of the valley lies Lake Victoria – Africa's largest and the world's third largest lake with an area of 69,500 km². West of the Rift Valley, the River Congo, Africa's second longest river, snakes through Congo and Democratic Republic of Congo, a distance of approximately 4,700 km. Central and east Africa's peoples have experienced varying fortunes since independence from colonial powers occurred mainly in the 1960s. Some nations such as the Central African Republic are poor, others like Rwanda have been torn apart by war, while some nations, including Kenya, are relatively stable.

▲ Central Africa is home to the gorilla, the largest of the world's apes. The region's gorilla population is under threat from hunting and habitat destruction.

▼ Refugees from the central African nation of Rwanda in a refugee camp in Tanzania. In the mid-1990s, a brutal civil war in Rwanda saw between half and one million Tutsi peoples killed in fighting.

CAMEROON

A heavily forested country, with the majority of its people living in the south, Cameroon has developed its industry and infrastructure since independence in 1961.

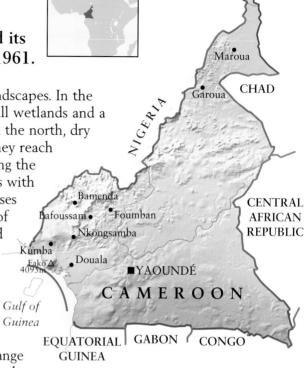

Area: 475,442 km²
Population: 15,085,000
Capital: Yaoundé (750,000)
Main languages: Fang, French, Bamileke, English
Main religions: Roman Catholic, traditional beliefs, Sunni Islam
Currency: CFA franc
Main exports: crude petroleum, timber, cocoa, coffee, aluminium, cotton
Type of government: republic; dictatorship

Cameroon is a country of varied landscapes. In the south there are coastal plains, small wetlands and a plateau mainly covered in rainforest. In the north, dry grasslands continue northwards until they reach the southern shores of Lake Chad. Along the country's northern and western borders with Nigeria, the land is mountainous and rises to an elevation of 4,095 m – the peak of the Cameroon mountain volcano called Fako. The western slopes of this mountain are one of the wettest places in the world with an average annual rainfall as high as 10,000 mm. Cameroon's population is very diverse with over 210 ethnic groups and no one dominant people. A large range of crops is grown for food and export and, for many years, the country has been self-sufficient in staple foods. Over 90 per cent of its electricity is generated through hydro-electric power, of which almost half is used to power a giant aluminium plant. Oil, although declining, still provides valuable export revenue while commercial fishing is on the increase.

CENTRAL AFRICAN REPUBLIC

Since independence in 1960, the landlocked and poor country of the Central African Republic has been largely governed by dictators and the military.

Area: 622,436 km²
Population: 3,577,000
Capital: Bangui (535,000)
Main languages spoken: Sango, French, Baya
Main religions: traditional beliefs, Baptist, Roman Catholic
Currency: CFA franc
Main exports: diamonds, coffee, timber and timber products, cotton
Type of government: republic; limited dictatorship

Most of the Central African Republic consists of a plateau which ranges in elevation between 600 and 800 m. The plateau is flanked by highland areas to the northeast and hill ranges to the north. Dense rainforest covers much of the south of the country, some of which is in reserves to protect wildlife including gorillas and leopards. The remainder of the land is grassland with some trees. Less than four per cent of the country is cultivated and subsistence agriculture dominates the lives of the people. Deposits of uranium, iron and copper exist, but mining focuses on diamonds which comprise just over half the country's exports.

▶ These Baaka pygmies in the rainforests of the Central African Republic make simple shelters from bent tree branches covered in bark and foliage.

EQUATORIAL GUINEA

The small country of Equatorial Guinea consists of the mainland called Rio Muni and five islands, the largest of which, Bioko, is the site of the country's capital.

Area: 28,051 km²
Population: 453,000
Capital: Malabo (30,000)
Main languages spoken: Fang, Bubi, Spanish, English Creole
Main religions: Roman Catholic, traditional beliefs
Currency: CFA franc
Main exports: petroleum products, timber, cocoa
Type of government: republic; dictatorship

Surrounded by Gabon and Cameroon, the small mainland region of Equatorial Guinea is a land of few extremes in height. Inland from the coastal plain and hill ranges, over half the land is heavily forested. The country's varied wildlife includes elephants, gorillas, leopards, crocodiles and chimpanzees. However, many creatures are endangered as a result of extensive and uncontrolled logging operations. In contrast to the landscape of the mainland, Equatorial Guinea's largest island, Bioko, has a dramatic and rugged terrain. Of volcanic origin, the island contains a number of crater lakes and extinct volcanic cones, one of which, Pico de Basilé, is the country's highest point at 3,008 m elevation. Bioko is the centre of the country's cacao bean production, the country's main export crop. Coffee is grown for export on the mainland while rice, yams and bananas are among the key staple foods. The country became independent in 1968 after a long period of Spanish rule and remained largely undeveloped until the discovery of oil in the late 1980s. Oil production today is around 115,000 barrels per day, small by Arab nation standards but enough to comprise almost 80 per cent of its exports and almost two-thirds of its GDP.

SÃO TOMÉ & PRÍNCIPE

Lying off the coast of west Africa, the smallest country in Africa consists of one large island, São Tomé, one smaller island, Príncipe, and a small number of islets.

Area: 1,001 km²
Population: 147,000
Capital: São Tomé (42,000)
Main languages spoken: Portuguese, Lungwa-Crioulu (Portuguese Creole)
Main religion: Roman Catholic
Currency: dobra
Main exports: cocoa (over 95 per cent of exports)
Type of government: republic; democracy

Separated by 144 km of ocean, both islands were formed by volcanic activity and have high mountains in the south and west, and lowland areas to the north. Lying on the Equator, São Tomé & Príncipe has a warm tropical climate and dense forests cover around half of both islands. A former Portuguese colony, the people are mainly of African descent with a minority being of Portuguese origin. The majority are Roman Catholics although some are Protestant or practise traditional African beliefs. The country is dependent on cocoa exports to pay for food and fuel imports, and is reliant on foreign aid. However, oil exploration, tourism and fisheries offer hope of future economic development.

Príncipe • Santo António

Gulf of Guinea

SÃO TOMÉ & PRÍNCIPE

São Tomé
Pico de São Tomé △ ■ SÃO TOMÉ
2024m

ATLANTIC OCEAN

CHAD

A poor, landlocked nation in northern central Africa, Chad lies more than 1,600 km from the ocean and its northern region is part of the Sahara desert.

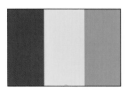

Area: 1,284,000 km²
Population: 7,651,000
Capital: N'Djamena (531,000)
Main languages spoken: Arabic, French, Sara
Main religions: Sunni Islam, Roman Catholic, various Protestant churches
Currency: CFA franc
Main exports: cotton, live cattle, meat, animal hides
Type of government: republic; dictatorship

Chad's landscape is dominated by the large basin which surrounds Lake Chad. This lake varies in size, swelling from an area of less than 10,000 km² up to 25,000 km² during a heavy rainy season. Stretching away from the basin are plateaus which rise to mountains in the north, south and east. Chad's climate is hot and extremely dry to the north where the land is desert, while rainfall is relatively heavy in the south where the majority of the country's people live. The south is mainly savannah and is the chief farming region of the country. Since independence from France, Chad has been beset by internal conflict and civil war which has prevented the country's development. Oil reserves have recently been discovered in the southwest which may help the country's outlook.

LIBYA
Tibesti
△ Emi Koussi 3415m
Sahara
NIGER
CHAD
Sahel
Lake Chad
Abéché •
SUDAN
■ N'DJAMENA
CAMEROON
Chari
Sarh
• Moundou
CENTRAL AFRICAN REPUBLIC

▼ Located 790 km northeast of N'Djamena, Faya is one of the largest oasis towns in the Sahara desert and relies on underground water to grow dates, wheat and figs.

GABON

Containing some of Africa's largest original rainforests and an array of wildlife, Gabon is a sparsely populated nation whose people are relatively prosperous.

Area: 267,667 km²
Population: 1,226,000
Capital: Libreville (420,000)
Main languages spoken: Fang, French, Punu-Sira
Main religions: Roman Catholic, traditional beliefs
Currency: CFA franc
Main exports: petroleum and petroleum products (accounting for over 80 per cent of exports), wood, manganese ore, uranium
Type of government: republic; limited democracy

Gabon consists of a coastal plain which rises inland to form a series of mountains, valleys and plateaus mostly covered in virgin rainforest. Unlike many African countries, Gabon has not been troubled by conflict since independence from France in 1960. Although many Gabonese live in poverty, the country is wealthy in comparison to much of Africa, largely due to its oil revenues – the country produces 325,000 barrels per day. Gabon has large, unexploited, reserves of metals including iron ore and manganese.

CONGO

The Republic of the Congo is a tropical country which was Africa's first communist state from 1970 to 1991. More than half of the land is covered in rainforest.

Area: 342,000 km²
Population: 2,943,000
Capital: Brazzaville (938,000)
Main languages spoken: Monokutuba, Kongo, French
Main religions: Roman Catholic, traditional beliefs, various Protestant Churches
Currency: CFA franc
Main exports: petroleum and petroleum products, wood and timber products
Type of government: republic; limited democracy

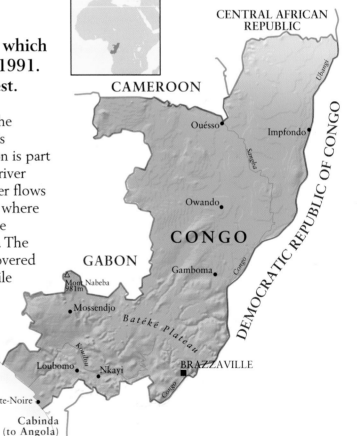

Much of the country's northern region is part of the Congo river basin. This river flows along the country's eastern frontier where it forms most of the border with the Democratic Republic of the Congo. The northern region of the country is covered with swamps and dense forests, while there are grasslands to the south. Oil, first discovered in the 1970s and largely found offshore, is the country's key resource and is responsible for 90 per cent of its export earnings. Other major industries are mining, timber, coffee and cocoa. Most farmland is devoted to producing food for local consumption, with women traditionally the farm workers. Congo's transport, energy and communications are underdeveloped, and much of the country is isolated, using only dirt roads or the large river network for transport. Two hydro-electric dams have been built with aid from China. A third is under construction.

DEMOCRATIC REPUBLIC OF CONGO

The Democratic Republic of Congo, formerly Zaire, is Africa's third largest country. Despite rich natural resources, its people are among Africa's poorest.

Area: 2,344,856 km²
Population: 51,654,000
Capital: Kinshasa (4,655,000)
Main languages spoken: Lingala, Swahili, French, Luba, Mongo
Main religions: Roman Catholic, various Protestant churches, traditional beliefs
Currency: Congolese franc
Main exports: diamonds, crude petroleum, coffee, copper
Type of government: republic; dictatorship

The Democratic Republic of Congo is almost landlocked save for a thin strip of land on the north bank of the Congo river which gives the country a 37 km-long Atlantic coastline. The Congo's giant river basin dominates the country's landscape covering an area of almost one million km² and is largely covered in rainforest. The basin rises to form mountain plateaus to the west while, to the south, there are grassland plains. The country's highest mountains are found in the east. Lying on the Equator, the country has a tropical climate with the hottest temperatures in the central region. The southern highlands are cooler and drier, while the eastern highlands are cooler and wetter. Over 60 per cent of this large country is covered in rainforests which account for approximately half of Africa's woodlands and around six per cent of the world total. The country's underdeveloped transport network has prevented massive clearance by large logging businesses. However, deforestation is occurring to supply local people with firewood and farmland. Most of the population farm the land growing rice, cassava, peanuts and fruit trees. The Democratic Republic of Congo is extremely rich in natural resources and is one of the world's leading producers of copper, cobalt and diamonds. Yet the wealth from these resources has been squandered through decades of colonial exploitation, civil war and corrupt government.

▼ A small settlement in the Democratic Republic of Congo's Ruwenzori Mountains. This rugged mountain range straddles the country's border with its neighbour, Uganda.

UGANDA

Uganda is a land of fertile uplands and mountains which border Africa's largest lake. It is recovering after 25 years of ethnic conflict under dictators.

Area: 241,040 km²
Population: 24,749,000
Capital: Kampala (1,273,000)
Main languages spoken: Swahili, English, Ganda, Teso
Main religions: Roman Catholic, Anglican, traditional beliefs
Currency: Uganda shilling
Main exports: coffee (nearly 70 per cent of exports), cotton, tea
Type of government: republic; limited democracy

▼ This Ugandan fisherman hauls in a freshwater fish from the waters of Lake Victoria. Uganda has one of the largest freshwater fishing catches in the world, nearly all of which is consumed within the country. In 2001, the total fish catch was over 218,000 tonnes.

Much of Uganda consists of a plateau which rises gently from an elevation of around 900 m in the north to 1,500 m in the south. Surrounding this elevated plateau on most sides are large valleys or mountainous areas. The mountain range, to the west, is the location of the country's highest peaks. Uganda is a land of abundant freshwater sources. Many rivers flow through the country, while nearly one-fifth of the country's area is made up of lakes. These include Lake Kyoga in the centre of the country and Lake Albert which lies in the Rift Valley to the west. Uganda has a long shoreline with Africa's largest lake, Lake Victoria. Uganda has an essentially tropical climate, but average temperatures are cooler due to its relatively high altitude. Rainfall varies with the wettest areas in the south receiving around 1,500 mm per year and the driest in the northeast receiving just over half that figure.

UGANDA'S RESOURCES

Compared to some of its neighbours, Uganda is not heavily forested. The country had around 6,500 km² of forests in 1960, but this has been reduced by over a quarter. While clearing land for farming has contributed to deforestation, the major cause has been the use of trees to burn as fuel by Uganda's mainly rural population. Around 85 per cent of the country's total energy consumption is provided by wood fuel. Nearly all of Uganda's electricity is generated by hydro-electric power. Uganda is not an oil producer nor does it have large mining or manufacturing industries. The cost of transporting goods to seaports in Kenya and Tanzania is high. The country is blessed with fertile farmland and the country's largely rural population grows a range of crops for domestic use and also for export. Coffee beans provide over 70 per cent of the country's export income.

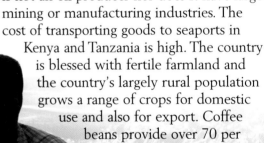

RWANDA

Called the 'land of 1,000 hills', Rwanda is heavily populated with about 90 per cent of its people living in rural areas and involved in farming.

Area: 26,338 km²
Population: 8,163,000
Capital: Kigali (608,000)
Main languages spoken: Rwanda, French
Main religions: Roman Catholic, traditional beliefs
Currency: Rwanda franc
Main exports: coffee (accounts for over 70 per cent of exports), tea, hides and skins
Type of government: republic; dictatorship

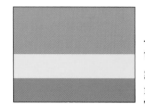

A centuries-old conflict between two major ethnic groups, the Hutu majority and the Tutsi minority, has dominated Rwanda since independence from Belgium in 1962. In 1994, violence led to the deaths of about half a million people, while around two million fled the country as refugees. The economy was devastated in the civil war. Attempts have been made to reconcile the two peoples, but poverty and disease are widespread, and Rwanda depends

on foreign aid. It plans to develop natural gas reserves under Lake Kivu and increase tourism in the northern forests – home to the world's largest population of mountain gorillas.

BURUNDI

A small, landlocked and mountainous country just south of the Equator, Burundi has been troubled by ethnic conflict between the Tutsi and Hutu peoples.

Area: 27,834 km²
Population: 6,695,000
Capital: Bujumbura (225,000)
Main languages spoken: Rundi, French
Main religions: Roman Catholic, non-religious, traditional beliefs
Currency: Burundi franc
Main exports: coffee, tea, cotton, animal hides
Type of government: republic; dictatorship

Lush hills and low mountains cover much of Burundi, while a large plain which neighbours Lake Tanganyika rises to form a plateau in the south. On the lake's northern shore is the country's largest city and chief port, Bujumbura. The fertile hill slopes are heavily farmed with coffee the most important cash crop followed by tea and cotton. Tropical fruits are grown in the country's valleys. Burundi is one of the most densely populated countries in Africa with 240.5 people per km². Birth rates are high and families tend to have a lot of children. Although the Tutsi comprise just 14 per cent of the population, they retain much political and military control of the country. This has led to conflict with the majority Hutus which has seen over 200,000 deaths and as many as one million refugees.

KENYA

After independence in 1963, Kenya successfully developed its economy, but recent political and economic troubles have afflicted the country.

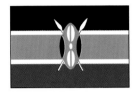

Area: 582,646 km²
Population: 28,687,000
Capital: Nairobi (2,143,000)
Main languages spoken: Swahili, English, Kikuyu, Luhya
Main religions: Roman Catholic, various Protestant Churches, traditional beliefs
Currency: Kenya shilling
Main exports: tea, coffee, fruit and vegetables, petroleum products, cement
Type of government: republic; limited democracy

Kenya's dramatic landscape is dominated by the Great Rift Valley, which cuts through the country from north to south. The valley, which in some places is over 600 m deep, varies in width from 14 km to over 85 km. A number of lakes are found along the valley in Kenya including Lake Turkana, the country's largest. The Rift Valley divides Kenya into two areas, unequal in size. A narrower western area consisting of plains and plateaus borders Uganda and the northeastern shore of Lake Victoria. The far larger eastern region starts with a large area of central highlands in which Kenya's loftiest peak, the 5,199 m-high Mount Kenya, is located. This extinct volcano is the second highest mountain in Africa. The highlands slope down towards grassy plains before reaching the coast, which is lined with long beaches and is the home of Kenya's major port and second largest city, Mombasa. The former British colony of Kenya has 55 national parks or reserves which help protect large numbers of its rich array of native wildlife. Although numbers have declined since the 1980s, Kenya still receives close to a million visitors, and tourism still remains Kenya's single largest foreign income earner.

▲ A group of Masai warriors in the Masai Mara National Park, Kenya.

▼ The Samburu National Reserve is one of many large nature reserves in Kenya. Animals that roam the Samburu include elephants, lions, giraffes, zebras and leopards.

About two-thirds of Kenyans are mostly from three ethnic groups: the Kikuyu, Luhya and Kamba. Many other minority groups exist including Kenyan Asians and Kenyan Arabs, who although small in number, tend to hold much commercial power. Most Kenyans are employed in agriculture with herding livestock important in the drier regions particularly to the north. Although they tend to be on a small scale, Kenya also has some of the most developed industries in east Africa. These include processing of foodstuffs, textiles, beer brewing, furniture, plastics and building materials.

TANZANIA

Tanzania is home to some of the most spectacular features on Earth including Africa's highest mountain, Mount Kilimanjaro.

Area: 945,037 km²
Population: 31,271,000
Capitals: Dodoma (189,000) – legislative capital and capital designate; Dar es Salaam (1,747,000) – administrative capital
Main languages spoken: Swahili, English, Nyamwezi, Hehet
Main religions: traditional beliefs, Sunni Islam, Roman Catholic
Currency: Tanzania shilling
Main exports: coffee, cotton, cashew nuts, tobacco
Type of government: republic; limited democracy

▼ Located in northeastern Tanzania, Kilimanjaro consists of three separate extinct volcanic peaks: Kibo, Mawensi and Shira. Kibo, the youngest and the highest, has a crater almost two km in diameter. Despite lying near the Equator, Kibo's 5,895 m high peak has a year-round cap of snow and ice.

Tanzania's landscape varies from its low, flat coastal plain heavily covered in tropical vegetation to its rugged volcanic mountain tops. Much of the country, though, is located on a plateau averaging 1,200 m in elevation which is largely covered in savannah grasslands and woodlands, but is more arid in the north. Isolated mountain groups rise in the southwest and the northeast while both branches of the Great Rift Valley run through the country. The eastern branch divides the northeastern highlands and contains a series of small lakes. The western branch contains Lakes Malawi and Tanganyika, and acts as a natural border separating Tanzania from nations to the west. A little over half of Africa's largest lake, Lake Victoria, lies in the north of the country. Offshore from Tanzania's Indian Ocean coastline lie a number of islands including Pemba and Zanzibar. Many of these merged with the mainland of Tanganyika in 1964 to form Tanzania. Around one-third of the country is protected as either national parks or game reserves. These include the world-renowned Serengeti National Park which contains over 200 species of birds and 35 species of land animals including cheetahs, lions, elephants and the extremely rare black rhinoceros. Tourists drawn to the country's parks and reserves and to its spectacular geography number almost half a million every year. Although Tanzania has gold and diamond mines and some 44 per cent of the country is forested, farming provides most of the country's exports and employs nearly 80 per cent of the workforce.

MALAWI

The landlocked country of Malawi contains most of the giant Lake Malawi within its territory. It is one of the least developed and poorest countries in Africa.

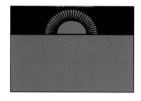

Area: 118,484 km²
Population: 10,925,000
Capital: Lilongwe (441,000)
Main languages spoken: Chichewa, English, Lomwe
Main religions: Sunni Islam, Roman Catholic, Presbyterian
Currency: Malawi kwacha
Main exports: tobacco (which accounts for over 60 per cent of exports), tea, sugar, cotton
Type of government: republic; limited democracy

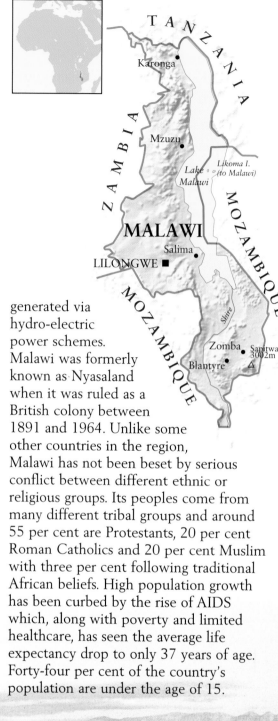

Malawi is bordered by Zambia, Mozambique and Tanzania. The Great Rift Valley runs along the eastern region of the country from north to south. Contained within the valley and occupying almost a third of Malawi's territory is Africa's third largest lake, Lake Malawi. Much of the country consists of highland plateaus and mountains. South of Lake Malawi lies the Shire Highlands home of the country's highest peaks. The vast majority of Malawi's people live in the countryside where farming is the chief occupation. An almost solely agricultural nation, Malawians rely totally on their domestic food crop and, when droughts strike, they devastate the country. When adequate rainfall does occur, Malawi is Africa's second largest producer of tobacco only behind Zimbabwe. Other major exports include tea, sugar and peanuts while maize, sorghum and a wide range of fruit and vegetables are grown for local food. The country also has a growing fishing industry, based on the shores of Lake Malawi, which catches 56,500 tonnes of fish per year. Malawi has few industries beyond small local concerns and few mineral resources. Over 90 per cent of its electricity is generated via hydro-electric power schemes. Malawi was formerly known as Nyasaland when it was ruled as a British colony between 1891 and 1964. Unlike some other countries in the region, Malawi has not been beset by serious conflict between different ethnic or religious groups. Its peoples come from many different tribal groups and around 55 per cent are Protestants, 20 per cent Roman Catholics and 20 per cent Muslim with three per cent following traditional African beliefs. High population growth has been curbed by the rise of AIDS which, along with poverty and limited healthcare, has seen the average life expectancy drop to only 37 years of age. Forty-four per cent of the country's population are under the age of 15.

▼ Malawian fishermen bring in their boats and catch. Nearly all of Malawi's 56,500 tonnes of fish caught every year are found in the waters of Lake Malawi (Lake Nyasa).

ZAMBIA

Zambia, formerly known as Northern Rhodesia, is one of Africa's most urbanised nations with around 44 per cent of people living in towns and cities.

Area: 752,614 km²
Population: 10,286,000
Capital: Lusaka (982,000)
Main languages spoken: Bemba, English, Tonga
Main religions: various Protestant churches, traditional beliefs
Currency: Zambian kwacha
Main exports: copper (over 70 per cent of exports), cobalt
Type of government: republic; limited democracy

▼ The 128 m high Kariba Dam on Zambia's border with Zimbabwe was completed in 1959. The 579 m long dam is is part of a giant hydroelectric power station.

Zambia's northern border is divided by land belonging to the Democratic Republic of Congo. The territory extends deep into the middle of Zambia, partly dividing the country into eastern and western regions. The eastern region is more sparsely populated. Running to the west and parallel to the Luangwa river are mountains that are the home of Zambia's highest hills. The western region of Zambia is where most of the country's population and industry reside. Zambia sits on a high plateau crossed by deep river valleys and occasional lakes and swampland. The country has a tropical climate with temperatures moderated due to its relatively high altitude. The natural vegetation is mainly savannah grassland with areas of woodland. Despite poaching, which has slashed rhino and elephant herds, Zambia's land supports a large number of wild animals, many now in protected game reserves. The climate and some of the land supports farming which is the nation's biggest employer. Maize is the most frequently grown staple food while large amounts of cassava, sugarcane, wheat and peanuts are also harvested.

THE ZAMBEZI, ENERGY AND MINERALS

Winding its way from northwestern Zambia to the Indian Ocean, the Zambezi river forms much of the country's southern border. The river drops 108 m as it flows over one of the world's most famous waterfalls, the Mosi-oa-Tunya or Victoria Falls, on Zambia's border with Zimbabwe: 480 km east of the Victoria Falls, the river flows into the Kariba lake, a giant artificial lake built to generate hydro-electric power shared by Zambia and Zimbabwe. Zambia derives 99 per cent of its electricity from hydro-electric power. Zambia has traditionally relied on just two products to generate exports: copper and cobalt. Giant reserves in the north of the country saw the formation of an urban and industrial mining region known as the Copper Belt in which minerals are mined and processed. However, several decades of falling copper prices on the world markets and lower levels of production have caused serious economic problems.

SOUTHERN AFRICA

Southern Africa's geography is dominated by the Southern Plateau which crosses much of the region at an elevation of between 900 and 1,500 m. Around the edges of the plateau is a series of mountains and cliffs called the Great Escarpment, while further mountainous areas lie in places along the southern and eastern coastlines. Large stretches of the region are grasslands with both forested area and two deserts, the Kalahari in the centre and the Namib along the western coast. Southern Africa is one of the world's most mineral-rich areas. A large proportion of the world's copper, uranium, gold and diamonds come from the area which has had an impact on regional economies.

▲ A maize store in Mozambique. Southern Africa has a long history of migration to its lands and has an ethnically varied population, most of whom works in agriculture.

Politically and economically, the region is dominated by South Africa, the most populous and most industrialized of the region's eight nations.

▼ Lions roam parts of the grasslands of southern Africa. Many are now found in protected reserves including Namibia's Etosha Park and South Africa's Kalahari and Kruger Parks.

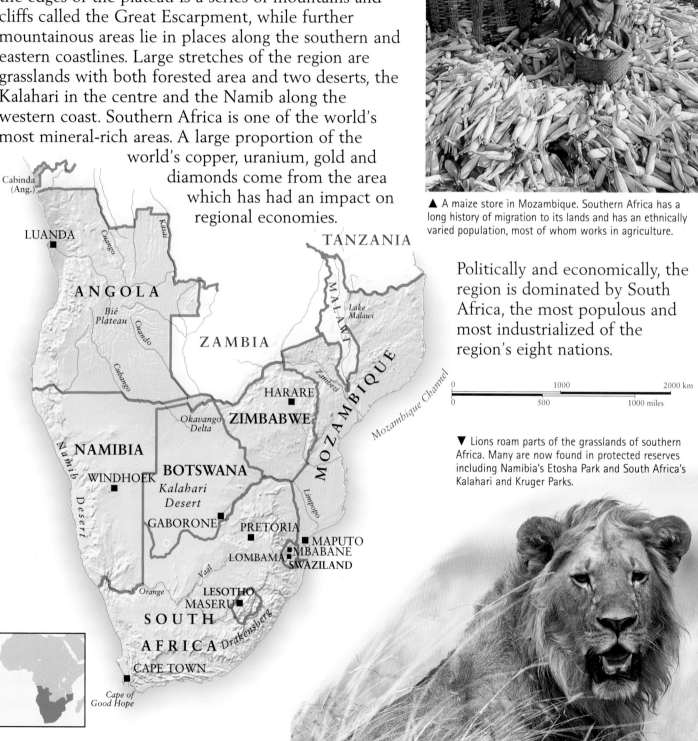

Cabinda (Ang.)

LUANDA

ANGOLA

Bié Plateau

Cuango

Kasai

Cuanza

Cubango

TANZANIA

MALAWI

Lake Malawi

ZAMBIA

Zambezi

HARARE

ZIMBABWE

Okavango Delta

MOZAMBIQUE

Mozambique Channel

NAMIBIA

Namib Desert

WINDHOEK

BOTSWANA

Kalahari Desert

GABORONE

Limpopo

PRETORIA

MAPUTO

MBABANE

LOMBAMA

SWAZILAND

Vaal

Orange

LESOTHO

MASERU

SOUTH

AFRICA

Drakensberg

CAPE TOWN

Cape of Good Hope

0   500   1000   2000 km
0   500   1000 miles

ANGOLA

Rich in oil and diamonds, Angola suffered an almost continual civil war from its independence from Portugal in 1975 until 2002.

Area: 1,246,700 km²
Population: 12,878,000
Capital: Luanda (2,000,000)
Main languages spoken: Portuguese, Umbundu, Kimbundu, Kongo
Main religions: Roman Catholic, traditional beliefs, various Protestant churches
Currency: new kwanza
Main exports: petroleum, diamonds
Type of government: republic; dictatorship

▼ The Benguela Railroad is a vital transport link connecting Angola to both the Democratic Republic of Congo and Zimbabwe. It is currently undergoing renovation after being seriously damaged during the long civil war.

Angola's landscape is diverse. The land stretches from a coastal plain which varies in width between 25 km in the south and between 100 and 200 km in the north. Inland from the plain, the land rises towards mountains and a plateau which covers almost two-thirds of the country. The plateau undulates and varies in average height between 1,200 and 1,600 m. Angola has no large lakes but many rivers, most of which begin in the central mountains and either flow west to the Atlantic or north. Angola's climate is essentially tropical but relatively dry. In the southwest, the country is extremely dry and desert-like. Close to the coast, the climate is more temperate while the northern half of the central plateau is tropical and receives a little more rainfall. Vast rainforests cover the northern part of the country while grasslands are found in the central and south-central regions. Angola has large oil deposits, particularly offshore of the enclave of Cabinda, producing around 730,000 barrels per day. The country also has large reserves of diamonds, iron and many other minerals, as well as great hydro-electric potential. Along with fertile farmland, Angola has many resources and should be relatively prosperous, but a civil war between two major groups, UNITA and the MPLA, was fought for many years. The result was a shattered economy with mines, industries and transport links destroyed and as many as ten million unexploded mines left across its land.

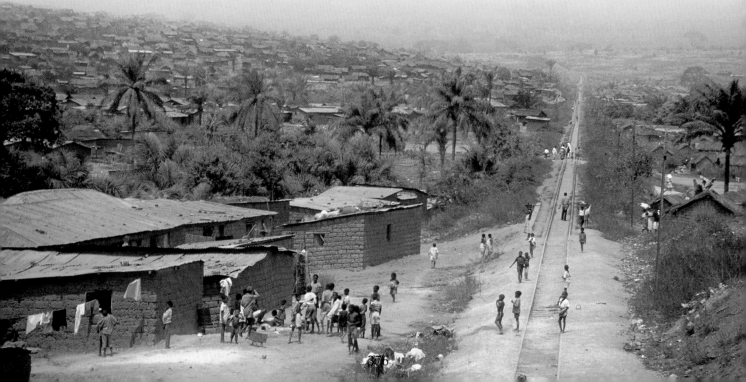

BOTSWANA

Landlocked and dry, much of Botswana's territory is part of the red soil, sand and scrubland of the vast Kalahari Desert.

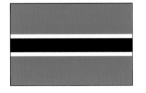

Area: 581,730 km²
Population: 1,679,000
Capital: Gaborone (186,000)
Main languages spoken: Tswana, English, Shona
Main religions: traditional beliefs, various Protestant churches, Roman Catholic
Currency: pula
Main exports: diamonds, copper-nickel, textiles
Type of government: republic; democracy

Botswana's land is largely a broad, flat plateau with some hills to the east. In the northwest, the Okavango river empties inland creating the largest inland river delta in the world. The swamplands and flood plains of the Okavango Delta are a haven for wildlife, particularly birds. Farming is the main occupation, although water is often scarce. In 1967, a year after independence from Britain, enormous diamond reserves were discovered. Botswana is now the world's third largest producer of diamonds and also has huge reserves of coal, copper and nickel. The Tswana peoples make up over 95 per cent of the country's population. Around 60,000 San people live a nomadic life in the Kalahari, hunting and gathering as well as tending small herds of livestock. Despite much economic growth, the country's people are poor and beset by diseases particularly AIDS/HIV. An estimated 40 per cent of all Botswana's adults are believed to be HIV positive, the highest rate in the world.

NAMIBIA

Lying on the southwestern coast of Africa, sparsely populated but mineral-rich Namibia gained independence from South Africa in 1990.

Area: 824,269 km²
Population: 1,827,000
Capital: Windhoek (243,000)
Main languages spoken: English, Ovambo, Nama, Kavango, Afrikaans
Main religions: Lutheran, Roman Catholic
Currency: Namibia uses South African currency
Main exports: diamonds, fish and fish products, copper, lead
Type of government: republic; democracy

▲ The Namib desert is a dry, largely barren region where temperatures can reach 49°C.

Namibia consists of a central plateau region which occupies around half of the country with an elevation of between 970 and 2,000 m. Either side of this plateau lie deserts: to the east the Kalahari desert extends into the country, while the whole western coast is occupied by the Namib desert. Namibia's climate is hot and dry and only the central plateau supports a large amount of vegetation. Despite the hostile environment, Namibia has much wildlife, some of which is protected in reserves. Eighty per cent of the population are black African with around six per cent white. Namibia is Africa's fourth largest producer of non-fuel minerals.

ZIMBABWE

As a British colony, the landlocked nation of Zimbabwe was known as Southern Rhodesia and, between 1965 and 1980, as Rhodesia.

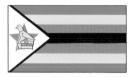

Area: 390,757 km²
Population: 11,163,000
Capital: Harare
(1,486,000)
Main languages spoken: Shona, English, Ndebele
Main religions: Anglican, traditional beliefs, Roman Catholic
Currency: Zimbabwe dollar
Main exports: gold, ferro-alloys, nickel, cotton, asbestos, tobacco, cut flowers
Type of government: republic; dictatorship

▼ Straddling the border between Zimbabwe and Zambia, Victoria Falls (Mosi-oa-Tunya) is around twice as high and twice as wide as Niagara Falls in North America.

Most of Zimbabwe lies on the Southern Plateau of Africa and is above 300 m in elevation. The Zambezi river flows along Zimbabwe's northern border and generates almost 40 per cent of the country's electricity via hydro-electric power. Despite large-scale migration to the country's towns and cities, about two-thirds of the population still live in rural areas. Farming is practised on a large commercial scale, with tobacco the leading export crop. The growing of cotton and the rearing of cattle are also conducted on a large scale. In contrast, many Zimbabweans work their own small farms growing just enough to feed their families. Vast mineral reserves exist in Zimbabwe including gold, nickel and asbestos. Zimbabwe also has one of the widest range of industries in Africa – from steel, chemicals and cement to motor vehicles, footwear and textiles. Ruled by an increasingly oppressive government, Zimbabwe has attracted international criticism for human rights abuses. Redistribution of land and wealth from the wealthy white minority to the black majority has occurred, sometimes using force, but many black Zimbabweans are still poor. Around one-quarter of the population are believed to be HIV positive.

MOZAMBIQUE

Mozambique is a large, ethnically diverse nation trying to rebuild after a lengthy civil war and devastating droughts and floods.

Area: 801,590 km²
Population: 17,242,000
Capital: Maputo (1,430,000)
Main languages spoken: Makua, Portuguese, Tsonga
Main religions: traditional beliefs, Sunni Islam, Roman Catholic
Currency: metical
Main exports: prawns, cotton, cashew nuts, sugar, copra
Type of government: republic; limited democracy

Two-fifths of Mozambique's land is coastal lowlands which end in a 2,470 km-long shoreline with the Indian Ocean. Further inland, the land rises to a series of hill ranges with mountains in the west and north. Mozambique has a tropical climate but much of its soil is poor. Despite this, most of its people work as farmers growing maize and cassava for themselves or working for plantations growing coconuts, cashew nuts, cotton or sugarcane. The country's fishing industry is vital, with prawns the most important export. Mining is underdeveloped and the country is seeking investment to tap its large reserves of copper and also of iron, uranium, coal and natural gas. Following independence from Portugal in 1975, a violent civil war erupted. Mozambique has struggled to rebuild after the war ended in the early 1990s. Apart from the legacy of destroyed towns, transport systems and industries, there are between two and three million unexploded land mines. Clearing land of these weapons has been a slow process. In addition, the country has suffered from floods and droughts which have killed thousands of people, while diseases, especially AIDS, are common.

▲ Zebras are one of a number of large mammals that live within Mozambique's borders. 40,000 km² of the country is part of the Greater Limpopo Park which also extends into South Africa and Zimbabwe.

► A large cooking pot, made from an oil drum, is stirred at a Mozambique orphanage. Civil war, diseases including AIDS, and land mines have created approximately 1.2 million orphans in the country – one in six of all the country's children.

SOUTH AFRICA

South Africa occupies the southernmost lands of Africa. A multi-ethnic society and a country of great mineral wealth, it has the largest economy in Africa.

Area: 1,224,691 km²
Population: 40,377,000
Capitals: Pretoria (1,080,000) – administrative capital; Cape Town (2,350,000) – legislative capital
Main languages spoken: English, Zulu, Afrikaans, Xhosa, Sotho, Tswana
Main religions: traditional beliefs, various Protestant churches, Roman Catholic
Currency: rand
Main exports: gold, base metals, diamonds, food (particularly fruit and wine)
Type of government: republic; democracy

South Africa borders six nations including Lesotho, which it completely surrounds, and is the only nation with both Atlantic and Indian ocean coastlines. Fishing in the coastal waters brings in over half a million tonnes of fish every year. The lands close to the coast are low-lying, fertile plains which tend to occupy a relatively narrow strip between 30 and 100 km in width. The coastal plains give way to a mountainous region known as the Great Escarpment which separates the coast from the high inland plateau on which most of the country is situated. The Drakensberg Mountains are the highest part of the Great Escarpment and run in an arc inland from the Indian Ocean coast.

THE VELDS AND WILDLIFE

Most of the plateau region of South Africa is called the Highveld and consists of rolling grasslands mostly above 1,500 m in elevation. The western portion of the plateau is known as the Middle Veld. Lying at an average elevation of 920 m, the land here is dry and mostly used for herding livestock. The Middle Veld merges with the Namib and Kalahari deserts to the west and northwest. To the northeast, the High Veld descends into a large lowland area called the Bushveld which consists mainly of savannah grasslands and scattered trees. South Africa has a highly varied wildlife, with over 200 species of mammals including elephants, hippos, zebras and lions. Hunting has slashed herd numbers, but many of these creatures are

▲ A gold miner at work, drilling, in Savuka Gold Mine, approximately 80 km southwest of Johannesburg. Savuka along with its sister mine, Mponeng, are among the deepest gold mines in the world, over 3,500 m in depth.

ZIMBABWE

MOZAMBIQUE

Limpopo

BOTSWANA

Kalahari

PRETORIA
Johannesburg
Soweto • Benoni
Carltonville • Vereeniging
Klerksdorp • Vaal

SWAZILAND

NAMIBIA

Namib Desert

Orange

Vaal

• Welkom

Kimberley •

Botshabelo •
Bloemfontein •

LESOTHO
Injasuri 3408m △

• Pietermaritzburg

• Durban

Orange

SOUTH AFRICA

Drakensberg

INDIAN OCEAN

ATLANTIC OCEAN

Great Karoo

• East London

CAPE TOWN ■

Cape of Good Hope

Cape Agulhas

• Port Elizabeth

now protected in the country's 30 national parks and game reserves. In addition, South Africa is incredibly rich in flowering plants with over 20,000 different species.

CLIMATE

South Africa lies in the temperate zone but its climate varies greatly throughout the country. The highest temperature recorded was 51.7°C in the Kalahari desert. Sutherland, 270 km northeast of Cape Town, regularly sees winter temperatures drop to -15°C. Elevation, wind and ocean currents influence the regional differences in climate. For example, the cold Benguela Current, which flows northwards along the west coast, cools temperatures and also reduces rainfall levels. South Africa is a semi-arid country and around half the land receives between 200 and 600 mm of rainfall a year, while a further quarter receives less than 200 mm. Rainfall levels tend to increase from west to east with the eastern coast benefiting from the warm Mozambique Current which raises temperature and rainfall levels.

WATER AND AGRICULTURE

South Africa has no large lakes and only a small number of major rivers. These include the Vaal and the Limpopo which flow in the north and form much of the country's border with Botswana and Zimbabwe. South Africa's longest river is the Orange which travels some 2,090 km from Lesotho west through the Highveld before forming all of South Africa's border with Namibia and flowing into the Atlantic. With water at a premium, South Africa relies on large irrigation systems to water croplands. Despite only a small percentage of the land being suitable for crop growing, South Africa is usually self-sufficient in many crops including cereals, vegetables and sugarcane. The country is renowned for its high quality fruit crops including grapes which form the basis of a large and profitable wine industry.

▲ Native bushmen in the Kgalagadi Transfrontier Park study animal tracks. This protected reserve has a huge area of 36,000 km².

▼ The rugged and spectacular Drakensberg Mountains are found in the Royal Natal National Park. Peaks in this mountain chain exceed 3,000 m in places.

▲ Founded in 1886 as a gold mining town, Johannesburg has grown into South Africa's largest urban area with a population of four million.

▼ Cape Town is the law-making capital of South Africa and one of its major ports and commercial centres. A fast-growing city, it is overlooked by the majestic Table Mountain.

INDUSTRY

South Africa is the most industrially powerful country in the African continent. Cape Town, Johannesburg, Port Elizabeth and Durban are large industrial centres producing a vast range of goods from chemicals, textiles and paper to motor vehicles, electronic goods and weapons. Much of South Africa's development has stemmed from huge reserves of valuable minerals which lie within its borders. Despite a decline in gold production, South Africa remains the world's biggest producer. It is also a world leader in platinum, manganese, chrome and diamond production. The country has no major oil deposits but has massive reserves of coal. This is burned to generate most of the country's electricity. A huge challenge facing the country's government is how to provide electricity to the 80 per cent of black South African homes which currently are not on the national electricity grid.

THE RAINBOW NATION

South Africa is a multi-racial nation in which there are 11 officially recognized languages and many more spoken. Approximately three-quarters of the population belong to one of nine black African ethnic groups. The Zulu peoples are the largest group, comprising around 21 per cent of the country's total population. The next largest are the Xhosa

▲ This family live in Nyanga township close to the city of Cape Town. Township dwellers often have to contend with poor living conditions, poor sanitation and water supplies and high unemployment.

followed by Tswana, Sotho, Venda, Tsonga, Ndebele, Swazi and Pedi peoples. Around 12 per cent of South Africa's people are white and divided into two principal groups. Afrikaners or Boers are descendants of Dutch and sometimes German or French settlers. They speak Afrikaans and make up around 60 per cent of the white population. Most of the remainder speak English and are of British origin. One in ten of South Africa's people has a mixed ethnic background and three

classified by race. It kept people of different racial groups apart on public transport, schools, jobs and in most walks of life. Many black people were forced to live in townships outside major cities or in 'homelands' in rural areas. In these areas, the growing land, schools and facilities were often far worse than in whites-only areas. Condemnation of South Africa's racist apartheid policy occurred around the world and was followed by trade sanctions and boycotts which prevented the country from taking part in many sporting and cultural events. Apartheid's grip was finally loosened in the late 1980s and early 1990s, and in 1994, elections involving all peoples, regardless of race or colour, occurred, returning a black president, Nelson Mandela, for the first time. Since then, governments have tried to chart a peaceful path to a multi-racial society but with great difficulties. Large inequalities in education, income and living conditions between many blacks and whites remain, and violent crime, especially in the cities, is among the highest in the world.

▲ Workers harvest the grapes in the Nuy Valley vineyards in the Western Cape. South Africa is one of the world's leading wine producers. Approximately one billion litres are produced each year. The wine industry employs over 300,000 people.

per cent are of Asian, mainly Indian, descent. Over half of South Africans live in cities and nine in ten live in the eastern half of the country or along the southern coast. Apart from the area around Cape Town, the west is very sparsely populated.

APARTHEID AND RECONCILIATION
South Africa's black population had been oppressed for decades before the government policy of apartheid was introduced in 1948. Meaning 'apartness', apartheid was a country-wide policy until the 1990s designed to look after the interests of a white minority. Under apartheid people were

SWAZILAND

Landlocked between South Africa and Mozambique, Swaziland's traditional society and customs are in contrast to its many more modern industries.

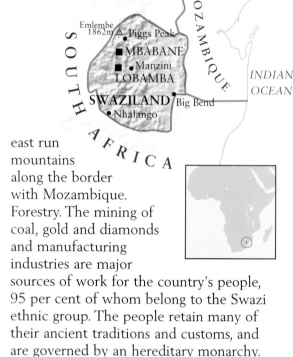

Area: 17,363 km²
Population: 1,008,000
Capitals: Mbabane (52,000) – administrative capital; Lobamba (6,000) – royal and legislative capital
Main languages spoken: Swazi, English
Main religions: various Protestant churches
Currency: lilangeni
Main exports: wood and wood products, sugar
Type of government: kingdom; dictatorship

Swaziland is divided into three regions: the mountainous high veld in the west, the grassy middle veld in the centre and the low bushveld in the east. The high veld is humid and temperate with warm wet summers and cold dry winters. Originally largely treeless, there are now large plantations of pine and eucalyptus trees – part of the country's extensive forestry industry. The middle veld has a subtropical climate and has the most fertile soils. The majority of the population live in this region. Many herd cattle or grow maize or work on large plantations growing sugarcane and other crops. The low veld is dry and hot in summer and receives less rainfall than the other regions. To the far east run mountains along the border with Mozambique. Forestry. The mining of coal, gold and diamonds and manufacturing industries are major sources of work for the country's people, 95 per cent of whom belong to the Swazi ethnic group. The people retain many of their ancient traditions and customs, and are governed by an hereditary monarchy. Despite pressures for reform, political parties remain banned.

LESOTHO

Lesotho is surrounded by South Africa, from which it gained independence in 1966. Its people are mainly farmers and reliant on South Africa for trade.

Area: 30,355 km²
Population: 2,153,000
Capital: Maseru (129,000)
Main languages spoken: Sotho, English
Main religions: Roman Catholic, traditional beliefs, Presbyterian
Currency: maluti
Main exports: clothing, furniture, footwear, food and live animals, wool
Type of government: kingdom; limited democracy

▶ Like most of her country's population, this Lesotho woman makes a living from raising small herds of livestock and subsistence crop growing.

Known as the Roof of Africa, Lesotho is a mountainous land. Its lowest point is some 1,380 m in elevation rising to almost 3,500 m in the mountains to the east. Rolling lowlands mainly to the west are the main agricultural area. Maize, wheat, root vegetables, beans and peas are grown, while more land is used as grazing pasture for cattle, sheep and goats. Unrestricted grazing has caused much soil erosion. Apart from some diamond mining, the country has few mineral resources. Lesotho's rugged landscape does, however, allow it to generate all the electricity it needs from hydro-electric power. Large quantities of electricity are exported to South Africa. Lesotho has few industries and many male adults move to South Africa to seek work in mines and other industries. Its people are poor; 49 per cent of the population are believed to live below the poverty line.

OCEANIA & ANTARCTICA

OCEANIA

Oceania is a vast region of scattered islands lying across most of the Pacific Ocean. Covering approximately one-third of the entire planet's surface, the Pacific occupies a total area of over 165 million km^2. The continent of Oceania has a land area of just over 8.5 million km^2 and consists of the continental land mass of Australia, larger islands including New Zealand's North and South islands, New Guinea and Tasmania, and more than 20,000 smaller islands. This latter group, often referred to as the Pacific islands, are often clustered in groups and separated by vast stretches of ocean. Most of the smaller islands have been created through coral formation or through volcanic activity. Many of Oceania's islands lie on or near the edges of the Pacific tectonic plate which is also the location of many of the world's volcanoes. The Pacific islands of Oceania are often divided into three distinct groups. Polynesia is the most easterly and consists of a huge, roughly triangular expanse of the Pacific, extending north of Hawaii, south of New Zealand and eastwards past Easter Island. Micronesia is the region west of Polynesia and nearest to southeast Asia, while Melanesia is considered the region containing New Guinea, Fiji, the Solomon Islands, Vanuatu and a small number of other island groups. While Aboriginal peoples reached Australia over 50,000 years ago and New Guinea has a long history of settlement, other parts of Oceania were the last places in the world to be settled by people.

In waves of migrations, which are estimated to have started between 6,000 and 7,000 years ago, different peoples from southeast Asia reached the most westerly and northerly islands. Long voyages, made in simple vessels, saw peoples travel across much of the Pacific reaching the most outlying islands between 2,000 and 1,000 years ago. Today, Oceania's people number fewer than 31 million – less than half a per cent of the total world population. Over half of the continent's people are found in Australia, a giant land mass and the most developed and economically powerful nation in the continent. In contrast, neighbouring Papua New Guinea and many of the smaller island nations are among the least developed countries in the world. The majority of the people of these countries are reliant on fishing and forms of agriculture which have altered little for many centuries.

▲ The scattered Pacific islands of Oceania tend to experience tropical or subtropical climates with heavy rainfall. Many of the islands are covered in lush vegetation including palm trees.

Philippine
Sea

Pagan
Anatahan

Northern
Mariana
Islands
(to US)

M

i

Guam (to US)

Yap Islands

Chuuk

C A R O L I N E

I

Babelthuap △

PALAU

FEDERATED STAT
OF MICRONESIA

M

e

l

Admiralty
Islands

New Ire

Bismarck
Sea

New
Britain

Bougain

New
Guinea

Mt Wilhelm 4509m

PAPUA NEW
GUINEA

Solomon
Sea

Arafura
Sea

Cape York

Timor
Sea

Cape
York
Peninsula

Co
Se

Gulf of
Carpentaria

Great Barrier R

Barkly
Tableland

Great Dividing Range

Tanami
Desert

Great Sandy
Desert

AUSTRALIA

Gibson
Desert

Lake Eyre

Great Victoria
Desert

Lake
Torrens

Darling

Nullarbor Plain

Great
Australian
Bight

Murray

△
Mt Kosciu
2230m

Tasmania

▲ Polynesian men paddle a type of canoe with a
balancing float known as an outrigger in the Pacific
Ocean. Outrigger canoes or double canoes were used by
many Pacific peoples, including the Melanesians and
Polynesians, to complete amazingly long journeys
between islands dwarfed by the ocean around them.

◄ These Aboriginal people live in Arnhem Land, a region in
northeastern Australia which has been continuously settled by
them for at least 40,000 years. Aboriginal Australians were among
the first settlers in Oceania and are believed to have reached
Australia at least 50,000 and possibly even 70,000 years ago.

PACIFIC

OCEAN

Hawaiian
Islands
(US)

Palmyra *(to US)*

Tabuaeran

Kiritimati

MARSHALL
ISLANDS

Ratak Chain

Ralik Chain

n
e
s
i
a

D
S

Gilbert
Islands

Howland I. *(to US)*

Baker I. *(to US)*

Phoenix Is.

NAURU

K I R I B A T I

Line Islands

SOLOMON
ISLANDS

Malaita

Makira

*Santa
Cruz Is.*

e

s

i

a

Ellice
Islands

TUVALU

Tokelau
(to NZ)

P

o

l

y

n

e

s

i

a

Marquises
Islands

American
Samoa
(to US)

Espiritu
Santo

VANUATU

Malakula

Éfaté

a

Vanua
Levu

Vitu
Levu

Kadavu

Wallis
& Futuna
(to Fr.)

SAMOA
Savai'i

Cook Islands
(to NZ)

Tuamotu Islands

Society Islands

Tahiti

Lau
Group

TONGA

Niue
(to NZ)

New
donia
Fr.)

New
Caledonia

Loyalty Is.

FIJI
ISLANDS

Tongatapu

French
Polynesia

Rarotonga

Îles Australes

Norfolk I.
(Aust.)

Kermadec Is.
(to NZ)

Pitcairn Is.
(to UK)

Pitcairn I.

Lord Howe I.
to Aust.)

asman
Sea

NEW
ZEALAND

North
Island

PACIFIC

OCEAN

Mt Cook
3754m

South
Island

Chatham Is.
(to NZ)

Stewart I.

International Date Line

► Part of the complex of New Zealand's national
government buildings known as the Beehive
which was opened in 1977. It is located in New
Zealand's capital city, Wellington, which lies on
the southern coast of the country's North Island.

PAPUA NEW GUINEA

A land of rich resources and traditional cultures, Papua New Guinea occupies half of the island of New Guinea as well as numerous other smaller islands in the Pacific.

Area: 462,840 km²
Population: 5,191,000
Capital: Port Moresby (254,000)
Main languages spoken: English, Tok Pisin, over 800 other languages
Main religions: traditional beliefs, Roman Catholic, Lutheran
Currency: kina
Main exports: petroleum, gold, copper, timber, coffee, cocoa, crayfish and prawns
Type of government: dominion; democracy

Papua New Guinea consists of over 600 islands. These include New Britain, its second largest land mass, and the archipelago of islands located in the Bismarck Sea. Four-fifths of its land area are made up of the eastern half of New Guinea. From a low-lying, often swampy coastline, the land of New Guinea rises to rugged mountains. Although some of the country's smaller islands are formed from coral, many are of volcanic origin and also feature mountainous interiors. Papua New Guinea's varied landscape provides habitats for large numbers of plants and animals. Recent surveys show that some five per cent of the world's living species are found within its borders. Located just south of the Equator, Papua New Guinea's climate is tropical, with its rainy season occurring between December and March.

▲ A Papua New Guinea tribesman paints his face in traditional decoration. Many highland tribes and groups were not discovered until the mid or late 20th century and have lived in ways largely unchanged for thousands of years.

Ninigo Islands

Mussau

Manus I.

New Hanover

Wewak

Bismarck Sea

PACIFIC OCEAN

Sepik

Rabaul

Kokopo

New Ireland

Central Range

Madang

INDONESIA

Mount Wilhelm 4509m

Mount Hagen

Goroka

New Britain

New Guinea

Lae

P A P U A

Arawa

Lake Murray

N E W

Solomon Sea

Bougainville I.

Fly

G U I N E A

Trobriand

Gulf of Papua

Woodlark I.

Fergusson I.

PORT MORESBY

Owen Stanley Range

Normanby I.

Alotau

Coral Sea

Tagula

RICH IN RESOURCES

Over 80 per cent of Papua New Guinea is covered in dense tropical rainforest, although this is declining due to large scale logging. One-third of its forests is open to timber companies, and forestry is a major industry. This is eclipsed in importance, though, by the mining sector. It is rich in many minerals including copper, gold, silver, nickel and cobalt, while oil and natural gas reserves are also exploited. The mining sector makes the largest contribution to the country's economy. Eighty-five per cent of the workforce are subsistence farmers despite less than two per cent of the land being suitable for crops. Larger farms grow coffee and other export crops.

PEOPLE AND LANGUAGE

Settled for around 50,000 years, the geography of the country has acted as a barrier to movement, isolating many different groups of people who have developed their own language and culture. As a result, Papua New Guinea has one of the most culturally varied populations on Earth with over 800 languages spoken.

A distinction is often made between those people who live in lowland areas near the coasts, who tend to have frequent contact with other groups, and the more isolated highlanders. Although the majority of Papua New Guinea's people are nominally Christian, traditional beliefs and customs are still widely practised. Since independence in 1975, some of these ethnic groups have pressed for further change and to break away from the country.

▲ A highland area near Goroka, close to the highest point on Papua New Guinea, Mt Wilhelm. The highland areas are cooler than on the coast, where temperatures rise to 32°C or higher in summer.

▼ Port Moresby, the capital of Papua New Guinea, is the manufacturing centre of the country with food processing being the main industry.

AUSTRALIA

Australia's vast arid interior is sparsely populated. But its rich mineral resources and highly developed agricultural base have made it a prosperous nation.

Area: 7,682,300 km²
Population: 19,485,000
Capital: Canberra (353,000)
Main language spoken: English
Main religions: Roman Catholic, Anglican, Uniting Church
Currency: Australian dollar
Main exports: food and live animals (particularly cereals and cereal preparations and meat and meat preparations), metallic ores, mineral fuels and lubricants (particularly coal and petroleum), basic manufactures
Type of government: dominion; democracy

▼ Sydney Harbour Bridge and Sydney Opera House are world famous symbols of Australia's prosperity. The bridge was opened in 1932 and its total length is 1,149 m with a single arch span of 503 m. It carries eight vehicle lanes, two railway lines, a footway and a cycleway. The more modern opera house was completed in 1973 and its unique concrete roofs were designed by the Finnish architect, Ove Arup.

Situated between the Indian and South Pacific oceans, Australia includes in its territory the large island of Tasmania and many other islands dotted around its 25,760 km long coastline. Considered a continental land mass rather than an island, Australia has been geologically stable for over 300 million years with few earthquakes, volcanoes or upthrusts of land to create mountains. As a result, erosion by wind and water has created large flat plains. Under seven per cent of its huge area is above 600 m in elevation. Much of Australia is extremely dry; two-thirds of the country are desert or semi-desert. Situated to the east of the country, the Great Dividing Range runs roughly north to south and separates the eastern coastline from the dry interior of Australia, known as the outback. Most of the population live in cities and towns along this eastern coast including the country's largest and most cosmopolitan city, Sydney. Other major cities include Brisbane, Melbourne, Perth, Adelaide and Canberra, the country's capital. Separating from other continental land masses around 65 million years ago, Australia's isolation from the rest of the world has meant that many creatures have evolved which are not found elsewhere. Most famous are

▲ Also known by its Aboriginal name of Uluru, Ayers Rock is the world's largest monolith. Located in the Uluru-Kata Tjuta National Park, it rises 348 m above the desert floor and has a circumference of 8 km.

creatures such as the kangaroo, koala and duck-billed platypus. Australia's first human inhabitants arrived at least 40,000 years ago. The Aboriginals settled throughout much of Australia. They lived off the land and developed a rich culture before the arrival of European settlers in the 18th century onwards. Today, Aboriginals make up less than two per cent of Australia's population, most of whom are of European descent.

INDIAN
OCEAN

Timor
Sea

Arafura Sea

Melville
Island

Cape
York

Joseph
Bonaparte
Gulf

Arnhem
Land

Gulf of
Carpentaria

Cape
York
Peninsula

Kimberley
Plateau

Great Barrier Reef

Coral
Sea

North
West Cape

Great Sandy
Desert

Hamersley Range

Lake
Disappointment

Lake
MacLeod

WESTERN
AUSTRALIA

Gibson
Desert

Lake
Carnegie

Tanami
Desert

NORTHERN
TERRITORY

Lake
Mackay

Macdonnell Ranges

AUSTRALIA

Uluru
△ (Ayers Rock)
867m

Simpson
Desert

Mitchell

Flinders

Georgina

QUEENSLAND

Diamantina

Thomson

Buckland
Tableland

Barkly
Tableland

Great Dividing Range

Lake
Barlee

Great Victoria
Desert

SOUTH AUSTRALIA

Lake
Eyre North

Lake
Eyre South

Cooper

Sturt
Stony
Desert

Warrego

Nullarbor plain

Lake
Torrens

Flinders Ranges

Lake
Frome

Lake
Gairdner

Darling

NEW SOUTH
WALES

Lachlan

Dividing Range

Great
Australian Bight

Tasman
Sea

Cape Leeuwin

Kangaroo
Island

Murray

VICTORIA

CANBERRA
AUSTRALIAN
CAPITAL TERRITORY
△ Mt. Kosciuszko
2230m

SOUTHERN OCEAN

0   300   600 km
0   150   300 miles

Bass Strait

Furneaux
Group

TASMANIA

EASTERN AUSTRALIA

The region of Australia first settled by Europeans, eastern Australia is a land of rich mineral and natural resources and the centre of industry and commerce.

▲ The Royal Flying Doctor Service treats a patient in Queensland. Founded in 1928, its aircraft fly over 11 million km each year to isolated communities all over Australia.

Australia is divided into six states and two territories. Eastern Australia consists of the states of Queensland, Victoria and New South Wales as well as the Australian Capital Territory (ACT) in which the country's capital city, Canberra, is located. Australia became a federation of states on its independence in 1901 and Canberra was chosen as the seat of government shortly afterwards. It is the only major Australian city not to lie on the country's huge coastline. Australia has a 25,760 km long coastline, of which Eastern Australia has 30 per cent. However, the country's fishing catches are relatively modest at around 215,000 tonnes per year. Over half of the income from fishing comes from shellfish such as lobsters, prawns and oysters. Inland from eastern Australia's coast lies a series of coastal plains which form much of the region's farmland. Eastern Australia's most dominant land feature is the Great Dividing Range. This broken chain of mountains runs almost the entire length of eastern Australia from the north of Queensland to the southern coast of Victoria. Averaging around 1,200 m in height, the Great Dividing Range has the highest peaks in the Snowy Mountains in New South Wales with Australia's tallest, Mount Kosciuszko, rising to 2,230 m. These highlands have some of the country's largest coal deposits enabling Australia to be one of the world's largest coal exporters. West of the Great Dividing

Range, the land slopes down to plains heading westwards into the country's mainly flat and dry interior. A major feature of this portion of eastern Australia is the Great Artesian Basin, one of the largest regions of underground water springs, many of which are tapped for irrigation. Eastern Australia's largest river system is the Murray-Darling river system to the south of the region. It has a total length of 3,750 km and drains an area of over one million km².

THE GREAT BARRIER REEF

One of the natural wonders of the world, the Great Barrier Reef lies off the Queensland coast. It consists of more than 3,000 reefs along with a number of small islands which extend some 2,000 km. Covering an area close to 350,000 km² it is the planet's largest coral reef system. More than 350 species of coral make up the Great Barrier Reef and the region provides habitats for a staggering array of wildlife including 1,500 species of fish and more than 200 species of birds. It is also a breeding ground for several species of turtles and home to dolphins, large, endangered sea mammals called dugongs and humpback whales. A region of great natural beauty, some two million visitors travel to the reef system every year, but such large numbers are one of the threats that the fragile reef faces. Coral is delicate and can be easily broken by divers, tourists' feet and shipping. It also suffers from pollution and rises in sea temperature. In addition, the reef faces damage from the crown of thorns starfish which eats living coral.

▲ Parliament House lies in the centre of Canberra and was completed in 1988. Canberra was chosen as the seat of government in 1908, seven years after Australia's independence.

▼ The tropical rainforests of Cape Tribulation National Park stretch right down to the shoreline facing Queensland's Great Barrier Reef. Much of the rainforest in the 1,600 km2 protected area has existed unchanged for around 100 million years.

▲ The beautiful living coral and the breathtaking array of marine life draw millions of tourists to dive and snorkel in the waters of the Great Barrier Reef.

▼ The Canberra Space Communications Complex features giant antennae, the largest 70 m in diameter, which are used to communicate with spacecraft. The centre was the first to receive images of the first man on the Moon in 1969.

INTRODUCED ANIMALS

Many species of animals have been introduced to Australia by humans. Among the earliest was a wild Asian dog known as a dingo which arrived with Aboriginals at least 40,000 years ago. Some creatures have been introduced which have had a damaging effect on the environment. Creatures such as the cane toad and the rabbit, for example, have multiplied into populations of millions and become major pests to farming while disrupting fragile natural ecosystems. Other introduced species have formed the backbone of Australian farming in eastern Australia and elsewhere. Australia has over 110 million sheep and around 29 million head of beef and dairy cattle. These graze grasslands in almost all of the states of

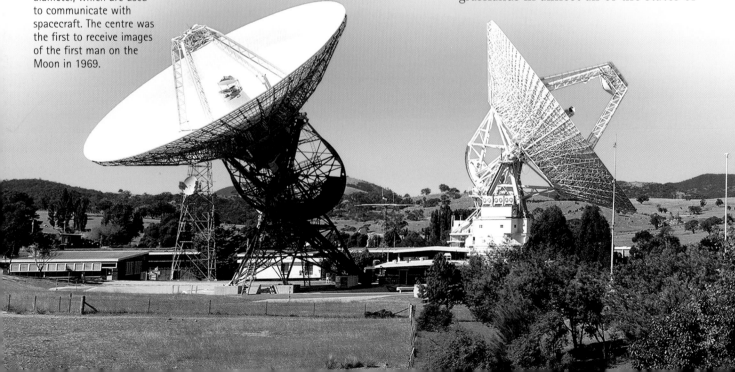

Australia. Grazing lands make up more than 90 per cent of Australia's farmed areas. Queensland is home to over a third of all cattle while 40 million head of sheep are found in New South Wales. Many of these herds are kept on vast farms called stations, with the largest over 12,000 km² in area. Australia is the world's largest exporter of beef and its vast sheep herds make it the world's leading wool producer.

THE AUSTRALIAN PEOPLE

Australia was reached by Dutch explorers in the mid-17th century and by the Englishman, William Dampier, in 1688 and 1699. In 1770, James Cook claimed the land for Britain and in 1788, a British prison colony was established in Australia at the site of what is now the country's largest city, Sydney. From that time until 1853, the policy of transportation saw approximately 160,000 British convicts transported to Australia. Most arrived at one of eastern Australia's settlements. In 1851, gold was discovered in the state of Victoria and a major gold rush attracted thousands of free settlers hoping to make a fortune. After World War II, the Australian government promoted an extensive immigration programme and around 5.5 million people emigrated to the country. Over half of the migrants who arrived were British, with large numbers of Germans, Dutch, Italians, Greeks and Yugoslavs. Australia adopted a whites-only immigration policy until 1973. Today, over 90 per cent of the population are of European descent with growing minorities from Asia and the Middle East. The country's population of just under 20 million represents over 150 different nationalities. Around 68 per cent of the population are Christians while over 13 per cent of the population are non-religious. Australia's climate and wide, open spaces have encouraged people to live an outdoor lifestyle and many sports including cricket, rugby and swimming are avidly played and watched. The Australian people generally have a high standard of living although downturns in the economy have led to an increase in the gap between rich and poor. With its former major trading partner, the UK, now part of the European Union, Australia has increased its trade links with the USA and many Asian nations. Although a 1999 referendum was in favour of keeping the United Kingdom monarch as the head of state, large numbers of Australians, particularly the younger generation, want their country to become a republic.

▲ Part of the Great Dividing Range, the Blue Mountains are so named due to the blue appearance given by the leaves of the large forests of eucalyptus trees which cover their slopes.

ABORIGINAL RIGHTS AND WELFARE

As many as one million Aboriginals lived in Australia before the arrival of European settlers. These immigrants brought new diseases with them against which the Aboriginals had no natural protection. Thousands died from smallpox, tuberculosis and the common cold virus. Many more were killed in fights over land with the settlers, many of whom treated the Aboriginals as if they were savages. They were discriminated against, their lands seized and, in many cases, forced to change their way of life, moving to cities or housed in reservations. An estimated 100,000 Aboriginal children, known as the 'Stolen Generation', were taken from their families and placed in institutions or with white families. Until the mid-1960s, adult Aboriginals were not even allowed to vote in elections. Since that time, much progress has been made. Aboriginal culture has been increasingly embraced, welfare and education schemes have been introduced and native rights to land have started to be recognized. Despite many initiatives, Aboriginal peoples still tend to be the most disadvantaged and poverty-stricken of all Australians with a life expectancy over 15 years lower than the rest of the population.

▲ Australia has an illustrious sporting heritage and the 2000 Oympics held in Sydney was the largest Olympics yet, with 10,651 athletes competing in 300 events.

▼ The Gold Coast is a 50 km stretch of resorts, hotels and apartments in southern Queensland attracting over two million tourists every year.

EASTERN AUSTRALIAN CITIES

Australia's three largest cities are found on eastern Australia's coast: Melbourne, the capital of Victoria, Brisbane, the capital of Queensland, and Sydney, the capital of New South Wales. Built on a spectacular natural harbour, Sydney has become the country's most populous city and is also its commercial centre and the Australian city which draws more of the 4.9 million foreign visitors each year than any other.

TASMANIA

Separated from mainland Australia by the Bass Strait, the island of Tasmania is Australia's smallest state. Home to 473,000 people, it has a dramatic and beautiful landscape.

▲ A small boat nudges a salmon pen into position at the Port Esperance fish farm, 50 km southwest of the state capital, Hobart.

▼The New River Lagoon lies in the Tasmanian Wilderness World Heritage Area which covers a region 13,000 km². More than one-fifth of Tasmania is covered in national parks designed to protect its unique landscape and wildlife.

Tasmania's 67,800 km² territory, including the smaller islands of Flinders, King and Cape Barren, is less than one per cent of Australia's total land area. Tasmania was linked to Australia until as little as 9,000 years ago and, geologically, it is part of Australia's Great Dividing Range. Much of the main island consists of a plateau over 900 m in height and a series of mountain peaks. The land is crossed with many fast-flowing streams and rivers, a number of which have been harnessed to provide hydro-electric power. Rolling farmland and meadows and many vineyards occupy large parts of the north, east coast and the central midlands of the island. However, to the west, the landscape is less cultivated and includes large tracts of native forests of many different trees, including the blue gum

eucalyptus, the state symbol. Tasmania's logging and mining industries are economically important, but the state is now trying to conserve as much of the natural landscape as possible. Much of the workforce is engaged in farming, with apples, grapes and livestock the key products. Most of the state's limited industries are based in the southeast, close to Hobart, Australia's second-oldest city and the state's chief port. Tasmania was originally settled more than 35,000 years ago by Aboriginals when it was part of the Australian mainland but, after European settlement, disease and conflict dramatically reduced the number of native people, they now comprise no more than three per cent of the population.

CENTRAL AUSTRALIA

Consisting of Northern Territory and the state of
South Australia, Central Australia is a largely flat and
arid land with isolated hill and mountain ranges.

▲ Goods are often moved
through central Australia
by road train – a high-
speed truck carrying a
number of linked trailers.

▼ A bush fire rages in
Kakadu National Park,
approximately 250 km
east of Darwin. Famous
for its Aboriginal art sites
and its abundant wildlife,
Kakadu is home to 1,200
plant, 100 reptile, 200 bird
and 50 mammal species.

Much of central Australia
is part of the hot, dry
scrublands and deserts that
constitute the country's Great
Red Centre. The Simpson,
Tanami and Great Victoria
deserts occupy large areas of
the region. In the centre, close
to the border between
Northern Territory and South
Australia, lie several mountain
ranges – the MacDonnell
Ranges which extend over
200 km to the west of Alice Springs and
rise to heights of over 1,500 m, and the
Musgrave Ranges just south of Uluru
(Ayers Rock). The northernmost region of
Northern Territory is known as the Top
End and is a region of savannah woodlands
and smaller areas of rainforest with
swamps along the coast. South Australia is
generally low-lying with the heavily
forested Flinders Ranges, the largest area
of highlands. Lying relatively close to the
Flinders Ranges is a series of huge lakes
which are salt basins most of the time, and
are only occasionally filled
with water. The
largest of these,
Lake Eyre, lies

▲ Two Aboriginal men wear ceremonial body paint made
from crushed rocks and soil. Aboriginal gatherings called
Corroborees are held to celebrate Aboriginal culture and
feature music and dance.

north of the Flinders Range and sometimes covers an area of over 8,900 km². It drains an area of over one million km². South Australia's major river is the 2,520 km long Murray which flows mainly through New South Wales before entering South Australia and emptying into the ocean, east of Adelaide.

CLIMATE AND FARMING

South Australia is considered the driest state in Australia. Its coast experiences higher rainfall and a temperate climate but, inland, around 80 per cent of the state is arid, receiving less than 300 mm of rain per year. The same hot, dry conditions prevail throughout most of Northern Territory. However, on and near the coast the climate is tropical and can receive more than 1,600 mm of rain per year, much of it in the monsoon season from November to April. Tropical vegetable and fruit crops are grown in the Top End of Northern Territory. With poor soils and a dry climate in the centre and the south, farming there is largely restricted to cattle grazing, particularly beef cattle. Cattle and sheep herds are also found in the northern and central area of South Australia. The south of its territory is more fertile and large amounts of wheat, barley and fruit are grown here, as well as oats, flax and vegetables. Irrigation is widely practised here. South Australia produces more grapes than any other state and its wine industry has grown greatly in the past 20 years.

▲ South Australia's Lake Eyre is fed by occasional rivers and evaporation often reduces the bed to a dry, salt-crusted area. At 16 m below sea level, it is the lowest point in Australia.

▼ Located 50 km northeast of Adelaide, the Barossa Valley is a fertile wine-growing area flanked by the Barossa Range to the east. The 30 different wine-making companies located in the Barossa Valley are responsible for around a third of Australia's total wine production, much of which is exported.

SPARSELY POPULATED LANDS

Central Australia is a sparsely settled region with most of the population concentrated in small areas. Vast tracts of land are largely empty. Although Northern Territory is over 1.34 million km^2 in area it is only home to around 200,000 people – around one per cent of the total Australian population. Small numbers of people are found in mining towns, farming communities and Aboriginal towns, but the majority of the region's population live in either Alice Springs or in Darwin. Northern Territory's major port and its capital city, Darwin has had to be rebuilt on five separate occasions after tropical cyclones have devastated the city. Today, fuelled by the development of mining industries, government and defence jobs and a growing tourist trade, it is a prosperous and growing city with a population of 109,000 people. South Australia is smaller, at around 984,000 km^2, but its population is over seven times as large as Northern Territory's. Around 95 per cent of South Australia's inhabitants live within 45 km of the coast. Most are concentrated in a small number of settlements, the biggest of which is the state capital of Adelaide. Australia's fifth most populous city, it is surrounded by parkland, while its roads are designed on a grid system. The mining of metals, exploiting of natural gas reserves, and some manufacturing industries, particularly in and around Adelaide, supplement farming and tourism as the state's major sources of income.

▲ The low-lying, spacious town of Alice Springs lies in Northern Territory and is the headquarters of the country's flying doctor service. The town has also become a tourist base as it is the nearest main settlement to the Uluru (Ayers Rock) monolith.

ANIMALS IN ISOLATION

Australia was once part of a super-continent known as Gondwanaland. Continental drift saw Australia break away from the rest of the continent and, over a period of between 55 and 60 million years, move gradually towards its current position. Isolation has meant that Australia's animals have

century for use as pack animals in the central Australian deserts. There are now more than 60,000 wild camels in Australia, mainly in Northern Territory. Australia lacks large land predators but does have some highly venomous insects, jellyfish and reptiles, including the taipan snake, which produces the most powerful poison in the world.

▲ South Australia is home to over three million kangaroos of several species. Kangaroos are the world's largest marsupials, with male red kangaroos growing to over 1.8 m in height and weighing 85 kg.

evolved separately from the rest of the world, generating dozens of unique species. Many of its mammals are either marsupials – creatures such as kangaroos, koala bears, wombats and wallabies which nurture their young in a pouch – or monotremes, egg-laying mammals such as the duck-billed platypus and the echidna or spiny anteater. Many marsupials and monotremes are found in central Australia while Australia's largest bird, and the second largest in the world, the emu, is found in South Australia. Camels were introduced in the 19th

ABORIGINAL CULTURE

Aboriginal peoples live throughout Australia but they make up a higher proportion of the population of Northern Territory than any other region of the country. The first human arrivals to Australia's shores, many different Aboriginal tribal groups with their own cultures and languages developed throughout the country. There are an estimated 250 different Aboriginal languages or dialects. All lived a nomadic or semi-nomadic life in harmony with their environment, gathering seeds, fruits and berries, and hunting and fishing. Aboriginal culture is rich and varied with traditional painting, stories, music and dance. Much of their art and story-telling concerns the origins of the land, people and Ancestors in a complex set of beliefs known as The Dreaming or Dreamtime. Each tribe had its own territory granted by the Ancestors, the mythical creators of the world and people. This territory could not be sold or given away, and many sites within the land were considered sacred.

WESTERN AUSTRALIA

The largest state of Australia, Western Australia has a mainly dry, desert landscape. The state has massive mineral resources and fertile lands to the southwest.

▲ A match between the Western Australian cricket team and a touring England side takes place at the WACA cricket ground in Perth.

▼ The sun sets over a beach at Broome in the Kimberley region of Western Australia. One of the few towns in northern Western Australia, Broome was once a traditional centre of pearl fishing and now raises oysters on pearl farms.

Western Australia is a vast, arid land area bordering the Indian Ocean to the northwest, west and south, and the Timor Sea to the north. The state has an area of around 2.5 million km². Most of it is a sandy, dry plateau with an elevation of between 300 and 600 m and with little vegetation. Three large deserts cover much of its territory: the Great Sandy in the north, the Gibson in the centre, and the Great Victoria in the southeast. All three contain some scrub grasslands as well as salt marshes and lakes. However, they are arid and hostile areas with average annual rainfall below 200 mm and temperatures of over 30°C.

Western Australia's highland areas are isolated from each other. There are high peaks in the Hamersley Range in the northwest, while the most extensive area of uplands is the rugged Kimberley region in the northeast. Damming in the Kimberley region has created Western Australia's largest lake, Lake Argyle, in the far north of the state.

CLIMATE AND FARMING

Western Australia is mainly hot and dry but, over such a large area, there are climate variations. The extreme north has a tropical climate and is sometimes affected by tropical cyclones, while the extreme south has a Mediterranean climate. Both these areas receive rainfall as high as 1,400 mm per year. In general, rainfall dwindles rapidly away from these areas and from the coast. Average daily temperatures rise above 30°C in summer and, in winter, temperatures often fall to below zero.

◄ Despite being one of the most remote cities in the world, Perth's business centre flourishes with office blocks dominating the skyline. Rapid growth since the 1970s has meant that Perth has overtaken Adelaide to become Australia's fourth most populous city.

A series of low-lying mountains just north of Albany is the only place which receives snowfall. To the southwest there is a fertile region where most of the state's crop-growing is concentrated. There is around 28,000 km² of farmland in the state, on which oats, oilseeds and wheat are grown. Western Australia is the country's biggest wheat producer. Livestock herding is also a major part of farming. Timber, largely from state-controlled forests in the southwest, and coastal fishing also make major contributions to the economy.

▼ Aboriginal children sit in the flat, dry landscape of the Gibson Desert which lies in the centre of Western Australia and occupies an approximate area of 155,500 km².

MASSIVE MINES AND RESERVES

Australia is very rich in mineral resources and has one of the largest and most important mining industries in the world. Large deposits of certain minerals exist in different parts of Australia, enabling major mining industries to exist in all of the country's states and territories. For example, around 70 per cent of the country's copper is extracted from giant mines in Queensland, while uranium mines exist in both Northern Territory and South Australia. Western Australia, however, leads the way in mineral production with around 38 per cent of all mining and two-thirds of all metals mined in the country. The state has massive

▲ A huge open-cut gold mine in Western Australia. Gold makes up around 17 per cent of the total mining income of the state and is its leading export ahead of iron ore, oil, natural gas, wheat and wool.

▼ Located in the centre of Nambung National Park, a short distance north of Perth, the Pinnacles Desert comprises thousands of limestone pillars rising out of yellow quartz sand. It is part of over 200,000 km² of parks and protected areas in Western Australia.

reserves of minerals such as bauxite, used to make aluminium, and nickel. Some 97 per cent of all of Australia's iron ore is mined in Western Australia. Over two-thirds of Australia's gold output, equivalent to about eight per cent of the world's production, is mined in the state. Diamond deposits were discovered in the northern Kimberley region in the 1970s, and Australia is now one of the top five diamond producers in the world. In addition to this, Western Australia has major oil and natural gas deposits, particularly offshore on the northwest continental shelf.

A FAST DEVELOPING ECONOMY

Western Australia has had the fastest-growing economy of all Australian states since the 1960s onwards. Its economy is based on agriculture and mining, which contributes over a quarter of the state's income. More recently, tourism has also boomed to become a major source of revenue. The manufacturing industry, mostly based around Perth, has grown rapidly in recent decades and largely involves the processing of the region's raw materials into usable materials such as sheet steel, or finished goods such as woollen clothing. Perth has become a major business and commerce centre and, situated closer to Singapore than to Sydney, has looked to strengthen trading links with southeast Asian nations.

MANY SMALL SETTLEMENTS AND ONE CITY

Western Australia is sparsely populated with an average density of fewer than one person per km^2. Despite agriculture playing a large role in the region, less than 15 per cent of the population live in rural areas. Western Australia's first permanent colony was established in the late 1820s. Its people struggled to prosper until larger farmlands were found and a workforce of around 10,000 male convicts were transported to the region in the 1850s. In the late 1880s and 1890s, a series of large gold finds generated a gold rush and the population of the region increased dramatically. Revenue from gold wealth saw ambitious public works projects completed, including an artificial harbour for the town of Fremantle in 1899. Today, Fremantle has been swallowed up by the sprawling city of Perth, Western Australia's single major settlement and the state capital. Perth's urban area is home to 1,340,000 of Western Australia's total population of 1,906,000. In contrast, no other town in Western Australia has a population larger than 35,000. It is Australia's fourth most populous city.

▲ An iron ore bulk carrier approaches the docks at Port Hedland in northwest Western Australia. Australia is the third-largest iron ore producer in the world with 15 per cent of total output, almost all of which comes from Western Australia.

NEW ZEALAND

Similar in size to Japan, New Zealand is geographically isolated from the rest of the world. Its small population lives in a varied and often spectacular landscape.

Area: 270,534 km²
Population: 3,821,000
Capital: Wellington (343,000)
Main languages spoken: English, Maori
Main religions: non-religious (nearly one quarter), Anglican, Presbyterian, Roman Catholic
Currency: New Zealand dollar
Main exports: meat and dairy products, wood and wood products, fish, machinery, basic manufactures, minerals
Type of government: dominion; democracy

New Zealand lies around 1,600 km southeast of Australia. It consists of two large islands, North and South islands, divided by the 20 km wide Cook Strait, and a number of far smaller islands. Of these, mountainous Stewart Island off the south coast of South Island is the largest with an area of 1,685 km². New Zealand has strong links with a number of island territories. The Cook Islands and Niue, for example, are self-governing territories in free association with New Zealand. Tokelau is a separate territory dependent on New Zealand. It consists of three coral atolls almost 500 km north of Samoa. These islands provide homes to around 1,500 Pacific islanders who fish, farm and export woven handicrafts.

VOLCANIC NORTH ISLAND, MOUNTAINOUS SOUTH ISLAND

For a relatively small nation, New Zealand has an incredible variety of landscapes including fjords, glaciers, mountains, beaches, plains, swamps and gently rolling hills. New Zealand's North Island has been shaped greatly by volcanoes. The country's largest lake, Lake Taupo, extends to over 600 km² in area and is the crater of a huge extinct volcano. New Zealand's longest river, the Waikato, flows north and west from this lake before emptying into the Tasman Sea. Rising steeply from Lake Taupo is North Island's central plateau on which there are four active volcanoes. The central plateau is an area of much heat

▲ Located in New Zealand's Southern Alps in west-central South Island, Mount Cook is New Zealand's highest mountain at 3,754 m above sea level. Known to the Maoris as Aoraki, meaning Cloud Piercer, the mountain is surrounded by a further 22 peaks exceeding 3,000 m in elevation.

and activity beneath the Earth's surface, with many hot springs, geysers and frequent small earth tremors and occasional larger earthquakes. Away from the plateau, North Island's landscape includes rolling plains and chains of low mountains with coastal lowlands. The North Island's coast is heavily indented and both of its largest cities, Auckland and Wellington, are built around large natural harbours.
The Northland region, north of Auckland, has vast sandy beaches, subtropical vegetation and mangrove swamps. South Island's landscape is mostly mountainous, dominated by a

▼ Auckland lies on a large natural harbour. Piercing the skyline is the 328 m high Sky Tower which, on its completion in 1997, was the tallest building in New Zealand and the entire southern hemisphere.

PACIFIC
OCEAN

North Cape

Whangarei

*Kaipara
Harbour*

*Hauraki
Gulf*

*Great
Barrier
Island*

Waitakere
North Shore
Auckland
Manukau
Manukau Harbour
Pukekohe

*Coromandel
Peninsula*

*Bay of
Plenty*

*North
Island*

Hamilton
Cambridge

Tauranga

*East
Cape*

Tokoroa

*Lake
Rotorua*
Rotorua

Lake
Taupo

Taupo

Gisborne

*North Taranaki
Bight*

New Plymouth

*Cape
Egmont*

*Hawke
Bay*

*Mahia
Peninsula*

Napier

**NEW
ZEALAND**

*South Taranaki
Bight*

Hastings

Wanganui

Fielding
Palmerston North
Levin

Cape Farewell

*D'Urville
Island*

Porirua
Lower Hutt
WELLINGTON

*Tasman
Bay*

Cook Strait

Cape Palliser

*Karamea
Bight*

Nelson

*Cape
Foulwind*

Blenheim

large mountain chain, the Southern Alps,
which runs almost the full length of the
island. The large Tasman glacier is
located in the Southern Alps on the
slopes of the country's highest peak,
Mount Cook, known to the Maoris as
Aoraki meaning Cloud Piercer. The
scouring action of glaciers has created
many features on the South Island
including long lakes and deep
valleys. Much of the island's
rugged coastline is
broken up by many
fjords and bays.

Greymouth

*South
Island*

Southern Alps

*Tasman
Sea*

Aoraki
(Mount Cook)
3754m△

Christchurch

*Pegasus
Bay*

*Canterbury
Plains*

Ashburton

*Lake
Ellesmere*

*Banks
Peninsula*

*Lake
Tekapo*

Timaru

*Canterbury
Bight*

*Lake
Wanaka*

*Lake
Hawea*

PACIFIC
OCEAN

Fiordland

*Lake
Te Anau*

*Lake
Wakatipu*

Oamaru

*Resolution
Island*

Waiau

*West
Cape*

Dunedin
*Otago
Peninsula*

Invercargill

Mataura

▶ The Champagne Pool is a
crater lake filled with bubbling
mineral-rich waters at
temperatures of over 60°C. It
is found in Wai-o-tapu
Thermal Reserve, an area of
great geothermal activity,
about 20 km south of Rotorua.

Foveaux Strait

Stewart I.

*South West
Cape*

▲ Maori men, wearing traditional dress, perform a version of the traditional war dance known as the Haka.

▼ A handful of New Zealand's 42 million sheep graze pastures close to the city of Dunedin. The country also has 9.5 million cattle and over 13 million chickens.

A TEMPERATE CLIMATE

New Zealand experiences a temperate climate with regular rainfall all year round. No part of the country is more than 120 km from the ocean which tends to moderate the climate, so that extremes of temperature are rare. Summers tend to be mild to warm except in the cooler southern mountains, while winter temperatures in lowland areas rarely fall below zero. Rainfall averages 750 mm per year but varies greatly, mainly due to the country's mountain ranges. Rainfall is highest on the mountain slopes, with the Southern Alps receiving some of the world's highest annual rainfall levels (over 8,000 mm in some places). East of the mountains on South Island and north of the Otago Peninsula lies New Zealand's driest region, receiving an average of only 330 mm of rainfall.

NATURE AND FARMING

New Zealand is geographically isolated and, as a result, many of its native plant and animal species are unique, including a number of species of flightless birds such as the kiwi and the kakapo. The country has a wide range of plant species, but relatively few large native animals. Forests cover over a quarter of New Zealand, with native kauri trees, some of the tallest trees in the world, found in the north of North Island. Around half of the land supports either crop-growing or livestock-rearing and New Zealand is the world's biggest exporter of butter and one of the leading exporters of wool, cheese and meat products. A large range of different crops are grown including cereals, vegetables, hops – used for brewing beer – and grapes. New Zealand is one of the world's largest exporters of fruit. The country's farming industry has been overhauled and modernized in the past 30 years and is one of the most advanced in the world.

A MIXED ECONOMY

While agriculture is still a major part of the New Zealand economy, the country has developed other industries in the past 30 years. The cost of transporting raw materials to New Zealand has limited the development of heavy industries. Instead, the country has concentrated on working with natural and mineral materials found in its own lands. The processing of farm products is the country's leading industrial sector with food processing companies, large wool mills and textiles, clothing and leatherwear businesses. Forestry and associated industries, such as timber, paper, printing and furniture-making, form an

important part of the economy. In the past, much of New Zealand's dense forests have been cleared but today, most of the remaining native forests are protected. Over 90 per cent of the trees felled for timber and paper are tree species introduced especially for the timber industry. Over a third of the workforce is employed in service industries including banking, insurance and tourism. The tourist industry has grown to become the single largest earner of foreign currency in the economy. Around 1.8 million visitors arrive every year. Most are drawn to the country's beautiful scenery, the heritage of its Maori people, and its reputation as a quiet, uncrowded, friendly nation.

ENERGY AND TRANSPORT

New Zealand has significant deposits of certain minerals, particularly coal, while gas and oil were discovered in the 1970s. Around four-fifths of the country's electricity is generated by renewable methods including geothermal and hydro-electricity. Much of the hydro-electricity is generated in South Island but supplied to North Island which houses around three-quarters of the country's population. New Zealand has a large road network but only 150 km of major motorways. Car ownership is high, with over 2.5 million motor vehicles and there are many small aircraft services and ferries linking the two islands and communities along the coast.

▲ The peaceful waters and dramatic landscape of Milford Sound, a deep fjord in New Zealand's South Island, attract many tourists. The 19 km long fjord is an inlet of the Tasman Sea and is one of the wettest places on Earth receiving more than 8,000 mm average annual rainfall in some places.

▲ Intricate wood carvings are an important part of Maori art. The Maori are of Polynesian origin and their wood carvings are more complex than those of any other Polynesian people.

NEW ZEALAND'S PEOPLE

New Zealand is a country of old and new settlers. Around 12 per cent are the oldest arrivals – the Maori who live predominantly in North Island. The Maori are greatly outnumbered by people of European, particularly British, descent who arrived in New Zealand mainly after 1840. European peoples comprise three-quarters of the population and have traditionally held most of the power and commercial positions in the country. Around six per cent of the country's population originally come from other Pacific Islands, such as Tonga, the Cook Islands and Samoa. They were drawn to New Zealand by the need to find work and by the expansion of the New Zealand economy after World War II. Waves of more recent immigrants have come from parts of Asia, particularly Malaysia and Hong Kong. These more recent arrivals also make up around six per cent of the population. New Zealanders tend to enjoy a high standard of living, although the Maori tend to suffer higher levels of unemployment and poverty. Changes to the economy since the 1980s have meant that welfare services are less generous than in the past. Despite the importance of agriculture, around 85 per cent of New Zealanders live in towns and cities.

THE MAORI CULTURE

The Maori are the indigenous people of New Zealand and are of Polynesian origin. They are believed to have reached New Zealand, possibly from the Cook Islands, from the 9th century. The Maori developed a rich culture which included intricate wood carvings and full-face tattooing, called moko, common among male warriors. Dutch explorer Abel Tasman made the first European contact with the Maori in 1642, but it was the British explorer, James Cook, who first landed on New Zealand soil in 1769 and claimed the country for Britain. The arrival of waves of European settlers from the early 19th century onwards resulted in wars and disease which reduced the Maori population to under 50,000. The Maori were forced to give up large areas of land for no more than token payments. Conflicts between Maori and Europeans continued throughout the 19th century. Recently, New Zealand has begun to address its past and awarded some compensation and land returns to the Maori, and their children now have access to education in their own language, Maoritanga.

POLITICS AND INTERNATIONAL RELATIONS

Although Auckland is the biggest and most populous city, and the financial centre of New Zealand, the seat of national government is in Wellington. Modelled along British lines, the country

▼ Located on the north coast of the South Island, the beautiful 49 km long Queen Charlotte Sound with its many bays is a popular haven for pleasure boating. The waterway was named by Captain Cook in the 1770s.

has no written constitution and its head of state is the British monarch. In 1893, New Zealand was the first country in the world to give women the vote and, in 2003, the country's Prime Minister and the leader of the main opposition party were both women. Most New Zealanders are firmly in favour of staying in the Commonwealth and keeping strong ties with Britain, which was traditionally its most important trading partner. However, the UK's entry into the European Union has forced New Zealand to strengthen its ties with other nations, particularly Australia, its largest trading partner, the USA, Japan and southeast Asian nations. Around a quarter of the entire country is part of the 13 national parks and other protected areas. New Zealand strongly opposed French nuclear testing in the Pacific and has banned nuclear-powered shipping and submarines from docking in its ports.

▲ The Wairakei Valley steam pipeline carries steam, superheated by geothermal activity under the Earth's surface, to a nearby geothermal power station which generates electricity. The Wairakei Valley lies just north of Lake Taupo, the largest lake on New Zealand's North Island.

▼ An international rugby union match in progress between New Zealand, known as the All Blacks, and South Africa held in Auckland. Rugby Union is the most popular sport in New Zealand and the All Blacks have a long and illustrious history.

GUAM & NORTHERN MARIANAS

Territories of the USA, Guam and the Northern Mariana Islands are small island nations which have both developed successful service industries.

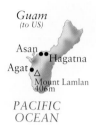

Guam
(to US)

Asan
Agat
Hagatna
Mount Lamlan
406m

PACIFIC OCEAN

Guam

Area: 541 km²
Population: 155,000
Capital: Hagatna (27,000)
Main languages spoken: English, Chamorro
Main religion: Roman Catholic
Currency: US dollar
Principal exports: re-exported petroleum, construction materials, foodstuffs, fish
Type of government: dependency of the USA

Northern Mariana Islands

Area: 477 km²
Population: 69,000
Capital: Garapan (7,000)
Main languages spoken: English, Chamorro
Main religion: Roman Catholic
Currency: US dollar
Principal exports: clothing, agricultural and fishing products
Type of government: self-governing dependency of the USA

Guam was formed through the uplift of undersea volcanoes. The northern half of the island is a plateau of coral limestone. The southern half is a collection of volcanic hills and valleys. Guam's native wildlife, particularly its bird life, has been decimated by the brown tree snake which has killed off the island's nine native bird species. A major military outpost for the USA in the Pacific, military bases cover one-third of the island. Its palm-fringed beaches encourage visitors, and tourism is the single largest industry on Guam and accounts for over half of the country's income. Along with the spending of US military personnel stationed on the island, this has enabled Guam to develop its services and give its people one of the highest standards of living in the Pacific islands.

The Northern Marianas has also developed tourist resorts particularly on the three largest islands of Saipan, Tinian and Rota. Agriculture plays an important role in the Northern Marianas, which has a tropical climate. Cattle and pigs are kept, while sugarcane, taro, cassava, coconuts and vegetables are grown in the fertile volcanic soil. A number of the islands' volcanoes are still active.

Agrihan
Pagan
Philippine Sea
Northern Mariana Islands (to US)
Saipan
Tinian
Garapan
Rota
PACIFIC OCEAN

► Over 1.5 million tourists, particularly from Japan and some from the USA, visit Guam every year. Visitors are attracted by the island's tropical climate and duty-free shopping.

FEDERATED STATES OF MICRONESIA

A scattered collection of 607 small tropical islands, the Federated States of Micronesia was settled over 3,500 years ago and has a culturally diverse people.

Area: 701 km²
Population: 119,000
Capital: Palikir (5,000)
Main languages spoken: English, Chuukese, Pohnpeian
Main religions: Roman Catholic, Congregational
Currency: US dollar
Principal exports: fish, clothing, bananas, black pepper
Type of government: republic; democracy

The Federated States of Micronesia consists of four states: Yap, Pohnpei, Kusaie and Chuuk, which retain close ties and trade links with their former ruler, the United States. Part of the widely spread Caroline Islands archipelago, Micronesia experiences a tropical climate. The largest island, Pohnpei, is also the wettest, receiving as much as 5,500 mm of rainfall per year. Although the islands stretch across a vast area of the Pacific – over 1.6 million km² – the total land area is small, no more than 701 km². Apart from deposits of phosphates, there are no

mineral reserves and just 42 km of paved roads while many homes outside of the small towns have no electricity or running water. The islanders rely on subsistence farming, growing crops such as taro, coconuts, bananas and yams, fishing, and keeping poultry, pigs and, sometimes, dogs for food. US aid makes up more than half of the country's income. The islands have a variety of different Pacific peoples with their own distinct cultures and languages despite Western customs being imposed by European whalers, missionaries and traders from the early 19th century onwards. Situated on Pohnpei, the giant ruins of Nan Madol are the largest ancient archaeological site to be found throughout the Pacific islands.

► A woman plaits palm fronds into thatching for the roof of a home on Satawal Island. The most easterly of Yap's inhabited islands with a population of around 560, Satawal had electricity installed for the first time in 2001.

MICRONESIA

Yap

Caroline Islands

Chuuk Islands

PALIKIR ■ Pohnpei

PACIFIC OCEAN

Kusaie

MARSHALL ISLANDS

Consisting of 1,150 coral islands of which only 20 are inhabited, the Marshall Islands were United Nations Trust Territories under US administration until 1986.

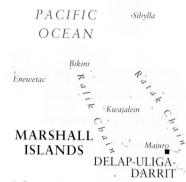

Area: 181 km²
Population: 51,000
Capital: Delap-Uliga-Darrit (16,000)
Main languages spoken: Marshallese, English
Main religions: Congregational, Roman Catholic
Currency: US dollar
Main exports: copra, coconut oil, handicrafts, fish
Type of government: republic; democracy

The Marshall Islands consist of two chains of coral islands and islets: the Ralik, meaning sunset, to the west and the Ratak, meaning sunrise, to the east. The chains lie about 200 km apart and are around 1,300 km long. Many of the islands are atolls consisting of a narrow fringe of coral-based land encircling lagoons. The largest atoll, Kwajalein, is one of the largest in the world. It encircles a lagoon of some 1,700 km² in area yet its actual land area is only 16 km². Several of the atolls, including Bikini atoll, were used for the testing of nuclear weapons in the 1940s and 1950s and radioactive fallout made these and neighbouring islands uninhabitable for many years. Kwajalein atoll is the current home of a US missile testing range and rent from this base along with US aid form the majority of the country's income. Around one in ten of the workforce is employed in tourism, while the atoll of Majuro is the commercial centre of the Marshall Islands and home to 45 per cent of its population. Life away from Majuro and Kwajalein is dominated by subsistence agriculture, growing coconuts, breadfruit and taro, and fishing. Copra and dried coconut meat is the island's major export, while many goods have to be imported.

NAURU

A small, oval-shaped, raised coral island and the world's smallest republic, Nauru's economy is based almost solely on phosphate mining.

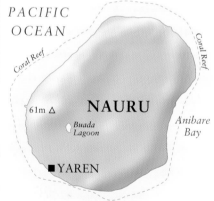

Area: 21 km²
Population: 12,000
Capital: Yaren (700)
Main languages spoken: Nauruan, English, Kiribati
Main religions: Congregational, Roman Catholic
Currency: Australian dollar
Main export: phosphates
Type of government: republic; democracy

A central plateau approximately 60 m in elevation covers the majority of the tropical island of Nauru. This plateau contains the island's phosphate reserves and phosphate mining has traditionally been Nauru's sole industry. However, reserves are depleted and attempts to diversify have led the economy into bankruptcy. Nauru has no natural harbour, docking is conducted offshore and all drinking water, fuel and many foodstuffs have to be imported. Most of the island's people live around the narrow, but fertile, coast of the island. The population includes groups of other Pacific islanders and people of Chinese and European origin. Many younger Nauruans migrate to Australia or New Zealand for work or education.

▶ Nauru has been mined for phosphates, used to make chemicals and fertilizers, for over 100 years. However, its reserves of phosphates are nearly exhausted.

SOLOMON ISLANDS

The third largest island chain in the Pacific Ocean, the Solomon Islands consist of a mixture of rugged, mountainous islands and low-lying coral atolls.

Area: 28,370 km²
Population: 444,000
Capital: Honiara (44,000)
Main languages spoken: English, various Melanesian languages
Main religions: Anglican, Roman Catholic, Evangelical
Currency: Solomon Islands dollar
Main exports: timber products, fish, palm oil, copra, cocoa
Type of government: dominion; limited democracy

▼ Many of the islands in the Solomon Islands group are fringed by coral reefs. The waters around the islands are rich in marine life including many brightly marked species of tropical fish, sharks and dugongs – large sea mammals also known as sea cows.

The tropical islands of the Solomons are a haven for plant life. The islands are home to over 4,500 plant species, many of which are used for building, food, medicine and clothing. Copra, cacao and palm oil are important cash crops, while people grow sweet potatoes, yams, taro, rice and tropical fruits for food. The timber industry is the country's largest and, as a result, more than one-tenth of the land has been cleared of trees. People have settled on around a third of the islands with the majority living on one of the six largest islands: Malaita, Guadalcanal, New Georgia, Makira (formerly San Cristobal), Isabel and Choiseul. The larger islands are volcanic and mountainous, with vast forests. Guadalcanal is the biggest of the islands and home of the capital, Honiara, which is also the islands' major port. First settled approximately 3,000 years ago, the

Solomon Islands have seen waves of arrivals from many parts of the Pacific over the centuries. Different peoples, societies and cultures developed on many of the islands with their own distinct ways of life. Most Solomon Islanders are Melanesian and there are an estimated 115 different languages spoken. The differences between certain ethnic groups spilled over into conflict between 1998 and 2000 and, again, in 2002.

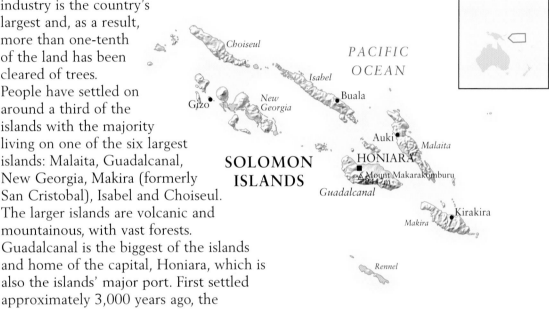

VANUATU

Vanuatu consists of 80 islands located in a Y-shaped archipelago, 2,170 km northeast of the Australian city of Sydney. The island group is renowned for its scenery.

Area: 12,190 km²
Population: 190,000
Capital: Vila (34,000)
Main languages spoken:
Bislama, English, French
Main religions:
Presbyterian, Roman Catholic
Currency: vatu
Main exports: copra, beef and veal, timber, cocoa, coffee
Type of government:
republic; democracy

▼ A man from Tanna island prepares for a traditional ceremony involving the drinking of kava. The traditional drink of chiefs in many Pacific Island cultures in the Melanesian part of the Pacific, kava is made from the root of a plant related to the pepper tree.

Vanuatu was formerly known as the New Hebrides and was ruled jointly by France and Britain until 1980. The islands experience a tropical climate with rainfall averaging around 2,400 mm per year but as high as 3,900 mm in the northern islands. Tropical cyclones visit the islands from December to March. Vanuatu's islands are a mixture of coral and volcanically formed land masses. They contain a number of active volcanoes and experience relatively frequent, but usually minor, earthquakes. Subsistence agriculture employs the majority of the workforce, but tourism and offshore banking services contribute most money to the economy. Vanuatu's scenery including deep ravines, heavily rainforested mountains, clear seas, beaches and cave systems attract an increasing number of tourists. Although almost all of Vanuatu's islands are inhabited, 80 per cent of people live on 11 main islands. The population is one of the most culturally diverse of all Pacific nations.

The native Ni-Vanuatu peoples make up over 90 per cent, but different languages and cultures have developed separately on many islands. Vanuatu has 105 native languages. There are also small communities of French, British, Australian, New Zealand, Vietnamese, Chinese and other Pacific island peoples. Ethnic strife is rare but until very recently, women tended to have a lower status.

NEW CALEDONIA

New Caledonia is a French overseas territory. It consists of one large island, New Caledonia, on which 90 per cent of the population live, and many smaller islands.

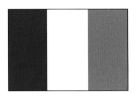

Area: 18,576 km²
Population: 214,000
Capital: Nouméa (119,000)
Main language spoken: French
Main religion: Roman Catholic
Currency: French Pacific franc
Main exports: refined ferro-nickel and nickel, nickel ore, fish
Type of government: dependency of France

The island of New Caledonia is a little over 320 km long and around 50 km wide, and has a mountainous landscape with areas of grasslands. Tourism and agriculture are the biggest employers of New Caledonians, but mining, particularly of nickel, is the most economically important industry. New Caledonia has around 25 per cent of the world's reserves of nickel and over 85 per cent of the islands' income comes from nickel exports. Sighted in 1774 by the British explorer, James Cook, the island came under French control in the middle of the 18th century. The native Kanak people form over two-fifths of the population, with a large and significant minority of French origin

known as the Caldoches. Tensions between the two groups have remained for many years.

▶ A traditional home on Lifou, New Caledonia's second largest island. Lifou is part of the Loyalty islands group which also includes Ouvéa, Maré and other smaller islands.

KIRIBATI

The republic of Kiribati is a series of 33 small islands spread out over five million km² of the Pacific Ocean.

Area: 717 km²
Population: 83,000
Capital: Bairiki (25,000)
Main languages spoken: English, Kiribati
Main religions: Roman Catholic, Congregational
Currency: Australian dollar
Main exports: copra, re-exports, fish and fish products
Type of government: republic; democracy

Kiribati's terrain is extremely low with its highest point just 87 m and almost all of its land only metres above sea level. Rising sea levels, caused by global warming, are a major concern to Kiribati and other low-lying island groups in the Pacific. Kiritimati is the country's largest island, making up over half of the land area, but Tarawa is the most populous. A part of the British Gilbert and Ellice Islands colony until 1979, the people of Kiribati still refer to themselves as Gilbertese and nearly all practise Christian religions. Most are relatively poor relying on farming and fishing to feed their families. The majority of the islands' soil is of poor quality and supports little

vegetation. Islanders grow a variety of tropical crops including bananas, pawpaw and breadfruit. The islands can also suffer from low rainfall, such as in 1999 when a drought emergency was declared. Phosphate mining was the principal industry until reserves of this mineral ran out in 1980. Organized resettlement from densely populated Tarawa to other less populated islands occurred during the 1990s.

PALAU

The Republic of Palau consists of 260 islands, nearly all of which lie in a large lagoon enclosed by a barrier reef that stretches a distance of over 100 km.

PALAU
Babelthuap
Peleliu · KOROR
· Angaur

PACIFIC
OCEAN

Sonsorol
Is.

· Pulo Anna
· Merir

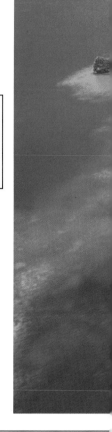

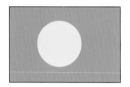

Area: 458 km²
Population: 19,000
Capital: Koror (11,000) – a new capital (Melekeiok) is under construction on Babelthuap island
Main languages spoken: Palauan, English, Filipino
Main religions: Roman Catholic, Modekngei
Currency: US dollar
Main exports: shellfish, tuna, copra, clothing
Type of government: republic; democracy

Palau is a small nation with the fourth smallest population in the world. Many of its people live on Babelthuap, the largest island, or on Koror, its administrative centre. The two islands are linked by a concrete bridge. Palau has one of the smallest economies in the world. Its small population, however, has a higher than average standard of living among the Pacific islanders. Tourism is the fastest growing part of the economy. Palau is considered to have some of the most spectacular underwater diving sites in the world. Agreements between Palau and the USA have allowed US military bases to be located in the islands in return for aid and trade deals. While the majority of Palauans are Christians, around a third follow a native religion called Modekngei.

▶ Palau's famed Rock Islands are humps of rounded, coralline limestone, thickly covered with dense forest, which have been undercut by erosion. The waters and reefs around Palau's islands are home to more than 1,400 species of fish.

TUVALU

Lying 1,000 km north of Fiji, the nine coral atolls of Tuvalu were formerly known as the Ellice Islands. In 2000, it became one of the newest members of the UN.

· Nanumea
Islands
· Niutao
Nanumaga

· Nui Atoll

· Vaitupu
Vaitupu

TUVALU

PACIFIC
OCEAN

Funafuti Atoll · FONGAFALE

Nukulaelae Atoll ·

Area: 24 km²
Population: 12,000
Capital: Fongafale (3,800)
Main languages spoken: Tuvaluan, English
Main religion: Congregational
Currency: Australian dollar
Main exports: copra, fish, clothing, fruit and vegetables
Type of government: dominion; democracy

Tuvalu's land is low-lying with generally poor, salty soils in which only certain plants, such as coconut palms, flourish. The tending and harvesting of coconuts and keeping ducks, pigs and chickens are key farming activities. Copra – dried coconut flesh – is the only agricultural export of note and even this is in limited quantities. Much food has to be imported, most arriving by ship at the islands' main port on Funafuti atoll. Tuvalu's land is very low-lying and under severe threat from rising sea levels due to global warming. Opportunities for work on these tiny islands are limited and many younger Tuvaluans work overseas and send money back to help support their families. Tuvalu's major resource are the fish-rich seas around its islands, and the

Tuvaluan government has sold licences to foreign trawler companies, particularly from Taiwan, South Korea and the USA. Foreign aid is also important, especially for new projects, including solar energy schemes. Sales of postage stamps also support the economy. Tuvalu's internet country identifying code is .tv and rights to use this for websites has been sold to a Canadian media company bringing in many millions of pounds. In contrast, the islands themselves have no television service or daily newspapers, only a single radio service and bi-monthly newspapers.

WALLIS & FUTUNA ISLANDS

Made up of two volcanic island archipelagos, Wallis & Futuna Islands are a French overseas territory, and are among the least developed of all Pacific island groups.

Mata'utu • *Wallis* (Uvéa)

Wallis and Futuna (to France)

Futuna
Alofi

PACIFIC
OCEAN

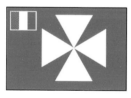

Area: 274 km²
Population: 15,000
Capital: Mata-Utu (1,100)
Main languages spoken: French, Wallisian, Futunan
Main religion: Roman Catholic
Currency: French Pacific franc
Main exports: copra and coconuts, construction materials
Type of government: dependency of France

The Wallis archipelago is made up of over 20 small islands and islets that are found on a barrier reef which encircles the one main island of Wallis. It is a volcanic island but relatively low-lying with a highest point of 145 m. Its terrain includes sharp sea cliffs and a number of water-filled craters. The Futuna archipelago is made up of two main islands, Futuna and Alofi, which is uninhabited. Futuna consists of a narrow coastal plain that rises sharply to heights above 500 m. The islands have a tropical climate with heavy rainfall of over 3,000 mm per year. The Wallis Islands take their name from English navigator Samuel Wallis, who claimed possession of them for England in 1767. Both the Wallis and Futuna island groups have been under French control since 1842, and became an overseas territory of France in 1961. The economy is limited to traditional subsistence farming, growing mostly coconut palms, breadfruit, mangoes and vegetables. Pigs and chickens are reared, and fishing from small boats is also important. These activities engage over 80 per cent of the workforce. A further five per cent are employed by local government, which receives aid from France and sells licences for fishing rights to Japan and South Korea. Over 15,000 Wallisians work in New Caledonia, another French territory, sending back part of their income to their families.

FIJI

Lying 2,000 km north of New Zealand, Fiji is the most populous and most developed of all the Pacific island nations.

Area: 18,272 km²
Population: 817,000
Capital: Suva (168,000)
Main languages spoken: Fijian, Hindi, English
Main religions: Hinduism, Methodist
Currency: Fijian dollar
Main exports: sugar, clothing, gold, fish, timber, coconuts
Type of government: republic; limited democracy

▼ A casual game of rugby, one of Fiji's major sports, takes place in Albert Park in the capital city of Suva. Over 168,000 Fijians live in or around Suva making it one of the largest settlements in the Pacific islands.

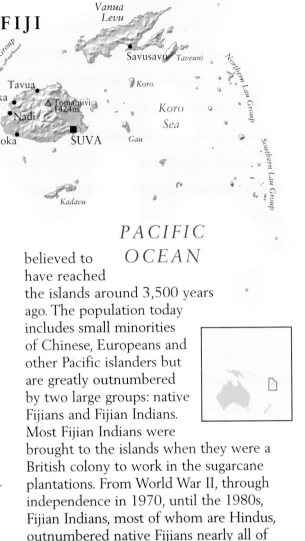

Fiji consists of around 330 islands of which 106 are inhabited. A majority of the population live on the two largest islands, Viti Levu and Vanua Levu. These islands and a number of others are of volcanic origin with mountainous interiors. Agriculture employs over 70 per cent of the workforce with major crops including bananas, cocoa beans, maize, coconuts, rice and sugarcane. Fiji exports around one and a half times the amount of food it has to import. Sugar processing is the country's biggest industry and is largely government controlled. Sugar accounts for over half of all exports. Forestry and fishing are important industries, while tourism was the fastest-growing industry until the country's troubles in 2000. Fiji has no fossil fuels but a large hydro-electricity plant on Viti Levu generates over three-quarters of the country's electricity. Viti Levu is also the location for Fiji's largest private industry – the Vatukoula gold mine which employs around 1,600 workers. Fiji is sometimes known as the 'Crossroads of the Pacific' and has seen a number of waves of settlement stretching back to the Lapita peoples who are believed to have reached the islands around 3,500 years ago. The population today includes small minorities of Chinese, Europeans and other Pacific islanders but are greatly outnumbered by two large groups: native Fijians and Fijian Indians. Most Fijian Indians were brought to the islands when they were a British colony to work in the sugarcane plantations. From World War II, through independence in 1970, until the 1980s, Fijian Indians, most of whom are Hindus, outnumbered native Fijians nearly all of whom are Christian. Tensions between the two groups have dominated Fijian politics with civil disorder, outbursts of violence and a series of military coups occurring between 1987 and 2000. This has led to economic problems, and a great number of Fijian Indians leaving the country.

SAMOA

Consisting of nine islands and a number of small islets, Samoa is one of the most traditional of the Pacific island nations. It used to be known as Western Samoa.

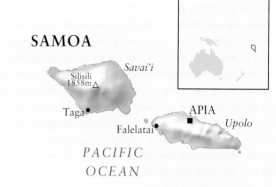

Area: 2,831 km²
Population: 180,000
Capital: Apia (34,000)
Main languages spoken: Samoan, English
Main religions: Mormon, Congregational, Roman Catholic
Currency: tala, local issue of New Zealand currency
Main exports: coconut oil, coconut cream, copra, fish, clothing, beer
Type of government: elective monarchy; democracy

▼ The interior of Samoa's major islands tend to be covered in lush plant life and cut by short, shallow and fast-moving streams and rivers.

Samoa's land is dominated by two large islands, Savai'i and Upolo, and seven smaller islands of which only two are inhabited. Savai'i and Upolo both have narrow coastal plains, coral reefs around their coasts and volcanically formed, mountainous centres much of which is densely covered in tropical forests. Samoa is a nation of farmers, with 78 per cent of its people living in the countryside, mostly in the islands' 400 coastal villages. Agriculture is mainly on a small scale, although larger plantations of hardwood trees, coconut palms and bananas provide products for export. Fishing is largely conducted using traditional outrigger canoes. Samoans tend to live in communal family groups who own 80 per cent of the land and which they are not allowed to sell. Each extended family is headed by a matai, or elected male chief, who wields much power. Samoa faces major

environmental problems, particularly deforestation and soil erosion. More than half of its original forests have been cleared, destroying habitats of many native wildlife species. Government replanting schemes and strict logging laws are helping to keep the timber industry working while protecting some of the islands' land. Samoa generates over 35 per cent of its electricity through hydro-electric power, but has to import the rest along with many other goods and supplies. Despite a flourishing tourist industry, Samoa has large foreign debts and very high unemployment. Thousands of Samoans have migrated to other nations particularly to New Zealand, the USA and American Samoa to seek a living abroad.

TONGA

Lying 640 km east of Fiji, the kingdom of Tonga consists of 172 islands, many of which are covered in thick vegetation while less than 40 are inhabited.

Area: 748 km²
Population: 99,000
Capital: Nuku'alofa (34,000)
Main languages spoken: Tongan, English
Main religions: Methodist, Roman Catholic
Currency: pa'anga
Principal exports: squashes, fish, vanilla beans, root crops
Type of government: kingdom; limited democracy

▼ A sentry stands guard in front of the Royal Palace of the King of Tonga. Political power lies with the monarch. King Taufa'ahau Tupou IV has ruled since 1965 and oversaw Tongan independence from the UK in 1970.

Tonga's three main island groups – Tongatapu, Ha'apai and Vava'u lie just west of the Tonga Trench, the second deepest part of the Pacific Ocean floor. The eastern islands are mainly low-lying and formed of coral. Many of the western islands were formed from volcanic activity, and are more rugged and mountainous, with four active volcanoes. Tonga lies over 2,200 km south of the equator and has more variation in summer and winter temperatures than many Pacific islands. Winter temperatures average between 17°C and 22°C with summer temperatures between 25°C and 33°C. The islands are located within the South Pacific's cyclone belt and tropical storms regularly strike the islands. Tonga's largest island is called Tongatapu and is home to around two-thirds of the islands' people. Over half of all Tongans work in agriculture growing vanilla beans, coconuts and squash for export and

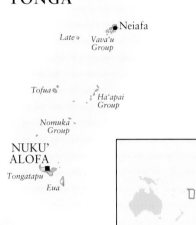

vegetables, such as cassava, for food. Fishing, tourism and the sale of handicrafts contribute to the economy. Tonga has no mineral resources and mostly generates its energy needs from imported fuel.

AMERICAN SAMOA

American Samoa consists of six volcanic islands and two coral atolls. The largest island is Tutuila where the capital, Pago Pago, is located.

Area: 199 km²
Population: 57,000
Capital: Pago Pago (4,300)
Main languages spoken: Samoan, English
Main religions: Congregational, Roman Catholic
Currency: US dollar
Principal exports: tuna, other fish
Type of government: dependency of the USA

American Samoa's volcanic-formed islands, which include Tutuila, Tau and Olosega, have rugged landscapes rising to eroded mountains in their centre and with a mixture of cliffs and scooped out bays on their coast. The mountain interiors of these islands are heavily covered in rainforests which provide homes for many bird species as well as flying foxes, lizards, rats and snakes. American Samoa experiences a tropical climate with heavy rainfall. Pago Pago tends to receive an average of 5,000 mm per year. The islands are susceptible to heavy storms between December and March. Unlike many Pacific island groups, American Samoa has relatively few tourists and the economy relies on tuna canneries which process tuna fish caught in local waters. Textiles and

handicrafts, such as woven mats are also exported. The largest island, Tutuila, is where the majority of the territory's population live. The people of American Samoa often still live in large extended family groups called aiga but younger Samoans are becoming more Westernized and abandoning traditional ways of life.

► One of the finest deep water harbours in the Pacific, Pago Pago harbour was formed from a volcanic crater that collapsed and was submerged millions of years ago.

NIUE

One of the largest coral islands and smallest self-governing states in the world, Niue is separately governed in free association with New Zealand.

Area: 259 km²
Population: 1,800
Capital: Alofi (620)
Main languages spoken: English, Niuean
Main religion: Congregational
Currency: New Zealand dollar
Principal exports: coconut cream and copra, honey, fruit
Type of government: self-governing dependency of New Zealand

Niue is a roughly oval-shaped island with broken and sharp cliffs facing the sea and an inland plateau rising to around 60 m. The most fertile part of the island, where the majority of the people live, is the land approaching the coast which contains wooded areas of palms and banyan trees. Almost a quarter of the island is capable of supporting some form of farming although the soils are not of good quality. Niue lacks streams or rivers and water tends to filter through the soil and the porous coral out into the ocean. Rainfall, which averages 2,000 mm per year, has to be collected and stored. Niue's economy is tiny with the income from

fewer than 800 tourists per year making a major contribution. The sale of postage stamps to foreign collectors, and the exporting of copra, limes and honey bring in further revenue. Aid, particularly from New Zealand, has enabled Niue to build a relatively extensive infrastructure, including television and telephone links. Yet, opportunities for work on the island are limited and around 15,000 Niueans have migrated to New Zealand to seek work. Niue's people are mainly descended from Samoans and Tongans who settled on the island and have developed their own Pacific language, Niuean.

COOK ISLANDS

Lying east of Tonga, the Cook Islands consist of two groups of small volcanic and coral islands scattered over some 2.2 million km² of the Pacific Ocean.

Area: 237 km²
Population: 20,000
Capital: Avarua (3,000)
Main languages spoken: English, Cook Islands Maori
Main religion: Cook Islands Church, Roman Catholic
Currency: New Zealand dollar
Main exports: copra, fresh fruit (particularly papayas), tinned fruit, fish, clothing
Type of government: self-governing dependency of New Zealand

The Cook Islands is a self-governing dependency of new Zealand. It is made up of a northern group of six coral atolls and nine islands of volcanic origin in the southern group. The majority of the population live in the southern group, especially on the largest island, Rarotonga where its capital, Avarua, is based. Surrounded by a coral reef, Rarotonga's land rises from a coastal plain to a volcanic peak. The Cook Islanders are mostly descended from Polynesians related to the Maori peoples who settled New Zealand. The Maori language, along with English, is widely spoken. While fishing and growing pineapples and other tropical crops occupy many of the small workforce, the most lucrative activities are tourism and offshore banking. Marine farms producing cultured pearls have recently been established. The expansion of New Zealand's economy has drawn many Cook Islanders to seek work there. An estimated 32,000 Cook Islanders live and work in

▶ Traditional dancing on the Cook Islands tells stories handed down from generation to generation. Usually accompanied by beating drums, the dancers wear traditional costumes made from palm fronds, tree bark, sea shells, feathers and flowers.

New Zealand. The islands are self-governing but heavily linked to New Zealand which donates aid and is the islands' major trading partner.

FRENCH POLYNESIA

A collection of island archipelagos made up of over 115 islands, French Polynesia sprawls across the Pacific and is the most eastern of the Pacific island nations.

French Polynesia (to France)
Marquesas Islands
Tuamotu Islands
Bora-Bora
Society Islands
Papeete
Tahiti
Tubuai Islands
Gambier Is.

Area: 4,000 km²
Population: 235,000
Capital: Papeete (113,000)
Main languages spoken: French, Tahitian
Main religion: Roman Catholic
Currency: French Pacific franc
Main exports: pearls, copra and other coconut products, mother-of-pearl, vanilla
Type of government: dependency of France

▼ Scattered over an enormous area of the Pacific Ocean – there is over 2,000 km distance between the northernmost and southernmost islands – French Polynesia attracted over 200,000 tourists in 2001. Fringed by coral reefs, the tropical paradise island of Bora Bora, in the Society Islands group, is a popular destination for the wealthier tourists.

French Polynesia is divided into five island archipelagos: the Society Islands, the Gambier Islands, the Tubuai Islands, the Marquesas Islands and the Tuamotu Archipelago. The larger islands, which are of volcanic origin, support an array of natural life including large tiare flowers often worn by islanders. Many of the islands' plant and animal species, including wild pigs and sheep, were introduced by human settlers and have since flourished. The islands are also home to around 100 species of birds. While farming and fishing provide some employment on the outer islands, tourism is the most important industry. French Polynesia is the world leader in creating cultured pearls, particularly on the Tuamotu and Gambier islands. French Polynesia's economy, government and transportation network are dominated by the island of Tahiti in the Society Islands. Encircled by a fertile coastal plain, Tahiti's land rises sharply to spectacular volcanic mountains. Over two-thirds of

▲ Located in the Society Islands, Raiatea occupies 238 km² and is a mountainous island surrounded by palm-fringed beaches and coral reefs.

the islands' population live on Tahiti which is also home to the main port at Papeete. French military presence in the islands has provided much income and employment, but French nuclear tests on Muroroa atoll in the mid-1990s provoked opposition and outrage among the islanders, some of whom want more independence from France.

ANTARCTICA

Lying undiscovered until the early 19th century, the continent of Antarctica is a largely icy wasteland whose interior has been barely touched by human impact or by the activities of plants and animals. The continent, whose name means the opposite of Arctic, encircles the geographic South Pole and with an approximate land area of 14 million km² is larger than the continent of Europe. The giant Transantarctic Mountain Range, almost 5,000 km long and containing peaks over 4,000 m in elevation, splits the continent into two regions: a larger eastern region and the western region which includes the Antarctic Peninsula. This peninsula extends 1,300 km northwards towards the southernmost tip of South America and is covered in mountain ranges. Its loftiest peak, the 4,897 m high Vinson Massif, is also the highest point on the continent. Around 90 per cent of the world's freshwater is contained in Antarctica, locked together as ice. All except around five per cent of its land surface is covered by a thick ice sheet, averaging 2.3 km in depth. It is the coldest, windiest region on Earth and also one of the driest. With a temporary human population of around 4,000 in summer and less than 1,000 in winter, Antarctica is the most unspoilt and hostile environment on the planet.

South Orkney Islands (to UK)

South Shetland Islands

James Ross I.

Antarctic Peninsula

Anvers I.

Adelaide I.

Palmer L

Alexander I.

Bellingshausen Sea

El.

Thurston I.

Amunsden Sea

Carne

◀ An icebreaker ship travels slowly through an open but narrow sea lane in the ice off the continent of Antarctica.

ANTARCTICA

SOUTHERN OCEAN

Fimbul
Ice Shelf

Riiser-Larsen
Peninsula

Queen
Maud
Land

Enderby
Land

Riiser-Larsen
Ice Shelf

Weddell
Sea

Coats
Land

Kemp
Land

Cape Darnley

Berkner I

Filchner
Ice Shelf

Amery
Ice Shelf

Ronne
Ice Shelf

Henry
Ice Rise

ANTARCTICA

Princess
Elizabeth
Land

Vinson Massif
4897m

South Pole

Greater
Antarctica

Willhelm II
Land

Shackleton
Ice Shelf

Davis
Sea

Lesser
Antarctica

Transantarctic Mountains

Queen Mary
Land

Ross
Ice Shelf

Roosevelt I.

Vincennes
Bay

Cape Poinsett

Wilkes Land

Ross
Sea

Ross I.

Victoria
Land

SOUTHERN
OCEAN

Adélie
Land

Porpoise Bay

George V
Land

Oates
Land

South Magnetic
Pole (1990)

Cape Adare

Dumont
d'Urville
Sea

0	1000	2000 km

0	500	1000 miles

including most of the Antarctic Peninsula, Wilkes Land, Southern Victoria Land and much of Ross Island. The peaks and some valleys in parts of the Transantarctic Mountain Range and the Ellsworth Mountains are also exposed rock and, because of global warming, Antarctica's ice cap appears to be receding in places. Despite the harsh climate, the continent draws around 13,000 tourists during its summer months who travel on organized tours to experience Antarctica. Most visit the Antarctic Peninsula or travel through the Ross Sea which contains Ross Island, the home of one of Antarctica's two active volcanoes, the 3,794 m high Mt Erebus.

COLD AND DRY

Antarctica is the location of the coldest known temperature on Earth. In 1983, the former Soviet Union's Vostok scientific station recorded a temperature of -89.2°C. The warmest temperatures recorded on the continent are in the northern part of the Antarctic Peninsula which has seen summer temperatures of 11°C. However, temperatures for the majority of the continent most of the time remain below zero. Average temperatures during the winter vary from between -40 and -70° C in the interior to between -20 and -30°C on the coast. These temperatures can feel colder to creatures due to the wind-chill

▲ The largest of all penguins, the Emperor penguin journeys up to 100 km inland on Antarctica to its breeding ground. Dense layers of fat and thick waterproof feathers enable these birds to survive the incredibly harsh Antarctic winter on land, the only large creature to do so.

▼ The rugged, icebound, Mount Lister has a height of 4,025 m. The mountain is part of the giant Transantarctic Mountain Range which cuts across the continent, dividing it into two distinct halves.

Antarctica is dominated by its giant ice cap which is over 4,000 m in depth in some places, while thinning to 1,500 m near the coast. The weight of the ice cap is phenomenal, enough to push parts of the continent's rocky base down below sea level. Antarctica doubles its effective size in winter when a massive build-up of sea ice surrounds the coastline. Some of this ice calves, or breaks off, to form icebergs. In other places, the floating sea ice stays attached to the land and builds up to form an ice shelf. Ice shelves make up around ten per cent of the continent's area, with the Ross Ice Shelf and the Ronne Ice Shelf the two largest examples. Not all of Antarctica is covered in ice. Around 280,000 km² of land is ice-free,

factor brought about by the powerful, sweeping winds which scour the continent. In the interior, winds as high as 320 km/h have been recorded. The interior of Antarctica is a desert in which annual rainfall averages less than 50 mm per year. This increases at the coast to around 300 mm per year.

BARREN LANDS – FOOD-RICH SEAS

Antarctica's climate is so severe that few species of living thing can survive there. The continent's plant life consists mainly of different types of simple algae, lichens and mosses. These provide food for some small insects and micro-organisms as well as Antarctica's 43 different species of seabirds, including albatross and many species of penguin. In contrast to the barren land, the waters around Antarctica hold vast amounts of marine life. The ocean abounds with microscopic plants and animals known as plankton which is fed upon by a small shrimp-like creature called krill. Krill live in giant swarms and provide rich feeding grounds for fish and larger marine creatures including squid, seals, penguins and whales. Many species of whales migrate to Antarctica in the summer to feed off the rich krill stocks. Trawlers from many nations fish the seas surrounding the continent but a ban on whaling in the region was agreed in 1994.

▲ This 50 m wide, 16 m high dome covers part of the Amundsen-Scott research station located close to the South Pole. Named after the two explorers who memorably raced to reach the South Pole over 90 years ago, it is home to over 130 people in the summer months but just 28 people in winter. Work on a new, enlarged South Pole research station is currently underway.

EXPLORATION AND RESEARCH

Antarctica was first discovered in the 1820s.
Gradually, expeditions began to cross parts
of the continent and, in 1911, the
Norwegian, Roald Amundsen, was
the first person to reach the South
Pole. Antarctica has no permanent
human population. Its residents
are temporary and are mainly
scientists, and researchers from
25 nations working at over 70
research stations. Many of
these research stations study
aspects of the continent, its
geology, its ice sheets and its
impact on world weather
systems. With its clear
skies and isolated location,
Antarctica is also used as a base
for radio astronomy studying distant
galaxies and deep space. Geological
surveys have shown that the
Transantarctic Mountain Range may be
part of the world's biggest coalfield, while
reserves of a number of valuable minerals
including iron ore, gold, chromium and
uranium have also been found. Large
deposits of oil and natural gas are believed
to exist in Antarctica's continental shelf.
However, in 1990, the international
community agreed to ban mining and
mineral exploitation on Antarctica for
50 years. A greater threat to Antarctica's
environment comes from pollution and
particularly global warming. The depletion
in the atmosphere's ozone layer over
Antarctica was discovered by an Antarctic
research station in 1985.

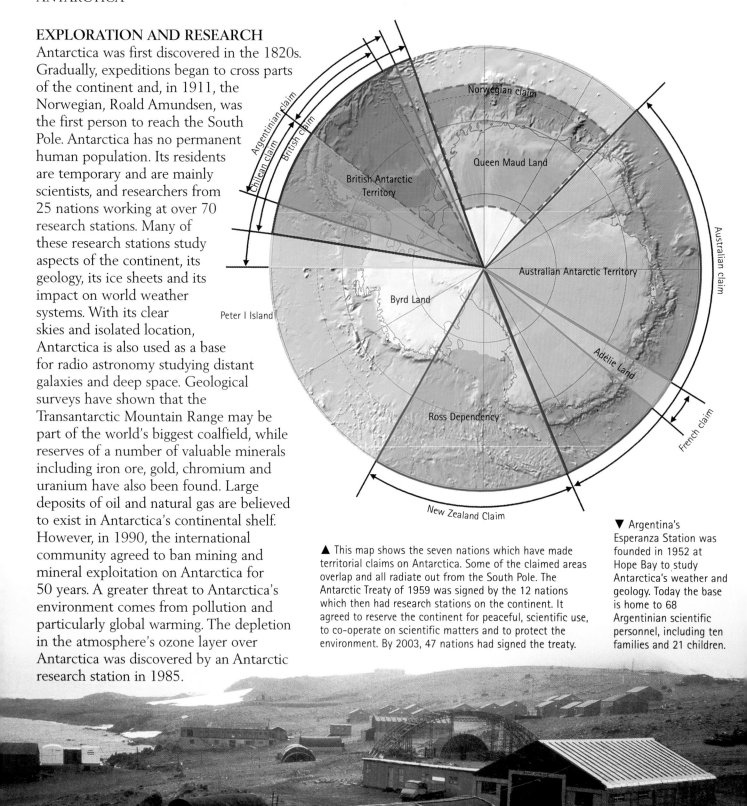

▲ This map shows the seven nations which have made
territorial claims on Antarctica. Some of the claimed areas
overlap and all radiate out from the South Pole. The
Antarctic Treaty of 1959 was signed by the 12 nations
which then had research stations on the continent. It
agreed to reserve the continent for peaceful, scientific use,
to co-operate on scientific matters and to protect the
environment. By 2003, 47 nations had signed the treaty.

▼ Argentina's
Esperanza Station was
founded in 1952 at
Hope Bay to study
Antarctica's weather and
geology. Today the base
is home to 68
Argentinian scientific
personnel, including ten
families and 21 children.

READY REFERENCE

WORLD BIOMES

Plants and animals rarely live in isolation. They live in their natural home or habitat, and exist as part of an interdependent community of different living things. The world's large general habitats are called biogeographical regions or biomes.

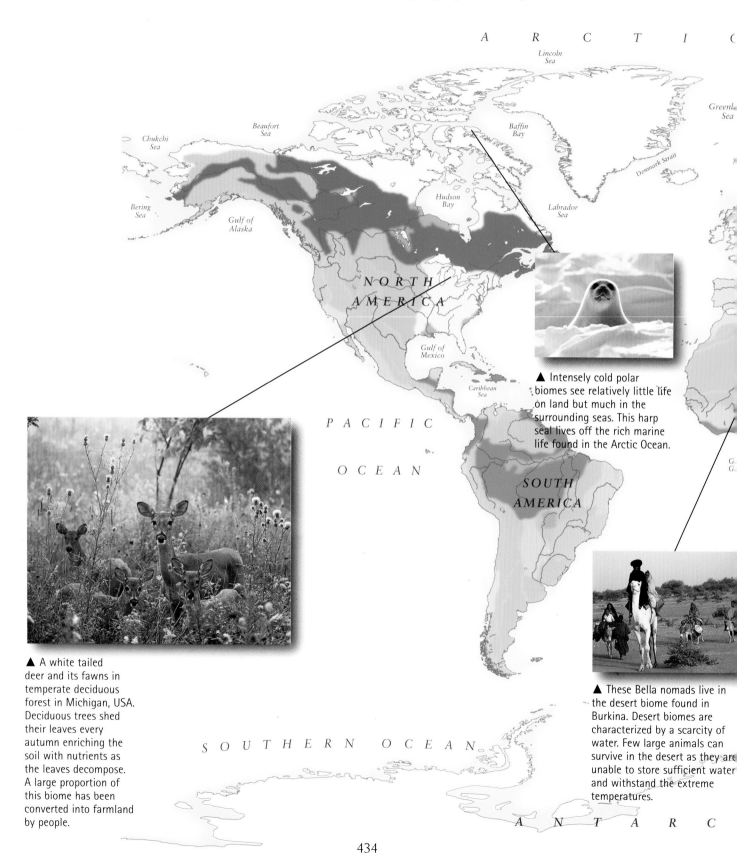

▲ Intensely cold polar biomes see relatively little life on land but much in the surrounding seas. This harp seal lives off the rich marine life found in the Arctic Ocean.

▲ A white tailed deer and its fawns in temperate deciduous forest in Michigan, USA. Deciduous trees shed their leaves every autumn enriching the soil with nutrients as the leaves decompose. A large proportion of this biome has been converted into farmland by people.

▲ These Bella nomads live in the desert biome found in Burkina. Desert biomes are characterized by a scarcity of water. Few large animals can survive in the desert as they are unable to store sufficient water and withstand the extreme temperatures.

KEY TO WORLD MAP

- ☐ Polar
- ☐ Tundra
- ☐ Mountain
- ■ Needleleaf forest
- ☐ Broadleaf forest
- ☐ Temperate grassland
- ☐ Mediterranean
- ☐ Hot and cold desert
- ▨ Wetland
- ☐ Dry woodland
- ■ Tropical rainforest
- ☐ Temperate rainforest

Except for Antarctica, a number of different biomes exist on each continent. Biomes vary in what natural life they support and in factors such as the wind, soil quality, rainfall, light intensity and temperature. Biomes are constantly changing both in extent and content. The cutting down of large numbers of trees has seen forest biomes shrink in size while desertification has seen deserts grow faster than other biomes.

O C E A N

Kara Sea

Laptev Sea

East Siberian Sea

Barents Sea

ROPE

Black Sea

Caspian Sea

erranean Sea

A S I A

Sea of Okhotsk

The Gulf

Red Sea

FRICA

Arabian Sea

Bay of Bengal

Sea of Japan

Yellow Sea

East China Sea

South China Sea

Philippine Sea

Mozambique Channel

I N D I A N

O C E A N

Timor Sea

Arafura Sea

Coral Sea

AUSTRALASIA AND OCEANIA

Tasman Sea

▲ These tribesmen live in the tropical rainforests of Papua New Guinea. Tropical rainforests are hot, wet regions found close to the Equator. They feature the greatest biodiversity – the number and range of plant and animal species – of any biome. Despite being home to an estimated 90 per cent of the world's living species, half of all the world's rainforests have been destroyed.

S O U T H E R N   O C E A N

▲ The savannah biome consists of tropical or subtropical grasslands with few trees. Savannah covers over 40 per cent of Africa as well as large areas of Australia, South America and India. This biome supports many large land animals including the African elephant, shown living in Kenya's Amboselli National Park.

C   A

WORLD WATER

Water is the most precious resource on Earth. Despite vast quantities existing, water supplies are often scarce and are distributed unevenly around the planet.

BOTTOM 20 COUNTRIES WITH LEAST ACCESS TO SANITATION FACILITIES By percentage of population	
China	38%
The Gambia	37%
Togo	34%
Solomon Islands	34%
Mauritania	33%
India	31%
Mongolia	30%
Burkina	29%
Sierra Leone	28%
Haiti	28%
Nepal	27%
Benin	23%
Gabon	21%
Niger	20%
D R Congo	20%
Cambodia	18%
Ethiopia	15%
Eritrea	13%
Afghanistan	12%
Rwanda	8%

▲ Sanitation is essential to prevent the spread of disease and to prevent water supplies becoming contaminated. The list of nations above illustrates how many nations still struggle to offer adequate sanitation to their people.

Although people require only a small amount of drinking water each day to survive, water is also vital in ensuring public health and hygiene through sanitation systems. People in more developed nations tend to use between 150 and 400 litres of water each day for cooking and cleaning tasks. Flushing a toilet can use between 10 and 25 litres, a washing machine 75 litres and a bath as much as 80 litres of fresh water. In contrast, in nations where water is not so easily available, consumption is far lower. The domestic use of water is dwarfed by the amount used in agriculture; some 70 per cent of all water used in human activity is consumed by farming. Without adequate water supplies, crops fail, livestock die, and food supplies shrink drastically. Cheap, plentiful supplies of water are also essential to industry, which uses almost a quarter of all water consumed. Industries use water as a coolant, a solvent, in washing and cleaning applications as well as an ingredient in many chemical, food and drink products.

NOT JUST FOR CONSUMPTION
Water is exploited in other ways to benefit people and nations besides being consumed directly by people, or used in public health, agriculture or industry. Water is a rich habitat for many forms of

life that, in turn, provides important sources of food for millions of people. Natural inland waterways provide important transport routes through many regions enhanced by the construction of artificial waterways or canals. The power held in moving water is exploited in many nations to generate electricity through hydro-electric power plants.

WATER SUPPLIES
Over three-quarters of the planet is covered in water, but the vast majority of this is salt water found in the seas and oceans. Only 2.5 per cent of the world's water is freshwater and over 70 per cent of this freshwater is locked up in the polar

► A sudden excess of water in the form of a flood can kill people, destroy villages and ruin crops, crippling an area's economy. Bangladesh is considered one of the most flood-prone regions in the world. This Bangladeshi village has been flooded by the rising waters of the River Jamuna.

▲ An Omani worker examines part of a desalination plant. Desalination removes the salts from seawater in order to make it drinkable. Desalination is expensive but is used in many of the wealthier Middle Eastern nations.

ice caps. Rivers and lakes are an important water source while a huge amount of fresh water is stored as groundwater beneath the Earth's surface in the soil, in the pores between particles of sedimentary rocks and in the cracks and fissures between other rock. Approximately one-tenth of the world's groundwater supplies are easy to reach and, increasingly, groundwater is being tapped by countries in order to fulfil the demand for water. Over 1.5 billion people rely on groundwater supplies for their drinking water, but groundwater levels take a relatively long time to

replenish and can become exhausted if used at a rapid rate. In the southern Indian state of Tamil Nadu, for example, the level of groundwater has fallen by more than 20 m over ten years due to so much of the water being tapped.

THE WATER CRISIS

The water cycle which sees water circulate between the Earth and the atmosphere is a finely balanced natural cycle which produces enough clean water to support life in many regions. Yet, the increasing demands of a booming human population and, with it, many forms of pollution, from domestic sewage and dumped industrial chemicals to poisonous agricultural pesticide, are reducing the levels of fresh water available in many places in the world. In large regions of Africa, the Middle East and Asia, the problem is considerably more acute. Over one billion people currently lack access to clean water. Thousands die from hunger, frequently caused by a lack of water to sustain local crops. Even more people – between 1.5 and 2 billion – lack safe sanitation. As a result, as many as three million people die every year from avoidable water-related diseases.

THE 20 COUNTRIES WITH LEAST ACCESS TO IMPROVED DRINKING WATER
By percentage of population

Congo	51%
Kiribati	48%
Guinea	48%
Madagascar	47%
Fiji	47%
Haiti	46%
Eritrea	46%
D R Congo	45%
Equatorial Guinea	44%
Papua New Guinea	42%
Burkina	42%
Rwanda	41%
Oman	39%
Angola	38%
Mauritania	37%
Laos	37%
Cambodia	30%
Chad	27%
Ethiopia	24%
Afghanistan	13%

▲ In many wealthy countries every person has access to clean and safe drinking water. This is not the case in many poor countries.

▼ The Cabora Bassa dam in Mozambique is the country's largest hydro-electric power dam generating thousands of megawatts of electricity.

WINDS AND OCEAN CURRENTS

Our climate is influenced by two systems of currents: the circulation of moving air in the atmosphere and the circulation of water in the oceans. Together, these generate a region's climate and weather as well as helping to form the distinct features of the world's biomes.

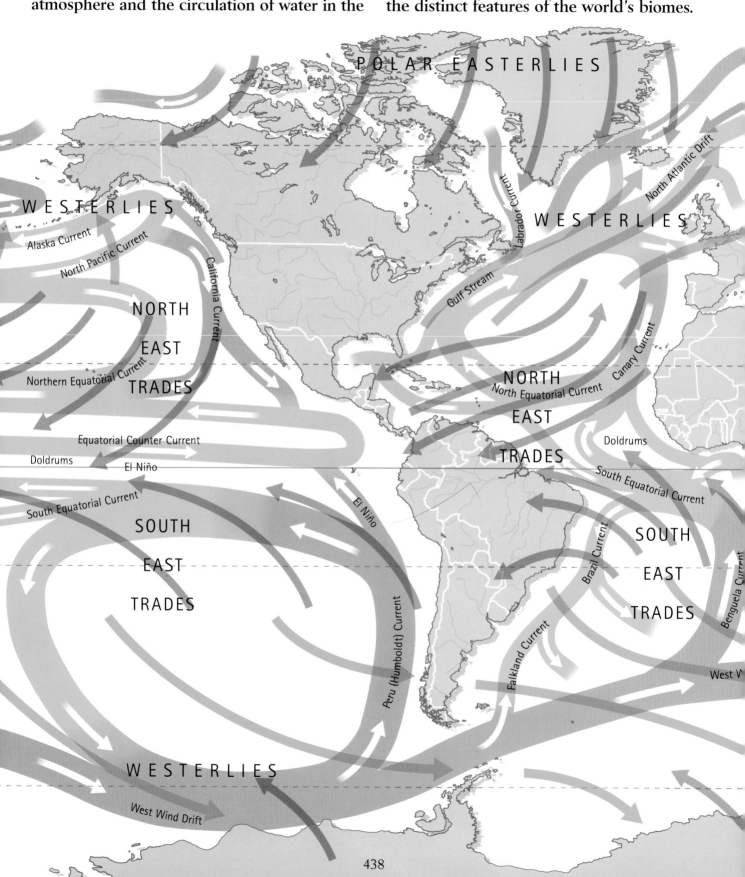

POLAR EASTERLIES

WESTERLIES

WESTERLIES

North Atlantic Drift

Alaska Current

North Pacific Current

Labrador Current

Gulf Stream

California Current

NORTH

EAST

TRADES

Canary Current

NORTH

North Equatorial Current

EAST

Northern Equatorial Current

TRADES

Equatorial Counter Current

Doldrums

Doldrums

El Niño

South Equatorial Current

South Equatorial Current

SOUTH

EAST

TRADES

El Niño

Brazil Current

SOUTH

EAST

TRADES

Benguela Current

Peru (Humboldt) Current

Falkland Current

West W

WESTERLIES

West Wind Drift

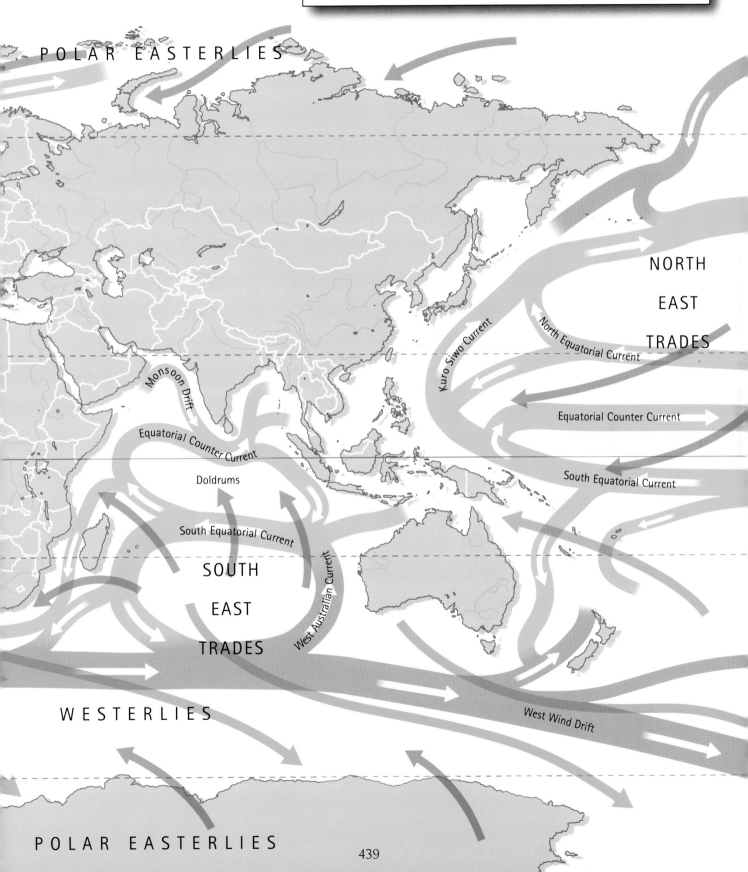

KEY TO WORLD MAP

warm ocean currents   warm winds

cold ocean currents   cold winds

This map depicts the world's major wind and ocean current systems. Winds are named according to the direction from which they blow and those shown are the usual, or prevailing, winds. Ocean currents circulate in paths which are called gyres. These move in an anti-clockwise direction in the southern hemisphere. In the northern hemisphere, they move in a clockwise direction. When these currents move towards the poles, they carry warm water away from the equatorial regions. Currents returning towards the Equator carry cold water from the polar regions.

POLAR EASTERLIES

NORTH EAST TRADES

North Equatorial Current

Kuro Siwo Current

Monsoon Drift

Equatorial Counter Current

Equatorial Counter Current

Doldrums

South Equatorial Current

South Equatorial Current

SOUTH EAST TRADES

West Australian Current

WESTERLIES

West Wind Drift

POLAR EASTERLIES

WORLD POLLUTION

Pollution is the introduction of waste energy or a substance, called a pollutant, into an environment which has a harmful effect.

Human impact on the planet has generated many different forms of pollution which affect the air, seas and oceans and land.

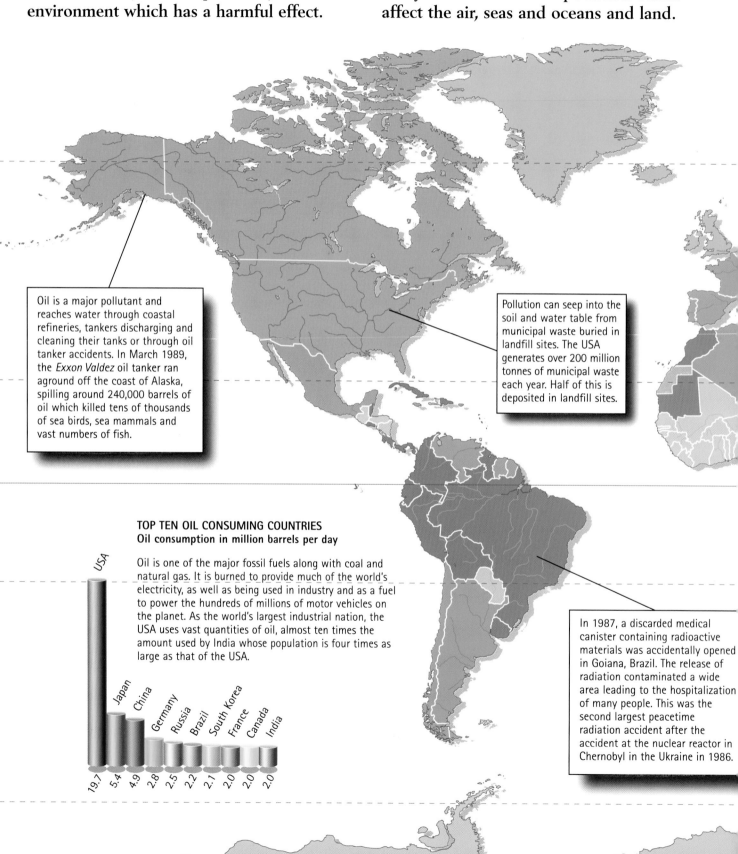

Oil is a major pollutant and reaches water through coastal refineries, tankers discharging and cleaning their tanks or through oil tanker accidents. In March 1989, the *Exxon Valdez* oil tanker ran aground off the coast of Alaska, spilling around 240,000 barrels of oil which killed tens of thousands of sea birds, sea mammals and vast numbers of fish.

Pollution can seep into the soil and water table from municipal waste buried in landfill sites. The USA generates over 200 million tonnes of municipal waste each year. Half of this is deposited in landfill sites.

TOP TEN OIL CONSUMING COUNTRIES
Oil consumption in million barrels per day

Oil is one of the major fossil fuels along with coal and natural gas. It is burned to provide much of the world's electricity, as well as being used in industry and as a fuel to power the hundreds of millions of motor vehicles on the planet. As the world's largest industrial nation, the USA uses vast quantities of oil, almost ten times the amount used by India whose population is four times as large as that of the USA.

USA	Japan	China	Germany	Russia	Brazil	South Korea	France	Canada	India
19.7	5.4	4.9	2.8	2.5	2.2	2.1	2.0	2.0	2.0

In 1987, a discarded medical canister containing radioactive materials was accidentally opened in Goiana, Brazil. The release of radiation contaminated a wide area leading to the hospitalization of many people. This was the second largest peacetime radiation accident after the accident at the nuclear reactor in Chernobyl in the Ukraine in 1986.

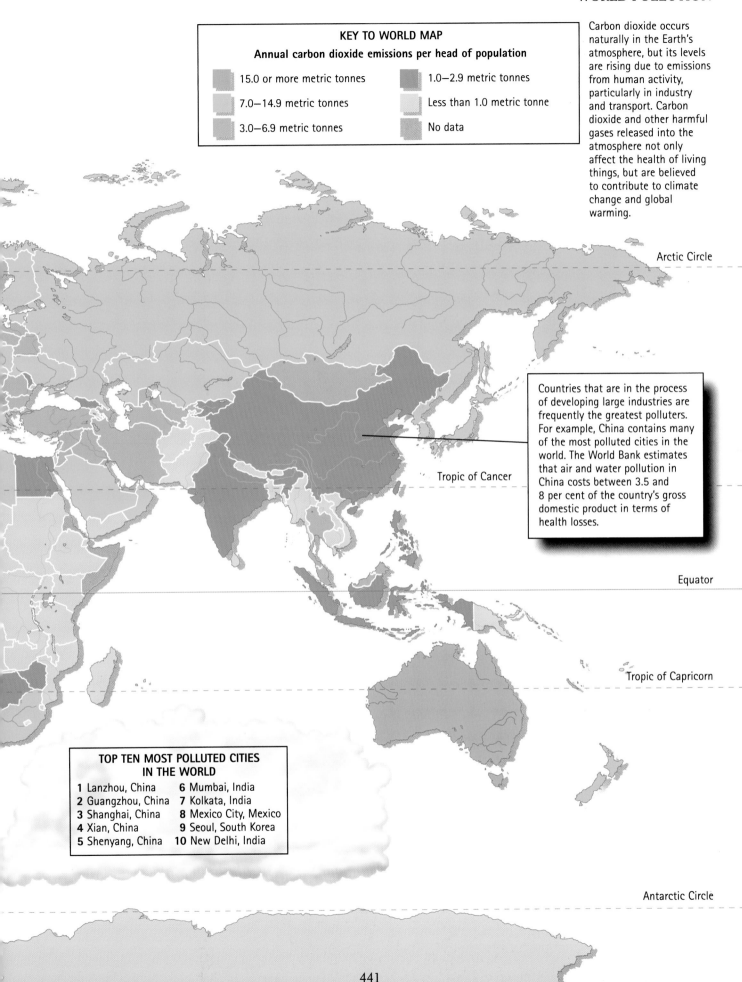

KEY TO WORLD MAP
Annual carbon dioxide emissions per head of population

- 15.0 or more metric tonnes
- 7.0–14.9 metric tonnes
- 3.0–6.9 metric tonnes
- 1.0–2.9 metric tonnes
- Less than 1.0 metric tonne
- No data

Carbon dioxide occurs naturally in the Earth's atmosphere, but its levels are rising due to emissions from human activity, particularly in industry and transport. Carbon dioxide and other harmful gases released into the atmosphere not only affect the health of living things, but are believed to contribute to climate change and global warming.

Arctic Circle

Countries that are in the process of developing large industries are frequently the greatest polluters. For example, China contains many of the most polluted cities in the world. The World Bank estimates that air and water pollution in China costs between 3.5 and 8 per cent of the country's gross domestic product in terms of health losses.

Tropic of Cancer

Equator

Tropic of Capricorn

**TOP TEN MOST POLLUTED CITIES
IN THE WORLD**

1 Lanzhou, China   6 Mumbai, India
2 Guangzhou, China   7 Kolkata, India
3 Shanghai, China   8 Mexico City, Mexico
4 Xian, China   9 Seoul, South Korea
5 Shenyang, China   10 New Delhi, India

Antarctic Circle

BIODIVERSITY AND EXTINCTION

A region's biodiversity is the range and number of animal and plant species it supports. The Earth is home to many millions of different species, yet thousands are under threat from extinction – their permanent disappearance from the planet.

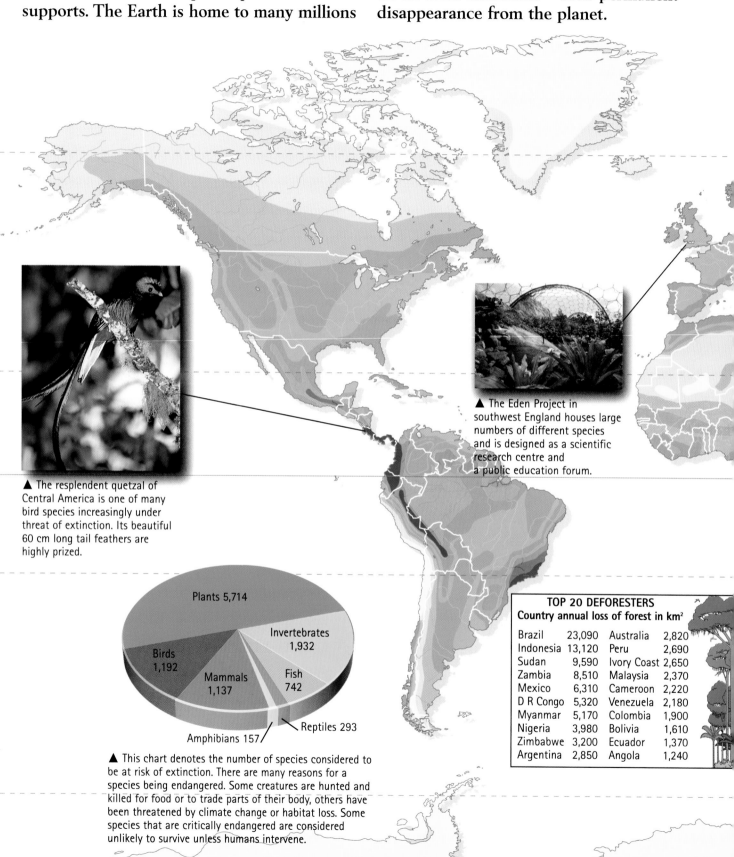

▲ The resplendent quetzal of Central America is one of many bird species increasingly under threat of extinction. Its beautiful 60 cm long tail feathers are highly prized.

▲ The Eden Project in southwest England houses large numbers of different species and is designed as a scientific research centre and a public education forum.

Plants 5,714
Invertebrates 1,932
Birds 1,192
Mammals 1,137
Fish 742
Amphibians 157
Reptiles 293

▲ This chart denotes the number of species considered to be at risk of extinction. There are many reasons for a species being endangered. Some creatures are hunted and killed for food or to trade parts of their body, others have been threatened by climate change or habitat loss. Some species that are critically endangered are considered unlikely to survive unless humans intervene.

TOP 20 DEFORESTERS
Country annual loss of forest in km²

Country		Country	
Brazil	23,090	Australia	2,820
Indonesia	13,120	Peru	2,690
Sudan	9,590	Ivory Coast	2,650
Zambia	8,510	Malaysia	2,370
Mexico	6,310	Cameroon	2,220
D R Congo	5,320	Venezuela	2,180
Myanmar	5,170	Colombia	1,900
Nigeria	3,980	Bolivia	1,610
Zimbabwe	3,200	Ecuador	1,370
Argentina	2,850	Angola	1,240

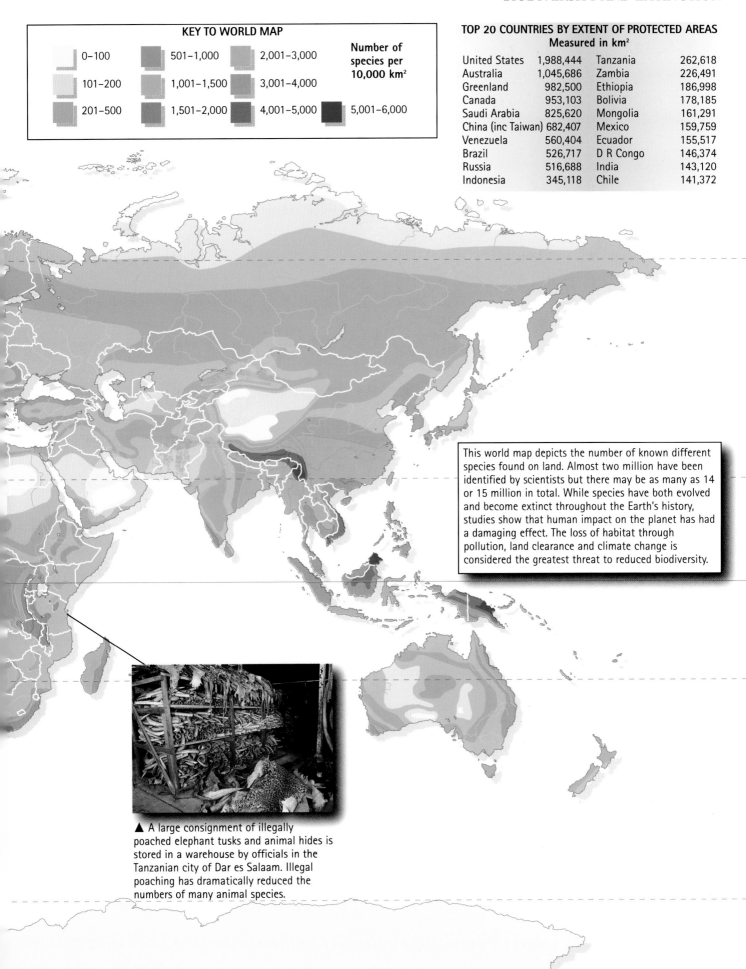

KEY TO WORLD MAP

0–100	501–1,000	2,001–3,000
101–200	1,001–1,500	3,001–4,000
201–500	1,501–2,000	4,001–5,000

5,001–6,000

Number of species per 10,000 km²

TOP 20 COUNTRIES BY EXTENT OF PROTECTED AREAS
Measured in km²

United States	1,988,444	Tanzania	262,618
Australia	1,045,686	Zambia	226,491
Greenland	982,500	Ethiopia	186,998
Canada	953,103	Bolivia	178,185
Saudi Arabia	825,620	Mongolia	161,291
China (inc Taiwan)	682,407	Mexico	159,759
Venezuela	560,404	Ecuador	155,517
Brazil	526,717	D R Congo	146,374
Russia	516,688	India	143,120
Indonesia	345,118	Chile	141,372

This world map depicts the number of known different species found on land. Almost two million have been identified by scientists but there may be as many as 14 or 15 million in total. While species have both evolved and become extinct throughout the Earth's history, studies show that human impact on the planet has had a damaging effect. The loss of habitat through pollution, land clearance and climate change is considered the greatest threat to reduced biodiversity.

▲ A large consignment of illegally poached elephant tusks and animal hides is stored in a warehouse by officials in the Tanzanian city of Dar es Salaam. Illegal poaching has dramatically reduced the numbers of many animal species.

WORLD HEALTH

Many major advances have been made in ways of improving the health of the world's human population in the past century.

However, access to ways of improving health, from a good diet to drugs and healthcare, varies greatly all over the world.

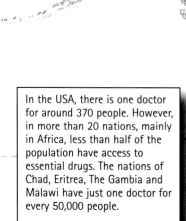

In the USA, there is one doctor for around 370 people. However, in more than 20 nations, mainly in Africa, less than half of the population have access to essential drugs. The nations of Chad, Eritrea, The Gambia and Malawi have just one doctor for every 50,000 people.

▲ A patient is surrounded by advanced monitoring and life-support systems in an intensive care unit in Hamburg, Germany.

LIFE EXPECTANCY AT BIRTH

TOP 20 COUNTRIES		BOTTOM 20 COUNTRIES	
Andorra	83.5 years	Somalia	46.6 years
San Marino	81.2 years	Burkina	46.4 years
Japan	80.8 years	Afghanistan	46.2 years
Singapore	80.2 years	Burundi	46.1 years
Australia	79.9 years	Guinea	45.9 years
Sweden	79.7 years	Sierra Leone	45.6 years
Switzerland	79.7 years	Ivory Coast	44.9 years
Canada	79.6 years	Ethiopia	44.7 years
Iceland	79.5 years	Cen Af Rep	43.8 years
Italy	79.1 years	Uganda	43.4 years
Liechtenstein	79.0 years	Niger	41.6 years
Monaco	79.0 years	Namibia	40.6 years
France	78.9 years	Rwanda	39.0 years
Spain	78.9 years	Angola	38.6 years
Norway	78.8 years	Swaziland	38.6 years
Israel	78.7 years	Zambia	37.3 years
Greece	78.6 years	Botswana	37.1 years
Netherlands	78.4 years	Malawi	37.1 years
Malta	78.1 years	Zimbabwe	37.1 years
Belgium	78.0 years	Mozambique	36.5 years

TOP 20 COUNTRIES AIDS ORPHANS

Nigeria	1,000,000	Mozambique	420,000
Ethiopia	990,000	Ivory Coast	420,000
D R Congo	930,000	Thailand	290,000
Kenya	890,000	Burkina	270,000
Uganda	880,000	Rwanda	260,000
Tanzania	810,000	Burundi	240,000
Zimbabwe	780,000	Cameroon	210,000
South Africa	660,000	Ghana	200,000
Zambia	570,000	Haiti	200,000
Malawi	470,000	Cen Af Rep	210,000

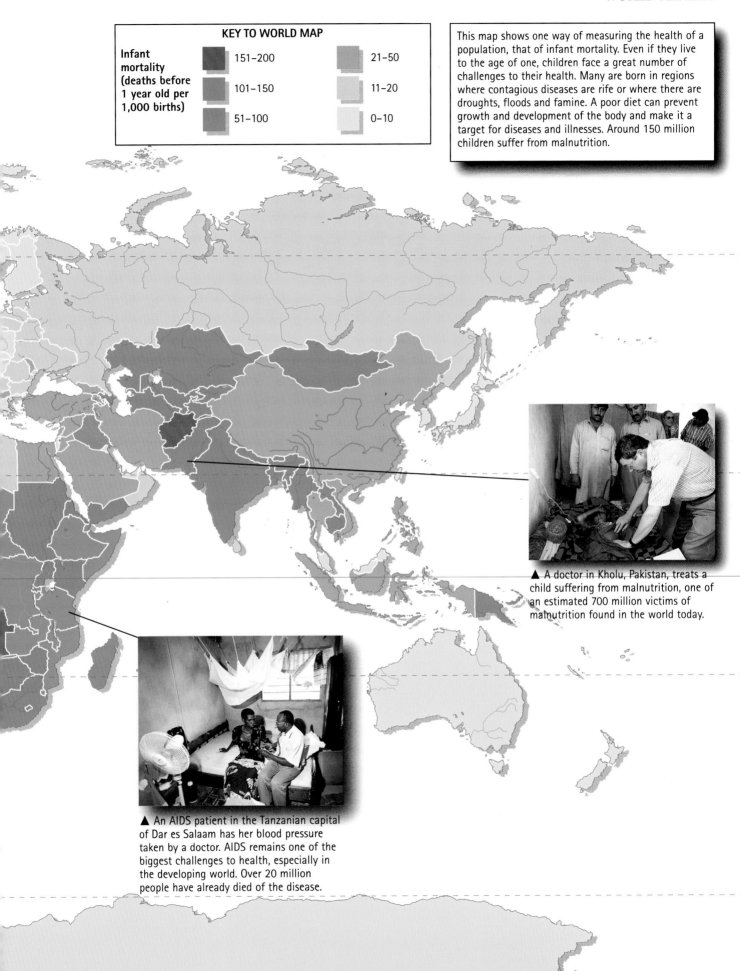

KEY TO WORLD MAP

Infant mortality (deaths before 1 year old per 1,000 births)

151–200
101–150
51–100
21–50
11–20
0–10

This map shows one way of measuring the health of a population, that of infant mortality. Even if they live to the age of one, children face a great number of challenges to their health. Many are born in regions where contagious diseases are rife or where there are droughts, floods and famine. A poor diet can prevent growth and development of the body and make it a target for diseases and illnesses. Around 150 million children suffer from malnutrition.

▲ A doctor in Kholu, Pakistan, treats a child suffering from malnutrition, one of an estimated 700 million victims of malnutrition found in the world today.

▲ An AIDS patient in the Tanzanian capital of Dar es Salaam has her blood pressure taken by a doctor. AIDS remains one of the biggest challenges to health, especially in the developing world. Over 20 million people have already died of the disease.

WORLD EDUCATION

Education enables people to read, write and communicate with others. It also provides people with the opportunity to work and the potential to improve their lives. The standard and quantity of education people receive varies greatly across the world.

Literacy is frequently used as a measure of how successful basic education has been in a country. The USA has an adult literacy rate of 99 per cent meaning that only one in 100 adults cannot read or write. Other nations, particularly in Africa, have far lower literacy rates.

▲ Students in wealthier countries, such as Germany, benefit from modern teaching facilities in classrooms.

PERCENTAGE OF GIRLS AS A TOTAL OF SECONDARY SCHOOL POPULATION

In many societies, especially in less developed countries, girls have fewer opportunities than boys to pursue education beyond primary level.

Chad	21%	China	45%
Afghanistan	25%	Australia	49%
Guinea	26%	France	49%
Yemen, Rep.	26%	Germany	49%
Benin	31%	Italy	49%
Iraq	35%	Japan	49%
India	38%	Spain	50%
Nepal	38%	Bangladesh	51%
Papua New Guinea	40%	United Kingdom	52%
Russia	40%	Namibia	53%
United States	41%	Sweden	55%

▲ Bolivia has one of the lowest literacy rates in South America. This adult literacy class seeks to educate adult Bolivians who missed out on education as children.

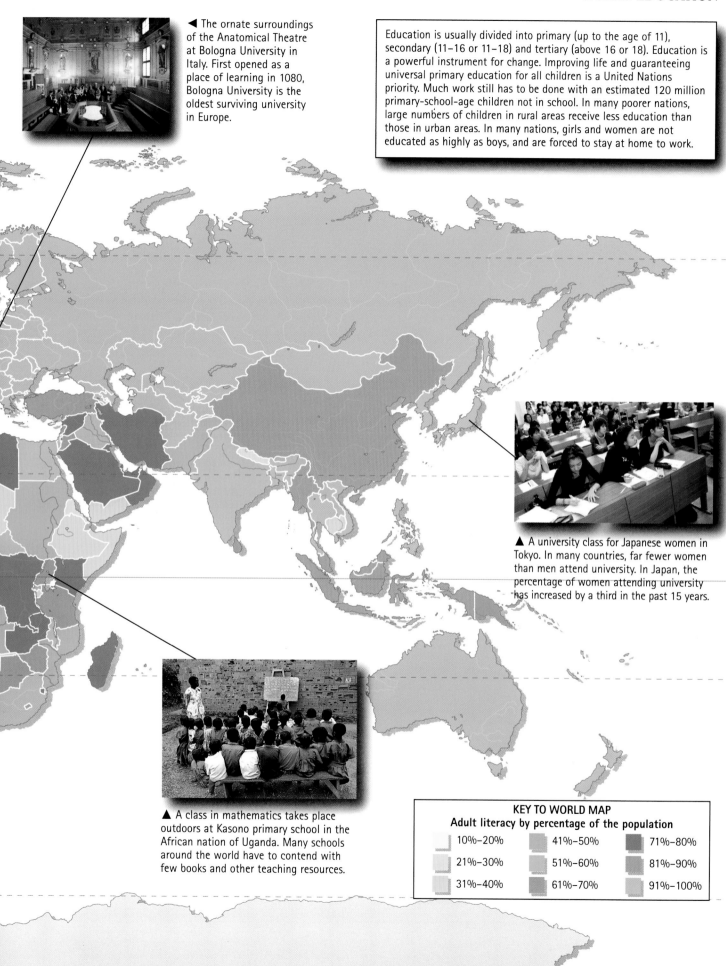

◄ The ornate surroundings of the Anatomical Theatre at Bologna University in Italy. First opened as a place of learning in 1080, Bologna University is the oldest surviving university in Europe.

Education is usually divided into primary (up to the age of 11), secondary (11–16 or 11–18) and tertiary (above 16 or 18). Education is a powerful instrument for change. Improving life and guaranteeing universal primary education for all children is a United Nations priority. Much work still has to be done with an estimated 120 million primary-school-age children not in school. In many poorer nations, large numbers of children in rural areas receive less education than those in urban areas. In many nations, girls and women are not educated as highly as boys, and are forced to stay at home to work.

▲ A university class for Japanese women in Tokyo. In many countries, far fewer women than men attend university. In Japan, the percentage of women attending university has increased by a third in the past 15 years.

▲ A class in mathematics takes place outdoors at Kasono primary school in the African nation of Uganda. Many schools around the world have to contend with few books and other teaching resources.

KEY TO WORLD MAP
Adult literacy by percentage of the population

10%–20%	41%–50%	71%–80%
21%–30%	51%–60%	81%–90%
31%–40%	61%–70%	91%–100%

WORLD WEALTH

The world's nations vary enormously in the size and wealth of their economies and so do the world's people. While millionaires exist in many countries, over a fifth of the total world population has a standard of living which is estimated at less than 1.5 US dollars a day.

The USA is the world's greatest economic power in terms of gross national product (GNP), and is sixth highest in terms of gross national income per capita behind Luxembourg, Switzerland, Japan, Norway and Liechtenstein. The country has abundant natural resources producing almost one-fifth of the world's oil and coal and almost half its maize. The USA owes its economic position to its massive and highly developed industries.

The wealth found in a country does not necessarily reach many of its people. However, Sweden is an exception with relatively high taxes on wealth and an extensive welfare state. It distributes its national wealth more equally than many nations around the world.

Exploitation by their former colonial rulers, internal conflict and wars with neighbours, a lack of resources, famines and droughts have blighted many sub Saharan nations making their people the poorest in the world. Guinea-Bissau's people have a gross national income of just US$160 per year. Twelve of the 13 nations with the lowest gross national income are found in sub Saharan Africa.

THE DEVELOPMENT GAP

The development of industries and economies around the world has not occurred at an even pace or brought equal benefits to all people. The massive difference in conditions found in many of the more developed nations compared to many of the less developed is known as the development gap. This gap can be seen in terms of income. According to World Bank estimates, the citizens of Luxembourg enjoy the highest gross national income per person estimated in 2001 at US$41,771 per year. In contrast, the African nations of Burundi and Ethiopia have a gross national income of just US$100 per person per year. The gap is also apparent in the

▲ French doctors tend patients in an oasis in Mauritania.

quality of diet, sanitation and health which leads to vast differences in life expectancy. The development gap can also be seen in the way resources are used unequally around the world. For example, around 20 per cent of the world's population use 65 per cent of the energy.

KEY TO WORLD MAP
Gross national income per capita (2000)

- High (US$9,266 or more)
- Upper middle (US$2,996–9,265)
- Lower middle (US$756–2,995)
- Low (US$755 or less)
- No data

▶ TOP TEN COUNTRIES WITH LARGEST EXTERNAL DEBT

A country's balance of trade is determined by its amount of imports and exports. Countries that import more than they export build up a negative balance of trade and often borrow money from abroad to finance new industries, services or to pay off exisiting debts. Over time, heavily indebted nations slip further into debt.

Turkey $118.8 billion
South Korea $131.3 billion
Indonesia $133.1 billion
Mexico $148 billion
Argentina $155 billion
Russia $157 billion
China $157.3 billion
Australia $176 billion
Brazil $230 billion
USA $2.3 trillion

Some of the most startling changes in wealth have occurred in a number of Pacific Rim countries – nations such as South Korea, Singapore, Thailand, Taiwan and Malaysia. Developing large manufacturing industries based particularly on computing and electronics, the economies of these nations grew rapidly throughout the 1980s and early 1990s. Between 1980 and 1993, for example, South Korea's economy more than doubled in size. As a result, the country is now the 13th wealthiest nation in terms of gross domestic product (GDP).

TOP TEN WEALTHIEST ECONOMIES
In terms of absolute gross domestic product in millions of US dollars

Gross domestic product (GDP) is a measure of the total value of finished goods and services which are produced by a national economy. This chart shows how the USA far outstrips all other economies in size. The smallest world economies are found in the Pacific Island nations such as Kiribati with a GDP of around US$50 million.

USA $10,171,400
Japan $4,245,191
Germany $1,873,854
UK $1,406,310
France $1,321,669
China $1,302,793
Italy $1,090,910
Canada $677,178
Mexico $617,817
Spain $577,539

WORLD ENERGY

Energy exists in many forms. Converting energy into types which can be used to provide heat, light and power is of vital importance to the world's human population. Chief among these forms are electricity and fuels that can be burned to provide power.

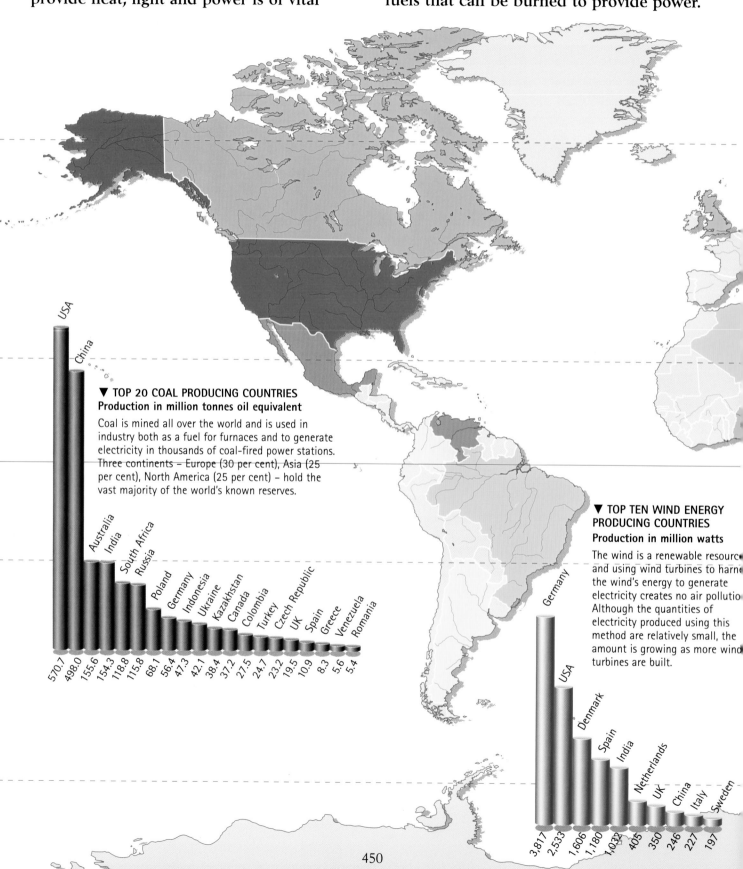

▼ TOP 20 COAL PRODUCING COUNTRIES
Production in million tonnes oil equivalent

Coal is mined all over the world and is used in industry both as a fuel for furnaces and to generate electricity in thousands of coal-fired power stations. Three continents – Europe (30 per cent), Asia (25 per cent), North America (25 per cent) – hold the vast majority of the world's known reserves.

USA 570.7
China 498.0
Australia 155.6
India 154.3
South Africa 118.8
Russia 115.8
Poland 68.1
Germany 56.4
Indonesia 47.3
Ukraine 42.1
Kazakhstan 38.4
Canada 37.2
Colombia 27.5
Turkey 24.7
Czech Republic 23.2
UK 19.5
Spain 10.9
Greece 8.3
Venezuela 5.6
Romania 5.4

▼ TOP TEN WIND ENERGY PRODUCING COUNTRIES
Production in million watts

The wind is a renewable resource and using wind turbines to harness the wind's energy to generate electricity creates no air pollution. Although the quantities of electricity produced using this method are relatively small, the amount is growing as more wind turbines are built.

Germany 3,817
USA 2,533
Denmark 1,606
Spain 1,180
India 1,032
Netherlands 405
UK 350
China 246
Italy 227
Sweden 197

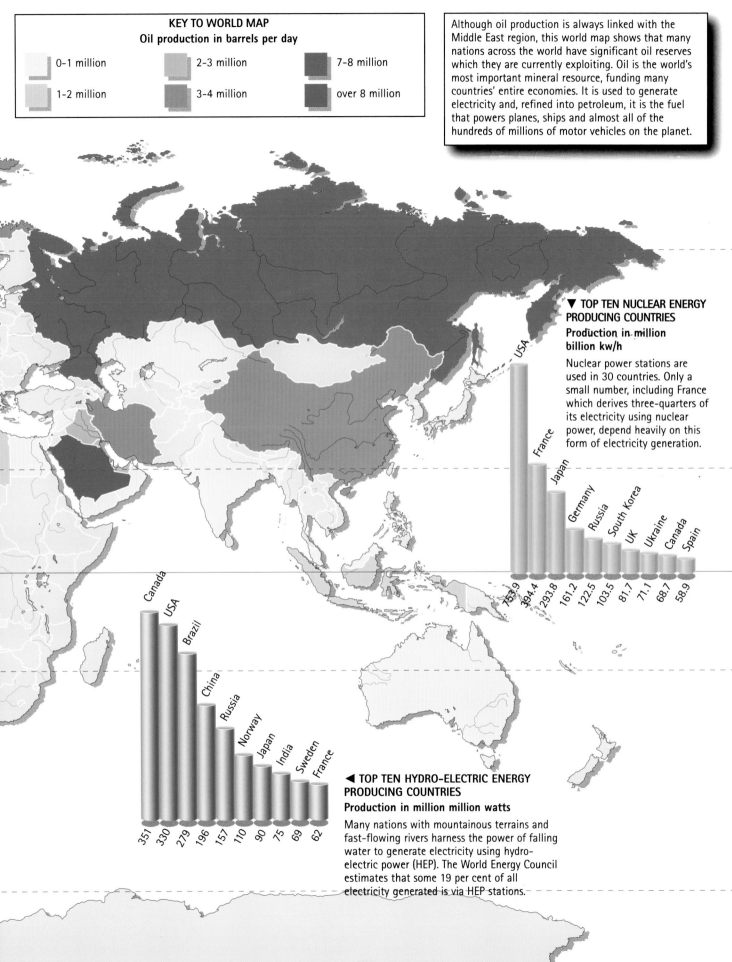

KEY TO WORLD MAP
Oil production in barrels per day

0-1 million	2-3 million	7-8 million
1-2 million	3-4 million	over 8 million

Although oil production is always linked with the Middle East region, this world map shows that many nations across the world have significant oil reserves which they are currently exploiting. Oil is the world's most important mineral resource, funding many countries' entire economies. It is used to generate electricity and, refined into petroleum, it is the fuel that powers planes, ships and almost all of the hundreds of millions of motor vehicles on the planet.

▼ TOP TEN NUCLEAR ENERGY PRODUCING COUNTRIES
Production in million billion kw/h

Nuclear power stations are used in 30 countries. Only a small number, including France which derives three-quarters of its electricity using nuclear power, depend heavily on this form of electricity generation.

Country	Production
USA	753.9
France	394.4
Japan	293.8
Germany	161.2
Russia	122.5
South Korea	103.5
UK	81.7
Ukraine	71.1
Canada	68.7
Spain	58.9

◄ TOP TEN HYDRO-ELECTRIC ENERGY PRODUCING COUNTRIES
Production in million million watts

Many nations with mountainous terrains and fast-flowing rivers harness the power of falling water to generate electricity using hydro-electric power (HEP). The World Energy Council estimates that some 19 per cent of all electricity generated is via HEP stations.

Country	Production
Canada	351
USA	330
Brazil	279
China	196
Russia	157
Norway	110
Japan	90
India	75
Sweden	69
France	62

WORLD COMMODITIES

Our planet has yielded vast quantities of many commodities – partly refined or raw materials – which are used to make goods or other materials.

TOP 12 SAWN SOFTWOOD PRODUCING COUNTRIES	
Production per annum in m³	
USA	84,000,000
Canada	70,000,000
Russia	19,000,000
Sweden	17,000,000
Japan	17,000,000
Germany	16,000,000
Finland	15,000,000
Austria	10,000,000
France	10,000,000
Brazil	10,000,000
Chile	8,000,000
Poland	4,000,000

▲▼ Timber is a valuable commodity in many forms, including paper. This giant paper-making operation is underway in Skutskar in Sweden. Sweden is the world's fourth largest exporter of paper-based products and the second largest exporter of sawn softwood products.

Commodities are valued according to the cost of finding, extracting or harvesting them as well as their relative scarcity. Today, many of the nations in the southern hemisphere are primarily occupied with the production of commodities that are mostly sold to nations in the northern hemisphere with more developed manufacturing industries. The value of commodities rises and falls, sometimes extremely sharply. This can bring additional wealth to a nation, such as when oil shortages and subsequent price rises boost the economies of many Middle Eastern nations. Yet, it more frequently creates major economic crises when price falls occur especially in nations which are over-reliant on one or a handful of commodities. Certain Central American nations, for example, are over-dependent on the value of coffee or cocoa creating economic difficulties when prices drop.

NATURAL COMMODITIES

Many commodities are natural products which are potentially renewable such as timber and natural rubber. Cotton, flax and silk are all natural commodities which provide much of the raw materials for the world's enormous textiles and clothing industries. Crops and livestock are often considered as commodities, which are sold and then processed into products with which to feed the six billion plus world human population. The trade in major food commodities such as cereal crops, rice, fruits and vegetables is immense. For example, rice is the staple food of around half the world's people – around 535 million tonnes of rice are grown worldwide every year.

TOP 20 STEEL PRODUCING COUNTRIES Production in million tonnes p.a.	
China	148.9
Japan	102.9
USA	90.1
Russia	59.0
Germany	44.8
South Korea	43.9
Ukraine	33.1
India	27.3
Brazil	26.7
Italy	26.7
France	19.3
Taiwan	17.2
Spain	16.5
Canada	15.3
Turkey	15.0
United Kingdom	13.7
Mexico	13.3
Belgium	10.8
South Africa	8.8
Poland	8.8

◄ Hot steel is cooled during the manufacturing process in a factory in Bochum, Germany. Steel is used in all forms of construction and the manufacture of many goods from motor vehicles to household goods.

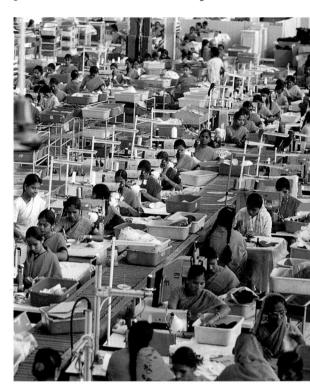

MINERAL COMMODITIES

Minerals tend to be valuable commodities because they do not occur everywhere and they are not renewable. Manufacturing industry depends on mineral commodities, especially metals, to produce many of the world's finished goods. Iron ore is the basis of the world's largest metals industry, steel manufacture. Bauxite, the ore from which aluminium is processed, is another valuable metal commodity which has generated large amounts of revenue for nations such as Australia – the world's largest bauxite exporter. The most financially important of all mineral commodities is oil which is not only used as a vital source of energy, but is also necessary for the manufacture of plastics, polymers and many artificial materials. The 20th century saw more mineral commodities extracted from the planet than in all other centuries put together. While no mineral commodity has yet been exhausted, there are fears that some are dwindling fast.

▲▼ A large textiles factory in India uses cotton as a raw material to make clothing. India is the third largest producer of cotton in the world and one of the world's greatest manufacturers of clothing. India's textiles industry is the country's second largest employer.

TOP TEN WHEAT PRODUCING COUNTRIES Production in tonnes p.a.	
China	94,000,000
India	68,800,000
USA	53,300,000
Russia	46,900,000
France	31,400,000
Australia	24,000,000
Germany	22,800,000
Ukraine	21,000,000
Canada	20,600,000
Pakistan	19,100,000

▲► Sacks of rice are loaded onto ships at Indonesia's Sunda Kelapa port on the island of Java. Rice, along with cereal crops such as wheat, are fundamental sources of food for much of the world's human population.

TOP 20 COTTON PRODUCING COUNTRIES Production in tonnes p.a.	
China	4,600,000
USA	4,092,000
India	2,450,000
Pakistan	1,530,000
Uzbekistan	1,150,000
Turkey	795,000
Australia	681,000
Brazil	370,000
Egypt	350,000
Greece	345,000
Argentina	270,000
Mali	216,000
Mexico	193,000
Turkmenistan	192,000
Benin	151,000
Ivory Coast	140,000
Burkina	138,000
Syria	132,000
Iran	132,000
Tajikistan	119,000

WORLD TRADE

Trading goods and services is vital in order for countries to prosper and progress economically. Many countries have joined regional trade blocs or international organizations to gain favourable treatment or to exert more influence on the world stage.

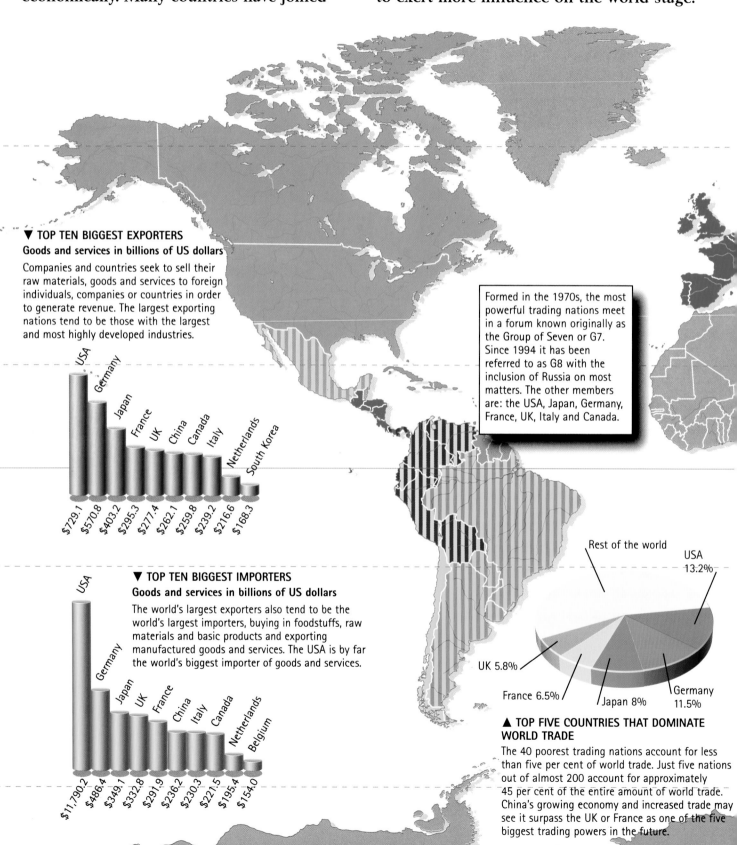

▼ TOP TEN BIGGEST EXPORTERS
Goods and services in billions of US dollars

Companies and countries seek to sell their raw materials, goods and services to foreign individuals, companies or countries in order to generate revenue. The largest exporting nations tend to be those with the largest and most highly developed industries.

USA $729.1
Germany $570.8
Japan $403.2
France $295.3
UK $277.4
China $262.1
Canada $259.8
Italy $239.2
Netherlands $216.6
South Korea $168.3

Formed in the 1970s, the most powerful trading nations meet in a forum known originally as the Group of Seven or G7. Since 1994 it has been referred to as G8 with the inclusion of Russia on most matters. The other members are: the USA, Japan, Germany, France, UK, Italy and Canada.

▼ TOP TEN BIGGEST IMPORTERS
Goods and services in billions of US dollars

The world's largest exporters also tend to be the world's largest importers, buying in foodstuffs, raw materials and basic products and exporting manufactured goods and services. The USA is by far the world's biggest importer of goods and services.

USA $11,790.2
Germany $486.4
Japan $349.1
UK $332.8
France $291.9
China $236.2
Italy $230.3
Canada $221.5
Netherlands $195.4
Belgium $154.0

Rest of the world
USA 13.2%
UK 5.8%
France 6.5%
Japan 8%
Germany 11.5%

▲ TOP FIVE COUNTRIES THAT DOMINATE WORLD TRADE

The 40 poorest trading nations account for less than five per cent of world trade. Just five nations out of almost 200 account for approximately 45 per cent of the entire amount of world trade. China's growing economy and increased trade may see it surpass the UK or France as one of the five biggest trading powers in the future.

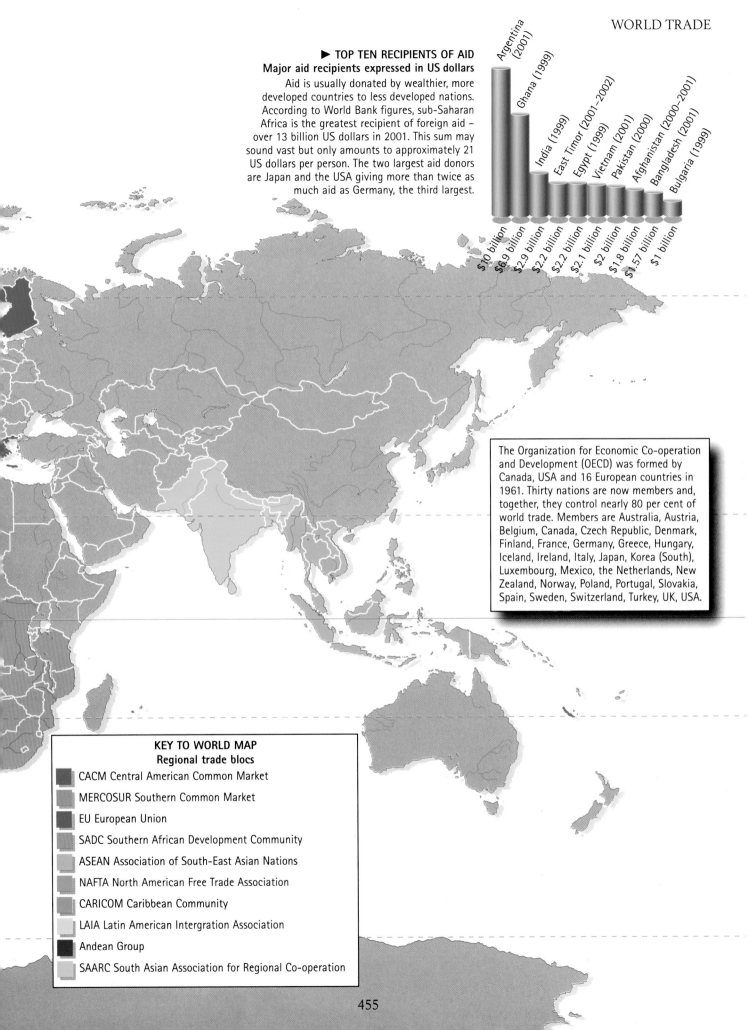

▶ **TOP TEN RECIPIENTS OF AID**
Major aid recipients expressed in US dollars

Aid is usually donated by wealthier, more developed countries to less developed nations. According to World Bank figures, sub-Saharan Africa is the greatest recipient of foreign aid – over 13 billion US dollars in 2001. This sum may sound vast but only amounts to approximately 21 US dollars per person. The two largest aid donors are Japan and the USA giving more than twice as much aid as Germany, the third largest.

Argentina (2001) — $10 billion
Ghana (1999) — $6.9 billion
India (1999) — $2.9 billion
East Timor (2001–2002) — $2.2 billion
Egypt (1999) — $2.2 billion
Vietnam (2001) — $2.1 billion
Pakistan (2000) — $2 billion
Afghanistan (2000–2001) — $1.8 billion
Bangladesh (2001) — $1.57 billion
Bulgaria (1999) — $1 billion

The Organization for Economic Co-operation and Development (OECD) was formed by Canada, USA and 16 European countries in 1961. Thirty nations are now members and, together, they control nearly 80 per cent of world trade. Members are Australia, Austria, Belgium, Canada, Czech Republic, Denmark, Finland, France, Germany, Greece, Hungary, Iceland, Ireland, Italy, Japan, Korea (South), Luxembourg, Mexico, the Netherlands, New Zealand, Norway, Poland, Portugal, Slovakia, Spain, Sweden, Switzerland, Turkey, UK, USA.

KEY TO WORLD MAP
Regional trade blocs

CACM Central American Common Market

MERCOSUR Southern Common Market

EU European Union

SADC Southern African Development Community

ASEAN Association of South-East Asian Nations

NAFTA North American Free Trade Association

CARICOM Caribbean Community

LAIA Latin American Intergration Association

Andean Group

SAARC South Asian Association for Regional Co-operation

TIME ZONES

Millions of people now travel the world using modern transport systems. Travelling long distances east to west or west to east means crossing up to 24 time zones – measured in hours ahead of, or behind, the time found at the Greenwich Meridian at 0° longitude.

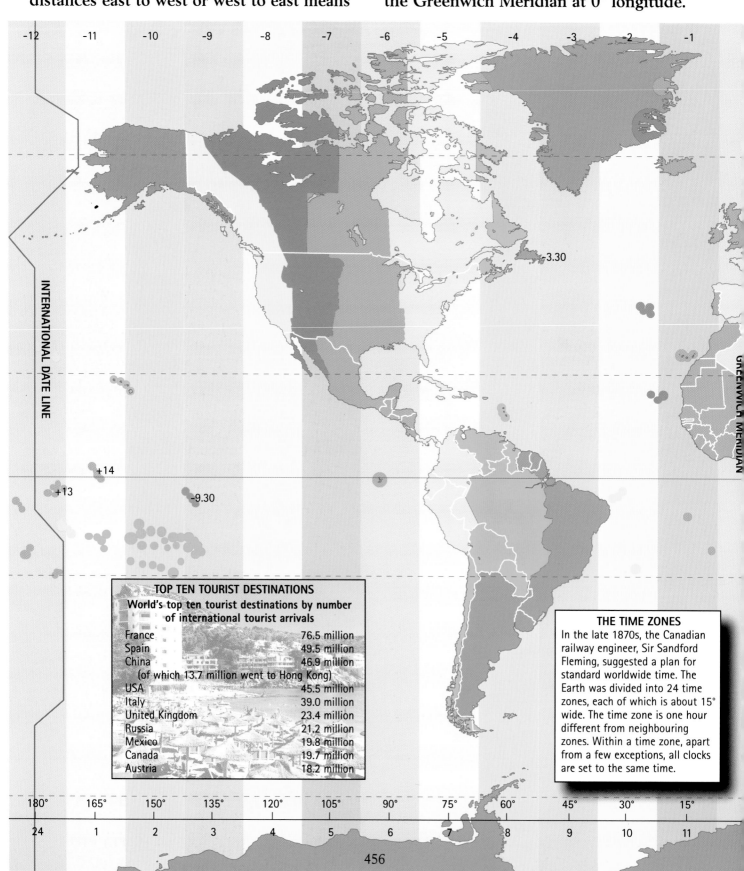

INTERNATIONAL DATE LINE

GREENWICH MERIDIAN

-3.30

+14

+13

-9.30

| -12 | -11 | -10 | -9 | -8 | -7 | -6 | -5 | -4 | -3 | -2 | -1 |

| 180° | 165° | 150° | 135° | 120° | 105° | 90° | 75° | 60° | 45° | 30° | 15° |

| 24 | 1 | 2 | 3 | 4 | 5 | 6 | 7 | 8 | 9 | 10 | 11 |

TOP TEN TOURIST DESTINATIONS

World's top ten tourist destinations by number of international tourist arrivals

France	76.5 million
Spain	49.5 million
China	46.9 million
(of which 13.7 million went to Hong Kong)	
USA	45.5 million
Italy	39.0 million
United Kingdom	23.4 million
Russia	21.2 million
Mexico	19.8 million
Canada	19.7 million
Austria	18.2 million

THE TIME ZONES
In the late 1870s, the Canadian railway engineer, Sir Sandford Fleming, suggested a plan for standard worldwide time. The Earth was divided into 24 time zones, each of which is about 15° wide. The time zone is one hour different from neighbouring zones. Within a time zone, apart from a few exceptions, all clocks are set to the same time.

TOP 20 AIRPORTS   World's busiest airports by passenger numbers

Atlanta, Hartsfield	75,849,375	Dallas/Fort Worth	55,150,689	Phoenix, Sky Harbor	35,481,950	Madrid	33,984,413
Chicago	66,805,339	Frankfurt-Main	48,559,980	Las Vegas	35,195,675	Hong Kong	32,553,000
Los Angeles	61,024,541	Paris, Charles de Gaulle	47,996,223	Minneapolis/St Paul	35,170,528	Detroit	32,294,121
London, Heathrow	60,743,154	Amsterdam, Schiphol	39,538,483	Houston	34,794,868	Miami	31,668,450
Tokyo, Haneda	58,692,688	Denver	36,086,751	San Francisco	34,626,668	London, Gatwick	31,182,361

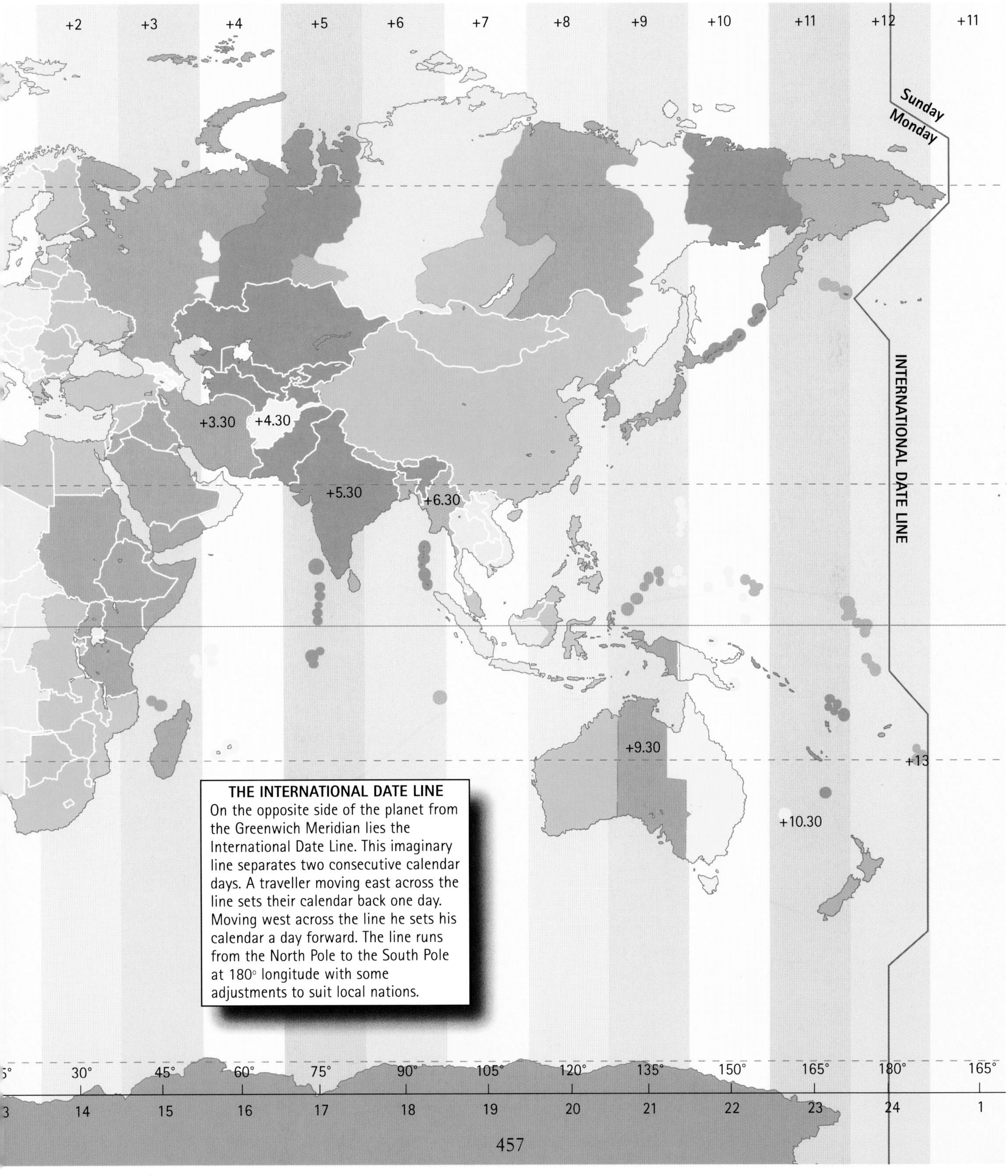

+2 +3 +4 +5 +6 +7 +8 +9 +10 +11 +12 +11

Sunday
Monday

INTERNATIONAL DATE LINE

+3.30 +4.30

+5.30 +6.30

+9.30

+10.30

+13

THE INTERNATIONAL DATE LINE
On the opposite side of the planet from the Greenwich Meridian lies the International Date Line. This imaginary line separates two consecutive calendar days. A traveller moving east across the line sets their calendar back one day. Moving west across the line he sets his calendar a day forward. The line runs from the North Pole to the South Pole at 180° longitude with some adjustments to suit local nations.

5° 30° 45° 60° 75° 90° 105° 120° 135° 150° 165° 180° 165°

3 14 15 16 17 18 19 20 21 22 23 24 1

WORLD ORGANIZATIONS

As the number of independent nations has risen, the need for countries to share information, conduct research, debate topics and settle disputes has grown.

▲ The flag of the European Union adopted on its formation under the Treaty of Maastricht in 1993. Ten more nations are expected to join the European Union in 2004.

▲ The distinctive five rings symbol of the Olympic Games movement. The International Olympic Committee (IOC) organizes the Winter and Summer Olympic Games, the latter is the world's single largest sporting event.

▼ Ethiopian refugees are cared for in a camp by the International Red Cross and Red Crescent Movement. Formed in the 19th century to look after the victims of wars, it also assists victims of natural disasters in peacetime.

Historically, nations aligned with each other in pacts to gain territory and for military reasons in the event of war. Security organizations, such as the North Atlantic Treaty Organisation (NATO) (1949–present day), were modern versions of international alliances of the past. After World War II, there was a large rise in international organizations devoted to issues other than military involvement. International organizations are often split into two types. Intergovernmental organizations such as the United Nations (UN) or NATO involve the governments of different countries. Nongovernmental organizations (NGOs) are private organizations which work on, or campaign for, often, single issues. For example, the International Whaling Commission conducts research into and seeks to conserve whales while the International Atomic Energy Agency (IAEA) promotes the peaceful use of nuclear energy. Many nongovernmental organizations are concerned with the welfare of the world's poor. There are over 500 intergovernmental and an estimated 5,500 nongovernmental organizations in the world today.

▲ The United Nations Security Council in session at its New York headquarters. The council consists of five permanent members: the USA, Russia, China, France and the UK, and ten further member states which are elected for two-year terms.

THE UNITED NATIONS

Since its formation in the aftermath of World War II, the United Nations has grown into the largest of all international organizations. Almost every nation of the world is a member of the UN although not all sign the UN's many agreements, treaties and conventions. The United Nations has a vast and complex structure with a General Assembly in which all members are represented, a Security Council and more than 30 programmes and

▲ Armoured vehicles of a UN peacekeeping force patrol and protect a convoy bringing humanitarian aid to Bosnia during the Balkans conflict in the 1990s.

specialized agencies such as the Food and Agriculture Organisation (FAO), the World Health Organisation (WHO) and the United Nations Children's Fund (UNICEF). One of the UN's fundamental aims is to put an end to war. UN peacekeeping forces, made up of civilian police and observers and soldiers volunteered by their governments, have

been employed around the world to restore and maintain peace. UN peacekeepers have helped to disarm former fighters, train and monitor civilian police, and organize and observe elections. Working with UN agencies and other organizations, they have helped refugees return home, monitored respect for human rights, cleared landmines and started the process of reconstructing a war-torn area.

REGIONAL ORGANIZATIONS

A number of international organizations have been formed by countries in a region to solve issues affecting their region or promote that region's interests. For example, ASEAN (the Association of South-East Asian Nations) promotes economic and military co-operation between ten nations in southeast Asia. The European Union (EU) is an organization of currently 15 European member nations. Its key goal is of greater economic union between its member states with free movement of people, goods and services within its borders and one currency, the euro, which was introduced in 1999 and adopted by most of the member states by 2003.

LEAGUE OF ARAB STATES

Algeria
Bahrain
Comoros
Djibouti
Egypt
Iraq
Jordan
Kuwait
Lebanon
Libya
Mauritania
Morocco
Oman
Palestine
Qatar
Saudi Arabia
Somalia
Sudan
Syria
Tunisia
United Arab Emirates
Yemen

▲ The League of Arab States, also known as the Arab League, was formed in 1945 to protect and promote the interests of many Arab-based nations in the Middle East region.

WORLD RELIGIONS

Many of the world's people live their lives according to sets of beliefs and practices that define their relationship with others, the Universe and its creation.

▲ The head of the Roman Catholic Church is the Pope, here seen blessing a crowd of followers, who resides in the independent city-state of the Vatican.

Religious beliefs first developed many thousands of years ago. Today, there are hundreds of different religions with a few that have hundreds of millions of followers. One of the oldest surviving major religions is Judaism, the religion of the Jewish people, which developed around 4,000 years ago. The state of Israel was established in 1948 as a homeland for the Jewish people but the largest community of Jews in a single country is found in the USA, numbering over five million. Religions have had a major impact on world history and continue to shape the world and its people to this very day.

THE SPREAD OF RELIGIONS

In the past, religious beliefs were spread by traders and missionaries and also imposed by conquering forces. The fastest-growing religion today is believed to be Islam whose followers are called Muslims. The largest communities of Muslims are found in Indonesia, Pakistan, Bangladesh and India with many of the nations of the Middle East also Islamic states. Migrations of peoples from one nation to another have seen many countries become multi-faith nations with sizeable minorities of many different religious persuasions. For example, the largest community of followers of the Sikh religion outside of India is found in the United Kingdom. Christianity is the most widely spread religion and is divided into many differing forms. A little over half of all Christians

▼ **LARGEST RELIGIONS By number of followers**
This chart shows the estimated number of people who follow each of the world's main religions. Almost all the major religions have different branches or sects. In addition, there are numerous other religions with smaller numbers of followers.

Christianity 2,000,000,000
Islam 1,300,000,000
Hindu 900,000,000
Agnostic and non-religious 860,000,000
Buddhist 360,000,000
Traditional beliefs in Africa, South America and Asia (includes Animism) 245,000,000
Chinese folk religions including Daoism 225,000,000
Sikhism 23,000,000
Judaism 14,000,000
Shamanism 14,000,000
Juche 14,000,000
Bahai 6,000,000
Jains 4,000,000
Shinto 4,000,000
Cao Dai 3,000,000

▲ This 13-year-old Jewish boy is undergoing his Bar Mitzvah ceremony in which he becomes an adult in Jewish religious life. Bat mitvah, a similar ceremony for girls, usually occur at age 12.

◄ Two Buddhist monks stand in front of Vat Xieng Thong royal temple in Laos. Buddhism is especially followed in the nations of southeast Asia and in China and Japan.

► Two Sikhs with their distinctive turbans attend the World Conference Unity of Man held in Punjab, India. The Punjab is the homeland of the Sikh religion and the one region on Earth where Sikhs are in the majority.

are Roman Catholics. There are large numbers of Catholics in South and Central America and Europe, while the Philippines is home to the world's fourth largest community of Catholics. The Protestant churches split from the Catholic Church around 500 years ago.

Today, a quarter of all Christians are Protestants, particularly in northern Europe and North America. The Eastern Orthodox churches of Russia and Eastern Europe account for a further ten per cent of all Christians. Some religions are less widely spread. Over 750 million of the world's 900 million Hindus live in India, with the second and third largest Hindu communities found in the neighbouring nations of Nepal and Bangladesh.

▼ Muslims at mid-day prayer in the Jami Masjid mosque in the Indian city of Delhi. Completed in 1650, it is the largest mosque in India and one of the largest in the world.

WORLD COMMUNICATIONS

The range of communication methods has increased dramatically, allowing people greater contact to share information and ideas with other parts of the world.

TOP 20 COUNTRIES WITH TV OWNERSHIP	
China	400,000,000
USA	219,000,000
Japan	86,500,000
India	63,000,000
Russia	60,500,000
Germany	51,400,000
Brazil	36,500,000
France	34,800,000
UK	30,500,000
Italy	30,300,000
Mexico	25,600,000
Canada	21,500,000
Ukraine	18,050,000
Spain	16,200,000
South Korea	15,900,000
Thailand	15,190,000
Indonesia	13,750,000
Poland	13,050,000
Malaysia	10,800,000
Australia	10,150,000

▼ Television has extended its reach into almost all parts of the world. These villagers in Tsatan Uul in northern Mongolia are among the most isolated peoples in Asia. Yet, with a portable electricity generator, they are able to watch television.

Communication comes in many forms from hand gestures and facial expressions to sophisticated electronic communication devices such as mobile phones. Spoken language is the most common form of communication while the development of written language has allowed peoples to record spoken language and ideas and to pass them on to others.

PRINTED COMMUNICATION

Despite the rise of radio, television and electronic media such as the Internet, the printed word, in the form of books, newspapers and journals, remains a major form of mass communication throughout the world. The United Kingdom has one of the world's largest book publishing industries. According to the International Publishing Association around 100,000 new titles are published in the UK every year, double that of France, Italy and Russia. More newspapers are sold daily in Japan than in any other nation – 72.2 million copies in 2000. India with 60 million and the USA with 56 million copies daily were second and third.

▲ Telecommunications and the Internet allow distance learning by children and adults in isolated areas. This young Australian pupil uses a CB radio to contact her teacher hundreds of kilometres away.

TELECOMMUNICATIONS

Much early communication was direct between people in the same place. As transport improved and people explored greater distances, a need for longer-distance communication devices arose. Telecommunications are types of media that enable communication over great distances. The first major telecommunications device was the telegraph, pioneered in Europe and the USA. This was followed by the telephone, radio and television. Television has had a profound impact on the way many people view the world; there are now over two billion TV sets in existence. Television audiences for major global events such as conflicts or sporting events are measured in their hundreds of millions. The past 15 years has seen the rise of mobile phone services. In 2001, 60 per cent of the French, 68 per cent of Germans, 58 per cent of Japanese and 57 per cent of Australians all had mobile phones. In contrast, just 11 per cent of the Chinese population, 2.4 per cent of Indonesians and 2.9 per cent of all Africans had a mobile phone.

▼ TOP 20 MOST COMMON FIRST LANGUAGES BY NUMBER OF USERS

Around 3,000 languages and dialects (versions of a language differing in some words and pronunciations) are spoken in the world today. This chart shows the most commonly spoken languages as the first language of peoples. The large number of Spanish speakers reflects Spain's historical impact in South and Central America. Some languages are far more widely spoken than is reflected by their number of first language users. Although less than one-tenth of the world has English as its first language, the number of people who speak English as their second or third language is far higher. English is often the language used internationally in business and information technology.

Chinese (Guoyo) 1,070,000,000
English 508,000,000
Hindu 497,000,000
Spanish 497,000,000
Arabic 246,000,000
Bengali 211,000,000
Portuguese 191,000,000
Malay-Bahasa Indonesia (includes Javanese) 159,000,000
German 128,000,000
French 128,000,000
Japanese 126,000,000
Urdu 105,000,000
Punjabi 94,000,000
Korean 78,000,000
Telegu 76,000,000
Tamil 74,000,000
Marathi 71,000,000
Cantonese 71,000,000
Wu 70,000,000
Vietnamese 67,000,000

▲ A Chinese newspaper stand selling some of the 50 million newspapers purchased every day in China. There are over 40 daily newspapers and, in some parts of the country, renting newspapers for one hour for a fraction of the cover price is practised to save money.

▼ The Main Reading Room of the Library of Congress in Washington DC, USA. The largest library in the world, it has over 28 million books in 470 different languages.

▼ Global mobile phone technology has evolved using geostationary satellites orbiting Earth to enable worldwide communication in even the remotest regions. This member of the Mount Vaughan Expedition is using a global satellite phone to make a call from the icy wastelands of Antarctica.

PERSONAL COMPUTING

The past 30 years has seen a dramatic change in communication powered by personal computing and, more recently, the Internet. Computers are now found in millions of people's homes all over the world enabling access to information stored on media such as CD-ROMs as well as new methods of communication and handling information such as word processing, spreadsheets and electronic books. Personal computer ownership has boomed since the mid 1980s – the USA leads the way with almost 60 per cent of its population having access to a personal computer. Australia, New Zealand and the nations of western Europe and southeast Asia are not far behind. In contrast, less than half of one per cent of the population in many African nations have access to a computer.

INTERNET COMMUNICATION

The linking of computers together in a network started in the 1960s in academic institutions and with the network of US defence computers called ARPAnet developed by the Pentagon in 1969. By 1990, about 160,000 computers around the world were linked to the Internet but it was the arrival of the World Wide Web with websites containing pages of linked

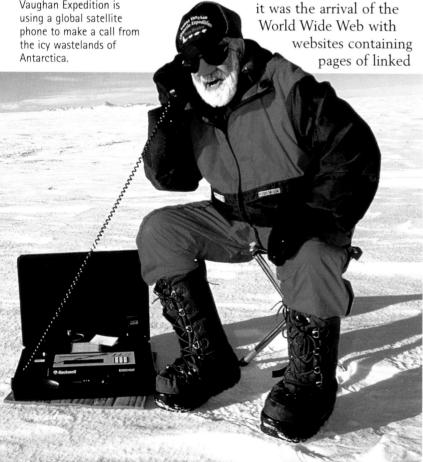

▲ Modern telecommunications allow businesses to span the globe. This call centre for a mobile phone company in the Indian city of Delhi deals with enquiries about its services from customers in the United Kingdom.

information that fuelled the boom in the Internet. Its growth has been explosive. The amount of access to it increased by 1,000 per cent in 1995 and 1996 and has doubled in almost every year since. Today, over one billion people have direct Internet access while many more use Internet facilities in schools and at Internet cafés. According to the International Telecommunications Union, Iceland is the country with the highest level of Internet usage among its population. The Internet is revolutionizing communications for many people. E-mails, Internet chat rooms and messaging allow people to make instant contact with people on the other side of the world.

Many governments and international organizations publish important documents on the World Wide Web, allowing access to increasing amounts of information. In the Dhar District of India, for example, the Gyandoot scheme provides 39 computer kiosks to farmers who can check produce prices and ship to whatever markets offer the best price. For small businesses in poorer countries, isolated a long distance away from potential markets, the Internet offers a chance to sell direct to consumers. Internet access is expected to continue to rise dramatically especially in developing countries. Some of the most powerful Pacific Rim nations are leading the way in upgrading Internet connections to allow fast business and information access. South Korea has the highest level of broadband Internet access with over 60 per cent of households linking up.

WORLD STATISTICS

AUSTRALIA
STATES AND TERRITORIES

NEW SOUTH WALES
Area: 801,600 km^2
Population: 6,609,000
Capital: Sydney

QUEENSLAND
Area: 1,727,200 km^2
Population: 3,635,000
Capital: Brisbane

SOUTH AUSTRALIA
Area: 984,000 km^2
Population: 1,515,000
Capital: Adelaide

TASMANIA
Area: 67,800 km^2
Population: 473,000
Capital: Hobart

VICTORIA
Area: 227,600 km^2
Population: 4,823,000
Capital: Melbourne

WESTERN AUSTRALIA
Area: 2,525,500 km^2
Population: 1,906,000
Capital: Perth

AUSTRALIAN CAPITAL TERRITORY
Area: 2,330 km^2
Population: 322,000
Capital: Canberra

JERVIS BAY TERRITORY
Area: 70 km^2
Population: 600
Capital: administered from Canberra

NORTHERN TERRITORY
Area: 1,346,200 km^2
Population: 200,000
Capital: Darwin

AUSTRIA
FEDERAL STATES

BURGENLAND
Area: 3,965 km^2
Population: 278,000
Capital: Eisenstadt

CARINTHIA (KÄRNTEN)
Area: 9,533 km^2
Population: 559,000
Capital: Klagenfurt

LOWER AUSTRIA (NIEDERÖSTERREICH)
Area: 19,174 km^2
Population: 1,546,000
Capital: Sankt Pölten

SALZBURG
Area: 7,154 km^2
Population: 515,000
Capital: Salzburg

STYRIA (STEIERMARK)
Area: 16,388 km^2
Population:1,183,000
Capital: Graz

TIROL
Area: 12,648 km^2
Population: 674,000
Capital: Innsbruck

UPPER AUSTRIA (OBERÖSTERREICH)
Area: 11,980 km^2
Population: 1,377,000
Capital: Linz

VIENNA (WIEN)
Area: 415 km^2
Population: 1,550,000
Capital: Vienna

VORARLBERG
Area: 2,601 km^2
Population: 351,000
Capital: Bregenz

BELGIUM
FEDERAL REGIONS

BRUSSELS (BRUXELLES OR BRUSSEL)
Area: 161 km^2
Population: 959,000
Capital: Brussels

FLANDERS (VLAANDEREN)
Area: 13,522 km^2
Population: 5,940,000
Capitals: Brussels and Ghent

WALLONIA (WALLONIE)
Area: 16,844 km^2
Population: 3,340,000
Capital: Namur

BRAZIL
STATES

ACRE
Area: 153,150 km^2
Population: 557,000
Capital: Rio Branco

ALAGOAS
Area: 27,933 km^2
Population: 2,820,000
Capital: Maceió

AMAPÁ
Area: 143,454 km^2
Population: 476,000
Capital: Macapá

AMAZONAS
Area: 1,577,820 km^2
Population: 2,841,000
Capital: Manaus

BAHIA
Area: 567,295 km^2
Population: 13,067,000
Capital: Salvador

CEARÁ
Area: 146,348 km^2
Population: 7,417,000
Capital: Fortaleza

ESPÍRITO SANTO
Area: 46,194 km^2
Population: 3,093,000
Capital: Vitória

GOIÁS
Area: 341,289 km^2
Population: 4,995,000
Capital: Goiânia

MARANHÃO
Area: 333,366 km^2
Population: 5,639,000
Capital: São Luís

MATO GROSSO
Area: 906,807 km^2
Population: 2,298,000
Capital: Cuiabá

MATO GROSSO DO SUL
Area: 358,159 km^2
Population: 2,075,000
Capital: Campo Grande

MINAS GERAIS
Area: 588,384 km^2
Population: 17,835,000
Capital: Belo Horizonte

PARÁ
Area: 1,253,165 km^2
Population: 6,189,000
Capital: Belém

PARAÍBA
Area: 56,585 km^2
Population: 3,437,000
Capital: João Pessoa

PARANÁ
Area: 199,709 km^2
Population: 9,558,000
Capital: Curitiba

PERNAMBUCO
Area: 98,938 km^2
Population: 7,911,000
Capital: Recife

PIAUÍ
Area: 252,379 km^2
Population: 2,841,000
Capital: Teresina

RIO DE JANEIRO
Area: 43,910 km^2
Population: 14,367,000
Capital: Rio de Janeiro

RIO GRANDE DO NORTE
Area: 53,307 km^2
Population: 2,771,000
Capital: Natal

RIO GRANDE DO SUL
Area: 282,062 km^2
Population: 10,179,000
Capital: Pôrto Alegre

RONDÔNIA
Area: 238,513 km^2
Population: 1,378,000
Capital: Pôrto Velho

RORAIMA
Area: 225,116 km^2
Population: 324,000
Capital: Boa Vista

SANTA CATARINA
Area: 95,443 km^2
Population: 5,333,000
Capital: Florianópolis

SÃO PAULO
Area: 248,809 km^2
Population: 36,967,000
Capital: São Paulo

SERGIPE
Area: 22,050 km^2
Population: 1,780,000
Capital: Aracaju

TOCANTINS
Area: 278,421 km^2
Population: 1,155,000
Capital: Palmas

FEDERAL DISTRICT
Area: 5,822 km^2
Population: 2,043,000
Capital: Brasilia

CANADA
PROVINCES AND TERRITORIES

ALBERTA
Area: 661,190 km²
Population: 2,975,000
Capital: Edmonton

BRITISH COLUMBIA
Area: 947,800 km²
Population: 3,908,000
Capital: Victoria

MANITOBA
Area: 649,950 km²
Population: 1,120,000
Capital: Winnipeg

NEW BRUNSWICK
Area: 73,440 km²
Population: 729,000
Capital: Fredericton

NEWFOUNDLAND
Area: 405,720 km²
Population: 513,000
Capital: St John's

NOVA SCOTIA
Area: 55,490 km²
Population: 908,000
Capital: Halifax

ONTARIO
Area: 1,068,580 km²
Population: 11,410,000
Capital: Toronto

PRINCE EDWARD ISLAND
Area: 5,660 km²
Population: 135,000
Capital: Charlottetown

QUÉBEC
Area: 1,540,680 km²
Population: 7,237,000
Capital: Québec

SASKATCHEWAN
Area: 652,330 km²
Population: 979,000
Capital: Regina

NORTHWEST TERRITORIES
Area: 1,305,220 km²
Population: 37,000
Capital: Yellowknife

NUNAVUT TERRITORY
Area: 2,121,100 km²
Population: 27,000
Capital: Iqaluit

YUKON TERRITORY
Area: 483,450 km²
Population: 29,000
Capital: Whitehorse

CHINA
PROVINCES AND REGIONS

ANHUI
Area: 139,900 km²
Population: 59,860,000
Capital: Hefei

BEIJING
(municipal province)
Area: 16,800 km²
Population: 13,820,000
Capital: Beijing

CHONGQING (CHUNGKING)
(municipal province)
Area: 82,000 km²
Population: 30,900,000
Capital: Chongqing

FUJIAN
Area: 123,100 km²
Population: 34,710,000
Capital: Fuzhou

GANSU
Area: 366,500 km²
Population: 25,620,000
Capital: Lanzhou

GUANGDONG
Area: 197,100 km²
Population: 86,240,000
Capital: Guangzhou (Canton)

GUANGXI ZHUANG
(autonomous region)
Area: 220,400 km²
Population: 44,890,000
Capital: Nanning

GUIZHOU
Area: 174,000 km²
Population: 36,690,000
Capital: Guiyang

HAINAN
Area: 34,300 km²
Population: 7,870,000
Capital: Haikou

HEBEI
Area: 202,700 km²
Population: 67,440,000
Capital: Shijiazhuang

HEILONGJIANG
Area: 463,600 km²
Population: 36,890,000
Capital: Harbin

HENAN
Area: 167,000 km²
Population: 92,560,000
Capital: Zhengzhou

HONG KONG (OR XIANGGANG)
(autonomous special administrative region)
Area: 1,076 km²
Population: 6,930,000
Capital: Xianggang (Hong Kong) City

HUBEI
Area: 187,500 km²
Population: 60,280,000
Capital: Wuhan

HUNAN
Area: 210,500 km²
Population: 64,400,000
Capital: Changsha

JIANGSU
Area: 102,600 km²
Population: 74,380,000
Capital: Nanjing

JIANGXI
Area: 164,800 km²
Population: 41,400,000
Capital: Nanchang

JILIN
Area: 187,000 km²
Population: 27,280,000
Capital: Changchun

LIAONING
Area: 151,000 km²
Population: 42,380,000
Capital: Shenyang

MACAU
(autonomous special administrative region)
Area: 18 km²
Population: 473,000
Capital: Macau

NEI MONGGOL (INNER MONGOLIA)
(autonomous region)
Area: 1,177,500 km²
Population: 23,730,000
Capital: Hohhot

NINGXIA HUI
(autonomous region)
Area: 66,400 km²
Population: 5,620,000
Capital: Yinchuan

QINGHAI
Area: 721,000 km²
Population: 5,180,000
Capital: Xining

SHAANXI
Area: 195,800 km²
Population: 36,050,000
Capital: Xian

SHANDONG
Area: 153,300 km²
Population: 90,790,000
Capital: Jinan

SHANGHAI
(municipal province)
Area: 6,200 km²
Population: 16,740,000
Capital: Shanghai

SHANXI
Area: 157,100 km²
Population: 32,970,000
Capital: Taiyuan

SICHUAN
Area: 487,000 km²
Population: 83,290,000
Capital: Chengdu

TIANJIN (TIENTSIN)
(municipal province)
Area: 11,300 km²
Population: 10,010,000
Capital: Tianjin

XINJIANG UYGUR (SINKIANG)
(autonomous region)
Area: 1,646,900 km²
Population: 19,250,000
Capital: Ürümqi

XIZANG (TIBET)
(autonomous region)
Area: 1,221,600 km²
Population: 2,620,000
Capital: Lhasa

YUNNAN
Area: 436,200 km²
Population: 42,880,000
Capital: Kunming

ZHEJIANG
Area: 101,800 km²
Population: 46,770,000
Capital: Hangzhou

FRANCE
REGIONS

ALSACE
Area: 8,280 km²
Population: 1,734,000
Capital: Strasbourg

AQUITAINE
Area: 41,309 km²
Population: 2,908,000
Capital: Bordeaux

AUVERGNE
Area: 26,013 km²
Population: 1,309,000
Capital: Clermont-Ferrand

BRITTANY (BRETAGNE)
Area: 27,209 km²
Population: 2,906,000
Capital: Rennes

BURGUNDY (BOURGOGNE)
Area: 31,582 km²
Population: 1,610,000
Capital: Dijon

CENTRE-VAL DE LOIRE
Area: 39,151 km²
Population: 2,440,000
Capital: Orléans

CHAMPAGNE-ARDENNE
Area: 25,606 km²
Population: 1,342,000
Capital: Reims

CORSICA (CORSE)
Area: 8,681 km²
Population: 260,000
Capital: Ajaccio

FRANCHE-COMTÉ
Area: 16,202 km²
Population: 1,117,000
Capital: Besançon

ÎLE DE FRANCE
Area: 12,011 km²
Population: 10,952,000
Capital: Paris

LANGUEDOC-ROUSSILLON
Area: 27,376 km²
Population: 2,296,000
Capital: Montpellier

LIMOUSIN
Area: 16,942 km²
Population: 711,000
Capital: Limoges

LORRAINE
Area: 23,547 km²
Population: 2,310,000
Capital: Nancy

LOWER NORMANDY (BASSE-NORMANDIE)
Area: 17,589 km²
Population: 1,422,000
Capital: Caen

MIDI-PYRÉNÉES
Area: 45,349 km²
Population: 2,552,000
Capital: Toulouse

NORD-PAS-DE-CALAIS
Area: 12,413 km²
Population: 3,997,000
Capital: Lille

PAYS DE LA LOIRE
Area: 32,082 km²
Population: 3,222,000
Capital: Nantes

PICARDY (PICARDIE)
Area: 19,399 km²
Population: 1,858,000
Capital: Amiens

POITOU-CHARENTES
Area: 25,809 km²
Population: 1,640,000
Capital: Poitiers

PROVENCE-ALPES-CÔTE-D'AZUR
Area: 31,400 km²
Population: 4,506,000
Capital: Marseille

RHÔNE-ALPES
Area: 43,698 km²
Population: 5,646,000
Capital: Lyon

UPPER NORMANDY (HAUTE NORMANDIE)
Area: 12,318 km²
Population: 1,780,000
Capital: Rouen

GERMANY
STATES (LÄNDER)

BADEN-WÜRTTEMBERG
Area: 35,751 km²
Population: 10,601,000
Capital: Stuttgart

BAVARIA (BAYERN)
Area: 70,548 km²
Population: 12,330,000
Capital: Munich (München)

BERLIN
Area: 889 km²
Population: 3,388,000
Capital: Berlin

BRANDENBURG
Area: 29,481 km²
Population: 2,593,000
Capital: Potsdam

BREMEN
Area: 404 km²
Population: 660,000
Capital: Bremen

HAMBURG
Area: 755 km²
Population: 1,726,000
Capital: Hamburg

HESSE (HESSEN)
Area: 21,114 km²
Population: 6,078,000
Capital: Wiesbaden

LOWER SAXONY (NIEDERSACHSEN)
Area: 47,606 km²
Population: 7,956,000
Capital: Hannover

MECKLENBURG-WEST POMERANIA (MECKLENBURG-VORPOMMERN)
Area: 23,169 km²
Population: 1,760,000
Capital: Schwerin

NORTH RHINE-WESTPHALIA (NORDRHEIN-WESTFALEN)
Area: 34,072 km²
Population: 18,052,000
Capital: Düsseldorf

RHINELAND-PALATINATE (RHEINLAND-PFALZ)
Area: 19,845 km²
Population: 4,049,000
Capital: Mainz

SAARLAND
Area: 2,570 km²
Population: 1,066,000
Capital: Saarbrücken

SAXONY (SACHSEN)
Area: 18,409 km²
Population: 4,384,000
Capital: Dresden

SAXONY-ANHALT (SACHSEN-ANHALT)
Area: 20,446 km²
Population: 2,581,000
Capital: Magdeburg

SCHLESWIG-HOLSTEIN
Area: 15,739 km²
Population: 2,804,000
Capital: Kiel

THURINGIA (THÜRINGEN)
Area: 16,175 km²
Population: 2,411,000
Capital: Erfurt

INDIA
STATES AND TERRITORIES

ANDHRA PRADESH
Area: 275,068 km²
Population: 75,728,000
Capital: Hyderabad

ARUNACHAL PRADESH
Area: 83,743 km²
Population: 1,091,000
Capital: Itanagar

ASSAM
Area: 78,438 km²
Population: 26,638,000
Capital: Dispur

BIHAR
Area: 94,163 km²
Population: 82,879,000
Capital: Patna

CHHATTISGARH
Area: 135,191 km²
Population: 20,796,000
Capital: Raipur

GOA
Area: 3,702 km²
Population: 1,344,000
Capital: Panaji

GUJARAT
Area: 196,024 km²
Population: 50,597,000
Capital: Gandhinagar

HARYANA
Area: 44,212 km²
Population: 21,083,000
Capital: Chandigarh

HIMACHAL PRADESH
Area: 55,673 km²
Population: 6,077,000
Capital: Simla

JAMMU AND KASHMIR
Area: 222,236 km², of which 121,667 km² are occupied by China and Pakistan
Population: 10,070,000 in Indian-administered areas
Capital: Srinagar

JHARKHAND
Area: 79,714 km²
Population: 26,909,000
Capital: Ranchi

KARNATAKA
Area: 191,791 km²
Population: 52,734,000
Capital: Bangalore

KERALA
Area: 38,863 km²
Population: 31,839,000
Capital: Thiruvananthapuram (Trivandrum)

MADHYA PRADESH
Area: 308,245 km²
Population: 60,385,000
Capital: Bhopal

MAHARASHTRA
Area: 307,690 km²
Population: 96,752,000
Capital: Mumbai (Bombay)

MANIPUR
Area 22,327 km²
Population: 2,389,000
Capital: Imphal

MEGHALAYA
Area: 22,429 km²
Population: 2,306,000
Capital: Shillong

MIZORAM
Area: 21,081 km²
Population: 891,000
Capital: Aizawl

NAGALAND
Area: 16,579 km²
Population: 1,989,000
Capital: Kohima

ORISSA
Area: 155,707 km²
Population: 36,707,000
Capital: Bhubaneshwar

PUNJAB
Area: 50,362 km²
Population: 24,289,000
Capital: Chandigarh

RAJASTHAN
Area: 342,239 km²
Population: 56,473,000
Capital: Jaipur

SIKKIM
Area: 7,096 km²
Population: 540,000
Capital: Gangtok

TAMIL NADU
Area: 130,058 km²
Population: 62,111,000
Capital: Madras (Chennai)

TRIPURA
Area: 10,486 km²
Population: 3,191,000
Capital: Agartala

UTTARANCHAL
Area: 53,483 km²
Population: 8,480,000
Capital: Dehra Dun

UTTAR PRADESH
Area: 240,928 km²
Population: 166,053,000
Capital: Lucknow

WEST BENGAL (BANGLA)
Area: 88,752 km²
Population: 80,221,000
Capital: Kolkata (Calcutta)

ANDAMAN AND NICOBAR ISLANDS UNION TERRITORY
Area: 8,249 km²
Population: 356,000
Capital: Port Blair

CHANDIGARH UNION TERRITORY
Area: 114 km²
Population: 901,000
Capital: Chandigarh

DADRA AND NAGAR HAVELI UNION TERRITORY
Area: 491 km²
Population: 220,000
Capital: Silvassa

DAMAN AND DIU UNION TERRITORY
Area: 112 km²
Population: 158,000
Capital: Daman

DELHI UNION TERRITORY
Area: 1,483 km²
Population: 13,783,000
Capital: Delhi

LAKSHADWEEP UNION TERRITORY
Area: 32 km²
Population: 61,000
Capital: Kavaratti

PONDICHERRY UNION TERRITORY
Area: 492 km²
Population: 974,000
Capital: Pondicherry

ITALY
REGIONS

ABRUZZI
Area: 10,794 km²
Population: 1,244,000
Capital: L'Aquila (although Pescara shares with L'Aquila some of the functions of capital)

BASILICATA
Area: 9,992 km²
Population: 596,000
Capital: Potenza

CALABRIA
Area: 15,080 km²
Population: 1,993,000
Capital: Catanzaro

CAMPANIA
Area: 13,595 km²
Population: 5,652,000
Capital: Naples (Napoli)

EMILIA-ROMAGNA
Area: 22,123 km²
Population: 3,961,000
Capital: Bologna

FRIULI-VENEZIA GIULIA
Area: 7,845 km²
Population: 1,180,000
Capital: Trieste

LAZIO
Area: 17,203 km²
Population: 4,976,000
Capital: Rome (Roma)

LIGURIA
Area: 5,418 km²
Population: 1,561,000
Capital: Genoa (Genova)

LOMBARDY (LOMBARDIA)
Area: 23,857 km²
Population: 8,922,000
Capital: Milan (Milano)

MARCHE
Area: 9,693 km²
Population: 1,464,000
Capital: Ancona

MOLISE
Area: 4,438 km²
Population: 317,000
Capital: Campobasso

PIEDMONT (PIEMONTE)
Area: 25,399 km²
Population: 4,167,000
Capital: Turin (Torino)

PUGLIA
Area: 19,348 km²
Population: 3,983,000
Capital: Bari

SARDINIA (SARDEGNA)
Area: 24,090 km²
Population: 1,599,000
Capital: Cagliari

SICILY (SICILIA)
Area: 25,709 km²
Population: 4,866,000
Capital: Palermo

TUSCANY (TOSCANA)
Area: 22,992 km²
Population: 3,461,000
Capital: Florence (Firenze)

TRENTINO-ALTO ADIGE
Area: 13,618 km²
Population: 937,000
Capital: Bolzano-Bozen (Trento shares some of the functions of capital)

UMBRIA
Area: 8,456 km²
Population: 816,000
Capital: Perugia

VALLE D'AOSTA
Area: 3,262 km²
Population: 119,000
Capital: Aosta

VENETIA (VENETO)
Area: 18,364 km²
Population: 4,491,000
Capital: Venice (Venezia)

MALAYA
STATES AND TERRITORIES

JOHORE (JOHOR)
Area: 18,986 km²
Population: 2,741,000
Capital: Johore Bahru (Johor Baharu)

KEDAH
Area: 9,426 km²
Population: 1,650,000
Capital: Alor Star (Alor Setar)

KELANTAN
Area: 14,943 km²
Population: 1,313,000
Capital: Kota Bahru (Kota Baharu)

MALACCA (MELAKA)
Area: 1,650 km²
Population: 636,000
Capital: Malacca (Melaka)

NEGERI SEMBILAN
Area: 6,643 km²
Population: 860,000
Capital: Seremban

PAHANG
Area: 35,965 km²
Population: 1,288,000
Capital: Kuantan

PERAK
Area: 21,005 km²
Population: 2,051,000
Capital: Ipoh

PERLIS
Area: 795 km²
Population: 204,000
Capital: Kangar

PENANG (PULAU PINANG)
Area: 1,031 km²
Population: 1,313,000
Capital: Penang (Pinang)

SABAH
Area: 73,620 km²
Population: 2,603,000
Capital: Kota Kinabalu

SARAWAK
Area: 124,449 km²
Population: 2,072,000
Capital: Kuching

SELANGOR
Area: 7,916 km²
Population: 4,189,000
Capital: Shah Alam

TRENGGANU (TERENGGANU)
Area: 12,955 km²
Population: 899,000
Capital: Trengganu Bahru (Terengganu Baharu)

FEDERAL CAPITAL TERRITORY (WILAYAH PERSEKUTUAN)
Area: 243 km^2
Population: 1,379,000
Capital: Kuala Lumpur

LABUAN TERRITORY
Area: 91 km^2
Population: 76,000
Capital: Victoria

PUTRAJAYA TERRITORY
Area: 40 km^2
Population: 7,000
Capital: Putrajaya

MEXICO
STATES AND TERRITORIES

AGUASCALIENTES
Area: 5,471 km^2
Population: 944,000
Capital: Aguascalientes

BAJA CALIFORNIA NORTE
Area: 69,921 km^2
Population: 2,488,000
Capital: Mexicali

BAJA CALIFORNIA SUR
Area: 73,475 km^2
Population: 424,000
Capital: La Paz

CAMPECHE
Area: 50,812 km^2
Population: 690,000
Capital: Campeche

CHIAPAS
Area: 74,211 km^2
Population: 3,921,000
Capital: Tuxtla Gutiérrez

CHIHUAHUA
Area: 244,938 km^2
Population: 3,048,000
Capital: Chihuahua

COAHUILA
Area: 149,982 km^2
Population: 2,296,000
Capital: Saltillo

COLIMA
Area: 5,191 km^2
Population: 541,000
Capital: Colima

DURANGO
Area: 123,181 km^2
Population: 1,446,000
Capital: Durango

GUANAJUATO
Area: 30,491 km^2
Population: 4,657,000
Capital: Guanajuato

GUERRERO
Area: 64,281 km^2
Population: 3,075,000
Capital: Chilpancingo

HIDALGO
Area: 20,813 km^2
Population: 2,231,000
Capital: Pachuca

JALISCO
Area: 80,836 km^2
Population: 6,321,000
Capital: Guadalajara

MÉXICO
Area: 21,355 km^2
Population: 13,083,000
Capital: Toluca

MICHOACÁN
Area: 59,928 km^2
Population: 3,979,000
Capital: Morelia

MORELOS
Area: 4,950 km^2
Population: 1,553,000
Capital: Cuernavaca

NAYARIT
Area: 26,979 km^2
Population: 920,000
Capital: Tepic

NUEVO LEÓN
Area: 64,924 km^2
Population: 3,826,000
Capital: Monterrey

OAXACA
Area: 93,952 km^2
Population: 3,432,000
Capital: Oaxaca

PUEBLA
Area: 33,902 km^2
Population: 5,070,000
Capital: Puebla

QUERÉTARO
Area: 11,449 km^2
Population: 1,402,000
Capital: Querétaro

QUINTANA ROO
Area: 50,212 km^2
Population: 874,000
Capital: Chetumal

SAN LUIS POTOSÍ
Area: 63,068 km^2
Population: 2,296,000
Capital: San Luis Potosí

SINALOA
Area: 58,328 km^2
Population: 2,535,000
Capital: Culiacán

SONORA
Area: 182,052 km^2
Population: 2,213,000
Capital: Hermosillo

TABASCO
Area: 25,267 km^2
Population: 1,889,000
Capital: Villahermosa

TAMAULIPAS
Area: 79,384 km^2
Population: 2,747,000
Capital: Ciudad Victoria

TLAXCALA
Area: 4,016 km^2
Population: 962,000
Capital: Tlaxcala

VERACRUZ
Area: 71,699 km^2
Population: 6,901,000
Capital: Jalapa

YUCATÁN
Area: 38,402 km^2
Population: 1,656,000
Capital: Mérida

ZACATECAS
Area: 73,252 km^2
Population: 1,351,000
Capital: Zacatecas

FEDERAL DISTRICT (DISTRITO FEDERAL)
Area: 1,479 km^2
Population: 8,591,000
Capital: Mexico City

RUSSIA
REPUBLICS

ADYGEA
Area: 7,600 km^2
Population: 449,000
Capital: Maykop

ALTAY
see GORNO-ALTAY

BASHKORTOSTAN
Area: 143,600 km^2
Population: 4,111,000
Capital: Ufa

BURYATIA
Area: 351,300 km^2
Population: 1,038,000
Capital: Ulan-Ude

CHECHNYA
Area: 14,300 km^2
Population: 780,000
Capital: Grozny (called Dzhokhar-Ghala by the Chechens). De facto capital: Gudermes (Grozny is largely ruined)

CHUVASHIA
Area: 18,300 km^2
Population: 1,362,000
Capital: Cheboksary

DAGESTAN
Area: 50,300 km^2
Population: 2,119,000
Capital: Makhachkala

GORNO-ALTAY
(also known as Altay)
Area: 92,600 km^2
Population: 203,000
Capital: Gorno-Altaisk

INGUSHETIA
Area: 5,000 km^2
Population: 317,000
Capital: Magas

KABARDINO-BALKARIA
Area: 12,500 km^2
Population: 786,000
Capital: Nalchik

KALMYKIA (KHALMG TANGCH)
Area: 76,100 km^2
Population: 316,000
Capital: Elista

KARACHAY-CHERKESSIA
Area: 14,100 km^2
Population: 434,000
Capital: Cherkessk

KARELIA
Area: 172,400 km^2
Population: 771,000
Capital: Petrozavodsk

KHAKASSIA
Area: 61,900 km^2
Population: 581,000
Capital: Abakan

KOMI
Area: 415,900 km^2
Population: 1,152,000
Capital: Syktyvkar

MARI-EL
Area: 23,200 km^2
Population: 761,000
Capital: Yoshkar-Ola

MORDVINIA
Area: 26,200 km^2
Population: 937,000
Capital: Saransk

NORTH OSSETIA (SEVERO-OSSETIYA)
Area: 8,000 km^2
Population: 663,000
Capital: Vladikavkaz

RUSSIA (ROSSIYA)
Area: 12,198,300 km²
Population: 130,620,000
Capital: Moscow (Moskva)
Russia has no government. It is divided into autonomous regions, districts, territories and cities, each with its own administration

SAKHA (FORMERLY YAKUTIA)
Area: 3,103,200 km²
Population: 1,001,000
Capital: Yakutsk

TATARSTAN
Area: 68,000 km²
Population: 3,784,000
Capital: Kazan

TYVA (FORMERLY TUVA)
Area: 170,500 km²
Population: 311,000
Capital: Kyzyl-Orda

UDMURTIA
Area: 42,100 km²
Population: 1,633,000
Capital: Izhevsk

SPAIN
AUTONOMOUS COMMUNITIES (REGIONS)

ANDALUSIA (ANDALUCÍA)
Area: 87,599 km²
Population: 7,358,000
Capital: Seville

ARAGÓN
Area: 47,720 km²
Population: 1,204,000
Capital: Zaragoza

ASTURIAS
Area: 10,604 km²
Population: 1,063,000
Capital: Oviedo

BALEARIC ISLANDS (BALEARES)
Area: 4,992 km²
Population: 842,000
Capital: Palma de Mallorca

BASQUE COUNTRY (PAÍS VASCO OR EUSKADI)
Area: 7,234 km²
Population: 2,083,000
Capital: Vitoria (Gasteiz)

CANARY ISLANDS (ISLAS CANARIAS)
Area: 7,447 km²
Population: 1,694,000
Joint capitals: Santa Cruz de Tenerife and Las Palmas

CANTABRIA
Area: 5,321 km²
Population: 535,000
Capital: Santander

CASTILE-LA MANCHA (CASTILLA-LA MANCHA)
Area: 79,461 km²
Population: 1,761,000
Capital: Toledo

CASTILE AND LEÓN (CASTILLA Y LEÓN)
Area: 94,224 km²
Population: 2,457,000
Capital: Valladolid

CATALONIA (CATALUÑA OR CATALUNYA)
Area: 32,112 km²
Population: 6,343,000
Capital: Barcelona

CEUTA Y MELILLA (CEUTA AND MELILLA)
Area: 33 km²
Population: 138,000
Joint capitals: Ceuta and Melilla

EXTREMADURA
Area: 41,634 km²
Population: 1,059,000
Capital: Mérida

GALICIA (GALIZA)
Area: 29,575 km²
Population: 2,696,000
Capital: Santiago de Compostela

LA RIOJA
Area: 5,045 km²
Population: 277,000
Capital: Logroño

MADRID
Area: 8,028 km²
Population: 5,423,000
Capital: Madrid

MURCIA
Area: 11,314 km²
Population: 1,198,000
Capital: Murcia (regional parliament Cartagena)

NAVARRE (NAVARRA)
Area: 10,391 km²
Population: 556,000
Capital: Pamplona

VALENCIA
Area: 23,255 km²
Population: 4,163,000
Capital: Valencia

SWITZERLAND
CANTONS

AARGAU
Area: 1,404 km²
Population: 547,000
Capital: Aarau

APPENZELL AUSSER-RHODEN
(half-canton)
Area: 243 km²
Population: 54,000
Capital: Herisau

APPENZELL INNER-RHODEN
(half-canton)
Area: 173 km²
Population: 15,000
Capital: Appenzell

BASEL-LANDSCHAFT
(half-canton)
Area: 517 km²
Population: 259,000
Capital: Liestal

BASEL-STADT
(half-canton)
Area: 37 km²
Population: 188,000
Capital: Basel

BERN (BERNE)
Area: 5,961 km²
Population: 957,000
Capital: Bern

FRIBOURG
Area: 1,671 km²
Population: 242,000
Capital: Fribourg

GENEVA (GENÈVE)
Area: 282 km²
Population: 414,000
Capital: Geneva

GLARUS
Area: 685 km²
Population: 38,000
Capital: Glarus

GRAUBÜNDEN (GRISONS)
Area: 7,105 km²
Population: 187,000
Capital: Chur

JURA
Area: 836 km²
Population: 68,000
Capital: Delémont

LUCERNE (LUZERN)
Area: 1,493 km²
Population: 351,000
Capital: Lucerne

NEUCHÂTEL
Area: 803 km²
Population: 168,000
Capital: Neuchâtel

NIDWALDEN
(half-canton)
Area: 276 km²
Population: 37,000
Capital: Stans

OBWALDEN
(half-canton)
Area: 490 km²
Population: 32,000
Capital: Sarnen

ST GALLEN (SANKT GALLEN)
Area: 2,026 km²
Population: 453,000
Capital: St Gallen

SCHAFFHAUSEN
Area: 299 km²
Population: 73,000
Capital: Schaffhausen

SCHWYZ
Area: 908 km²
Population: 129,000
Capital: Schwyz

SOLOTHURN
Area: 791 km²
Population: 244,000
Capital: Solothurn

THURGAU
Area: 991 km²
Population: 229,000
Capital: Frauenfeld

TICINO
Area: 2,812 km²
Population: 307,000
Capital: Bellinzona

URI
Area: 1,077 km²
Population: 35,000
Capital: Altdorf

VALAIS
Area: 5,225 km²
Population: 272,000
Capital: Sion

VAUD
Area: 3,212 km²
Population: 641,000
Capital: Lausanne

ZUG
Area: 239 km²
Population: 100,000
Capital: Zug

ZÜRICH
Area: 1,729 km²
Population: 1,248,000
Capital: Zürich

UNITED KINGDOM,
COUNTRIES

ENGLAND
Area: 130,422 km²
Population: 49,139,000
Capital: London

NORTHERN IRELAND
Area: 13,576 km²
Population: 1,685,000
Capital: Belfast

SCOTLAND
Area: 77,925 km²
Population: 5,062,000
Capital: Edinburgh

WALES
Area: 20,779 km²
Population: 2,903,000
Capital: Cardiff

USA
STATES

ALABAMA
Area: 133,915 km²
Population: 4,447,000
Capital: Montgomery

ALASKA
Area: 1,530,693 km²
Population: 627,000
Capital: Juneau

ARIZONA
Area: 295,259 km²
Population: 5,131,000
Capital: Phoenix

ARKANSAS
Area: 137,754 km²
Population: 2,673,000
Capital: Little Rock

CALIFORNIA
Area: 411,407 km²
Population: 33,872,000
Capital: Sacramento

COLORADO
Area: 269,594 km²
Population: 4,301,000
Capital: Denver

CONNECTICUT
Area: 12,997 km²
Population: 3,406,000
Capital: Hartford

DELAWARE
Area: 5,294 km²
Population: 784,000
Capital: Dover

FLORIDA
Area: 151,939 km²
Population: 15,982,000
Capital: Tallahassee

GEORGIA
Area: 152,576 km²
Population: 8,187,000
Capital: Atlanta

HAWAII
Area: 16,760 km²
Population: 1,212,000
Capital: Honolulu

IDAHO
Area: 216,430 km²
Population: 1,294,000
Capital: Boise

ILLINOIS
Area: 149,885 km²
Population: 12,419,000
Capital: Springfield

INDIANA
Area: 94,309 km²
Population: 6,081,000
Capital: Indianapolis

IOWA
Area: 145,752 km²
Population: 2,926,000
Capital: Des Moines

KANSAS
Area: 213,096 km²
Population: 2,688,000
Capital: Topeka

KENTUCKY
Area: 104,659 km²
Population: 4,042,000
Capital: Frankfort

LOUISIANA
Area: 123,677 km²
Population: 4,469,000
Capital: Baton Rouge

MAINE
Area: 86,156 km²
Population: 1,275,000
Capital: Augusta

MARYLAND
Area: 27,091 km²
Population: 5,297,000
Capital: Annapolis

MASSACHUSETTS
Area: 21,455 km²
Population: 6,349,000
Capital: Boston

MICHIGAN
Area: 251,493 km²
Population: 9,938,000
Capital: Lansing

MINNESOTA
Area: 224,329 km²
Population: 4,920,000
Capital: St Paul

MISSISSIPPI
Area: 123,514 km²
Population: 2,845,000
Capital: Jackson

MISSOURI
Area: 180,514 km²
Population: 5,595,000
Capital: Jefferson City

MONTANA
Area: 380,847 km²
Population: 902,000
Capital: Helena

NEBRASKA
Area: 200,349 km²
Population: 1,711,000
Capital: Lincoln

NEVADA
Area: 286,352 km²
Population: 1,998,000
Capital: Carson City

NEW HAMPSHIRE
Area: 24,032 km²
Population: 1,236,000
Capital: Concord

NEW JERSEY
Area: 20,168 km²
Population: 8,414,000
Capital: Trenton

NEW MEXICO
Area: 314,924 km²
Population: 1,819,000
Capital: Santa Fe

NEW YORK
Area: 136,583 km²
Population: 18,977,000
Capital: Albany

NORTH CAROLINA
Area: 136,412 km²
Population: 8,049,000
Capital: Raleigh

NORTH DAKOTA
Area: 183,117 km²
Population: 642,000
Capital: Bismarck

OHIO
Area: 115,998 km²
Population: 11,353,000
Capital: Columbus

OKLAHOMA
Area: 181,185 km²
Population: 3,451,000
Capital: Oklahoma City

OREGON
Area: 251,418 km²
Population: 3,421,000
Capital: Salem

PENNSYLVANIA
Area: 119,251 km²
Population: 12,281,000
Capital: Harrisburg

RHODE ISLAND
Area: 3,139 km²
Population: 1,048,000
Capital: Providence

SOUTH CAROLINA
Area: 80,582 km²
Population: 4,012,000
Capital: Columbia

SOUTH DAKOTA
Area: 199,730 km²
Population: 755,000
Capital: Pierre

TENNESSEE
Area: 109,152 km²
Population: 5,689,000
Capital: Nashville

TEXAS
Area: 691,027 km²
Population: 20,852,000
Capital: Austin

UTAH
Area: 219,887 km²
Population: 2,233,000
Capital: Salt Lake City

VERMONT
Area: 24,900 km²
Population: 609,000
Capital: Montpelier

VIRGINIA
Area: 105,586 km²
Population: 7,079,000
Capital: Richmond

WASHINGTON
Area: 176,479 km²
Population: 5,894,000
Capital: Olympia

WEST VIRGINIA
Area: 62,758 km²
Population: 1,808,000
Capital: Charleston

WISCONSIN
Area: 171,496 km²
Population: 5,364,000
Capital: Madison

WYOMING
Area: 253,324 km²
Population: 494,000
Capital: Cheyenne

DISTRICT OF COLUMBIA
Area: 179 km²
Population: 572,000
Capital: Washington DC

GLOSSARY

abrasion physical wearing and grinding of a surface through friction and impact by material carried in air, water or ice.

acid rain rain and snow containing poisonous or harmful chemicals such as sulphur dioxide released by burning fossil fuels.

aquaculture the farming of freshwater and saltwater species including fish, shellfish and seaweed.

archipelago a chain or set of islands grouped together often in a curving arc.

arid dry with little rainfall.

atmosphere the collection of different gases that surrounds the Earth.

atoll a coral reef, usually circular, that encloses a shallow lagoon.

avalanche a downwards slide of snow, ice and debris.

bay an area of the sea enclosed by a curved section of the coast.

bedrock the solid rock that underlies all soil or other loose material; the rock material that breaks down to form soil eventually.

biodiversity short for biological diversity, the range of different species of living thing. The greater the biodiversity of an area, the greater the number of species it contains.

biome a large, general habitat which covers a region of the Earth, such as tundra or desert.

biosphere the name given to all parts of the Earth where living things are found.

caldera a bowl-shaped circular depression caused by the destruction of the peak of a volcano.

cartography the art and science of making maps.

census an investigation or count of a population.

cirque a bowl-shaped depression on a mountain that is carved out by a glacier. Also known as a cwm.

climate the general weather conditions of a region or the entire Earth over a long period of time.

colonialism the system by which one country controls and dominates another country or territory politically and economically.

confluence the place at which two streams join to form one larger stream.

conifer a plant that reproduces by making cones. Conifers are mainly evergreen trees and bushes which keep their leaves throughout the year.

continent one of the large, continuous areas of the Earth into which the land surface is divided.

continental climate the type of climate found in the interior of major continents in the temperate latitudes. The climate is characterized by a great seasonal variation in temperature, four distinct seasons, and relatively low annual rainfall.

continental shelf the extension of the continents into the ocean.

contour map a map that shows points of equal elevation as a line.

conurbation several towns and cities that adjoin or run into one another. *See also* **metropolitan area**.

core the metallic centre of the Earth made of a molten outer core and a solid inner core.

crust the outermost part of the Earth.

cyclone *see* **hurricane**.

deciduous trees which shed their leaves in autumn.

decomposer a living thing that gains nutrients by breaking down dead bodies releasing the minerals they contain into the environment.

deforestation the cutting down of large numbers of trees for fuel or timber, or to clear the land for settlements or farming.

delta the often triangular-shaped area at the mouth of a river.

demography the study of population statistics and trends, such as births, deaths and disease.

desert an area with little precipitation or where evaporation exceeds precipitation, and thus includes sparse vegetation.

desertification the way a desert expands and spreads reducing the land's ability to support life. Desertification is brought about by the planet's changing climate, by over-farming, over-grazing and removing trees and plants which hold the soil in place.

dictatorship a form of government where the ruler, known as a dictator, has absolute power.

earthquake a large, sudden movement of the Earth's crust.

ecology the branch of science that studies the relationships between different living things and living things and their environment.

economy the way in which natural resources are used and goods and services are produced, distributed (sold or passed on to people) and consumed (used by organizations or people).

ecosystem a collection of all living things and their non-living surroundings in a defined area.

El Niño a periodic warming of the ocean waters in the eastern Pacific Ocean which affects global weather patterns.

elevation the height of a point on the Earth's surface above sea level.

emissions harmful gases released into the air by industry, fires and motor vehicles.

enclave a territory of one nation enclosed within another state or country.

endangered species species of living thing that is seriously threatened with extinction.

enhanced greenhouse effect the build-up of carbon dioxide, methane and other gases in the atmosphere, trapping the Sun's heat and affecting the climate.

epicentre the point on the Earth's surface directly above the hypocentre, where the energy of an earthquake is first released.

Equator the imaginary line drawn around the centre of the Earth an equal distance from the South and North Poles.

equinox the beginning of autumn and spring, the two days each year when the Sun is directly overhead at the Equator.

escarpment a long cliff or steep slope separating two comparatively level or more gently sloping surfaces and resulting from erosion or faulting.

estuary the wide end of a river when it meets the sea.

evaporation the process where a liquid changes into a gas. The warming of the air by the Sun causes water to evaporate and change into water vapour.

extinction the permanent disappearance of a species.

fault a fracture or crack in the Earth's crust where blocks of rock slip past each other.

fauna animal life.

federation a form of government in which powers and functions are divided between a central government and a number of political subdivisions which have significant control over their own affairs.

fjord a coastal valley which was sculpted by glacial action.

flood plain a flat, low-lying area near a river or stream which is subject to flooding.

flora plant life.

fold a bend in the layers of rock which makes up the Earth's crust.

food chain the links between different animals that feed on plants and each other. Food chains show how energy is passed up through the chain.

fossil fuels materials which were formed from living things which have decayed and been buried in the ground for millions of years and which can now be burned to generate energy.

geological time the calendar of the Earth's history since its birth. Geological time is divided into eras, epochs and periods.

geyser a fountain of hot water and steam found in volcanic areas.

glacier a mass of ice carrying rocks and soil formed from densely packed snow which does not melt. Pressure forces the glacier to move slowly downhill.

greenhouse gases gases such as carbon dioxide, methane, water vapour and nitrous oxide in the atmosphere that trap heat from the Sun and warm the Earth.

gross domestic product (GDP) a common measure of a country's economic strength and wealth. It represents the total value of all goods and services produced by a nation during a given year.

habitat the surroundings that a particular species needs to survive. Habitats include coral reefs, grasslands, freshwater lakes and deserts. Some creatures can live in more than one habitat.

hemisphere one of the halves of the Earth. The Equator divides the Earth into the southern hemisphere and northern hemisphere.

humidity the amount of water vapour in the air.

humus partially decomposed organic soil material.

hurricane a tropical storm which contains winds of at least 119 km/h. Hurricanes are also known as cyclones in the northern Indian Ocean and as typhoons in the western Pacific Ocean.

hydrography the study of the surface waters of the Earth.

hydroponics the growing of plants, especially vegetables, in water containing essential mineral nutrients rather than in soil.

hypocentre the point under the Earth's surface where the energy of an earthquake is first released.

ice sheet a large, thick layer of ice covering an area of land.

igneous rock a rock formed from the cooling and hardening of hot liquid magma or lava.

indigenous the earliest known inhabitants of a country.

industrialization the process in which more and more emphasis is placed upon industry and manufacturing in a country's economy.

International Date Line an imaginary line near 180° longitude that separates the two simultaneous days that exist on Earth at the same time.

introduced species a species that people have taken from one part of the world and released into another.

irrigation a human-made system of watering the land using pipes and ditches to channel water.

jet stream a narrow band of fast-moving winds which is found at high altitudes.

karst a landscape composed of limestone features including sinkholes, caves and underground streams.

lagoon a small, shallow body of water between a barrier island or a coral reef and the mainland; also a small body of water surrounded by an atoll.

latitude an imaginary line around the Earth parallel to the Equator and used to measure distance from the Equator.

lava magma that reaches the Earth's surface through a volcanic vent or fissure.

life expectancy the length of time people can expect to live on average from when they are born. Life expectancy is affected by factors such as disease, nutrition, poverty and living conditions.

literacy the ability to read and write.

lithosphere the soil and rock layer of the Earth.

longitude an imaginary line around the Earth from the North Pole to the South Pole. Lines of longitude are used to measure distances east and west.

magma hot liquid rock that lies beneath the surface of the Earth.

mantle the rocky middle layer of the Earth between the core and the outer crust.

manufacturing industry industry which brings together materials or products in order to offer them for sale.

map a graphic representation of the Earth's surface.

map projection a mathematical formula which assists in representing the curved surface of the Earth onto the flat surface of a map.

map scale the relationship between distance on a map and the distance on the Earth's surface.

maritime climate a climate strongly influenced by an ocean, found on islands and the windward shores of continents. It is characterized by small daily and yearly temperature ranges and high humidity.

meander a curve in the course of a river.

meridian a line of longitude.

mesa a large flat-topped but steep-sided landform.

Mestizo a person of mixed European and native Indian descent.

metamorphic rock a type of rock formed when igneous or sedimentary rock is altered by great heat and pressure.

metropolitan area a large city and its surrounding suburbs forming one built-up area.

microclimate the climate of a small, defined area such as a valley.

migration a move by people or animals from one location to another.

monarchy a country whose head of state is a king, queen or prince who usually inherits the position rather than being elected.

monsoon a wind system in southeast Asia which changes direction seasonally, creating wet and dry seasons.

moraine the rocks and soil carried and deposited by a glacier.

multilingual the ability to use more than one language when speaking or writing.

municipal waste unwanted by-products generated by people living in an urban area.

nomadic people who do not have a fixed home and usually keep on the move travelling to wherever food can be found.

nutrient any material taken in by a living thing to help it sustain life.

oasis a fertile area with a good water supply found in a desert.

ocean current a regular movement of seawater in or near the surface of a sea or ocean.

ore a type of mineral which contains useful metals such as iron, copper or zinc which can be extracted.

ozone layer a thin layer of the atmosphere consisting of ozone gas which absorbs the majority of the harmful ultraviolet rays from the Sun.

parallel a line of latitude.

parasite an animal that feeds on or inside another living animal, which is called its host. Parasites are usually much smaller than, and do not necessarily harm, their hosts.

peninsula a narrow area of land which stretches out into the sea or into a lake.

permafrost ground that is permanently frozen below the surface.

photosynthesis the process by which plants make food from water and sunlight.

physical geography the branch of geography dealing with the natural features of the Earth.

plateau a raised area of largely flat ground usually surrounded by steep slopes.

pollution waste products or heat which damages the environment in some way.

population density of the number of people per unit of area, often per km^2.

porous something through which water can pass.

prairie a type of largely treeless, grassy plain found in the centre of the North American continent.

precipitation any form of water that falls from the atmosphere to the surface of the Earth such as rain, snow or hail.

predator an animal that kills and feeds on another animal which is known as its prey.

prevailing wind the wind which blows in an area most often.

quarry an open pit made by digging for rocks or minerals.

rapids fast-flowing parts of a river.

recycling recovering waste material to make new products. Can also mean to re-use discarded products.

reef a line of hard rocks or coral at or near the surface of the sea.

republic a country that has an elected government but no monarch.

reservoir an artificial lake built to store water.

resources natural things found on Earth such as water, rocks, wood and coal which can be used in some way.

ridge a narrow, raised stretch of land.

rift valley a long, deep valley formed when part of the Earth's crust collapses along a fault line. The Great Rift Valley in Africa is the world's largest rift valley.

runoff the part of rainfall that reaches streams or rivers. The remainder either evaporates back into the atmosphere or seeps below ground.

rural belonging to the countryside.

salinity a measure of the amount of salt dissolved in water.

savannah a type of lowland plain covered in grasses with occasional trees.

scree a collection of loose rocks and stones on the side of a mountain.

sea level the average height of the surface of the sea.

seamount a single volcanic mountain rising up from the seabed but which does not break the surface of the sea.

sediment the solid that settles at the bottom of a liquid.

sedimentary rock a type of rock formed from sediment which is compressed to form a solid over time.

seismic waves waves of energy which travel through the Earth following an earthquake.

seismology the study of seismic waves in order to learn about earthquakes and the structure of the Earth.

service industries types of work activity which provide services for people such as banking, retailing, education and tourism.

sewage liquid and solid wastes which are channelled into the ground, rivers or the ocean.

silt a dust-like substance made up of tiny particles of rock.

sinkhole a crater formed when the roof of a cavern collapses; usually found in areas of limestone rock.

soil erosion the process by which loose soil is washed or blown away.

soluble capable of being dissolved.

source the place where a stream or river begins to flow.

species a set of organisms that can be grouped together due to their similarity and their potential ability to breed with each other.

spit a long, narrow stretch of sand or gravel running out into the sea.

spring a place where a stream or river rises out of the ground.

stalactite a pointed piece of limestock rock hanging down from the roof of a cave like an icicle.

stalagmite a spike or mound of limestock rock rising up from the floor of a cave.

strait a narrow strip of sea connecting two seas or oceans.

strata layers of sedimentary rock.

subduction the process by which one of the Earth's plates is forced beneath another as they collide.

subsistence farming a form of agriculture in which farmers aim to produce enough food to feed just their families.

subterranean something which is below the surface of the ground such as a cave or underground river.

summit the highest point of a hill or mountain.

tableland a large area of high, flat land.

taiga a moist subarctic coniferous forest that begins where the tundra ends and is dominated by spruces and firs.

temperate term used to describe a region or a climate that is neither very hot nor very cold. Temperate zones lie between the tropics and the polar regions.

thaw the melting of a substance which has been previously frozen.

thermal a rising column of warm air.

tide a regular movement of seawater towards and away from the land. Tides are caused by the gravity exerted by the Sun and Moon.

topography the surface feature of a landscape including its slopes, soils and vegetation.

tor a small area of exposed rock on the top of a round hill.

tornado a fast-moving, potentially destructive wind which moves in a circular pattern.

toxic any substance that is poisonous or harmful to life.

tree line a limit in elevation on a mountain above which trees cannot grow. Also used as a limit in latitude towards the North and South Poles beyond which trees cannot grow.

trench a long, deep valley on the ocean floor.

tributaries streams or small rivers which flow into larger rivers.

tropics the region around the Equator which remains warm all year round.

tsunami a huge ocean wave, often known as a tidal wave, usually generated through movements of the sea floor.

tundra a treeless plain characteristic of the arctic and subarctic regions.

typhoon *see* **hurricane**.

urban belonging to the city or town.

urbanization an increase of people moving to urban areas.

valley a trough-shaped dip in the landscape. Many valleys contain a river.

vegetation the total plant cover of an area.

veld a type of dry, open grassland found in southern Africa.

wadi a dried-up river in a desert.

water cycle the continual flow of the Earth's water. Water vapour from the sea and land rises into the atmosphere becoming rain, snow or hail and then falls back to Earth.

water table the level below the land surface which is fully saturated with water.

weathering the gradual breaking down of rocks and minerals into sand and soil.

wetland an area or region which is usually flooded such as a swamp, marsh or bog.

INDEX

D

The publishers wish to thank the following for their contribution to this book:

Photographs (*t* = top; *b* = bottom; *m* = middle; *l* = left; *r* = right)

Page i *b* Corbis; ii/iii *b* Corbis; iv *tl* NASA; iv *bl* Robert Glusic/PhotoDisc; iv *m* Philip Coblentz/Brand X Pictures; iv *mr* Philip Coblentz/Brand X Pictures; v *tl* David Lorenz Winston/Brand X Pictures; v *m* Corbis; v *mr* Corbis; v *b* Corbis; vi *tl* Herbert Maeder/Still Pictures; vi *m* Steve Allen/Brand X Pictures; vi *b* Corbis; vii *b* MediaFocus International; 1 NASA; 2 *b* NASA; 3 *br* Adalberto Rios Szalay/Sexto Sol/PhotoDisc; 4 *tr* MediaFocus Interrnational; 5 *tl* Emanuele Taroni/PhotoDisc; 6 *tr* Chris Madeley/Science Photo Library; 7 *tr* US Geological Surveys/Science Photo Library; 8 *b* Jeremy Horner/Panos Pictures; 11 *tl* Bernhard Edmaier/Science Photo Library; 11 *br* Rob Huibers/Panos Pictures; 12 *tl* Photo 24/Brand X Pictures; 13 *tl* Photo 24/Brand X Pictures; 13 *l* John Mead/Science Photo Library; 15 *tl* Photo 24/Brand X Pictures; 15 *b* Corbis; 16/17 MediaFocus International; 16 *tl* MediaFocus International; 16/17 *t* Lyndon Harvey; 17 *br* Bernhard Edmaier/Science Photo Library; 18/19 MediaFocus International; 19 *t* MediaFocus International; 19 *br* Photo 24/Brand X Pictures; 20 *tl* Glen Allison/PhotoDisc; 20 *b* Tom Van Saint, Geosphere Project/Planetary Visions/Science Photo Library; 22 *tl* Julian Holland; 22/23 *t* Photo 24/Brand X Pictures; 23 *br* MediaFocus International; 24/25 *t* MediaFocus International; 25 *br* MediaFocus International; 26 *tl* MediaFocus International; 26 *tr* MediaFocus International; 26 *b* MediaFocus International; 27 *tr* Charles O'Rear/Corbis; 28 *tr* NASA; 28 *b* NASA/Science Photo Library; 31 *bl* Photo 24/Brand X Pictures; 31 *br* Corbis; 32 *tl* Photo 24/Brand X Pictures; 32 *bl* MediaFocus International; 33 *bl* Amanda Clement/PhotoDisc; 33 *tr* David Lorenz Winston/Brand X Pictures; 33 *mr* Alain Le Garsmeur/Panos Pictures; 33 *r* MediaFocus International; 33 *br* Photo 24/Brand X Pictures; 34 *tl* Rouxaime & Jacana/Science Photo Library; 34 *tr* Philip Coblentz/Brand X Pictures; 35 *r* Julian Holland; 35 *b* NASA; 36 *tr* Bernhard Edmaier/Science Photo Library; 36 *b* Edouard Parker/Hutchison Library; 37 *t* Michael S. Yamashita/Corbis; 40 *tl* Trygve Bolstad/Panos Pictures; 41 *tr* Liba Taylor/Panos Pictures; 41 *br* John Mead/Science Photo Library; 42 *tr* Julian Holland; 43 *br* NASA; 49 PhotoDisc/Robert Glusic; 50 *b* B & C Alexander/Still Pictures; 51 *b* B & C Alexander/Still Pictures; 52/53 Photo 24/Brand X Pictures; 52 *tr* MediaFocus International; 52 *b* John Wang/PhotoDisc; 54 *b* Corbis; 54/55 *t* Corbis; 55 *r* Gerry Ellis/DigitalVision; 56 *tl* Ron Watts/Corbis; 56 *b* Steve Allen/Brand X Pictures; 57 *tl* David Lorenz Winston/Brand X Pictures; 58 *tl* Alain Le Garsmeur/Panos Pictures; 58 *bl* Bob Krist/Corbis; 58/59 *b* Glen Allison/PhotoDisc; 60 *tl* Gerry Ellis/DigitalVision; 60 *b* Steve Allen/Brand X Pictures; 61 *t* Corbis; 62 *tl* Trevor Page/Hutchison Library; 62 *b* Robert Glusic/PhotoDisc; 63 *tr* Gerry Ellis/PhotoDisc; 63 *bl* Staffan Widstrand/Corbis; 64 *tr* Gerry Ellis/PhotoDisc; 64 *b* Steve Allen/Brand X Pictures; 65 *t* Corbis; 65 *br* Photo 24/Brand X Pictures; 66 *tl* Steve Allen/Brand X Pictures; 66 *tr* David Lorenz Winston/Brand X Pictures; 66 *b* Steve Allen/Brand X Pictures; 67 *b* Jim Wark/Still Pictures; 68 *tl* Steve Allen/Brand X Pictures; 68/69 *t* Photo 24/Brand X Pictures; 68/69 *b* Jeremy Woodhouse/PhotoDisc; 69 *tr* Steve Allen/Brand X Pictures; 69 *r* Joseph Sohm; ChromoSohm Inc./Corbis; 70 *tl* Sandy Felsenthal/Corbis; 70 *tr* Photo 24/Brand X Pictures; 70 *bl* Jeri Gleiter/Still Pictures; 71 *tr* Gerry Ellis/PhotoDisc; 71 *br* Jeff Greenberg/Still Pictures; 72 *tl* Glen Allison/PhotoDisc; 72 *l* Photo 24/Brand X Pictures; 72 *b* Photo 24/Brand X Pictures; 73 *t* Photo 24/Brand X Pictures; 73 *br* Ken Redding/Corbis; 74 *tl* Bob Krist/Corbis; 74 *tr* Photo 24/Brand X Pictures; 74 *b* Corbis; 75 *b* Bob Rowan; Progressive Image/Corbis; 76 *t* Photo 24/Brand X Pictures; 76 *bl* Richard Weiss/Still Pictures; 77 *tr* NASA; 77 *b* Richard Hamilton Smith/Corbis; 78 *tl* Photo 24/Brand X Pictures; 78 *b* Steve Allen/Brand X Pictures; 78/79 *t* Robert Glusic/PhotoDisc; 79 *bl* MediaFocus International; 79 *br* Rick Doyle/Corbis; 80/81 Photo 24/Brand X Pictures; 80 *tl* Philip Coblentz/Brand X Pictures; 80 *l* Steve Allen/Brand X Pictures; 80 *bl* Jeff Greenberg/Still Pictures; 80/81 *t* Gunter Marx Photography/Corbis; 81 *tr* Gerry Ellis/PhotoDisc; 81 *br* Photo 24/Brand X Pictures; 82 *tl* Kevin Schafer/Still Pictures; 82 *r* Gerry Ellis/PhotoDisc; 82 *b* MediaFocus International; 83 *ml* Philip Coblentz/Brand X Pictures; 84 *b* Mark Henley/Panos Pictures; 85 *tr* Philip Coblentz/Brand X Pictures; 85 *bl* Philip Coblentz/Brand X Pictures; 86 *tr* Philip Coblentz/Brand X Pictures; 86 *b* Adalberto Rios Szalay/Sexto Sol/PhotoDisc; 87 *tr* MediaFocus International; 87 *br* Neil Beer/PhotoDisc; 88 *tl* IMS Communications; 88 *b* Edward Parker/Hutchison Library; 89 *tl* Phil Schermeister/Corbis; 89 *tr* Gerry Ellis/PhotoDisc; 89 *br* Adalberto Rios Lanz/Sexto Sol/PhotoDisc; 90 *b* Sean Sprague/Panos Pictures; 91 *tl* Nigel Dickinson/Still Pictures; 91 *bl* Gerry Ellis/PhotoDisc; 91 *br* Steve Allen/Brand X Pictures; 92 *ml* Philip Coblentz/Brand X Pictures; 92 *b* Mike Kolloffel/Still Pictures; 93 *r* David Reed/Panos Pictures; 93 *bl* S. Sprague/Panos Pictures; 94 *bl* Nik Wheeler/Corbis; 95 *ml* Philip Coblentz/Brand X Pictures; 95 *b* Philip Coblentz/Brand X Pictures; 95 *r* Philip Coblentz/Brand X Pictures; 96 *l* IMS Communications; 96 *br* Gerard & Margi Moss/Still Pictures; 97 Philip Coblentz/Brand X Pictures; 98 Philip Coblentz/Brand X Pictures; 99 *t* Mark Edwards/Still Pictures; 99 *b* Philip Coblentz/Brand X Pictures; 100 *tr* Klaus Andrews/Still Pictures; 100 *b* Mark Edwards/Still Pictures; 101 *mr* Rolando Pujol/South American Pictures; 102 *b* Marc French/Panos Pictures; 103 *m* Hisham F. Ibrahim/PhotoDisc; 104 *mr* Marc French/Panos Pictures; 105 *mr* Philip Wolmuth/Panos Pictures; 106/107 *b* Catherine Karnow/Corbis; 108 *b* Neil Cooper/Panos Pictures; 109 *mr* Philip Coblentz/Brand X Pictures; 110 *mr* Jonathan Blair/Corbis; 110 *br* Veronica Garbutt/Panos Pictures; 111 *tr* Philip Wolmuth/Panos Pictures; 111 *br* Philip Coblentz/Brand X Pictures; 112 *tr* Hubert Stadler/Corbis; 112/113 *b* Graham Neden; Ecoscene/Corbis; 113 *tr* Corbis; 113 *br* David Lorenz Winston/Brand X Pictures; 114 *tr* Corbis; 114/115 *b* Philip Coblentz/Brand X Pictures; 115 *bl* Philip Coblentz/Brand X Pictures; 115 *br* Philip Coblentz/Brand X Pictures; 116/117 *b* Tony Morrison/South American Pictures; 116/117 *t* Caroline Penn/Panos Pictures; 117 *br* Kevin Schafer/Still Pictures; 118 *t* Alfredo Cedeño/Panos Pictures; 118 *bl* IMS Communications; 119 *bl* Jonathan Kaplan/Still Pictures; 119 *br* Staffan Widstrand/Corbis; 120 *b* James L. Amos/Corbis; 121 *bl* Philip Coblentz/Brand X Pictures; 121 *br* European Space Agency; 122 *bl* IMS Communications; 123 *t* Jon Spaull/Panos Pictures; 123 *bl* Clive Gifford; 124 *bl* IMS Communications; 124/125 *b* Jeremy Horner/Panos Pictures; 125 *tl* Julian Holland; 125 *tr* Corbis; 126/127 *b* Tony Morrison/South American Pictures; 127 *tr* David Lorenz Winston/Brand X Pictures; 127 *br* Glen Allison/PhotoDisc; 128 *bl* Ron Giling/Still Pictures; 129 *tl* Mark Edwards/Still Pictures; 129 *b* Jeremy A. Horner/Panos Pictures; 130 *tr* MediaFocus International; 130 *b* Mark Edwards/Still Pictures; 132 *tl* Ricardo Azoury/Corbis; 132/133 *b* Richard T. Nowitz/Corbis; 133 *tr* Philip Coblentz/Brand X Pictures; 133 *br* MediaFocus International; 134/135 *t* Ernesto Rios Lanz/Sexto Sol/PhotoDisc; 134/135 *b* Chris Sattlberger/Panos Pictures; 136 *b* Tony Morrison/South American Pictures; 137 *b* Nick Haslam/Hutchison Library; 137 *mr* Philip Coblentz/Brand X Pictures; 138 *b* Philip Coblentz/Brand X Pictures; 138/139 *t* Jeremy Horner/Panos Pictures; 138/139 *m* Philip Coblentz/Brand X Pictures; 139 *br* Philip Coblentz/Brand X Pictures; 140 *bl* Philip Coblentz/Brand X Pictures; 141 *tl* Frank Nowikowski/South American Pictures; 141 *tr* Javier Pierini/PhotoDisc; 141 *b* MediaFocus International; 142 *tl* Kit Houghton/Corbis; 142 *b* MediaFocus International; 143 *tl* Gerry Ellis/DigitalVision; 143 *b* John Farmar; Ecoscene/Corbis; 144 *b* John Noble/Corbis; 145 Philip Coblentz/Brand X Pictures; 146 *bl* Charles & Josette Lenars/Corbis; 146 *tr* MediaFocus International; 147 *br* Ellerbrock & Schaft/Network; 148 *tr* MediaFocus International; 148 *b* Gavin Hellier/Robert Harding Picture Library; 149 *br* Steve Allen/Brand X Pictures; 150 *bl* Yann Arthus-Bertrand/Corbis; 151 *t* Galen Rowell/Corbis; 151 *b* Chris Lisle/Corbis; 152 *b* W. Herbert/Robert Harding Picture Library; 153 *t* Duncan Maxwell/Robert Harding Picture Library; 153 *mr* Pal Hermansen/Still Pictures; 153 *b* Bengt Andreasson/Robert Harding Picture Library; 154 *l* Dylan Garcia/Still Pictures; 155 *t* Wally Herbert/Robert Harding Picture Library; 155 *mr* K. Gillham/Robert Harding Picture Library; 155 *b* Robert Harding Picture Library; 156 *ml* MediaFocus International; 156 *b* MediaFocus International; 157 *tr* Adam Woolfitt/Corbis; 158 *ml* MediaFocus International; 158 *mr* Bob Krist/Corbis; 158 *b* Dave G. Houser/Corbis; 159 *b* Steve Allen/Brand X Pictures; 160 *ml* David Toase/PhotoDisc; 160 *b* Stephanie Maze/Corbis; 161 *tl* Christopher Tordai/Hutchison Library; 161 *tr* Christopher Tordai/Hutchison Library; 161 *br* Tuck Goh/Hutchison Library; 162/163 *b* Roger Ressmeyer/Corbis; 163 *ml* Julian Holland; 163 *bl* Julian Holland; 163 *t* Pawel Libera/Corbis; 163 *mr* Julian Holland; 164 *tl* David Toase/PhotoDisc; 164/165 *t* Robert Laberge/Getty Images; 164 *b* Michael St. Maur Sheil/Corbis; 165 *tr* Philip Coblentz/Brand X Pictures; 165 *mr* Philip Coblentz/Brand X Pictures; 165 *br* R. Rainford/Robert Harding Picture Library; 166 *ml* MediaFocus International; 166 *b* MediaFocus International; 167 *t* MediaFocus International; 168 *b* Sylvain Grandadam/Robert Harding Picture Library; 169 *t* Thomas Raupach/Still Pictures; 169 *br* MediaFocus International; 170/171 *b* Thomas Raupach/Still Pictures; 171 *t* MediaFocus International; 171 *br* MediaFocus International; 172 *tl* Emanuele Taroni/PhotoDisc; 172 *bl* John Wang/PhotoDisc; 172/173 *t* David Turnley/Corbis; 173 *tr* MediaFocus International; 173 *b* Hartmut Schwarzbach/Still Pictures; 174 *t* MediaFocus International; 174 *bl* MediaFocus International; 175 *b* Andy Williams/Robert Harding Picture Library; 176 *tl* MediaFocus International; 176/177 *b* MediaFocus International; 177 *tr* Martial Colomb/PhotoDisc; 177 *mr* Michael Busselle/Corbis; 178 *t* MediaFocus International; 178 *bl* Michael Short/Robert Harding Picture Library; 179 *tr* Philip Coblentz/Brand X Pictures; 179 *br* Martial Colomb/PhotoDisc; 180/181 *t* Tamas Revesz/Still Pictures; 180/181 *b* Ray Juno/Corbis; 182 *b* MediaFocus International; 183 *tr* Reuter Raymond/Corbis Sygma; 183 *b* Roy Rainford/Robert Harding Picture Library; 184 *b* S. Grandadam/Robert Harding Picture Library; 185 *t* Mike McQueen/Impact; 186/187 *b* Corbis; 187 *t* Barry Lewis/Corbis; 187 *br* Philip Coblentz/Brand X Pictures; 188 *b* Emma Lee/Life File/PhotoDisc; 189 *tr* Liba Taylor/Hutchison Library; 189 *b* Jan Hacad/Woodfall Wild Images; 190 *b* John Hatt/Hutchison Library; 191 *tl* Ron Giling/Still Pictures; 191 *tr* Phil Robinson/Robert Harding Picture Library; 191 *b* David Hoffman/Still Pictures; 192 *b* Liba Taylor/Hutchison Library; 193 David Lorenz Winston/Brand X Pictures; 194/195 *b* MediaFocus International; 195 *br* Edward Parker/Hutchison Library; 196 *bl* Philip Coblentz/Brand X Pictures; 197 *tr* Jose Fuste Raga/Corbis; 197 *b* Fin Costello/Robert Harding Picture Library; 198 *tl* Ryan MacVay/PhotoDisc; 198 *b* Philip Coblentz/Brand X Pictures; 199 *tr* Mark Henley/Impact; 200 *b* MediaFocus International; 201 *t* MediaFocus International; p.201 *r* Philip Coblentz/Brand X Pictures; 201 *br* Joerg Boethling/Still Pictures; 202/203 *b* Marco Cristofori/Still Pictures; 203 *t* Corbis; 203 *br* Explorer/Robert Harding Picture Library; 204 *tl* MediaFocus International; 204 *b* Martyn Goddard/Corbis; 205 *br* Philip Coblentz/Brand X Pictures; 206 *b* Janez Stock/Corbis; 207 *b* MediaFocus International; 208 *bl* Colin Paterson/PhotoDisc; 208 *tr* Marc French/Panos Pictures; 209 *b* MediaFocus International; 210 *b* Michael Short/Robert Harding Picture Library; 211 *b* Ed Kashi/Corbis; 212 *b* Leif Skoogfors/Corbis; 213 *b* Melanie Friend/Hutchison Library; 214/215 *b* Toma Babovic/Still Pictures; 215 *t* Mark Henley/Impact; 215 *br* Mark Henley/Impact; 216/217 *b* MediaFocus International; 216/217 *t* Christopher Bluntzer/Impact; 218 *ml* Gregory Wrona/Panos Pictures; 218 *b* Dean Conger/Corbis; 219 *bl* Steve Raymer/Corbis; 220 *b* Chris Lisle/Corbis; 221 *b* Nik Wheeler/Corbis; 222/223 *b* Peter Turnley/Corbis; 223 *tr* Gyori Antoine/Corbis Sygma; 224 *ml* Jeff Greenberg/Robert Harding Picture Library; 224 *b* Barry Lewis/Corbis; 225 *b* C. Bowman/Robert Harding Picture Library; 226 *b* Sandro Vannini/Corbis; 227 *tr* David B. A. Jones/Robert Harding Picture Library; 228 *tl* Dave G. Houser/Corbis; 228/229 *b* Michael Nicholson/Corbis; 229 *br* Janet Wishnetsky/Impact; 230 *tl* David Turnley/Corbis; 230 *b* Gregor Schmid/Corbis; 231 *tl* Wolfgang Kaehler/Corbis; 232 *tl* Bojan Vrecelj/Corbis; 232/233 *b* Christina Dodwell/Hutchison Library; 233 *tr* Paul A. Souders/Corbis; 234 *tr* Rhodri Jones/Panos Pictures; 235 *b* Heidi Bradner/Panos Pictures; 236 *b* Rhodri Jones/Panos Pictures; 237 *ml* Heidi Bradner/Panos Pictures; 237 *b* Jon Spaull/Panos Pictures; 238/239 *t* MediaFocus International; 239 *tr* Adam Woolfitt/Robert Harding Picture Library; 239 *b* Joan Klatchko/Hutchison Library; 240 *b* Philip Woolmuth/Hutchison Library; 241 Corbis; 242 *tr* Jochen Tack/Still Pictures; 242 *b* Giacomo Pirozzi/Panos Pictures; 243 *bl* Lindsay Hebberd/Corbis; 244 *tr* Jean-Léo Dugast/Panos Pictures; 244 *b* Robin Constable/Hutchison Library; 245 *br* MediaFocus International; 246/247 *t* K. M. Westermann/Corbis; 246/247 *b* K. M. Westermann/Corbis; 247 *mr* Dave Bartruff/Corbis; 248 *bl* Ricki Rosen/Corbis; 248/249 *b* Ricki Rosen/Corbis; 249 *t* Mike Schroder/Still Pictures; 250 *ml* Edward Parker/Hutchison Library; 250 *b* Alan Keohane/Impact; 251 *ml* Toby Adamson/Still Pictures; 251 *b* Charles & Josette Lenars/Corbis; 252 *ml* Caroline Penn/Panos Pictures; 252 *b* Michael S. Yamashita/Corbis; 253 *tr* Mohamed Ansar/Impact; 253 *b* John Isaac/Still Pictures; 254 *tr* Robin Laurance/Impact; 254/255 *b* Marcus Rose/Panos Pictures; 255 *tr* Charles & Josette Lenars/Corbis; 256 *tr* Hutchison Library; 257 *tr* Hutchison Library; 256/257 *b* Bernard Gerard/Hutchison Library; 258 *tl* Alex Majoli/Magnum; 258 *b* Mohamed Amin/Robert Harding Picture Library; 259 *b* Adrian Arbib/Still Pictures; 260 *mr* Guy Mansfield/Panos Pictures; 261 *ml* Romano Cagnoni/Still Pictures; 261 *br* MediaFocus International; 262 *b* Nick Haslam/Hutchison Library; 263 *tr* John Miles/Panos Pictures; 263 *ml* John Miles/Panos Pictures; 264 *tr* Klaus Reisinger/Still Pictures; 264/265 *b* Dieter Telemans/Panos Pictures; 265 *br* John McDermott/Panos Pictures; 266 *tr* Liba Taylor/Corbis; 266 *l* ESA/Starsem; 267 *tr* John Spaull/Panos Pictures; 267 *b* Marcus Rose/Panos Pictures; 268 *b* Brian Goddard/Panos Pictures; 270/271 *b* Dr Petocz/Still Pictures; 271 *tr* Joe Raedle/Getty Images; 272 *tr* Alain Le Garsmeur/Panos Pictures; 272/273 *b* Hartmut Schwarzbach/Still Pictures; 273 *br* Fred Hoogervorst/Panos Pictures; 274 *tr* Friedrich Stark/Still Pictures; 275 *tr* Henning Christoph/Still Pictures; 275 *br* Dermot Tatlow/Panos Pictures; 276/277 *t* Ingo Jezierski/PhotoDisc; 276 *b* Hutchison Library; 277 *tr* Jeremy Horner/Corbis; 277 *br* Gerry Ellis/DigitalVision; 278 *tl* Jeremy Horner/Panos Pictures; 278 *bl* Corbis; 278/279 Mark Henley/Panos Pictures; 278/279 *t* Bob Krist/Corbis; 278/279 *b* Wolfgang Schmidt/Still Pictures; 280 *tl* Daniel O'Leary/Panos Pictures; 280/281 *t* Piers Cavendish/Impact; 281 *tr* Jochen Tack/Still Pictures; 280/281 *b* Christopher Cormack/Corbis; 282 *b* Shehzad Nooran/Still Pictures; 283 *mr* David Lorenz Winston/Brand X Pictures; 284 *b* Chris Stowers/Panos Pictures; 285 *b* MediaFocus International; 286 *b* Thierry Thomas/Still Pictures; 287 *b* MediaFocus International; 288 *b* Sarvottam Rajkoomar/Still Pictures; 289 Corbis; 290 *b* Corbis; 291 *br* B.S.P.I/Corbis; 292/293 *t* Corbis; 292 *b* Corbis; 293 *tr* Gerry Ellis/DigitalVision; 294/295 *t* Corbis; 294/295 *b* Glen Allison/PhotoDisc; 295 *tr* Corbis; 295 *br* Ron Giling/Still Pictures; 296 *tl* MediaFocus International; 296/297 *b* Adam Crowley/PhotoDisc; 296/297 *t* Liu Liqun/Corbis; 297 *br* SETBOUN/Corbis; 298 *t* Adam Crowley/PhotoDisc; 298 *bl* Corbis; 299 *bl* Chris Stowers/Panos Pictures; 300/301 *t* Mark Henley/Impact; 301 *bl* Toby Adamson/Still Pictures; 301 *br* PERN/Hutchison Library; 302 *b* Friedrich Stark/Still Pictures; 303 *t* Jeremy Horner/Panos Pictures; 303 *b* Friedrich Stark/Still Pictures; 304 *b* R. Ian Lloyd/Hutchison Library; 305 *t* Jim Holmes/Panos Pictures; 305 *br* Friedrich Stark/Still Pictures; 306 *b* Corbis; 306/307 *t* Dean Conger/Corbis; 307 *br* Akira Kaede/PhotoDisc; 308 *tl* Roger Ressmeyer/Corbis; 308 *b* Corbis; 308/309 *t* Corbis; 309 *br* Akira Kaede/PhotoDisc; 310 *b* Philip Coblentz/Brand X Pictures; 311 *tl* Philip Coblentz/Brand X Pictures; 311 *tr* Philip Coblentz/Brand X Pictures; 311 *br* Chris Stowers/Panos Pictures; 312 *bl* Philip Coblentz/Brand X Pictures; 313 *t* Amanda Leung/Panos Pictures; 313 *b* Ingo Jezierski/PhotoDisc; 314 *bl* Jeremy Horner/Hutchison Library; 315 *t* Philip Coblentz/Brand X Pictures; 315 *br* Jean-Léo Dugast/Panos Pictures; 316/317 *b* Sarah Murray/Hutchison Library; 317 *tr* Caroline Penn/Panos Pictures; 318/319 *b* Glen Allison/PhotoDisc; 319 *tr* Hartmut Schwarzbach/Still Pictures; 320/321 *b* J. Holmes/Panos Pictures; 321 *t* Jorgen Schytte/Still Pictures; 321 *br* Jorgen Schytte/Still Pictures; 322 *bl* Jim Olive/Still Pictures; 323 *ml* R. Ian Lloyd/Hutchison Library; 323 *br* Corbis; 324 *tr* Steve Allen/Brand X Pictures; 325 *tl* Gerard & Margi Moss/Still Pictures; 325 *r* Macduff Everton/Corbis; 326 *tl* Fred Hoogervorst/Panos Pictures; 326 *bl* Mark Edwards/Still Pictures; 326/327 *t* Nigel Dickinson/Still Pictures; 327 *tr* Corbis; 327 *b* Robert Francis/Hutchison Library; 328/329 *t* Russell Gordon/Still Pictures; 329 *br* Chris Stowers/Panos Pictures; 330 *tl* Mark Edwards/Still Pictures; 330 *b* Philip Coblentz/Brand X Pictures; 331 *t* Dani & Jeske/Still Pictures; 331 *br* Michael Macintyre/Hutchison Library; 332 *tl* Johann Scheibner/Still Pictures; 332 *b* Mark Edwards/Still Pictures; 333 *t* Robert Francis/Hutchison Library; 333 *br* T. Turner/Times Picayune/Still Pictures; 334 *bl* Friedrich Stark/Still Pictures; 335 *bl* IMS Communications; 336 *tl* Dean Conger/Corbis; 336 *b* Yann Arthus-Bertrand/Corbis; 337 Herbert Maeder/Still Pictures; 338 *tr* Betty Press/Panos Pictures; 338/339 *b* M & C Denis-Huot/Still Pictures; 339 *br* Gerry Ellis/DigitalVision; 340 *tr* Adrian Arbib/Still Pictures; 341 *b* Ron Giling/Still Pictures; 342 *b* Georges Lopez/Still Pictures; 343 *bl* Mark Henley/Impact; 344 *b* Voltchev-Unep/Still Pictures; 345 *tr* Markus Matzel/Still Pictures; 346/347 *b* MediaFocus International; 347 *tr* Tibor Bognar/Corbis; 348 *b* Paul O'Driscoll/Impact; 349 *br* Dan Charlish-Christian Aid/Still Pictures; 350 *b* Maya Kardum/Panos Pictures; 351 *tr* Henning Christoph/Still Pictures; 352 *b* Mark Edwards/Still Pictures; 353 *mr* Clive Shirley/Panos Pictures; 354 *b* Ron Giling/Still Pictures; 355 *tr* Friedrich Stark/Still Pictures; 356 *b* Caroline Penn/Corbis; 357 *mr* Eldad Rafaeli/Corbis; 357 *br* Betty Press/Panos Pictures; 358 *b* Sebastian Bolesch/Still Pictures; 359 *b* Gallo Images/Corbis; 360/361 *t* Bruce Paton/Panos Pictures; 360/361 *b* Mark Edwards/Still Pictures; 362 *mr* Knut Müller/Still Pictures; 363 *tr* Julian Holland; 363 *bl* Liba Taylor/Panos Pictures; 365 *b* Genevieve Renson/Still Pictures; 366 *b* Edgar Cleijne/Still Pictures; 368 *b* James Sugar/Still Pictures; 369 *b* Ron Giling/Still Pictures; 370/371 *b* Fred Hoogervorst/Panos Pictures; 371 *ml* Anthony Bannister; Gallo Images/Corbis; 372 *b* Yann Arthus-Bertrand/Corbis; 373 *b* Brian Moser/Hutchison Library; 374 *bl* Michael Busselle/Corbis; 375 *tr* Trygve Bolstad/Panos Pictures; 375 *br* Gerry Ellis/DigitalVision; 376 *b* Hjalte Tin/Still Pictures; 377 *mr* Jeremy Woodhouse/PhotoDisc; 378 *b* Gerard & Margi Moss/Still Pictures; 379 *ml* Gerry Ellis/DigitalVision; 379 *b* Friedrich Stark/Still Pictures; 380 *tr* Michael S. Lewis/Corbis; 380/381 *b* Roderick Johnson/Panos Pictures; 381 *tr* Roger de la Harpe/Still Pictures; 382 *tl* IMS Communications; 382/383 *b* Jeremy Woodhouse/PhotoDisc; 382/383 *t* Friedrich Stark/Still Pictures; 383 *tr* Caroline Penn/Panos Pictures; 384 *b* Billie Rafaeli/Hutchison Library; 385 Steve Allen/Brand X Pictures; 386/387 Philip Coblentz/Brand X Pictures; 388 *tl* Bob Abraham/Corbis; 388 *bl* Penny Tweedie/Corbis; 389 *br* Paul A. Souders/Corbis; 390/391 *t* Corbis; 391 *tr* Michael Macintyre/Hutchison Library; 391 *b* Michael Macintyre/Hutchison Library; 392 *tr* Glen Allison/PhotoDisc; 392/393 *b* Steve Allen/Brand X Pictures; 394 *tl* Patrick Ward/Corbis; 394/395 *t* MediaFocus International; 394/395 *b* Corbis; 396 *t* Bill Ross/Corbis; 396/397 *b* Corbis; 397 *tr* Paul A. Souders/Corbis; 398 *tl* Nick Wilson/Getty Images; 398 *b* MediaFocus International; 399 *tl* Paul A. Souders/Corbis; 399 *b* Martin Hawes/Still Pictures; 400 *tl* O. Alamany & E. Vicens/Corbis; 400 *tr* Penny Tweedie/Corbis; 400/401 *b* Corbis; 402 *tl* Ted Spiegel/Corbis; 402/403 *t* L. Clarke/Corbis; 402/403 *b* Dave G. Houser/Corbis; 403 *tr* Gerry Ellis/DigitalVision; 404 *tl* Nick Wilson/Getty Images; 404/405 *t* Paul A. Souders/Corbis; 404/405 *b* Corbis; 405 *br* Robert Garvey/Corbis; 406 *t* Roger Garwood & Trish Ainslie/Corbis; 406/407 *b* Massimo Mastrorillo/Corbis; 407 *tr* Robert Garvey/Corbis; 408 *b* Steve Allen/Brand X Pictures; 408/409 *t* Pat O'Hara/Corbis; 409 *br* Steve Allen/Brand X Pictures; 410 *tl* Anders Ryman/Corbis; 410/411 *b* Corbis; 411 *t* Robert Dowling/Corbis; 412 *tl* Steve Allen/Brand X Pictures; 412 *b* Steve Allen/Brand X Pictures; 413 *t* Paul A. Souders/Corbis; 413 *br* Scott Barbour/Getty Images; 414 *b* J. G. Fuller/Hutchison Library; 415 *m* Anders Ryman/Corbis; 416 *br* Andy Crump/Still Pictures; 417 *b* Stephen Frink/Corbis; 418 *b* Roger Ressmeyer/Corbis; 419 *mr* Glen Allison/PhotoDisc; 420/421 Norbert Wu/Still Pictures; 422 *b* Jan Butchofsky-Houser/Corbis; 423 *b* Michael Macintyre/Hutchison Library; 424 *b* Patricio Goycoolea/Hutchison Library; 425 *mr* Jack Fields/Corbis; 426 *mr* Philipp Hympendahl/Still Pictures; 426/427 *b* Glen Allison/PhotoDisc; 427 *mr* Philip Coblentz/Brand X Pictures; 428 *b* W. Perry Conway/Corbis; 430 *tl* Fritz Polking/Still Pictures; 430/431 *b* Galen Rowell/Corbis; 431 *tr* Galen Rowell/Corbis; 432 *b* Mark Carwardine/Still Pictures; 434 *ml* Carl R. Sams II/Still Pictures; 434 *r* Gerry Ellis/DigitalVision; 434 *br* Mark Edwards/Still Pictures; 435 *mr* Corbis; 435 *bl* Diane Blell/Still Pictures; 436/437 *t* Bojan Brecelj/Still Pictures; 436/437 *b* Gil Moti/Still Pictures; 437 *br* Rui Vieira/Panos Pictures; 442 *ml* Kevin Schafer/Still Pictures; 442 *mr* Caron Philippe/Corbis; 443 *bl* Sabine Vielmo/Still Pictures; 444 *mr* Mike Schroder/Still Pictures; 445 *mr* Shehzad Noorani/Still Pictures; 445 *bl* Jorgen Schytte/Still Pictures; 446 *mr* Wolfgang M. Weber/Still Pictures; 446 *br* Ron Giling/Still Pictures; 447 *tl* Robert Holmes/Corbis; 447 *mr* Tom Wagner/Corbis; 447 *bl* Caroline Penn/Panos Pictures; 448 *bl* Pierre Gleizes/Still Pictures; 452/453 *t* Manfred Voller/Corbis; 452 *b* Claes Lofgren/Still Pictures; 453 *tr* Ron Giling/Still Pictures; 453 *br* Chris Stowers/Panos Pictures; 458 *tr* Ron Giling/Still Pictures; 458/459 *b* Heine Pedersen/Still Pictures; 459 *t* Nigel Dickinson/Still Pictures; 460 *tl* Bettmann/Corbis; 460/461 *t* Jorgen Schytte/Still Pictures; 460 *br* Robert Mulder/Still Pictures; 461 *tr* Sabine Sauer/Still Pictures; 461 *b* Hartmut Schwarzbach/Still Pictures; 462 *tr* Penny Tweedie/Panos Pictures; 462 *bl* Adrian Arbib/Still Pictures; 463 *tr* John Van Hasselt/Corbis Sygma; 463 *b* Catherine Karnow/Corbis; 464 *tr* Mark Henley/Panos Pictures; 464 *bl* Gordon Wiltsie/Still Pictures

Additional artwork: Julian Baker